# Handbook of Family Therapy

# Handbook
# of
# Family Therapy

*The Science and Practice of Working
with Families and Couples*

*Edited by*

Thomas L. Sexton
*Indiana University*

Gerald R. Weeks
*University of Nevada, Las Vegas*

Michael S. Robbins
*University of Miami*

BRUNNER-ROUTLEDGE
New York and Hove

Published in 2003 by
Brunner-Routledge
29 West 35th Street
New York, NY 10001
www.brunner-routledge.com

Published in Great Britain by
Brunner-Routledge
27 Church Road
Hove, East Sussex
BN3 2FA
www.brunner-routledge.co.uk

10 9 8 7 6 5 4 3 2 1

Library of Congress Cataloging-in-Publication Data

Handbook of family therapy : the science and practice of working with families and couples /
edited by Thomas L. Sexton, Gerald R. Weeks, Michael S. Robbins.
     p. cm.
Includes bibliographical references and index.
  ISBN 1-58391-325-4 (hbk. : alk. paper)
  1. Family psychotherapy—Handbooks, manuals, etc.  I. Sexton, Thomas L., 1953- II. Weeks,
Gerald R., 1948- III. Robbins, Michael S.

  RC488.5.H333 2003
  616.89′156—dc21

                                                                                    2003002718

# Contents

# About the Editors

**Thomas L. Sexton, PhD,** is a professor in the Department of Counseling and Educational Psychology at Indiana University where he is the Director of the Clinical Training Center, Director of the Center for Adolescent and Family Studies, and teaches in the APA accredited Counseling Psychology Program. Dr. Sexton has written extensively in the areas of outcome research and its implications for clinical practice and training. He is a national expert on family-based treatment interventions for at-risk adolescents and regularly presents workshops nationally and internationally. Dr. Sexton is the author of four books and over 50 professional articles and chapters in the areas of marriage and family therapy and counseling outcome research. Among his publications are: *Constructivist Thinking in Counseling Research, Practice and Training* and *Utilizing Counseling Outcome Research to Improve Counseling Effectiveness: Implications for Practice, Research, and Training.* He is a licensed psychologist, member of the American Psychological Association (APA), the American Counseling Association (ACA), and an approved supervisor in the American Association of Marriage and Family Therapy (AAMFT).

**Gerald Weeks, PhD, ABPP,** is professor and chair of the Department of Counseling at UNLV. He is an approved supervisor, and clinical member of the American Association of Marriage and Family Therapy, and is board-certified by the American Board of Professional Psychology and the American Board of Sexology. He is currently completing his 16th professional textbook having published in the fields of sex, marital, and family therapy. Among his publications are *Couples in Treatment, Paradoxical Psychotherapy, Erectile Dysfunction,* and *Treating Hypoactive Sexual Desire.*

**Michael S. Robbins, PhD,** received his doctorate in clinical psychology from the University of Utah in 1995. Since receving his degree, Dr. Robbins has worked as a faculty member in the University of Miami School of Medicine's Department of Psychiatry and Behavioral Sciences. Dr. Robbins's primary research interest is in examining process and outcome of family therapy with adolescents with behavior problems. He is specifically interested in identifying clinical processes that are linked to successful family therapy outcomes. Dr. Robbins has also been involved in conducting clinical research examining processes in drug abuse prevention with parents of urban, poor Hispanic children and in studies evaluating the efficacy of family-based interventions for HIV-positive, African-American women and their families.

# Contributors

**Harlene Anderson, PhD**
Harlene Anderson is a consultant, psychotherapist, educator, clinical theorist, and author. She is a founding member of the Houston Galveston Institute and the Taos Institute, specializing in postmodern collaborative practice. She received the Outstanding Contribution to Marriage and Family Therapy Award from the American Association for Marriage and Family Therapy in 2000.

**David C. Atkins, PhD**
David C. Atkins is an assistant professor in the School of Psychology at Fuller Seminary. He recently completed a clinical internship in the Department of Psychiatry and Behavioral Sciences and his doctorate in clinical psychology in the Department of Psychology at the University of Washington. His research focuses on couples, couple therapy, and the application of advanced statistical techniques.

**Dorothy S. Becvar, PhD**
Dorothy S. Becvar is a licensed marital and family therapist and a licensed clinical social worker in private practice in St. Louis, Missouri. She is also president and CEO of the Haelan Centers, a not-for-profit corporation dedicated to promoting the growth and wholeness of clients in body, mind, and spirit.

**Andrew Christensen, PhD**
Andrew Christensen is professor of psychology in the Department of Psychology at the University of California, Los Angeles. He has published widely on couple conflict and couple therapy. He is co-author of the influential scholarly work *Close Relationships* (Freeman, 1983; reprinted in 2002). For therapists, he authored *Acceptance and Change in Couple Therapy: A Therapist's Guide for Transforming Relationships* (1996, Norton), with Neil S. Jacobson. He recently completed a trade book for couples, *Reconcilable Differences* (2000, Guilford), also with Jacobson.

**Frank M. Dattilio, PhD, ABPP**
Frank M. Dattilio holds a dual faculty position in psychiatry at Harvard Medical School and the University of Pennsylvania School of Medicine. A licensed psychologist, Dr. Dattilio is also board certified in both behavioral and clinical psychology with the American Board of Professional Psychology and is a clinical member and approved supervisor of the American Association for Marriage and Family Therapy.

**Rita DeMaria, PhD**
Rita DeMaria is a senior staff member at Council for Relationships in Philadelphia, PA.

She is director of the PAIRS program and the author of several texts. She is a member and an approved supervisor of AAMFT.

**Sona Dimidjian, MSW**
Sona Dimidjian is a doctoral candidate in clinical psychology at the University of Washington. Her research and clinical work focus on the areas of depression and couple therapy.

**Karen M. Donahey, PhD**
Karen M. Donahey is an associate professor in the Department of Psychiatry and Behavioral Sciences and director of the Sex and Marital Therapy Program at Northwestern University Medical School in Chicago, IL.

**Barry L. Duncan, PsyD**
Barry L. Duncan is codirector of the Institute for the Study of Therapeutic Change, has over 75 publications, including 10 books. The latest are *The Heroic Client* (with Scott Miller [Jossey-Bass, 2000]) and *Heroic Clients, Heroic Agencies* (with Jacqueline Sparks [ISTC Press, 2002]), which offer outcome-based alternatives to mental health business as usual.

**Norman B. Epstein, PhD**
Norman B. Epstein is professor of family studies at the University of Maryland, College Park. He is a fellow of the American Psychological Association, a clinical member of the American Association for Marriage and Family Therapy, and a founding fellow of the Academy of Cognitive Therapy.

**Celia Jaes Falicov, PhD**
Celia Falicov is Clinical Professor in the Department of Psychiatry at the University of California, San Diego. She has published extensively on issues of migration, culture and life cycle transitions in families and has received awards for these contributions to theory and practice from the American Psychologi-

cal Association, the Association of Marriage and Family Therapy and the American Family Therapy Academy. She is a fellow and approved supervisor of AAMFT and past president of AFTA. Currently, she is Visiting Professor at the Tavistock Clinic in London, England.

**Scott W. Henggeler, PhD**
Scott W. Henggeler is professor of Psychiatry and Behavioral Sciences and Director of the Family Services Research Center, Medical University of South Carolina. His research interests include mental health and substance abuse services for disadvantaged children and their families, and effective redistribution of mental health resources to preserve family integrity.

**Amy S. Hollimon, MS, NCC**
Amy Hollimon is a counseling psychology doctoral student at Indiana University. She is a national consultant for Functional Family Therapy, providing clinical supervision and implementation of the model, and she is the assistant director of the training clinic for the Department of Counseling and Educational Psychology at IU.

**Susan M. Johnson, EdD**
Dr. Johnson is professor of psychology at Ottawa University and Director of the Ottawa Couple and Family Institute. She is an approved supervisor for the American Association of Marriage and Family Therapy and a recipient of the 2000 Outstanding Contribution to the Field Award from AAMFT. She is the main proponent of Emotionally Focused Couple Therapy, an APA empirically validated treatment.

**Luciano L'Abate, PhD**
Professor emeritus of psychology at Georgia State University, and president of Workbooks

for Better Living. He has published over 200 papers and chapters in professional and scientific journals, as well as authored, co-authored, edited, and coedited 33 books. He also has 4 books in press and 2 others submitted for publication.

## Jay L. Lebow, PhD, ABPP

Jay Lebow is a member of the senior staff at the Family Institute at Northwestern and adjunct associate professor at Northwestern University. He is a fellow of the American Psychological Association and president-elect of its Division of Family Psychology and an approved supervisor of AAMFT.

## Janie K. Long, PhD

Janie Long teaches MFT at Purdue University. Dr. Long is on the board of directors of AAMFT and the editorial board of the *Journal of Feminist Family Therapy*. She is the author of several book chapters and articles on supervision and has made numerous national presentations in this area.

## Carla C. Mayorga, BA

Carla C. Mayorga is a research assistant at the Center for Family Studies in the University of Miami School of Medicine. She currently works on projects examining in-session processes in family-based prevention and intervention of adolescent behavior problems.

## Susan H. McDaniel PhD

Susan H. McDaniel is professor of psychiatry and family medicine, and director of the Wynne Center for Family Research at the University of Rochester School of Medicine and Dentistry, Rochester, NY. She is coeditor of the journal *Families, Systems & Health* and is known for her books and articles on medical family therapy and collaborative family health care.

## Teresa McDowell, MA

Teresa is a visiting professor in the MFT department at Pacific Lutheran University. She has supervised and taught in MFT master's level programs for the past 10 years. Teresa's research and scholarship are primarily in the area of training and supervision, including an emphasis on race and social justice.

## Alyson L. Mease, MA

Alyson Mease has her master's degree in counseling psychology and is currently in her 4th year of a doctoral program at Indiana University in the same field. She has been conducting research and practicing within a family-based, empirically-supported treatment protocol. Alyson has also co-authored chapters regarding the status of couple and family therapy research and functional family therapy as a school-based mental health intervention.

## Scott D. Miller, PhD

Scott D. Miller is a cofounder of the Institute for the Study of Therapeutic Change. He is the author, co-author, and coeditor of several books, including *Handbook of Solution-Focused Brief Therapy: Foundations, Applications, and Research* (with Mark Hubble [Jossey-Bass, 1996]), and *The Heart and Soul of Change: What Works in Therapy* (APA Press, 1999)

## Victoria Behar Mitrani, PhD

Victoria B. Mitrani is research assistant professor at the University of Miami School of Medicine in the Center for Family Studies. She has been an investigator on numerous clinical research studies involving family therapy for minority populations, including behavior-problem and drug-abusing adolescents, HIV-seropositive women, and caregivers of persons with dementia.

**William C. Nichols, EdD, ABPP**
William C. Nichols is an adjunct professor of child and family development, University of Georgia; former professor, Florida State University and elsewhere; editor, *Contemporary Family Therapy*; past president, International Family Therapy Association and American Association for Marriage and Family Therapy; and a diplomate in clinical psychology, American Board of Professional Psychology.

**Timothy J. Ozechowski, PhD**
Tim Ozechowski is an associate scientist at the Oregon Research Institute where he specializes in family therapy outcome and process research, and quantitative longitudinal data analysis. He received his masters and doctoral degrees from accredited marriage and family therapy training programs (Purdue University Calumet and Purdue University, respectively). In addition, he completed a post-doctoral research fellowship at the University of Miami in the area of in family-based adolescent substance abuse treatment. He is a clinical member of the American Association for Marriage and Family Therapy.

**Maria A. Perez, BA**
Maria A. Perez is a research associate at the University of Miami School of Medicine's Center for Family Studies. Ms. Perez has been involved in the development and implementation of family therapy process and outcome studies, including intensive collaboration on projects examining brief strategic family therapy with families of drug-using, behavior-problem adolescents.

**S. Michael Plaut, PhD**
Dr. Plaut is associate professor of psychiatry at the University of Maryland School of Medicine. A licensed psychologist, he is certified as both a sex therapist and an educator. He has served as president of the Society for Sex

Therapy and Research and as editor of the *Journal of Sex Education and Therapy*.

**Nancy Breen Ruddy, PhD**
Nancy Breen Ruddy received her PhD in child clinical psychology from Bowling Green State University in 1991. She was on faculty at the University of Rochester from 1991 to 2000 in Family Medicine and Psychiatry. She currently is on faculty at the Hunterdon Family Practice Residency in Flemington, New Jersey.

**David E. Scharff, MD**
David E. Scharff is co-director of the International Institute of Object Relations Therapy, Chevy Chase, Maryland; clinical professor of psychiatry at Georgetown University and at the Uniformed Services University of the Health Sciences; and a teaching analyst at Washington Psychoanalytic Institute.

**Jill Savege Scharff, MD**
Jill Savege Scharff is co-director of the International Institute of Object Relations Therapy, Chevy Chase, Maryland; clinical professor of psychiatry at Georgetown University; and a teaching analyst at Washington Psychoanalytic Institute.

**Sonja K. Schoenwald, PhD**
Sonja K. Schoenwald is associate professor of psychiatry and behavioral sciences and associate director of the Family Services Research Center, Medical University of South Carolina. Her research focuses on the development, empirical validation, and dissemination of clinically and cost-effective mental health services for youths with complex clinical problems and their families.

**Ashli J. Sheidow, PhD**
Ashli J. Sheidow is assistant professor of psychiatry and behavioral sciences, Medical University of South Carolina. Her research inter-

ests focus on the development, prevention, and treatment of adolescent psychopathology and juvenile delinquency from an ecological perspective, with a concentration in quantitative methods.

**Jacqueline A. Sparks, PhD, LMFT**
Jacqueline A. Sparks is an adjunct faculty member at the Department of Family Therapy, Graduate School of Humanities and Social Sciences, Nova Southeastern University, where her interests are critical theory and the social construction of mental illness. An AAMFT clinical member, she has worked as a therapist, trainer, supervisor, and administrator. She is currently director of special projects at the Center for Family Services of Palm Beach County.

**Cheryl L. Storm, PhD**
Cheryl L. Storm is chair of the Department of Marriage and Family Therapy, Pacific Lutheran University. She is editor of the *Journal of Systemic Therapy,* where she edited a special issue on postmodern supervision. She also coedited (with Thomas Todd) a book on supervision, *The Systemic Superior: Context, Philosophy, & Pragmatics.* She has served as chair of the Commission of Supervision, was editor of the *Supervision Bulletin,* and taught supervision institutes for the American Association for Marriage and Family Therapy.

**José Szapocznik, PhD**
José Szapocznik is director of the University of Miami Center for Family Studies, a flagship program on Hispanic family therapy research. He serves on the National Institute on Drug Abuse National Advisory Council and has served on the National Institute of Mental Health National Advisory Council, and the U.S. Center for Substance Abuse Prevention National Advisory Council.

**Charles Turner, PhD**
Dr. Turner received his PhD in Psychology from the University of Wisconsin, Madison in 1970. He was at the University of Utah from 1970 until 2002, when he retired. He is now with the Oregon Research Institute, where he investigates family-based interventions to reduce child and adolescent drug abuse.

**Holly B. Waldron, PhD**
Dr. Waldron is a research scientist at the Oregon Research Institute in Eugene, Oregon and directs the ORI Center for Family and Adolescent Research in Albuquerque, New Mexico. Her primary research and clinical interests include the development and evaluation of behavioral and family-based interventions for adolescent alcohol and drug use disorders, HIV risk, and other problem behaviors. Dr. Waldron is also actively involved in cross-cultural research and the development of culturally sensitive interventions for Hispanic, First Nations, and Native American youth.

# Foreword

## *Ushering in a New Era*

ALAN S. GURMAN, PHD

*University of Wisconsin Medical School*

Somewhere along the way in the process of being invited to write this foreword, the title "Ushering in a New Era" was suggested to me by the editors. Though no one had ever before supplied me with a title for anything I wrote, I did not bristle at the novelty of the suggestion. I thought that the wording of the proposed title—simple and direct, on the face of it—disguised an interesting array of meanings. Or, at least, it evoked an array of meanings and associations in me.

First, I thought of the role of ushers in a theater. In some theaters, ushers help ticketholders find the seats to which they have already been assigned. In other theatres, ushers help ticketholders find any seats that are available. So, who are the select ticketholders who have been invited to the "performance" of this handbook? Do the invitees already know their places, or will they be content just to find any space for themselves? In a comprehensive undertaking of a multimethod textbook such as this handbook, not everyone can be invited along. So, it is always interesting to note who the "hosts" invite and to see who

gets left at home. With an ever-increasing number of purportedly new approaches to family and couple therapy, it will be eye-opening to see, over time, just who can maintain their "reserved seats," who will get front row seats, who will get balcony seats, and who will be simply left outside, waiting in line for admission. For example, will some of the historically important methods of family therapy lose their places as perpetual "season ticketholders" because they fail to provide empirically adequate evidence of their efficacy to policy makers, academic teachers of psychotherapy, and health insurance providers? Will some of the newer, "empirically supported" approaches eventually not be invited to the gathering, not because they don't deserve invitations on the merits of their efforts, but because significant numbers of clinicians just don't find them to be flexible and inclusive enough to be useful in everyday clinical practice situations?

As I pondered the matter of who gets to be an honored guest in the theater of (and that is) family therapy, a strange fantasy came to me.

Might it not be a thought-provoking and provocative experience for teachers of family therapy to have their students predict and debate which family therapy approaches will still be receiving invitations to such noble gatherings 5, 10, or 20 years from now? What factors would influence such predictions? The accumulation of empirical support? The conceptual coherence of different approaches? The simplicity of some models? The complexity of others? Certainly, the next edition of this handbook will not be identical to this one. Imagine similar debates happening among senior leaders in the field, if they would dare to take the risk of actually disagreeing with each other!

The other type of ushers that came to mind, not surprisingly, are those who serve as official members of wedding parties. Although these ushers' roles are more honorific than functional, such ushers serve as witnesses to marriage ceremonies. This, I suppose, is my role in this foreword, to welcome and acknowledge the "marriage" of two quite different domains of the field of family and couple therapy. The editors of this important handbook have taken on the matchmaker role in a most challenging context. They have drawn together a most interesting gathering of authors, some of whom focus on the "state of the science" of family therapy, some of whom focus on the "state of the art" of family therapy. I applaud the editors' matchmaking efforts. Indeed, I have been trying to foster such relationships between research and practice, and among different styles of practice, for many years. But, one must ask, can such a marriage be consummated? If it is, will it last? Would this be a marriage of convenience; a marriage of mutual caring, respect, and passion; or, indeed, an arranged marriage, organized not by the central parties to the wedding, but by those larger social entities that seek to gain by their exchanging vows? Can the field of family therapy, as the editors put

it, "savor the dialectic . . . and embrace the inevitable tensions" inherent in such a pairing of science and practice? Can the parties to such a wedding find enough commonality between them that affirms the identity and worthiness of each to allow them to be compatible? Can they live with their irreducible differences? And what of their offspring? Can the parties to this wedding cooperatively seek to create a truly scientific practice, while also seeking to create a truly practical science? Over 20 years ago, David Barlow, a prominent behavior therapist, lamented that there was "a growing acceptance of the proposition that clinicians will not do science and that very few scientists will engage in clinical practice." And Morris Parloff, a former chief of the Psychotherapy Section of the National Institute of Mental Health, observed that "No new technique was ever invented in the laboratory, and none was ever discarded because of laboratory findings." Have the times changed? Will they change?

Noted marital researcher John Gottman has written eloquently about the importance of couples' continuing dialogues over what he calls "perpetual problems," that is, core differences between the partners that do not go away or get "resolved." Here are some of my nominations of topics for such ongoing dialogues in the field of family and couple therapy:

1. How do we maintain the conceptual connection between family therapy and couple therapy?
2. How do we bring together the proponents of empirically supported therapies with the advocates of empirically supported therapeutic relationships? And where do empirically supported *therapists* fit into the mix?
3. How do we bring together quantitative research and qualitative research? A scholarly positivistic perspective and a scholarly postmodern perspective? Researchers and clinicians?

4. How do we assimilate or integrate different, indeed competing, approaches to therapy without a loss of identity for the methods thus integrated, and without a loss of face, as well?

Quite honestly, I am not sure if the appearance of this handbook signifies the "launching of the new paradigm shift" for family therapy, or whether it embodies inevitable paradigm clashes. Perhaps both. Certainly, few previous comprehensive textbooks in the field have ever even attempted to introduce the potential partners of science and practice to each other, let alone lead them to the matrimonial altar. I don't know if the extended family of the field of family therapy will think that science and practice are "right for each other." But, speaking for myself, I sure hope they make it. They could have beautiful children.

# Acknowledgments

THOMAS L. SEXTON, PhD
GERALD R. WEEKS, PhD
MICHAEL S. ROBBINS, PhD

Each of us has devoted our professional careers to furthering the science, theory, and practice of family and couple therapy. When the opportunity to participate in this project presented itself, we agreed with both anticipation and a sense of tremendous responsibility. We knew the volume would be a reflection of an entire field. In finishing the task, each of us has come to an even greater appreciation of our chosen profession. Couple and family therapy is a dynamic and evolving field with the potential to have an important and positive impact on the world around us. We are honored to have the opportunity to represent this important work in this volume. Our initial thanks go out to the field that has taught us, supported us, and challenged us to think differently.

A volume like this does not happen without the hard work and dedication of many. Tim Juliet, a former editor with Brunner-Routledge, had the vision for this volume and was relentless in helping us initiate this book. George Zimmar, the current editor, and the editorial staff at Brunner-Routledge, made the work come to fruition. Our advisory board helped guide our ideas and focus our vision. Our contributing authors provided the "real" substance about the current status of couple and family therapy. The external reviewers pushed us to explore areas we had not considered. However, we can't acknowledge enough the contribution of Lynn Gilman (Indiana University) for her dedication and hard work. She went far beyond the call of duty. Thanks to Elizabeth Alonso and Carla Mayorga for their assistance in reviewing and editing multiple drafts of chapters. Finally, each of us had help, assistance, and support from our own families. Sue, always patient, supportive, and understanding, and Jen, Michael, and Matt, who saw much more of the handbook than they ever wanted (TS). Mindy, for her patience and support during the many weekends and evenings that I shirked my familial roles to focus on tasks for the handbook (MR).

# Preface

## *A New Era of Couple and Family Therapy*

THOMAS L. SEXTON, PHD
GERALD R. WEEKS, PHD
MICHAEL S. ROBBINS, PHD

Two decades ago, Gurman and Kniskern launched what became classic volumes in the field of marital and family therapy: *The Handbook of Family Therapy*. These two volumes, one in 1981 and one in 1991, chronicled the emerging theoretical ideas and research trends in the field of marital and family therapy (MFT). The first volume (1981) portrayed an emerging field with a "first generation" of theoretical models that was built on a set of founding constructs that represented a relationally and systemically based way of thinking about clients, therapy, and the mechanisms of clinical change. In this first volume, the emerging trends regarding the efficacy of these approaches were hopeful but only at a very broad level. At that time, the best we could say was that in general MFT seemed to help some clients. The second volume (1991) captured the expansion of the field, including "second generation" theoretical models as, well as stronger research trends from more studies, which produced emerging support for MFT as a clinical enterprise. This volume chronicled new theoretical developments, new approaches, specialized treatment approaches,

and advances in understanding basic issues in the field of marital and family therapy. Based upon the work presented in the second volume, we could now state with certainty that MFT does work, but we were not quite sure what about it was effective, who it might work best for, or in which contexts might specific MFT approaches be particularly effective. The work contained in the Gurman and Kniskern handbook quickly became a primary source of knowledge about the field. Just as important, these volumes became symbols of the paradigm shift from individual to relational focus on the complex systems of the "family."

During the ensuing 2 decades, the field of MFT continued to dynamically evolve in regard to the complexity of our founding constructs, our theoretical perspectives, the application of these principles in clinical practice, and the complexity and clinical validity of the supporting research. The theoretical foundations of family therapy have become increasingly integrative, research-based, and multisystemic. The initial research found little evidence for the efficacy of "theoretical approaches" in treating clinical problems. These findings led later researchers to suggest that global therapeutic orientations do not represent the important and distinguishing characteristics that differentiated effective and ineffective interventions (Alexander, Holtzworth-Munroe, & Jameson, 1994; Sexton, Alexander, & Mease, in press). Over the last number of years the "schools" of therapy have given way first to "Common Factors" and now to more specific, systematic, and well-articulated clinical models. According to Liddle, Santisteban, Levant, and Bray (2002), these approaches represent the emergence of "family intervention science," which is predicated on the growing body of outcome and process research studies that meet the highest standards of research methodology. Alexander, Sexton, and Robbins (2002) suggest that these models represent "mature" clinical models of practice.

The landscape of clinical practice has also changed. The context of clinical practice is now one steeped in accountability, with a focus on outcome and specific mechanisms of change. Communities, government agencies, and health-care policy developers are increasingly focused on the successful outcomes of clinical practice (Surgeon General, 1999, 2001). In many arenas (e.g., juvenile justice, managed health care) the concept of "best practice" has become the criterion upon which decisions are made regarding funding for treatment programs (Elliott, 1998). Professional organizations are developing practice guidelines (Alexander et al., 2002; Sexton & Alexander, 2002), as well as evidence-based practice guidelines identifying the scientific basis for psychological treatments (e.g., American Psychological Association, American Psychiatric Association). *Empirically Supported Treatment* (Chambless & Hollon, 1998) and *Principles of Empirically Supported Interventions* (Wampold, Lichtenberg, & Waehler, 2002) are both attempts to set a standard for what is "enough" research support

for a psychological intervention to be reliable enough to be implemented by practitioners. These efforts have brought empirical evidence and systematic treatment models into the forefront of consideration in MFT. The changing context of practice ushered in by an era of accountability has dramatically altered the way that MFT is practiced.

The research foundations of MFT have also grown in the last 2 decades. Early efforts responded to the need to demonstrate that the approaches to MFT worked and adopted traditional "gold standard" research approaches, typified by randomized clinical trials (RCT) and well controlled research designs. These methods were critical to establish the field as an empirically grounded, scientifically respected discipline. Without these efforts, MFT could easily have become a hot trend that then dissipated when the next hot trend emerged (Pinsof & Wynne, 2000). This early research path increasingly resulted in conflict with the systematic practice of MFT. Clinicians and theorists openly questioned whether traditional methods could capture phenomena thought to be recursive, dynamic, multidirectional processes of openness and growth; interdeterminate dynamic system trajectories; and interpersonal transactions that absolutely could not be "dismantled" in a manner that represented the tradition of "good science." These tensions have helped the clinical research of MFT evolve into what today is a comprehensive and systematic body of clinical research that can and does capture the complexity of the relational and clinical practice of MFT. The field has moved well beyond the early outcome studies to complex investigations of actual clinical processes and community-based outcome investigations of MFT practices with "real" therapists, in actual clinical settings, with diverse clients, in many specific contexts. In fact, over the last 2 decades family therapy has developed a rich research foundation built on ecologically valid, clinically relevant process and outcome research. MFT researchers now "set the bar' for clinically relevant and multisystemic, community-focused, diversity-oriented clinical research (Sexton, Alexander, & Mease, in press).

Despite the reliable and informative results of the cumulative research knowledge documented in these presentations, the gap between the established findings of marital and family research and the practice and training of marital and family therapy continues. Indeed, it is not uncommon, now more than 3 decades since the publication of the first research findings in the field, to encounter concerns about the role of research in practice. For example, practitioners continue to argue that researchers are not clinically responsive, whereas the researchers argue that practitioners are not systematic. The gap is also reflected in the fact that it is common to find new "hot" ideas being touted in practice publications and on the lecture circuit that have no support in either the rich theory or research of the field. As Gurman et al. (1986) noted, "Despite numerous attempts at seduction and mutual courtship, it remains the case that clinicians and therapy researchers have failed to consummate a 'meaningful' and lasting relationship, as has been observed, commented on, and lamented repeatedly" (p. 490). There is no doubt that much needs to be done to overcome the practice and research gaps in the field of MFT.

The theoretical framework of family therapy has evolved since its beginnings in the late 1940s and early 1950s in very distinct ways. The early founding constructs of systems theory/cybernetics focused on recursion, or circular causality and behavior influenced by feedback. Theoretical constructs of boundaries, communication and information processing, entropy and negentropy, equifinality and equipotentiality, morphostasis and morphogenesis, openness and closedness, and positive and negative feedback, all emerged

as ways to understand the "system." Traditional focus on systemic constructs has, in many ways, been challenged by the emerging era of postmodern epistemological perspectives. The postmodern movement has shifted attention from the relationship to the "meaning" of events and situations within individuals in an attempt to recognize the role of self-reference and the individual in the systemic process. The postmodern epistemology has, like other philosophical approaches before, spawned a number of models of schools of practice (e.g., narrative therapy). More recently, there has been an emerging interest in approaches that focus on the integration of older models, as well as the emergence of a variety of new approaches. Furthermore, the notions of "common factors" has replaced integrated theory as the basis of practice for some. Finally, we are only now experiencing the beginning of what some have labeled "mature clinical models" or those approaches that are by definition integrative, clinically responsive, and meaning focused, with attention directed to multiple systems (individual, family, and environment).

## THE HANDBOOK OF FAMILY THERAPY: THE SCIENCE AND PRACTICE OF WORKING WITH FAMILIES AND COUPLES

Out of this changing context, the *Handbook of Family Therapy: The Science and Practice of Working with Families and Couples* emerges. In that regard, this volume comes at a historic time—a new era, if you will—in the evolution of marriage and family theory, practice, and research. Many of the primary practice models used to approach work with couples and families have undergone significant refinements as a result of both theory development and clinical research. Some of these refinements are based upon new epistemological perspectives that are having a major impact on practice by expanding on and further developing the early systemic notions that initially underpinned the field. In addition, the theoretical models of understanding family dynamics and clinical problems have evolved from the founding concepts of systems theory into more refined notions of family functioning, adaptability, and resiliency. As a result, the focus of therapy has broadened to a true multisystemic focus that includes individuals, families, and the social context in which they exist. The maturation of couple and family work is also represented by the fact that there are now clinical models that have more than 30 years of sustained, systematic, and theoretically guided outcome and process research available to inform clinical practice. It is a field poised to move well beyond the general principles of common factors to integrated, systematic models of effective practice. The field has also ventured into increasingly specialized arenas, slowly expanding its realm of practice. These various developments represent significant advances in the field of couple and family therapy. These advances also represent a developmental trajectory from the early period of revolutionaries and theoretical zealots to the current era of mature multisystemic clinical models (although not very many) that integrate research, theory, and clinical wisdom in a systematic way.

We suggest that the current era of family therapy, presented in this volume, represents a paradigm shift that is unique across all of the helping professions. The paradigm shift is built upon the convergence of three powerful and sometimes independent "threads" in (1) clinical practice, (2) ecologically valid clinical research into the change mechanisms and outcomes of therapy, and (3) a broadening of systemic theory and epistemological development. In a new era it is possible to embrace the diversity (from the postmodern to the traditional approaches), to promote a diversity of science (from qualitative to quantitative methods), and to integrate science, practice, and systemic theory to produce clinical interventions in which we have confidence. To do so, we must appreciate and value our history, acknowledge our foundational constructs, build on our founding theoretical models, and include diverse perspectives.

The promise of this new era is to take advantage of these advances in order to "seize the day" and build a new generation of mature clinical approaches and new conceptual ideas that will stand the test of time. The challenge of this era is to "savor the dialectic" within our complex field and accept and embrace the inevitable tensions that emerge when integrating theoretical perspectives (e.g., postmodern and manualized protocols) and science in clinical settings (e.g., randomized clinical trials vs. community effectiveness and case study methods). In a sense we are suggesting that if we can "savor the dialectic," we can accept that putting science into practice and practice into science is an inevitable and enduring quality of our profession. From our perspective, this era is one in which we can accept that the only true functional perspective is that experienced by the clients, and that our different epistemological perspectives are united by a common purpose that demands a more inclusive embodiment of methodologies, perspectives, and conceptual models. Inclusiveness and respect for different perspectives have been central themes of MFT that were lost in the struggle of the last 2 decades. We suggest that an inclusive acceptance of difference and "savoring the dialectic" represent themes of a maturing field that will include all good ideas, while the field distances itself from unscientific and atheoretical approaches to family therapy. The challenge of the new era will be whether or not we have the courage to question the foundational ideas that are part of our history, in order to forge a new future. This volume can serve as both a marker of and a stimulus to pursue the new era.

We intend this volume to be more than a compendium of information on family and couple therapy. The handbook is a developmental marker that describes what family therapy has become by chronicling the newest developments of the field. More important, the book launches the new paradigm by laying out the future agenda for theory development, clinical practice, and family research for the next 2 decades. As such, this text follows the three major threads that are powering the evolution of family therapy: family therapy practice, clinical research, and systemic theory.

Our goal in developing the *Handbook of Family Therapy: The Science and Practice of Working with Families and Couples* is to move the newest information of family and marital therapy into the forefront of both educational and practice settings. We intend for the book to review the major theoretical approaches and break new ground by identifying and describing the new era of evidence-based models and current areas of application. As such, it is intended to be the primary desk reference for theory, practice, and research in the field. It will function as a reference book for all couple and family therapy practitioners seeking the most current knowledge in the field; for couple and family therapy researchers interested in identifying the current research trends, current status, or both of our empirical knowledge base; and for training professionals who are looking for content resources. The use of this volume will be as a text in graduate courses in couple and family therapy programs and as a secondary text in counseling, social work, and family psychology graduate programs and courses. As such, the *Handbook of*

*Family Therapy* is, a historical event, as well as an important reference.

## DEVELOPMENT AND ORGANIZATION OF THE VOLUME

Because the handbook is intended to be representative of the field, we established an advisory board, composed of leaders in the field, who provided guidance, comments, and advice on the overall direction and content of this volume. The advisory board consisted of James F. Alexander, PhD (former president of Division 43-Family Psychology of APA); Froma Walsh, PhD (former editor of the *Journal of Marital and Family Therapy*); Karen Wampler, PhD (current editor of the *Journal of Marital and Family Therapy*); Terry Trepper, PhD (*Journal of Family Psychotherapy* editor); and Terence Patterson, Ed.D., ABPP (current president of Division 43-Family Psychology of APA). Along with the editors, the advisory board helped develop content areas and identify chapter authors who are expert in the specific area and who represent the most current thinking on the topic. In addition, the advisory board helped in developing chapter outlines that facilitate the best dissemination of the topic at hand. We are grateful for the input, guidance, and support from our advisory board.

In producing a volume like this, we, along with the advisory board, had to make a number of assumptions in order to best represent the diverse domain of family and couple therapy in a way that was both inclusive and yet systematic. First, it is now more common to talk about couple, rather than marital, therapy. This change reflects and acknowledges an evolution of our ideas of what constitutes a committed dyadic relationship. In this volume we refer, whenever possible, to couple, rather than marital, relationships.

Second, we find a field in which overlap between couple and family therapy is minimal; research and model builders seem to restrict themselves to one or the other domain. This trend is apparent in reviews and meta-analyses and the many theoretical publications of recent times. In this volume we include both but approach them as two domains that are different but overlapping, sharing common constructs, with different recent histories and current developmental trajectories, but as representatives of a common field of practice. Finally, after long debate we decided to use the name *Handbook of Family Therapy*. This decision is based in our belief that the title reflects a volume that will be an important marker in the current and future development of the field of family and couple therapy. We added the subtitle, The Science and Practice of Working With Families and Couples, to differentiate it from the work of Gurman and Kniskern.

This volume is organized into five major sections. *Part I: Understanding Families and Couples: The Foundations of Practice* lays the groundwork for the sections that follow. These chapters are intended to review the developmental status of the field and the current status of both our traditional and our more mature models of family and couple practice and science. This section begins with a review of our epistemological history or the history of our ideas. These ideas are the foundation of the new era that faces the profession. A multisystemic perspective is provided to capture the complex understanding of individuals and family members in their social context that guides current couple and family interventions. Finally, we revisit the notions of culture, gender, and ethnicity as threads that reach through the fiber of each model and intervention in the field. Our hope is that these constructs lay the groundwork for the theories and models of practice that follow in later sections.

*Part II: Major Theoretical Models of Couple and Family Therapy* provides an overview of the traditional theoretical models of family therapy. These models serve either directly or indirectly as guides to practice. Our goals were to provide chapters that not only identify the primary theoretical constructs of each theory but also highlight the ideas that have emerged during the last 2 decades. Although there are many theories, these were chosen for inclusion because they best represent the range of traditional theory of the field. To provide continuity in the presentation of information, all chapter authors were asked to organize their content using the following outline:

1. History and background of the approach
2. Major theoretical constructs
3. Proposed etiology of clinical problems
4. Methods of clinical assessment
5. Clinical change mechanisms/curative factors
6. Specific therapeutic interventions
7. Effectiveness of the approach
8. Future developments/directions

The chapters in *Part III: Evidence-Based Couple and Family Intervention Programs* look at the current status of outcome and process research in the field and the specific clinical models that have emerged from this work. In a way the clinical models presented here show how the advances in clinical research have an impact on practice through systematic, comprehensive, research-based clinical treatment models. These research-based models are examples of the potential future directions (thus, the new paradigm) of evidence-based couple and family therapy practice. This section is not intended to be a comprehensive list of the "evidence-based approaches" but instead is intended to provide the best examples of family and couple therapy (two illustrative approaches of each area) approaches that illustrate how clinical models can be theoretically integrative, evidence-based, and clinically responsive. To provide continuity, all chapter authors were asked to organize their presentations using the following outline:

1. History and background of the approach
2. Major theoretical and research-based constructs
3. Research evidence that supports the model
4. Research-based treatment protocol
5. Methods of model evaluation
6. Implementation of the model in community/practice settings.

*Part IV: Special Applications/Special Populations* represents the application of these research and theoretical trends in the special populations in which couple and family therapy is practiced. Again, this is not an exhaustive presentation of all the areas in which MFT is successfully practiced. Instead, this section represents the ways in which MFT continues to push the limits of practice. To provide continuity in the presentation, all chapter authors were asked to organize their contributions using the following outline:

1. Nature/extent of the special problem—what is unique in this area?
2. Special needs of the problem/area—why does it require a special approach?
3. Special approaches that work—demonstrated approaches that "work"
4. Evaluation/research evidence of the approach
5. Future developments/directions in the specific area

*Part V: The Future of Couple and Family Therapy* is a look toward future trends that may guide the next decade in couple and family therapy. In the final chapter we (Sexton, Weeks, and Robbins) give our perspective on what is presented in this volume. Our goal in the chapter is to look to the future through the identification of trends that we might build upon for the next era of MFT.

## REFERENCES

Alexander, J. F., Holtzworth-Munroe, A., & Jameson, P. (1994). The process and outcome of marital and family therapy: Research review and evaluation. In A. E. Bergin & S. L. Garfield (Eds.), *Handbook of psychotherapy and behavior change* (4th ed., pp. 595-630). Oxford, England: Wiley.

Alexander, J. F., Sexton, T. L., & Robbins, M. S. (2002). The developmental status of family therapy in family psychology intervention science. In H. Liddle, D. Santisteban, R. Levant, & J. Bray (Eds.), Family psychology intervention science. Washington, DC: American Psychological Association.

Chambless, D. L., & Hollon, S. D. (1998). Defining empirically supported therapies. *Journal of Consulting & Clinical Psychology, 66*(1), 7–18

Gurman, A. S., & Kniskern, D. P. (Eds.). (1981). *Handbook of family therapy*. New York: Brunner/Mazel.

Gurman, A. S., & Kniskern, D. P. (Eds.). (1991). *Handbook of family therapy* (Vol. 2). New York: Brunner/Mazel.

Liddle, H. A., Santisteban, D. A., Levant, R. F., & Bray, J. H. (2002). *Family psychology: Science-based interventions*. Washington, DC: American Psychological Association.

Pinsof, W. M., & Wynne, L. C. (2000). Toward progress research: Closing the gap between family therapy practice and research. *Journal of Family and Marital Therapy 26*, 1–8.

Sexton, T. L., & Alexander, J. F. (2002). Family-based empirically supported interventions. *The Counseling Psychologist, 30*(2), 238–261.

Sexton, T. L., Alexander, J. F., & Mease, A. L. (in press). Levels of evidence for the models and mechanisms of therapeutic change in couple and family therapy. In M. Lambert (Ed), *Handbook of psychotherapy and behavior change*. New York: Wiley.

U.S. Public Health Service. (1999). Mental health: A report of the Surgeon General. Rockville, MD: U.S. Department of Health and Human Services, National Institutes of Health, National Institute of Mental Health.

U.S. Public Health Service. (2001). Youth violence:

A report of the Surgeon General. Washington, DC: Author.

Wampold, B. E., Lichtenberg, J. W., & Walhler, C. A. (2002). Principles of empirically supported interventions in counseling psychology. The Counseling Psychologist, 30(2), 197–217.

# PART I

# Understanding Families and Couples

## *The Foundations of Practice*

### SECTION INTRODUCTION

The current family and couple therapy intervention models and theories are a product of the dynamic evolution of epistemological foundations of the field. The ways in which we think about the families we work with, their problems, and change are inexorably tied to our concepts of family functioning and family dynamics. Systems theory was the early foundation for family therapy, but we have made significant advances in our understanding of how families work since the application of this general theory to the family. The field has increasingly turned its attention to include a focus on successful "functioning" of families. Thus, increasingly, the foundations of our practice have moved toward family strengths and resiliency and understanding problems with a consideration of social and ecological context, as well as an appreciation of the specific meanings of family members in their unique settings. In changing perspectives the field is increasingly informed by the postmodern and constructivist epistemologies that emphasize meaning. Within the evolution

of thinking in this field, a focus on culture and ethnicity has continued to be a primary guide.

Three chapters make up Part I of the handbook. In Chapter 1, Becvar describes how the dynamic evolution of the ideas that form the foundation of the field is also the foundation of the techniques and perspectives of practice. This evolution represents a series of changing eras of thinking and of our own belief systems. The current multisystemic, systemic, and evidence-based ideas are increasingly the foundation of current practice. In Chapter 2, Szapocznik and Robbins present a multisystemic perspective on family functioning and strength-based approaches to family developmental and relational functioning. Couple and family theory is now multisystemic or multilayered, considering individual dynamics, family functioning, and context. In Chapter 3, Falicov presents an integrative picture of the role of culture, gender, and race as a foundation of practice, research, and theory. These three presentations are intended to be the foundation of the theory, research, and special applications that follow in later sections.

1

CHAPTER 1

# Eras of Epistemology

## A Survey of Family Therapy Thinking and Theorizing

DOROTHY S. BECVAR, PhD

*The Haelan Centers, St. Louis, MO*

## INTRODUCTION

The idea of working with entire families was a unique aspect of a transformation in thinking and theorizing that ushered in a new discipline in the field of mental health—that of family therapy. Moving away from a strict focus on individuals and their psyches, consideration began to be given to relationship systems and the contexts in which people live, problems emerge, and solutions may be found. Often perceived as merely a different technique, this shift to working with families, in fact, signaled the beginning of a scientific revolution and the emergence of an alternative paradigm (Kuhn, 1970).

A paradigm, according to Thomas Kuhn (1970), is a set of presuppositions regarding the nature of the world, the problems within that world worthy of investigation, and the appropriate methods for investigating the par-

ticular problems thus identified. It is a coherent belief system by means of which scientists know and attempt to understand reality, providing a relatively inflexible framework within which solutions are sought during periods of normal science. The appearance of anomalies not explainable by the rules of the paradigm initiates a crisis characterized by a search for new explanations and a period of extraordinary science in which basic beliefs are subject to reconstruction. A paradigm shift occurs with the establishment of an alternative belief system, by means of which the world is seen from a different perspective and old events take on new meaning.

Gregory Bateson (1972), anthropologist and major contributor to the paradigm shift represented by systems theory/cybernetics and family therapy, used the term *epistemology* synonymously with *paradigms*, applying it not only to the theoretical frameworks of scientists

3

but also to the personal interpretive systems used by individuals. Epistemology, in a more general sense, is a branch of philosophy concerned with studying how people know and the ways in which valid knowledge claims based on a particular theoretical framework may or may not be made. Included in such study is the consideration of assumptions underlying a theoretical framework and the degree to which assertions derived from the framework are consistent with these assumptions.

When used to denote personal belief systems, epistemology describes internalized theories that enable people to give order and predictability to their lives, the means by which individual realities are created. Although generally outside of conscious awareness, personal theories are learned in families of origin, in school, and from other meaningful events and encounters in each person's life. Like scientific theories, such personal theories rest on a set of assumptions regarding the nature of the world, and they guide and limit the way in which one both perceives and creates experience.

The theoretical framework upon which much of family therapy initially was based and according to which the world, including individuals and families, came to be understood is perhaps this discipline's most distinctive feature. For, from the systemic/cybernetic perspective, more crucial than who is in the therapy room is how the therapist thinks about who is in the therapy room. Indeed, what family therapy ultimately is about, at many levels, is epistemology. And as the field has evolved since its beginnings in the late 1940s and early 1950s, so has its epistemology evolved in terms of philosophy, practice, and research, although often at different rates and in different ways. Thus we may define three epistemological domains and seek to understand the eras of epistemology within each. At the same time, it is important to recognize them as overlapping eras, as explorers in all

three domains mutually influenced and were influenced by one another and yet retained a degree of separation by virtue of their focus. Therefore, although appearing to be linear for purposes of the following discussions in which we survey the evolution of epistemology relative first to philosophy, next to practice, and then to research, the developmental process described must be recognized as one that is totally recursive.

## PHILOSOPHY

In Western society, the prevailing paradigm is based on the belief system proposed by John Locke and those who followed him. Described as the modernistic worldview (Gergen, 1991), this framework assumes linear causality, with reality understood as a phenomenon whose order is recognized rather than created. The world is believed to be deterministic and to operate according to law-like principles. Scientific study is reductionistic and individualistic, the appropriate methodology is empirical and quantitative, and knowledge must be pursued by means of observation and experimentation. Subjects are separate from the objects of observations, and reality and related theories are viewed primarily in terms of either/or, right or wrong explanations. In contrast to the Lockean paradigm, systems theory is consistent with the tradition labeled Kantian (Rychlak, 1981) and at the level of second-order cybernetics, with postmodernism (Becvar & Becvar, 2003). Rather than focusing on the individual and individual problems viewed in isolation, attention is given to relationships, relationship issues between individuals, and the contexts within which these issues emerge. The observer is understood to be part of the observed, with subjectivity inevitable as the one who is observing perceives, acts on, and participates in the co-creation of realities. Interactions are described in terms of a noncausal, dialectical process of mutual influence in which all parties are involved. An understanding of systems is derived from the assessment, or inference, of patterns of interaction, with an emphasis on what is happening in the here and now, rather than on why it is happening or in terms of a historical focus.

### Era I: The Paradigm Begins to Shift

The change in epistemology represented by systems theory/cybernetics emerged in the context of research related to weaponry and technology improvement during World War II (Heims, 1975). The new science, named cybernetics by mathematician Norbert Wiener and dating from approximately 1942, was unique in its focus on organization, pattern, and process, rather than on matter, material, and content. Cyberneticians were concerned with feedback mechanisms, information processing, and patterns of communication, studying inanimate machines and comparing them with living organisms in an effort to understand and control complex systems.

Bateson, an early investigator of cybernetic processes, provided the philosophical bridge from the physical to the behavioral sciences, with a particularly significant impact on the development of family therapy. His goal was the creation of a framework for understanding human behavior more adequate than those currently in use in the social sciences. To that end, his thinking was influenced significantly (Bateson & Mead, 1976) by the ideas of recursiveness and of teleology described by Rosenblueth, Wiener, and Bigelow (1943, p. 22), "as synonymous with 'purpose controlled by feedback.'"

Further explorations led to Bateson's integration of the theory of logical types (Whitehead & Russell, 1910) with communication and information processing within a cybernetic perspective (Ruesch & Bateson, 1951).

Accordingly, he began to view various psychological constructs as informational processes. Indeed, cybernetics had resolved for him the ancient problem posed by dualistic thinking about mind and body; rather than being considered transcendent, mind could now be described as immanent in systems. Next, Bateson began to focus his research on the paradoxes of human communication in general and on schizophrenic communication in particular. By 1949, he and his research team were hypothesizing about the appropriateness of family therapy, questioning the traditional concept of psychosis as an illness, and considering the possibility of defining a schizophrenic episode as a "spontaneous initiation ceremony" (Heims, 1977, p. 153).

The double-bind hypothesis evolved toward the end of 1954 and 2 years later the landmark paper "Toward a Theory of Schizophrenia" (Bateson, Jackson, Haley, & Weakland, 1956) was published. This theory proposed that an inability to discriminate between levels of communication was the result of repeated experiences of a double bind in intense relationships. In the context of a relationship between mother and child, the outcome of such a situation was likely to be a pathology in communication and "symptoms whose formal characteristics would lead the pathology to be classified as schizophrenia" (Bateson, 1972, pp. 202–203). Although retaining aspects of a linear epistemology and focusing primarily on mothers as part of the problem, the basic message was revolutionary. At the time, psychodynamic theories were predominant, with insight the only means of change (Simon, 1982). By contrast, the Bateson group had described schizophrenia as an interpersonal, relational phenomenon, rather than as an intrapsychic disorder of the individual that secondarily influences interpersonal relationships.

As we discuss later, Bateson was not alone in proposing similar new ways of thinking. In addition, despite his preference for the term *cybernetics*, generally in the United States it was systems theory, following biologist Ludwig von Bertalanffy's (1968) use of "general system theory," with which family therapy became identified. Although considered by many to be less mechanistic than cybernetics, which is derived from an engineering perspective, systems theory, with its biological roots, shares a concern with feedback mechanisms and recursion.

### Era II: Paradigm Shift Completed

The fundamental and radical assumption of systems theory/cybernetics is recursion, or circular causality and behavior influenced by feedback. However, in the earlier era of the development of this perspective relative to family therapy, the notion of recursion was applied from a black box perspective, with observers outside a system attempting to observe what was going on inside the system. Using such constructs as boundaries, communication and information processing, entropy and negentropy, equifinality and equipotentiality, morphostasis and morphogenesis, openness and closedness, and positive and negative feedback, the goal was to assess and understand the system. Despite its relational and holistic focus, lacking was recognition of the role of self-reference, and thus the scientific revolution was not yet complete.

Only as a distinction was made between first-order and second-order cybernetics, with acknowledgment in the latter of the influence of observers on their observations, could we say that the paradigm shift truly had occurred. Bateson's particular contributions included his use of language, focus on logical types, recognition of the importance of metaphor, and the idea that information is the difference that makes a difference. In addition, Heinz von Foerster outlined the idea of observing systems; a related specific concern for ethics,

understood as the property of the observer; and the notion of constructivism, that in drawing distinctions the mind constructs reality (Glanville, 2001). Chilean biologists Humberto Maturana and Francisco Varela (1987) were responsible for describing the concepts of organizational closure, autopoiesis, and autonomy.

As family therapists began including such concepts in their thinking and theorizing (Keeney, 1983), recognition began to be given to the influence of therapists and their role in the definition of problems, as well as in the outcome of therapy. Also significant was the concept of a multiverse and the deconstruction of the idea of family as a unitary concept. Rather, each family member's perception of the system was acknowledged as valid and important, however different it might be from others'. The notion of a storied reality grew in acceptance, with awareness that minds construct reality and the process of such construction influences and is influenced by the larger societal context. Not only had the paradigm shift occurred, but it was consistent with further developments in the philosophical realm that also had an impact on family therapy.

### Era III: Postmodernism

Described variously as a critique (Anderson, 1997), "the principal intellectual issue of our time" (Lowe, 1991, p. 41), a perspective, and an era, postmodernism, like systems theory/cybernetics, calls into question the assumptions and beliefs fundamental to a modernist perspective. Accordingly, within many disciplines, the idea of certainty, as well as of the totalizing discourses, or metanarratives, by means of which society traditionally has been organized, is receiving close scrutiny. And family therapy is one of the fields affected significantly in terms of postmodern thinking and theorizing.

The primary challenge of postmodernism is offered by "the notion that our 'reality' is inevitably subjective and that we do indeed dwell in a multiverse that is constructed through the act of observation" (Becvar & Becvar, 2003, p. 91). Rather than discovering facts, we give recognition to perspectives and framework relativity. The idea of arriving at statements of absolute truth is no longer considered possible, nor can one make recourse to any "transcendent criterion of the correct" (Gergen, 1991, p. 111). Given this awareness, the power and privilege ascribed to those who previously were presumed to possess knowledge has been undermined, with the perspectives of all individuals understood as having validity in terms of personal truth.

A major focus of postmodernism is discourse and the role of language (Lowe, 1991). German philosopher Ludwig Wittgenstein proposed that language acquires meaning as a function of social practice, rather than as a referential base; French theorist Michel Foucault explored the power that culturally embedded languages have to expand or oppress; and philosopher Richard Rorty invited his colleagues to participate in the dialogues of society, rather than pursue their search for absolute truth (Gergen, 1994a, 1994b). What emerged from this alternative form of inquiry were both a caution against reifying the language of a community as true for any other than the members of that community and a focus on the limitations of local languages relative to what they exclude.

Language thus has come to be understood as the means by which the world is both known and constructed by each individual. Consistent with a constructivist emphasis, it is recognized that a description of reality is a function of one's beliefs and that all we can know are our interpretations of other people and things. From a radical constructivist perspective (von Glasersfeld, 1988), it is proposed further that, although a real reality may exist,

there is no way we may know it or represent it in any absolute sense. And with a social constructionist focus, greater consideration is given to the context within which language is created and becomes a defining framework for those who make recourse to it. As suggested by French theorist Jacques Derrida, the notion of an internal mind bounded by the skin is replaced by the concept of a nonlocal mind that is universal and empowering of all creatures and things. What is more, one's knowing is experienced and expressed through a system of language considered to have a separate existence (Gergen, 1985).

As postmodern thought penetrated the family therapy world, the use of terms such as *individual responsibility, homeostasis, resistance, pathology,* and *objectivity* were called into question (Piercy & Sprenkle, 1990). There was also increasing recognition that the predominant metanarratives in the social sciences and mental health practice were deficit-focused and pathology-based and that such narratives were a reflection more of their creators than of those about whom they theoretically were created. For postmodernism brings with it greater acceptance both of a storied reality and of a higher-order consciousness, an epistemology that has a conscious awareness of itself (Keeney, 1983).

With knowledge viewed as framework-relative, the assumption of hierarchy based on so-called experts with privileged information, and thus power, is undermined. Rather, everyone is understood to have expertise, the client on content and the therapist on process (Anderson, 1997). Relationships, which are of central importance, are understood to be co-created, and therapy becomes "an exercise in ethics; it involves the inviting, shaping, and reformulating of codes for living together" (Efran, Lukens, & Lukens, 1988, p. 27). The goal is the creation through dialogue of a context that accommodates the needs and desires of all participants.

Social constructionism also emphasizes the importance of context, of the way individuals and problems are created in relationship (Gergen, 1991). There is a dedication to understanding knowledge generation and the way in which strength-based and solution-focused narratives may participate in the creation of more humane realities for all individuals (Gale & Long, 1996). As "facts" are deconstructed by delineating the assumptions, values, and ideologies on which they are based, professionals are encouraged to take themselves and their constructions less seriously. Also encouraged is respect for the uniqueness of each client and client system. Indeed, "Constructivist models, with their emphasis on differing individual perspectives of reality, have led to models of therapy that have underscored the importance of conversation, of co-construction of problems and proposed solutions, of respect for individual differences" (Steinglass, 1991, p. 268).

The idea of second-order therapies emerged as a distinction, derived from the work of Maturana and Varela (1980), was made (Hoffman, 1985) between first-order, allopoietic, control models and second-order, autopoietic, autonomy models of living systems. True to a prediction that new models would be forthcoming, the final decades of the 20th century saw the appearance of several approaches to family therapy consistent with a second-order or postmodern stance. The thinking of creators of such approaches is discussed in the next section. However, as we move to a consideration of the eras of epistemology within the practice domain, we first must return to the early days of family therapy and the then current worldview.

## PRACTICE

As the assumptions of Lockean epistemology were translated from the physical sciences into the behavioral sciences, they became the foundation for a variety of theories and therapies focused on the individual. Accordingly, human behavior was considered to be determined either by internal events or by external environmental influences to which people react—or both. Approaches based primarily on either Freudian notions or reactions to them proliferated throughout the first half of the 20th century. By contrast, family therapy was not yet widespread. However, many clinicians and researchers, along with the theorists discussed previously, had adopted or were moving toward a systemic framework, including a focus on families, and had begun expanding their knowledge, delineating concepts, and enlarging the repertoire of techniques logical to the basic assumptions of the new perspective. And by the 1960s family therapy had gained considerable recognition.

### Era I: Early Explorations in Family Therapy

In the clinical world several key figures questioned the effectiveness of the prevailing focus on individuals for dealing with mental illness. In this realm, Nathan Ackerman represented the primary link between the intrapsychic and interactional approaches to therapy. Ackerman, author of the earliest publication in the field (1937), focused on "nonpsychotic disorders in children as related to the family environment" (Ackerman, 1967). By the 1940s, he was experimenting with having both mother and child seen in therapy together, rather than splitting their treatment as consistent with more traditional models. He also began sending staff members on home visits in order to understand the families with whom they were working (Guerin, 1976).

During family therapy's early years, there was a division along ideological lines between those intrapsychically oriented and those more systemic. Ackerman, the leading proponent of the former position, combined psychodynamic theory and the concept of social role to understand the ongoing interaction between heredity and environment, as well as the maintenance of homeostasis within and between the person, the family, and society. Rather than emphasizing interactional sequences and patterns of communication, his primary focus was the psychological impact of families on individuals (Nichols & Schwartz, 2001). Thus, his most significant contributions to the field included a shift in focus from individuals to interpersonal interactions, as well as clinical artistry, rather than the construction of theory or creation of a school of thought.

Murray Bowen's major contribution was one of the most complete and elegant theories of family therapy to emerge from this discipline. By 1950, he was focusing on mother–child symbiosis, on the assumption that "schizophrenia was the result of an unresolved tie with the mother" (Hoffman, 1981, p. 29). The next year he began having children diagnosed with schizophrenia reside with their mothers for several months in a clinical setting. In 1954, Bowen instituted and directed the classic study in which entire families of patients diagnosed with schizophrenia were hospitalized for observation and research. He then directed his attention to the articulation of his approach. Among the more important contributions of Bowenian family therapy, or natural systems theory, are the concepts of *triangulation*, *intergenerational transmission*, *differentiation of self*, and *undifferentiated family ego mass*, as well as the *genogram* (Bowen, 1978).

Carl Whitaker, also a psychiatrist by training and psychodynamic in original orientation, assumed a stance diametrically opposed to that of Bowen in his advocacy of an atheoretical approach to family therapy. As a function of circumstances, he began doing co-therapy, which became a trademark of his work; included the spouses and children of patients in therapy; and eventually insisted on the presence of three generations. Particularly interested in the treatment of schizophrenia, he evolved what he ultimately defined as an experiential symbolic approach, or a "psychotherapy of the absurd" (Whitaker, 1975). Accordingly, the therapist goes crazy so that the client may become sane, with a concurrent focus on growth for everyone involved.

Ivan Boszormenyi-Nagy also emphasized the impact of intergenerational processes in families. Particularly significant in terms of its introduction of an ethical dimension, Nagy's contextual therapy centers around the notion that trust and loyalty are the crucial dimensions in relationships. Families must have *balanced ledgers* relative to these dimensions, and the goal of therapy is the ethical redefinition of the relational context such that trustworthiness is a mutually merited phenomenon and concern for future generations provides the impetus for health (Boszormenyi-Nagy, 1966).

John Elderkin Bell, one of the first to see entire families, based his approach on the theory of group dynamics and group psychotherapy (1961). Christian Midelfort (1951) included family members in outpatient therapy and had the relatives of hospitalized patients act as nurses' aides and companions who supervised various therapies, took part in patient interviews, and served to minimize the risk of problematic behaviors.

## Era II: The Creation of Models

A variety of models and more complete approaches to family therapy appeared during the 1960s and 1970s. The communications and strategic approaches grew out of work at the Mental Research Institute (MRI) in Palo Alto. The MRI was opened in 1959 by Don Jackson, a psychiatrist, who contributed the notion of balance in families, as well as descriptions of the basic rules of communication. The MRI may be credited with such fundamental assumptions as all behavior is communication at some level; communication has both a report, or digital, level and a command, or analog, level and it is the latter that defines the nature of a relationship; to understand behavior, one must consider it in context; systems are characterized by rules, by means of which balance is maintained; relationships may be described as symmetrical, with exchanges of similar behavior, or complementary, with exchanges of opposite behaviors; each person has a personal belief system according to which reality is experienced and understood and which is that person's truth; and problems are maintained in the context of recurrent patterns of communication (Watzlawick, Beavin, & Jackson, 1967). With these basic principles in mind, therapy involves a process that includes (1) defining the problem in clear, concrete terms; (2) investigating all previous attempted solutions; (3) defining the desired change in clear, concrete terms; and (4) formulating and implementing a strategy for change (Watzlawick, 1978).

Virginia Satir added to an initial focus on communication, and particularly on incongruencies between the levels of messages, an emphasis on emotional growth and self-esteem. Hers is a process model (Satir, 1982), one that also might fit in the experiential category. Satir focused primarily on helping to enhance the lives of those with whom she worked, both clients and trainees. She saw families as balanced, rule-governed systems that provide the context for the natural movement toward growth and development of all members. Therapy, which is necessitated by an impasse in the growth process, aims to facilitate the ability of family members to access their inherent physical, intellectual, emotional, sensual, interactional, contextual, nutritional, and spiritual resources. Important

to this process is the recognition of mutual influence and shared responsibility, as clients move toward wholeness in the supportive context of therapy. Specific constructs that are the hallmarks of Satir's model include the *primary survival triad* of parents and child; the triad of *body, mind, and feelings*, with recognition that body parts and problems may be metaphors for emotional distress; and the communication stances of *placating, blaming, superreasonable, irrelevant,* and *congruent.* Her therapeutic strategies included the *family life fact chronology,* sculpting, modeling effective communication, humor, and games, all aimed at helping clients to grow.

Jay Haley (1963) also focused first on the levels of communication but shifted to a consideration of relationships, emphasizing the power tactics he felt were an inevitable aspect of human interaction. Building on the MRI's four-step process for change, Haley concentrated on families, with an emphasis on the importance of hierarchy and recognition that it is the triad by means of which family stability is maintained. He was concerned with behavior sequences, communication patterns, and symptoms as control mechanisms. He labeled himself strategic, based on his method-oriented and problem-focused approach to designing unique strategies to attain clients' goals. He encouraged interventions, by means of either directives or paradoxical injunctions or both, to shift the covert hierarchical structure, as well to replace symptomatic metaphors with those that were more adaptive.

The focus of Salvador Minuchin was the family's patterns of interaction, understood as providing information about the *structure* and *organization* of the system. According to his theory, structure is constrained by those characteristics generic to all families, as well as by the characteristics unique or idiosyncratic to each family. Important aspects of the organization of a family are its subsystems, including the spousal, the parental, and the sibling.

Crucial to the functioning of these subsystems are their boundaries and the degree to which they are clear, rigid, or diffuse and by means of which an appropriate hierarchy is or is not being maintained. In therapy, the goal is to facilitate structural change so that new, more functional patterns may emerge. This goal is achieved through observation of spontaneous behavioral sequences or enactments of problematic interactions. The therapist acts as a director, using intensity to enable clients to understand important information and shaping competence to foster more functional behavior (Minuchin, 1974).

Behavioral family therapists applied the principles of learning theory to their work with client systems. Emerging in the middle to late 1960s, the goal of this approach is to provide a safe environment for learning new and expanding old behavioral alternatives, developing skills, and enabling individuals to deal more effectively with each other and with relationship problems. Crucial aspects include research and evaluation, with a focus in such areas as behavioral marital therapy, behavioral parent training, and conjoint sex therapy. Behavioral/cognitive approaches to family therapy also consider the thought processes and worldview of individuals, as well as the impact of feelings on behavior.

## Era III: Challenge, Controversy, Integration, and Innovation

The period of model creation saw the establishment of distinct schools of family therapy, each with its respected leaders and proponents. By the late 1970s and early 1980s, the field was coming of age and the excitement it generated was palpable. However, family therapists soon found themselves facing challenges and controversy on several fronts. And by the end of the era, their thinking and theorizing had changed dramatically, with a focus on the integration of older models and the emergence of a variety of new approaches.

The feminist critique, one of the first and most significant challenges, focused on the lack of attention previously paid to gender-related issues in both theory and therapy. Rachel Hare-Mustin (1978) and others criticized family therapists for failing to consider the larger context in their descriptions of family dysfunction, adhering to the notion of mutual responsibility for the formation of problems, perceiving mothers as the source of family pathology, and assuming a neutral stance in therapy. Much of this critique was directed specifically at systems theory, considered problematic, given its use of mechanistic metaphors to describe family dysfunction and the belief that it blinded adherents to the influence of the larger social, political, and economic context.

With its rejection of the idea of unilateral control, systems theory was censured for its failure to acknowledge the power relationships inherent in our patriarchal society. Family therapists thus were chastised for their participation, however inadvertent, in maintaining a sexist status quo. Even more repugnant was the idea of circular causality as applied particularly to such problems as battering, rape, and incest. Accordingly, rather than the therapist looking for cause or placing blame, it was perceived that the family therapist "subtly removes responsibility for his behavior from the man while implying that the woman is co-responsible, and in some ways plays into the interactional pattern which results in violence and abuse" (Avis, 1988, p. 17). To remedy this situation, feminists suggested that family therapists discuss with clients gender-related issues, self-disclose their biases, and emphasize the strengths, needs, and specific ways in which women may be empowered (Avis, 1988). The challenge was to accept "gender as an irreducible category of clinical observation and theorizing" (Goldner, 1985,

p. 22). Also called for was an ongoing self-examination relative to honesty, responsibility, and integrity and a consideration of whether the practice of the family therapist "is the most ethical, effective, and humane treatment for women" (Wheeler, 1985, p. 55).

By the early 1990s, following years of conflict, a more collegial dialogue between feminists and their family therapy colleagues had been established, with the emergence of postmodernism a significant aid in this regard. Nevertheless, though agreeing with radical constructivists that families may not be "real" in the same sense that a living organism is real, feminists continued to remind therapists that people and societies live and act as if families were real. Furthermore, they noted the crucial need to recognize that quality of life may be determined by political categories and that the social consequences of therapeutic conversations cannot be ignored. Therapists, therefore, were advised to become sensitive to their use of language and to avoid participation in the maintenance of prevailing ideologies, especially given their perceived expertise, and thus power, relative to the implicit hierarchy that always exists, despite efforts to the contrary. Indeed, the issue of hierarchy (Simon, 1993) was also an important catalyst for the revision of old models and the creation of newer, second-order or postmodern, approaches to family therapy.

Prior to their emergence, however, there was recognition by the early 1980s that in order to be truly effective, therapists needed to have at least some knowledge of all the therapies, rather than being single-theory practitioners. Concurrently, there was a growing interest in the creation of eclectic and integrative approaches to therapy, categorized as either (1) pluralism, or the peaceful coexistence of models, with an understanding that each offers something meaningful and useful; (2) theoretical integration, or the creation of an umbrella theory or metatheory that captures the central aspects of a variety of theories; or (3) technical/systematic eclecticism, or the use of techniques whose effectiveness with specific problems or clients has been demonstrated (Held, 1995).

For many reasons (Lebow, 1997), integration found much support from family therapists. Arising initially within the discipline, they focused first on merging various models (e.g., Bischof, 1993; Fraser, 1982). Other formats included those that crossed disciplines and integrated, for example, individual and family approaches (e.g., Braverman, 1995; Pinsof, 1994) or family therapy and family medicine (Doherty & Baird, 1983). However, perhaps their most significant contributions are metaframeworks that acknowledge the wider systemic contexts within which individuals and families live (e.g., Breunlin, Schwartz, & MacKune-Karrer, 1992; Rigazio-Digilio, 1994). One of the earliest and most evidence-based examples is functional family therapy (Alexander & Parsons, 1973, 1982; Alexander & Sexton, 2002; Barton & Alexander, 1981; Morris, Alexander, & Waldron, 1988; Sexton & Alexander, 2002).

Indeed, consistent with a postmodern awareness, theorists, therapists, and researchers are challenged to become sensitive to one-size-fits-all approaches to problem resolution. Integrative approaches and metaframeworks attempt to respect the uniqueness of each client system, considering such factors as race, gender, class, socioeconomic status, and developmental stage in the design of interventions. Accordingly, various older techniques and models are subsumed under the umbrella of a larger organizing theory. In addition, revisions within the field have also taken the form of several newer approaches whose explicit intent was the incorporation of the basic assumptions of a postmodern perspective.

Tom Andersen, a Norwegian family physician, became curious about the social context of illness, experimenting with many of the concepts of the seminal models of family therapy. However, he did not achieve the desired results and was bothered particularly by the stance of therapist as expert, whose deliberations were hidden from the client. He thus developed a reflecting team approach (Andersen, 1992), according to which therapy includes the therapist, the client, and a team of silent observers, whose members at some point are invited to share their reflections on what they saw taking place. Such reflections are offered respectfully and tentatively, with the intent of expanding the ways in which a situation may be viewed, leading to new understandings and new views of self.

William O'Hanlon also focuses on the framework of meaning according to which problems are defined and solutions are thus limited. Building on the work of Milton Erickson, O'Hanlon is pragmatic, emphasizes the way in which perception and meaning are embedded in language, and encourages the search for newer, more useful perspectives. Therapy is a conversational process that involves joining with the client, allowing the client to describe the problem, uncovering exceptions to the problem, normalizing, and goal-setting (O'Hanlon & Weiner-Davis, 1989). The therapist is active, directing the conversation toward goal-oriented solutions, validating clients' experiences, moving clients toward actions that lead to their goals, and emphasizing solution-oriented stories.

Similarly, Steve de Shazer (1991) has created a solution-focused approach according to which clients' goals, rather than their problems, are emphasized. Clients are encouraged to understand that a single situation may be given many different meanings and that their lives are filled with exceptions during which the problem does not exist. The therapist utilizes language games, sometimes creatively misunderstanding and always preferring progressive narratives that stress solution themes. Clients are asked the miracle question, in response to which they are to articulate the changes desired in their lives, and it is the achievement of these changes that is the focus of therapy.

Narrative family therapy has evolved from the work of Australian family therapist Michael White and his colleague from New Zealand David Epston. Particularly focused on helping clients to create and live their own personal stories, rather than being lived by the more generic, metanarratives of society, both seek to *externalize,* or separate the problem from the person; search for unique outcomes that reveal gaps in clients' stories; and facilitate the reauthoring of their lives (White & Epston, 1990). Particularly highlighting language, the emphasis on stories takes both oral and written forms. For example, Epston (1994) makes use of letters describing his thinking about the therapy process that he sends to clients. Clients thereby are encouraged to understand the storied nature of reality in the process of resolving the problems that brought them to therapy.

Harlene Anderson and Harry Goolishian (1988) developed a language system approach to working with clients, in an effort to move away from the extreme focus of earlier models on intervention and change. In their view, an attitude of not-knowing and the facilitation of caring, empathic conversations that are respectful and collaborative are the means for assisting in the co-creation of new stories that enable clients to live more meaningful lives. Believing that it is the problem that creates the system, they encourage conversations in which problems are dis-solved and one's sense of self is re-constructed.

Such approaches emphasize collaboration, respect for the expertise of both clients and therapist, and the idea that there may be many meanings or ways that people may be. Above all, there is a focus on ethics and a reminder of the degree to which therapists may participate in the creation of problems, as well as of solutions. With their emergence, however, has come a variety of tensions, many of them centered in the research domain. And once again, we return to an earlier era and work our way forward.

## RESEARCH

The scientific methodology consistent with a Lockean, modernist epistemology emphasizes the importance of objectivity and values most highly measurable, quantifiable data. Root causes are the focus, and attention is directed toward history or previous events in an effort to understand human behavior and find solutions to current problems. The goal is to reduce behavior to the lowest common denominator, considering either the individual and the individual's specific behaviors or the internal events of the human mind.

Much of the early thinking and theorizing that led to the development of family therapy emerged in the context of research based on this methodology. As the field evolved, the focus shifted from etiology to demonstrating the effectiveness of various approaches. Currently, there are yet other movements, one toward more clinically relevant research and the other toward empirically validated therapy that meets the requirements for greater accountability. At the same time, and almost from its inception, the field has been characterized by an ongoing tension and debate between proponents of the traditional quantitative methodologies and those who prefer more qualitative approaches.

### Era I: Etiologic Research

As was evident in previous discussions, research, particularly on schizophrenia, was a catalyst for much of the early thinking and theorizing about the influence of families and

relationships on the causes and treatment of mental illness. In addition to those approaches already discussed, the work of Theodore Lidz and Lyman Wynne is also particularly worthy of note. Both had as their primary focus the research and treatment of schizophrenia, were psychodynamic in original orientation, and are identified more with specific conceptual contributions than with comprehensive models.

Lidz concluded from his studies of families in which a member was diagnosed with schizophrenia that the influence of fathers could be equal to that of mothers (Lidz & Lidz, 1949). He rejected the Freudian notion that schizophrenia is caused by fixation in the oral stage, followed by stress-induced regression in young adulthood. He also refuted the belief that schizophrenia is caused by maternal rejection and included in his observations the entire maturation period, rather than just infancy. And Lidz was responsible for defining the concepts of *marital schism* and *marital skew*. Marital schism is characterized by an inability to achieve role reciprocity or complementarity of purpose, as each member of a couple attempts to coerce the other into meeting his or her expectations. As part of this process, each may distrust the motivation and attempt to undermine the position of the other, particularly in the realm of parenting. Marital skew occurs when there is one strong and one weak spouse and the strong spouse allows the weak spouse to dominate. In this case, conflict is masked, with a lack of acknowledgment of discrepancies between what is felt and what is admitted (Simon, Stierlin, & Wynne, 1985). Lidz's focus was relational and holistic, emphasizing the interaction of family communication patterns and role relationships with individual developmental processes. He thus moved from a belief in individual pathology to a consideration of family dynamics as the matrix out of which pathology may emerge, a foundational idea in the development of family therapy.

Wynne similarly concluded that the significance of the family must be recognized, that role relationships are of vital importance, and that understanding pathology requires a focus on communication patterns. In addition to a program of research on schizophrenia that has continued throughout his career, Wynne's major conceptual contributions include the notions of *pseudomutuality, pseudohostility,* and the *rubber fence.* Pseudomutuality refers to "a predominant absorption in fitting together at the expense of the differentiation of identities of the persons in the relation" (Wynne, Ryckoff, Day, & Hirsch, 1958, p. 207). In families characterized by a pseudomutual pattern, the members are focused on the whole and family-centeredness is maintained by a flexible but nonstable boundary known as a rubber fence. This boundary is composed of rules that are in continual flux, as the family opens to admit what it considers acceptable and closes in an unpredictable manner to exclude what is not acceptable. The context is one of confusion and enmeshment, and communication, individual perceptions, and identity formation all become problematic. By contrast, pseudohostility refers to a superficial alienation of family members that masks their needs for intimacy and affection, as well as a deeper level of chronic conflict and alienation. A distortion of communication and perceptual impairment is reflected, as rational thinking about relationships is obstructed.

## Era II: Early Efficacy and Evidence-Based Research

As various models and approaches to family therapy were created and continued to evolve, it became appropriate to provide evidence to support their proponents' claims for success. Accordingly, throughout the 1970s and 1980s attention was directed to research questions regarding whether family therapy was effective; which approaches were most effective; how effectiveness was influenced by therapist, client, or treatment factors, or any combination of these; and the problems of measurement relative to family therapy research, as well as future research issues in need of attention (Piercy, Sprenkle, & Associates, 1986, p. 330). The use of the randomized, clinical trial was considered the ideal methodology, providing scientific legitimacy through the use of rigorous definitions, or operationalization, of the therapy process.

When a host of studies ultimately was reviewed (Gurman & Kniskern, 1978, 1981; Gurman, Kniskern, & Pinsof, 1986; Pinsof, 1981; Todd & Stanton, 1983), it was possible to conclude that family therapy was as effective and in some cases more so than individual therapy. Further conclusions were that effective communication was the key to success in marital therapy and that the outcome was likely to be more positive when the members of a couple were seen together, rather than in individual therapy. The rate of success for family therapy was found to be comparable with that of individual therapy, and certain therapist styles were reported to be most salient relative to negative outcomes.

The many analyses of family therapy research now available also have revealed much greater specificity in terms of approaches appropriate for different types of problems, different age groups, and so forth. At the same time, as we have moved into an era of managed care and reimbursement by third-party payers, the need to expand research and demonstrate efficacy has grown in importance. Fortunately, recent studies (Pinsof & Wynne, 1995; Pinsof, Wynne, & Hambright, 1996) continue to validate effectiveness, and it has been noted that relative to family therapy, "outcomes have been found as good as or better than other approaches to psychotherapy" (Pinsof & Wynne, 1995, p. 342).

*Era III: Current Trends and Issues*

Despite the wealth of information available from a multitude of research studies and reviews, clinicians consistently have found these results to be less than helpful. There thus have been repeated calls over the years for more relevant research, with a particular emphasis on the specifics of the therapeutic process (Hawley, Bailey, & Pennick, 2000). Some have advocated for a research emphasis on utility, or what works in therapy (Amundson, 2000), whereas others support inclusion of the perspectives of clients, as well as of clinicians (Miller & Duncan, 2000). Indeed, although traditional outcome research results may offer direction in broad general terms, their impact on the way that most marriage and family therapists practice has been minimal (Pinsof & Wynne, 2000). For when the process of family therapy is structured to fit the model of the clinical trial, it loses most of its resemblance to what actually happens in practice. And the more that methodology is the focus, the less relevant are the results.

To meet this need, the development of progress research, based on understanding therapy as an educational process, has been suggested (Pinsof & Wynne, 2000). This approach is intended to accommodate the improvisational nature of therapy, characterized as it is by ongoing mutual influence and feedback between therapist and client. The goal is the delineation of theories that describe how clients learn and change, both in and out of therapy, and the way that therapists can best support this process.

Also currently receiving considerable attention is the creation of empirically validated treatments (EVT), or approaches to therapy whose efficacy has been experimentally tested (Chambless & Ollendick, 2001). The goal is to replace claims based on anecdotal evidence with those that are scientifically based, thus maximizing benefits and minimizing risks. A more specific approach utilizes the Principles of Empirically Supported Interventions (PESI) to integrate theory and practice (Sexton & Alexander, 2002). Seen by some as the wave of the future, EVT also has been criticized in terms of its ability to define efficacy in any absolute sense (Hubble, Duncan, & Miller, 1999).

Indeed, postmodernists urge researchers to recognize that subjectivity is inevitable and thus their theories are always biased relative to political, economic, and cultural contexts. Also advised is a shift in emphasis from a search for representation, as well as an awareness that demonstration of utility is not the same as evidence of truth (Longino, 1990). Such ideas are inherent in qualitative approaches, which are also more consistent with systems theory/cybernetics.

Qualitative approaches focus on discovery (Chenail, 1994), on understanding individual human experience in depth (Gerhart, Ratliff, & Lyle, 2001). Subjectivity is acknowledged, with recognition that research can be performed only on representations of reality. While seeking commonalties across human experience, study designs are dictated by the questions of interest and may change midstream. All variables are considered part of the context and are included in the investigation. Subjects may be invited to participate with the researcher throughout the project. The data and interpretations are assumed to be valid only relative to the unique conditions of a particular project at a particular time and place. Qualitative research also may be "praxis oriented," aiming to "combat dominance and push toward thoroughgoing change in the practices of . . . the social formation" (Benson, 1983, p. 338), raising questions about the results of professional discourses on such issues as mental illness or marriage and family dysfunction.

Although both quantitative and qualitative research can inform clinical practice, the latter does not have the legitimacy of the former. The dilemma is that if marriage and family therapy is to avoid marginalization and maintain a status comparable to the other mental health professions, information about its efficacy must be presented in a form acceptable to the institutions and agencies paying for services. However, from the perspective of both second-order cybernetics and postmodernism, quantitative approaches tend to provide support for the ideas, institutions, and practices that may, as a function of the research questions that are likely to get funded for investigation, paradoxically create increasing incidence of "mental illness" and marriage and family "dysfunction." Although interest in qualitative studies appears to be increasing (Gerhart, Ratliff, & Lyle, 2001), research from and theories about this approach are generally much less available than are reports on quantitative research (Faulkner, Klock, & Gale, 2002).

## CONCLUSION

As noted at the outset, family therapy is ultimately about epistemology. Given an epistemology inconsistent with the worldview of mainstream Western society, controversy and conflict have been inherent in its evolution and promise to continue in the future. However, throughout the history of family therapy, such conflict often has been a catalyst for thinking and theorizing that has produced more effective and more ethical ways to help clients.

The first family therapists were mavericks, choosing to see the world and act within it differently. That has been our legacy and our tradition. Consistent with the systemic/cybernetic logic that change equals a change in context, it also may be the key to understanding the effectiveness of family therapy. It thus may be a sign of health that the members of this profession continue to debate and to push one

another, both to achieve self-referential consistency and to explore new frontiers, searching always for better ways to write the family therapy story.

## REFERENCES

Ackerman, N. W. (1937). The family as a social and emotional unit. *Bulletin of the Kansas Mental Hygiene Society, 12*(2).

Ackerman, N. W. (1967). The future of family psychotherapy. In N. Ackerman, F. Beatman, & S. Sherman (Eds.), *Expanding theory and practice in family therapy* (pp. 3–16). New York: New York Family Association of America.

Alexander, J., & Parsons, B. (1973). Short-term behavioral interventions with delinquent families: Impact on family process and recidivism. *Journal of Abnormal Psychology, 81,* 219–225.

Alexander, J. F., & Parsons, B. V. (1982). *Functional family therapy.* Pacific Grove, CA: Brooks/Cole.

Amundson, J. K. (2000). How narrative therapy might avoid the same damn thing over and over. *Journal of Systemic Therapies, 19*(4), 20–31.

Andersen, T. (1992). Reflections on reflecting with families. In S. McNamee & K. J. Gergen (Eds.), *Therapy as social construction* (pp. 54–68). Newbury Park, CA: Sage.

Anderson, H. (1997). *Conversation, language, and possibilities.* New York: Basic Books.

Anderson, H., & Goolishian, H. A. (1988). Human systems as linguistic systems: Preliminary and evolving ideas about the implications for clinical theory. *Family Process, 27,* 371–393.

Avis, J. M. (1988). Deepening awareness: A private study guide to feminism and family therapy. In L. Braverman (Ed.), *A guide to feminist family therapy.* New York: Harrington Park Press.

Barton, C., & Alexander, J. (1981). Functional family therapy. In A. Gurman & D. Kniskern (Eds.), *Handbook of family therapy* (pp. 403–443). New York: Brunner/Mazel.

Bateson, G. (1972). *Steps to an ecology of mind.* New York: Ballantine.

Bateson, G., Jackson, D. D., Haley, J., & Weakland, J. (1956). Toward a theory of schizophrenia. *Behavioral Science, 1,* 251–264.

Bateson, G., & Mead, M. (1976, Summer). For God's sake, Margaret. *The Co-Evolution Quarterly,* 32–43.

Becvar, D. S., & Becvar, R. J. (2003). *Family therapy:*

*A systemic integration* (5th ed.). Boston: Allyn & Bacon.

Bell, J. E. (1961). *Family group therapy.* Public Health Monograph No. 64. Washington, DC: U.S. Government Printing Office.

Benson, J. (1983). A dialectical method for the study of organizations. In G. Morgan (Ed.), *Beyond method: Strategies for social research* (pp. 331–346). Beverly Hills, CA: Sage.

Bertalanffy, L. von. (1968). *General system theory.* New York: George Braziller.

Bischof, G. P. (1993). Solution-focused brief therapy and experiential family therapy activities. An integration. *Journal of Systemic Therapies, 12,* 61–73.

Boszormenyi-Nagy, I. (1966). From family therapy to a psychology of relationships: Fictions of the individual and fictions of the family. *Comprehensive Psychiatry, 7,* 406–423.

Bowen, M. (1978). *Family therapy in clinical practice.* New York: Jason Aronson.

Braverman, S. (1995). The integration of individual and family therapy. *Contemporary Family Therapy, 17,* 291–305.

Breunlin, D., Schwartz, R., & MacKune-Karrer, B. (1992). *Metaframeworks: Transcending the models of family therapy.* San Francisco: Jossey-Bass.

Chambless, D. L., & Ollendick, T. H. (2001). Empirically supported psychological interventions: Controversies and evidence. *Annual Review of Psychology, 52,* 685–716.

Chenail, R. (1994). Qualitative research and clinical work: "Privat-ization" and "Public-ation." *The Qualitative Report, 2*(1), 1–12.

de Shazer, S. (1991). *Putting difference to work.* New York: W. W. Norton.

Doherty, W. J., & Baird, M. A. (1983). *Family therapy and family medicine: Toward the primary care of families.* New York: Guilford Press.

Efran, J. A., Lukens, R. J., & Lukens, M. D. (1988). Constructivism: What's in it for you? *Family Therapy Networker, 12*(5), 27–35.

Epston, D. (1994). Extending the conversation. *Family Therapy Networker, 18*(6), 30–37, 62–63.

Faulkner, R. A., Klock, K., & Gale, J. (2002). Qualitative research in family therapy: Publication trends from 1980 to 1999. *Journal of Marital and Family Therapy, 28*(1), 69–74.

Fraser, J. S. (1982). Structural and strategic family therapy: A basis for marriage, or grounds for divorce? *Journal of Marital and Family Therapy, 8*(2), 13–22.

Gale, J. E., & Long, J. K. (1996). Theoretical foundations of family therapy. In F. P. Piercy, D. H. Sprenkle, J. L. Wetchler, & Associates (Eds.), *Family therapy sourcebook* (pp. 1–24). New York: Guilford Press.

Gergen, K. J. (1985). Social constructionist movement in psychology. *American Psychologist, 40,* 266-275.

Gergen, K. J. (1991). *The saturated self.* New York: Basic Books.

Gergen, K. J. (1994a). Exploring the postmodern: Perils or potentials? *American Psychologist, 49*(5), 412–416.

Gergen, K. J. (1994b). *Realities and relationships.* Cambridge, MA: Harvard University Press.

Gerhart, D. R., Ratliff, D. A., & Lyle, R. R. (2001). Qualitative research in family therapy: A substantive and methodological review. *Journal of Marital and Family Therapy, 27*(2), 261–274.

Glanville, R. (2001). Second order cybernetics. Unpublished paper.

Goldner, V. (1985). Feminism and family therapy. *Family Process, 24,* 31–47.

Guerin, P. J. (1976). Family therapy: The first twenty-five years. In P. J. Guerin (Ed.), *Family therapy: Theory and practice.* New York: Gardner Press.

Gurman, A. S., & Kniskern, D. P. (1978). Research on marital and family therapy: Progress, perspective and prospect. In S. Garfield & A. Bergin (Eds.), *Handbook of psychotherapy and behavior change: An empirical analysis* (2nd ed., pp. 817–902). New York: Wiley.

Gurman, A. S., & Kniskern, D. P. (1981). *Handbook of family therapy.* New York: Brunner/Mazel.

Gurman, A. S., Kniskern, D. P., & Pinsof, W. M. (1986). Research on the process and outcome of marital and family therapy. In S. Garfield & A. Bergin (Eds.), *Handbook of psychotherapy and behavior change: An empirical analysis* (3rd ed., pp. 525–623). New York: Wiley.

Haley, J. (1963). *Strategies of psychotherapy.* New York: Grune & Stratton.

Hare-Mustin, R. T. (1978). A feminist approach to family therapy. *Family Process, 17,* 181–194.

Hawley, D. R., Bailey, C. E., & Pennick, K. A. (2000). A content analysis of research in family therapy journals. *Journal of Marital and Family Therapy, 26*(1), 9–16.

Heims, S. P. (1975). Encounter of behavioral sciences with new machine-organism analogies in the 1940's. *Journal of the History of the Behavioral Sciences, 11,* 368–373.

Heims, S. P. (1977). Gregory Bateson and the mathematicians: From interdisciplinary interaction to societal functions. *Journal of the History of the Behavioral Sciences, 13,* 141–159.

Held, B. S. (1995). *Back to reality.* New York: W. W. Norton.

Hoffman, L. (1981). *Foundations of family therapy.* New York: Basic Books.

Hoffman, L. (1985). Beyond power and control. *Family Systems Medicine, 4,* 381–396.

Hubble, M. L., Duncan, B. L., & Miller, S. D. (1999). *The heart & soul of change: What works in therapy.* Washington, DC: American Psychological Association.

Keeney, B. P. (1983). *Aesthetics of change.* New York: Guilford Press.

Kuhn, T. (1970). *The structure of scientific revolutions.* Chicago: University of Chicago Press.

Lebow, J. (1997). The integrative revolution in couple and family therapy. *Family Process, 36,* 1–18.

Lidz, R. W., & Lidz, T. (1949). The family environment of schizophrenic patients. *Journal of Psychiatry, 106,* 332–345.

Longino, H. (1990). *Science as social knowledge.* Princeton, NJ: Princeton University Press.

Lowe, R. N. (1991). Postmodern themes and therapeutic practices: Notes towards the definition of "Family Therapy: Part 2." *Dulwich Center Newsletter, 3,* 41–42.

Maturana, H., & Varela, F. J. (1980). *Autopoiesis and cognition.* Dordrecht, Holland: D. Reidel.

Maturana, H., & Varela, F. J. (1987). *The tree of knowledge.* Boston: New Science Library.

Midelfort, C. (1957). *The family in psychotherapy.* New York: McGraw-Hill.

Miller, S. D., & Duncan, B. L. (2000). Paradigm lost: From model-driven to client-directed outcome informed clinical work. *Journal of Systemic Therapies, 19*(1), 20–34.

Minuchin, S. (1974). *Families and family therapy.* Cambridge, MA: Harvard University Press.

Morris, S., Alexander, J., & Waldron, H. (1988). Functional family therapy. In I. R. Falloon (Ed.), *Handbook of behavioral family therapy* (pp. 107–127). New York: Guilford Press.

Nichols, M. P., & Schwartz, R. C. (2001). *Family therapy: Concepts and methods.* Boston: Allyn & Bacon.

O'Hanlon, W. H., & Weiner-Davis, M. (1989). *In search of solutions: A new direction in psychotherapy.* New York: W. W. Norton.

Piercy, F. P., & Sprenkle, D. H. (1990). Marriage and family therapy: A decade review. *Journal of Marriage and the Family, 52,* 1116–1126.

Piercy, F. P., Sprenkle, D. H., & Associates. (1986). *Family therapy sourcebook.* New York: Guilford Press.

Pinsof, W. M. (1981). Family therapy process research. In A. S. Gurman & D. P. Kniskern (Eds.), *Handbook of family therapy* (pp. 669–674). New York: Brunner/Mazel.

Pinsof, W. M. (1994). An overview of integrative problem-centered therapy: A synthesis of family and individual psychotherapies. *Journal of Family Therapy, 16*(1), 103–120.

Pinsof, W. M., & Wynne, L. C. (1995). The effectiveness and efficacy of marital and family therapy: Introduction to the special issue. *Journal of Marital and Family Therapy, 21,* 341–343

Pinsof, W. M., & Wynne, L. C. (2000). Toward progress research: Closing the gap between family therapy practice and research. *Journal of Marital and Family Therapy, 26*(1), 1–8.

Pinsof, W. M., Wynne, L. C., & Hambright, A. B. (1996). The outcomes of couples and family therapy: Findings, conclusions, and recommendations. *Psychotherapy, 33,* 321–331.

Rigazio-Digilio, S. R. (1994). A co-constructive developmental approach. *Journal of Mental Health Counseling, 16,* 43–74.

Rosenblueth, A., Wiener, N., & Bigelow, J. (1943). Behavior, purpose and teleology. *Philosophy of Science, 10,* 18–24

Ruesch, J., & Bateson, G. (1951). *Communication: The social matrix of society.* New York: W. W. Norton.

Rychlak, J. F. (1981). *Introduction to personality and psychotherapy.* Boston: Houghton Mifflin.

Satir, V. (1982). The therapist and family therapy: Process model. In A. M. Horne & M. M. Ohlsen (Eds.), *Family counseling and therapy* (pp. 12–42). Itasca, IL: F. E. Peacock.

Sexton, T. L., & Alexander, J. F. (2002). Family-based empirically supported interventions. *The Counseling Psychologist, 30*(2), 238–261.

Simon, G. (1993). Revisiting the notion of hierarchy. *Family Process, 32,* 147–155.

Simon, R. (1982). Behind the one-way mirror. *Family Therapy Networker, 6*(1), 18–59.

Simon, T. B., Stierlin, H., & Wynne, L. C. (1985). *The language of family therapy: A systemic vocabulary and sourcebook.* New York: Family Process Press.

Steinglass, P. (1991). An editorial: Finding a place for the individual in family therapy. *Family Process, 30*(3), 267–269.

Todd, T., & Stanton, M. (1983). Research on marital

therapy and family therapy: Answers, issues and recommendations for the future. In B. Wolman & C. Stracker (Eds.), *Handbook of family and marital therapy* (pp. 91–115). New York: Plenum Press.

von Glasersfeld, E. (1988). The reluctance to change a way of thinking: Radical constructivism and autopoiesis and psychotherapy. *Irish Journal of Psychology, 9,* 83–90.

Watzlawick, P. (1978). *The language of change.* New York: Basic Books.

Watzlawick, P., Beavin, J., & Jackson, D. D. (1967). *Pragmatics of human communication.* New York: W. W. Norton.

Wheeler, E. (1985). The fear of feminism in family therapy. *Family Therapy Networker, 9*(6), 53–55.

Whitaker, C. A. (1975). Psychotherapy of the absurd: With a special emphasis on the psychotherapy of aggression. *Family Process, 14*(1), 1–16.

White, M., & Epston, D. (1990). *Narrative means to therapeutic ends.* New York: W. W. Norton.

Whitehead, A. N., & Russell, B. (1910). *Principia mathematica.* Cambridge, UK: Cambridge University Press.

Wynne, L. C., Ryckoff, I. M., Day, J., & Hirsch, S. I. (1958). Pseudo-mutuality in the family relations of schizophrenics. *Psychiatry, 21,* 205–220.

CHAPTER 2

# The Ecosystemic "Lens" to Understanding Family Functioning

MICHAEL S. ROBBINS, PhD
CARLA C. MAYORGA, BA
JOSÉ SZAPOCZNIK, PhD

*University of Miami School of Medicine*

## INTRODUCTION

Context has always played a critical role in couple and family theory. Pioneers of CFT championed a view that expanded the focus from an individual level to the larger contexts that contain individuals—with, of course, a primary emphasis on the family. Even the use of the term *systems,* a central theoretical base of virtually every couple and family approach, is rich with an understanding of context and contextual influence. Historically, context in CFT has not been solely limited to the nuclear family. For example, early approaches often considered the role of multiple generations within a family, other extended family members, as well as other important systems in the individuals' and families' social ecology in the

evolution, maintenance, and treatment of a variety of problems (Boszormenyi-Nagy, 1987; Bowen, 1976; Framo, 1976; McGoldrick & Gerson, 1985; Speck & Attneave, 1973; Whitaker, 1975). Although this broader "ecological" focus has persisted over time, only recently has the "lens" been sharpened to include a more intensive focus on developing and testing integrated interventions that utilize social contextual frameworks for understanding and treating symptoms. Using this "ecosystemic lens," a base of empirically supported intervention strategies has begun to emerge in CFT.

The focus of this chapter is to capture the essence of the ecosystemic movement in CFT. In doing so, we start with a brief description of factors that have influenced the rise in importance of ecological theories and interventions. Next, we present Bronfenbrenner's theory of social ecology as a conceptual framework for organizing ecological intervention theories and implementation strategies. To Bronfenbrenner's theory, we add a developmental component to capture the complex, dynamic, and reciprocally influencing relationships of individuals, couples, and families over time. Examples of ecological interventions are presented, including general strategies and specific techniques of prominent interventions (such as multisystemic therapy), as well as unique strategies that utilize interdisciplinary frameworks to enhance the lives of family members. We conclude with a discussion of the role that CFT may (and maybe even should) play in the future to target change at all levels of the social ecology.

## THE EMERGENCE
## OF ECOSYSTEMIC APPROACHES

Many factors have influenced the emergence of an ecological focus in CFT. Obviously, the "systemic" foundation of CFT required sensitivity to all levels of influence on the lives of individual family members. Although intervention models typically created a boundary around the "family system" to understand family dynamics and organize intervention strategies, the systemic focus of early theorists required the inclusion of external influences on the family system. In fact, as we discuss in the next section on social ecology, the theoretical foundation of CFT in the past included an articulation of boundaries, communication flow, and the reciprocal influence of individual, family, and social contextual variables.

A sensitivity to context notwithstanding, there is no doubt that early approaches clearly emphasized the "family" as the primary unit for understanding and treating a variety of clinical problems. Some models focused on the nuclear family, whereas other approaches included diverse family compositions, such as extended family members or families of origin. Finally, some models excluded non–family members from interventions and excluded even a focus on external influences during intervention sessions, whereas other approaches included all of the relevant "players" in the lives of family members as part of treatment sessions. This rich diversity in the focus and delivery of interventions continues to persist in CFT. However, most approaches tend to be considerably more flexible in their focus and delivery, and, as noted throughout this volume, most CFT approaches explicitly include social ecological variables as a critical feature of treatment.

Many factors have contributed to the rise in importance of ecosystemic factors in CFT. One of the most powerful influences in the child and adolescent treatment arena was the emergence of the "family preservation" movement. This movement occurred in response to rising discontent about the system of child welfare practice that was common through the 1970s and '80s. Rejecting the old paradigm that tended to blame families for their failures in child rearing and viewed foster care or institutional placement as the best way to save children, the family preservation movement adopted the perspective that families were worth saving (Nelson & Landsman, 1992). The passage of the Adoption Assistance and Child Welfare Act of 1980 initiated the replacement of the old system with a new model of family-centered social services. Many fundamental aspects of family preservation are not unique (e.g., focus on the whole family, rather than on the "problem" child; a recognition of both the interdependence of family members and connections between the family and its environment); however, the formal inclusion of a systematic focus on the improvement of all aspects of family functioning—social, material, or psychological—and the mobilization of relevant systems in the child's and family members' treatment had a profound influence on shifting the lens to the broader contexts and systems that interfered with or enhanced family functioning (Nelson, 1991; Nelson & Landsman, 1992, p. 5). The lasting impact of this movement is evident in the fact that most current family-based programs now include a focus on empowering families through increasing families' coping skills and facilitating families' use of appropriate formal and informal helping resources. It is worth noting that the "do whatever it takes" mentality of the family preservation movement has also influenced the format of service delivery, with many approaches now adopting an approach where services are delivered in homes, schools, and other locations that are convenient for family members.

With respect to children and adolescents, research documenting the influence of multisystemic factors in the evolution and maintenance of disruptive behavior problems (c.f. Hawkins, Catalano, & Miller, 1992) has had a profound impact on the development of ecological intervention strategies. A core assumption of these approaches is that changing the risk to protection ratio in the child's social ecology can dramatically reduce the odds of problem-behavior development. In general, this philosophy is most evident in the arena of family-based preventive interventions; however, a notable exception in CFT is the theoretical, clinical, and empirical work of Scott Henggeler and colleagues with multisystemic therapy (see Chapter 13).

Many other factors have also contributed to the growing support for ecosystemic approaches in CFT. These influences include but are not limited to the following: (1) the challenges of adapting or developing "specific" models for working in diverse contexts with diverse populations, (2) interdisciplinary cross-fertilization and collaboration to provide comprehensive treatment addressing the full range of symptoms related to the "presenting problem," and (related to number 2) (3) an increased focus on modifying service delivery to provide a continuity of care, from intake to primary care to follow-up. Each of these factors has required an expansion/modification of existing approaches or the development of new approaches to provide services that meet the needs of complex problems and populations. The influence of these factors on the evolution of ecosystemic approaches has been fueled by the emergence of new theoretical frameworks (postmodernism) and a new era of accountability (efficacy, effectiveness, and transportability) in the health and mental health sciences and services.

## SOCIAL ECOLOGICAL THEORY

Despite the fact that most of the early clinical models in CFT considered ecosystemic factors, very few models included an articulation of ecological variables with the same focus and theoretical grounding that guided understanding family functioning and treatment. Typically, ecological factors were included as an afterthought to make sure that the therapist did not forget to account for "external" factors that may be influencing family functioning, family members' responsiveness to treatment, or the family's ability to maintain changes over time or generalize changes to new contexts. Couple and family therapists were thus provided with only minimal guidance about theories and strategies for working in the family's social ecology. Unfortunately, this situation has not been adequately addressed in CFT, and only a few comprehensive ecological intervention theories have been developed, refined, implemented, and evaluated.

*Bronfenbrenner's Theory
of Social Ecology*

Ecological approaches draw heavily from the theoretical work of Urie Bronfenbrenner (1977, 1979, 1986). Bronfenbrenner's theory organizes social ecological influence on individuals at four different levels. Each level contains and influences the prior level and directly or indirectly influences individuals. The four levels of systems are known as microsystems, mesosystems, exosystems, and macrosystems (see figure 2.1). *Microsystems* refer to systems that include the target individual directly. For children and adolescents, this might include the family, peers, the school, and the neighborhood. For an adult, microsystems might consist of the couple, the immediate family (of origin and of procreation), work, the neighborhood, and the health-care system (e.g., in the case of chronic disease). *Mesosystems* represent relationships between the members of the microsystems in which the individual participates but which do not involve the target individual. For children and adolescents, the primary mesosystemic relationships may involve parents' interactions with the youth's peer, school, and justice systems. For an adult, mesosystemic relationships might include interactions between the partner and the target individual's parents or siblings, or between the partner and friends or doctors. *Exosystems* are those systems that include a member of a microsystem but that do not involve the individual directly. For children and adolescents, exosystems may include the gang of a friend or the social support network or place of work of a parent. Both of these exosystems, through their impact on the friend (gang members support the antisocial behavior of the friend) and on the parent (the parent receives support from friends/extended family or is under stress from work), respectively, may have an indirect impact on the child. Szapocznik and Coatsworth (1999) suggest that this impact occurs through

the interactions between the youth and the other person. For an adult, important exosystems include the support network or place of work of the partner. Both of these relationships may serve as a critical buffer or stressor on the partner that, in turn, may dramatically influence couple interactions. Finally, at the broadest level are *macrosystems,* defined as the broad social forces and systems that have the most widespread impact, such as the law, as well as the cultural blueprints that pervade a family's social environment. An example of macrosystems is the societal belief that individuals who do not speak English are less valuable to society because they do not speak English. At this broadest level, cultural factors are important in the development and maintenance of problems for individuals and families, for example, the differential levels of acculturation among parents and children in immigrant families (Szapocznik & Kurtines, 1993).

*Cross-Domain "Cascading" Effects*

Ecological interventions may address problems at all four levels of the social ecology. For example, as suggested by figure 2.1, therapists might intervene to improve family relationships (family microsystem), a partner's relationship with his or her in-laws (family-extended family mesosystem), a behavior-problem child's parent's connection to Alcoholics Anonymous (exosystem), and a therapist serving on committees to shape sentencing and treatment practices for victims and perpetrators of domestic violence (macrosystem). However, it is import to note that changes often have a "cascading" effect (Szapocznik & Coatsworth, 1999). These "cross-domain effects" must be considered in planning and implementing ecological interventions. For example, improvements in the spousal relationship can influence improve-

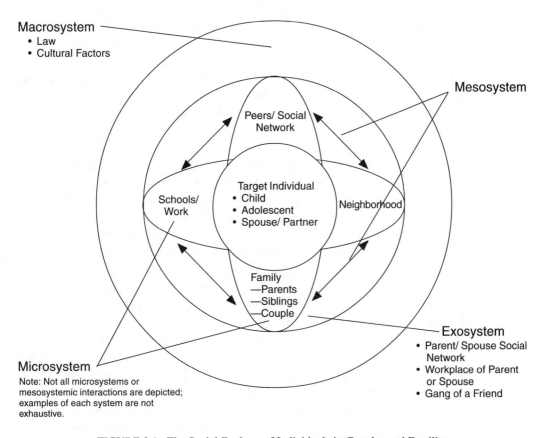

FIGURE 2.1.  The Social Ecology of Individuals in Couples and Families

ments in child behavior, a partner's work satisfaction, and the relationship to extended family members. Likewise, patterns of child–parent relations may influence patterns of child-peer interactions developmentally over time. Understanding and anticipating cross-domain effects will dramatically influence treatment planning in ecological intervention strategies. Cross-domain effects are particularly valuable because they increase targets for intervention.

*Influences Within and Between Systems: Boundaries and Communication Flow*

CFT's historical and current foundation is social contextualism. What this implies is that family approaches consider larger units or contexts as a focus of intervention. CFT is rich with theoretical articulations defining the boundary between individuals and dyads, and even in definitions of the boundary separating the family from its context. An ecological focus thus adds other important contexts to understanding the functioning of each of these smaller units (individual, dyads, family). In doing so, the assumption is that the boundaries at each level may be punctuated or defined in a relatively concrete way. This assumption is important because operationalizing boundaries ultimately defines membership at each level (e.g., sibling subsystem, family, neighborhood), as well as the parameters of communication/interactions between these levels.

Thus, the systemic notion of "boundaries"

is essential for understanding how ecological approaches conceptualize etiology and treatment. Conventionally, boundaries have been seen as the metaphorical "walls" that separate people, denoting where one people or group of persons ends and where the next begins. However, a more complete view of boundaries recognizes that just as boundaries signify separateness, they also denote connectedness (Szapocznik & Coatsworth, 1999). For example, the parent–child boundary not only signifies the distinction between the parenting subsystem and the child subsystem, but it also signifies the precise point at which the two people come together to interact as parent and child. Take, for example, an analogy from biology. Initially, a cell membrane was viewed as a "wall" that helped contain the contents of the cell and that separated the inside of the cell from the outside of the cell. This view provided the membrane with a certain "concreteness." A more contemporary view of a cell membrane, however, reveals that the "wall" is constantly negotiating a transfer of biological components from inside to outside and vice versa. Thus, the cell membrane represents the cell's systematic mechanism for regulating transactions with its environment. This dynamic view of "boundaries" is reflected in the family systemic focus on the reciprocal process of interactions within the family, and between the family and its environment (Bronfenbrenner, 1979, 1986; Magnusson, 1995; Szapocznik & Coatsworth, 1999).

Most family approaches have developed extensive theories for understanding within family boundaries. With the rise of ecological approaches, increased attention has been paid to defining the *family–environment boundary* and the influence of this boundary on individual and family functioning. The simplest way of identifying the family–environment boundary is by examining biological relationships, by examining who lives together and shares daily household responsibilities, or both of these (Greenwood, Hervis, Mitrani, Taylor, & Szapocznik, 1995).

Like the boundaries that separate and connect individuals and subsystems within the family, the boundary between the family and the environment is more or less permeable. That is, much like the membrane of a cell, this boundary regulates communication between the family and its environment and represents the precise point at which they intersect and reciprocally influence each other.

The family–environment boundary is considered at several levels. For example, at the microsystem level the connection between a target child and the school or between a target adult and the place of work are important. At the mesosystemic level, the target child's relationship to the child's school or the target adult's partner's relationship to the adult's place of work should be considered. The family–environment boundary is critically related to the family's functioning and is frequently an indication of potential problems in the family's ability to function adaptively. For example, Alexander (1988) notes that in families in which there is incest, the boundary between the family and the environment is often rigid, resulting in increased insularity of the family and an inability of the family to receive and respond adaptively to "feedback" from the environment.

*Individuals in Context*

A fundamental assumption in ecological approaches is that an individual's behavior is quite different from what it would be if it were possible for that individual to act in isolation. That is, the behaviors of individual family members are linked in an interdependent fashion, and each family member is viewed as being responsible for contributing to, maintaining, or changing the system's interactions

(Szapocznik & Kurtines, 1989). As such, the family is at the core of ecological approaches. However, ecological approaches also appreciate the full range of systemic influences that affect the individual. For example, these approaches acknowledge the important influence of peers/support networks, school/work, and the neighborhood on children, parents/partners, and other family members.

Understanding individuals in context does not mean that "individual" factors are ignored. In fact, a fuller appreciation of the range of systems that influences family members also includes biological processes (i.e., genetics), as well as individual psychological processes (i.e., cognitions). For example, Magnusson (1995) proposes a modern, integrated, holistic model for individual functioning and development, in which "individual functioning is determined in a process of continuous, reciprocal interaction b/w mental factors, biological factors, and behavior—on the individual side—and situational factors" (p. 27). From this perspective, individuals develop through continuous reciprocal interactions among psychological, biological, and environmental factors. Likewise, Ceci and Hembrooke (1995) offer a bioecological perspective that considers context not only to be a basic ingredient of intellectual development but also to differentiate and actualize biological potential. Bronfenbrenner and Ceci (1994; Ceci, 1990) developed this theory, suggesting that proximal processes, defined as reciprocal interactions between the child and other people, objects, and symbols, are the mechanisms by which genotypes are translated to phenotypes (p. 308).

Despite rich articulations of the dynamic relationships between individual factors and contextual factors in the development and maintenance of adaptive and maladaptive behaviors, very little research has elucidated specific mechanisms in the dynamic relationship between intra-individual and contextual

factors that give rise to individual and systemic symptoms. As such, much treatment at this level relies on speculation and on research findings on individuals and contexts, rather than on research evidence for understanding the differential impact of specific contexts on specific individuals. Future research must expand on these limits to develop theories and intervention strategies that are specific to individuals in context.

*Developmental Considerations*

Ecosystemic approaches also consider the dynamic nature and mutual influence of systemic relationships over time. That is, to understand the evolution of individual, couple, or family problems requires an examination of individual and family development, as well as of the changing nature of broader social context influences in which development occurs. For example, Szapocznik and Coatsworth (1999) use the term *ecodevelopment* to capture the complex set of features that emerges within the target family member and in the target family member's social ecology and the nature of the interactions within and among these systems, as they change and influence each other reciprocally over time.

The ever-changing nature of the ecosystem makes it difficult to capture the essence of multisystemic influences. However, ecodevelopmental theory offers a framework for understanding the evolving relationship between individual and social ecological factors. Consistent with Rutter's (1987) transactional conceptions of risk and Cicchetti and Sroufe's (1978) organismic developmental theory, ecodevelopmental theory considers that functioning at one point in development will influence functioning in the next, and that functioning at any one point in time is also influenced by current interactions within and between multiple systems. Thus, identifying how individual and multisystemic risk trajectories have shaped the nature of current multisystemic interactions becomes important for understanding risk and protection within the social ecology and for implementing comprehensive and appropriate multisystemic interventions.

Figure 2.1 depicts a static view of the nesting of individuals in context, providing an organizational theory of the relevant systems that influence family members frozen at one point in time. However, this view does not adequately capture the nature of changes in individuals and the social ecology that mutually influence one another over time. For example, view figure 2.1 as traveling across time in such a way that each level of the ecosystem and each domain currently influences all other levels and domains, and that each level and domain is also influenced by the trajectory of change in every level or domain that has occurred up to the present. Likewise, each domain is influenced by its own trajectory over time. Figure 2.2 adds this developmental perspective to capture the transactional nature of ecological influences. In the next section, we describe how the ecodevelopmental perspective conveyed in figure 2.2 may be applied to understanding families with behavior-problem youths and individuals in couples.

## FAMILIES WITH BEHAVIOR-PROBLEM YOUTHS

The family is the primary context in which child development occurs, and, therefore, family functioning has a profound influence on young children. Problems in the family, such as high conflict or abuse, are related to a variety of behavioral and emotional problems manifested by the child. As shown in figure 2.2a, during infancy and early childhood, the family is the most proximal and influential system in the child's life. During early and middle childhood, the family is still in a very

influential role; however, other systems become increasingly important to the developing child, particularly the school system. During adolescence, the peer system emerges as perhaps the most salient influential system for youths with behavior problems

Several aspects of the nature of ecosystemic influences over time must also be considered. First, current interactions are influenced by the quality of experiences in prior stages, as well as by the ongoing pattern of interaction; Pathway A in figure 2.2b demonstrates this within-domain influence over time. For example, problems in the family, school, or peer systems often persist over time (as illustrated by Pathway A in figure 2.2b). Second, problems in one system may be directly related (or may even predict) problems in other systems. For example, family problems may lead to current or future problems in the school system (see Pathways C and B, respectively). (Note: Family–peer relations are discussed further on.) Likewise, problems in the school system may increase the likelihood of association with deviant peers, which in turn may lead to further problems at school. This reciprocal influence between the school and the peer systems is illustrated in Pathway D. Pathway E illustrates perhaps the most important mesosystemic relationship for adolescents with behavior problems, the family–peer mesosystem (Dishion, French, & Patterson, 1995; Patterson, Dishion, & Bank, 1984). In particular, this pathway captures how parenting practices (e.g., nurturance, discipline, and monitoring and supervision) influence the emergence, maintenance, or both of the adolescent's connection to a peer group that validates the adolescent's deviant behaviors. This influence is bi-directional, with considerable within-family conflict emerging as parents express discontent about the adolescent's selection of peers and as peers directly support the adolescent's rebellion against parents.

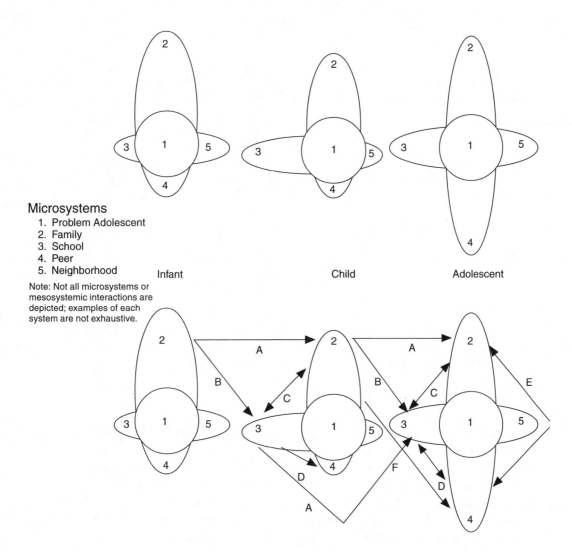

Microsystems
1. Problem Adolescent
2. Family
3. School
4. Peer
5. Neighborhood

Note: Not all microsystems or
mesosystemic interactions are
depicted; examples of each
system are not exhaustive.

FIGURE 2.2a. Differential Microsystemic Influences Over Time on Adolescents with Behavior Problems
FIGURE 2.2b. Within- and Cross-Domain Influences in the Social Ecology of Adolescents with Behavior Problems

## INDIVIDUALS IN COUPLES

Similarly, as context for a couple evolves, so does the nature of systems of influence (see figure 2.3). Early stages in a couple's relationship are marked by high levels of influence from each partner's family of origin. For many young couples, this period of time is also marked by the influence of schools (e.g., college) and job placement. However, over time, as the context of the couple changes (birth of a child, new home, job promotion), so does the nature of the couple system. For example, the influences of family of origin decrease as the couple creates and negotiates its own procreative developmental trajectory. So, as time investment toward a child increases, time spent alone as a couple often decreases and leads to changes in the quality and quantity of the couple's daily interactions. As figure 2.3 shows, such changes in context (birth of a

**Microsystems**
1. Depressed Spouse
2. Partner
3. Children/Procreative Family
4. Work/Career (Education)
5. Health-Care System

Note: Not all microsystems or mesosystemic interactions are depicted; examples of each system are not exhaustive.

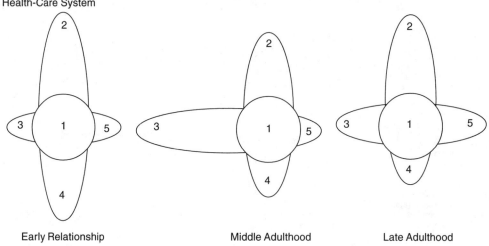

Early Relationship                    Middle Adulthood                    Late Adulthood

FIGURE 2.3. Differential Microsystemic Influences Over Time on Individual Couples

child) may lead to further changes in the couple system by increasing marriage dissatisfaction and negative interactions. Likewise, as the "family" system changes over time, the couple negotiates (1) changing parenting styles to deal with raising adolescents, (2) dealing with the loss associated with their children leaving for school or to form their own families, and (3) establishing new patterns as they "enjoy the golden years." Similar to the patterns depicted in figure 2.2b, over time the partnerships' interactions are influenced by the quality of experiences in prior stages as well as by the ongoing pattern of interaction within their social envelope. Likewise, the relationships between systems must also be considered, such as the impact of each individual's work/career trajectory on the couple and family. For example, an individual takes a job that requires extensive travel or long hours away from home. It is important to note that the systems of influence may also

change as individuals shift responsibilities and roles or as new roles emerge. For example, as individuals retire or as health status changes, systems that were important in prior stages may no longer have a primary influence, and new systems, such as health care, may become more influential.

## INTERVENTION STRATEGIES IN ECOSYSTEMIC APPROACHES

Ecological approaches primarily borrow intervention strategies from family systems models, extending interventions to the larger social context. In many ways, the only novelty of ecological interventions is the systematic focus on the family's social context. Further on, we discuss common issues involved in working in the ecology. The theoretical base for this discussion is described in more detail in Robbins, Schwartz, and Szapocznik (2002);

consequently, much of the information is presented in a manner that is consistent with an ecological version of brief strategic family therapy (Szapocznik & Kurtines, 1989). However, the areas that are covered are particularly accurate in describing the range of family-based ecological approaches for behavior problem adolescents. Although other approaches may vary in the specific nature of intervention strategies, the general information presented further on is consistent with Howard Liddle's multidimensional therapy (Liddle, Dakof, Diamond, Holt, Arojo, & Watson, 1992) and Scott Henggeler's multisystemic therapy (Henggeler & Borduin, 1990). For example, both multidimensional and multisystemic therapy include modules and procedures for working therapeutically with extrafamilial systems, such as the peer, school, and justice systems, as well as modules for facilitating adaptive family–mesosystemic relationships with each of these systems.

## Identifying Strengths and Weaknesses in the Ecosystem

Therapists must systematically examine the social ecology of individuals and the family to identify areas of difficulty or strength that may be critical to address or utilize in treatment. For example, with behavior-problem adolescents, therapists should assess the degree of parental monitoring and supervision of adolescent activities and the nature of the communication across systems. Or, in a couple in which one member has a chronic illness, therapists may seek to identify and engage a support network of the healthy partner.

Once relevant ecosystems have been identified, the therapist can work toward creating a therapeutic system that includes family members and individuals from the social ecology. In doing so, therapists must recognize that engaging ecosystems involves connecting with both individuals and the systems to which they belong. The first step in joining the ecosystem involves gaining family members' approval to contact members of the ecosystem. This step is critical because family members must understand and approve of any attempt to involve others in their treatment process, and they should decide on the amount of personal information they choose to share with others.

The second step in engaging the ecosystem is to identify the most influential members of a particular ecosystem and to obtain their permission and willingness to participate in treatment in support of individual family members or the whole family. The therapist must assess the aspects of other systems (such as their power structure) and enter the system with the permission, approval, and sanction of its power structure—without alienating individuals who may resent the power structure.

## Implementing Interventions in the Ecosystem.

In implementing ecological interventions, two kinds of interventions are typically used: those intended to enlarge positive informal social support networks and linkages with formal service delivery, on the one hand, and those intended to discourage damaging relationships, on the other (e.g., drug-using friends). Interventions aimed at enlarging systems are frequently accomplished by creating and assigning tasks to create a history of successful shared experiences on which more substantive experiences and relationships can be built. Interventions aimed at discouraging damaging relationships may utilize blocking and limit setting. Because ecological interventions usually emphasize building the system's (in this case, the family-ecology system) inner capacity to conduct and maintain changed behaviors, the therapist best accomplishes these kinds of interventions by allying with and strengthening those subsystems that have the competence, power, and interest to undertake the limit setting.

With behavior-problem adolescents, the most prominent ecological interventions involve creating or maximizing the positive influence of mesosystemic relationships, particularly parents' relationships with the systems that directly contain the adolescent (i.e., peer, school, and justice). In the peer system, for example, interventions systematically address parent supervision and monitoring of peer activities. Parents are encouraged to meet the child's friends, as well as the friends' parents, and are coached and supported in setting up procedures/rules for tracking their child's daily activities. Likewise, parents are coached on how to effectively negotiate with the school system. Parent–teacher conferences are conducted (with the therapist present), and plans are developed for maintaining consistent parent investment in the youth's school activities. Similarly, parents and adolescents are encouraged to interact to discuss the youth's current criminal charges, and a plan is developed for interacting with the justice system, which will maximize the likelihood that the family's goals will be met. Parents are coached on how to interact with the justice system, and the therapist attends these meetings to work with parents and juvenile justice representatives to facilitate interactions that ensure that the parent is able to have some influence on the judicial decision-making process. A benefit of conducting sessions with parents and justice system representatives is that a new pattern of interaction is established in the family–juvenile justice mesosystem. A secondary benefit of these types of interventions is that parents learn valuable skills that they may generalize to future interactions within important microsystems.

Exosystemic interventions typically include enhancing or supporting the connection of parents with a supportive extended network. The focus of interventions in this domain is to facilitate the enlargement of boundaries to establish a parent support system. With such supports, parents are better able to carry out their leadership and their nurturing role within the family. This may involve enlisting the support of extended family, friends, and employers, and in instances where a parent figure (or figures) has a history of drug abuse, therapists may encourage the parent(s) to attend appropriate support groups.

## MULTISYSTEMIC THERAPY

The most recognized and well-researched ecological approach is the multisystemic therapy approach developed by Scott Henggeler and colleagues (Henggeler & Borduin, 1990; see Chapter 13 of this handbook). Adopting Bronfenbrenner's (1979) social-ecological model of human development, MST proposes that behavior problems are often "maintained by problematic transactions within and across multiple systems of the social ecology of the child" (Huey, Henggeler, Brondino, & Pickrel, 2000, p. 452). Consistent with social-ecological theory, MST aims to reduce antisocial behavior and promote prosocial behavior by altering the youth's familial and social context. For example, core principles of MST (Henggeler & Borduin, 1990; Henggeler, Melton, Brondino, Scherer, & Hanley, 1997) include (1) understanding the fit between identified problems and the broader systemic context, (2) emphasizing the positive and using the systemic strengths as levers for change, (3) intervening to target the sequences of behavior within or between multiple systems, (4) promoting change by empowering caregivers to address family members' needs across multiple systemic contexts, and (5) implementing interventions that are developmentally appropriate and fit the developmental needs of the youths.

## WORKING IN THE SOCIAL ECOLOGY: WHAT DOES THE FUTURE HOLD?

Certainly, the future will continue to generate more elaborate models for understanding and treating couples and families. We believe that just as this research will shed light on individual and familial processes, research will also provide a clearer understanding of processes in the family's social ecology. In part, the rise of ecological work will occur as existing treatment models add ecological components to further enhance treatment outcome. However, we expect that with increased understanding of social ecological processes, new theories of intervention and change process are likely to emerge as well.

The expansion of ecosystemic work is also likely to occur, as ecological theories and interventions are generalized to new clinical and nonclinical populations. For example, in our own work at the University of Miami's Center for Family Studies, we have expanded our ecological work to include interventions for HIV+ African American women and their families, as well as for primary caregivers in families with an Alzheimer's patient or a developmentally disabled adult. In doing so, we have expanded our clinical theory to address the primary systems that influence the lives of each treatment population.

As noted earlier, interdisciplinary cross-fertilization and collaboration to provide comprehensive treatments for couples and families have also given rise to unique ecological intervention strategies. One of the most interesting and novel areas of cross-fertilization has occurred at the interface of architecture and family psychology, where new interventions have been developed to address the neighborhood context. Evidence indicating that microsystemic characteristics of neighborhoods affect individuals and families, such as social connectedness and collective efficacy of the neighborhood (Sampson, Raudenbush & Earls, 1997), has led to theories about how the "built environment" can be (re)designed to increase or decrease individual family members' social connectedness and perceptions of collective efficacy. Based on these theories, interventions can be implemented at many levels, including the macrosystemic level that is governed largely by policies and cultural beliefs.

Several aspects of the "built environment" have been linked to social processes that increase or decrease youths' risk for developing behavior problems (c.f., Gorman-Smith, Lombard, Martinez, Mason, & Szapocznik, 2002). For example, neighborhoods in which buildings are used for multiple purposes, *diversity of use,* ensures that streets are occupied throughout the day and night, thereby increasing supervision and monitoring of neighborhood activities (Duany & Plater Zyberk, 1992). Also, the extent to which adult residents of the community function as *"eyes on the street"* (Jacobs, 1992) serves to provide additional protection against youth problem behavior. Aspects of the built environment, such as the number, size, and location of windows, as well as the structure and organization of a residential building can either enhance or hinder monitoring of neighborhood activities and social interaction among residents in the neighborhood. Likewise, the *character* of a neighborhood can either invite or discourage social interaction among residents. Whereas poor maintenance creates concern for safety and may reduce interaction, aesthetically attractive buildings create a desire to gather outside (Jacobs, 1992; Katz, 1994). Duany, Plater Zyberk, Speck, & Langdon (2000) and Kay (1998) found that narrow streets tend to slow automotive traffic and that sidewalks also enhance pedestrian safety, thus increasing *walkability*. The *use of open space* can also reduce risk. For example, large parks that are well maintained and patrolled by police and park workers can be a very positive influence on residential interactions and can serve as a deterrent against problem behaviors. However, maintaining large parks requires considerable resources (Jacobs, 1992). For communities with limited resources, smaller plots work well. Lots that are affiliated with an institution or that are located between two buildings have a more favorable impact on youths and neighborhood residents because they increase the likelihood of adult monitoring and supervision.

Examples such as the collaboration between architecture and family psychology demonstrate that the future holds considerable promise for couple and family therapists, as clinical theorists and researchers continue to identify and integrate ecological variables into comprehensive intervention theories. The range of factors will likely be influenced by theory and research from a variety of disciplines, including family psychology; psychology; individual, couple and family therapy practice and research; developmental psychology and psychopathology; social psychology; architecture; and biological sciences, to name a few. Such diversity of findings will raise many challenges for training and research programs, as well as for practicing clinicians. For example, there will be a need for new theories (or refinements to existing approaches) and intervention strategies to address these ecological processes. At the very least, couple and family therapists will be faced with the challenge of learning to collaborate effectively across disciplines to implement integrated and comprehensive treatment programs to systematically address a full range of ecological risk and protective factors.

Central in this process will be the need to redefine the roles and responsibilities of couple and family therapists as agents of ecological change. For example, does an increased understanding of complex multisystemic factors put couple and family therapists in a position to systematically address these factors? Does CFT as a discipline have an ethical obligation to develop specific plans or policies to address these factors? These considerations quickly, but appropriately, spin off into discussions of the role that CFT should play in dealing with issues of social inequity, particularly as research identifies ecological factors that perpetuate the status quo, which is particularly problematic for minority groups and women. Undoubtedly, within CFT there will continue to be a movement to "take on" systems that support one group of people at the exclusion of others; consequently, the clinical focus of couple and family therapists will likely expand to the macrosystemic level to target social policies and systems that impact (directly or indirectly) individuals, couples, and families.

## REFERENCES

Alexander, P. C. (1985). A systems theory conceptualization of incest. *Family Process, 24,* 79–88.

Borduin, C. M., & Henggeler, S. W. (1990). A multisystemic approach to the treatment of serious delinquent behavior. In R. J. McMahon & R. DeV. Peters (Eds.), *Behavior disorders of adolescence: Research, intervention, and policy in clinical and school settings* (pp. 63–80). New York: Plenum Press.

Boszormenyi-Nagy, I. (1987). *Foundations of contextual therapy: Collected papers of Ivan Boszormenyi-Nagy, M.D.* New York: Brunner/Mazel.

Bowen, M. (1976). Theory in the practice of psychotherapy. In P. J. Guerin, Jr. (Ed.), *Family therapy: Theory and practice.* New York: Gardner Press.

Bowen, M. (1978). *Family therapy in clinical practice.* New York: Aronson.

Bronfenbrenner, U. (1977). Toward an experimental ecology of human development. *American Psychologist, 32*(7), 513–531.

Bronfenbrenner, U. (1979). *The ecology of human development: Experiments by nature and design.* Cambridge, MA: Harvard University Press.

Bronfenbrenner, U. (1986). Ecology of the family as a context for human development. *American Psychologist, 32,* 513–531.

Ceci, S. (1990). A sideways glance at this thing called LD: A content X process X person framework. In H. L. Swanson, & B. K. Keogh (Eds.), *Learning disabilities: Theoretical and research issues* (pp. 59–73). Hillsdale, NJ: Erlbaum.

Ceci, S. J. (1994). Education, achievement, and general intelligence: Whatever happened to the psycho in psychometrics? *Psychological Inquiry, 5*(3), 197–201.

Ceci, S. J., & Hembrooke, H. A. (1995). A bioecological model of intellectual development. In P. Moen, G. H. Elder, & K. Luescher (Eds.), *Examining lives in context: Perspectives on the ecology of human development* (pp. 303–345). Washington, DC: American Psychological Association.

Cicchetti, D., & Sroufe, L. A. (1978). An organizational view of affect: Illustration from the study of Down's syndrome infants. In M. Lewis & L. Rosenblum (Eds.), *The development of affect.* New York: Plenum.

Dishion, T. J., French, D. C., & Patterson, G. R. (1995). The development and ecology of antisocial behavior. In D. Cicchetti & D. J. Cohen (Eds.), *Developmental Psychopathology, Vol. 2: Risk, disorder, and adaptation. Wiley series on personality processes* (pp. 421–471). Oxford, UK: Wiley.

Duany, A., & Plater Zyberk, E. (1992). The second coming of the American small town. *The Wilson Quarterly, 16,* 19–50.

Duany, A., Plater Zyberk, E., Speck, J., & Langdon, P. (2000). Suburban nation. *American Enterprise, 11*(7), 57–58.

Framo, J. L. (1976). Family of origin as a therapeutic resource for adults in marital and family therapy: You can and should go home again. *Family Process, 15*(2), 193–210.

Greenwood, D., Hervis, O., Mitrani, Taylor, D., & Szapocznik, J. (1995, August). *Family definition in low income, HIV-1 seropositive African American women.* Paper presented at the Annual Meeting of the American Psychological Association, New York, NY.

Gorman-Smith, D., Lombard, J., Martinez, F., Mason, C., & Szapocznik, J. (2002). *Neighborhoods and risk: A link between social organization and the built environment?* Manuscript in preparation, University of Miami.

Hawkins, J. D., Catalano, R. F., & Miller, J. Y. (1992). Risk and protective factors for alcohol and other drug problems in adolescence and early adulthood: Implications for substance abuse prevention. *Psychological Bulletin, 112*(1), 64–105.

Henggeler, S. W., & Borduin, C. M. (1990). *Family therapy and beyond: A multisystemic approach to treating the behavioral problems of children and adolescents.* Pacific Grove, CA: Brooks/Cole.

Henggeler, S. W., Melton, G. B., Brondino, M. J., Scherer, D. G., & Hanley, J. H. (1997). Multisystemic therapy with violent and chronic juvenile offenders and their families: The role of treatment fidelity in successful dissemination. *Journal of Consulting and Clinical Psychology, 65*(5), 821–833.

Huey, S. J., Henggeler, S. W., Brondino, M. J., & Pickrel, S. G. (2000). Mechanisms of change in multisystemic therapy: Reducing delinquent behavior through therapist adherence and improved family and peer functioning. *Journal of Consulting and Clinical Psychology, 68*(3), 451–467.

Jacobs, J. (1992). *The death and life of great American cities.* New York: Vintage Books.

Katz, P. (1994). *The new urbanisim: Toward an architecture of community.* New York: McGraw-Hill.

Kay, J. H. (1998). *Asphalt nation: How the automobile took over America and how we can take it back.* Berkeley: University of California Press.

Liddle, H. A., Dakof, G., Diamond, G., Holt, M., Arojo, J., & Watson, M. The adolescent module in multidimensional family therapy. In G. W. Lawson & A. W. Lawson (Eds.), *Adolescent substance abuse: Etiology, treatment, and prevention* (pp. 165–186). Gathersburg, MD: Aspen.

Magnusson, D. (1995). Individual development: A holistic, integrated model. In P. Moen, G. H. Elder, & K. Luscher (Eds.), *Examining lives in context: Perspectives on the ecology of human development* (pp. 19–60). Washington, DC: American Psychological Association.

McGoldrick, M., & Gerson, R. (1985). *Genograms in family assessment.* New York: W. W. Norton.

Nelson, K. E. (1991). Populations and outcomes in five family preservation programs. In K. Wells & D. E. Biegel (Eds.), *Family preservation services: Research and evaluation* (pp. 72–91). Newbury Park, CA: Sage.

Nelson, K. E., & Landsman, M. J. (1992). *Alternative models of family preservation: Family-based services in context* (pp. 3–20). Springfield, IL: Charles C. Thomas.

Patterson, G. R., Dishion, T. J., & Bank, L. (1984). Family interaction: A process model of deviancy training. *Aggressive Behavior, 10*(3), 253–267.

Robbins, M. S., Schwartz, S., & Szapocznik, J. (2002). Structural ecosystems therapy with adolescents exhibiting disruptive behavior disorders. In J. Ancis (Ed.), *Culturally based interventions: Alternative approaches to working with diverse populations and culture-bound syndromes.* New York: Brunner-Routledge.

Rutter, M. (1987). Psychosocial resilience and protective mechanisms. *American Journal of Orthopsychiatry, 57,* 316–331.

Sampson, R. J., Raudenbush, S. W., & Earls, F. (1997). Neighborhoods and violent crime: A multilevel study of collective efficacy. *Science, 277*(5328), 918–924.

Speck, R. V., & Attneave, C. L. (1973). *Family networks.* New York: Pantheon.

Szapocznik, J., & Coatsworth, D. (1999). An ecodevelopmental framework for organizing the influences on drug abuse: A developmental model of risk and protection. In M. D. Glantz & C. R. Hartel (Eds.), *Drug abuse: Origins & Interventions* (pp. 331–366). Washington, DC: American Psychological Association.

Szapocznik, J., & Kurtines, W. (1989). *Breakthroughs in family therapy with drug abusing problem youth.* New York: Springer.

Szapocznik, J., Kurtines, W. M. (1993). Family psychology and cultural diversity: Opportunities for theory, research and application. [Invited article] *American Psychologist, 48*(4), 400–407. (Reprinted in N. Goldberger & J. Veroff (1995), *Essential papers in psychology and culture.* New York: NYU Press).

Whitaker, C. A. (1975). Psychotherapy of the absurd: With a special emphasis on the psychotherapy of aggression. *Family Process, 14,* 1–16.

# CHAPTER 3

# Culture in Family Therapy

## *New Variations on a Fundamental Theme*

CELIA JAES FALICOV, PhD

*University of California, San Diego*

*The first thing you do is to forget that I am black. Second, you must never forget that I am black.*
—from Pat Parker's poem, "For the White Person Who Wants to Know How to Be My Friend" (1990)

## HISTORICAL CONTEXTS FOR MULTICULTURALISM

The call for cultural sensitivity in mental health services is not new. The civil rights movement demanded that institutions be more responsive and less discriminatory toward minority clients, and the nationwide development of community mental health programs in the 1970s attempted to expand services to economically disadvantaged and culturally marginalized groups. The multicultural movement of the 1990s has revitalized these concerns within newer, postmodern epistemologies that stress a social constructionist lens, a strength-based orientation, and a collaborative engagement with clients.

Among health disciplines, family therapy has emphasized contextual issues since its earliest days. With its foundation in systems theory, family therapy has always regarded the behavior of families as contextual and ecological (Auerswald, 1968). Early research and scholarly writings that focused on economically disadvantaged families highlighted the importance of sociocultural context in understanding family life (Aponte, 1976; Minuchin, Montalvo, Guerney, Rosman, & Schumer, 1967; Montalvo & Gutierrez, 1983, 1988; Sluzki, 1969). Other notable contributions include the work of Spiegel (1971) and Papajohn and Spiegel (1975), which compared value orientations of various ethnic groups; McGoldrick, Pearce, and Giordano's (1982) examination of ethnicity in families; Boyd-Franklin's (1989) multisystemic approach in *Black Families in Therapy;* the feminist critique of family therapy (Goldner, 1985; Hare-Mustin, 1978; Luepnitz, 1988; McGoldrick, Anderson, & Walsh, 1989; Walters, Carter,

Papp, & Silverstein, 1988); the attention paid to gay and lesbian families (Johnson & Keren, 1998; Laird, 1998); or the use of "cultural consultants" in the New Zealand "Just Therapy" approach (Waldegrave, 1990); and my own work, which proposes a more comprehensive definition of culture and challenges the assumed universality of family therapy concepts and interventions (Falicov, 1983, 1995, 1998a, 1998b). The historical progression of these concerns places family therapy squarely within the multicultural movement.

*Collective Identities: A World of Variation*

Defining specific "collective identities," such as ethnic, class, gender, or social identities, appears at first glance both possible and practical. We look at the worldviews, values, and customs of certain groups and assume these traits to be normative and stable. We talk about how Latinos value family closeness and interdependence, how Anglos are time-conscious and schedule-oriented, how the Irish like to tell stories and drink. However, on close examination, deciding about sameness and difference isn't so simple.

Even if one could describe characteristics that make up something like "Jewishness" or "Mexicanness" or "blackness," ethnic identities are profoundly modified by other variables that affect behavior, experience, and worldviews. The cultural experiences of African American women are very different from those of African American men. A Puerto Rican elder who practices *espiritismo*—a belief in the ability of invisible spirits to materialize—as a way of coping with the loss of her granddaughter to cancer, has a different connection to her heritage than does the Puerto Rican mother who trusts only her Roman Catholic priest for advice about her drug-addicted son.

Gender, race, class, religion, nationality, and

even cohort (the historical generation into which a person is born) all contribute to cultural identities. Consistencies of language, meaning or belief systems, worldviews, and experiences often lend a sense of familiarity and community for people who share the same culture. But inconsistencies, variabilities, and novelties along some of those dimensions exist as well. Cultural identities are also influenced by the constructs supplied by the dominant discourses. Taking these influences into account, and the myriad cultural blends that result, helps us avoid treating cultures as static. Given this incredibly complex, moving construct that we vaguely call the "culture" of a person or a family, how do we address its relevance and place for families that seek psychotherapy?

## MULTICULTURALISM AND PSYCHOTHERAPY

Two constructs encompass family therapy's current focus on multiculturalism: (1) a *cultural diversity* practice that respects cultural preferences among clients and critically examines existing models of the family and theories and techniques used in psychotherapy; and (2) a *social justice* practice that focuses on the effects of power differentials (due to gender, economic, and racial inequities) on individual and family well-being and on the relationship between clients and therapists.

*A Cultural Diversity Lens*

One of the first effects of bringing culture into the therapy room is that it upsets our theoretical applecart. Multiculturalism challenges what traditional schools of thought—psychoanalytic, systemic, structural, strategic, and so on—consider universal. Views about how families function, how problems develop, and how change is facilitated by those approaches may be "local" ideas originated by various "schools of thought" or "cultures"(Fancher, 1995) within the professional standard clinical practices. It follows from this that clients' beliefs or behaviors that are part of a cultural meaning system other than the one in which the therapist has been schooled could potentially be judged as dysfunctional or at least problematic. In the newer modes of family therapy, where a respect for or a consideration of differences is at the core of the principle of therapeutic respect, we see families as all different, all uniquely organized, and all needing description, rather than categorization, in order for us to understand them (Anderson & Goolishian, 1992; Alexander & Sexton, 2002; Freedman & Combs, 1996; Madsen, 1999; Penn & Frankfurt, 1994; Sexton & Alexander, 2002; White, 1989).

To avoid confusing other cultural ways with dysfunction, a multicultural therapist needs to incorporate a critically questioning attitude toward the Euro-American biases inherent in most professional training. This means accepting that theories and interventions stem from one local cultural niche and are not the standard by which families can be evaluated. Instead, a practice based on curiosity and respect for cultural diversity explores the healing resources within the client's culture and develops a stance of empathic "sociological imagination" (Wright Mills, 1959). When we attend to issues of race, ethnicity, social class, gender, religion, or sexual orientation, critical questions are raised about the customary assumptions of mainstream psychotherapy. In family therapy, issues of boundaries, hierarchies, communication styles, or life-cycle norms may come into question and lead to transformations and accommodations of taken-for-granted therapy concepts and techniques (Gergen, Gulerce, Lock, & Misra, 1996; Sampson, 1993; Taylor & Gutmann, 1994).

## A Sociopolitical Lens

Multiculturalism consists of more than a respect for multiple meanings or diverse values about family life. A component of social justice is essential to the multiculturalist lens. Members of collective-identity political movements—African Americans, Latinos, gay rights advocates, or feminists—have been denied their own voice in determining the conditions of their lives and (Sampson, 1993; Young, 1990) seek redress not only by having the legitimacy of their own worldviews recognized but also by obtaining equal rights and access to resources.

In the clinical arena, this social justice position directs the attention to life conditions, power differentials, and prejudice that limit social and economic opportunities, promote internalized racism, and affect psychological development and mental health for those who are poor or marginalized. Without a lens that includes social inequities, cultural preferences may be used as "explanations" for economic failure, domestic violence, or poor school performance, whereas the larger negative effects of poverty and social discrimination are downplayed.

A sociopolitical lens is not limited to impoverished clients. For example, in the past, a case of anorexia nervosa was viewed as "idiosyncratically" linked to an "overinvolved" mother and a "peripheral" father, without awareness of the social demand for the gender specialization of each parent and the social demands for thinness in young women (Bordo, 1997). More recently, a large number of therapists are considering cultural and sociopolitical discourses to be central to the treatment of anorexia and other eating disorders (Epston, 1993). A social justice practice connects mental health issues with experiences of social oppression and aims to empower families in their interactions with larger systems and cultural discourses, including those in the psychotherapy field. (Hardy & Laszloffy, 1994; Korin, 1994)

In addition to attending to cultural diversity and social justice issues, a fundamental part of the multicultural equation consists of the therapist attitudes that incorporate beliefs about individual and family resilience, and support clients' personal agency and creativity. Therapy must not become a form of social and cultural reductionism, whereby a client's gender, race, or social class automatically explains that person's beliefs, attitudes and behavior. Although interlaced with historical moments, cultural discourses, and sociopolitical forces, the client's biography is always unique.

## MECA: A Multilevel/Multidimensional Approach

One answer to the questions of how therapists can orient themselves in the array of issues related to cultural diversity and sociopolitical realities is provided by the Multidimensional-Ecosystemic-Comparative Approach (MECA), (Falicov, 1995, 1998a). MECA encompasses the ability to hold various levels of consideration: the "universal" similarities, the idiosyncratic particulars, and the sociopolitical level. It offers a multidimensional definition of culture, a method for making meaningful comparisons across groups, and room for multiple and evolving cultural narratives. Rather than making culture marginal and an add-on to theory, practice, or training, a multidimensional-ecosystemic-comparative approach takes culture into the *mainstream* of all teaching, thinking, and intervening in therapy (Falicov, 1988, 1995).

MECA is based on the idea that we are all multicultural persons, rather than belonging to a single group that can be summarized with a single label: Latino, lesbian, Lutheran, or Black. In reality, each person belongs to, participates in, and identifies with multiple groups that provide particular experiences and bestow particular values. Furthermore, people are denied access or are excluded from certain settings, and these exclusions also shape their experiences.

## THE CONSTRUCT OF ECOLOGICAL NICHE

Taken altogether, these participations and exclusions make up a client's and also a therapist's *ecological niche*. Including culture in therapy requires that therapists and other service providers locate individuals and families in terms of race, class, religion, sexual orientation, occupation, migration experiences, nationality, and ethnicity. Likewise, all service providers must locate themselves in the same variables. Describing an ecological niche is equally important for "mainstream" clients who are White, middle class, and Protestant. Cultural location should not be described only for minority groups and should not imply that culture and society influence only the marginalized groups, whereas the dominant groups are regarded implicitly as the standard norm.

Another related idea underlying MECA is that the therapy encounter is really an encounter between the therapist's and the family's cultural and personal constructions. Therapists' views about family and family problems and resources stem from their ecological niche, which includes their own cultural variables, as well as their preferred brand of theory and professional subculture.

The construct of ecological niche makes it apparent that human beings share *cultural borderlands* (Anzaldúa, 1987; Rosaldo, 1989) or zones of overlap with others. By virtue of sharing the experiences of contexts such as race, social class, occupation, religion, or ethnicity, discrete groups dissolve and partial groupings and bridges of human connectedness emerge.

A middle-class first-generation Vietnamese agnostic biologist may have more in common with another university-educated biologist, even though the latter is White, than with a Vietnamese immigrant who is Roman Catholic and is employed in a beauty salon. The first two share a greater number of cultural borderlands than the second two, in spite of the fact that they are both Vietnamese. The notion of ethnic or racial matching between therapist and client becomes more complex within this framework, because therapists and clients can share other forms of connectedness through their cultural borderlands.

With MECA, therapists make a holistic assessment of all the contexts to which the family belongs and draw from the family members their understanding of the resources, the constraints, and the cultural dilemmas those multiple contexts create. These types of collaborative explorations render a picture closer to what the anthropologist Clifford Geertz (1973) dubbed a "thick" description, rather than relying on identity labels and a priori knowledge about collective groups. Aiming for thick descriptions, the observer draws conclusions based on the people's descriptions of their own complex locations, using their own cultural categories of understanding, rather than utilizing the labels and categories of the observer.

## A CULTURAL GENERALIST FRAMEWORK

MECA attempts to arrive at a "cultural generalist" framework because it focuses only on those dimensions that family therapists generally use to orient themselves about basic aspects of relational life to be taken into account when trying to understand a presenting problem. The four dimensions identified by MECA are migration, ecological context, family organization, and family life cycle. MECA is based on the belief that the contents of these dimensions are culturally constructed, but that the dimensions themselves as general categories probably exist in all societies. In the clinical situation, an assessment includes conversations about possible connections between the presenting concerns that bring the family to therapy and the various cultural dimensions covered in MECA. The assessment should be relevant to the family's concerns, so the question revolves around the family's and client's views and theories about the problem, who is most affected, and what has been done about it. From these assessments a contextual picture of the family emerges that includes cultural dilemmas that may be connected with the presenting problems or cultural and personal strengths that may be helpful in finding solutions.

## MIGRATION AND ACCULTURATION

Much of the current emphasis on cultural competence is based on the demographic changes of the past 20 years. Statistics show that 1 out of 6 people in the United States are foreign born and 1 out of 4 is the offspring of foreign-born parents. Many immigrants leave their countries reluctantly. Their motivations primarily include improving their desperate economic situation or escaping political oppression and organized violence. Another language was spoken in their homes when they were children, and cultural dissonance permeates their lives.

### The Uprooting of Meaning Systems

Personal stories, views of reality, and adaptive behaviors are all anchored in the lived experiences of one's race, ethnicity, or social class *within national contexts*. Perhaps the most fundamental dislocation of migration is the uprooting from known structures of cultural meanings tied to those national contexts. These structures of meanings and beliefs have been likened to the roots that sustain and nourish a plant (Marris, 1980). The uprooting of established meaning systems and exposure to new life constructs have been linked to various types of psychological distress for immigrants, including culture shock (Garza-Guerrero, 1974); marginality, social alienation, and psychological conflict (Grinberg & Grinberg, 1989; Shuval, 1982); psychosomatic symptoms, such as palpitations, dizziness, and insomnia; and anxiety and depression (Warheit, Vega, Auth, & Meinhardt, 1985). Post-traumatic stress may occur if migration involved trauma, for example, for asylum seekers or for political refugees who have witnessed or have been victims of mass destruction.

## AMBIGUOUS LOSS

The experiences of loss, grieving, and mourning that accompany migration have been likened to the processes of grief that accompany other types of losses, particularly the death of loved ones. However, the experience of migration loss seems to be better captured by the construct of ambiguous loss (Boss, 1991, 1999). Migration is a stressful event that brings with it losses of all kinds: gone is the support of family, friends, and community; gone is the ease of the native language, the customs, the foods, and the multiple connections with one's own country itself. These physical absences are real, yet unlike the losses of death, with migration it is always possible to fantasize an eventual return or a forthcoming reunion with loved ones. Immigrants also hope that the added burdens will be lifted when their hard work is rewarded with improved economic or educational conditions or new political or cultural freedoms. The contradictory elements create a persistent mix of emotions: sadness and elation, absence and

presence, despair and new hope, which make grieving incomplete or postponed. Ambiguity becomes inscribed in immigrants' lives, an ambiguity that they must constantly learn to live with.

## A MIGRATION NARRATIVE

Obtaining a *migration narrative* provides the therapist entrée into the individual members' migratory experiences, their dreams and hopes and their strategies for coping with massive changes. To assess the changes in family composition and the meaning of the migration, the therapist might ask how long each family member has resided in the United States; who immigrated first, who was left behind, who came later, or who is yet to be reunited; what motivated the migration and how they went about planning for it; what stresses and joys were experienced by various family members at various stages; and what strengths and resources they discovered. It is important to inquire about who was left behind and their reactions to the migration because they are also members of a social system in transformation, affected by and affecting those who migrated.

Although ambiguity permeates the immigrant's experience, the degree of agency people experience in making the decision to migrate may have important consequences for psychological distress. The migration narrative should start temporally in the premigration stage, to clarify various members' participation and feelings about the decision. Immigrants who feel coaxed, forced, or manipulated to migrate may display more symptoms of anxiety and depression than so those who were fully cognizant and accepting of their decisions. In telling a migration narrative, family members may find meaning in their uprooting in terms of their unique personal history, which incorporates gains as well as losses.

## RESILIENT ADAPTATIONS AND RITUALS

Most immigrants and refugees demonstrate enormous capacity for resilient adaptations. The need to reestablish a sense of coherence and make meaning out of adverse circumstances is manifested in the emergence of what may be thought of as spontaneous rituals, which renew presences across absences by recreating the familiarity of old spaces, sounds, faces, smells, and other cultural rituals in the new land (Falicov, 2002, and in press). These rituals of connection, recreation, memory, and preservation illustrate the ambiguous and conflictual nature of immigrants' losses and continued attachments. Yet, embedded in these spontaneous rituals, there are resilient both/and dual visions or "solutions" that symbolize learning to live with the ambiguity of never putting a final closure to migration. Work with immigrants can greatly profit from an exploration of the place of rituals in their lives. It seems possible that the abandonment of cultural rituals or excessive reliance on their performance at the expense of new adaptations may signal difficulties around migration. The creation of therapeutic rituals to deal with migration issues holds promise of dealing with migration impasses (Falicov, 2002; Imber-Black, Roberts, & Whiting, 1988; Woodcock, 1995).

## ACCULTURATION AND ALTERNATION THEORIES

In time, new cultural and social contexts generate new meanings and accommodations or hybrid mixes between the dominant and the local cultures. Acculturation theory assumes that immigrants gradually shed their original culture and language in favor of a better "fit" that correlates with mainstream culture and mental health. Acculturation theory has been challenged recently, after several studies indicated that immigrants who try to "Ameri-canize," or assimilate, actually have *more* psychological problems and drug use than those who retain their language, cultural ties, and rituals, at least partially (Escobar, 1998; Portes & Rumbaut, 1990). Furthermore, social ills such as drugs, alcohol, teen pregnancy, domestic violence, gangs, and AIDS, which affect discriminated groups, appear more frequently in the second and third generations than in the first (Padilla, 1994), presumably because the initial protection of a firm cultural and family identity was still intact in the immigrant generation.

A recent model, alternation theory, is based on a different assumption than acculturation theory, in other words, that it is possible to know two languages and two cultures and to appropriately use this knowledge for different contexts (La Framboise, Coleman, & Geron, 1993), without giving up one for the other. Communications made possible by globalization have transformed immigration into a two-home, trans-context lifestyle for many immigrants (Bustamante, 1995; Schiller, Basch, & Blanc-Szanton, 1992; Turner, 1991). Studying Mexicans in Redwood City, California, Rouse (1992) observed a "cultural bifocality," that is, the capacity to see the world through two different value lenses, such as maintaining language and ethnic values within the family, while also learning and using English and American values when dealing with larger systems. Intrafamily conflict may emerge as family members acquire the new values or retain the old ones at different rates. Dilemmas of cultural meanings, beliefs, and expectations are often the subtext of many individual and family consultations and may also cause misunderstandings with larger systems, including with therapists' discourses. Dual visions of continuity and change or double discourses appear also in the sociopolitical arena. Double consciousness, DuBois's (1903) description of the awareness of African Americans about who they really are in their own group, in contrast with the prejudicial ways in which they are seen by others, is helpful in understanding the feelings and experiences of living in two worlds.

## STRUCTURAL DILEMMAS

In addition to dilemmas of cultural meanings, beliefs, and expectations, migration precipitates family structural dilemmas, primarily because of separations and reunions between extended and nuclear family members but also among nuclear family members, such as when the father or the mother migrates first alone, to be reunited later with the children (Suarez-Orozco & Suarez-Orozco, 2001). Both men and women experience difficulties during migration, and both use mechanisms that appear to follow gender socialization, such as depression or psychosomatic problems in women and alcohol dependency and violent behaviors in men.

Separations are tied to practical reasons and economic limitations, but there may be other powerful, less conscious, reasons, such as loyalty toward the family of origin. Regardless of the reasons, separations at migration may differentially affect individuals and families. For example, separations may increase closeness between some family subsystems, whereas it weakens bonds among other family groupings, both among those who left and among those who stayed. Increased nuclear closeness cushions from culture shock and supplements role functions left vacant, but, ultimately, these reorganizations may limit the reincorporation of separated family members, as it happens with children who become closer to their grandmothers than to their biological parents. Individual development may also be curtailed through either excessive closeness or excessive distance from significant figures.

The process of reunification is often traumatic for all involved, especially children, who may present with stomach pains, sleep distur-

bances, and temper tantrums or defiant behaviors that become the precipitant for therapy consultations. A therapeutic ritual that can be used at the time of reunion to help the family bridge the absences and temporal gaps of the separations is a "catching-up life narrative" (Falicov, 1998a). It consists of a family storytelling, whereby all members present facts, anecdotes, photos, objects, or drawings of their lives apart. The therapist weaves all these elements into a written story form that is repeatedly read and modified until a final product is arrived at, sometimes adding a "feed-forward" section that predicts an affirming future family form. Apprehension about the future may be assuaged by previewing a possible more stable future, where the family will continue to be together rather than suffer new separations.

How immigrants cope with these separations and the ambiguities of losing so much, while hoping for a better future, is in part related to the meanings they attach to the separations. The attached meanings often reflect the culture's preferred ways of dealing with adversity and losses that are beyond one's control. The use of religion or spiritual resources is one example of a positive cultural mechanism for coping with suffering that should not be automatically attributed to passive fatalism (Boss, 1999; Comas-Díaz, 1989; Falicov, 1999a). Turning to spiritual solace can also be seen from a sociopolitical perspective. Fanon (1967) suggests that when self-determination is limited, as is the case with nondominant groups, placing oneself under the protection of benevolent and powerful figures may help counteract fear, powerlessness, and lack of agency.

Other structural dilemmas occur when wives remain isolated in their homes and do not learn English, or conversely, when they encounter economic and gender freedoms denied before. Both situations can unleash matrimonial conflicts. Generational hierarchies may also be overturned when children serve as language intermediaries with the host society and cultural translators for their parents. Often, this hierarchical reversal is limited to certain areas, but in some situations it may become pervasive and eventually weaken parental authority, particularly if the parents abdicate their cherished values.

A therapist who intervenes in these situations of cultural dilemmas or conflicts by quickly becoming an agent of acculturation into the mainstream may create more, rather than less, emotional distress. Maintaining continuity, that is, supporting the "wisdom of no-change" and thus not overburdening an already unstable situation with more suggestions for "adaptive" change, may be more therapeutic for overstressed families (Falicov, 1993). Promoting acculturation goals may in effect colonize clients by "imposing" values without awareness of cultural biases, as, for example, when the therapist supports the "Americanized" second generation against "old-fashioned" parents.

## ECOLOGICAL CONTEXT

Migration or social disadvantage transports families to a social terrain different from the exposure to the mainstream messages of the dominant cultural discourses. Bombarded with differences, families re-create elements of their own culture and class in urban ethnic neighborhoods that serve as a buffer against culture shock and discrimination, while providing a continuity of faces, voices, smells, and foods. But the illusion of a safe haven may be offset by the fear of persecution, physical threat, and social unrest in inner-city neighborhoods. Middle-class families have their own set of stresses in isolated suburbs, with pressures of competition and maintaining affluent and overworked lifestyles.

In the case of immigrants, relocation can disrupt the emotional support, advice, and ma-

terial aid that social networks provide. Enduring intimate relationships, whether husband-wife or parent–child, are taxed with many more requests for companionship from each other than before (Sluzki, 1969). Lacking the watchful eye of nearby relatives, parents compensate with restrictions on adolescents' activities, which may aggravate intergenerational conflicts. Because social networks are essential for physical and emotional well-being (Sluzki, 1993), particularly in situations of stress, therapists must assess the family's social interactions and sources of support and community involvement.

Religion and spirituality are the most transportable elements in the immigrant's knapsack. In fact, the performance of soothing rituals, such as prayer, may contain elements of resilience for many impoverished groups. The church or temple in the ethnic neighborhood also provides community support in the form of a sanctuary for undocumented immigrants, a center for crisis counseling, and a meeting place for activist groups and community celebrations. Priests, pastors, or rabbis who officiate at life-cycle celebrations, communions, baptisms, and weddings may become resources for stability and a sense of community.

For many ethnic groups, folk medicine and indigenous spirituality coexist with mainstream religion and medical practices. Folk healers are consulted for many maladies but are turned to the most for "folk illnesses," which are often thought to have psychological roots. It is important that therapists develop nonjudgmental ways of inquiring about these sources of help and assume a collaborative attitude toward them.

The notion that little in life is under one's control is a worldview more frequently attributed to cultural discourses other than the American view, which is that much in life can be modified through personal will or intervention. It is important for therapists to consider that the ecology of lower socioeconomic status can disempower individuals and limit their hopeful outlook. The belief in an external locus of control should not be taken as a deficit but rather as a realistic and philosophical form of coping by trying to accept circumstances that may be beyond one's control.

Externalizing conversations, that is, separating a client from a problem and stimulating personal agency or choice (White, 1989), also may be used, particularly in the form of "inner" rather than "outer" externalization. According to Tomm, Suzuki, and Suzuki (1990), an outer externalization involves talking about a problem as if it eventually could be defeated or escaped. Therefore, the conversation tends toward discussion about conflict and control over the problem. An inner externalization, on the other hand, encourages talking about a problem as if it will be necessary to "live with it." This latter formulation is more syntonic with cultural discourses that encourage accepting or being resigned to problems, rather than confronting or struggling against them.

Interactions with institutions, such as school, work, and health systems, are challenging experiences for many marginalized adults and children. They may experience incompatibility between home and institution in primary languages, difference in cognitive and relational styles, and meaning or belief systems, which may cause conflict, confusion, and a sense of inferiority. Teachers, employers, physicians, and therapists also experience dissonance when they struggle to understand and serve culturally diverse families. A shift from a positive to a disenchanted or oppositional attitude occurs after children and parents become aware of institutional marginalization or racism, increasing the possibility of school dropout or work unemployment (Ogbu, 1987; Suárez-Orozco & Suárez-Orozco, 1995a, 1995b). Therapists need to explore the family's experiences and evaluations of larger systems interactions, whether

these are teachers, priests, medical doctors, therapists, or employers, and the impact of these experiences in the family's outlook of the present help being offered.

Common constraints of immigrants are social and cultural isolation, ignorance about community resources, and tensions between home norms and those of the school, peer group, or work situation. To inquire about such ecological issues, the therapist may explore the family's neighborhood (housing, safety, crime, gangs); racial acceptance; employment (income, occupation, job stability); extended family and friendship networks; school and parent–teacher relationships; church attendance or other spiritual practices; and experiences with helping professions, including the present referral source.

It is revealing for the family and for the therapist to draw an "eco-map" that depicts family–environment relationships (Hartman & Laird, 1983). If this map reveals that ecological constraints and tensions zap the family's strengths to cope, the therapist may temporarily become a "social intermediary" or a "matchmaker" between the family and various communal institutions (Falicov, 1988; Minuchin et al., 1967). The therapist can help the family mobilize to use existing networks or facilitate building new reciprocal ones. Priests may offer spiritual support, particularly when dealing with physical illness, old age, and death. Relatives or compatriots can be advocates for a child or for the family in dealing with institutions, as well as a temporary relief for parents. The aim is to collaborate in empowering the family to deal with larger systems and to insist on receiving adequate services.

### Family Organization

Cultural preferences and limited financial resources have traditionally motivated families from impoverished countries (many Latin

American and Asian countries) and discriminated groups (African Americans or single mothers) to live in close proximity to extended family networks that can provide emotional and practical support. They form a larger kin and kith network than the isolated nuclear middle-class family that has become the prototype of family psychology depictions of normal family life. It is important for therapists to help draw a genogram that includes the current family composition and, in the case of immigrants, the family network clients had in their countries. It is important to explore multigenerational patterns that might be related to the presenting complaint. Although the migration narrative can become a powerful magnet that absorbs all elements of family history for the protagonists and their therapists, immigrant families, like other families, have complex past life stories that preceded migration and might be implicated in their current concerns.

In traditional settings, intergenerational lifelong connectedness and respect for parental authority are valued greatly, sometimes creating structural and meaning conflicts with the contemporary egalitarian democratic ideologies based on the husband-wife bond. Certain dyads, like mother–eldest son or father–eldest son, may be very strong and may also run against notions of egalitarianism from parents towards all of their children, complicating sibling relationships. Traditional family organization affects family bonds along several dimensions of interaction: (1) collectivism and individualism, (2) gender and generation hierarchies, and (3) communication styles and emotional expressivity. Cultural preferences along these dimensions may remain over several generations, in some fashion, and may stir up dilemmas when younger generations incorporate Anglo-American discourses, or when the family comes in contact with the institutions of mainstream culture, such as the values upheld by psychotherapists.

## COLLECTIVISM AND INDIVIDUALISM

Family collectivism is embedded in the cultural discourse of many ethnic groups, such as Latinos, African Americans, Asians, and even many European groups, such as Italian or Greeks. Family inclusiveness may also be more typical among women than men. Under these values, family boundaries easily expand to include grandparents, uncles, aunts, or cousins. Children who are orphaned or whose parents have migrated or divorced may be incorporated into the family, along with adults who have remained single or have become widowed or divorced. Strong sibling ties are stressed from a young age and throughout life. Any member of this large network can be involved in the problem or can become part of the solution. A family may bring a relative to a psychotherapy session, providing an entrée for therapists to understand the social network around the family and expand their professional definitions of family composition and family life.

Family interdependence involves sharing the nurturing and disciplining of children, shared financial responsibility, companionship for lonely or isolated members, and communal problem-solving. Concomitantly, there is a low reliance on institutions and outsiders. The idea of a "familial self" (Roland, 1988) is useful in understanding many individuals' dedication to family unity and family honor and the celebration of family rituals. Adult sons or daughters who may unwittingly curtail their chances for marriage in order to take care of an ailing parent may be responding to their familial selves and not necessarily be inappropriately self-sacrificing.

The process of separation/individuation, so highly regarded in American culture may be de-emphasized in other cultures in favor of close family ties. Deficit views tend to pathologize this type of family closeness and label it enmeshment. However, family closeness may reflect cultural interactional preferences that contribute to resilient adaptations. Furthermore, in traditional settings, individuation also takes place, along with family closeness, via marriage, work, or simply having personal opinions and a sense of personal self, along with a familial self. Therapists who insist on stressing the client's individual, as pitted against family, needs may run counter to internalized cultural specifications.

## GENDER AND GENERATION HIERARCHIES

When family loyalty and collective cooperation are culturally stressed, usually there is also an emphasis on clear family hierarchies. Child-rearing practices of ethnic or disadvantaged groups may reflect this emphasis on hierarchies. Punishment, shaming, belittling, deception, promises, and threats may be used in response to young people's misbehavior.

Unquestioned respect for authority runs counter to the democratic, egalitarian discourses of psychotherapists, who may negatively judge parents who show concern and caring according to their cultural ways. The parents may also react and judge negatively the "permissiveness" of American society, perhaps unwittingly personified in the individualistic democratic discourses of the therapist. Transparency in the therapeutic dialogue helps clarify the benevolent intent on both sides. Even in patriarchal systems, a child's well-being is the responsibility of both parents, and, therefore, even traditional men can be persuaded to participate in conversations about children's well-being.

Although a patriarchal view of gender roles persists among many Asian, Latin American, and other immigrants, more complex transitional dynamics are evolving. For example, a double standard of gender socialization and sexuality persists (Falicov, 1992), yet decision making is often shared by both parents or in-

volves a process in which the mother alone or the father alone commands much authority (Kutsche, 1983; Ybarra, 1982). Increasingly, immigrant and ethic family life is characterized by a wide range of structures and processes, from patriarchal to egalitarian, with many combinations in-between. Given the centrality of the parent–child dyad and the generational conflicts that may take place in immigrant families with adolescent children, it is not unusual to encounter situations where the father tries to exert authority by disciplining the children and compelling them to obey the mother, whereas she tends to defend and protect them. This interactional pattern may generate father-mother-child triangulations that need to be seen culturally and contextually, rather than simply regarded as "pathological" (Falicov, 1998b). Often, triangulations may be successful in resolving conflicts indirectly, in ways that are culturally syntonic even if they run counter to family therapy notions about generational boundaries, as when a family member asks another to intercede in a conflict, rather than confronting her opponent directly.

## COMMUNICATION AND EMOTIONAL EXPRESSIVITY

Indirect, implicit, or covert communication is consonant with some groups' collectivistic emphasis on family harmony, on "getting along" and not making others uncomfortable. For other traditional groups, assertiveness and open differences of opinion may be the norm. From their own cultural discourses about communication, therapists may regard the first cultures as too stifling of individual expression and the second as too dismissive of the feelings of others. Yet both are legitimate ways of handling interpersonal relationships.

Because of power differentials and respect for authority, clients may feel that it is impolite to disagree with the therapist. Encouraging the family members to express their reactions, both positive and negative, to the therapist's opinions helps to establish a tone of mutuality. Manifesting real interest in the client, rather than gaining data via referral sheets or obtaining many behavioral details about a problem, is essential to build personal relationships that carry emotional expressivity. Similarly, a therapist who suggests an explicit contract about the number of sessions or the treatment goals may be too task-oriented, rather than person-oriented, increasing the cultural distance clients may already be feeling.

The three elements of traditional cultural discourses—collectivism, hierarchies, and indirect communication—discussed previously, can appear to be constraining to individual development, but therapists should not assume that a position of cultural resistance to those cultural preferences is in order. Professional discourses are often based on mainstream values, such as individualism, that should not be privileged or imposed. Changes in discourse are valid only if they stem from a true and informed collaboration with the clients.

*Family Life Cycle*

Families from diverse cultures may approach family and sociocultural life in ways that may differ from the dominant interpretations of the life cycle. The meaning of the stages and transitions, the developmental tasks, and the rituals of the individual and the family life cycle may all be heavily guided by culture, custom, and traditional practice (Falicov, 1998a, 1999b). Many groups may differ from the dominant culture's view of the life cycle by experiencing a longer state of interdependence between mother and children and a more relaxed attitude about children's achievement of self-reliance skills (these attitudes are often mistaken for overprotection); the absence of an independent living situation for unmarried

young adults; the absence of an "empty nest" syndrome or a middle-age crisis and a refocusing on marital issues; and the continuous involvement, status, and usefulness of elders in the family. These traditional developmental expectations may persist alongside the new considerations of individual pursuits and romantic love espoused by the younger generations, sometimes causing intergenerational tensions.

For many traditional families, leaving home occurs primarily through marriage, and boundary or loyalty issues with families of origin are common, particularly because the second generation has begun to stress husband-wife exclusivity. The relationship between the mother-in-law and the daughter-in-law may enter into conflict, given the differences in cultural codes.

Some developmental impasses can be linked to the stresses of migration. Leaving home can become more problematic when parents have depended on their older children to be intermediaries with the larger culture. Younger siblings, too, may cling to an older one who appears to be more culturally understanding than the parents are. Normal-life cycle events, such as the death of a loved one, either in the country of origin or the adoptive country, may precipitate additional stress by rekindling the ambiguities of migration and the questioning about the wisdom of being so far away from loved ones (Falicov, 2003).

Because professional discourses tend to be based in taken-for-granted but nevertheless culture-bound expectations about how to navigate life-cycle stages and transitions, therapists need to be aware and self-reflexive about their own normative evaluations about age-appropriate behaviors in their clients. Once the life-cycle dilemmas within the family or with other institutions are deconstructed and discussed, the therapist may attempt to become a "cultural mediator," encouraging conversation between parents and offspring about developmental expectations and their loyalties to both cultures.

The presence of two or three generations, each speaking a different language and holding different cultural values while partaking in some common customs and traditions, is both very enriching and resourceful. The challenge is how to merge and blend differing cultural codes about family life. It is not unusual for a Latino, a Greek, or an Italian group of adult siblings to have arrived at vastly different connections to their parents' language and cultural rituals and to also have varied degrees of adherence to the mainstream culture and language.

Gender differences appear as well in perceptions of life-cycle meanings. Although studies of 20 years ago reported a slower pace of language-cultural change in immigrant women than in men, more recent studies indicate that women adapt to cultural changes faster than men do. Women are more likely to adopt new life-cycle values and gains in greater personal freedoms (Hondagneu-Sotelo, 1994).

## A Method for Deconstructing Cultural Meaning Systems

In a rapidly evolving multicultural society many family problems may be related to several conflicting cultural experiences and perspectives, often those regarding generational and gender perspectives. The method is one

attempt to deal with dilemmas of intersecting cultural views by constructing integration, alternations, and other hybrid solutions between cultural meanings (Turner, 1991; Falicov, 1998a; see Table 3.1).

The first step is to "draw attention to differences" in ideologies and meanings. It involves simply naming the differences: the husband may feel that women's work is at home, whereas the wife feels ready and willing to work outside the home; the son may feel that the father is overly strict in his discipline, but the father feels that his disciplinary approach is correct.

The second step is to "contextualize the differences." By inquiring about the experiences behind the differences, an appreciation emerges that each person's thoughts, preferences, and feelings are influenced by his or her ecological niche–the combination of institutional contexts and social settings from which the person has been included or excluded. Polarizations soften and are replaced for greater respect or appreciation for each other's views.

The third step is to "reframe the presenting concern as a dilemma of coexisting meanings." The discussion focuses on how family members' differences about collectivism and individualism, gender and generation hierarchies, and communicative directness and indirectness pose dilemmas for the adults, the children, the men, and the women in the family. The presenting problem is looked at as being connected to the stresses of these dilemmas

**TABLE 3.1**
Deconstructing Cultural Meaning Systems

1. Drawing attention to **DIFFERENCES** within the family and with larger systems (individualism and collectivism; gender and generational hierarchies)
2. **CONTEXTUALIZING** the differences (understand socialization forces and search for similarities that transcend differences)
3. **DILEMMAS** of coexistence of conflicting meanings (how these relate to the presenting problem)
4. Previewing **FUTURE** family shapes, narratives, solutions (alternation, integration, metatexts)

or as an attempted solution, albeit a problematic one.

The fourth step, that of "previewing future family patterns and cultural blends," introduces a future-oriented dimension. What kinds of alternation or blends of meaning systems are possible? Can each be used, depending on the context at hand? Are there overarching meanings, such as universal needs for freedom or justice, that can transcend differences? Therapists have an opportunity here to be transparent with clients about their own personal or professional belief systems. Asking these questions can orient the family toward a future in which multiple cultural meanings coexist or are integrated. Each family will find its own solutions of blending and living with cultural differences.

The therapist might note similarities and contrasts with dominant cultural meanings, as well as the possible dilemmas and enrichments precipitated by the meeting of different beliefs and meaning systems. These explorations should set a tone of respect, curiosity, and collaboration in understanding the philosophical and behavioral consequences of a cultural way of life as part of American society.

## TOWARD BOTH/AND INTEGRATIVE ATTITUDES

An ethnically focused position encourages therapists—though always mindful that families never fit stereotypes—to inform themselves of as many details as possible about particular cultures, views in family life, and beliefs about health and the process of change that lead to cures. This position can be contrasted to a "not-knowing" stance in therapy. "Not-knowing" approaches are based on curiosity and on dialogue that takes into account all meanings—cultural and personal—as they emerge in the therapeutic situation. Yet there

are families where "credibility" and direction from a "knowing" agent "fits."

These two positions seem to be unnecessarily polarized. A dialectic, both/and approach, which combines a "not-knowing" stance with "some-knowing" or information about specific cultures, including the therapist's own, allows for more complexity and effectiveness. This integration of attitudes can provide the most beneficial means of working with diverse client families, as the following case illustrates.

Behind the one-way mirror, an emerging power struggle was brewing between a family therapy trainee at a well-known training institution and the Bernals, a Puerto Rican immigrant family. The therapist insisted that the father's delusions should be treated with psychotropic medication. But the family politely refused pharmacotherapy and could not answer why. Suspecting there was a plausible cultural belief or practice behind the resistant behavior, I suggested to the therapist that she ask the family members if they had other health or religious resources that might be helpful to the husband's condition. The wife then said she believed her husband would get better because prayer would help him. I suggested the therapist adopt a curious stance by asking the family, "How does prayer work?" To this, the mother replied that she met twice a week with her friends to pray at a local storefront church, and all of their prayers together swelled up to a powerful, luminous energy that could counteract the dark forces that had overtaken her husband's psyche. The family's refusal to accept could now be understood positively as linked to their belief systems about effective treatment of delusions. Furthermore, their "cure" connected the mother to her social network of co-nationals, which was clearly supportive and helpful. This new meaning decreased the polarization with the therapist and opened the door for collaboration in stages.

Having some knowledge of cultural details attuned the consultant to the possibility that religion and ecological context may be playing a role in the family's resistance to the therapist's "local" medical cure for delusions. A therapist with a "not-knowing" approach toward culture might have eventually arrived at the same place. The family members, meanwhile, conscious of difference with the dominant culture views, might not ever have volunteered their prayer practice unless asked. One might be tempted to say that the first therapist would have done better. Not necessarily. The ethnic-focused therapist may have stopped at simple respect for the family's cultural solution once the family mentioned prayer. A "not-knowing," curious stance was very helpful in taking the inquiry further by asking how prayer works concretely in the family's particular subculture of religion. Weaving back and forth between these stances—one informed by some cultural knowledge and the other guided by curiosity—could clarify the family's fears that medication would preclude the prayers from working. The therapist could then ally with the family members to better define what kind of help they needed and would be willing to accept from the clinic.

In a both/and position, involving "some-knowing" and "not-knowing," the therapist must be comfortable with other "double discourses"—an ability to connect with the universal human similarities that unite us beyond color, class, ethnicity, or gender—yet simultaneously recognize and respect culture-specific differences due to color, class, ethnicity, and gender. This "double discourse" may be explicit or implicit, foreground or background, expanding or shrinking, the cultural empha-

sis depending on the case at hand. Consistent with the reality of shifting multiple contexts, there is no list of "do's" and "don'ts" when working with ethnic, gender, racial, or religious groups. There is only one "do" and one "don't"—*do* ask, and *don't* assume. Like the lines of the Pat Parker (1990) poem at the beginning of this chapter, we must relate to each other's universal humanity, yet not forget about each other's remarkable cultural contexts. The borderlands we share can be a meeting place for these conversations to begin.

## REFERENCES

Alexander, J. F., & Sexton, T. L. (2002). Functional family therapy: A model for treating high-risk, acting-out youth. In J. Lebow (Vol. Ed.), *Comprehensive handbook of psychotherapy, Vol. 4: Integrative/eclectic.* New York: Wiley.

Anderson, H., & Goolishian, H. A. (1982). Human systems as linguistic systems: Preliminary and evolving ideas about the implications for clinical theory. *Family Process, 27,* 371–393.

Anzaldúa, G. (1987). *Borderlands/La frontera: The new mestiza.* San Franscisco: Spinsters/Aunt Lute.

Aponte, H. J. (1976) The family school-interview: An eco-structural approach. *Family Process, 15,* 303–311.

Auerswald, E. H. (1968) Interdisciplinary versus Ecological Approach. *Family Process, 7,* 202–215.

Bordo, S. (1997). Anorexia nervosa: Psychopathology as crystallization of culture. In M. M. Gergen & S. N. Davis (Eds.), *Toward a new psychology of gender: A reader.* New York: Routledge.

Boss, P. (1991). Ambiguous Loss. In F. Walsh & M. McGoldrick (Eds.), *Living beyond loss: Death in the family.* New York: W. W. Norton.

Boss, P. (1999). *Ambiguous loss: Learning to live with unresolved grief.* Cambridge, MA: Harvard University Press.

Boyd-Franklin, N. (1989). *Black families in therapy.* New York: Guilford Press.

Bustamante, P. (1995). *The socioeconomics of undocumented migration flood.* Presentation at the Center for U.S. Mexican Studies, University of California, San Diego.

Comas-Díaz, L. (1989). Culturally relevant issues and treatment implications for Hispanics. In D. R. Koslow & E. Salett (Eds.), *Crossing cultures in mental health.* Washington, DC: Society for

International Education Training and Research.

DuBois, W. E. B. (1903). *The souls of black folk*. Chicago: McClurg.

Epston, D. (1993). Internalizing discourses versus externalizing discourses. In S. G. Gilligan & R. Price (Eds.), *Therapeutic conversations*. New York: Norton.

Epston, D. (1994). Extending the conversation. *Family Therapy Networker, 18*, 31–37, 62–23.

Escobar, J. I. (1998). Immigration and mental health: Why are immigrants better-off? *Archives of General Psychiatry, 55,* 781–782.

Falicov, C. J. (Ed.). (1983). *Cultural perspectives in family therapy*. Rockville, MD: Aspen.

Falicov, C. J. (1988). Learning to think culturally. In H. A. Liddle, D. C. Breunlin, & R. C. Schwartz (Eds.), *Handbook of family therapy training and supervision* (pp. 335–357). New York: Guilford Press.

Falicov, C. J. (1988 a). *Latino families in therapy: A guide to multicultural practice*. New York: Guilford Press.

Falicov, C. J. (1992). Love and gender in the Latino marriage. *American Family Therapy Association Newsletter, 48,* 30–36.

Falicov, C. J. (1993). Continuity and change: Lessons from immigrant families. *American Family Therapy Newsletter, Spring,* 30–34.

Falicov, C. J. (1995). Training to think culturally: A multidimensional comparative framework. *Family Process, 34,* 373–388.

Falicov, C. J. (1996). Mexican families II. In M. McGoldrick, J. Giordano, & J. K. Pearce (Eds.), *Ethnicity and family therapy* (2nd ed.). New York: Guilford Press.

Falicov, C. J. (1998a). *Latino families in therapy: A guide to multicultural practice*. New York: Guilford Press.

Falicov, C. J. (1998b). The cultural meaning of family triangles. In M. McGoldrick (Ed.), *Re-visioning family therapy: Race, culture, and gender in clinical practice*. New York: Guilford Press.

Falicov, C. J. (1999a). The value of religion and spirituality in immigrant Latinos. In F. Walsh (Ed.), *Spirituality and family therapy*. New York: Guilford Press.

Falicov, C. J. (1999b). Cultural variations in the family life cycle: The case of the Latino family. In B. Carter & M. McGoldrick (Eds.), *The changing family life cycle: A framework for family therapy* (3rd ed.). New York: Gardner Press.

Falicov, C. J. (2002). Ambiguous loss: Risk and resilience in Latino immigrant families. In M. Suarez Orozco & M. Paez (Eds.), *Latinos: Remaking America*. Berkeley, CA: University of California Press.

Falicov, C. (2003). Immigrant family processes. In F. Walsh (Ed.), *Normal family processes* (pp. 280–300). New York: Guilford Press.

Falicov, C. J., & Brudner-White, L. (1983). The shifting family triangle: The issue of cultural and contextual relativity. In C. J. Falicov (Ed.), *Cultural perspectives in family therapy* (pp. 52–67). Rockville, MD: Aspen.

Fancher, R. T. (1995). *Cultures of healing: Correcting the image of mental health care*. New York: Freeman.

Fanon, F. (1967). *Black skins, white masks*. New York: Grove.

Freedman, J., & Coombs, G. (1996). *Narrative therapy: The social construction of preferred realities*. New York: W. W. Norton.

Garza-Guerrero, A. C. (1974). Culture shock: Its mourning and the vicissitudes of identity. *Journal of American Psychoanalytic Association, 22,* 408–429.

Geertz, C. (1973). *The interpretation of cultures*. New York: Basic Books.

Gergen, K. J., Gulerce, A., Lock, A., & Misra, G. (1996). Psychological science in cultural context. *American Psychologist, 51*(5), 496–503.

Goldner, V. (1985). Feminism and family therapy. *Family Process, 24,* 31–47.

Grinberg, L., & Grinberg, R. (1989). *Psychoanalytic perspectives on migration and exile. Handbook of stress: Theoretical and clinical aspects* (2nd ed., pp. 641–657). New York: Free Press.

Hardy, K., & Laszloffy, T. (1994). Deconstructing race in family therapy. *Journal of Feminist Family Therapy, 5*(3/4), 5–33.

Hare-Mustin, R. C. (1978). A feminist approach to family therapy. *Family Process, 17,* 181–194.

Hartman, A., & Laird, J. (1983). *Family-centered social work practice*. New York: Free Press.

Hondagneu-Sotelo, P. (1994). *Gendered Transitions*. Berkeley: University of California Press.

Imber-Black, E., Roberts, J., & Whiting, R. (Eds.). (1988). *Rituals in families and family therapy*. New York: Norton.

Johnson, T., & Keren, M. (1998). The families of lesbian women and gay men. In M. McGoldrick *Re-visioning Family Therapy: Race, culture and gender in clinical practice*. New York: Guilford Press.

Korin, E. C. (1994). Social inequalities and therapeutic relationships: Applying Freire's ideas to clinical practice. *Journal of Feminist Family Therapy, 5*(3/4), 75–98.

Kutsche, P. (1983). Household and family in Hispanic northern New Mexico. *Journal of Comparative Family Studies, 14*, 151–165.

LaFramboise, T., Coleman, H. L., & Gerton, J. (1993). Psychological impact of biculturalism: Evidence and theory. *Psychological Bulletin, 114*(3), 395–412.

Laird, J. (1998). Theorizing culture: Narrative ideas and practice principles. In M. McGoldrick (Ed.), *Revisioning family therapy: Race, culture, and gender in clinical practice.* New York: Guilford Press.

Luepnitz, D. A. (1988). *The family interpreted: Psychoanalysis, feminism, and family therapy.* New York: Basic Books.

Madsen, W. C. (1999). *Collaborative therapy with multi-stressed families: From old problems to new futures.* New York: Guilford Press.

Marris, P. (1980). The uprooting of meaning. In G. V. Coelho & P. I. Ahmed (Eds.), *Uprooting and development: Dilemmas of coping with modernization.* New York: Plenum Press.

McGoldrick, M., Anderson, C., & Walsh, F. (1989). *Women in families: A framework for family therapy.* New York: Basic Books.

McGoldrick, M., Pearce, J., & Giordano, J. (Eds.). (1982). *Ethnicity and family therapy.* New York: Guilford Press.

Minuchin, S., Montalvo, B., Guerney, B., Rosman, B., & Schumer, F. (1967). *Families of the slums: An exploration of structure and treatment.* New York: Basic Books.

Montalvo, B., & Gutierrez, M. (1983). A perspective of the use of the cultural dimension in family therapy. In C. J. Falicov (Ed.), *Cultural perspectives in family therapy.* Rockville, MD: Aspen.

Montalvo, B., & Gutierrez, M. (1988). The emphasis on cultural identity: a developmental-ecological constraint. In C. J. Falicov (Ed.), *Family rransitions: Continuity and change over the life cycle.* New York: Guilford Press.

Ogbu, J. (1987). Variability in minority school performance: A problem in search of an explanation. *Anthropology and Education Quarterly, 18*(4), 312–334.

Padilla, A. M. (1994). Bicultural development: a theoretical and empirical examination. In R. G. Malgady & O. Rodriguez (Eds.), *Theoretical and conceptual issues in Hispanic mental health.* Melbourne, FL: Krieger.

Papajohn, J., & Spiegel, J. (1975). *Transactions in families.* San Francisco: Jossey-Bass.

Parker, P. (1990). For the white person who wants to know how to be my friend. In G. Anzaldua (Ed.), *Making faces, making soul: Haciendo cara.* San Francisco: An Aunt Lute Foundation Book.

Penn, P., & Frankfurt, M. (1994). Creating a participant text: Writing, multiple voices, narrative multiplicity. *Family Process, 33*(3), 217–231.

Portes, A., & Rumbaut, R. G. (1990). A foreign world: Immigration, mental health and acculturation. In *Immigrant America: A portrait.* Berkeley: University of California Press.

Roland, A. (1988). *In search of self in India and Japan: Toward a cross-cultural psychology.* Princeton, NJ: Princeton University Press.

Rosaldo, R. (1989). *Culture and truth: The remaking of social analysis.* Boston: Beacon Press.

Rouse, R. (1992). Making sense of settlement: Class transformation, class struggle and transnationalism among Mexican immigrants in the U.S. In N. G. Schilller, L. Basch, & C. Blanc-Szanton (Eds.), *Towards a transnational perspective on migration.* New York: New York Academy of Sciences.

Sampson, E. E. (1993). Identity politics: Challenges to psychology's understanding. *American Psychologist, 48*(12), 1219–1230.

Schiller, N. G., Basch, L., & Blanc-Szanton, C. (Eds.). (1992). *Towards a transnational perspective on migration: Race, class, ethnicity and nationalism reconsidered.* New York: New York Academy of Sciences.

Sexton, T. L., & Alexander, J. F. (2002). Functional family therapy for at-risk adolescents and their families. In T. Patterson (Vol. Ed.), *Comprehensive handbook of psychotherapy, Vol. 2: Cognitive-behavioral approaches.* New York: Wiley.

Shuval, J. T. (1982). Migration and stress. In L. Golderger & S. Breznitz (Eds.), *Handbook of stress: Theoretical and clinical aspects* (2nd ed., pp. 641–657). New York: Free Press.

Sluzki, C. (1969) Migration and family conflict. *Family Process, 18*(4) 379–390.

Sluzki, C. (1993). Network disruption and network reconstruction in the process of migration/relocation. *The Berkshire Medical Center Department of Psychiatry Bulletin, 2*(3), 2–4.

Spiegel, J. (1971) *Transactions: The interplay between individual, family and society.* New York: Science House.

Suárez-Orozco, M. M., & Suárez-Orozco, C. E. (1995a). *Transformations: Immigration, family life and achievement motivation among Latino ado-lescents.* Stanford, CA: Stanford University Press.

Suárez-Orozco, M. M., & Suárez-Orozco, C. E. (1995b). Migration: Generational discontinuities and the making of Latino identities. In L. Romanucci-Ross & G. DeVos (Eds.), *Ethnic identity: Creation, conflict, and accommodation* (3d ed.), Walnut Creek, CA: Alta Mira Press.

Suárez-Orozco, C. E., & Suárez-Orozco, M. M. (2001). *Children of immigration.* Cambridge, MA: Harvard University Press.

Taylor, C., & Gutmann, A. (Eds.). (1994). *Multiculturalism: Examining the politics of recognition.* Princeton, NJ: Princeton University Press.

Tomm, K., Suzuki, K., & Suzuki, K. (1990). The Ka-No-Mushi: An inner externalization that enables compromise? *Australian Journal of Family Therapy, 11*(2), 104–107.

Turner, J. (1991). Migrants and their therapists: A trans-context approach. *Family Process, 30,* 407–419.

Waldegrave, C. (1990). Social justice and family therapy. *Dulwich Centre Newsletter, 1,* 15–20.

Walters, M., Carter, B., Papp, P., & Silverstein, O. (1988). *The invisible web: Gender patterns in family relationships.* New York: Guilford Press.

Warheit, G., Vega, W., Auth, J., & Meinhardt, K. (1985). Mexican-American immigration and mental health: A comparative analysis of psychosocial stress and dysfunction. In W. Vega & M. Miranda (Eds.), *Stress and Hispanic mental health* (pp. 76–109). Rockville, MD: National Institute of Mental Health.

White, M. (1989). The externalizing of the problem and the reauthoring of lives and relationships. In M. White (Ed.), *Selected papers* (pp. 5–28). Adelaide, Australia: Dulwich Centre.

Woodcock, J. (1995). Healing rituals in families in exile. *Journal of Family Therapy, 17,* 397–410.

Wright Mills, C. (1959). *The sociological imagination.* London: Oxford University Press.

Ybarra, L. (1982). Marital decision making and the role of machismo in the Chicano family. *De Colores, 6,* 32–47.

Young, I. M. (1990). *Justice and the politics of difference.* Princeton, NJ: Princeton University Press.

# PART II

# Major Theoretical Models of Couple and Family Therapy

## SECTION INTRODUCTION

The task of providing a comprehensive "snapshot" of CFT in a single textbook (that has a page limit) is impossible. So many intervention theories and models, as well as manuals, training programs, books, chapters, articles, and journals, are devoted to this topic that there is no way that everyone in the field can be satisfied that his or her work has been presented—let alone, adequately presented. As such, with feedback from external reviewers, we narrowed the focus of this section to those theoretical models that have had and that continue to have the broadest impact on CFT practice. Although many theories and models were left out, the group that we finally selected was chosen because we believed it best represented the range of traditional and current theories of the field.

Authors for the chapters in this section were given the challenge of presenting the primary theoretical constructs of each theory and were instructed to integrate the most recent developments/evolutions in their areas. To provide continuity in the presentation, authors were asked to organize their presentation using the following outline:

1. History and background of the approach
2. Major theoretical constructs
3. Proposed etiology of clinical problems
4. Methods of clinical assessment
5. Clinical change mechanisms/curative factors
6. Specific therapeutic interventions
7. Effectiveness of the approach
8. Future developments/directions

Establishing a common framework was necessary for a variety of reasons, particularly to increase the readability of this section for consumers of this handbook. Nonetheless, because the models described in this section are so richly diverse and complex, we created some philosophical and practical dilemmas for our contributors by forcing all of them to present their work in the same manner. For example, there is considerable variability in the field about the appropriateness of (1) framing etiology from a problem perspective, (2) using traditional methods of formal and clinical assessment, and (3) using quantitative research methods in model evaluation and development. This variability is evident in the presentation of chapters in this section. Some sections are larger in one chapter than in others.

Some authors specifically point out the challenges and limitations of this framework as applied to their respective models. Some chapters focus on presenting a "state of the science," whereas others seem to focus on a "state of the art." Such variability ensures that each contributor remains true to his or her philosophical and theoretical perspectives, but more important, this variability represents the current complexity of the "cutting edge" of CFT.

# CHAPTER 4

# Object-Relations and Psychodynamic Approaches to Couple and Family Therapy

JILL SAVEGE SCHARFF, MD
DAVID E. SCHARFF, MD

*International Institute of Object Relations Therapy*

## INTRODUCTION

Object-relations couple and family therapy is a group-analytic approach built from psychoanalytic object-relations theory and technique, developmental theory, attachment theory, sexuality research, systems theory, group theory, and chaos theory.

Fairbairn's systematic, relational theory of psychic structure has had the greatest impact on the object relations approach to couple and family therapy (D. Scharff & Birtles, 1994; D. Scharff & J. Scharff, 1987, 1991). Other important influences are (1) Winnicott's ideas on the mother–infant relationship, (2) Klein's concept of projective identification accounting for unconscious communication between two individual personalities, and (3) Bion's theories of mental processing and group func-

tioning (D. Scharff, 1996). Taken together, these theories show how one personality interacts with another in the intimate relationships of family life.

In this chapter, we will review and integrate the basic building blocks of object-relations, couple, and family therapy (ORCFT) and will present vignettes to show how ORCFT is applied in clinical practice.

## HISTORY AND BACKGROUND OF THE APPROACH

Some couple and family therapists read the word *psychoanalytic* and close the book. To them, it implies a silent, blank screen approach to the individual patient, with too much emphasis on sexual and aggressive instincts as the driving force for development and little relevance to therapy for family relationships. Nevertheless, classical analytic theory has served as the base on which couple and family therapy developed. For example, many of the early family therapists were graduates of analytic training programs—Ackerman, Bowen, Cooklin, Lidz, Minuchin, Selvini-Palazzoli, Stierlin, Shapiro, Watzlawick, Wynne, Zilbach, and Zinner (J. Scharff, 1995). Jackson, Riskin, Andolfi, Byng-Hall, and Jackson had analytic training; Satir was influenced by the Chicago Institute of Psychoanalysis; and Ryckoff and Wynne (both analysts) were influenced by the interpersonal theory of Harry Stack Sullivan. Framo and Paul were exposed to analytic theory, and Skynner, who applied Freud's concept of fixation and regression to family functioning, was trained as a group analyst. Although some had to turn their backs on their analytic origins to develop their family therapy style, the influence of their analytic roots is evident in their theories of functioning and change.

Freud's instructions on technique offer excellent guidance for couple and family therapists. Freud advised listening to the unconscious, working with resistance, following affect as a guide to conflict in the person's history, working with dreams and fantasy, interpreting transference, and working through as critical aspects of securing change. Although systems therapists may not acknowledge the importance of these factors, couple and family therapy has been profoundly affected by Freud's views on affect and family history. In fact, the developmental aspects of psychoanalytic theory provided classically trained analysts and couple and family therapists alike with a foundation for understanding family life.

Nevertheless, several aspects of classical analytic theory interfere with its widespread acceptance in relational/systemic intervention practice: (1) its intense focus on the intra-

psychic, which keeps it from lending itself to the study of relationships and systems; (2) its primary focus on human development in terms of instinctual energies that must be released to gratify the individual or tamed to suit the demands of society; and (3) its emphasis on the infant's instincts as sexual and aggressive or death-driven in nature. This perspective loses the importance of the mother, without whom the infant could not survive, and the interactions with her and the family, all of which shape the developing personality. Unfortunately, although early classical analysts did work with family experiences, as revealed in the transference, their theory was blind to the family group and therefore did not have more influence on the field of family therapy. Revisions of classical theory provided by object-relations theory are much more readily incorporated into the practice of couple and family therapists.

## MAJOR THEORETICAL CONSTRUCTS OF OBJECT-RELATIONS THEORY

### Infant Development

In object-relations theory, the mother is not simply an object on which the infant's energies happen to fall. A mother is crucial to a child's survival, nurturing and loving the child, presenting the child to the family group and fostering their relationships, and helping the child to self-regulate. She gives meaning to the child's existence, and the child does the same for her. Including the father, brothers, sisters, and the wider family group, a complex matrix of important reciprocal relationships influences the infant's growth, development, character structure, and capacity for relating.

At birth, infants are in for a shock, as they take their first breath and separate from nurturing processes that were automatic in the uterus. The infant must seek nurturance and learn to recognize the person who gives food and safety. The infant is born with competencies to engage the mothering person. These include the following fixed action patterns: (1) rooting to find the breast; (2) interacting with the mother in gazing and cooing sequences that the infant starts and stops to maintain appropriate levels of stimulation and connection; (3) grasping, reaching, clinging, and following (as soon as the infant develops mobility), all of which secure proximity to the person who protects and provides safety; (4) crying to communicate distress and get a response that brings relief; (5) and smiling to engage and form family bonds (Bowlby, 1969). In short, the infant is born able to use relationships for survival and for the pleasure that relatedness brings.

Pathways for emotional experience and expression are created, refined, and solidified through the effects of interactions between the infant, the mother, and other important family members. The baby's unformed mind is being entrained by the mother's already developed mind. When the mother is chronically unable to respond, the baby misses the connection, and interruption in the formation of brain pathways reflects this lack of nurturance (Schore, 1994). The baby feels the pain of rejection and tries hard to engage the mother. If a mother is too depressed to respond, eventually the baby loses hope. In contrast, the healthy mother has moments of exhaustion that are painful to her baby, but overall she is responsive. The healthy baby copes with these frustrations, but the constitutionally challenged baby is more readily overwhelmed.

## FAIRBAIRN'S THEORY OF PSYCHIC STRUCTURE

Fairbairn's model of the mind holds that internal structure is built from personal experience across phases of development (Fairbairn, 1952, 1963). This model fully accepts the impact of the child's fantasy life and limited cognitive capacities on perception of experience during development. At the same time, this perspective leaves open the possibility of growth and change as a function of both external influences and internal changes in perceptual ability. The child is born with a fully formed, undifferentiated ego, having the capacity both to relate and to seek autonomy, to be both an individual and a member of a family group. When the infant's needs are no longer met automatically after birth, the ensuing frustration drives the differentiation of the ego into conscious and unconscious parts (Fairbairn, 1944). If the degree of frustration is overwhelming to the self, either because the mother is unresponsive or because the baby's ego is weak, then defensive measures must be taken against painful feelings. The baby has an experience of the mother (called the external object) that feels sometimes ideally good and sometimes awfully bad. The infant lays down traces of these experiences (now internal objects) in the developing ego, and psychic structure begins to form.

The ideal object resides in the ego in consciousness, infusing the self with feelings of satisfaction and confidence. Inevitably, however, the infant is faced with personally frustrating ("bad") experiences. To deal with the "bad" experiences, the ego copes by splitting off the bad from the good, to keep the good feeling safe. The bad is pushed out of mind by the ego and is repressed as an internal bad object. The ego also splits off parts of itself and represses them, along with the repressed bad object. This repressed bad object is sorted into two categories of badness, depending on whether that bad experience had been too rejecting of need (the rejecting object) or too exciting of need (the libidinal object).

The developing self is now composed of three internal object relationships, each con-

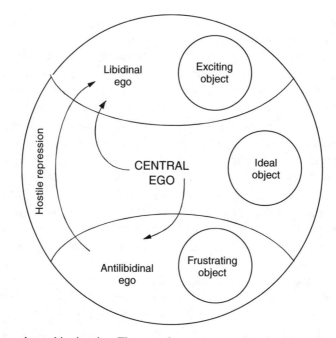

FIGURE 4.1. The endopsychic situation. The central ego represses the rejecting and exciting internal object relationships, and they press for their return to consciousness. Reprinted from *The Sexual Relationship: An Object Relations View of Sex and the Family*, courtesy of Jason Aronson Inc., 1992. Copyright © David E. Scharff, 1982.

sisting of part-ego, part-object, and the affect that enjoins them (figure 4.1).

In the *unconscious* area of the mind, the two parts of the ego are

1. The *libidinal ego,* connected to the *need-exciting object* and feelings of emptiness, neediness, longing, and craving, and
2. The *antilibidinal ego,* connected to the *rejecting object,* filled with feelings of outrage, anger, and hurt.

In the *conscious* area of the mind, the original ego retains only

3. The *central ego*—the largest part, it is hoped—which is connected to the *ideal object* and feelings of satisfaction.

In consciousness, there is the ideal object relationship, and in unconsciousness, the ex-

citing object relationship and the rejecting object relationship. Fairbairn thought that the ideal object relationship represses the other two and, in addition, the rejecting object relationship represses the exciting object relationship—a situation seen in couple therapy when partners' actions, such as fighting to the death and threatening to divorce over small issues, disguise how much they long to be together and feel loved. From an ORCFT perspective, the exciting object relationship is just as likely to repress the rejecting one, such as when partners use sex to make up after a disagreement instead of resolving their conflicts. Both kinds of repressed object relationships are always pressing back to consciousness because the self seeks to be whole again, but the central ego continues the repression to protect itself from pain. This is a view of the self as a dynamic system of parts, like an interactive group inside the person.

This dynamic system of the self influences and is influenced by outside relationships. If a large part of the ego remains in consciousness, available for learning and interaction with others, future experience creates new traces that modify the original objects. The system of internal object relationships remains open to shaping by new events and relationships. If splitting and repression are severe and there is not enough of the central ego left for interaction, the old objects aren't exposed to modifying influences, and a relatively closed inner-world system develops. ORCFT breaches the closed system and opens it to learning from experience, in relationship to the couple and family therapist.

As the child moves into the oedipal phase and becomes aware of being excluded from adult privileges that the parents enjoy together, the child experiences conflicts of ambivalence. The mechanism of splitting comes into play again as the child assigns the bad object category to one parent who is then rejected. At the same time, the other parent is represented as the exciting object, which creates intense longing. This splits the parental couple—as if this would improve the child's chances of possessing the desired parent. Fairbairn thought that this happened in an attempt to resolve conflicts of ambivalence about the parents having a relationship that partly excluded the child. Keeping this theory in mind helps the couple and family therapist, who feels excluded like a child from a tightly knit couple, to find words for her experience, and so helps the partners recognize their avoidance of their own painful experiences of exclusion in their families of origin.

## WINNICOTT'S THEORY OF INFANT DEVELOPMENT

Winnicott was emphatic that there is "no such thing as an infant"—meaning that without maternal care, the infant dies (1960, p. 39 fn.). He described the mother–infant relationship as a partnership of mind and body, in which love and personal significance are conveyed to the infant through the parents' holding and handling (1971). ORCFT believes that the physical and emotional quality of this early relationship is reflected in the intimate relationship later created with a partner in adulthood. Winnicott noted two aspects of the mother: (1) the environment mother, holding the baby in her arms and in her mind, providing the context for the baby's continued existence; and (2) the object mother, engaging in direct-gaze interactions, eye-to-eye with the baby. These two aspects of parental functioning provide a model for adult intimate relating (D. Scharff, 1982, 1992) and are recreated in the therapist's providing a secure treatment contract and engaging emotionally but responsibly with the couple and the family as a group and as individuals for the benefit of the whole.

Within the environmental envelope and beyond direct object relating, there lies a potential space that is filled with possibility for creative exchanges in transition between self and other—seen in play, imagination, dreaming, creative expression, and autonomous development (Winnicott, 1951). This space collapses, however, when the context is unsafe and the direct object relating is intrusive, sexualized, or absent (Scharff & Scharff, 1994). This happens, for instance, when the couple splits up and the children are left with a depressed single mother who has to be absent while working to provide for them and no longer has the energy to engage with them as she did before the divorce. The space also collapses in cases of incest, when the parent exploits the child's dependency and oedipal longings. In such instances, the space for imagining is invaded with fearfully concrete action, with no promise for the future. ORCFT works to clear and enlarge this space so that the family has more room to explore new options and solutions.

## KLEIN'S THEORY OF EGO DEVELOPMENT IN RESPONSE TO INSTINCTS

Klein reached into the unconscious fantasy life of babies, using her knowledge as a therapist of young children and her intuition as a mother. Klein (1946) noted that infants are anxious and that they live in the early months in a paranoid-schizoid state of mind, in which they experience the mother as a part-object that is alternately either good or bad, the primacy of the life and death instincts coloring the infant's perceptions of being mothered. Under the force of the death instinct, the infant, fearing for its life, projects its annihilation anxiety into the mother and then misidentifies the mother as the source of the potential for annihilation. The infant then defends against the persecutory experience by identifying with the bad object. At the same time, under the force of the life instinct, the infant projects life-affirming qualities into the mother, perceives her as loving, and identifies with her as a good object. Klein gave the term *projective identification* to summarize this complex process of unconscious communication and defense. Intimate partners communicate by projective identification too, creating a feeling of at-oneness within which there is a continuum of effects, from empathy for the position of the partner to obliteration of the reality of that other person.

Klein was interested in the infant's splitting the object and, secondarily, the ego, under the influence of the instincts. In contrast, Fairbairn thought that the ego split itself primarily in reaction to the need to manage contradictory impressions of the object. Klein wrote about the infant's aggression, greed, and envy spoiling the good mother, whereas Fairbairn thought that the good mother was felt to be periodically bad because of inevitable delays in satisfaction after birth. Fairbairn was also in touch with the effects of truly bad, abusive mothers and fathers, whose children desperately tried to make their parents seem good by blaming themselves for the parents' badness. Dick's (1967) integration of Fairbairn's theory of internal object relationships in personality and Klein's concept of projective identification in child development is shown in figure 4.2.

### BION'S GROUP THEORY

Bion (1970) took Klein's ideas beyond the infant's unconscious mental life to the interpersonal level. His studies of thinking led him to imagine the effects of the infant's unconscious anxiety on the mother and the influence of her thought processes on the child. The mother contains the infant's anxiety and emotion in the realm of thought, processes them in her mind, and returns them metabolized to the child. The infant thus gets anxiety back in a more structured, manageable form. More than that, the infant identifies with the mother's containing (or processing) function and builds psychic structure for coping with adversity.

Bion (1959) became interested in group dynamics. He noted that every work group has subgroup formations that meet emotional needs of the group, sometimes working to the advantage of the group's task performance, other times disrupting the work. There are three main types of these subgroupings: dependency subgroups, fight–flight formations, and exclusive pairings. The dependency group wants the leader to take care of its members and tell them what to do; the fight–flight group wants to flee from or fight against the authority of the leader; and the pairing group is dominated by the coupling of two members, which, it is imagined, may bring forth a replacement for the frustrating leader who will not meet the needs of the subgroup formations.

The family group may be helped or hindered by subgroup formations, as it carries out its work of supporting its members through the life cycle. For example, a dependency subgroup is useful for raising a lap-baby, but it may get in the way of sending a child off to college successfully. A fight against parental authority may be useful in arriving at autonomy for the toddler or the adolescent, but in late adulthood it may result in a lack of investment in one's own family. Exclusive pairing is useful to the couple in conceiving children and in promoting a vigorous sexual life, which makes for a vital center to the family, but it is destructive when parent and child create an incestuous pair. ORCFT helps couples and families recognize the subgroup formations and analyze their adaptive and defensive functions.

## SYSTEMS THEORY OF VON BERTALANFFY AND PRIGOGINE

An organic system is an open system that changes as it interacts and receives positive feedback from the environment, and that constantly aspires to higher levels of organization (von Bertalanffy, 1950; Prigogine, 1976). Similarly, the structures of the self are systems of relationships inside the self that are reflected in and influence relationships between the self and others. Freud believed that the organism responds principally to negative feedback, governed by the principle of homeostasis driving its return to the resting state for conserving energy. Nature, however, does not behave with linear simplicity. Thus, in ORCFT, individuals and relationships are seen to change in complex, nonlinear patterns as they grow over time.

## CHAOS THEORY

Chaos theory is a theory of nonlinear systems brought from the world of physics and mathematics (Gleick, 1987). Chaos theory is well suited to understanding human development in the family (Scharff & Scharff, 1998). From this perspective, the organism enters a state of disequilibrium when affected by positive feedback. New processes are needed for recalibrating. Then the organism is open to the possibility of a new arrangement of defenses and psychic structures. Parts of the system may revert to the old way of functioning and remain stuck there, but as a whole the organism moves forward. The state of chaos is generative and leads to the development of new forms.

The system in chaos shows particular sensitivity to changes in initial conditions; for instance, a grass seedling is dependent on water and sunlight, without which it will not grow, but mature grass can survive a period of drought. A baby's brain is so sensitive to the nurturing environment that if the mother's emotional attunement is not there at the right moment, development is not encouraged. The system in chaos is moved forward to a state of higher organization by coming close to a more organized system. This is what happens when the baby is moved forward by emotional proximity to the mother's mind and continues to grow and develop in association to the larger system of the family. In a family, members living close together influence each others' ways of being and together create a family group mentality that is greater than that of any individual. Similarly, in therapy, the family comes into contact with a therapist who, after years of training, clinical experience, supervision, and personal treatment, should have a more flexible yet stable self system, which has a positive influence on the family's unconscious organization.

## ATTACHMENT THEORY

Young children show specific patterns of behavior with particular family members when they seek comfort under stress (Ainsworth, Blehar, Waters, & Wall, 1978). These patterns convey the level of security the child experiences in relation to that caregiver. Some are securely attached, and others are not. Of those who are insecurely attached, some are avoidant of attachment, rejecting offers of comfort; some are resistant to being separated, showing anxious, clingy behavior and at other times refusing to be comforted; and others are totally disorganized by separation and reunion. The attachment style of the child varies from one caregiver to another and is profoundly influenced by the attachment style of that caregiver. From the ORCFT perspective, attachment behaviors reflect the relational context within which the child's personality engages directly with that family member and therefore influences the nature of the internal object-relations set.

Attachment styles have been measured in adults (Main & Goldwyn, in press). They, too, may be secure, autonomous, and freely expressive. Or they may be insecure in various ways—preoccupied with and dependent on close relationships, dismissing of the need for closeness and compulsively self-reliant, or downright fearful of rejection. The secure and preoccupied adults have positive views of intimate partners, whereas dismissing and fearful adults tend to have more negative views of their partners. Attachment styles in the family affect the psychological development of the children and influence the quality of the marital relationship. The concept of attachment style helps us to view the family members' behaviors upon entering treatment as attempts at creating a secure base or at avoiding recreating an insecure one.

## THE OBJECT RELATIONS APPROACH TO COUPLE AND FAMILY SYSTEMS

The couple relationship stands at the center of the family group. The couple relationship is constructed from the melding of two personalities into a marital joint personality, analogous to the mother-infant relationship

(see figure 4.2). It is greater than the sum of its parts and may be valued more than each of them (Dicks, 1967). This new joint marital personality consists of (1) a central ego system in which each partner is represented as a satisfactory, maturely functioning partner; and (2) two split-off and repressed internal object-relationship systems, in which one partner is represented as (a) the exciting object, for which the other partner provides the libidinal ego; or (b) the rejecting object, for which the other partner provides the antilibidinal ego. In other words, an aspect of the partner is dealt with as if it were a part of the self.

The individual's conscious and unconscious internal object relationships are projected into the spouse who has been chosen for having the capacity to resonate with, fit, and identify with the projection. In the healthy marriage, the spouse also has the capacity to separate from the unconscious projections and modify them, but in the unhealthy marriage the projections are confirmed and form a closed system that stifles the growth of the individuals.

If the spouses do not create an open system, they tend to further project unwanted aspects of their personalities and their relationship out of the marital system and into one or more of their children. The children to whom this happens then have the role of scapegoats, carrying the burden of the couple relationship. Child scapegoats protect the marriage and the family of procreation from demise, at the cost of their own personal development.

ORCFT aims to modify the projective identificatory system by reducing the need for splitting and repression. This is achieved through containment, the process in which the therapist bears the family's anxiety, reflects on the experience of being with that family, and puts anxiety into words. Therapists help to transform anxiety into an emotional experience that can be borne and thought about and therefore managed differently in the future. The therapist provides a safe psychological

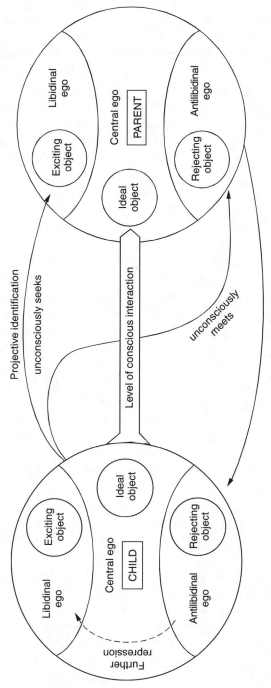

FIGURE 4.2. Projective and introjective identification. The mechanism here is the interaction of the child's projective and introjective identifications with the parent as the child meets frustration, unrequited yearning, or trauma. The diagram depicts the child longing to have his needs met and identifying with similar trends in the parent via projective identification. If he meets with rejection, he identifies with the frustration of the parent's own antilibidinal system via introjective identification. In an internal reaction to the frustration, the libidinal system is further repressed by the renewed force of the child's antilibidinal system. Reprinted from *The Sexual Relationship: An Object Relations View of Sex and the Family*, courtesy of Jason Aronson, Inc., 1992. Copyright © David E. Scharff, 1982.

space for revealing the usual defensive patterns of family behavior and underlying anxieties. Working with the therapist, the family members arrive at an improved ability to work together as a group to understand conflict, solve current problems, and deal with future developmental challenges.

## PROPOSED ETIOLOGY
## OF CLINICAL PROBLEMS

### Unconscious Factors in Marital Choice

Factors that were out of awareness when the couple fell in love often emerge later to cause discord and stress. Partners in love find each other to be the ideal mate: physically attractive, emotionally compatible, intellectually equal, and similar in background and aspiration—or charmingly different but committed to the same principles. This attraction happens at the central ego level. But attraction at the unconscious level, based on the interaction between repressed internal object relationships, determines the long-term quality of the marriage (Dicks, 1967). These features are so repressed that the lovers are not aware of the pathological potential of their mating. Troubling interactions may be displayed after commitment is solidified—for instance, when the honeymoon is over or the first child is born. Over time, the committed couple may find that behaviors that were delightful at first have become sources of conflict. This occurs as central ego functioning is invaded by the return of the repressed object relationships, which elicit feelings of rejection by, or craving for a better relationship with, the partner.

### EXAMPLE: A COUPLE PROJECTS
### POWER INTO THE MATERNAL IMAGE

A shy, timid man always felt inferior because, although he was tall and handsome, he was not athletic, didn't have male friends, and could never get a date for the prom. He met a small but assertive, opinionated, athletic woman who was his company's softball coach. He saw in her qualities that he would have liked to have himself. She felt much less attractive than he was, but she enjoyed a challenge and invited him out on a date. She soon recognized that he had problems with self-esteem. She disavowed them in the same way that she pushed past her own vulnerabilities. It turned out that they were attracted to each other physically and felt happy together and sexually fulfilled, but they stayed together for unconscious reasons. Both shared the unconscious assumption that the woman was more important, stronger, and more dependable than the man. In his close-knit, Old World immigrant family, the man continued to revere the mother, even though he wanted distance from the old-fashioned family culture. The woman was close to her mother, a modern, divorced, professionally achieving woman, and she had been deeply hurt by her father's abandonment. In marriage, the man found another woman to adore and serve, and the woman found a father who would stay with her.

Then she became pregnant, and their sex life stopped. He thought that his male role was to stay out of the way so that she could carry out her supremely maternal function. She felt that he had abandoned her now that she was to have a child, just as her father had done to her mother. The more passive and withdrawn he became, the more she overfunctioned, recreating with her daughter the exclusive relationship she had with her mother and hating her husband for abandoning her emotionally, as her father had done. All her rage at her father came out in relation to her husband. Envious of the exclusive attention given to the baby, he felt inferior and unworthy of love, and his self-esteem plummeted.

The projective identificatory system, in which the strong woman was admired and which was the basis for their bond during courtship, became a divisive force in the child-rearing years of their marriage. In ORCFT, the couple learned about this basic assumption and how disabling it had been. The husband and wife reviewed their family histories and let go of the working models they had developed in their families of origin. They freed each other to create a more equal appreciation of mother and father, traditional and contemporary lifestyles, and male and female contributions to their marriage and family.

## Unmetabolized Marital Conflict and Sexual Incompatibility

As we have noted, unmetabolized marital conflict can spill over into children. It may also be projected out of the mind of the couple and into their own bodies in the form of psychosomatic pain in any part of the body. The part of the body affected may be the tissues of the erogenous zones (D. Scharff, 1982). A rejecting object relationship may reside in the breasts of the woman who can't bear to be touched there. An exciting object relationship may be conveyed by the man who repeatedly seeks the stimulation of intercourse—whether or not his partner wants more—because he is unable to feel satisfaction. The bored wife who has an affair finds an exciting object in the lover with whom she is obsessed and simultaneously becomes a rejecting, abandoning object to her husband. The straight or gay man who has multiple partners makes sexual gratification an object that is more exciting than the possibility of a life partner in whom sexuality and intimacy coincide.

In the treatment of sexual dysfunction, an excellent strategy is to combine ORCFT with behavioral desensitization. In the behavioral component, a series of graded exposures to sexual intimacy with the partner in the privacy of the bedroom produces sexual encounters that can be discussed in the next ORCFT

session. The encounters cause anxiety that connects to earlier experiences of sexuality and nonsexual intimacy that were problematic in the family of origin. ORCFT examines defensive avoidance of doing the exercises and looks at the underlying anxieties located in the sexual interactions. Repeated examination of them delivers the repressed internal object relationships that bedevil the couple relationship into the therapeutic space, where they can be understood and worked through in both the emotional and the physical realm.

## Projective Identification in Families and Couples

Projective identification is a form of unconscious communication that is the basis for empathy and a feeling of at-oneness in the healthy marriage, but in the unhealthy marriage it leads to serious distortion in the perception of self and other, and it obliterates individual boundaries and stifles autonomy. When parents projectively identify a child as the repository for unwanted aspects of themselves, the child either rebels against the projection or accepts it and acts accordingly. The combination of constitutional vulnerability, child-rearing practices, and, most important of all, unconscious fantasy about the child, communicated by projective identification, combine to create pathology.

## Loss—of Person, Place, Motivating Fantasy, or Self-Esteem in Trauma, Relocation, Death, Divorce, and Infidelity

Loss of a loved one, especially one who was loved ambivalently, whose demise was sharply traumatic, or whose deterioration was troubling over time, can throw the family into depression or can create a symptomatic child. Loss of a loved one occurs in ways other than death. For example, a family may react to the parents' divorce as if it were the death of one of the parents. An affair can throw a couple into turmoil, in which the one who has the lover becomes manic and the betrayed spouse becomes depressed. If divorce follows, the loss of being together is painful, and the loss of the house itself removes the family's context of support and safety and aggravates that feeling of personal loss. Any loss of the home by fire, invasion, or vandalism uproots the family and disturbs the family's equilibrium. Frequent relocations of the sort the military family must cope with can lead to feelings of anxiety about moves, alienation in new locations, and grief about lost friendships and familiar surroundings. Sometimes a family becomes depressed at the loss of a motivating fantasy—for instance, when the dream of adult children and grandchildren remaining close by is wrecked by the children's ambition to work for a global corporation.

## EXAMPLE: LOSS AND TRAUMA DESTABILIZING THE PROJECTIVE IDENTIFICATORY SYSTEM OF THE MARRIAGE

A 14-year-old girl was referred for treatment of social phobia (J. Scharff, 1992). In family therapy, it emerged that the phobia had developed 2 years earlier when she became anxious about her elder sister's out-of-wedlock pregnancy. She conspired to keep the pregnancy a secret and was traumatized when the pregnancy resulted in a massive hemorrhage. Her mother became very depressed, which was exacerbated by her memories of having considered whether to abort a pregnancy early in her own marriage. The 14-year-old daughter stayed home because she was afraid of social behavior that might lead to sexual experimentation. She was afraid of learning and having sexual knowledge because

of its association to a secret that had led to damage. She imagined her own potential for sexual knowledge as especially dangerous. Staying home was also driven by using the pleasure of her company to regulate her mother's depression.

The shared depression and anxiety of mother and daughter were also driven by their grief about various losses stemming from the father's chronic illness. Previously a strong father and leader of the family unit, he now suffered from scleroderma, which made it hard for him to walk and to breathe. He had lost his health, his occupational identity, and his main leisure pursuit of sailing. He had worked hard and saved toward a retirement dream of sailing around the coast of the United States with his family. The family members did not lose their father, but they lost him as the figure they had relied on. They also lost their motivating fantasy of the family boat trip.

These family-wide losses were built on losses in the marriage. The mother had chosen her husband because he had good morals and could take care of her. This was important to her because she had been sexually abused by a grandfather. This having occurred during second grade, she had been too upset to learn to read, and so she chose a man who could cover for her illiteracy and on whom she could depend. She had lost self-esteem in childhood, and with marriage she lost her autonomy and all confidence in her ability to function outside a domestic role. To protect her daughters from her irrational fear of their being abused, she would not allow their father to be alone with them. He lost the pleasure of caring for his children, and they lost the opportunity to learn ordinary trust in an intimate situation with a man.

Illness upset the projective identificatory system of their marriage. The husband was supposed to be the dependable leader and the wife the weak and dependent one. He could no longer protect her and provide for her, and she was faced with having to provide for herself and cope in the world of work.

## Sexual and Physical Trauma, Including Medical Illness

A couple's intimate life may be seriously compromised by sexual abuse, whether or not the victim of abuse has memory of the incident. For example, in one couple a man complained of his wife's lack of interest in sex and failed to recognize that his loss of erection was a contributing factor to her low desire. He turned his sexual attention to his daughter and did not admit that this was sexual abuse until years later. He said that genital stimulation was a soothing technique used when he was a boy. A woman who had been sexually abused in childhood could not let her husband diaper their baby girls or read to them in their room in case he abused them, even though she believed that he was protective of her and the girls. In reaction to the idea that intimacy with a man is harmful, one girl became prematurely sexually active, as if to prove this idea wrong, only to find that intimacy did bring her harm; the other girl became socially phobic.

Medical interventions such as urethral dilatation, stomach tubes, and multiple injections that are traumatic to a girl may also induce a fear of bodily penetration that interferes with her later pleasure in intercourse. In adulthood, medical illness after marriage may force an unexpected shift in the couple's projective identificatory system. For instance, the family may fall apart when the at-home mother on whom everyone relies is debilitated by chemotherapy.

The mind deals with trauma by dissociation and encapsulation. This appears to defend against pain and to allow one to go on living. But various scenarios that occur in ordinary family life can trigger an explosion of irrational behavior, as traumatic material escapes from the capsule. This leads to conflict-avoidant patterns of behavior. Alternatively, the traumatized person's need to maintain a tight boundary around the capsule may ensure that there will be no activation of the trauma in this generation. Nevertheless, it drives the trauma by projective identification into members of the next generation, and they may then become symptomatic. Narcissistic personality disorder and substance abuse frequently cover a trauma history, and both conditions have an enormous effect on a family system.

For instance, the son of a father who died of chronic alcohol poisoning, when the son was only 3 years old, may learn not to drink so as to provide a stable home environment for himself and his child. When the son's own child experiments with alcohol, the child may not avoid it as his father does. Instead, the child rebels against his father's rigid defense against the dangers of drinking and identifies with his father's projective identification of him as having qualities like his grandfather—and then the child becomes like the grandfather. Without a negative image of drinking behavior, the young man is not made aversive to alcohol, at which point genetic loading may combine with unconscious predilections so that compulsive alcohol consumption takes over.

Problems with narcissism secondary to trauma lie at the root of many couple dynamics (Scharff & Bagnini, 2003). Difficulties in regulating self-esteem mean that feedback leaves the narcissistic partner feeling humiliated. The other partner feels pushed away. Withdrawal into a defensive cocoon prevents communication and intimate interaction, which are essential to the establishment of a sustaining marriage. The other partner retreats or pursues, either approach causing further pain for both partners.

## Attachment Disorder

In marriage, a couple creates a complex attachment, in which the partners are attachment figures for each other. Secure attachment in individual partners predicts for reciprocity in the couple relationship, whereas insecure attachment leads to fixed, rigidly defensive positions. For example, Kirkpatrick and Davis (1994) found that a couple in which both partners score as securely attached is most likely to create a stable, lasting bond. In contrast, a relationship between a man whose attachment style is classed as anxious/ambivalent and a woman whose attachment style is classed as avoidant, or between a man whose style is avoidant and a woman who is anxious/ambivalent about attachment, is most likely to lead to an unstable bond that does not last.

## Temperamental Fit

One mother's perfect baby is another mother's nightmare. The naturally active baby may be highly stressful for the calm and slow-moving mother, but lots of fun for the mother who is high energy. The passive, flaccid baby may suit the temperamentally low-key mother, but the high-energy mother will be bored. If the bored mother overstimulates her infant, she creates a situation of stress for the child. The child may respond by developing a false self to entertain the mother or by withdrawing even more. The child deals with the overwhelming aspects of the experience by introjection of a negative experience connected to the mother, identifies with it inside the self, and creates an internal object relationship filled with affects of painful excitement.

## Holding and Containment

The mother (or primary caretaker) holds the child, the father holds the mother and their baby, the marriage holds the spouses, and the circle of the family holds its members as they move through the life cycle. Of these, the most important is the marriage. The couple relationship has to be able to deal with challenge and confrontation, loss, deprivation, and temptation. A flexible, respectful, forgiving, and sexually vital couple relationship is the strength at the center of the family. It provides holding, safety, and nurturing and is the children's primary model for being in a couple. The cooperative functioning of the couple conveys the integration of male and female elements in experience, thought, feeling, intimacy, and sex. The privacy of the couple relationship establishes clear limits against which the children find their own autonomy and then, as young adults, develop sexual desire for a significant other outside the family. Without firm holding, the family is at sea.

Within the context of good holding, the parents also have a containing function in which they mentally process the children's experience at each developmental stage, imagining their distress, putting themselves in the children's shoes, talking with them about their anxieties and putting these into perspective, and developing a way of thinking about and solving problems. When the parents do not have a good experience of containment in their families of origin, they carry forward a reduced containing function. Then, anxiety in the family group leads to a continuum of defensive postures. These may take various forms: (1) enmeshment or splintering, (2) dependency on one overfunctioning individual, (3) rebellion against authority or fleeing the family prematurely, or (4) the formation of a substitute pair, such as an incestuous union, in which to find gratification of component drives, rather than a real relationship for fostering mental stability, healthy development, and growth.

*Substance Abuse*

Flight from the family group may take the form of substance abuse. A repressed exciting internal object relationship, full of longing, propels the individual toward an available object—drugs, alcohol, or excess food— which is found to be a reliable source of satisfaction, at least at first. It does many things: it soothes anxiety, facilitates social interaction, blots out awareness of conflict, emboldens the timid to protest, permits sexual expression, and exposes aggression. In excess, substance use interferes with the family's processing of experience. Tiptoeing around the parent so as not to set off a drinking bout, denial of the abuse problem, secrecy to avoid shame, codependent behaviors, impoverishment, and criminal behaviors all complicate the children's upbringing. Substance abuse leads to addiction for the individual who is constitutionally vulnerable. At that point, the person's relationship to the chosen substances overshadows all human relationships and develops autonomy from the family dynamics that propelled the person toward the use of substances.

## METHODS OF CLINICAL ASSESSMENT

*Establishing a Frame*

ORCFT works within the structure of a prearranged time period, usually of one to four assessment sessions. A flexible frame is tailored to the needs of the family or the couple, but once agreed on, it is firm. Any attempts to bend the frame are viewed as examples of problematic behaviors. For instance, pressure to run over at the end of the session might indicate difficulty in being satisfied, greed, or dependent longings. Wishes to take time from the

next appointment might express envy of siblings and their families. The therapeutic relationship is a professional relationship, and the family's way of dealing with the business transactions is open to examination. Within this frame, how the family members or marital partners engage in the treatment situation, how they deal with therapists as authority figures and as helping professionals, and how they accept or bend the frame can be examined and compared to how they react to parental authority.

*Establishing an Alliance*

The couple and family therapist's professional demeanor is one of calm helpfulness and friendly concern. Although ORCFT is psychoanalytic, the therapist's behavior conforms to socially appropriate standards and not to the classic blank-screen approach to neutrality. The focus is on relationships within the family and between the family and the therapist, not on individuals. Within that group orientation, the therapist is equally partial to hearing from one or another family member in each generation. In the first session, attention is given to identifying transference manifestations of resistance to treatment and to using these for understanding underlying anxieties about meeting with a therapist. Speaking about distrust brings the issue into the open, where it can be dealt with, and if the therapist does this without defensiveness, trust usually increases. The goal is to secure a second session, in which there can be greater confidence for expression of anxieties.

*Nonstructured Interview*

ORCF therapists follow the discourse of the couple or the family, instead of asking a series of questions (Scharff & Varela, 2000). It is more instructive to notice how the story comes out and who tells it. Therapists should notice any pauses in the narrative, because these often indicate conflict or troublesome memories of attachment difficulties. If an important area is not mentioned, it is forgotten or overlooked for an unconscious reason. Therefore, the family is asked to think about the meaning of the omission. The primary interest is in all communications from the unconscious—in gestures, tones of voice, fantasies, dreams, and play.

### Connecting Core Affective Exchanges to Object Relations History

The emergence of affect in a couple or family session is used as a guide to assessing underlying conflict. By the therapist's asking if this feeling is like anything that happened earlier, current affect is connected to experiences in the families of origin. At certain moments, the therapist feels the drawing force of a powerful feeling state that takes hold of the couple or the family. This intense affect in a current relationship signals the replay of an important early experience that hasn't been understood or even consciously recalled, and that can only be repeated instead of being remembered. These are called core affective exchanges. Bringing them to consciousness allows the family to come to terms with its past and to detoxify its emotional flashpoints.

### Creating a Psychological Space

The firm frame, with a commitment from the therapist to be there over time, creates an environment where the couple or family feels willing to discuss intimate details of its private family life. Therapists create psychological space by being ready to hear whatever the couple or the family needs to say and by be-

ing nonjudgmental. The therapist's ability to bear anxiety opens the space for thinking, understanding, and problem solving.

### Beginning With Symptoms and How Each Member Thinks About Them

Therapists start with hearing about what each family member thinks about the presenting problem. As this proceeds, the problem tends to be enacted in the session. How the problem is connected to life as a family now and in the previous generation is then available for exploration.

### Observing Defensive Patterns

Patterns of behavior typically recur in therapy. These patterns are defensive structures to protect the family or the couple from recognizing anxiety-provoking or frustrating aspects of existence: unmet wishes for depending on others, being intimate, or feeling important; unexpressed emotions of a sexual, aggressive, or murderous nature; unmetabolized trauma; family secrets; and, ultimately, fear of the end of the couple or the family. Having identified defensive interaction patterns, the therapist has a base in personal experience from which to work on making the anxieties conscious. Once this is achieved, the family has less automatic reversion to defensive patterns, becomes more functional, and is better prepared for future developmental challenges.

### Working with Transference and Countertransference

The key to therapeutic action is working with transference and countertransference. This means that the ORCF therapist gathers how the couple's or the family's feelings about life affect the therapist directly (the family transference). Therapists monitor their own reactions (countertransference) and use it to guide interventions. Having experienced difficulty in the session, therapists can work on it from inside their own experience and comment on their own difficulty. This is more acceptable to the family and more effective than pronouncing an interpretation based on an intellectual formulation.

## Assessing Sexual Adjustment of the Couple

In ORCFT with families, therapists don't ask for intimate details of parents' intimacy. Parents may indicate difficulty in this area directly, or their children's symptoms may point to it. Parents whose sexual problems spill over into the family may discuss their sexual life and its impact on the family in a family therapy session. When this occurs, therapists create an opportunity to study the couple's difficulty in privacy. A separate session with the couple to deal with intimacy issues and establishing appropriate boundaries is recommended.

In ORCFT with couples, therapists directly ask about the sexual life of a couple. Sexuality may reflect the tone of the relationship, be immune from relational difficulties, or contradict the essence of the relationship. Where there is specific sexual dysfunction, ORCFT is integrated with a behavioral analytic approach, in which pleasuring exercises and a gradual approach to full sexual intercourse are prescribed, and then the couple reports on and analyzes difficulties with the assignments.

## Testing response to interpretation and making recommendation and referral

As treatment progresses, therapists begin to make interpretations of family interactions and evaluate how family members respond to these views. In short, the therapist is evaluating whether the couple or the family comes to value thinking about problems in a psychological way. If the fit is not good, either because of distance, appointment time options, fee, religious differences, or personal incompatibility, or because the family wants a quick fix and not growth through understanding and insight, the family should be referred to a suitable colleague.

## CLINICAL CHANGE MECHANISMS/ CURATIVE FACTORS

### The Therapeutic Method

All the features of the assessment phase continue after a commitment to proceeding in therapy is made: providing a good psychological environment within a firm frame, following the affect, and working with unconscious material in play, fantasies, and dreams.

### Developing Negative Capability

As the couple or the family proceeds, uncharted territory is being explored, and the therapist may feel lost or unsure of where the treatment is going. This is when the therapist's willingness to tolerate confusion and uncertainty becomes increasingly important. In ORCFT, this tolerance is called "negative capability" and is viewed as the crucial element of the therapist's holding capacity, the ability to let things emerge without constricting experience by imposing a form on it too soon.

### Working With Transference and Countertransference

In the assessment phase and at the beginning of treatment, the transference is toward the therapist. We call this the "contextual transference" because it reflects attitudes toward the parents as providers of a good holding environment for the family (Scharff & Scharff, 1987, 1991; J. Scharff & Bagnini, 2002). In response to this contextual transference, therapists experience a set of feelings specific to each couple or family. This "contextual countertransference" provides valuable information about the transference that evoked it. For instance, when therapists feel appreciated, they might believe that the families think of them as good providers, but if they feel exalted, they might begin to feel unworthy or likely to disappoint. Checking this out, a therapist might find that there was ambivalence about parenting in the families of origin, leading to a split in which the parents of the husband are idealized and those of the wife are presented as inadequate in comparison. When therapists' arrangements are found unfair or their office furnishing unacceptable, they may pick up a clue about inadequate emotional provisions in the previous generation. These countertransference experiences put the therapist in touch with the projection of anxiety into the present family system from the internalization and reprojection of parental expectations, based on the needs of childhood.

The couple also has a focused transference, as each member of the couple finds aspects to love and hate in the therapist over time. In family therapy the contextual transference tends to be predominant, and in individual therapy focused transferences become the meat of the work, but in couple therapy transference oscillates between focused and contextual transferences (Scharff & Scharff, 1991, 1997).

## Making Interpretations

There are clarifying comments, comments that lead to more information, comments that link one event or thought with another, and interpretations that lead to insight, which produce a change in perspective and ultimately a change in behavior within couple and family relationships. The most effective interpretation includes a *because clause,* which addresses the required relationship and the avoided relationship, and the calamity that they defend against (Ezriel, 1952). At the surface level, ORCF therapists point out the behavior that keeps the partner or other family members in a required relationship that defends against another way of relating that is more feared. Therapists then point out an avoided relationship that the required relationship covers. Finally, at the deepest level lies the calamity that is feared if an avoided relationship were to be allowed. For instance, a young wife continually nagging her ambitious, workaholic husband to clean up the mounds of paper in his home office seems to want order and space for herself (the required relationship), instead of expressing her longing for sexual intimacy and fertility (the avoided relationship), which fends off the prospect of death of the family when the couple does not procreate (the calamity).

## Ending the Session

At the end of sessions, couples or families lose face-to-face contact with the therapist. This is the moment when they return to the confines of their couple or family group. If some of the space for thinking that the therapist provides has been internalized, family members are less anxious about leaving. In the case of family therapy, because children are less aware of time, a few minutes before the end of each session, therapists should alert them that it is time to begin the clean-up of the toys. Some families balk at this and need more time than others. It's an opportunity to help them with the task of working together.

## Terminating Treatment

In consultation with the therapist, the couple or the family sets a date for terminating. This sets in motion a phase of the treatment process in which all the previous work gets recapped and revised. As they face being without the help of therapy, couples and families become temporarily anxious, and so old transference issues arise again. Because of what they have learned in therapy there is less sense of threat. Because there is now a deadline, there is more of a push to understand issues even more completely. Couple, family, and therapist must mourn the loss to achieve a successful separation from the therapeutic relationship.

## Specific Therapeutic Interventions

*Empathic listening* means waiting for whatever the couple or the family wants to say and imagining each person's situation. An *inquiry* into a detail may be made to facilitate understanding. One of the most useful questions is simply, "Can anyone tell me more about that?" Therapists ask for comments on children's play as a way of reaching past the family's conscious portrayal of its functioning to explore the unconscious life of the family. The therapist may *ask the family to draw a picture* of the family in interaction, and this provides the family and the therapist with a shared image the family can then elaborate.

Similarly, the therapist may *ask for a dream as a narrative of the shared unconscious.* When one member gives a dream, admittedly a construction of the individual unconscious, associations are gathered by the ORCF therapist from all present, because the dream is viewed as a product of the couple or the family system. The dream springs from the unconscious aspects of the family relationships and is a means of conveying the transference

to the therapist. Therapists' *clarifying comments* ensure that all those at the session hear the various views expressed and appreciate the nuances in the family's various communications, and the therapists' *shaping comments* pull together the process to date. Therapists give *support* through commitment and empathic listening, *negotiate* a shared point of view, and give *advice about child rearing and sexual behavior,* when asked.

*Therapists put conflict into words* to begin the process of developing a *shared narrative of experience.* By pointing out repetitive patterns of interaction, they address defenses and figure out with the family what purpose the defenses serve. Gradually, the couple and the family are helped to *face the underlying anxieties.* Using countertransference in relation to the couple and the family group, therapists detect these anxieties and then *interpret* them. They show that the defensive aspects express resistance and defend against anxiety and change, especially against sexual development, aging, and illness, which threaten the death of the couple or the family.

In ORCFT, therapists *look for unconscious projective identifications.* For example, these are found in the marriage of a methodical accountant and a flamboyant actress. She loves the order and steadiness he brings to her life, but she hates his rituals. He loves the emotional expressiveness that she brings, but it drives him crazy that her clothes and costumes are spread out on various chairs and beds in the house. He thinks that she is bad for being so messy, and she thinks he is accusing her unfairly. She thinks he is bad for being so controlling and self-righteous.

The next step is *re-owning projective identifications.* The couple investigates why each partner feels so adoring and judgmental at the same time. He cherishes emotional freedom, but he can't allow it to himself because he repressed his tears about losing his baby sister. He refinds that lost object in his wife, and he tries to control it in her, and in so doing he controls her so that he doesn't face losing her in the mess. She cherishes order, but she can't keep order because she preferred to thwart her controlling mother so as to retain her creativity. Now he criticizes her like his mother did to him so as to get compliance. She fights against him because she hasn't solved her conflict with her mother. When her father died, she felt abandoned to her mother, and so she found a man who would keep things going. Learning about these histories, partners can stop seeing each other as a part of their own selves. Recognizing how their internal conflicts mesh in the couple joint personality, they can stop replaying them in the interpersonal setting.

ORCFT recommends *adjunctive methods*, such as Alcoholics Anonymous and Al-Anon, for substance abusers. When family interpretation cannot relieve a well-established mental illness, such as psychosis, mania, or major depression, hospitalization or psychopharmacological medication (or both) of an individual or a family is recommended. ORCT has been useful in dealing with the heterosexual couple struggling to adjust to the homosexuality of one of the partners and in helping gay and lesbian couples maintain long-term couple relationships and raise families.

The Silvers, a single-parent mother and her two sleepy daughters, attend their early morning family therapy session with the first author (J. Scharff, 1992). Suddenly energized, the children start drawing at the play table. Liz and Ruth talk sadly of how they miss their mother when she works late. The discussion leads usefully to Mrs. Silver's feelings of exclusion by her family. She had paid for herself to go to a prestigious school in the Northeast. Her self-sufficiency, which stood her in good stead when her husband became ill and died, had been taken as a rejection of Southern values in her youth. Her commitment to therapy was perceived as a criticism of her parents' lifestyle.

As often happens, the children's play helps us along. Liz's drawing is signed and entitled "Good Which" (*sic*). When I ask about her drawing, of a witch with long red nails, I get a noncommittal response. I say, "I am interested in the title of the drawing. It seems to me to ask, 'Which witch is this?'"

Liz does not know that she has misspelled *witch*. Mrs. Silver and Ruth find this odd because Liz is normally an excellent speller. That's why Mrs. Silver thinks that I must be right and asks me to elaborate on what I meant. Because of her Southern phrasing, I hear her question as: "What—do you mean Dr. Scharff?"

After some dialogue, I say, "I don't mean that this drawing is proof that Liz thinks of me as a witch. I think that her drawing of the 'which' and what you have all said about the 'witch' raises the question: Are there ways in which all of you feel me to be a dangerous, mean woman?"

Summoning all the spunk that so annoyed her family of origin and her daughter, Mrs. Silver reminds the girls that they hadn't wanted to come today. Ruth explains that she wanted to go to school early instead, because she has a test today. But Mrs. Silver is not to be interrupted. She is just getting around to me. She leans forward in her seat, her body tense as if about to spring. Ruth looks anxious. Mrs. Silver looks me straight in the eye, venomously, and argues at length that I am mean for charging for a missed appointment.

"I know that my policy is hard for you," I acknowledged. "And I know it takes a lot to come here. It takes a lot to tell me how angry you are about it." Mrs. Silver confirms that she is angry, then relaxes and smiles. I realize that she isn't requiring me to do anything, after all. She just wants to be taken seriously and not avoided. She thanks Liz for doing the drawing that helped her to say what she was thinking and feeling. Liz beams for the first time. Often it was her role in the family to whine and echo her mother's complaint about things being unfair. Here, she is doing something that enables her mother to speak for herself.

As a family, the Silvers are worried that angry feelings, as well as feelings and questions about maturing sexually, cannot be respected and dealt with in the family. This session has gone well. This family, whose anger usually circles around between them, defeating their family goals and lowering their self-esteem, has been able to express some rage in the transference to me as the person like their mother, who leaves them to go after money, and like their father, from whom they are separated. I was able to introjectively identify with the family's projective identification of me as a cruel object, which will help Mrs. Silver and the children face the witch they see in each other and in themselves.

## EFFECTIVENESS OF THE OBJECT-RELATIONS APPROACH

The complexity of ORCFT concepts makes it hard to operationalize and reduce key concepts to manageable bits for testing. As a result, clinical outcome research is regrettably sparse. However, tests for measuring object relations do exist and could be applied to the study of therapeutic change. The Object Relations Test (ORT) was developed by Phillipson at the Tavistock Clinic and revised with the author's permission for use in measuring the internal object relations set of an individual (Shaw, 2000). Administering the test to both members of a couple before and after couple therapy holds potential for documenting internal change.

Adult attachment research is the most promising and widely used method for studying couple relationships and therapeutic progress (Scharff & Scharff, 1998). Internal working models of attachment have been shown to in-

fluence the construction of intimate relationships in adult life, to affect perceptions of emotional availability in the partner (Sroufe & Fleeson, 1986) and to influence internal representations of relationships (Morrison, Urquiza, & Goodlin-Jones, 1997a) and the sense of satisfaction in a relationship, especially in a short-term one (Morrison et al., 1997b). At the Tavistock Marital Studies Centre, the Couple Attachment Joint Interview (CAJI) has been used to study how secure and insecure internal working models of attachment influence the complex attachment of partners in long-term marriages (Clulow, 2001; Fisher & Crandell, 1997).

At the Maudsley, Birtchnell (1993) has pioneered a set of questionnaires and software for entering the data, the results of which yield the *octagon*, a visual-spatial representation of the partners' relatedness in terms of upperness and lowerness, closeness and distance. At the end of therapy the questionnaire is repeated and the results again plotted in the octagon. Change in these dimensions of relatedness can be demonstrated when the octagons are compared at the end of therapy.

In terms of research into training in object-relations couple therapy, the ORT is in use at the International Institute of Object Relations Therapy (IIORT), before and after an immersion course in working with couples, children, and families. To the traditional multichannel teaching method with lectures, videos, readings, and case presentation, IIORT adds experiential workshops on play and a small group that meets twice a day to discuss the concepts and cases, personal reaction to the material, and the group process that inevitably develops as therapists work together to learn about couples and families in depth. The concepts under study are displayed in the group interaction, and this allows them to be thoroughly internalized and then more confidently applied in the clinical situation. The ORT measures change in the student therapist's object relations set in response to this type of intensive continuing education.

## FUTURE DEVELOPMENTS AND DIRECTIONS

Living with managed care has been difficult for the ORCF therapist. The pressure to proscribe the treatment to meet goals accepted by insurance companies has played havoc with the flexible, thoughtful attitude so essential to real change. Faced with people who can afford only six sessions, ORCF therapists choose to show them what they can learn in object-relations therapy, rather than set a simple goal and switch a symptom temporarily in order for the therapist to look effective and for the treatment to appear complete. For those cases of well-functioning families where a sudden crisis throws the family off balance, a brief therapy adaptation, dealing with both the symptom and the dynamic focus, is effective.

Families in transition have special need of family therapy. ORCFT has been adapted to suit the needs of divorcing families by seeing the children with one parent one week and with the other parent the next. This treatment model reflects the living arrangements of divorced and blended families. From the early 20th to the 21st century, the family norm has changed from the traditional heterosexual nuclear family, where divorce and homosexual marriage were unusual. Now the family may be headed by a heterosexual or a homosexual couple or by an individual at any one time, and the family is often in transition regarding membership, leadership, and location. As the concept of marriage and the form of the family continue to evolve, ORCFT has the flexibility, adaptability, tolerance of ambiguity, and comprehension of complexity to remain a relevant treatment option.

## REFERENCES

Ainsworth, M. D. S., Blehar, M. C. Waters, E., & Wall, S. (1978). *Patterns of attachment: A psychological study of the strange situation.* Hillsdale, NJ: Erlbaum.

Bertalanffy, L. von. (1950). The theory of open systems in physics and biology. *Science, 111*, 23–29.

Bion, W. (1959). *Experiences in groups.* New York: Basic Books, 1961.

Bion, W. (1970). *Attention and interpretation.* London: Tavistock.

Birtchnell, J. (1993). The interpersonal octagon. In *How humans relate: A new interpersonal theory* (pp. 215–229). Westport, CT: Praeger.

Bowlby, J. (1969). *Attachment and loss* (Vol. I). New York: Basic Books.

Clulow, C. (2001). *Adult attachment and couple psychotherapy.* London: Routledge.

Dicks, H. V. (1967). *Marital tensions: Clinical studies towards a psychoanalytic theory of interaction.* London: Routledge & Kegan Paul.

Ezriel, H. (1952). Notes on psycho-analytic group therapy II: Interpretation and process. *Psychiatry, 15*, 119–126.

Fairbairn, W. R. D. (1944). Endopsychic structure considered in terms of object-relationships. In *Psychoanalytic studies of the personality* (pp. 82–136). London: Routledge.

Fairbairn, W. R. D. (1952). *Psychoanalytic studies of the personality,* reprinted as *An object relations theory of the personality* (pp. 82–136). New York: Basic Books, 1954.

Fairbairn, W. R. D. (1963). Synopsis of an object-relations theory of the personality. *International Journal of Psycho-Analysis, 44*, 224–226. Reprinted in D. E. Scharff & E. F. Birtles (Eds.), *From instinct to self: Selected papers of W. R. D. Fairbairn* (Vol. 1, pp. 155–156). Northvale, NJ: Jason Aronson.

Fisher, J., & Crandell, L. (1997). Complex attachment: patterns of relating in the couple. *Sexual and Marital Therapy, 12*(3), 211–223.

Gleick, J. (1978). *Chaos.* New York: Viking Penguin.

Kirkpatrick, L. A., & Davis, K. E. (1994). Attachment style, gender, and relationship stability: A longitudinal analysis. *Journal of Personality and Social Psychology, 66*, 502–512.

Klein, M. (1946). Notes on some schizoid mechanisms. *Envy and gratitude and other works: 1946–1963* (pp. 1–24). London: Hogarth, 1975.

Main, M., & Goldwyn, R. (in press). Interview based adult attachment classification: Related to infant-mother and infant–father attachment. *Developmental Psychology*.

Morrison, T., Goodlin-Jones, B. L., & Urquiza, A. J. (1997a). Attachment and the representation of intimate relationships in adulthood. *Journal of Psychology, 131*, 57–71.

Morrison, T., Urquiza, A. J., & Goodlin-Jones, B. L. (1997b). Attachment, perceptions of interaction, and relationship adjustment. *Journal of Social and Personal Relationships, 14*, 627–642.

Prigogine, I. (1976). Order through fluctuation: Self-organization and social system. In C. H. Waddington & E. Jantsch (Eds.), *Evolution and Consciousness: Human Systems in Transition* (pp. 93–126, 130–133). Reading, MA: Addison-Wesley.

Scharff, D. (1982). *The sexual relationship: An object relations view of sex and the family*. London: Routledge & Kegan Paul. Reprinted 1998, Northvale, NJ: Jason Aronson.

Scharff, D. (1992). *Refinding the object and reclaiming the self*. Northvale, NJ: Jason Aronson.

Scharff, D. (Ed.). (1996). *Object relations theory and practice*. New York: Aronson.

Scharff, D. (in press). Couple and family therapy. Special issue. *Journal of Applied Psychoanalytic Studies*.

Scharff, D., & Scharff, J. S. (1991). *Object relations couple therapy*. Northvale, NJ: Jason Aronson.

Scharff, D. E., & Birtles, E. (1994). *From instinct to self, Vol. 1: Clinical and theoretical*. Northvale, NJ: Jason Aronson.

Scharff, D. E., & Scharff, J. S. (1987). *Object relations family therapy*. Northvale, NJ: Jason Aronson.

Scharff, J. S. (1992). *Projective and introjective identification and the use of the therapist's self*. Northvale, NJ: Jason Aronson.

Scharff, J. S. (1995). Psychoanalytic marital therapy. In A. Gurman & N. Jacobsen (Eds.), *Clinical handbook of couple therapy* (pp. 164–193). New York: Guilford Press.

Scharff J. S., & Bagnini, C. (in press). Narcissistic disorder. In D. K. Snyder & M. A. Whisman (Eds.), *Treating emotional, behavioral, and health problems in couple therapy*. New York: Guildford Press.

Scharff J. S., & Bagnini, C. (2002). Object relations couple therapy. In A. Gurman & N. Jacobsen (Eds.), *Clinical handbook of couple therapy* (3rd Ed.). New York: Guilford Press.

Scharff, J. S., & Scharff, D. E. (1994). *Object relations therapy of physical and sexual trauma*. Northvale, NJ: Jason Aronson.

Scharff, J. S., & Scharff, D. E. (1997). Object relations couple therapy. *American Journal of Psychotherapy, 51*(2), 141–173.

Scharff, J. S., & Scharff, D. E. (1998). *Object relations individual therapy*. Northvale, NJ: Jason Aronson.

Scharff, J. S., & Varela, Y. de (2000). Object relations therapy. In *Comparative treatments for relationship dysfunction* (pp. 81–101). New York: Springer.

Schore, A. (1994). *Affect regulation and the origin of the self: The neurobiology of emotional development*. Hillsdale, NJ: Erlbaum.

Shaw, M. (2002). *The object relations technique: Assessing the individual*. Manhasset, NY: O.R.T. Institute.

Sroufe, L. A., & Fleeson, J. (1986). Attachment and the construction of relationships. In *Relationships and development* (pp. 51–71). Hillsdale, NJ: Erlbaum.

Winnicott, D. W. (1951). Transitional objects and transitional phenomena. In *Through paediatrics to psycho-analysis* (pp. 229–242). London: Hogarth, 1975.

Winnicott, D. W. (1960). *The theory of the parent-infant relationship: The maturational processes and the facilitating environment* (pp. 37–55). London: Hogarth Press and the Institute of Psycho-Analysis.

Winnicott, D. W. (1971). *Playing and reality*. London: Tavistock.

# CHAPTER 5

# Family-of-Origin Treatment

WILLIAM C. NICHOLS, EdD, ABPP

*Athens, Georgia*

## INTRODUCTION

Family-of-origin treatment is an approach that takes several different forms and modes of intervention, rather than a single, distinctive model of therapy. It generally consists of several ways of making therapeutic interventions under certain circumstances and for certain purposes, rather than being the sole way of doing therapy, even for those therapists who regard interventions with the family of origin as an exceedingly important element in family therapy.

## Terminology

*Family-of-origin therapy* is used as a broad term in this chapter but one with some specific meanings. Family therapy that involves, whatever the particular forms of intervention, working with two or more generations, including an adult client's family of origin, to change the relationship between the client and his or her family of origin, is regarded here as family-

of-origin therapy. The terms *family-of-origin therapy, intergenerational family therapy,* and *multigenerational therapy* are used here somewhat interchangeably. Some theorists and therapists, as noted by Fine and Hovestadt (1987), would prefer to restrict the term *family-of-origin* because of concerns over whether the focus is on two-generational or three-generational families. Working with either two-generational or three-generational families would in a strict sense be family-of-origin therapy. This use of the term family-of-origin therapy is done with the recognition that the intergenerational concept has carried specific meanings in contextual family therapy, such as the theoretically and clinically rich concept of intergenerational loyalties (Boszormenyi-Nagy & Spark, 1973). Similarly, multigenerational has embodied particular meanings—for example, Bowen's concept of multigenerational transmission process (Boszormenyi-Nagy & Spark, 1973; Bowen, 1978; Kerr, 1981).

Whatever the terminology, Carr (2000) notes that "all transgenerational therapists are

83

united by their belief that family problems are multigenerational phenomena and that often this is because patterns of family interaction or relationships are replicated from one generation to the next" (p. 159).

## WHAT IS THE FAMILY?

Family of origin refers to one's natural family, the family into which one is born (Foley & Everett, 1982) or adopted (Sauber, L'Abate, Weeks, & Buchanan, 1993). However, the term *family,* as the field is beginning to recognize, has different meanings in different cultures and with different ethnic groups. As McGoldrick (1982, 1996) has emphasized, among the long-dominant WASP (White, Anglo-Saxon, Protestant) definition in the United States, family referred to an intact nuclear family. African Americans focused on a wide network of kinspeople and community. Italians included three or four generations of kin, godparents, and old friends.

Others go beyond those definitions. A tribal definition of family has been used in Speck and Attneave's (1973) social network intervention method, in which the nuclear family, extended family, neighbors, other significant acquaintances of individual family members, and some professionals meet in therapy sessions of as many as 50–100 participants. This approach, however, commonly referred to as "network therapy," is not aimed at family-of-origin work as such but specifically at providing psychotherapy for the network of a family in a time of extreme crisis (Rueveni, 1979).

Determining what constitutes a family of origin is becoming increasingly more difficult. As Lita Schwartz has pointed out:

> We have single-parent families, remarried families (formerly called step-families), blended families, foster families, adoptive families, and combinations of some of these, each with a legal under-pinning. There are those who wish to be perceived as families, such as homosexual couples who perform activities normally regarded as functions of a family, but who may not be legally recognized as such for parenting or legal purposes. (1993, pp. 429–430)

The increasing complexity results in growing difficulties, not only in defining the family of origin but also in dealing with the kinds of issues therapeutically that typically have been the agenda for family-of-origin therapy. Some of these forms of families, such as found in some instances of adoption, for example, embody intricate and perplexing issues regarding an ill-defined or elusive family of origin for the client. The psychological image of one's family carried by the client sometimes provides a better guide to troubling issues or potential supports in the perceived "family of origin" than does the legal definition.

After growing up as an only child in a family in which her mother was married four times, twice for short periods to the biological father, a woman who sought out therapy had major difficulties in deciding what constituted her family. For instance, who was included? Who was really "family" when she was growing up? With whom did she have "unfinished business" that she needed to complete so that she could move on with her life? She had little emotional investment in her biological father who had been merely perfunctory in his limited parenting behaviors. The woman recalled the loss of contact with her biological father's stepdaughter (whom she regarded as her "sister"), when that child moved away, as one of life's more traumatic events. She clearly regarded her nurturant and supportive stepfather as her "real" father.

## HISTORY AND BACKGROUND OF THE APPROACH

After psychotherapy's long background and struggles with rigid family structures in Western culture, family therapists today are faced with a greater and more universal need to try to understand and intervene effectively with clients regarding various, often ambiguous, family backgrounds. Aponte (1976) characterized some poor families as underorganized; similarly, the growing number of stepfamilies in Western society may be underorganized, rather than rigidly structured (Nichols, 1980). Always there seems to have been a need to help families find a balance between integrating individuals into the family and assisting them in differentiating themselves, in balancing elements of sameness and difference, as Ackerman (1961) put it. Given the rate and extent of change in the past few decades, assisting families today to assimilate their members may be at least as important as focusing on differentiation/individuation.

Today's therapists are often faced with the task of making pragmatic decisions regarding family of origin by carefully considering both theoretical orientations and the client's personal feelings regarding important persons, relationships, and factors in determining what constitutes the family of origin and where remedial work is needed.

## Sources of Family-of-Origin Work

Even when the strictures imposed by elements of the psychoanalytic movement against seeing more than one troubled person from a family at a time and the 19th-century views of personality and physics that long prevailed are acknowledged, it is amazing that it took psychotherapists so long to discover or to overtly admit that there were strong benefits to be gained from bringing together two or more generations of a family to work on problems that are manifested in human adaptation, mental health, intimate interactions, and relationships. Psychiatry, as Nathan Ackerman (1954, 1956) noted, traditionally was concerned with the individual personality and not with the

family. Working with family groups, often including members of three generations, for example, appears to have been a relatively common occurrence with some social workers and with clergy when members of their flock were experiencing trouble long before the family therapy revolution burst on the scene in the United States in the 1950s. Working without the theoretical orientations of professional psychotherapists, such as diagnostic categories and concern with pathology, clergy and educators, along with pioneer family-oriented social workers, were on the right track when they intuitively and with common-sense guidance sought to bring together troubled family members to facilitate change.

The emergence of the field of family therapy from its lengthy roots in concerns with child behavior problems, marital problems, and relationships and its somewhat shorter but intensive focus on schizophrenia has been described elsewhere (Broderick & Schrader, 1981, 1991; Nichols, 1996; Nichols & Everett, 1986).

## MAJOR PURPOSES OR OUTCOMES

Family-of-origin work has two different, though often interrelated, purposes or outcomes. One may be described as an individual approach. "Historically" oriented therapists traditionally worked to help clients uncover conflicts carried over from the past and to understand their internal conflicts as a basis for effecting positive change. In brief, the purpose of an individual focus is to help clients change and to become free of crippling conflicts carried over from their developmental years.

The other wing of family-of-origin therapy, labeled here an interpersonal approach, is concerned with not only changes in the individual client but also changes in interactions among family members. It goes beyond altering perceptions of and reactions to past events and earlier relationships, and it involves interventions in current patterns. This is not to imply that the therapist necessarily regards members of the family of origin other than the specified client/s as being in therapy, but to acknowledge that any kinds of interventions into the relationships of the client and the family of origin produce systemic changes as well as alterations in the client.

## MAJOR THEORETICAL CONSTRUCTS

Describing the major theoretical constructs of family-of-origin therapy is not an easy matter, largely because of the variety of theoretical approaches advanced by transgenerational therapists. Some of the constructs mentioned further on are identified with a particular approach, whereas others are coin of the realm for most intergenerational, multigenerational, and transgenerational therapists.

### *Differentiation Constructs*

A number of constructs are associated with the notion of differentiation of self from the family of origin.

#### DIFFERENTIATION OF SELF

This refers to the psychological separation of intellectual and emotional systems within the self, which permits the concurrent separation of self from others within the family of origin and elsewhere (Bowen, 1978).

#### FUSION

The opposite of differentiation of self, fusion refers to a person's tendency to become so emotionally attached to another that his or her own sense of self and boundaries become blurred with the other person, resulting in an intense interdependency (Bowen, 1978).

#### UNDIFFERENTIATED EGO MASS

Bowen's term to describe the quality of "stuck togetherness" or lack of differentiation of self manifested by family members when the level of anxiety in a family has led to a confusion of the emotional and intellectual systems within an individual, resulting in a similar confusion in other family members so that identities and boundaries have become diffuse (Bowen, 1978).

#### EMOTIONAL CUTOFF

This refers to the establishment of emotional or physical distance or both from one's family of origin by an individual in response to an unresolved family-of-origin attachment relationship. "The greater the degree of cutoff, the greater the probability of replicating the problematic family-of-origin relationship in the family of procreation" (Carr, 2000, p. 181). In dramatic forms the pattern may not last very long because the isolation resulting from the cutoff may lead to intense fusion with others (e.g., spouses) outside of the family-of-origin system (Bowen, 1978; Kerr & Bowen, 1988).

#### EMOTIONAL DIVORCE

This is a term referring to the distance between two persons on the basis of their emotional reactivity to one another; this essentially automatic process results in the avoidance of certain subjects or events because they produce too much anxiety and corresponding emotional reaction (Everett, 1992).

#### MULTIGENERATIONAL TRANSMISSION PROCESS

This is a general term used in several family systems approaches to refer to the transmission of certain roles, myths, and interactional or structural family patterns across several generations (Boszormenyi-Nagy & Spark, 1973; Bowen, 1978; Everett, 1992). These roles, rules, and routines from the family of origin are inadvertently organized in ways that prevent differentiation (Carr, 2000).

## FAMILY PROJECTION PROCESS

This construct refers to the level of differentiation of parents and how it is passed on to their children, resulting in a given child becoming the symptom carrier for the family when the parents project their immaturity onto him or her (Carr, 2000; Everett, 1992).

## Family Development/Family Life-Cycle Constructs

### PERSONAL AUTHORITY IN THE FAMILY SYSTEM

Although a variant of the construct of differentiation of self, Williamson's personal authority in the family construct goes a step beyond differentiation of the self from one's family of origin. The Personal Authority in the Family System construct is intended to be a "synthesizing construct, connecting differentiation and intimacy" (Williamson, 1982a, 1982b, 1991). It theoretically applies to the 4th decade of life (the 30s, or perhaps the 40s, in some cases).

### INTERLOCKING PATHOLOGIES

Ackerman's early effort to integrate the complex levels of intrapsychic and interpersonal dynamics within family systems includes three dimensions: (1) group dynamics of the family, (2) the emotional integration of an individual within the family, and (3) the internal organization and development of individual members. A complete clinical picture requires an analysis of all three dimensions (Ackerman, 1956; Everett, 1992).

## Object-Relations Constructs

Reference here is to psychodynamics and object-relations theory from the work of W. R. D. Fairbairn (1952), which explains psychological functioning, particularly psychological difficulties, in terms of the influence of unconscious processes.

### OBJECT RELATIONS

This term from psychodynamic theory is utilized to describe the early interpersonal relationships between the child and the primary caretakers, who are internalized within the child and serve as the model for subsequent interpersonal relations in the family of origin, mate selection, family of procreation, and other intimate relationships (Everett, 1992; Framo, 1982; Scharff & Scharff, 1987).

### SPLITTING

Derived from a primitive defense reaction, in which an individual splits the good from the bad in an external object and then internalizes this split perception, this construct has been used in family therapy to describe an interaction style within families and among their members in which positive and negative feelings and thoughts are split and experienced in isolation from one another. The maneuver distorts the family's perception and experience of reality and tends to perpetuate diffusion of personal boundaries, rigid roles within the family, and rigid external family boundaries. In this process, one member is perceived as good or gratifying and another as depriving or bad (good/bad objects) (Everett, 1992; Framo, 1982; Skynner, 1976, 1981).

### INTROJECTION

This term refers to the identification process by which the child incorporates into his or her psyche simplified representatives of major aspects of parental figures (such as the "good" parent [object] or the "bad" parent [object]. These primitive mental representations of part of a person are referred to as introjects (Carr, 2000).

## PROJECTIVE IDENTIFICATION

This construct is the label given to a defense mechanism whereby one projects unacceptable parts of his or her personality onto another member of the family, who reciprocally accepts the projection and behaves in accordance with it (Everett & Volgy-Everett, 1988; Feldman, 1982; Middelberg, 2001; Skynner, 1981; Zinner & Shapiro, 1972).

## MODELS OF RELATIONSHIP

This construct refers to the patterns of interaction between one's parents, and perhaps grandparents, and patterns in other marriages that a person was exposed to over an extended period of time during his or her childhood and growing-up period. The construct includes the idea that influences of those models were absorbed both consciously and unconsciously and tend to play a significant role in one's own marriage and other important close relationships (Nichols, 1988; Nichols, 1996; Nichols & Everett, 1986; Skynner, 1976).

## Contextual Constructs

Although identified primarily with Ivan Boszormenyi-Nagy (Boszormenyi-Nagy, 1965; Boszormenyi-Nagy, Grunebaum, & Ulrich, 1991; Boszormenyi-Nagy & Krasner, 1986; Boszormenyi-Nagy & Spark, 1973), the constructs mentioned in this section have been widely adopted by other clinicians and have become a general part of the field, as have constructs initially developed by Bowen. (A more complete glossary of contextual family therapy definitions is found in Boszormenyi-Nagy & Krasner, 1986, pp. 413–422.)

## RELATIONAL ETHICS

This idea, located at the heart of contextual therapy, is that family members have a duty to be fair in their relationships by meeting their obligations and are responsible for the consequences of their behavior.

## ENTITLEMENT

This refers to merit or a relational "credit" accumulated by an individual as a result of fulfilling ethical obligations to other family members. Evident in the balancing of parent–child relationships, entitlement can accumulate across generations.

## DEBT

Failure to meet ethical obligations to other family members results in an accumulation of costs deemed debts.

## LEDGER OF MERITS

This term is used to refer to the accumulated accounts of entitlements and debts within family relationships, that is, to the balance of what has been given and what is owed.

## INTERGENERATIONAL LOYALTY

The emotional commitments and obligations to one's family of origin and to broader dynamics that may cross multiple generations and that involve preferential attachment to relational figures. Vertical loyalties, which are imbedded inherently in early childhood attachments and parental attachments at marriage, must be rebalanced with horizontal loyalties to an adult peer (Boszormenyi-Nagy & Spark, 1973; Everett, 1992).

## INVISIBLE LOYALTIES

Invisible or indirect loyalty presents as attitudes or behaviors associated with past relationships that block commitment to a current relationship, for example, the unconscious commitment to a parent or parents that blocks commitment to a marital partner (Boszormenyi-Nagy & Krasner, 1986; Boszormenyi-Nagy & Spark, 1973; Everett, 1992).

## LEGACY

This refers to expectations associated with the parent–child relationships arising from the family's history. The present generation, according to Boszormenyi-Nagy, has the imperative to sort out in life what is beneficial to posterity's quality of survival (Boszormenyi-Nagy & Krasner, 1986; Carr, 2000).

## INTERGENERATIONAL ACCOUNTING

This term refers to the intergenerational accounting that monitors the discharge of obligations due prior and subsequent generations, marital partners, and peers and keeps account of the balance of obligations among members in the system (Boszormenyi-Nagy & Krasner, 1986; Boszormenyi-Nagy & Spark, 1973; Everett, 1992).

## PARENTIFICATION

A process where, typically, a child is assigned responsibilities beyond age-appropriateness, such as a caretaking role for one or both parents or siblings. The result may be either negative or positive. This role serves not only to diffuse marital stress but, reciprocally, to reinforce the power of the child in the family. There is often an associated effect of sibling rivalry, and the parentified child may be more vulnerable to incidents of incest or physi-

cal abuse (Boszormenyi-Nagy, 1965; Boszormenyi-Nagy & Spark, 1973; Everett, 1992).

## SCAPEGOATING

A term sometimes used to refer to negative aspects of parentification, scapegoating denotes the process by which a family designates a member to carry and act out the stress and dysfunction for other members or subsystems, for example, a child may engage in delinquent behavior as a way of acting out stress in the parents' marriage (Everett, 1992; Vogel & Bell, 1960).

## OPERATIONAL MOURNING

This construct refers to a clinical technique that is aimed at involving a family in dealing with a delayed grief reaction. Norman Paul (Paul, 1967; Paul & Grosser, 1965; Paul & Paul, 1975) has maintained that incompleted mourning serves as a defense against suffering additional losses and often is unconsciously passed on to other family members, resulting in a freezing of symbolic relationships in the family. Paul's operational mourning approach—which involved introducing a delayed grief reaction and using empathic intervention and such procedures as "stresser stimuli" confrontations—is intended to break up the old patterns and help to resolve the grief and the resultant fixed family relationships.

## Sibling Position Constructs
## Ordinal positions

The relative birth order position of each individual within his or her sibling subsystem, for example, oldest daughter, youngest son, may affect personality formation and role development within the family of origin in a relatively predictable fashion and may influence the relative comfort levels between parents and children, based on the parents' own ordinal positions, as well as create other alliances and identifications within the family system and influence subsequent adult mate selection (Everett, 1992; Toman, 1976).

## FAMILY RECONSTRUCTION

This refers to a therapeutic tool developed by Virginia Satir for integrating a person into the historical and psychological matrix of his or her family of origin. This approach is still widely used and has continued to be expanded by Satir model adherents (Banmen, 2002; Nerin, 1985; Taylor, 2002).

## PROPOSED ETIOLOGY
## OF CLINICAL PROBLEMS

Family-of-origin approaches share the common idea that many problems are rooted in relationships and interactions that are spread across generational boundaries and that require alteration in those relationships and interactions, in order to produce meaningful and lasting change. Dealing with an individual's intrapsychic conflict as the sole focus of therapy is only infrequently a successful way to cope with the difficulties that plague the person. Ackerman's (1958) view that pathology in the family started with interpersonal conflict and led to intrapsychic conflicts and that these two levels of conflict existed in a reciprocal relationship with a circular feedback system carries the implication that interventions generally should be aimed at two or more generations. The point sometimes advanced that having a problematic child—for example, a developmentally disabled, physically ill, or genetically impaired youngster—may lead to family conflict does not change the fact that attention to multiple generations is indicated; how the parents in such families

react and attempt to deal with the problems is intricately shaped by the experiences and relationships in their own families of origin.

The dynamic picture of individual and family life is concerned with very significant transgenerational processes. Through "nongenetic transmission" (Nichols & Everett, 1986), patterns of thinking, feeling, fearing, and so forth are transmitted through the generations. Thus, parent–child problems need to be examined from at least a three-generational perspective. What would the parent's own parents expect of him or her? How would they behave in circumstances similar to those the parent is currently facing with the child?

Failure of a client to differentiate adequately from his or her family of origin is the source of many conflicts and failures to adapt successfully in adult life (Bowen, 1978). A variant of this is continuing tension and loss of intimacy between the adult person and his or her parents (Williamson, 1991). Continuing pathological interaction with one's family of origin and sources of pathological influence takes many other forms, including continuing loyalty conflicts, imbalances between entitlements and debts in the relational ethics area (Boszormenyi-Nagy & Krasner, 1986), unresolved grief reactions that affect marital and personal adaptation (Paul & Paul, 1975), family secrets (Pincus & Dare, 1978), and others.

Several different processes and sources of problems are found in borderline conditions, which are identifiable through several generations of a family system (Everett & Volgy-Everett, 1998). Assessment generally turns up patterns of splitting, good/bad object attachments, and reciprocal projective identification, which typically produce coexisting triangles, that is, two central triangles in the family in which children are involved as "good" and "bad" objects and thus moderate the intensity of parental conflict by deflecting it from the parental couple (Everett, Halperin, Volgy, & Wissler, 1989).

Increasingly, it seems, family therapists are giving attention to the roles of ethnicity, gender, and other context/setting issues in dealing with clients and their families. Hence, many issues that appear in family settings need to be interpreted in light of cultural values and behaviors before a decision is made that pathology exists and before interventions are planned or launched.

## METHODS OF CLINICAL ASSESSMENT

Many, perhaps most, family-of-origin therapists apparently use clinical interviewing as the basic mode for assessing clients and their needs. This approach may or may not be supplemented by the use of clinical aids such as measurement instruments.

### The Interview and Clinical Exploration With Clients

The interview can be broken down into two different but overlapping processes, interactive inquiry and observation of process.

#### INTERACTIVE INQUIRY

The therapist explores pertinent issues and areas with the clients, asking questions and examining the information for himself or herself for significant conclusions regarding personal/marital and family-of-origin matters.

#### OBSERVATION OF PROCESS

The therapist notes such factors as the ease with which the clients report on family-of-origin relations and other data, the areas of sensitivity, or repetitive role patterns. Areas of ambivalence, the presence of parentified or scapegoated roles on the part of the client, the

existence of projective collusion in the marriage, and other important matters can be checked out or noted for future work.

### The Use and Interpretation of Genograms

#### GENOGRAM

This refers to the use of a diagram of extended family relationships that includes at least three generations. Constructing a genogram maps out recurring patterns of behavior, for example, alcoholism, and includes critical events such as deaths, births, and rites of passage. The therapist gains specific information from family members regarding ongoing family patterns. Family members sometimes gain an awareness of patterns and reactions for the first time in the process of genogram formation. Genograms are sometimes used not only in assessment but also as important instruments in treatment (Everett, 1992; McGoldrick, Gerson, & Shellenberger, 1999).

#### DEVELOPMENTAL TRANSGENERATIONAL GENOGRAM

A developmental transgenerational genogram model for assessment has been offered that is useful, especially in relating the symptomatology to the patterns and history of the family system and in locating the symptoms within the family system's natural growth and development. This puts the immediate stress of the presenting problem in a broader and more understandable context that diffuses the crisis for the family and "normalizes" the conflict, rendering the situation more manageable (Nichols & Everett, 1986).

#### CULTURAL GENOGRAM

A cultural genogram has been devised by Hardy and Laszloffy (1995) for use in helping family therapy students and trainees to become aware of their cultural baggage and the roles it plays in their therapeutic work. Recent extensions by Demaria, Weeks, and Hof (1999) are described further on.

## AFRICAN-AMERICAN GENOGRAM

Declaring that the standard genogram used by family therapists is not adequate for work with African American families, primarily because it carries an underlying assumption that family is composed entirely of biological relationships, Watts-Jones (1997) has proposed an African American genogram. This genogram conceptualizes family as a kinship based on both biological and functional ties. Watts-Jones suggests that the African American genogram may also be useful with other families in which functional kinship relationships occupy a major position.

## PROJECTIVE GENOGRAM

Another approach to the use of genograms is as a projective device. This use is viewed as providing such benefits as helping clients to become aware of the intergenerational transmission process (Bowen, 1978) and what some of us have termed nongenetic transmission of psychological and emotional elements from one's family of origin, as well as helping them to become aware of triangulation tendencies in their family. Specific suggestions for using projective genograms effectively and for helping clients make good use of what they discover have been provided by Florence Kaslow (1995).

## MULTIFOCUSED GENOGRAMS

The most extensive form of genogram is the multifocused genogram for the intergenerational assessment of individuals, couples, and

families, developed by Demaria, Weeks, and Hof (1999). Grounded in attachment theory, this combination of the basic genogram, the family map, and a time line has significantly expanded the cultural genogram (Hardy & Lazloffy, 1995) to include such factors as race, religion, gender, socioeconomic status, and others. Outlining specific or focused genograms for many of the common difficulties of family life, the authors list more than 50 possible topics that can be focused on in assessment and therapy.

## *Measurement Scales*

Two scales focused specifically on the family of origin and related concepts have been rather widely used and cited, the Family-of-Origin Scale (Hovestadt, Anderson, Piercy, Cochran, & Fine (1985) and the Personal Authority in the Family System (PAFS) scale (Bray, Williamson, & Malone, 1984a).

## FAMILY-OF-ORIGIN SCALE

This scale developed out of efforts to measure the perceived health of one's family of origin. Evaluators of the Family-of-Origin Scale have given it mixed reviews. Piercy and associates state that it is easy to administer, has acceptable reliability and validity data, and is a useful measure for conducting family-of-origin research (Piercy, Sprenkle, Wetchler, & Associates, 1996). On the other hand, Lee, Gordon, and O'Dell (1989) found that the FOS differentiated between patients and nonpatients, but it measured only one general factor and provided little usable information. L'Abate and Bagarozzi concluded that "At this time, the best that can be said for the FOS is that much more research needs to be done to establish it as a valid instrument" (L'Abate & Bagarozzi, 1993, p. 186).

## PERSONAL AUTHORITY IN THE FAMILY (PAFS) QUESTIONNAIRE

A self-report measure that assesses three-generational family relationships that have been identified in the intergenerational family theory of Bowen (1978), Boszormenyi-Nagy and Ulrich (1981), Paul and Paul (1975), and Williamson (1981, 1982b) has been developed by Bray, Williamson, and Malone (l984a, 1984b, 1986). The instrument, termed the Personal Authority in the Family System Questionnaire, measures several key concepts and contains eight scales: (1) spousal fusion–individuation, (2) intergenerational fusion–individuation, (3) spousal intimacy, (4) intergenerational intimacy, (5) nuclear family triangulation, (6) intergenerational triangulation, (7) intergenerational intimidation, and (8) personal authority. Bray describes the PAFS-Q as "a reliable and valid measure of intergenerational family relationships and processes" (Bray, 1991, p. 285). L'Abate and Bagarozzi (1993) have concluded that the PAFS "shows much promise and has the potential for becoming a valuable tool for family assessment and outcome evaluation" (p. 198).

## CLINICAL CHANGE MECHANISMS/ CURATIVE FACTORS

The most general change mechanism and curative factor in the perspective of family-of-origin therapists is the opportunity clients have to deal directly with members of their family of origin and with the effects and relationships that cause them intrapsychic and interpersonal conflict. Within this broad framework, there are a number of other more specific and limited factors that contribute to change and improvement in the life of clients. Some of the more salient are described further on.

### Detriangulation

This process is useful in changing triangles, which were formed when a relationship became too intense or too distant so that a third person or object was triangulated into the relationship in order to give the system stability. By identifying the triangulation process and how it is being used to stabilize the family's dysfunction and by gradually separating one or more persons from the triadic interaction, the therapist can effect more change than by dealing directly with the presenting issues (Bowen, 1978; Everett, 1992; Kerr & Bowen, 1988).

### Corrective Intellectual and Emotional Experiences

Family-of-origin sessions can provide clients with corrective intellectual and emotional experiences that include discovering previously unknown information about the family, clarifying old misunderstandings rooted in childhood misperceptions, demystifying magical meanings that family members have for one another, and getting to know one's parents as real people (Framo, 1981, 1982). What happens in these experiences, according to Framo, is "that the internal objects are usually stimulated, re-enacted, and recontoured by the transactions with the parents, the original representatives of those introjects, during the family-of-origin sessions" (Framo, 1992, p. 119). The outcome of such face-to-face work with one's parents and siblings is the possibility of establishing adult-to-adult relationships with one's aging parents, as well as more appropriate peer relationships with siblings and less pathological relationship patterns in general.

*Exploration and Balancing the Ledger*

Knowledge and awareness obtained through identification of the broad range of relational determinants, including individual and transactional systems, intergenerational patterns, and relational ethics can help clients to drop feelings of blame and to determine how they can deal with transgenerational entitlements and indebtedness and go about balancing the ledger or obligations to past, present, and future generations (Boszormenyi-Nagy & Krasner, 1986; Boszormenyi-Nagy & Spark, 1973; Everett, 1992).

*Apology*

The specific act of apologizing to members of the family, including perhaps the ritual of telling each other member what one likes and appreciates about them, can result in a letting go of old grievances and a reorganization of one's internal world, with an accompanying rise in self-esteem (Framo, 1992). The self-esteem of both the child to whom a parent apologizes and of the parent offering the apology can be elevated in the process (Boszormenyi-Nagy & Krasner, 1986).

*Operationalizing Mourning
and Cross-Confrontation*

Long-term mourning, often hidden in marital and family difficulties, can be neutralized by use of operational mourning, which involves the family in a delayed grief reaction through cross-confrontation. The creation of therapist empathy and understanding of the sources of contemporary relational problems from the shared affective experience are powerful factors in loosening the strictures imposed by the previously unresolved grief (Paul, 1967; Paul & Grosser, 1965; Paul & Paul, 1975).

## SPECIFIC THERAPEUTIC INTERVENTIONS

Once again, as was the case in earlier sections, the attempt to cover issues in this section will be illustrative and selective, rather than exhaustive and total. The essential purpose, of course, will be to help clients deal with family-of-origin factors in their lives. It should be noted that the specific focus taken will be related to the theoretical orientation of the therapist—whether systems, psychodynamic-object relations, contextual, or other—and his or her assessment of the needs of the client and situation.

*Exploration of Family Background
and Experience*

Dealing with family-of-origin issues logically starts with explorations with the client, in which the therapist gains some perspectives on the structure of the client's family, on what has happened with the client during his or her formative years, and, subsequently, on the structure of the family and on the client's attitudes about and perspectives on the family and its members. This can be done in conjunction with the construction of a genogram and an exploration of issues and implications that emerge from that experience. Other instruments, such as a background information form completed by the client before the first session, can provide information and leads for the therapist to follow in the interview. Experience has also shown that having one client's spouse present when a family history or exploration is undertaken with the other can be invaluable on occasion, when the listening/observing spouse can provide insights that the partner could not give regarding his or her own family of origin (Nichols, 1988, 1996).

## Viewing/Interpreting Family Photographs, Videos, Movies

Another source of serendipitous insights and information is the use of family-of-origin photographs, video recordings, or home movies provided by the client during office interviews. Careful, sensitive questioning and observations by the therapist not only can result in new awareness on the part of the client but also can open up sometimes dramatic new avenues for treatment planning, interpretations, and recommendations for client actions (Nichols, 1985).

## Client Writing Letters/Preparing Recordings for Family of Origin

When clients are not ready for face-to-face contact and frank interchanges with members of their family of origin and need a considerable amount of support in thinking through and preparing what they wish to say to family members, they can be encouraged to put their thoughts and wishes into a letter or an audio recording, which they subsequently examine in therapy. Sometimes the client needs to draft several letters, discussing the content and what he or she feels about the message and the family member to whom it is directed. Clients also may audiotape telephone messages or letters sent to the parent or other family members (Headley, 1977; Williamson, 1991).

At times, the act of writing the letter results in significant liberation for the client, a shedding of long-held and not always conscious feelings. Particularly when the letter consists of venting strong emotions or a tirade against a parent or sibling, throwing the message away and drafting another one later is indicated and should be encouraged by the therapist. The possibility of dramatic breakthroughs in awareness on the part of the cli-

ent is even stronger when he or she listens to an audiotape of a message to a family member. "I didn't know I sounded that harsh" or "Boy, do I sound angry" (or childish, as the case may be) are not uncommon reactions upon hearing one's own voice in a recording.

Writing down the issues clients wish to address, the points they desire to make, and what they wish to accomplish in contacts with their family of origin can have the double benefit of both altering some of their feelings, perceptions, and understandings before the contact and also clarifying what they wish to say and do, thus enhancing the possibilities of a productive encounter and interchange with family members.

## Clients Going Home to Deal with Their Family of Origin

Some therapists plan from the beginning of treatment to send the client back home to deal with the important unresolved issues with the family of origin that are troublesome. One role conceived for the therapist is that of a coach, much like an athletic coach who does not play the game but teaches the players how to play and what to do. Typically, following a period of preparation that may include exploration of issues, role play of stances and steps to be taken by the client in "going home," and a declaration that he or she is ready, the client is coached and supported in taking the step of meeting with a parent, parents, or a sibling, as the case may be. Although trying to maintain an objective but personal position with the family, the coach/therapist acts both as a role model for individual family members in the differentiation process and as a facilitator of family-of-origin exploration (Everett, 1992). With the therapist acting in a supervisory role, a careful debriefing is indicated after the visit home has been made.

## Bringing Family Members into the Client's Session

Several patterns can be used in terms of bringing family-of-origin members into the client's sessions with the therapist. A common one is to isolate with the client an issue or issues that need to be dealt with and then, with the client's acquiescence, to invite the pertinent family member or members to attend one or more sessions for the limited purpose that has been predetermined with the client. It seems exceedingly important to be explicit with the invited participants—the parents, for example—as to why they are being invited and what they can expect. Having indicated what the focus will be and that the visitors are there as consultants only, it is deemed important to restrict the session to that item, or if the invited persons start to deal with other areas, to point out that they are going beyond the original agreement and to proceed no further unless a new agreement is made. This attention to "keeping the faith" with them can be a powerful factor in building trust with both the family members and the client. Among the outcomes frequently is a significant shifting of attitudes and a lowering of anxiety or resentment after the client perceives and accepts the parent's explanation and possible apology for something that occurred in the distant past. Witnessing the parent's complete amazement at the impact of a past event or pattern on the client or recognizing for the first time in this live encounter with the parent as a fellow adult the humanity of the parent often brings for the client more change than would be likely in months or years of individual examination of client memories and feelings.

A crucial step in the change process is the formalization or cementing of the new feelings and openness to alteration of the relationship through new actions and behavior con-sistent with what has been opened up. When the family members are amenable to continuing work toward new patterns, the therapist has a critical and sensitive role to perform in "midwiving" the emergent relationship (Nichols, 1988; Nichols & Everett, 1986) in order to help consolidate the gains. In addition, it is important to give encouragement and support to the client, including coaching where appropriate, in facilitating contact and interaction with the family members in subsequent days.

## Conducting Family-of-Origin Sessions/Consultations

Several different patterns and purposes are found in family-of-origin sessions with the client and all or portions of the client's family. All patterns should involve adequate preparation and clear understandings regarding the purpose and ground rules of the sessions. One pattern consists of two multi-hour meetings with the client and all members of the client's family of origin, typically conducted on a weekend, with an overnight break between them. The parents and siblings are present as consultants, and the sessions are not regarded as therapy (Framo, 1992).

Another pattern, which is focused on aiding the client to achieve personal authority in the family system and to become able to deal with his or her parents as peers and to achieve a new level of intimacy with them as part of personal differentiation, includes sessions spread over 3 days. Siblings and grandparents are not included, only the client and the parents. The client's preparation to deal directly with the parents involves several tasks, including writing an autobiography, audiotaping letters to each parent, and audiotaping telephone calls to each parent (Williamson, 1991).

## Sending Clients to the Graveyard

Limitations in changing relationships and interactions with family-of-origin members certainly exist when those relatives are deceased. Changes in perceptions, attitudes, and behaviors in the living client are still possible. One can go to the graveyard and "deliver a message" to deceased parents or siblings, for example, and gain freedom from formerly crippling memories and feelings, although there are no living relatives with whom to change present relationships (Williamson, 1978). The reworking activities are carried out by the client, instead of between the client and family members in vivo. Careful preparation and appropriate coaching regarding the letter, videotape, or other form of message to be delivered are essential in maximizing benefits of this approach.

## EFFECTIVENESS OF THE APPROACH

Does the family-of-origin approach work under "normal therapy" field conditions? Is it effective? Much of the support for the effectiveness of family-of-origin therapy appears to rest on anecdotal descriptions of process and outcome and the expressed beliefs of practitioners, primarily because there is little available research on effectiveness. Probably the best source of information on the effectiveness of marital and family therapy, a special issue of the *Journal of Marital and Family Therapy,* guest edited by William M. Pinsof and Lyman Wynne, emphasized primarily efficacy research rather than studies of effectiveness. Also, the reviews cited in the special issue of the journal "set aside the critical issue of the processes that lead to specific outcomes" (Pinsof & Wynne, 1995, p. 341). Despite the lack of attention to effectiveness and process research, authors in the issue were optimistic about the general effectiveness of family therapy in dealing with specific conditions. In additional, Piercy and colleagues assert, "Virtually no experimental research has been conducted on the effectiveness of transgenerational family therapies" (Piercy, Sprenkle, Wetchler, & Associates, 1996).

The outlook for future research possibilities depends on which part of transgenerational, intergenerational, multigenerational therapy theory and practice is considered. Gurman (1988) has encouraged research on psychodynamically based therapy in general, with the proviso that unique features of methods need to be disentangled from those widely shared with other approaches, and has indicated that some patterns of therapist intervention in Bowen's approach certainly are testable. He was much less optimistic about the possibilities of conducting empirical research on symbolic-experiential therapy and contextual therapy. Piercy and colleagues (Piercy et al., 1996) consider transgenerational therapies researchable at both the micro- and macrolevels and suggest a number of questions that could be addressed.

## FUTURE DEVELOPMENTS/ DIRECTIONS

At least two sets of factors are likely to have a major impact on the future use of family-of-origin therapy: future developments in family systems and future developments in family therapy practice. Given the continued high incidence of martial breakup and family reorganization, leading to confusion regarding questions of "What is my family?" and "Who am I?" among a major segment of the population, family therapists likely will need to adopt a more flexible definition of family than simply the biological kinship unit that has traditionally been considered the family of origin.

Client definitions and preferences in emotional attachment will be more important than ever. The extent to which the focus will be on family of origin, however defined, certainly will be affected by the theoretical orientation of therapists and the extent to which they focus with clients on the here-and-now and the extent to which they recognize and work with the client's current and past family attachments.

# REFERENCES

Ackerman, N. W. (1954). Interpersonal disturbances in the family: Some unresolved problems in psychotherapy. *Psychiatry: Journal for the Study of Interpersonal Processes, 17,* 359–368.

Ackerman, N. W. (1956). Interlocking pathology in family relationships. In S. Rado & G. Daniels (Eds.), *Changing concepts of psychoanalytic medicine* (pp. 135–150). New York: Grune & Stratton.

Ackerman, N. W. (1958). *The psychodynamics of family life.* New York: Basic Books.

Ackerman, N. W. (1961). Symptom, defense and growth in group process. *International Journal of Group Psychotherapy, 21*(2), 131, 140–142.

Aponte, H. J. (1976). Underorganization in the poor family. In P. J. Guerin (Ed.), *Family therapy: Theory and practice* (pp. 432–448). New York: Gardner Press.

Banmen, J. (Guest Ed.). (2002). Satir today (Entire Issue). *Contemporary Family Therapy, 24*(1), 3–239.

Boszormenyi-Nagy, I. (1965). A theory of relationships: Experience and transaction. In I. Boszormenyi-Nagy & J. L. Framo (Eds.), *Intensive family therapy: Theoretical and practical aspects* (pp. 33–86). New York: Harper & Row.

Boszormenyi-Nagy, I., Grunebaum, J., & Ulrich, D. (1991). Contextual family therapy. In A. S. Gurman & D. P. Kniskern (Eds.), *Handbook of family therap, Vol. 2,* (pp. 200–238). New York: Brunner/Mazel.

Boszormenyi-Nagy, I., & Krasner, B. R. (1986). *Between give and take: A clinical guide to contextual therapy.* New York: Brunner/Mazel.

Boszormenyi-Nagy, I., & Spark, G. (1973). *Invisible loyalties: Reciprocity in intergenerational family therapy.* New York: Harper & Row.

Boszormenyi-Nagy, I., & Ulrich, D. (1981). Contextual family therapy. In A. S. Gurman & D. P. Kniskern (Eds.), *Handbook of family therapy* (pp. 159–186). New York: Brunner/Mazel.

Bowen, M. (1978). *Family therapy in clinical practice.* New York: Jason Aronson.

Bray, J. H. (1991). The personal authority in the family system questionnaire: Assessment of intergenerational family relationships. In D. S. Williamson, *The intimacy paradox: Personal authority in the family system* (pp. 273–286). New York: Guilford Press.

Bray, J. H., Williamson, D. S., & Malone, P. E. (1984a). Personal authority in the family system: Development of a questionnaire to measure personal authority in intergenerational family processes. *Journal of Marital and Family Therapy, 10,* 167–178.

Bray, J. H., Williamson, D. S., & Malone, P. E. (1984b). *Manual for the personal authority in the family system questionnaire.* Houston: Houston Family Institute.

Bray, J. H., Williamson, D. S., & Malone, P. E. (1986). An evaluation of the effects of intergenerational consultation process to increase personal authority in the family system. *Family Process, 25,* 423–436.

Broderick, C. C., & Schrader, S. S. (1981). The history of professional marriage and family therapy. In A. S. Gurman & D. P. Kniskern (Eds.), *Handbook of family therapy* (pp. 5–35). New York: Brunner/Mazel.

Broderick, C. C., & Schrader, S. S. (1991). The history of professional marriage and family therapy. In A. S. Gurman & D. P. Kniskern (Eds.), *Handbook of family therapy* (Vol. 2, pp. 3–40). New York: Brunner/Mazel.

Carr, A. (2000). *Family therapy: Concepts, process and practice.* New York and Chichester: Wiley.

DeMaria, R., Weeks, G. R., & Hof, L. (1999). *Focused genograms: Intergenerational assessment of individuals, couples, and families.* (1999). New York: Brunner/Routledge.

Everett, C. A. (Ed.). (1992). *Family therapy glossary.* Washington, DC: American Association for Marriage and Family Therapy.

Everett, C. A., Halperin, S., Volgy, S., & Wissler, A. (1989). *Treating the borderline family: A systemic approach.* New York: The Psychological Corporation: Harcourt Brace Jovanovich.

Everett, C. A., & Volgy-Everett, S. (1998). *Short-term therapy with borderline patients and their families.* Iowa City, IA: Geist & Russell.

Fairbairn, W. R. D. (1952). *Psycho-analytic studies*

*of the personality.* New York: Basic Books.

Feldman, L. B. (1982). Dysfunctional marital conflict: An integrative interpersonal-intrapsychic model. *Journal of Marital and Family Therapy, 8,* 417–428.

Fine, M., & Hovestadt, A. J. (1987). What is family of origin therapy? In A. J. Hovestadt & M. Fine (Eds.), *Family of origin therapy* (pp. 11–19). Rockville, MD; Aspen.

Foley, V. D., & Everett, C. A. (Eds.). (1982). *Family therapy glossary.* Washington, DC: American Association for Marriage and Family Therapy.

Framo, J. L. (1981). The integration of marital therapy with sessions with family of origin. In A. S. Gurman & D. P. Kniskern (Eds.), *Handbook of family therapy* (pp. 13–158). New York: Brunner/ Mazel.

Framo, J. L. (1982). *Explorations in marital and family therapy:. Selected papers of James L. Framo, PhD.* New York: Springer.

Framo, J. L. (1992). *Family-of-origin therapy: An intergenerational approach.* New York: Brunner/ Mazel.

Gurman, A. S. (1988). Issues in the specification of family therapy interventions. In L. C. Wynne (Ed.), *The state of the art in family therapy research* (pp. 125–137). New York: Family Process.

Hardy, K. V., & Laszloffy, T. A. (1995). The cultural genogram: Key to training culturally competent family therapists. *Journal of Marital and Family Therapy, 21,* 227–237.

Headley, L. (1977). *Adults and their parents in family therapy.* New York: Plenum.

Hovestadt, A. J., Anderson, W. T., Piercy, F. P., Cochran, S. W., & Fine, M. (1985). A family of origin scale. *Journal of Marital and Family Therapy, 11,* 287–297.

Kaslow, F. W. (1995). *Projective genogramming.* Sarasota, FL: Professional Resource Press.

Kerr, M. E. (1981). Family systems theory and therapy. In A. S. Gurman & D. P. Kniskern (Eds.), *Handbook of family therapy* (pp. 226–264). New York: Brunner/Mazel.

Kerr, M. E., & Bowen, M. (1988). *Family evaluation.* New York: Norton.

L'Abate, L., & Bagarozzi, D. A. (1993). *Sourcebook of marriage and family evaluation.* New York: Brunner/Mazel.

Lee, R. E., Gordon, N. G., & O'Dell, J. W. (1989). The validity and use of the family-of-origin scale. *Journal of Marital and Family Therapy, 15,* 19–27.

McGoldrick, M. (1982) Ethnicity and family therapy: An overview. In M. McGoldrick, K. Pearce, & J. Giordano (Eds), *Ethnicity and family therapy* (pp. 3–30). New York: Guilford Press.

McGoldrick, M. (1996). Ethnicity and family therapy: An overview. In M. McGoldrick, J. K. Pearce, & J. Giordano (Eds), *Ethnicity and family therapy* (2nd ed., pp. 1–27). New York: Guilford Press.

McGoldrick, M., Gerson, R., & Shellenberger, S. (1999). *Genograms: Assessment and intervention.* New York: Norton.

Middelberg, C.V. (2001). Projective identification in common couple dances. *Journal of Marital and Family Therapy, 27,* 341–352.

Nerin, W. F. (1985). *Family reconstruction: Long day's journey into light.* New York: Norton.

Nichols, W. C. (1980). Stepfamilies: A growing family therapy challenge. In L. R. Wolberg & M. L. Aronson (Eds.), *Group and family therapy 1980* (pp. 335–344). New York: Brunner/Mazel.

Nichols, W. C. (1985). A differentiating couple: Some transgenerational issues in marital therapy. In A. S. Gurman (Ed.), *Casebook of marital therapy* (pp. 199–228). New York: Guilford Press.

Nichols, W. C. (1988). *Marital therapy: An integrative approach.* New York: Guilford Press.

Nichols, W. C. (1996). *Treating people in families: An integrative framework.* New York: Guilford Press.

Nichols, W. C., & Everett, C. A. (1986). *Systemic family therapy: An integrative approach.* New York: Guilford Press.

Paul, N. L. (1967). The role of mourning and empathy in conjoint marital therapy. In G. H. Zuk & I. Boszormenyi-Nagy (Eds.), *Family therapy and disturbed families* (pp. 186–205). Palo Alto, CA: Science and Behavior Books.

Paul, N. L., & Grosser, G. (1965). Operational mourning and its role in conjoint family therapy. *Community Mental Health Journal, 1,* 339–345.

Paul, N. L., & Paul, B. B. (1975). *Marital puzzle.* New York: Norton.

Piercy, F. P., Sprenkle, D. H., Wetchler, J. L., & Associates. (1996). *Family therapy sourcebook* (2nd ed.). New York: Guilford Press.

Pincus, L., & Dare, C. (1978). *Secrets in the family.* New York: Pantheon.

Pinsof, W. M., & Wynne, L. C. (1995). The effectiveness and efficacy of marital and family therapy: Introduction to the special issue. W. M. Pinsof & L. C. Wynne (Guest Eds.), Special issue: The effectiveness of marital and family therapy (Entire Issue). *Journal of Marital and Family Therapy, 21*(4).

Rueveni, U. (1979). *Networking families in crisis.* New York: Human Sciences Press.

Sauber, S. R., L'Abate, L., Weeks, G. R., & Buchanan, W. L. (1993). *The dictionary of family psychology and family therapy* (2nd ed.). Newbury Park, CA: Sage.

Scharff, J. S., & Scharff, D. (1987). *Object relations family therapy.* Northvale, NJ: Jason Aronson.

Schwartz, L. L. (1993). What is a family? A contemporary view. *Contemporary Family Therapy, 15,* 429–442.

Skynner, A. C. R. (1976). *Systems of family and marital therapy.* New York: Brunner/Mazel.

Skynner, A. C. R. (1981). *An open-systems, group-analytic approach to family therapy.* New York: Brunner/Mazel.

Speck, R., & Attneave, C. (1973). *Family networks.* New York: Pantheon.

Taylor, G. (2002). Family reconstruction. *Contemporary Family Therapy, 24,* 129–138.

Toman, W. (1976). *Family constellation* (3rd ed.). New York: Springer.

Vogel, E., & Bell, N. W. (Eds.). (1960). *The family.* Glencoe, IL: Free Press.

Watts-Jones, D. (1997). Toward an African American genogram. *Family Process, 36,* 375–383.

Williamson, D. S. (1978). New life at the graveyard: A method of individuation from a dead parent. *Journal of Marriage and Family Counseling, 4,* 93–101.

Williamson, D. S. (1981). Personal authority via termination of the intergenerational hierarchical boundary: A "new" stage in the family life cycle. *Journal of Marital and Family Therapy, 7,* 441–452.

Williamson, D. S. (1982a). Personal authority in family experience via termination of the intergenerational hierarchical boundary: Part II. The consultation process and the therapeutic method. *Journal of Marital and Family Therapy, 8,* 23–37.

Williamson, D. S. (1982b). Personal authority in family experience via termination of the intergenerational hierarchical boundary: Part III. Personal authority defined and the power of play in the change process. *Journal of Marital and Family Therapy, 8,* 309–323.

Williamson, D. S. (1991). *The intimacy paradox: Personal authority in the family system.* New York: Guilford Press.

Zinner, J., & Shapiro, R. (1972). Projective identification as a mode of perception and behavior in families of adolescents. *International Journal of Psychoanalysis, 53,* 523–530.

CHAPTER 6

# Interactional and Solution-Focused Brief Therapies

## Evolving Concepts of Change

BARRY L. DUNCAN, PsyD
SCOTT D. MILLER, PhD
JACQUELINE A. SPARKS, PhD, LMFT

*Institute for the Study of Therapeutic Change*

## INTRODUCTION

In this chapter, the term *brief therapy* refers to two distinct, yet interrelated, approaches of intervention in family therapy—the interactional approach outlined by the Mental Research Institute (MRI) and solution-focused brief therapy (SFBT) of the Brief Family Therapy Center (BFTC). Included in this discussion is a third perspective—an overarching conceptual framework based on common factors, arguably logical heir to the rich MRI and SFBT heritage. Rather than present an exhaustive treatise on these approaches, our aim is to link concepts of relationship and change espoused by each with current outcome research. In addition, we argue that an increas-ing reliance on the medical model as a foundation for research and practice undermines brief therapy traditions and their relevance to family therapy's future.

## HISTORICAL OVERVIEW

*"It's a poor sort of memory that only works backwards," the Queen remarked.*

—Lewis Carroll

The history of brief therapy is, in many ways, the history of family therapy. Family therapy diverged into a distinct professional paradigm within a climate of theoretical and practical skepticism and intense interest in the mechanics of therapeutic change. There was a growing disillusionment with psychodynamic therapy, and out of this dissatisfaction emerged a desire to find new ways of doing therapy briefly. This search eventually evolved into the cadre of brief, systemic, contextual approaches that comprise much of the field of family therapy.

Despite diverse influences, common themes connect family therapy, including the brief approaches: (1) a shift from the individual to relationship, interaction, and context; (2) a shift toward active, responsive intervention in the present; (3) a shift toward client-specific versus theory-specific intervention; and (4) a gradual movement toward therapy as an evolving, co-constructed conversation.

Although these themes defined an entire field, it is worth taking note of persons and ideas that inspired the more specific models that are the subject of this chapter. The Bateson project's double-bind theory of schizophrenia (Bateson, Jackson, Haley, & Weakland, 1956) suggested that the communication of people considered schizophrenic "made sense" in the context of multiply conflicting and paradoxical injunctions prevalent in the person's significant social system, the family. The Bateson project contributed the cornerstone of a burgeoning brief therapy movement—that problems can be understood in the context of communicative interaction in significant relationships.

Jay Haley and John Weakland's prolific study of Milton Erickson's work spawned strategic brief therapy (Haley, 1973), and significantly influenced both MRI (Watzlawick, Weakland, & Fisch, 1974) and SFBT (de Shazer, 1982). Chief among these influences were Erickson's insistence that therapists should tailor their approach to fit the client's unique worldview, expectations, and preferred method of working. Second, rather than approaching psychological distress as deficit,

Erickson highlighted the client's abundant storehouse of resources, challenging therapists to pursue and magnify resources, rather than disabilities. Third, Erickson demonstrated that change can happen quickly and often in dramatic, unexpected ways.

Brief therapies represent the best of both worlds. They encompass the formative ideas of family therapy's past, generated and taught by the field's most prominent scholars. At the same time, they serve as a bridge to therapies of a different era, including those interested in the possibility of change through language and relationship. Despite brief therapy's commitment to a pragmatic, here-and-now approach, the early reliance on context, language, and relationship paved the way for an eventual questioning of objectivity and mental health discourse and a trend toward privileging the client's experiences and resources in the resolution of problems.

## THE MENTAL RESEARCH INSTITUTE

*That so few dare to be eccentric marks the chief danger of the time.*

—John Stuart Mill

### Major Theoretical Constructs

The interactional approach of the MRI is a simple, elegant theoretical perspective of both human problems and change. It is foremost a systems view, but without the encumbrances of the constructs of invariant family structures, functionality of symptoms, or homeostasis. Instead, the MRI approach is based on an understanding of any selected bit of human behavior in terms of its place in a wider, ongoing, organized system of communicative interaction (Fisch, Weakland, & Segal, 1982,

p. 9). In addition, the MRI brought forth the original constructivist perspective in family therapy. This perspective posits that reality is invented, not discovered, and does not exist as a phenomenon separate from the constructs of the observer-describer (Watzlawick, 1984). This theoretical foundation permits a focus on both behavior and meaning.

The following principles of the MRI approach, delineated by Weakland, Fisch, Watzlawick, and Bodin (1974, pp. 147–150), are now taken-for-granted ideas within the family therapy field. However, at the time, they were considered revolutionary. They include: (1) the approach is symptom oriented; (2) problems that bring people to therapy are difficulties *between* people in human interaction; (3) problems are primarily an outcome of everyday difficulties, usually involving adaptation to some life change that has been mishandled; (4) problems develop usually by overemphasis or underemphasis on difficulties in living; (5) once a difficulty begins to be seen as a problem, the continuation and exacerbation of it results from the creation of a positive feedback loop, most often centering on those very behaviors of individuals in the family intended to resolve the difficulty; (6) long-standing problems, or symptoms, are not viewed in terms of "chronicity" but as the persistence of a repetitive poorly handled difficulty; (7) resolutions of problems require a substitution of behavior patterns so as to interrupt the vicious, positive feedback circles; (8) means to such an interruption often may appear illogical or paradoxical; (9) accepting what the client offers and reversing usual treatment in a pragmatic fashion is the main focus of therapy; and (10) conceptions and interventions are based on direct observation of what is going on in systems of human interaction, how these continue to maintain the problem, and how they may be altered most effectively and efficiently.

## Proposed Etiology of Clinical Problems

The MRI holds that problems develop from chance or transitional circumstances encountered by individuals and families evolving through the life cycle. Only two conditions are necessary for these everyday difficulties to become a problem: (1) the mishandling of the difficulty and (2) upon failure of the original solution attempt, more of the same is applied, resulting in a vicious cycle (Watzlawick et al., 1974). The inter/intrapersonal interaction that surrounds the difficulty, the process by which individual and shared meaning related to the difficulty is constructed, and the interplay of both are seen as significant to the problem process. Based on the individual and shared meanings about the problem or how to solve it, people will try variations on a theme of the same solution pattern, over and over again. The problem will grow in size and importance, taking on a life of its own, and often will bear little resemblance to the original difficulty; the solution, in essence, becomes the problem (Watzlawick et al., 1974).

## Methods of Assessment

Assessment begins with a concrete, action-oriented description, specifically addressing the question, "Who is doing what that presents a problem, to whom, and how does such behavior constitute a problem?" (Fisch et al., 1982, p. 70). The therapist attempts to elicit information that is clear, explicit, and in behavioral terms; the therapist is interested in what each individual is specifically saying and doing in performing the problem, rather than in general statements or abstract explanations.

The next step in assessment asks what all persons closely involved with the problem have been doing to try to resolve it. Again, this inquiry focuses on actual behaviors. A full appreciation of solution attempts is crucial because, over time, the solutions themselves become the problem. Therefore, ineffectual solution attempts must be interrupted for problem resolution to occur. This line of inquiry can steer the therapist away from interventions that have already failed, as well as provide direction toward what may be helpful.

Following an assessment of attempted solutions, therapists inquire about the client's minimal goals of treatment. It is noteworthy that few approaches of the day attended to the client's idiosyncratic desires like the MRI. With respectful perseverance, the therapist elicits the client's description of a small step toward improvement that serves as an outcome criterion. Even if questions regarding specific goals bear no fruit, the pursuit itself serves an important function. At the least, the client will most likely perceive the therapist as interested in change and therapy as being about change (Fisch et al., 1982).

The final and perhaps most important part of an MRI assessment is the understanding of the client's "position." Position is defined as those strongly held beliefs, values, and attitudes that influence the client's behavior in relation to the presenting problem and affect participation in therapy (Fisch et al., 1982). Knowing a client's position about the problem, as well as about therapy, allows the therapist to frame a suggestion or alternative meaning the client is most likely to accept. Determining position does not require great attentiveness, because most useful client positions are those that are strongly held and readily determined in therapy conversation. To utilize position, a therapist must accept the client's statement, recognize the values it represents, and avoid making inflammatory or noncredible comments (Fisch et al., 1982). Just as the presenting problem offers in a concise package what the client wants to address, client position indicates a belief system that therapists can honor to enhance the change

process. This concept has profound alliance implications (see further on) and was critical to the development of the idea of the client's theory of change and client-directed work (Duncan, Solovey, & Rusk, 1992).

### Clinical Change Mechanisms/Curative Factors

The MRI suggests that any interruption of the solution pattern, be it stopping the client's current solution attempts or initiating a solution that is appreciably different from the solutions being employed, will result in a change or a shift in the problem cycle. Once started, the change will enjoy a ripple effect, allowing other areas of the client's life to benefit and new perspectives to arise. Consider the following example:

Ella, a 37-year-old woman, sought therapy because her husband, John, started coming home late from work. Ella responded by restricting her trips out of the home, questioning John about his whereabouts, and eventually accusing him of an affair. John angrily denied an affair and countered that Ella was trying to control him. A cycle of interaction evolved, in which Ella waited anxiously for her husband and, with increasing frequency, brought up the affair accusation upon his arrival. In response, John became increasingly angry and more vehement about his right to go where he pleased, to the point that he threatened divorce (MRI calls this an accuser-defender cycle). The therapist suggested that Ella become *less* available to her husband. Unavailability included making trips out of the house, particularly when her husband was home or about to arrive, and waiting for her husband to initiate discussion about where he had been. Becoming less available and avoiding initiation of conversation ran counter to Ella's previous solution attempts. In addition, Ella decided to invest herself in a civic group and exercise club. As the MRI approach would predict, John began coming home again and the conflict stopped. Ella concluded that she had become too reliant on him and continued her out-of-home activities.

In this example, the therapist made suggestions that took into account not only Ella's presenting complaint, but also her position that, above all, she wanted to save the marriage. Ella was relieved when the therapist accepted without question her desire to save the marriage, instead of, as some of her friends had done, accusing her of "codependency" if she did not make more of the affair or leave her husband.

*Specific Therapeutic Interventions*

### GENERAL INTERVENTIONS

General interventions, hallmarks of the MRI approach, consist of restraining strategies and the therapist stance of "taking a one-down." Restraining strategies are used to avert the following dilemma: Clients seek therapy voluntarily and with every intention to change their problem, but they are also quite ambivalent about changing and may be fearful of losing security or stability. The MRI approach postulates that no matter how much pain clients currently experience, the draw toward the familiar and hesitance to confront the unknown are present, at least to some degree, in every change process. Restraining interventions directly address this ambivalence and align with that part of the client that may be afraid or reluctant.

Restraining interventions consist of offering valid and credible rationales to clients to exercise caution in resolving the presenting complaint, ranging from the suggestion to "go slow" to the consideration of the "dangers of improvement." The "go slow" injunction can be helpful for clients who seem to be trying too hard to resolve a problem or for clients who press the therapist with urgent demands for problem improvement. "Go slow" may be helpful because it portrays the therapist as uncommitted to changing the client, certainly quickly, and removes a sense of urgency for the client that perhaps has helped maintain the problem. "Go slow" messages may also be used when rapid change is noted in therapy. This, paradoxically, can spur and consolidate even faster gains, while helping clients temper enthusiasm in order to realistically assess and withstand potential setbacks. When therapists are conservative about change, clients are allowed the freedom to explore and to express the risks associated with it. This creates a space for clients to reflect about their concerns. In this way, they can more confidently choose to make the changes they desire and at the pace most comfortable for them.

Considering the dangers of improvement with clients is especially helpful when previous therapy has failed, the problem is long-standing, or the current therapy is stuck. If clients can see that improvement is fraught with difficulties, they may feel less compelled to harass themselves to change and may thus relax their current ineffective solution attempts. If clients agree with the dangers, then the therapist can amplify these and ask whether there should be any more attempts at change, given the risks involved. If clients disagree and maintains that even considering the risks, they want to improve the problem, then it is likely they will be even more invested in therapist suggestions or in trying new avenues to resolve it (Fisch et al., 1982).

Both general and specific interventions are presented in a style that the MRI calls "taking a one-down." The MRI asserts that although some people may respond well to authority or expertise, many feel intimidated, demeaned, or embarrassed by a therapist position of "one up" and therefore will not share pertinent information or cooperate fully. "Taking a one-down," or assuming a nonexpert role, prevents the implication that the client has failed in seeing the appropriate solution already or that cooperation will be regarded as following orders (Fisch et al., 1982). "Taking a one-down" may be considered a precursor to later postmodern ideas such as a "not-knowing" therapist stance and a more collaborative style. Not always a deliberate or strategic move, the one-down position simply recognized that in many instances, a mutual, collaborative stance is more useful than an authoritarian one.

## SPECIFIC INTERVENTIONS

The MRI gained much attention with the interventions of reframing and symptom/task prescriptions. Both seek to disrupt behavioral sequences, as well as to alter cognitive frames or beliefs. To reframe means "to change the conceptual and/or emotional setting or viewpoint in relation to which a situation is experienced and to place it in another frame that fits the facts of the same concrete situation equally well or even better, and thereby changes its entire meaning" (Watzlawick et al., 1974, p. 95). There are many ways to reframe client circumstances, ranging from simple relabeling (e.g., depression as realistic pessimism), to positive connotation (e.g., troubling behavior as creative ways of meeting the individual's needs or altruistically motivated to help the family), to redefining (e.g., adolescent rebellion as necessary steps toward individuation).

Based on a constructivist perspective, reframing introduces a difference in the client's current "frame" regarding the problem. In this way, reframing reconstructs the problem such that remedial action is possible or it is no longer distressful. For example, a

therapist uses reframing to help a 42-year-old woman put the story of the sexual abuse she experienced at age 16 in a different light. By asking the woman to imagine her own 16-year-old daughter being seduced by a man the age her stepfather had been at the time of the abuse, the woman is able to feel the outrage that had been blocked by her sense of responsibility and shame for what had happened. Consequently, the abuse is no longer a problem for her, and she goes on with her life. Reframing is a precursor of many postmodern therapeutic activities that are interested in meaning and language, where new narratives are co-created to replace old problem-saturated stories

Symptom and task prescriptions, like reframes, have many client-specific variations. To make their counterintuitiveness acceptable and to overcome the desire to avoid the problem at all costs, symptom or task prescriptions are usually given with a variety of credible rationales. The usual rationales offered encourage clients to exercise some control over their problem or to learn more about the sequence of events that occurs before, during, and after symptoms. By virtue of prescribing the symptom, the context in which it occurs is changed—the client is now voluntarily engaged in a problem that, before, was believed to be outside his or her control. Contrary to popular belief, symptoms are not prescribed with the intent that the client will "resist" the suggestion, essentially being "tricked" out of the problem by the cleverness of the therapist. Tasks and prescriptions may be offered for a multitude of reasons, but the goal is to provide a competing experience to the presenting problem, interrupting current solution attempts and enabling clients to ascribe different meanings to it.

The following illustrates MRI symptom and task prescriptions:

Seventeen-year-old Sean's fear of flying prevents him from attending a college interview in another state. Instead of trying to convince him of the safety of air travel (the therapist has learned that this was part of everyone's failed, if sincere, attempt to help), the therapist honors his position. She comments that hurling through space at 600 miles an hour at 30,000 feet in a 30–ton metal cylinder is indeed a pretty frightening endeavor. She adds that although it may be statistically safer, there are no fender benders at 30,000 feet. The therapist then assigns several tasks. First, Sean is to schedule time during the week to consider the dangers of flying and, next, he is to visit the airport to observe various levels of anxiety in waiting passengers. Several weeks later, Sean, by continuing throughout the experience to note the anxiety of others, successfully boarded a plane and was able to complete his scheduled interview.

These specific interventions were designed to interrupt the current solutions and to create a context that enabled Sean to shift his view about flying. His, and his family's, solution attempts of avoidance were stopped, and he accepted his fear as both rational and an expected part of flying.

## SOLUTION-FOCUSED BRIEF THERAPY

*It will help us every day, it will brighten all the way if we'll keep on the sunny side of life.*

—A. P. Carter

### Major Theoretical Constructs

The hallmark of SFBT is theoretical and technical parsimony. Throughout his writings, co-developer de Shazer (1985) has cited 14th-century William of Ockham as a guide in the development of the model, to wit, "What can be done with fewer means is done in vain with many" (p. 58). Consistent with this emphasis, the entire approach can be summed up in three simple rules, known collectively as the "central philosophy" of SFBT (de Shazer, 1990):

1. If it ain't broke, DON'T FIX IT!

According to de Shazer (1990), this first rule means, "If the client is not actively complaining about it, then it is none of our [therapists'] business" (p. 93). In contrast to traditional models of practice, solution-focused therapists do not look "below the surface" or "read between the lines" for underlying illnesses or unrecognized problem states. Rather, therapy is entirely focused on the client's complaints, which are accepted at face value and considered resolved when the client says so (de Shazer, 1991, 1994).

2. Once you know what works, DO MORE OF IT!

In practical terms, this rule means that therapeutic work should be focused on identifying times when the problem is not happening. Once found, all efforts should then be aimed at helping the client repeat and maintain these exceptional periods. On a theoretical level, however, this rule sets SFBT apart from most traditional approaches, in that emphasis is placed on looking for "what works" and encouraging it to continue, rather than looking for what is "broken" and needs "fixing." De Shazer (1990) further notes that this rule also highlights *the* crucial distinction between SFBT and MRI models, "They [MRI] mistakenly think that the third rule (do something different) is the second and our second rule is the third " (p. 94).

3. If it doesn't work, then don't do it again, DO SOMETHING DIFFERENT!

As the MRI discovered, the solutions people use to solve problems are often part of the problem. Treatment is successful when therapists are able to help the client stop doing what is not working and do something different. "All that is necessary," de Shazer and colleagues (1986) maintained in the first paper setting out the core principles of SFBT, "is that the person involved in a troublesome situation does something different, even if that behavior is seemingly irrational, certainly irrelevant, obviously bizarre, or even humorous" (p. 210).

### Proposed Etiology of Clinical Problems/ Methods of Assessment

The SFBT model contains no theory of problem causation. Rather, "complaints," as practitioners of the approach refer to problems, are viewed as the "tickets clients use to begin therapy" (Turnell & Hopwood, 1994). If etiology plays any role in the SFBT model, it is in the area of solution development, where, as de Shazer (1988) notes, there has been a surprising dearth of interest: "Historically[,] psychotherapy has concerned itself with problems (variously defined and solutions (seldom defined at all) . . . In fact, solutions have been looked at so rarely that . . . psychotherapy has developed a blind spot" (p. 6).

In contrast to traditional therapeutic practice, the solution-focused therapist assumes no necessary link between the problems that people bring into treatment and any resulting solutions. As a result, therapists are free to dispense with conventional activities, such as intake and diagnosis. Indeed, little time is spent assessing or discussing the problem in SFBT. As de Shazer et al. (1986) note, "Effective therapy can be done even when the therapist cannot describe what the client is complaining about" (p. 210). Rather, solution-focused practitioners are free to move swiftly and directly to the process of solution-development, where the focus is on changes and solutions, rather than on difficulties and problems.

### Clinical Change Mechanisms/Curative Factors

Assumptions regarding the underlying mechanisms or curative factors have changed as the SFBT model has evolved. Early on, emphasis was placed on designing end-of-session interventions aimed at helping clients change their behavior. This carryover from the MRI approach and Milton Erickson was based on the belief that "any really different behavior in a problematic situation can be enough to prompt solution and to give the client the satisfaction he or she seeks from therapy" (de Shazer et al., 1986, p. 210). Over time, the focus of the model has shifted away from the end of the session and toward in-session process. Rather than seeing the interview as a time for gathering the information needed for developing a homework task, solution-focused therapists increasingly talk about the session as a time for "socially constructing new stories for clients' lives" (p. 365). In what amounts to a shift from behavioral to more cognitive processes, the interview is now viewed as *the* intervention.

### Specific Therapeutic Interventions

Recent writings have served to codify the solution-focused approach around a handful of specific techniques or "characteristic features" (de Shazer & Berg, 1997), which include (1) the miracle question, (2) scaling questions, (3) an intra-session break, and (4) a postsession message that includes (a) compliments, and (b) a homework task or suggestion. To this list, Gingerich and Eisengart (2000) add two additional "core components:" (1) a search for pretreatment change, and (2) a search for exceptions.

Each list of SFBT techniques was developed in conjunction with research on the model. In the first case, the treatment techniques specific to SFBT were spelled out to enable researchers to "demonstrate that the model of therapy being tested is indeed the model used by the therapists" (de Shazer & Berg, 1997, p. 123) and, in the latter, to identify existing studies of SFBT for inclusion in a review of outcome research on the approach (Gingerich & Eisengart, 2000). Those familiar with the approach will recognize that all of therapeutic strategies identified in these two references are employed in the first session of SFBT. Consistent with the emphasis on brevity and belief that "every session may be the last," less has been written about techniques for second and subsequent sessions. De Shazer (1991) simply indicates that "Beginning with the second session and continuing until the final session, the primary conversation activity focuses around the question 'What is better?'" (p. 130). Kral and Kowalski (1989) published the first article on the topic, focusing on two tactics: (1) cheerleading, and (2) positive blame.

## RAPPORT

Most solution-focused writers acknowledge the time spent at the outset of treatment establishing rapport, as well as listening to the complaint(s) that bring client(s) into treatment. True to the belief that the problem and the solution may not necessarily be related, however, a basic tenet of SFBT is that "effective therapy can be done even when the therapist cannot describe what the client is complaining about" (p. 210). Therefore, the typical solution-focused therapist is not inclined to "deepen the description of the problem nor make any particular empathic responses" (Turnell & Hopwood, 1994, p. 40). Rather, as described by de Shazer (1991), any number of SFBT techniques may be introduced "in an attempt to establish the solution-focused language game, with a progressive narrative" (p. 133).

## EXCEPTION QUESTIONS

Though not included in the current list of SFBT techniques compiled by de Shazer and Berg (1997), exception questions were one of the earliest strategies developed by the team in Milwaukee. De Shazer et al. (1986) reported that interviewing clients about times when their problem *did not* happen had proven useful in "creat[ing] the expectation that a future is possible which does not include the complaint" (p. 215). In addition, asking about times when the problem does not occur and how these exceptions happen may enable clients to repeat what might otherwise go unnoticed or be dismissed as a fluke (Berg & Miller, 1992).

Miller (1994) relates a prototypical example of using exceptions to generate solutions:

> [A] bright engaging eight year old female was brought by a family member to be treated for a "persistent" problem with bedwetting. After taking a few minutes to become acquainted with the two, the therapist . . . simply asked if there were already periods of time when bedwetting was not a problem. Both immediately agreed that bedwetting was not a problem when the girl slept on the hardwood floor rather than her bed. . . . At the end of the first session, the girl was instructed to "continue to have dry beds while sleeping on the hardwood floor." Plans for future session included gradually expanding the exception to include sleeping on a sheet on the hardwood floor, on a sleeping bag on the floor, a mattress on the floor, etc.

Though the number of methods is potentially endless, Berg and Miller (1992) identified many of questions that could be used to find exceptions. For example,

- I have a good picture of what happens when there are problems. In order to get a more complete picture, now I need to know more about when the problem does not happen.
- When do you notice you do *not* have that problem?

- What is different at those times when the problem does not happen?
- What will have to happen for that (e.g., times when the problem is not happening) to happen more often?

## PRETREATMENT CHANGE

When the first paper on SFBT appeared in 1986, de Shazer et al. noted an ongoing study that involved asking people who were scheduling their first appointment to be on the lookout for any changes for the better that occurred prior to attending their first session of therapy. When this exploratory study on pretreatment change was published a year later, the results indicated that fully two-thirds of the 30 clients queried reported having experienced change in the direction desired (Weiner-Davis, de Shazer, & Gingerich, 1987).

According to the authors of the original study, the search for "pretreatment change" began after the "accidental discovery that change frequently occurs prior to the first session" (p. 359, Weiner-Davis, de Shazer, & Gingerich, 1987). In the article, the authors relate the story of an adolescent male who was brought to therapy by his mother because of his deteriorating school performance. The mother attributed the boy's problems to her divorce and thought he might have a "deeply rooted depression." The session was organized around these themes until the end of the hour, when the Mother matter-of-factly reported "that for the 3 days prior to coming for therapy, her son 'had been trying in school.'" The therapist picked up this apparent anomaly, expressing surprise and praising the young man for having decided to "turn over a new leaf." The remaining two sessions were spent helping him identify and reinforce what he needed to do to keep the change going.

As may be evident, utilizing "pretreatment change" in therapy begins *prior* to the formal initiation of services (e.g., on the telephone,

at intake), when clients are told to look for improvement in the time leading up to their first visit. Therapists must also remember to invite conversation about the occurrence of such changes at the first appointment because clients often do not consider it relevant and therefore rarely mention it on their own (Beyebach, Morejon, Palenzuela, & Rodriguez-Arias, 1996).

## THE MIRACLE QUESTION

Of all of the techniques associated with the solution-focused model, "the miracle question" is most well known. De Shazer (1994) notes that the "miracle question is designed to allow clients to describe what *they* want out of therapy" (p. 273, emphasis added). The question asks clients to imagine

> Suppose . . . after we are through here, you go home and have dinner, do your chores, watch TV, and whatever else you do, and then you go to bed and go to sleep . . . and while you are sleeping . . . a miracle happens . . . and the problems that brought you into therapy are gone, just like that! . . . but this happens while you are sleeping, so you can't know that it has happened. . . . So, once you wake up in the morning, how will you discover that this miracle has happened? (Miller & de Shazer, 1998, p. 366)

## SCALING QUESTIONS

Although first utilized in the behavioral therapies, scaling questions have become a core component of solution-focused interviewing. Berg and Miller (1992) note that asking clients to put their "problems, priorities, successes, emotional investments in relationships, and level of self-esteem on a numerical scale . . . gives the therapist a much better assessment of things he [*sic*] has to know" (p. 82). Berg and de Shazer (1993) further indicate that such questions can also be used purposefully, "to motivate and encourage, and to elucidate the goals and anything else that is important to the individual client" (p. 10).

Berg and Miller (1992) identified several examples of scaling questions, all beginning with the common stem, "On a scale of 1 to 10, 10 being the highest, 1 being the lowest,"

- Where would you put yourself on how much you are committed to working on solving this problem?
- What would it take to move [1 point higher] on your scale?
- When you are [1 point higher] what would you be doing that you are not doing now? What else?

## THE INTRA-SESSION BREAK AND POSTSESSION MESSAGE

The purpose of taking a break near the end of each session of SFBT has undergone significant revision over the years. As described by de Shazer (1982) in his first book, the interview was originally seen as a time for collecting the data the team "need[ed] to design an intervention" (p. 43). A number of papers (Gingerich & de Shazer, 1991; Molnar & de Shazer, 1987) and de Shazer's (1985) entire second book, were devoted to identifying the appropriate conditions for assigning specific interventions. However, emphasis on mapping the interaction sequences leading to the development of homework tasks has disappeared in recent writings. As de Shazer (1994) notes, the "clever tasks" that were so much a part of the early work were "difficult to design," and "no more, perhaps even less, effective than simpler ones based principally on what the clients have already said they know how to do" (p. 272).

The only part of the end of session message to be retained from the early days is the "compliment." As stated then, "the team develops complimentary statements based on . . . reframing . . . details of the family's description" (de Shazer, 1982, p. 44). Nowadays, if any suggestions are made, they are generally taken from what clients say they are doing well.

## Effectiveness and Research

Weakland et al. (1974) cite their efforts to evaluate the MRI approach. This evaluation revolved around two key questions: (1) Has behavior changed as planned? and (2) Has the complaint been relieved? (p. 163). The researchers divided their results into three categories: (1) complete relief of the presenting complaint; (2) clear and considerable, but not complete, relief of the complaint; and (3) little or no change. Out of 97 reviewed cases, they reported 40% success, 32% significant improvement, and 28% failure (p. 164). The authors note, "These results appear generally comparable to those reported for various forms of longer-term treatment" (p. 164). Bodin (1981) describes goal attainment scaling used to assess treatment outcome for services by senior MRI staff to a local police department. This analysis indicated an 82% "success rate" for all completed cases within a 2-year period. A more recent outcome study involved 250 families. In this study, success was determined if (1) the client no longer had the complaint, (2) the client did not need further therapy by follow-up, and (3) no new problem arose (R. Fisch, personal communication, August 25, 2002). By these criteria, 75% of clients had achieved a favorable outcome.[1] Despite the shortcomings in rigorous empirical method of these studies (e.g., no comparison to untreated sample), their findings reflect the overall absolute efficacy of psychotherapy (an effect size of .85, meaning a success rate of 70% for the treatment group versus 30% for the control group; Wampold, 2001). In addition, the researchers note the comparative equivalence of MRI with other approaches.

Initial reports indicated the promise of solution-focused therapy. For example, in a widely cited, yet unpublished, master's thesis that utilized the same follow-up questions as those employed by MRI, Kiser (1988) reported a success rate of 80.4% (65.6% who met their goal, plus 14.7% reporting significant improvement), with a sample of 164 clients seen for an average of 4.6 sessions at BFTC. In his summary of this study, de Shazer (1991) further notes that "the success rate had *increased* to 86%" when the clients were recontacted at 18 months (p. 161, emphasis added). Results from a second study conducted at BFTC nearly a decade later were more modest. Using a combination of scaling and the MRI follow-up questions, de Jong and Hopwood (1996) reported an overall success rate of 77% (45% of participants reporting having met their goals, added to 32% who made "some progress") in a sample of 275 randomly selected clients, seen for an average of 2.9 sessions.

More recent studies have sought to address problems inherent in such "in-house" studies that limit their reliability and validity, most notably, the lack of random sampling, control groups, a specific disorder or well-defined target complaint, treatment manuals, and standardized outcome measures. In 2000, Gingerich and Eisengart gathered all of the controlled outcome studies on SFBT and categorized them according to the six standards of assessing empirical support for psychological treatments as set out by Division 12 of the American Psychological Association (Chambless, 1996). Of the 15 identified, no study met all of the criteria. However, 5 of the studies met 5 out of the 6 criteria and were designated "well controlled" by the researchers.

Of these, the first to employ a randomized control group design with a well-defined clinical sample, standardized outcome measures, and treatment manuals was Sundstrom (1993).

The sample in this as yet unpublished doctoral dissertation was composed of 40 female undergraduate students who scored in the mild to moderately severe range on the Beck Depression Inventory. The participants received one 90-minute session of either SFBT or interpersonal psychotherapy for depression (IPT). Outcome was assessed pre- and postintervention on four standardized measures. Statistical analysis found that SFBT and IPT produced significant changes but *no difference in outcome between the two treatments*.

The remaining studies compared the SFBT approach to either a wait list control or "treatment as usual" condition. One of those studies (Lindforss & Magnusson, 1997) will not be reviewed here, as it failed to define the nature of the treatment ("SFBT network intervention"), did not include a treatment manual, and had no means for testing treatment integrity. Of the others, Zimmerman, Jacobsen, MacIntyre, and Watson (1996) compared an SFBT-based parenting group to a no-treatment, wait list control. Although no pretreatment assessments were made, comparisons of post-treatment scores on the Parenting Skills Inventory found significant differences between the SFBT parenting group and the no-treatment comparison group on the total score, as well as on several subscales.

Cockburn, Thomas, and Cockburn (1997) compared standard rehabilitation services to the same services augmented with an SFBT counseling component. Participants who received counseling, in addition to standard rehabilitation services, had significantly better psychosocial adjustment and social support. More dramatically, the treatment group was much more likely to return to work (within 30 days, 92% versus 47%) and to return quickly (within 7 days, 68% versus 4%).

In another as yet unpublished dissertation, Seagram (1997) compared individual sessions of SFBT delivered by the author to a group of adolescent offenders in a secure facility to a matched control group receiving "standard services" at the same institution. Results were mixed. No significant differences were found on two of the scales. Results on two other measures indicated that the SFBT group was significantly more optimistic, had greater empathy, and had fewer antisocial tendencies, less chemical abuse, and less difficulty with concentration. At the 6-month follow-up, 42% of the matched controls (8), as compared to 20% (4) of the SFBT group, had re-offended.

Since the publication of the Gingerich and Eisengart (2000) review, one additional study has appeared that meets the criteria that was set out for "well-controlled." In an unpublished doctoral dissertation, Bozeman (1999) compared the effects of SFBT to "past-focused" counseling on measures of depression and hope. Consistent with the hopeful, forward-looking nature of SFBT, participants in the treatment group ended treatment significantly more hopeful than did those in the comparison group. However, there were no significant differences between the groups on the Beck Depression Inventory.

### Summary (and the Dilemma)

Research on the MRI model is quite sparse; on solution-focused therapy, growing. And herein lies the dilemma. In the best of all scenarios, any current or future studies showing the efficacy of the approaches will serve only to confirm an already well-known and established fact: therapy works. Indeed, in literally hundreds of studies conducted over the last 40 years, the average treated client is better off than 80% of the untreated sample (Miller, Duncan, & Hubble, 1997).

The existing studies on the MRI and solution-focused models already indicate that the two approaches are *more similar* than different from other extensively researched and established treatment approaches. On average, they work about as well, in roughly the same amount of time, with approximately the same types of people and presenting complaints as did every other bona fide treatment approach that has been investigated.

### BEING CLIENT-DIRECTED AND OUTCOME-INFORMED

*Until lions have their historians, tales of hunting will always glorify the hunter.*

—African proverb

The fires of the dilemma posed previously are further fanned by the wings of a bird—the dodo bird in *Alice's Adventures in Wonderland,* who said, "Everybody has won and all must have prizes." In 1936, Saul Rosenzweig first invoked the dodo's words to illustrate his observation of the equivalent success of diverse psychotherapies. Almost 40 years later, Luborsky, Singer, and Luborsky (1975) empirically validated Rozenzweig's conclusion in their now classic review of comparative clinical trials. They dubbed their findings of no differences among models, the "dodo bird verdict." It has proven to be the most replicated finding in the literature.

Confirming the notion that all models are created equal is the landmark Treatment of Depression Collaborative Research Project (TDCRP) (Elkin et al., 1989), widely viewed as the most methodologically sophisticated outcome study ever done. This NIMH-funded project randomly assigned 250 depressed participants to four different treatments: cognitive therapy, interpersonal therapy, antidepressants, and a placebo called "clinical management." After all the effort that went into designing a study that represented the state-of-the-art in outcome research, the investigators were stunned by their own findings. Overall, the four treatments—including placebo—worked with about the same effectiveness.

A recent meta-analyses, designed specifically to test the dodo bird verdict, reconfirmed the bird's astute judgment (Wampold, Mondin, et al., 1997). Given that the brief therapies often work with individuals, these findings are particularly relevant. Nevertheless, Shadish, Ragsdale, Glaser, and Montgomery (1995) and Sprenkle, Blow, and Dickey (1999) report that comparative clinical trials in family therapy have yielded similar results. Punctuating this point is an enormous study conducted by Human Affairs International of over 2,000 therapists and 20,000 clients. This real-world study of effectiveness revealed no differences in outcome among various approaches, including medication, as well as SFBT and other family therapy approaches (Brown, Dreis, & Nace, 1999). Although a handful of studies have found differences, the number is far less than would be attributable to chance (Wampold, 2001).

Despite extraordinary efforts, the preponderance of the data indicates that no one can declare any approach superior to any other. The fact that the dodo bird verdict was largely found by accident—while researchers were trying to prove the superiority of their own models—makes it particularly worthy to consider. But what does it mean? As Rosenzweig said some 66 years ago (and legions have said since, e.g., Frank, 1973), because all approaches appear equal in effectiveness, there must be pantheoretical factors in operation that overshadow any perceived or presumed differences among approaches. Therapy works, but our understanding of how it works cannot be found in the insular explanations found in the different theoretical orientations, but rather in the factors common to all approaches.

After extensive analyses of decades of outcome research, Lambert (1986) identified four therapeutic factors (see further on) as the principal elements accounting for improvement in psychotherapy. Lambert's review inspired an introduction of common factors implications to family therapy (Duncan et al, 1992), and later, specific ways to broaden their effects (Hubble, Duncan, & Miller, 1999; Miller et al., 1997). The common factors provide the empirical backdrop for what we call "client-directed, outcome-informed" ways of working with clients. A client-directed, outcome-informed approach contains no fixed techniques, no invariant patterns in therapeutic process, and no causal theory regarding the concerns that bring people to therapy. Any interaction with a client can be client-directed and outcome-informed. This comes about when therapists purposely partner with clients: (1) to enhance the factors across theories that account for successful outcome, (2) to use the client's theory of change to guide choice of technique and integration of various models, and (3) to inform the therapy with valid and reliable measures of the client's experience of process and outcome (Miller, Duncan, & Hubble, 2002).

### Enhancing Common Factors

#### CLIENT FACTORS

Tallman and Bohart's (1999) review of the research makes clear that the client is actually the single most potent contributor to outcome in psychotherapy—the resources clients bring into the therapy room and what influences their lives outside it (Miller et al., 1997). These factors might include persistence, openness, faith, optimism, a supportive grandmother, or membership in a religious community: all factors operative in a client's life before he or she enters therapy. They also include serendipitous interactions between such inner strengths and happenstance, such as a new job or a crisis successfully negotiated.

Assay and Lambert (1999) ascribe 40% of improvement during therapy to client factors, making clients the true heroes and heroines of the therapeutic drama (Duncan & Miller, 2000). Bergin and Garfield (1994) note, "As therapists have depended more upon the client's resources, more change seems to occur" (pp. 825–826). Whatever path the therapist takes, it is important to remember that the purpose is to identify not what clients need, but what they already have that can be put to use in reaching their goals (see Hubble et al., 1999, for practical suggestions for enrolling client factors).

## RELATIONSHIP FACTORS

The next class of factors accounts for 30% of successful outcome variance (Assay & Lambert, 1999) and represents a wide range of relationship-mediated variables found across therapies, now more generally referred to as the therapeutic alliance. The alliance speaks to both therapist and client contributions and emphasizes the partnership between the client and the therapist to achieve the client's goals (Bordin, 1979). Research on the power of the alliance reflects over 1,000 findings (Orlinsky, Grawe, & Parks, 1994) and is particularly noteworthy when taken from the client's perspective; client ratings of the alliance are far superior predictors of outcome than are therapists' (Bachelor & Horvath, 1999).

For example, Krupnick et al. (1996) analyzed data from the TDCRP and found that the alliance was most predictive of success for all conditions. Similarly, in family therapy, Johnson and Talitman (1997) reported that the alliance (particularly regarding the tasks of therapy) accounted for 29% of the variance of post-treatment satisfaction in their study of emotionally focused marital therapy. Sprenkle et al. (1999), after their review of the alliance literature in family therapy, assert that "the extant literature supports the conclusion that relationship factors exert a potent influence on MFT outcome" (p. 337).

This *robust* link between the client's rating of the alliance and successful outcome makes a strong case for a different emphasis—on tailoring therapy to clients' perceptions of the relationship and their ideas about the tasks required to accomplish their goals. Clearly, one-approach-fits-all is a strategy guaranteed to undermine alliance formation (see Hubble et al., 1999, for practical suggestions on enhancing relationship factors).

## PLACEBO, HOPE, AND EXPECTANCY FACTORS

Following client and relationship factors come placebo, hope, and expectancy. Assay and Lambert (1999) put their contribution to outcome at 15%. In part, this class of factors refers to the portion of improvement deriving from clients' knowledge of being treated and the assessment of the credibility of the therapy's rationale and techniques. These effects, therefore, are not thought to derive specifically from a given treatment procedure, but rather come from the hopeful expectations that accompany the implementation of the method. From this perspective, any technique from any model may be viewed as a healing ritual (Frank, 1973; Rosenzweig, 1936), rich in the possibility that hope can inspire.

## MODEL/TECHNIQUE FACTORS

Assay and Lambert (1999) suggest that model/technique, like expectancy, accounts for 15% of improvement in therapy. How exactly should models be viewed when so much outcome variance is controlled by other factors? The different models may be at their most helpful when they provide therapists with novel ways of looking at old situations, when they empower therapists to *change,* rather than *make up* their minds about clients (Miller et al., 1997). When considered as a common factor to all therapies, providing structure and novelty to both clients and therapists, so-called unique techniques cease being reflections of a particular model. Instead, they become simply different means to the same end; that is, their principal contribution to therapy comes about by enhancing the potency of the other common factors—client, relationship, and placebo (see Hubble et al., 1999, for a discussion of selecting techniques from a common factors perspective).

### The Client's Theory of Change

Because all approaches seem equivalent with respect to outcome, and technique pales in comparison to client and relationship factors, an evolving story casts the client as not only the star of the therapeutic stage, but also the director of the change process (Duncan & Miller, 2000; Duncan & Sparks, 2002). The clients' worldview, their map of the territory, is the determining "theory" for therapy (Duncan, Hubble, & Miller, 1997), directing both the destination desired and the routes of restoration. The client's theory of change is not a static entity like a psychiatric diagnosis. Rather, it is best understood as an "emergent reality" that unfolds throughout a conversation structured by the therapists' curiosity about the client's perceptions of the presenting complaint, its causes and potential solutions, and ideas and experiences with the change process in general (Duncan & Miller, 2000).

Honoring the client's theory occurs when the treatment offered fits with or is complementary to the client's preexisting beliefs about his or her problems and the change process. Though few references to the intentional use of clients' preferences in the selection of treatment approaches exist in the literature, studies in which the treatment offered was later found to have been congruent with client preferences point to increased client engagement and better treatment outcomes. For example, a post hoc analysis of the data from the TDCRP (the large-scale study of treatments for depression) found that congruence between a person's beliefs about the causes of his or her problems and the treatment approach offered resulted in stronger therapeutic alliances, increased duration of treatment, and improved outcomes (Elkin et al., 1999). Hubble et al. (1999) provided additional empirical support in a review of research findings from the attribution, expectancy, acceptability, and the therapeutic alliance literatures, as well as specific suggestions for co-mapping a theory of change.

### Becoming Outcome-Informed

Recall the evidence pointing to the importance of the *client's* rating of therapeutic alliance in successful treatment. Moreover, evidence from a variety of sources now points to the *client's* subjective experience of change in the early stages of therapy as one of the best predictors of positive results (Brown et al., 1999; Howard, Kopte, Krause, & Orlinksy, 1986). Rather than a focus on a priori searches for "what works for whom," these findings indicate that decisions about therapy may be best informed by partnering with clients in ongoing assessments of the fit and effect of any given therapeutic relationship—asking instead, "Is it working now?"

#### MEASURING FIT

*Process* measures assess the degree to which the session contains the elements known to engender a positive outcome, namely, the alliance. Any instrument that measures the therapeutic relationship will provide feedback therapists can use to tailor treatment to the individual needs and characteristics of their clients. The *Session Rating Scale—*

*Revised* (SRS-R) (Johnson, Miller, & Duncan, 2000) is one example of a reliable, valid, and feasible process measure specifically designed to be sensitive to clients' perceptions of the alliance and easily integrated into the therapeutic conversation.

## MEASURING PROGRESS

*Outcome* measures, as the name implies, assess the impact or result of the service therapists offer their clients. Research conducted over the last 40 years indicates that changes in an individual's level of distress, functioning in close interpersonal relationships, and performance at work, at school, or in settings outside the home are reasonable indicators, as well as strong predictors, of successful therapeutic work (Kazdin, 1994; Lambert & Hill, 1994). One example of a reliable, valid, and feasible outcome measure specifically designed to be sensitive to the changes that research suggests are likely in successful treatment is the *Outcome Rating Scale* (ORS) (Miller & Duncan, 2000). The ORS is brief and easily integrated into therapeutic process, is applicable to a broad range of clients, and is sensitive to change in those undergoing treatment but stable in nontreated populations.[2]

Results from the measurement process are continuously "fed back" into treatment (Duncan & Miller, 2000). In a typical outpatient setting, for example, clients would be given the outcome measure *prior* to each session and given the process scale toward the end. In their review of the literature on the therapeutic relationship, Bachelor and Horvath (1999) point out that clients rarely report their dissatisfaction with therapy until *after* they have decided to terminate. Other large-scale and meta-analytic studies strongly suggest that therapies in which little or no change (or even a worsening of symptoms) occurs *early* in the treatment process are at significant risk for a null or even negative outcome (e.g., Howard,

Moras, Brill, Martinovich, & Lutz, 1996). In the Brown et al. (1999) study of more than 20,000 clients, researchers found that clients who reported no improvement by the third visit typically showed no improvement over the entire course of treatment.

In terms both of process and outcome, therefore, the systematic and ongoing measurement of outcome can provide therapists with a critical "window of opportunity" to address client concerns and make any necessary modifications to what they are offering. Common sense suggests that it is simply not possible for therapists to form a successful working relationship with every person they encounter. Moreover, a recent study of over 6,000 clients at six different outpatient clinics found a paltry overall effectiveness rate of 35% (Hansen, Lambert, & Forman, in press).

Research demonstrates that variables such as diagnosis, severity, and type of therapy (including medication) are not as important in predicting outcome as knowing whether or not the treatment being provided is working. Being outcome-informed means measuring the effectiveness of services and using the collected information as a guide to enhance what's working and to modify or quit whatever is not working. Whipple, Lambert, et al. (in press) found that when therapists received reliable feedback about client progress, it up to doubled the effectiveness of those therapists. Partnering with clients to make therapy accountable opens options for both clients and therapists by providing immediate feedback when things are stuck (see Duncan & Sparks, 2002, and Duncan & Miller, 2000, for specific descriptions of this partnering process).

## FUTURE DIRECTIONS

*Whoever acquires knowledge and does not practice it resembles him who ploughs his land and leaves it unsown.*

—Sa'di Gulistan (1258)

Our field, in its quest to discover what therapists do to bring about change, has engaged in what MRI and SFBT would call "more of the same." Like a dog chasing its tail, researchers continue to attempt to confirm that one approach, by virtue of specific ingredients, outshines another. We believe it wise, therefore, to *do something different*. A common factors vision of therapy embraces change that is client-directed, not theory-driven; subscribes to a relational, rather than a medical, model; and is committed to successful outcome instead of competent service delivery (Duncan, 2002; Duncan & Miller, 2000).

The paradigm shift we are suggesting no longer emphasizes exclusive and expert-derived theory as a basis for practice. Instead, it is interested in client ideas of change, client-initiated topics, client priorities, and client views of therapy progress. It elevates, without reservation, local, client theories over all those previously held sacrosanct by the therapeutic community. Inherent in this stance is the fundamental faith that clients can and will realign the parts of their lives that are distressing, given the powerful context of a relationship that respects and follows clients' leads (even when their lead is for therapists to lead). It takes seriously research that, over and over, places clients as the prime movers in therapy.

The paradigm shift we envision supplants the medical model with a relational model as a basis for therapy. From a common factors perspective, the medical model transposed onto therapy is a seriously flawed project (Duncan, 2001). The medical equation consists of the following: diagnosis + prescriptive treatment = symptom alleviation or cure. The essential components of this equation are an expert and theory-based assessment, plus a specified treatment based on that assessment that when competently implemented by a trained professional, will produce changes the clinician's assessment deems most important. From its outset, the medical model seriously interferes with the most potent common factor, the client's free and active engagement in therapy.

In addition, the medical model application to therapy cannot stand the test of its own measure, empirical evidence. Diagnosis, via the *DSM*, has notoriously poor reliability and has yet to prove any substantial validity (Carson, 1997; Kirk & Kutchins, 1992). Diagnosis consistently fails to predict outcome or what will work (If no approach has shown superiority, how can diagnosis indicate a preferred treatment?) (Beutler, 1989; Duncan & Miller, 2000). Although it clearly falls short on empirical grounds, diagnosis, as early brief therapists noted, has an additional liability—the unfortunate potential to reify that which it is supposed to merely describe.

Evidence of the medical model's stronghold on therapy is the increasing privilege of evidence-based treatments (EBTs). EBTs are those treatments that have been shown, through randomized clinical trials (there are many inherent problems with randomized clinical trials beyond the scope of the current discussion; see Duncan, 2002), to be efficacious over placebo or no treatment. This is not big news—the absolute efficacy (efficacy over placebo or no treatment) of all bona fide approaches is now virtually an indisputable fact (Wampold, 2001). Efficacy over placebo is, of course, not differential efficacy over other comparable approaches.

For example, consider multisystemic therapy (MST), which has impressively shown that it is superior to no treatment or treatment as usual for the reduction of criminal acts of juveniles, as well as having other benefits (e.g., Henggeler, Melton, & Smith, 1992). To imply, however, that it has proven to be differentially better because of comparisons to individual therapy is analogous to male and female bikini wear—notable for what is concealed, rather than for what is exposed. An inspection of one such comparison involving serious juvenile offenders (Borduin, Mann, et al., 1995) reveals that MST was conducted in the home, involving parents and other interacting systems, by therapists regularly supervised by founders of the approach. MST was then compared with therapy of the adolescent only, with little to no outside input of parents or others, conducted in an outpatient clinic by therapists with no special supervision. This type of comparison falls into what Wampold (2001) calls an indirect comparison, a treatment as usual contrast, rather that a bona fide treatment comparison. If a comparison were made of MST and another home-based approach we suspect that it would support what Lambert and Bergin (1994) observed in other studies, "carried out with the intent of contrasting two or more bonafide treatments shows surprisingly small differences between the outcomes for patients that undergo a treatment that is *fully intended* to be therapeutic" (p. 158).

Our suggestion that efficacy over no treatment or treatment as usual is not front page news and our critical comment on MST's ability to claim differential efficacy over other approaches do not diminish the outstanding results that MST has achieved nor do they diminish the promise it has shown for ameliorating difficult clinical situations. Rather, we applaud the efforts of the investigators and suggest caution in interpreting the results as any particular privilege that should be given any approach over any other.

## From Service to Outcome-Informed

In the medicalized milieu of present-day practice, the greatest attention is paid to the competent provision of services. Service is now increasingly defined as the appropriate application of evidence-based treatments. Instead, we argue for "practice-based evidence" as an alternative to "evidence-based practice." If diagnosis does not predict either treatment or outcome, but the client and his or her perception of progress and of the therapy relationship does, then a system based on reliable feedback from clients can both enhance therapy effectiveness *and* contain costs. Using client feedback in the form of reliable outcome and process tools makes it possible for therapists and payers to know how they're doing—are they being effective in capitalizing on client factors, building relationships, and helping clients reach their goals? Becoming outcome-informed in this way enables therapists and clients to regain control of the clinical decision-making process, rendering obsolete treatment plans, psychiatric diagnoses, lengthy intake forms, "approved" therapeutic modalities, or any other practice that takes up time but fails to improve treatment outcome. Such a system, dependent as it would be on client self-report data, would finally give the users of therapy the voice in the treatment process that 40 years of data say they deserve.

## SUMMARY AND CONCLUDING REMARKS

*There is no new thing under the sun.*
—Bible, Ecclesiastes 1:9

The interactional and solution-focused approaches can only be praised for their enormous contributions to all brief therapies. At the same time, we particularly note their influence on our own present-day interest in client-directed, outcome-informed practice based on common factors research. Specifically, MRI's seminal idea that problems and symptoms are simply ineffective attempts to solve everyday life difficulties renders "the six Ds" (diagnosis, disease, dysfunction, disorder, disability, and deficit) virtually obsolete. The significance of removing psychotherapy's pathology blinders can hardly be overstated. Today's competency-oriented therapies owe a debt of gratitude rarely expressed to these pioneers of positive perspectives of clients.

MRI's and SFBT's interest in client resources and client goals proved remarkably on track with the most robust findings in outcome research—that client contributions and attending to client preferences and goals account for as much as 70% of the outcome of therapy. SFBT, introducing the notion that the solution need have no relationship to the problem, runs directly counter to the medical model's insistence that a discrete, diagnosed disorder then dictates a specific, matched intervention. At the same time, an understanding of solutions as non–problem specific frees therapists and clients to travel multiple paths in a more client-directed and creative search for problem resolution. In addition, SFBT's attention to the future provides a natural enhancement of hope and expectancy factors, replacing the dismal past with a possibility-filled future. Finally, MRI's conceptualization of client position led the way for an increased interest in learning and validating the client's theory of change as a critical component of strengthening the therapeutic alliance and enhancing positive outcome.

According to MRI and SFBT, change results not from the enforced prescription of therapeutic power, but from the somewhat mysterious joining of client and therapist in a dialogue responsive to the evolving nuances of the specific relationship. Before collaborative language systems and narrative therapies, MRI and SFBT had already conceptualized the therapy process as persons in conversation. Therapy, from MRI on, became an exercise in the creative use of language in relationship to transform beliefs and problems. It is our contention that the early interactional models of family therapy were almost prescient applications of what was later confirmed by the bulk of outcome research. We acknowledge, with gratitude, this contribution and suggest that the logical heir to the brief

therapy tradition is practice that put clients in the leading role of change.

## NOTES

1. The authors thank Richard Fisch, MD, founder and director of the Brief Therapy Institute, for his assistance with this information.
2. The SRS and ORS are available at www.talkingcure.com.

## REFERENCES

Assay, T. P., & Lambert, M. J. (1999). The empirical case for the common factors in therapy: Quantitative findings. In M. A. Hubble, B. L. Duncan, & S. D. Miller (Eds.), *The heart and soul of change: What works in therapy* (pp. 33–56). Washington, DC: APA Press.

Bachelor, A., & Horvath, A. (1999). The therapeutic relationship. In M. A. Hubble, B. L. Duncan, & S. D. Miller (Eds.), *The heart and soul of change: What works in therapy* (pp. 133–178). Washington, DC: APA Press.

Bateson, G., Jackson, D. D., Haley, J., & Weakland, J. (1956). Toward a theory of schizophrenia. *Behavioral Science, 1,* 251–264.

Berg, I. K., & de Shazer, S. (1993). Making numbers talk: Language in therapy. In S. Friedman (Ed.), *The new language of change* (pp. 5–24). New York: Guilford Press.

Berg, I. K., & Miller, S. D. (1992). *Working with the problem drinker: A solution-focused approach.* New York: Norton.

Bergin, A. E., & Garfield, S. L. (Eds.). (1994). *Handbook of psychotherapy and behavior change* (4th ed.). New York: Wiley.

Beutler, L. (1989). Differential treatment selection: The role of diagnosis in psychotherapy. *Psychotherapy, 26,* 271–281.

Beyebach, M., Morejon, A. R., Palenzuela, D. L., & Rodriguez-Arias, J. L. (1996). Research on the process of solution-focused therapy. In S. D. Miller, M. A. Hubble, & B. L. Duncan (Eds.), *Handbook of solution-focused brief therapy* (pp. 299–334). San Francisco: Jossey-Bass.

Bodin, A. M. (1981). The interactional view: Family therapy approaches of the Mental Research Institute. In A. S. Gurman & S. P. Kniskern (Eds.), *Handbook of family therapy* (Vol. I, pp. 267–309).

New York: Brunner/Mazel.

Bordin, E. S. (1979). The generalizability of the psychoanalytic concept of the working alliance. *Psychotherapy: Theory, Research, and Practice, 16*, 252–260.

Borduin, C., Mann, B., Cone, L., Henggeler, S., Fucci, B., Blaske, D., & Williams, R. (1995). Multisysemic treatment of serious juvenile offenders. *Journal of Consulting and Clinical Psychology, 63*, 569–578.

Bozeman, B. (1999). *The efficacy of solution focused therapy techniques on perceptions of hope in clients with depressive symptoms.* Unpublished dissertation. New Orleans Baptist Theology Seminary. New Orleans, LA.

Brown, J., Dreis, S., & Nace, D. K. (1999). What really makes a difference in psychotherapy outcome? Why does managed care want to know? In M. A. Hubble, B. L. Duncan, & S.D. Miller (Eds.), *The heart and soul of change: What works in therapy* (pp. 389–406). Washington, DC: APA Press.

Carson, R.C. (1997). Costly compromises: A critique of the *Diagnostic and Statistical Manual of Mental Disorders*. In S. Fisher & R. P. Greenberg (Eds.), *From placebo to panacea: Putting psychiatric drugs to the test* (pp. 98–114). New York: Wiley.

Chambless, D. L. (1996). Identification of empirically supported psychological interventions. *Clinicians Research Digest, 14*(6), 1-2.

Cockburn, J. T., Thomas, F. N., & Cockburn, O. J. (1997). Solution-focused therapy and psychosocial adjustment to orthopedic rehabilitation in a work hardening program. *Journal of Occupational Rehabilitation, 7*, 97–106.

de Jong, P., & Hopwood, L. (1996). Outcome research on treatment conducted at the Brief Family Therapy Center, 1992-1993. In S. D. Miller, M. A. Hubble, & B. L. Duncan (Eds.), *Handbook of solution-focused brief therapy* (pp. 272–298). San Francisco: Jossey-Bass.

de Shazer, S. (1982). *Patterns of brief family therapy.* New York: Guilford Press.

de Shazer, S. (1985). *Keys to solutions in brief therapy.* New York: Norton.

de Shazer, S. (1988). *Clues.* New York: Norton.

de Shazer, S. (1990). What is it about brief therapy that works? In J. K. Zeig & S. G. Gilligan (Eds.), *Brief therapy: Myths, methods, and metaphors* (pp. 90–107).

de Shazer, S. (1991). *Putting difference to work.* New York: Norton.

de Shazer, S. (1994). *Words were originally magic.* New York: Norton.

de Shazer, S., & Berg, I. K. (1997). "What works?" Remarks on the research aspects of solution-focused brief therapy. *Journal of Family Therapy, 19*, 121–125.

de Shazer, S., Berg, I. K., Lipchik, E., Nunnally, E., Molnar, A., Gingerich, W., & Weiner-Davis, M. (1986). Brief therapy: Focused solution-development. *Family Process, 25*, 207–222.

Duncan, B. L. (2001). The future of psychotherapy. *Psychotherapy Networker, 25*(4), 24–33.

Duncan, B. L. (2002). The legacy of Saul Rosensweig: The profundity of the dodo bird. *Journal of Psychotherapy Integration, 12*(1), 10–31.

Duncan, B. L. , Hubble, M. A., & Miller, S. D. (1997). *Psychotherapy with impossible cases: The efficient treatment of therapy veterans.* New York: Norton.

Duncan, B. L., & Miller, S. (2000). *The heroic client.* San Francisco: Jossey Bass.

Duncan, B. L., & Sparks, J. (2002). *Heroic clients, heroic agencies: Partners for change.* Ft. Lauderdale: Institute for the Study of Therapeutic Change.

Duncan, B., Solovey, A., & Rusk, G. (1992). *Changing the rules: A client-directed approach.* New York: Guilford Press.

Elkin, I., Shea, T., Watkins, J. T., Imber, S. D., Sotsky, S. M., Collins, J. F., Glass, D. R., Pilkonis, P. A., Leber, W. R., Docherty, J. P., Fiester, S. J., & Parloff, M. B. (1989). National Institute of Mental Health Treatment of Depression Collaborative Research Program: General effectiveness of treatments. *Archives of General Psychiatry, 46*, 971–982.

Elkin, I., Yamaguchi, J. L., Arnkoff, D. B., Glass, C. R., Sotsky, S. M., & Krupnick, J. L. (1999). "Patient-treatment fit" and early engagement in therapy. *Psychotherapy Research, 9*(4), 437–451.

Fisch, R., Weakland, J. H., & Segal, L. (1982). *The tactics of change: Doing therapy briefly.* San Francisco, Jossey-Bass.

Frank, J. D. (1973). *Persuasion and healing.* Baltimore: Johns Hopkins University Press.

Gingerich, W., & de Shazer, S. (1991). The BRIEFER project. *Family Process, 30*, 241–250.

Gingerich, W., & Eisengart, S. (2000). Solution-focused brief therapy: A review of the outcome research. *Family Process, 39*, 477–498.

Haley, J. (1973). *Uncommon therapy: The psychiatric techniques of Milton H. Erickson, M.D.* New York: W. W. Norton.

Hansen, N. B., Lambert, M. J., & Forman, E. V. (in press). The psychotherapy dose-response effect and its implications for treatment delivery services. *Clinical Psychology: Science and Practice.*

Henggeler, S., Melton, G., & Smith, L. (1992). Family preservation using multisystemic therapy. *Journal of Consulting and Clinical Psychology, 60,* 953–961.

Howard, K. I., Moras, K., Brill, P. L., Martinovich, Z., & Lutz, W. (1996). Evaluation of psychotherapy: Efficacy, effectiveness, and patient progress. *American Psychologist, 51*(10), 1059–1064.

Howard, K.I., Kopte, S. M., Krause, M. S., and Orlinsky, D. E. (1986). The dose-effect relationship in psychotherapy. *American Psychologist, 41*(2), 159–164.

Hubble, M. A., Duncan, B. L., & Miller, S. D. (1999). *The heart and soul of change: What works in therapy.* Washington, DC: APA Press.

Johnson, S., Miller, S. D., & Duncan, B. L. (2000). *Session Rating Scale.* Salt Lake City, UT: Author Publisher.

Johnson, S., & Talitman, E. (1997). Predictors of success in emotionally focused marital therapy. *Journal of Marital and Family Therapy, 23,* 135–152.

Kazdin, A. E. (1994). Methodology, design, and evaluation in psychotherapy research. In A. E. Bergin & S. L. Garfield (Eds.), *Handbook of psychotherapy and behavior change* (pp. 19–71). New York: Wiley.

Kirk, S. A., & Kutchins, H. (1992). *The selling of DSM: The rhetoric of science in psychiatry.* New York: Aldine.

Kiser, D. (1988). *A follow up study conducted at the Brief Family Therapy Center of Milwaukee, Wisconsin.* Unpublished manuscript. Brief Family Therapy Center, Milwaukee, WI.

Kral, R., & Kowalski, K. (1989). After the miracle: The second stage in solution-focused brief therapy. *Journal of Strategic and Systemic Therapies, 8,* 73–76.

Krupnick, J. L., Sotsky, S. M., Simmens, S., Moyher, J., Elkin, I., Watkins, J., & Pilkonis, P. A. (1996). The role of the therapeutic alliance in psychotherapy and pharmacotherapy outcome: Findings in the National Institute of Mental Health Treatment of Depression Collaborative Research Project. *Journal of Consulting and Clinical Psychology, 64,* 532–539.

Lambert, M. J. (1986). Implications for psychotherapy outcome research for eclectic psychotherapy. In J. C. Norcross (Ed.), *Handbook of eclectic psychotherapy* (pp. 436–462). New York: Brunner/Mazel.

Lambert, M. J., & Bergin, A. E. (1994). The effectiveness of psychotherapy. In A. E. Bergin & S. L. Garfield (Eds.), *The handbook of psychotherapy and behavior change* (4th ed. pp.143–189). New York: Wiley.

Lambert, M. J., & Hill, C. E.(1994). Assessing psychotherapy outcomes and processes. In A. E. Bergin, & S. L. Garfield (Eds.), *Handbook of psychotherapy and behavior change* (4th ed., pp. 72–113). New York: Wiley.

Lindforss, L., & Magnusson, D. (1997). Solution-focused therapy in prison. *Contemporary Family Therapy, 19,* 89–103.

Luborsky, L., Singer, B., & Luborsky, L. (1975). Comparative studies of psychotherapies: Is it true that "everyone has won and all must have prizes"? *Archives of General Psychiatry, 32,* 995–1008.

Miller, G., & de Shazer, S. (1998). Have you heard the latest rumor about . . . ? Solution-focused therapy as a rumor. *Family Process, 37,* 363–378.

Miller, S. D. (1994). The symptoms of solution. *Journal of Strategic and Systemic Therapies, 11,* 1–11.

Miller, S. D., & Duncan, B. L. (2000). Outcome Rating Scale. Chicago, IL: Author.

Miller, S. D., Duncan, B. L., & Hubble, M. A. (1997). *Escape from Babel.* New York: Norton.

Miller, S. D., Duncan, B. L., & Hubble, M. A. (2002). Client directed outcome informed clinical work. In J. Lebow (Ed.), *Comprehensive handbook of psychotherapy* (Vol. 4, pp. 185–212). New York: Wiley.

Molnar, A., & de Shazer, S. (1987). Solution-focused therapy: Toward the identification of therapeutic tasks. *Journal of Marital and Family Therapy, 13,* 349–358.

Orlinsky, D. E., Grawe, K., & Parks, B. K. (1994). Process and outcome in psychotherapy—Noch einmal. In A. E. Bergin & S. L. Garfield (Eds.), *Handbook of psychotherapy and behavior change* (4th ed., pp. 270–378). New York: Wiley.

Rosenzweig, S. (1936). Some implicit common factors in diverse methods of psychotherapy. *American Journal of Orthopsychiatry, 6,* 412–415.

Seagram, B. C. (1997). *The efficacy of solution-focused therapy with young offenders.* Unpublished doctoral dissertation. York University. New York, Ontario, Canada.

Shadish, W., Ragsdale, K., Glaser, R., & Montgomery, L. (1995). The efficacy and effectiveness of marital and family therapy: A perspective from meta-analysis. *Journal of Marital & Family Therapy, 21*(4), 345–360.

Sprenkle, D. H., Blow, A. J., & Dickey, M. H. (1999). Common factors and other nontechnique variables in marriage and family therapy. In M. Hubble, B. Duncan, & S. Miller (Eds.), *The heart and soul of change: What works in therapy* (pp. 329–359). Washington, DC: APA Press.

Sundstrom, S. M. (1993). *Single session psychotherapy for depression: Is it better to focus on problems or solutions?* Unpublished doctoral dissertation. Iowa State University. Ames, Iowa.

Tallman, K., & Bohart, A. (1999). The client as a common factor: Clients as self-healers. In M. Hubble, B. Duncan, & S. Miller (Eds.), *The heart and soul of change: What works in therapy* (pp. 91–131). Washington, DC: APA Press.

Turnell, A., & Hopwood, L. (1994). Solution-focused brief therapy: I. A first session outline. *Case Studies in Brief and Family Therapy, 8*(2), 39–51.

Wampold, B. E. (2001). *The great psychotherapy debate: Models, methods, and findings.* Mahway, N J: Erlbaum.

Wampold, B. E., Mondin, G. W., Moody, M., Stich, F., Benson, K., & Ahn, H. (1997). A meta-analysis of outcome studies comparing bona fide psychotherapies: Empirically, "All must have prizes." *Psychological Bulletin, 122*, 203–215.

Watzlawick, P. (Ed.). (1984). *The invented reality: How do we know what we believe we know? Contributions to constructivism.* New York: Norton.

Watzlawick, P., Weakland, J. H., & Fisch, R. (1974). *Change: Principles of problem formation and problem resolution.* New York: Norton.

Weakland, J. H., Fisch, R., Watzlawick, P., & Bodin, A. (1974). Brief therapy: Focused problem resolution. *Family Process, 13,* 141–168.

Weiner-Davis, M., de Shazer, S., & Gingerich, W. (1987). Building on pretreatment change to construct the therapeutic solution: An exploratory study. *Journal of Marital and Family Therapy, 13,* 359–363.

Whipple, J., Lambert, M., Vermeersch, D., Smart, D., Nielsen, S., & Hawkins, E. J. (in press). Improving the effects of psychotherapy. *Journal of Counseling Psychology.*

Zimmerman, T. S., Jacobsen, R. B., MacIntyre, M., & Watson, C. (1996). Solution-focused parenting groups: An empirical study. *Journal of Systemic Therapies, 15,* 12–25.

# CHAPTER 7

# Postmodern Social Construction Therapies

HARLENE ANDERSON, PhD

*Houston Galveston Institute and Taos Institute*

## INTRODUCTION

Family therapy, as we know it today, can be traced back to two main roots. One perspective—the etiology, insight, and family patterns view of Nathan Ackerman—focused on the individual in the family and viewed families as a collection of individuals. Coming from within the child guidance movement and drawing from psychodynamic and social theories, Ackerman was interested in family role relationships and their influence on the intrapsychic development and makeup of the individual (Ackerman, 1958, 1966). The other perspective, the rhetorical communication and interactional view, grew from the early works of Donald Jackson and Gregory Bateson and their later collaborative efforts with interdisciplinary colleagues at the Mental Research Institute in California (Watzlawick & Weakland, 1977). They reached out to the social sciences and the natural sciences to understand families, early on developing a theory

of communication and later focusing on the role of language in the construction of reality. They conceptualized families as cybernetic systems of interconnected individuals and questioned the concept of psychological problems as illness. They viewed psychosis, for instance, as an interpersonal relational problem, rather than as an intrapsychic problem or a disease of the mind (Bateson, 1972; Watzlawick & Weakland, 1977; Watzlawick, Beavin, & Jackson, 1967). The current therapies primarily based in postmodern and social construction philosophies that have evolved over the last 20-plus years represent a hybrid-like ideological shift that can be traced back to the California rootstock and to developments in philosophy and the social sciences.

During these years the world around us was fast changing, shrinking, and becoming enormously more complex and uncertain and was impacting human beings and our everyday lives. Familiar concepts such as universal

125

truths, knowledge and knower as independent, language as representative, and the meaning is in the word no longer seemed helpful in accounting for and dealing with the changes and complexities and their associated impact. The familiar systems concepts, whether first- or second-order, helped, but such concepts risked placing human behavior into frameworks of understanding that seduced therapists into hierarchical expert–nonexpert structures, into discourses of pathology and dysfunction, and into a world of the known and the certain. Among developments in philosophy and the natural and social sciences, postmodernism and social constructionism have emerged as more fitting, offering alternative ways to think of people and their problems and of therapists' relationship to both.

Broadly speaking, postmodern refers to a family of concepts that critically challenges the certainty of objective truths, the relevance of universal or metanarratives, and language as representative of the truth (Kvale, 1992; Lyotard, 1984). Postmodernism is not a metanarrative, but rather one among numerous others. Inherent in postmodernism is a self-critique of postmodernism itself; that is, it invites and demands continued analysis of its premises and their applications. Social construction, a particular postmodern theory, places emphasis on truth, reality, and knowledge as socially embedded and the role that language plays in the creation of these products. According to the foremost proponent of social constructionism, social psychologist Kenneth Gergen (1982, 1985, 1994, 1999), it is "principally concerned with explicating the processes by which people come to describe, explain, or otherwise account for the world (including themselves) in which they live" (1985, p. 266).

Language emerged as the meaningful and useful metaphor, especially its role in the creation of knowledge, in the power of discourse and transformation, and in human systems and interaction. This ideological and epistemological shift holds significant implications and challenges for therapists' thoughts, actions, and interpretations of others. It offers a broad challenge to the culture, traditions, and practices of the helping professions. It invites reexamination and reimagination of psychotherapy traditions and the practices that flow from them, including how problems are conceptualized, client–therapist relationships, the process of therapy, and therapists' expertise. For varying reasons, a focus away from the family as the limited target of treatment is inherent in this shift. Instead, the postmodern/social construction ideology-informed approaches are not limited to families but are applicable to individuals, couples, families, and groups. In the words of family therapist historian Lynn Hoffman (2002), the shift changed the definition of what needs to be changed: The target has moved from the unit to the situation. Problems are not believed to reside within the person, the family, or the larger system. Instead, problems are considered linguistic constructions, with various punctuations such as the local dialogical context and process of people's everyday lives and the subjugating and oppressing influence of dominant universal narratives. Thus, the aim of the therapist has changed: to set a context and to facilitate a process for change, rather than to change a person or a group of people.

### Common Premises

Postmodern social construction premises influence a dialogical and relational perspective on understanding human behavior, including the dilemmas of everyday life and a therapist's stance regarding these. Although there are significant variations among the postmodern social construction therapies, generally speaking, some common basic premises (although with slight variations and differences in emphasis) include

- The notion of objective discoverable knowledge and universal absolute truths is viewed skeptically.
- The world, our truths, is not out there waiting to be discovered.
- Knowledge and social realities are linguistically and communally constructed; reality, therefore, is a multiverse.
- Language is the vehicle through which people know and attribute meaning to their world, including realities about the people, events, and experiences of their lives. Neither problems nor solutions exist within a person or a family; they take shape and have meaning within a relational and dialogical context.
- The goal of therapy is to create a relational and dialogical context for transformation.
- Transformation—outcomes and solutions— is inherent and emerges in dialogue.
- Transformation is unique to the client and the participants in the therapy conversation and therefore cannot be predetermined ahead of time.
- The person and *self,* including development and human agency, are viewed as interdependent, communal, and dialogic entities and processes, rather than as isolated, autonomous interior ones.
- People have multiple identities and their Identities are shaped and reshaped in social interaction.

*Common Values*

Therapies based on these premises share common values (with slight variations and emphasis):

- Taking a nonpathological, nonjudgmental view.

- Appreciating, respecting, and utilizing the client's reality and uniqueness.
- Using story and narrative metaphors.
- Being collaborative in structure and process.
- Avoiding labeling and blaming classifications of individuals and families or their behaviors.
- Being more "public" or "transparent" with information and biases.

More so than others, the postmodern/social construction therapies have captured practitioners' interest in learning about the effectiveness of their therapy in their everyday settings (Andersen, 1997; Anderson, 1997a, 1997b). This interest has created a number of studies that provide in-depth first-person descriptions of the lived experience of therapy processes and the nuances of its effectiveness, or lack of, from both therapists' and clients' perspectives. What is learned from the "insiders" can have relevancy to both current and future practices and yields a more thorough story of the nuances of therapy than can be captured in "outsider" qualitative research. Together, these efforts join other family therapy approaches at the forefront of promoting multiple alternative research methodologies, particularly those categorized as qualitative, such as single case studies, ethnographic interviews, and narrative accounts (see Addison, Sandberg, Corby, Robila, & Platt, 2002).

A growing number of therapists place their practice under a postmodern/social construction umbrella or are heavily influenced by it. The author chose to discuss three therapies in this chapter: the collaborative approach of Harlene Anderson and Harry Goolishian (Anderson & Goolishian, 1988, 1992; Anderson, 1997a), the narrative approach of David Epston and Michael White (White, 1995; White & Epston, 1990), and the solution-focused approach of Insoo Berg and Steve de Shazer (Berg & de Shazer, 1993; de Shazer,

1982, 1985, 1988, 1991, 1993). This choice was made because these three therapies are often the core therapies that are typically found in graduate and postgraduate family therapy courses with titles such as postmodern/social construction, advanced systems, and narrative therapies. Other significant contributors to the emergence of postmodern social construction practices included in these courses, who must be acknowledged, are Tom Andersen in Norway and Lynn Hoffman and Peggy Penn in the United States (Andersen, 1987, 1991; Hoffman, 1981, 1998, 2002; Penn, 1985, 2001; Penn & Frankfurt, 1994) and Jaakko Seikkula in Finland (1993, 2002). Although each of the previous approaches is historically or currently influenced by the postmodern social construction perspectives to various extents, they are not necessarily limited to these influences and their originators might make different theoretical and practice application punctuations than this author.[i]

*Some Distinctions*

Comparing and contrasting can be helpful in learning. Readers, therefore, might want to do this as they read along. In doing so, they might note these possible distinctions among the three approaches regarding power, client–therapist relationships, the therapist's role, and the process of therapy.

- Collaborative and narrative therapies place importance on power. Similarly, they value client–therapist relationships and systems that are more egalitarian and less hierarchical; they are careful to be, respectively, public and transparent about their views and biases. Dissimilarly, narrative therapy holds an agenda to liberate people from constraining or oppressive dominant narratives; collaborative therapists pay attention to these narratives when the client thinks it is im-

portant; and solution-focused therapists do not find the issue relevant.
- Collaborative and narrative therapies place emphasis on the client–therapist relationship, although perhaps a different emphasis; solution-focused therapies do not accent the relationship.
- Therapists' expertise can be thought of as along a continuum, in terms of importance and intent. Collaborative therapists espouse that the clients are the experts on their lives, and the therapist is in a not-knowing position regarding it. Narrative therapists are experts in helping clients achieve preferred stories and living them, and solution-focused therapists use their expertise in helping to devise strategies toward goals.
- Collaborative therapists favor a process of mutual inquiry and are not invested in a content outcome; they view themselves as walking alongside their clients toward an unknown destination of new meaning and action. Narrative therapists favor a process that leads to preferred stories and people being able to live these; their role is like that of a narrative editor. Solution-focused therapists overtly steer clients toward solution-talk and a specified behavioral goal.
- Observers might notice a narrative or solution-focused therapist systematically, for instance, asking questions and making comments as if moving the conversation in a particular direction, whereas, a collaborative therapist might be described as wandering here and there.

## COLLABORATIVE THERAPY

*History and Background: A Search*

The collaborative approach evolved from the 20-year mutual work of Harlene Anderson and Harry Goolishian and their colleagues and students, beginning in the early 1970s within the context of a medical school and later in what is now the Houston Galveston Institute. Its roots can be traced back to Goolishian's participation in the early multiple impact therapy (MIT) family therapy research project at the medical school (MacGregor, Ritchie, Serrano, Schuster, McDanald, & Goolishian, 1964). Although the practice was quite innovative at the time, the theory used to describe and understand it was limited by the psychodynamic, psychoanalytic, and developmental theories available then. Soon deciding that these theories could not provide adequate descriptions of their clients and their experiences of therapy, Goolishian and his colleagues began what became a continuous search for new theoretical tools. Now, the stage was set for the important reflexive process of the interaction of practice and theory. That is, new practices led to new theories that influenced the practices, which in turn began to require new theories, and so forth. This early interest was influenced by the voices of clients and therapists—their experiences, descriptions, and understandings of successful and unsuccessful therapy— and has remained an important thread throughout the development of the collaborative approach.

## Major Theoretical Constructs: Human Systems as Linguistic Systems

As Anderson and Goolishian and their colleagues searched for new descriptions and understandings, they went down a meandering path to revolutions in the social, natural, and physical sciences; philosophy; and, eventually, to the postmodern philosophical movement and the works of thinkers such as Bakhtin, 1981; Bruner, 1986, 1990; Geertz, 1983; Gergen, 1985; Lyotard, 1984; Rorty, 1979; Schon, 1984; Shotter, 1993; Vygostsky, L. S., 1986, and Wittgenstein, 1953, who focused on the relational and generative nature

of knowledge and language. Anderson and Goolishian found contemporary hermeneutics and social constructionism primarily relevant: the concepts of a socially constructed world of truths and knowledge, language as the vehicle and product of human interchange, understanding as an interpretive process, and language as generative. These concepts took their interests in language, which had been inspired by the work of Bateson and his colleagues at the Mental Research Institute in Palo Alto, California, away from learning clients' language for use in a strategic sense and away from systems theories.

Specifically, knowledge—what we think we know or might know—is linguistically constructed. Furthermore, its development and transformation are communal processes, and the knower and knowledge are interdependent. Knowledge, therefore, is neither static nor discoverable; rather, it is fluid and created. Authoritative discourses from this perspective give way to knowledge constructed on the local level that has practical relevance for the participants involved. Language in this perspective—spoken and unspoken communication or expression—is the primary vehicle through which we construct and make sense of our world and ourselves. As philosopher Richard Rorty (1979) suggests, language does not mirror what is; for instance, it is not an outward description of an internal process and does not accurately describe what actually happened. Rather, language allows a description of what happened and an attribution of meaning to it. Language gains its meaning and its value through its use. Thus, it limits and shapes thoughts and experiences and expressions of them. What is created in and through language (realities such as knowledge, truth, and meaning) is multi-authored among a community of persons. That is, the reality that we attribute to the events, experiences, and people in our lives does not exist in the thing itself; rather, it is a socially constructed attribution that is created within a particular culture and is shaped and reshaped in language. What is created, therefore, is only one of multiple perspectives (realities such as narratives or possibilities).[ii] Language, therefore, is fluid and creative.

Combined, these perspectives influenced Anderson and Goolishian to move away from the familiar, general, and second-order cybernetic systems notions on which family therapy had been based, to the notion of human beings as systems in language or language systems (Anderson & Goolishian, 1988). Human systems are meaning-making systems. Therapy becomes one kind of language or meaning-making system. Originally, Anderson and Goolishian referred to their work as a collaborative language systems approach and, more recently Anderson has simplified it to collaborative therapy (Anderson, 2001a, 2001b, 2000).

## Etiology of Clinical Problems

A collaborative therapist takes the position that there is no such thing as an objective problem. Problems are a form of co-evolved meaning that exists in ongoing communication among others and self. Through our interpretations, we attribute meaning to others, events, actions, and ourselves. Problems cannot be separated from an observer's conceptualizations.

Problems are considered part of everyday living; they are not considered the product of pathological individuals or dysfunctional families. What is problematic to one person or family may not be problematic to another: "Each problem is conceived as a unique set of events or experiences that has meaning only in the context of the social exchange in which it happened" (Anderson, 1997a, p. 74). Problems can be perpetuated and escalated through conversational breakdowns, a failure to main-

tain generative conversations (Anderson, 1986, 1997a).

## Assessment

Traditional notions of diagnosis and assessment are based on the idea of objective reality, commonality across problems, and linear cause and effect. Inherent in the notion of assessment is a determination of what is: A problem can be defined, its cause can be located, and it can be solved. From a collaborative perspective each observation, problem description, and understanding is unique to the people involved and their context. Problems are collaboratively explored and defined through conversation. Because conversation or dialogue is generative, a problem is never fixed; it shifts as its definitions, meanings, and shapes change over time through conversation.

Although collaborative therapists seldom find traditional notions of diagnosis and assessment useful, they acknowledge that they and their clients live and work in systems in which these are important. This is simply a challenge for therapists to respect, be in conversation with, and navigate multiple realities. In other words, it is a challenge to be true to one's beliefs and act accordingly, whatever the situation or context.

## Clinical Change Mechanisms and Curative Factors: Collaborative Relationships and Dialogical Conversations

Therapy is a process or activity that involves collaborative relationships and dialogical conversations. It is a process of coexploring, clarifying, and expanding the familiar; therapy invites and forms the "unsaid": the newness. Although newness in some form or another—stories, self-identities, and so on—can be the result, the emphasis of therapy is on this process, not on content or product. Collaborative therapists strive to be aware of this essentialist trap.

Dialogical conversation is distinguished by shared inquiry. Shared inquiry is the mutual process in which participants are in a fluid mode and is characterized by people talking *with* each other as they seek understanding and generate meanings; it is an in-there-together, two-way, give-and-take, back-and-forth exchange (Anderson, 1997a; Anderson & Goolishian, 1988). Dialogical conversation begins with the therapist as a learner whose interest and curiosity about the client naturally invite the client into shared inquiry. This shift and the interpretive process of shared inquiry are transformational processes.

Language is the primary vehicle for therapy. Transformation (e.g., new knowledge, meanings, expertise, identities, agency, actions, and futures) is inherent in the inventive and creative aspects of language and, therefore, dialogue: "In dialogue, new meaning is under constant evolution and no 'problem' will exist forever. In time all problems will dissolve" (Anderson & Goolishian, 1988, p. 379). This transformative nature of language invites a view of human beings as resilient, and it invites an appreciation of each person's contributions and potentials.

*Specific Interventions:*
*A Philosophical Stance*

Like most other postmodern/social construction–oriented therapies, collaborative therapy does not consider the therapist's position or actions as techniques. Anderson and Goolishian (1988) distinguished their work as a philosophy of therapy, rather than a theory or a model. For them, philosophy involves questions and ongoing analysis about ordinary human life, such as self-identity, relationships, mind, and knowledge. Their conceptualizations of knowledge and language inform a worldview or *philosophical stance*—a way of being in the world that does not separate professional and personal. The stance characterizes a way of thinking about, experiencing, being in relationship with, talking with, acting with, and responding with the people whom therapists meet in therapy. Several interrelated characteristics partly define the stance.

## CONVERSATIONAL PARTNERS

The collaborative therapist and the client become conversational partners as they engage in *dialogical conversations* and *collaborative relationships*. Dialogical conversation and collaborative relationship refer to the shared inquiry process, in which people talk *with* each other, rather than *to* each other. Inviting this kind of partnership requires that the client's story take center stage. It requires that the therapist constantly learn—listening and trying to understand the client from the client's perspective.

This therapist-learning position acts to spontaneously engage the client as a co-learner or what collaborative therapists refer to as a mutual or shared inquiry as they coexplore the familiar and codevelop the new. In this inquiry, the client's story is told in such a way that it clarifies, expands, and shifts. Whatever newness is created is co-constructed from within the conversation, in contrast to being imported from outside of it. In this kind of conversation and relationship, all members have a *sense of belonging*. Collaborative therapists report that this sense of belonging invites participation and shared responsibility (Anderson, 1997a). Dialogical conversations and collaborative relationships go hand in hand: the kinds of relationships people have with each other form and inform the kinds of conversations they have and vice versa.

## CLIENT AS EXPERT

The collaborative therapist believes that the client is the expert on his or her life and as such is the therapist's teacher (Anderson, 1997b; Anderson & Goolishian, 1992). The therapist respects and honors the client's story, listens to hear what is important for the client, and takes seriously what the client says and how the client says it. This includes any and all knowledge—for instance, whether dominant cultural discourse or popular folklore informs the client's descriptions and interpretations—and it includes the many ways that the client may express his or her knowledge. For instance, the therapist does not hold expectations that a story should unfold in a chronological order or at a certain pace. The therapist does not expect certain answers and does not judge whether an answer is direct or indirect, right or wrong. Tom Andersen (1991) suggests just how challenging it is to respect the client's expertise, "What I myself found important, but extremely difficult, to do was to try to listen to what clients say instead of making up meaning about what they say. Just listen to what they say" (p. 321). Inherent in this approach is an appreciative belief that most human beings value, want, and strive toward healthy successful relationships and qualities of life.

Collaborative therapists often work with members of clients' personal or professional systems. The therapist appreciates, respects, and values each voice and each client's reality and strives to understand the multiple and unique understandings from each member's perspectives: the richness of these differences is found to hold infinite possibilities.

## NOT-KNOWING

The collaborative therapist is a not-knowing therapist. Not-knowing refers to the way therapists think about and position themselves with their knowledge and expertise. They do not believe they have superior knowledge or hold a monopoly on the truth. They offer what they know or think they might know but always hold it and present it in a tentative manner. That is, therapists offer their voice, including previous knowledge, questions, comments, opinions, and suggestions, as food for thought and dialogue. Therapists remain willing and able to have their knowledge (including professional and personal values and biases) questioned, ignored, and changed.

Not-knowing can be misunderstood as therapists knowing nothing, pretending ignorance, or forgetting what they have learned. Instead, it simply refers to how therapists position themselves with their knowledge, including the timing and the intent with which knowledge is introduced.

## BEING PUBLIC

Therapists often learn to operate from invisible private thoughts—whether professionally, personally, theoretically, or experientially informed. Such therapist thoughts include diagnoses, judgments, or hypotheses about the client that influence how therapists listen and hear and that form and guide their questions. From a collaborative stance, therapists are open and make their invisible thoughts visible. They do not operate or try to guide the therapy from private thoughts. For instance, if a therapist has an idea or an opinion, it is shared with the client, again offered as food for thought and dialogue. Important are the manner, attitude, and timing in which therapists offer opinions, not whether they can or cannot share them. Keeping therapists' thoughts public minimizes the risk of therapist and therapist–client monologue—being occupied by one idea about a person or situation. Monologue can subsequently lead to a therapist's participating in, creating, or maintaining external descriptions of clients such as "resistance" and "denial."

## MUTUAL TRANSFORMATION

The therapist is not an expert agent of change; that is, a therapist does not change another person. Rather, the therapist's expertise is in creating a space and facilitating a process for dialogical conversations and collaborative relationships. When involved in this kind of process, both client and therapist are shaped and reshaped—transformed—as they work together.

## UNCERTAINTY

Being a collaborative therapist invites and entails uncertainty. When a therapist accompanies a client on a journey and walks alongside that individual, the newness (e.g., solutions, resolutions, and outcomes) develops from within the local conversation, is mutually created, and is uniquely tailored to the person or persons involved. How transformation occurs and what it looks like will vary from client to client, from therapist to therapist, and from situation to situation. Put simply, there is no way to know for sure the direction in which the story will unfold or the outcome of therapy when involved in a generative process of dialogical conversation and collaborative relationship.

## EVERYDAY ORDINARY LIFE

Therapy from a collaborative perspective becomes less hierarchical and dualistic. It resembles the everyday ordinary conversations and relationships that most people prefer. This does not mean chitchat, without agenda, or a friendship. Therapy conversations and relationships occur within a particular context and have an agenda: simply, a client wants help and a therapist wants to help. Clients and problems are not categorized as challenging or difficult. Collaborative therapists believe that each client presents a dilemma of everyday ordinary life.

If therapists assume the described philosophical stance, they will naturally and spontaneously act and talk in ways that create a space for and invite conversations and relationships where clients and therapists *connect*, *collaborate*, and *construct* with each other. Because the philosophical stance becomes a natural and spontaneous way of being as a therapist, there are no therapist techniques and skills, as we know them. The stance is unique for each therapist, for each client, and each situation the therapist encounters.

### Effectiveness of Approach: Who Decides?

Collaborative therapy contrasts with therapy approaches in which professional knowledge externally defines problems, solutions, outcomes, and success, creating expert–nonexpert dichotomies. Collaborative therapists believe that one must ask the client to determine whether therapy was useful, and if so, how. Although therapists' experiences and opinions are valued, every effort is made to privilege clients' perceptions and evaluations of therapy and to pay attention to what therapists can learn from them. Research, so to speak, becomes part of everyday practice, with therapists and clients as co-researchers during the process of therapy, as well as at its conclusion (Andersen, 1997; Anderson, 1997a). Findings are used during the therapy process to make therapy more useful to the client and, of course, influence the further evolution of ideas and practices (see Andersen, 1997).

The strengths of the approach are in the relationships and conversations that are created between the client and the therapist and in their inherent possibilities. Consequently, therapy becomes less hierarchical and dualistic, less technical and instrumental, and more of an insider, rather than an outsider, endeavor. Clients report a sense of ownership, belonging, and shared responsibility. Therapists report an increased sense of appreciation for their clients, sense of enthusiasm, and sense of competency, creativity, flexibility, and hopefulness for their work. They also report a reduction in burnout.

Most evidence of the effectiveness of collaborative therapy is anecdotal: client and therapist stories about their experiences of therapy and the usefulness of the approach for them are included, for instance, in articles on child abuse and other types of domestic violence, eating disorders, substance abuse, and war trauma (Anderson, 1997a; Anderson, Burney, & Levin, 1999; Anderson & Levin, 1998; Chang, 1999; London, Ruiz, Gargollo, & Gargollo, 1998; St. George & Wulff, 1999; Swim, Helms, Plotkin, & Bettye, 1998). As in narrative therapy, it is not unusual for therapists to invite clients to participate in writing and professional presentations (London, Ruiz, Gargollo, & Gargollo, 1998; Swim, Helms, Plotkin, & Bettye, 1998). Qualitative research includes studies of the effectiveness of collaborative therapy and analysis of whether therapists' behaviors and attitudes were consistent with their therapy philosophy (Gehart-Brooks & Lyle, 1999; Swint, 1995) and with the application of the ideas in supervision and education (St. George, 1994).

The history of its development also supports its effectiveness. The collaborative approach evolved in practice settings with a variety of challenging clients. These included chronic treatment failures, patients in outpatient and inpatient psychiatric settings, and, later, public agency clients, such as those from children's protective services, women's shelters, and adult and juvenile probation, who were often mandated for therapy and from various cultures (Anderson, 1991; Anderson & Goolishian, 1986, 1991; Anderson & Levin, 1998; Levin, Reese, Raser, & Niles, 1986). Finnish psychologist Jaakko Seikkula and his colleagues have aptly demonstrated effectiveness of a dialogue approach through a research

project with a 5-year follow-up with psychotic patients and their families (Seikkula, 1993; Seikkula, Aaltonen, Alakare, Haarakangas, Keranen, & Sutela, 1995).

Often-asked questions about the effectiveness of the collaborative approach include (1) "What are its limits?" and (2) "It sounds so cognitive, how does it work with people who are not so verbal or bright or who are psychotic?" When limits are experienced, the therapist creates the limits, rather than the client or the kind or severity of their problem. Therapist-created limits are usually associated with slipping out of a collaborative mode. When clients are approached from a collaborative perspective, they talk, they are forthcoming, and they are active in addressing their problem.

## NARRATIVE THERAPY

### History and Background: Joint Efforts

Social workers Michael White at the Dulwich Centre in Adelaid, Australia, and David Epston in Auckland, New Zealand, became interested in each other's work in the early 1980s. Combining Epston's background in anthropology and his interest in storytelling and White's interest in interpretive methods, inspired by the writings of Gregory Bateson, they created what became known as narrative therapy (Epston & White, 1992; White & Epston, 1990). Several factors affected the development of narrative therapy. Contextually, it is not surprising that narrative therapy emerged in these geographic and cultural contexts during a period when social and governmental attention and commitment in both countries were drawn to the oppression of their indigenous cultures and efforts of restitution. Given this backdrop, Epston and White were naturally attracted to the relevance of European poststructural theory, particularly Foucault's position on constructed truths and the inseparability of power and knowledge. White's wife, Cheryl White, also influenced White and Epston's interest in feminist theory and analysis of power. Over the years, other important leaders and extenders of the narrative therapy movement have been Gene Combs and Jill Freedman (Freedman & Combs, 1996), Victoria Dickerson and Jeffrey Zimmerman (Zimmerman & Dickerson, 1996), Sallyann Roth (Roth & Epston, 1996), and Kathy Weingarten (1998) in the United States and Stephen Madigan (Madigan & Epston, 1995) in Canada.

*Major Theoretical Constructs: Narrative, Knowledge, and Power*

Narrative therapy is based in a narrative/story metaphor: people make sense of and give meaning to their lives, including the people and events in it, through their narratives, the stories they tell others and themselves, and the stories they are told. That is, narratives or stories about others and self shape experiences and thus lives. People's narratives are their realities. We are born into the dominant narratives or discourses of our unique cultures that are created by the culture's power brokers. These dominant discourses, or truths, influence local and personal narratives, affect the words we use and the knowledge we have, and become internalized truths. The lived experience of the person becomes lost or subjugated to the dominant narratives. Narrative therapy views problems—their formation and their resolution—from this dominant narrative perspective.

Based on this cultural-discourse problem-formation perspective, narrative therapy carries a political and social agenda: to help people deconstruct and liberate themselves from their culture-dominated problem stories and to construct stories about themselves that give more possibilities to their lives. This applies to therapists, as well as to clients. Therapists are also subject to being captives of cultural privileged truths and imposing them on their clients. To avoid this risk, narrative therapists examine the influence of larger cultural discourses on their own narratives, preferred truths, and actions, and they openly disclose, or are transparent about, their beliefs and biases about problems, therapy, and so forth.

In the development of narrative therapy, this perspective and this agenda were strongly influenced by the poststructuralism view of the French social philosopher Michel Foucault (1972), more so than by a postmodern perspective. Foucault's life work was committed to calling attention to and challenging the taken-for-granted and often invisible but pervasively influential social, political, and cultural institutional structures and practices in which people live. Foucault, persuaded by his studies of institutions such as justice-penal systems and medical-psychiatric systems, believed that the dominant discourses of these institutions gave power and influence to some people, usually to those deemed to have expert knowledge, and objectified, marginalized, or victimized others. This consciousness-raising became a guiding principle for narrative therapy in relation to the goal of therapy, the process of therapy, and the position of the therapist. Narrative therapy's commitment to social justice and the questioning of power influences outside and inside the therapy room drew many therapists who shared this commitment to it.

The works of French literary deconstructionist Jacques Derrida (1992), North American anthropologist Clifford Geertz (1983), and psychologist Jerome Bruner (1986) have also influenced the narrative approach. Derrida's work focuses on meaning and its relation to the texts. For Derrida, a text has no one true meaning. The reader, through reading and interpreting a text, creates a text and its meaning. It is a linguistic trap to assume that a certain text exists or that one can search for and find it. Narrative therapists have also adopted Derrida's concept of deconstruction: "the critical analysis of texts . . . how a text is given meaning by its author or producers" (Smith, Harre, & Langenhove, 1995, p. 52). For Epston and White, the text analogy "advances the idea that the stories or narratives that persons live through determine their interaction and organization, and that the evolution of lives and relationships occurs through the performance of such stories or narratives" (White & Epston, 1990, p. 12). Geertz introduced the concept of "context analysis": an interpretive process of looking into the meaning of talk and action in their social and cultural contexts. The analysis gives a local "native" (1983) understanding, or a fuller understanding that Geertz referred to as "thick description" (1973). Through these local understandings, access is gained to the human lived experience, rather than to normative objective descriptions, labels, and classifications. A common thread through the works of Foucault, Derrida, and Geertz is a strong plea to the human sciences to be aware of and not participate in the entrapping danger of normalization to subjugate and control. Narrative therapists borrowed from Bruner's narrative theory, including his ideas about the structure of stories, how people understand and give meaning to their experiences through them, and how they create realities for the writer (teller) and the reader (listener).

Combined, these conceptual works influenced the designation *narrative* therapy: the way that our narratives, our stories about others and ourselves, shape our experiences and thus our lives. They are our realities. And they influence the mission of a narrative therapist: to help people deconstruct the stories that guide their lives, emancipate themselves from limiting or oppressive stories, and live their preferred stories. The influence of these conceptual works on the premises and promises

of narrative therapy are apparent in the following sections.

*Etiology of Problems*

From the narrative perspective, dominant cultural discourses and institutions influence the problem stories that people bring to therapy. Discourses of pathology and causality that exist within our broader social and psychotherapy cultures are large influences and are easily internalized, inviting problem-saturated stories. Problem stories effect people's identities and generate blame and hopeless feelings. Problems persist because problem-saturated stories persist. Thoughts and experiences of others and the self become the interpreting and validating lens that fixes and perpetuates the problem story. In the words of Epston and White (1990), "Persons experience problems, for which they frequently seek therapy, when the narratives in which they are 'storying' their experience, and/or in which they are having their experiences 'storied' by others, do not sufficiently represent their lived experience, and that, in these circumstances, there will be significant aspects of their lived experience that contradict these dominant narratives" (p. 14).

A problem is not inside a person, a couple or a family; it is not found within family structures or interaction patterns. Instead, problems are viewed as external to each person, limiting or oppressing them and other members of their system. People, therefore, are not blamed for problems.

*Assessment*

Assessment assumes that there is something—for example, a structure, a pattern, a personality, or a relationship—to evaluate. And usually embedded in that assumption is that the something is static. Traditionally, in psychotherapy, assessment tends to focus on determining the correct diagnosis, which in turn informs the treatment. Narrative therapists do not use standardized assessment instruments or focus on quantifiable diagnoses. Like collaborative therapists, they value the local or the native description of the problem. People consulting the therapist are the best source of description of the problem and the best judge of what they want from therapy and the therapist and of whether the therapy is helpful. Assessment is not seen as a beginning phase of treatment that determines the goal and the strategies for reaching that goal. Rather, assessment, or learning about the problem, is part of the continuous process of telling and re-telling the story. Narrative therapists are interested in mapping the impact and effect of the problem on the individual and the family, rather than in finding its cause.

Because narrative therapists hold assumptions about limiting and oppressing dominant discourses, they would have ideas about which discourses these might be as they listen to the client's narrative. So, part of the assessment would include determining the discourse in which the client's problem is located and the restraints that it poses on the client's life. Although introducing the taken-for-granted or invisible discourse can be viewed as an intervention, it is also viewed as an opportunity to assess the client's response and to negotiate understanding.

## Clinical Change Mechanisms and Curative Factors

Narrative therapy is based on the assumption that resolution requires a change in story or narrative. Narrative therapists want to help people "re-author" (Meyerhoff, 1986) their lives and relationships and to form new identities that liberate them from limiting and op-

pressing narratives. Re-authoring involves re-envisioning both the past and the future. It also requires making the invisible constraining problem-supporting discourses visible and helping people "confront the discourses that oppress or limit people as they pursue their preferred directions in life" (Freedman & Combs, 2000). The new or alternative story is sometimes called a preferred outcome. The new story becomes the vehicle for a new self-identity.

The focus is not on the more usual techniques and goals of therapy, such as improving communication among family members or encouraging people to express their feelings. Instead, the primary therapist activity is deconstructing the problem story and its supporting assumptions and on externalizing the problem. Critical to change is the therapist's attitude of respectful confidence in the client and tenacious hope.

## Specific Interventions

The preferred position for a narrative therapist is one that exemplifies a worldview of a "way of living that supports collaboration, social justice and local, situated, context-specific knowledge rather than normative thinking, diagnostic labeling, and generalized (noncontextualized) 'expert' knowledge" (Freedman & Combs, 2000, p. 345). This decentered therapist position is critical to achieving the mission of narrative therapy, more so than seeming interventions and techniques.

Whether narrative therapists describe their work in the language of technique and intervention varies. For example, some speak of "practices" (Freedman & Combs, 2002, p. 350). Narrative therapists take several identifiable actions, regardless of what they call them, to help them achieve their mission to deconstruct the problem story, liberate people from it, and construct a preferred story.

Questions lead this agenda; that is, narrative therapists ask questions to influence the emergence of preferred outcomes.

## DECONSTRUCTING

A therapist asks questions to deconstruct the problem story—detail it, explore its context—and to reveal the dominant social, cultural, and political practices that have helped create and maintain the problem. Some therapists refer to the deconstructing process as unpacking.

## EXTERNALIZING

A therapist asks questions and makes comments that emphasize the problem as an outside influence on the person, rather than as a characteristic or a defect inside them or their actions. Externalizing separates the person from the problem and disrupts the idea that problems originate within people. To aid in this separation and to help people renegotiate their relationship with the problem and exercise control over it, the problem is often given a name or personified. Externalizing the problem challenges not only the location of the problem, but also the idea of it as fixed and as a totalizing entity.

## THICKENING STORIES

A therapist asks questions that help create fuller descriptions and understandings of the lived experience of the client and that invite new preferred life narratives. Deconstructing, unpacking, and externalizing are part of the thickening process.

## REALIZING UNIQUE OUTCOMES AND CREATING PREFERRED OUTCOMES

Critical aspects of creating external definitions of problems are what narrative therapists call realizing unique outcomes and creating preferred outcomes. A therapist asks questions that help elicit unique outcomes—instances or "sparkling events" that contradict or open the way for an alternate or preferred story. They identify, highlight, and reinforce these unique outcomes, inviting and supporting the client to have power over the problem and his or her life. In addition to focusing on past and present unique outcomes, a narrative therapist focuses on future unique and unexpected outcomes. Therapists ask questions, using their knowledge of the problem story and their imagination to help the clients construct a preferred or more useful story.

## BEING TRANSPARENT

As a way of minimizing the power differential between clients and therapists, narrative therapists offer information about themselves and invite clients to ask them questions about their experiences and beliefs. In the words of Freedman and Combs (1996), "We try to be transparent about our own values, explaining enough about our situation and our life experience that people can understand us as people rather than experts or conduits for professional knowledge" (p. 36).

## REFLECTING

Using Tom Andersen's notion of reflecting process (Andersen, 1995), a therapist gives a therapy client, a therapy team, or any observers of the therapy the opportunity to reflect on the conversation while the client and the therapist listen. The reflectors are thought of as a witness or as one kind of community of concern (discussed further on).

## WRITING LETTERS

A therapist or a team writes letters as another way of participating in a client's story, externalizing the problem, and creating unique outcomes. Letters are most often written and mailed to a client after a therapy session or at the end of a course of therapy. Letters are used to show therapists' recognition of the client's situation and to help support and sustain change during the course of therapy or at its end. A client will then have the letter to read and re-read long after therapy has concluded. Letters may take any creative form and their content may vary, all depending on the clients and their circumstances and what the therapist hopes to accomplish. Numerous examples of a variety of letters can be found in White and Epston's (1990) book *Narrative Means to Therapeutic Ends* (pp. 84–187).

Two other techniques, creating communities of concern and designing definitional ceremonies, serve as important aids to acknowledging, solidifying, and sustaining the new story. They create another way of telling and retelling the story or what Wolfgang Iser (1978) calls a "performance of meaning." They also invite a sense of ownership for the client and a sense of joint responsibility for all participants.

## CREATING COMMUNITIES OF CONCERN

A therapist invites clients to bring into the conversation, literally or figuratively, the voices of significant people in their lives to help counter the influence of the broader culture's restrictive narratives and to support and maintain new narratives and preferred outcomes. These voices are utilized throughout the therapy and at its conclusion. A therapist can also encourage and help the client to bring together or join groups of people with the same kind of problem. Examples include Anti-Anorexia/Anti-Bulimic Leagues (Madigan & Epston, 1995) and Internet websites (Weingarten, 2000).

## DESIGNING DEFINITIONAL CEREMONIES

To focus on the change, to witness it, to celebrate it, and to sustain it, narrative thera-

pists borrowed from anthropologist Barbara Meyerhoff's (1986) practice of definitional ceremonies. Therapists invite clients to create a ceremony or a ritual in which significant people in their lives can witness the change, thus highlighting it. The event can take any form or shape that acknowledges the accomplishment, such as a certificate, a declaration, an imagined public announcement, a song, and so forth. The options are limitless and depend only on the creativity of the participants.

### Effectiveness of Approach

Most of the dissemination of information on the effectiveness and in support of narrative therapy is found in anecdotal form at conferences, in books and journal articles, and in the Dulwich Centre Newsletter. In keeping with the narrative/story metaphor, narrative therapists invite present and former clients, individuals, and large groups to tell their stories in writing and in professional presentations. This allows the conference participants and readers to hear the clients' stories and therapy experiences directly from the source, rather than through therapists' filters. It also acknowledges the major role of clients in the therapy and the change.

The approach has demonstrated success in various contexts and with different presenting problems: Application in schools is partly demonstrated in a special section on "Narrative Work in Schools" in the *Journal of Systemic Therapies* (Zimmerman, 2001), including success with bullying (Beaudoin, 2001) dealing with the effects of terrorism (Shalif & Leibler, 2002), and the use of the teacher's knowledge to revive commitment and success in teaching (Kecskemeti & Epston, 2001). Application with custody evaluation has demonstrated a favorable outcome of a narrative-collaborative process in which all parties (clients and evaluators) felt more respected and heard and less traumatized and blamed. Furthermore, its application and effectiveness in home-based therapy have been demonstrated (Madison, 1999). The success of narrative therapy is also discussed in Freedman and Combs (2000) and Smith and Nylund (1997).

## SOLUTION-FOCUSED THERAPY

*History and Background*

Steve de Shazer is widely acknowledged as the principal originator of solution-focused therapy, although its development emerged from the collective work of de Shazer; his professional partner and wife, Insoo Kim Berg; and his colleagues in Milwaukee, Wisconsin, in the late 1970s. Well-known others, primarily William O'Hanlan, Eve Lipchik, Michele Weiner-Davis, Jane Peller, and John Walter, built on the early foundations and practices of solution-focused therapy, especially its focus on solutions and brevity, and developed their own unique versions and names for it (Lipchick, 1993; O'Hanlon & Weiner-Davis, 1989; Walter & Peller, 2000). De Shazer was strongly influenced by his early work with the Mental Research Institute (MRI) group in Palo Alto, California, and its brief problem-focused therapy.

De Shazer and Berg may not place solution-focused therapy under a postmodern social construction umbrella, for there are distinct differences between solution-focused and collaborative and narrative therapies. All three, however, share the centrality of language and its relationship to reality, and de Shazer and Berg also use the narrative metaphor to refer to the ways people talk about and construct their lives. Like the MRI group, they promote the simplicity of their theory and practice; however, solution-focused therapy does have a solid theoretical base.

*Major Theoretical Constructs*

Solution-focused therapy is historically rooted in a tradition that started with the influence of Milton Erickson, Gregory Bateson, and the MRI associates, and giving credit to Berg, de Shazer supplemented the MRI influence with the premises of Buddhism and Taoism (de Shazer, 1982). De Shazer and Berg basically flipped the problem-focused approach that suggested more of the same ineffective solutions maintain the problem, to more of the same effective solutions solve the problem. They continued the MRI group's commitment to a pragmatic, deliberate intervention and brief perspective, including the importance of what rather than why and the importance of the present rather than history, and they added an emphasis on the future. They referred to their early task- and goal-directed practice as an ecosystemic approach to brief family therapy (de Shazer, 1982). Later, de Shazer and Berg wove philosopher Ludwig Wittgenstein's notions of language and language games into the background of these earlier influences (de Shazer, 1991). Language creates and is reality. Therefore, a problem is a client's reality: to change a problem, one must change the reality by changing the language. In de Shazer's view, a shift from problem talk to solution talk is critical to this change. Solution-talk takes the form of what de Shazer (1991) refers to as progressive narratives, ones that lead toward goals by allowing "clients to elaborate on and 'confirm' their stories, expanding and developing exception and change [problem] themes into solution themes" (pp. 92–93).

Solution-focused therapy is a non-pathologizing, positive, and future-oriented approach. Therapists focus on the positive aspects and the potential of clients, as well as on empowering them. Solution-focused therapy revolves around the question "How do we construct solutions?" (Walter & Peller,

1992). The major premise is that information about problems is not necessary; for change, all that is necessary is solution or goal talk (Walter & Peller, 1992). Central assumptions that guide the therapist's thinking and activity include the belief that change and cooperation are inevitable, that everyone has the resources to change, and that clients succeed when their goals drive therapy (Selekman, 2002). Maintaining the early systems notions that a change in one relationship or a part of the system will effect change in others and that a small change can lead to a large change, solution-focused therapists believe it is necessary only to work with the complainant and to have modest goals. They are, however, flexible, depending on the requests of the referring person(s) or other customer or complainant. Early on, solution-focused therapists placed clients in one of three categories to designate their commitment and level of desire to change: visitors, complainants, and customers. Interestingly, when clients do not cooperate, therapists interpret this as helping the therapist find a better way to help them.

A later influence for de Shazer was the work of Austrian philosopher Ludwig Wittgenstein (Miller & de Shazer, 1998). Drawing on Wittgenstein's notion of language games and his and other philosophers' notion that realities and meanings are created in language, de Shazer speaks of the construction and action of problem-talk and solution-talk as language games. Solution-focused therapists prefer to play the solution-talk game, with its focus on solution consequences.

## Etiology of Clinical Problems

Problems from a solution-focused perspective are related to language: the way that people talk about and attribute meaning to what they call problems. The talk about the events, circumstances, and people in clients' lives defines a problem as a problem. In de Shazer's words (1993), "There are no wet beds, no voices without people, no depressions. There is only *talk* about wet beds, *talk* about voices without people, *talk about depression*" (p. 89). From this perspective, information about the problem, such as its root and cause, its patterns, or its frequency, is not important. To the contrary, as mentioned earlier, solution-focused therapists want to avoid talking about the problem.

## Assessment

Assessment is not a component of solution-focused therapy in the traditional sense. De Shazer challenges the relationship between problem and solution, making assessment of problems irrelevant. In his words, "The problem or complaint is not necessarily related to the solution" and "The solution is not necessarily related to the problem" (de Shazer, 1991, p. xiii). Again, solution-focused therapists hold a strong belief that neither therapists nor clients need to know the problem's etiology or to even understand the problem. Looking for causes and grasping for meanings of problems are viewed as little more than problem-talk. And problem-talk can perpetuate the clients' obsession with and immersion in their problems, can risk reifying problems, and can obstruct the development of solutions. This is believed to be true for both the therapist and the client.

Solution-focused therapists do want to know or assess the client's goal. They also want to know the exceptions to the problem, for these exceptions hold the seeds for solutions. Although, historically, they have maintained a strategic stance, some now strive for a collaborative construction of goals and solutions.

*Techniques*

Early in the development of solution-focused therapy, de Shazer used what he called "formula tasks" (de Shazer, 1985) and later included specific kinds of questions to help move people from problem-talk to solution-talk, to discover and create solutions. With the tasks and questions, therapists aim for specific concrete behavioral information and instructions. The approach is manualized, in the sense that all questions and tasks are based on the assumption that the solutions to clients' problems already exist in their lives; thus, the question and tasks are constructed to achieve the desired outcome: solutions. In spite of the manualization, early on, solution-focused therapists believed in the value of cooperative relationships with clients. The most popular questions and tasks include:

### EXCEPTION QUESTIONS

Establishing exceptions to the problem is intended and believed to be an important part of orienting people toward solutions. Exception questions search for, identify, and confirm times in the past and the present when the problem was not as problematic. This is a way of deconstructing the problem without searching for causes and understandings of it and of constructing the solution. Another way to consider this process is to think of the therapist as helping to deconstruct an unsatisfactory reality, and when the problem is no longer a problem, the therapist constructs a satisfactory one.

### MIRACLE QUESTIONS

Miracle questions are "hypothetical solution questions" (Walter & Peller, 1992, pp. 75–85). They help people set goals by coaching them to imagine what their life would be like if the problem were solved. As with other solution-focused questions, the intent is to focus on the solution and defocus on the problem. The miracle question is typically worded,

> Suppose that one night there is a miracle and while you were sleeping, the problem that brought you to therapy is solved: How would you know? What would be different? What will you notice different the next morning that will tell you that there has been a miracle? What will your spouse [for instance] notice? (de Shazer, 1991, p. 113)

### SCALING QUESTIONS

Scaling questions are used by solution-focused therapists much as they are used by other therapists; that is, to help clients be more specific and concrete and be able to quantify and measure problems and successes. These questions can note how and where clients perceive themselves and give the therapist clues for questions that can reinforce improvement, as well as suggest the possibility of or nudge extenuation of the improvement. For instance, a therapist might ask questions such as: "On a scale from 1 to 10, with 1 being the lowest, where would you place your depression when you first came in? Where are you now? How did you move from a 1 to a 3? What would it take to move from a 3 to a 5?"

### COPING QUESTIONS

de Shazer and Berg also use what they call coping questions. These are questions to help clients who fail to see any exceptions or forward movement. Such a question might be, "I'm curious to know why you're doing as well as you are?" Again, striving to find any sort of identifiable difference.

### CREATIVE MISUNDERSTANDING

de Shazer suggests that therapist misunderstanding is more likely to occur than is understanding, so use misunderstanding to the therapist's advantage (de Shazer, 1991). For example, what might typically be thought of as resistance is viewed as information or a message that therapists have misunderstood the client or erred in their interpretation. This provides therapists with the opportunity to learn more from the client and get back on the solution track.

## Effectiveness of Approach

Like collaborative therapy and narrative therapy, the effectiveness of solution-focused therapy is mostly found in anecdotal and specific case reports. Solution-focused therapists have been prolific writers and conference presenters. Berg and Dolan (2001) offer a collection of success stories by clients and therapists on a variety of presenting problems. Miller, Hubble, and Duncan (1996) offer a review of relevant outcome research and reports of numerous applications of solution-focused therapy in action. Its usefulness has been demonstrated with specific populations and presenting problems, such as alcohol abuse (Berg & Miller, 1992), child abuse (Berg & Kelly, 2000), groups (Metcalf, 1998; Sharry, 1999), adolescents (Seagram, 1977; Selekman, 2002), older people (Dahl, Bathel, & Carreon, 2000), marital therapy (Gale & Newfield, 1992), schools (Osenton & Chang, 1999), and client-perspective. Qualitative research supporting its effectiveness is reported by Miller (1996) and Gingerich and Eisengart (2000).

## FUTURE DEVELOPMENTS AND DIRECTIONS OF POSTMODERN/ SOCIAL CONSTRUCTION THERAPIES

These postmodern social construction therapies represent an ideological shift that has slowly evolved over the last 2-plus decades and do not represent a trend that will fade. A frequently asked question, however, is what are the limitations of these therapies? Most therapists would respond that there are not across-the-board limitations in respect to particular client populations, presenting problems, or cultures. To the contrary, most of these therapists report that the postmodern/social construction approaches permit them, more so than do other approaches, to engage and work with a variety of populations and problems, even if they have no or limited experience with the same. This freedom and this competence seem to be associated with the collaborative aspect of doing something together and pooling resources, whether the therapist calls it that or not. They also seem to be associated with therapists' ability to be creative when not constrained by diagnosing pathology and being the curing expert. Perhaps therapists limit themselves when they fall into these essentialist modes.

The implications of this shift stretch far beyond family therapy, to other therapies and contexts outside the mental health discipline. Common among these therapies is their continuous evolution. The so-called originators and their colleagues and other thinkers and practitioners around the world continue to explore and extend the vast possibilities for therapy, education, research, organizational consultation, and medicine, as well as the complex social and cultural circumstances that challenge the earth we inhabit.

## NOTES

i. Other therapies that are sometimes placed under the postmodern umbrella are constructivist therapies. The distinction is that they draw from constructivist rather or more than from social constructionist theory. These therapies are not discussed in this chapter; for comprehensive reviews, see Neimeyer, 1993.

ii. Anderson does not suggest that "nothing exists outside linguistic constructions. Whatever exists simply exists, irrespective of linguistic practices" (Gergen, 2001). Rather, the focus is on the meaning of these existencs and the actions they inform, once we begin to describe, explain, and interpret them.

## REFERENCES

Ackerman, N. W. (1958). *The psychodynamics of family life*. New York: Basic Books.

Ackerman, N. W. (1966). *Treating the troubled family*. New York: Basic Books.

Addison, S. M., Sandberg, J. G., Corby, J., & Roblia. (2002). Alternative methodologies in research literature review: Links between clinical work and MFT effectiveness. *American Journal of FamilyTherapy, 30*(4), 3399–371.

Andersen, T. (1991). Client-therapist relationships: A collaborative study for informing therapy. *Journal of Systemic Therapies, 16*(2), 125–133.

Andersen, T. (1995). Reflecting processes; acts of informing and forming: You can borrow my eyes, but you must not take them away from me! In S. Friedman (Ed.), *The reflecting team in action: Collaborative practice in family therapy, Guilford family therapy series* (pp. 11–37). New York: Guilford.

Andersen, T. (1997). Researching client-therapist relationships: A collaborative study for informing therapy. *Journal of Systemic Therapies, 16*, 125–133.

Anderson, H. (1997a). *Conversation, language and possibilities: A postmodern approach to therapy*. New York: Basic Books.

Anderson, H. (1997b). What we can learn when we listen to and hear clients' stories. *Voices: The Art and Science of Psychotherapy, 33*(1), 4–8.

Anderson, H. (2000). Becoming a postmodern collaborative therapist: A clinical and theoretical journey, Part I. *Journal of the Texas Association for Marriage and Family Therapy, 5*(1), 5–12.

Anderson, H. (2001a). Postmodern collaborative and person-centered therapies: What would Carl Rogers say? *Journal of Family Therapy, 23*, 339–360.

Anderson, H. (2001b). Becoming a postmodern collaborative therapist: A clinical and theoretical journey, Part II. *Journal of the Texas Association for Marriage and Family Therapy, 6*(1), 4–22.

Anderson, H., & Creson, D. L. (2002). *Psychosocial services for children impacted by complex emergencies and the traumatic effects of war: Training manuals*. Richmond, VA: Christian Children's Fund.

Anderson, H., & Goolishian, H.A. (1988). Human systems as linguistic systems: Evolving ideas about the implications for theory and practice. *Family Process 27*:371-393.

Anderson, H., & Goolishian, H. A. (1992). The client is the expert. In S. McNamee & K. J. Gergen (Eds.), *The social construction of therapy*. Newbury Park, CA: Sage.

Anderson, H., & Goolishian, H. A. (1996). Systems consultation to agencies dealing with domestic violence. In L. Wynne, S. McDaniel, & Weber, T. (Eds.), *The family therapist as systems consultant.* (pp. 284-299). NewYork: Guilford.

Anderson, H., & Levin, S. (1998). *Collaborative conversations with children: Country clothes and city clothes. Narrative therapy with children*. NewYork: Guilford.

Bahktin, M. (1981). The Dialogic Imagination. In M. Holquist (Ed.) (C. Emerson & M. Holquist, Trans.) Austin: University of Texas Press.

Bateson, G. (1972). *Steps to an ecology of mind*. New York: Ballantine Books.

Beaudoin, M-N. (2001). Promoting respect and tolerance in schools. *Journal of Systemic Therapies, 20*(3), 10–24.

Berg, I. K., & Dolan, Y. M. (2001). *Tales of solutions: A collection of hope-inspiring stories*. New York: Norton.

Berg, I. K., & de Shazer, S. (1993). Making numbers talk: A solution-focused approach. In S. Friedman (Ed.), *The new language of change* (pp. 5–24). NewYork: Guilford Press.

Berg, I. K., & Kelly, S. (2000). *Building solutions in child protective services*. New York: Norton.

Berg, I. K., & Miller, S.D. (1992). *Working with the problem drinker: A solution-focused approach*. New York: Norton.

Bruner, J. (1986). *Actual minds, possible worlds*. Cambridge, MA: Harvard University Press.

Bruner, J. (1990). *Acts of meaning*. Cambridge, MA: Harvard University Press.

Chang, J. (1999). Collaborative therapies with young children. *Journal of Systemic Therapies, 18*(2), 44–64.

Dahl, R., Bathel, D., & Carreon, C. (2000). The use of solution-focused therapy with an elderly population. *Journal of Systemic Therapies, 19*(4), 45–55.

Derrida, J. (1978). *Writing and difference*. (A. Bass, Trans.). Chicago: University of Chicago Press.

de Shazer, S. (1982). *Patterns of brief family therapy:*

*An ecosystemic approach.* New York: Guilford.

de Shazer, S. (1985). *Keys to solutions in brief therapy.* New Y0rk: W. W. Norton.

de Shazer, S. (1991). *Putting Differences to Work.* New York: W. W. Norton.

de Shazer, S. (1993). Creating misunderstanding: There is no escape from language. In S. Gilligan & R. Price (Eds.), *Therapeutic conversations* (pp. 81–90). New York: Norton.

Epston, D., & White, M. (1992). *Experience, contradiction, narratie, and imagination: Selected papers of David Epston & Michael White, 1989–1991.* Adelaide, Australia: Dulwich Centre Publications.

Freedman, J., & Combs, G. (2000). Narrative therapy with couples. In F. M. Datillo & L. J. Bevilacqua (Eds.), *Comparative treatments for relationship dysfunction* (pp. 342–361). New York: Springer Publishing.

Freedman, J., & Combs. G. (1996). *Narrative therapy: The social construction of preferred realities.* New York: Norton.

Foucault, M. (1972). *The archeology of knowledge.* New York: HarperCollins.

Gale, J., & Newfield, N. (1992). A Conversation analysis of a marital therapy session. *Journal of Marital & Family Therapy, 18*(2), 153–165.

Geertz, C. (1983). *Local knowledge: Further essays in interpretive anthropology.* New York: Basic Books.

Geertz, C. (1973). *The interpretations of cultures.* New York: Basic Books.

Gehart-Brooks, D. R., & Lyle, R. R. (1999). Client and therapist perspectives of change in collaborative language systems: An interpretive ethnography. *Journal of Systemic Therapies, 18*(4), 58–77.

Gergen, K.J. (1982) *Toward transformation in social knowledge.* New York: Springer-Verlag.

Gergen, K. J. (1985). The social constructionist movement in modern psychology. *American Psychologist, 40,* 255–275.

Gergen, K. J. (1991b). *The saturated self.* New York: Basic Books.

Gergen, K. J. (1994). *Realities and relationships.* Cambridge, MA: Harvard University Press.

Gergen, K. J. (1999). *An invitation to social construction.* Newbury Park, CA: Sage.

Gergen, K. J. (2001). Psychological science in a postmodern context. *American Psychologist, 56*(10), 803–813.

Gingerich, W. J., & Eisengart, S. (2000). Soltionfocused brief therapy: A review of outcome research. *Family Process, 39*(4), 477–498.

Hoffman, L. (1981). *Foundations of family therapy.* New York: Basic Books.

Hoffman, L. (1998). Setting aside the model in family therapy. *Journal of Marital and Family Therapy, 24*(2), 145–156.

Hoffman, L. (2002). *Family therapy: An intimate history.* New York: Norton.

Iser, W. (1978). *The act of reading.* Baltimore, MD: Johns Hopkins University Press.

Kecskemeti, M., & Epston, E. (2001). Practices of teacher appreciation and the pooling of knowledges. *Journal of Systemic Therapies, 20*(3), 39–48.

Kvale, S. (1992). *Psychology and postmodernism.* London: Sage.

Levin, S., Raser, J., Niles, C., & Reese, A. (1986). Beyond family systems-toward problem systems: Some clinical implications. *Journal of Strategic and Systemic Therapies, 5,* 62–69.

Lipchik, E. (1993). Both/and solutions. In S. Friedman, (Ed.), *The new language of change: Constructive collaboration in psychotherapy.* New York: Guilford Press.

Lyotard, J-F. (1984). *The post-modern condition: A report on knowledge.* Minneapolis: University of Minnesota Press.

London, S., Ruiz, G., Gargollo, M. & Gargollo, M. C. (1998). Clients' Voices: A collection of clients' accounts. *Journal of Systemic Therapies, 17*(4), 61–71.

Madigan, S., & Epston, D. (1995). From "spychiatric gaze" to communities of concern: From professional monologue to dialogue. In S. Friedman (Ed.), *The reflecting team in action.* New York: Guilford.

Madison, W. (1999). Inviting new stories: Narrative ideas in family-centered services. *Journal of Systemic Therapies, 18*(3), 23–36.

MacGregor, R., Ritchie, A. M., Serrano, A. C., Schuster, F. P., McDanald, E. D., & Goolishian, H. A. (1964). *Multiple impact therapy with families.* New York: McGraw-Hill.

Metcalf, L. (1998). *Solution-focused group therapy.* New York: Free Press.

Meyerhoff, F. (1986). "Life not death in Venice": Its second life. In V. W. Turner & E. M. Bruner (Eds.). *The anthropology of experience* (pp. 261–286). Chicago: University of Chicago Press.

Miller, G., & De Shazer, S. (1998). Have you heard the latest rumor about . . . ? Solution-focused therapy as a rumor. *Family Process, 37*(3), 363–378.

Miller, S. D., Hubble, M. A., & Duncan, B. L. (Eds.). (1996). *Handbook of solution-focused therapy.* San Francisco: Jossey-Bass.

O'Hanlon, W. H., & Weiner-Davis, M. (1989). *In search of solutions: A new direction in psychotherapy*. New York: Guilford.

Osenton, T., & Chang, J. (1999). Solution-oriented classroom management: Application with young children. *Journal of Systemic Therapies, 18*(2), 65–76.

Penn, P. (2001). Chronic illness: Trauma, language, and writing: Breaking the silence. *Family Process, 40*(1), 33–52.

Penn, P. (1985) Feed-forward: Future questions, future maps. *Family Process, 24,* 299–310.

Penn, P., & Frankfurt, M. (1994). Creating a participant text: Writing, multiple voices, narrative multiplicity. *Family Process, 33,* 217–231.

Riessman, C. (1993). *Narrative analysis*. Thousand Oaks, CA: Sage Publications.

Rorty, R. (1979). *Philosophy and the mirror of nature*. Princeton, NJ: Princeton University Press.

Roth, S., & Epston, D. (1996). Consulting the problem about the problematic relationship: An exercise for experiencing a relationship with an externalized problem. In M. F. Hoyt (Ed.), *Constructive therapies, vol. 2* (pp. 148–162). New York: Guilford.

Schon, D. (1984). *The reflective practitioner: How professionals think in action*. New York: Basic Books.

Seagram, B. C. (1997). *The efficacy of solution-focused therapy with young offenders*. Unpublished doctoral dissertation, York University, Ontario, Canada.

Seikkula, J. (1993). The aim of therapy is to generarate dialogue: Bakhtin and Vygotsky in family session. *Human Systems: The Journal of Systemic Consultation & Management, 4,* 33–48.

Seikkula, J. (2002). Open dialogues with good and poor outcomes for psychotic crises: Examples from families with violence. *Journal of Marital & Family Therapy, 28*(3), 263–274.

Seikkula, J., Aaltonen, J., Alakare, B., Haarakangas, K., Keranen, J., & Sutela, M. (1995). Treating psychosis by means of open dialogue. In S. Friedman (Ed.), *The reflecting team in action: collaborative practice in family therapy* (pp. 62–80). New York: Guilford.

Selekman, M. D. (2002). *Solution-oriented brief family therapy with self-harming adolescents*. New York: Norton.

Shalif, Y., & Leibler, M. (2002). Working with people experiencing terrorist attacks in Israel: A narrative perspective. *Journal of Systemic Therapies, 21*(3), 60–70.

Sharry, J. J. (1999). Toward solution group work: Brief solution-focused ideas in group training. *Journal of Systemic Therapies, 18*(2), 77–91.

St. George, S. A. (1994). *Multiple formats in the collaborative application of the "As If" technique in the process of family therapy supervision*. Dissertation Abstracts International.

St. George, S. (1994). Using "As If" process in family therapy supervision. *The Family Journal: Counseling and Therapy for Couples and Families, 4*(4), 357–365.

St. George, S., & Wulff, D. (1999). Integrating the client's voice within case reports. *Journal of Systemic Therapies, 18*(2), 3–13.

Smith, C., & Nylund, D. (1997). *Narrative therapies with children and adolescents*. New York: Guilford.

Smith, J.A., Harre, R., & Langenhove, L. (1995). *Rethinking psychology*. London: Sage.

Swim, S., Helms, S., Plotkin, S., & Bettye (1998). Multiple voices: Stories of rebirth, heroines, new opportunities and identities. *Journal of Systemic Therapies, 17*(4), 61–71.

Swint, J. A. (1995). *Clients' experience of therapeutic change: A qualitative study*. Unpublished doctoral dissertation, Texas Women's University, Denton, TX.

Vygotsky, L. S. (1986). *Thought and language* (rev. ed.). (A. Kozulin, Trans.). Cambridge, MA: MIT Press. (Original work published 1934).

Walter, J. L., & Peller, J. E. (1992). *Becoming solution-focused in brief therapy*. New York: Bruner/Mazel.

Watzlawick, P., Beaven, J. H., & Jackson, D. D. (1967). *The pragmatics of human communication*. New York: Norton.

Watzlawick, P., & Weakland, J. (1977). *The interactional view: Studies at the mental research institute Palo Alto 1965–1974*. New York: Norton.

Weingarten, K. (1998). The small and ordinary: The daily practice of a postmodern narrative therapy. *Family Process, 37*(1), 3–15.

Weingarten, K. (2000). Using the Internet to build social support: Implications for well-being and hope. *Families, Systems & Health, 18*(2), 157–160.

White, M. (1995). *Re-authoring lives: interviews and essays*. Adelaide, Australia: Dulwich Centre Publications.

White, M., & Epston, E. (1990). *Narrative means to therapeutic ends*. New York: Norton.

Wittgenstein, L. (1953). *Philosophical investigations*. (G. E. M. Anscombe, Trans.). New York: Macmillan.

Zimmerman, J. (2001). The discourse of our lives. *Journal of Systemic Therapies, 20*(3), 1–9.

Zimmerman, J., & Dickerson, V. (1996). *If problems talked: Adventures in narrative therapy*. New York: Guilford Press.

CHAPTER 8

# Cognitive-Behavioral Couple and Family Therapy

FRANK M. DATTILIO, PhD, ABPP

*Harvard Medical School*

NORMAN B. EPSTEIN, PhD

*University of Maryland, College Park*

## HISTORICAL DEVELOPMENT OF COGNITIVE-BEHAVIOR THERAPY WITH COUPLES AND FAMILIES

Even though cognitive-behavior therapies (CBT) were initially developed to treat depression and anxiety, their application to problems with intimate relationships began over 40 years ago in writings by Albert Ellis (Ellis & Harper, 1961). Ellis and his colleagues have emphasized the important role that cognition plays in marital problems, based on the premise that dysfunction occurs when partners maintain unrealistic beliefs about their relationship and make extreme negative evaluations about the sources of their dissatisfaction (Ellis, 1977; Ellis, Sichel, Yeager, DiMattia, & DiGiuseppe, 1989). Also in the 1960s and early 1970s, behavior therapists were utilizing principles of learning theory to address individual problematic behaviors of both adults and children. Many of the behavioral principles and techniques that were used in the treatment of individuals were soon applied to distressed couples and families. For example, Stuart (1969), Liberman (1970), and Weiss, Hops, and Patterson (1973) described the use of social exchange theory and operant learning strategies to facilitate more satisfying interaction in distressed couples. Similarly, Patterson (1971; Patterson, McNeal, Hawkins, & Phelps, 1967) applied operant conditioning and contingency contracting procedures to develop parents' abilities to control the behavior of aggressive children. Later, behaviorally oriented therapists added communication and problem-solving skills training components to their interventions with couples and families (e.g., Falloon, Boyd, & McGill, 1984; Jacobson & Margolin, 1979; Stuart,

1980). Research studies confirmed the premise of social exchange theory (Thibaut & Kelley, 1959), indicating that members of distressed couples exchange more displeasing and less pleasing behavior than do members of nondistressed relationships, and that behavioral interventions (e.g., behavioral contracts, communication training) designed to shift the balance toward more positive interactions increase partners' satisfaction (see Epstein & Baucom, 2002, for a review). Findings by researchers such as Christensen (1988) and Gottman (1994) have identified the importance of reducing distressing avoidant behaviors, in addition to aggressive acts.

Marital and family therapists recognized the importance of intervening with cognitive factors, as well as with behavioral interaction patterns, long before most major theories of family therapy came into existence (Dicks, 1953; Haley & Hoffman, 1968; Satir, 1967). However, it was not until the late 1970s that cognitions were introduced as an auxiliary component of treatment within a behavioral paradigm (Margolin & Weiss, 1978). During the 1980s, cognitive factors became an increasing focus in the couples research and therapy literature, and cognitions were addressed in a more direct and systematic way than in other theoretical approaches to family therapy (e.g., Baucom, 1987; Baucom, Epstein, Sayers, & Sher, 1989; Beck, 1988; Dattilio, 1989; Epstein, 1982; Epstein & Eidelson, 1981; Fincham, Beach, & Nelson, 1987; Weiss, 1984). Established cognitive assessment and intervention methods from individual therapy were adapted for use in couple therapy, to identify and modify distorted or inappropriate perceptions, inferences, and beliefs that partners experience about each other (Baucom & Epstein, 1990; Dattilio & Padesky, 1990; Epstein, 1992; Epstein & Baucom, 1989). As in individual therapy, cognitive-behavioral marital interventions were designed to enhance partners' skills for evaluating and modifying their own problematic cognitions, as well as skills for communicating and solving problems constructively (Baucom & Epstein, 1990; Epstein & Baucom, 2002; Rathus & Sanderson, 1999).

Similarly, behavioral approaches to family therapy were broadened to include members' cognitions about one another. Ellis (1982) was also one of the pioneers in introducing a cognitive approach to family therapy, with his rational-emotive approach, whereas Bedrosian (1983) wrote about the application of Beck's model of cognitive therapy (Beck, Rush, Shaw, & Emery, 1979) to understanding and treating dysfunctional family dynamics. During the 1980s and 1990s, the literature on cognitive-behavioral family therapy (CBFT) expanded rapidly (Alexander, 1988; Dattilio, 1993, 1994, 1997, 2001; Epstein & Schlesinger, 1996; Epstein, Schlesinger, & Dryden, 1988; Falloon, Boyd, & McGill, 1984; Huber & Baruth, 1989; Robin & Foster, 1989; Schwebel & Fine, 1994; Teichman, 1981, 1992), and it currently is included as a major form of treatment in family therapy textbooks (e.g., Goldenberg & Goldenberg, 2000; Nichols & Schwartz, 2001).

Substantial empirical evidence has accumulated from treatment outcome studies indicating the effectiveness of cognitive-behavioral couple therapy (CBCT), although most studies have focused on primarily behavioral interventions and only a handful examined the impact of cognitive restructuring procedures (see Baucom, Shoham, Mueser, Daiuto, & Stickle, 1998, for a review). There has been less research on generic CBFT, with the predominant literature focusing on applications with individual disorders such as schizophrenia and child conduct disorders. Outcome studies have demonstrated the effectiveness of behaviorally oriented family interventions (psychoeducation and training in communication and problem-solving skills) with such disorders (Baucom et al., 1998).

The growing adoption of CB methods by couple and family therapists appears to be due to several factors: (a) research evidence of their efficacy; (b) their appeal to clients, who value the proactive approach to solving problems and building skills that the family can use to cope with future difficulties; and (c) their emphasis on a collaborative relationship between therapist and clients. Recent enhancements of CBT (Epstein & Baucom, 2002) have broadened the contextual factors that are taken into account, such as aspects of the couple's or the family's physical and interpersonal environment (e.g., extended family, the workplace, neighborhood violence, national economic conditions). CBCT and CBFT have become mainstream theoretical approaches, but they continue to evolve through the creative efforts of their practitioners.

## PHILOSOPHY AND MAJOR THEORETICAL CONSTRUCTS

Conceptions of the cognitive processes that can influence the quality of close relationships have been informed by basic theory and research on human information processing. Piaget's (1960) observations about the cognitive processes that children use to learn about the world had a major impact on our understanding of cognitive processes in adults as well. George Kelly (1955) proposed that individuals develop "personal constructs" or basic concepts that they use to categorize life experiences (e.g., identifying people along dimensions such as friendly–unfriendly and assertive–meek), and these constructs help them interpret their world and anticipate future events. CB therapists have incorporated the models of Piaget and Kelly in their conceptions of cognitive processes involved in family members' development of schemas about each other and intimate relationships. More recently, information-processing models of cognition have been applied to conceptions of varied clinical disorders such as depression and anxiety (Hamilton, 1980; Ingram & Kendall, 1986), as well as interpersonal relationship problems (e.g., Fincham, Garnier, Gano-Phillips, & Osborne, 1995). For example, cognitive psychology research has shed light on processes through which individuals' existing schemas (relatively stable concepts about objects and events) can bias their perceptions of others' present actions. Cognitive psychology literature has contributed to CB therapists' awareness of potential sources of distortion in their clients' cognitions about events in their family relationships.

## ADLERIAN THEORY

The early theoretical work of Alfred Adler provided much of the basis for cognitive-behavioral therapy in general, and CBCT and CBFT in specific. Adler applied his theory of individual psychology (Adler, 1964) to understanding marital relationships. Adler's view of individual personality and behavior was holistic and systemic, looking at individual functioning within the larger social context in which it occurs. Many believe that it is unfortunate that Adler did not label his theory "system psychology" while the term was still available (Nicoll, 1989). Adler (1978) theorized that all people have a need to develop a close intimate relationship with at least one individual, for their own benefit, as well as ultimately for the benefit of the community, society, and humankind. Adler believed that the formation of marriages and families provides connections for society between the past and the future. He suggested that success in marriage is a task requiring attitudes in both spouses of equality, cooperation, and mutual responsibility, as well as skills for communication and problem solving in a cooperative manner. According to Adler, individuals commonly enter relationships with unrealistic beliefs based on societal myths (e.g., need to be in control), and these beliefs interfere with successful relationships. In therapy Adler focused on the purposeful nature of each family member's behavior and the consequences their actions have on other members. Dysfunctional interaction involves each person trying to obtain or maintain a more advantageous position over the other(s). Adler focused on shifting skewed interaction patterns that interfered with a couple's ability to develop an egalitarian relationship.

The role of an Adlerian therapist is to teach individuals and families how to function more constructively in life. CB therapists take this role a step further and collaborate with clients to facilitate change. The therapist strives to gain insight into the purposes that the presenting problem behavior has served for all family members. The therapist identifies constructive or dysfunctional attitudes or beliefs that each family member holds about the relationship and then gives the family feedback about the significant themes that seem to contribute to the family tension. Next, the therapist coaches the family in alternative ways for dealing with conflict, which modify the family's interaction patterns. Homework assignments between sessions facilitate lasting change. Although CB therapists have given insufficient credit to Adler's work, it clearly provided the groundwork on which much of cognitive-behavior therapy with couples and families is based.

## Principles of Social Learning Theory and Social Exchange Theory

CBCT and CBFT have a strong foundation in theory and research on the processes through which behavioral, cognitive, and emotional responses are learned. Work on classical conditioning by Pavlov (1927) and Watson (1925),

followed by Wolpe's (1958) application of classical conditioning principles to the treatment of phobias (assumed to be fear responses conditioned to objectively neutral stimuli) through systematic desensitization demonstrated the relevance of learning processes in human problems. Skinner's (1953) work on operant conditioning demonstrated how individuals' responses are also controlled by their consequences (punishment, reinforcement, and extinction). Operant conditioning principles have been applied in behavioral couple and family therapy when parents are trained to control their children's actions by systematically varying the consequences (e.g., Forehand & McMahon, 1981; Patterson, 1971; Webster-Stratton & Herbert, 1994) and when members of a couple are guided in reinforcing responses that they desire in each other (e.g., Jacobson & Margolin, 1979; Liberman, 1970; Stuart, 1969). Even when the explicit goal of parent training has been to modify a child's behavior, the interventions develop more constructive actions on the parents' part, so that they involve the entire family and have a systemic quality. Similarly, contingency contracting used by behavioral marital therapists (BMT) (Jacobson & Margolin, 1979; Liberman, 1970; Stuart, 1969) involves the mutual exchange of positive behavior and thus modifies the dyadic pattern in a couple's relationship.

Social learning theory (Bandura, 1977; Bandura & Walters, 1963; Rotter, 1954) integrates principles from social, developmental, and cognitive psychology, along with principles of learning theory derived from experimental psychology. In addition to classical and operant conditioning, social learning theory emphasizes the efficiency of observational learning, in which an individual learns how to perform both simple and complex responses by observing another person modeling the responses. An individual may not imitate a modeled behavior unless he or she anticipates receiving reinforcement for doing so or believes it is appropriate to behave in that manner. Social learning theorists focus on ways in which children learn interpersonal behavior patterns through their exposure to family-of-origin dynamics. They also propose that human learning is mediated by cognitive processes, such as expectancies concerning the probability that one's actions will be followed by particular consequences (reinforcement or punishment).

Social exchange theory (Thibaut & Kelley, 1959) posits that individuals' satisfaction in close relationships depends on the ratio of positive to negative behaviors they receive from their significant others. Members of a relationship tend to reciprocate levels of positive and negative behavior; for example, if one member of a couple acts negatively toward the other, the other person is likely to respond in kind. Sometimes people reciprocate negativity or positivity immediately (e.g., thanking a family member for doing a favor for them), whereas sometimes reciprocity is delayed (e.g., holding a grudge about the way one's partner behaved and retaliating later). Research on couple relationships (see Baucom & Epstein, 1990, and Epstein & Baucom, 2002, for reviews) has supported these aspects of social exchange theory, and CB therapists have used interventions such as behavioral contracts and communication training to maximize partners' positive exchanges and minimize negative ones.

*Systems Theory*

CB therapists often focus on specific instances of linear relations, such as an association between an individual's relationship standards (e.g., "Partners should spend most of their leisure time together, rather than pursuing individual interests") and his or her response to a partner's actions ("I'm furious that you made

plans with your friends instead of me!"). Nevertheless, current CB models address the interrelatedness and mutual influences among parts of a family. Circular causal aspects of recurring behavioral patterns among family members, which include all of the members' cognitions, emotional responses, and behavior, are of central concern (Epstein & Baucom, 2002). Understanding a couple's or a family's functioning involves attending to multiple layers of the relationship system, including characteristics of each individual (such as personality characteristics, motives, psychopathology, and unresolved issues from his or her family of origin), interaction patterns that the couple or the family has developed (e.g., mutual attack, demand–withdrawal, mutual avoidance), and aspects of the couple's or the family's interpersonal and physical environment (e.g., extended family, jobs) that influence the relationship(s). Thus, a systems perspective on family functioning has become an integral part of CB theory and therapy. When devising interventions, therapists must anticipate their potential impact on all members of the family. In addition, therapists must consider potential barriers to change that are based on characteristics of the individuals (e.g., depression), the established relationship patterns (e.g., escalating arguments that interfere with effective problem solving), and factors in the environment (e.g., intrusive in-laws) (Epstein & Baucom, 2002).

ETIOLOGY OF CLINICAL PROBLEMS

Within a CB model, etiological factors in the development of clinical problems commonly include aspects of the family members' cognitions, emotions, and behavioral responses (Baucom & Epstein, 1990; Dattilio, 1998; Epstein & Baucom, 2002). The following are major components of these factors.

*Automatic Thoughts, Underlying
Schemas, and Cognitive Distortions*

Baucom, Epstein, Sayers, and Sher (1989) developed a typology of cognitions that have been implicated in relationship distress. Although each type is a normal form of human cognition, each is susceptible to being distorted or extreme (Baucom & Epstein, 1990; Epstein & Baucom, 2002). These include (a) selective attention, an individual's tendency to notice particular aspects of the events occurring in his or her relationship and to overlook others; (b) attributions, inferences about the factors that have influenced one's own and the partner's actions (e.g., concluding that a partner failed to respond to a question because he or she wants to control the relationship); (c) expectancies, predictions about the likelihood that particular events will occur in the relationship (e.g., that expressing feelings to one's partner will result in the partner being verbally abusive; (d) assumptions, beliefs about the natural characteristics of people and relationships (e.g., a wife's generalized assumption that men do not have needs for emotional attachment); and (e) standards, beliefs about the characteristics that people and relationships "should" have (e.g., that partners should have virtually no boundaries between them, sharing all of their thoughts and emotions with each other). Because there typically is so much information available in any interpersonal situation, some degree of selective attention is inevitable, but the potential for family members to form biased perceptions of each other must be examined. Inferences involved in attributions and expectancies are also normal aspects of human information processing involved in understanding other people's behavior and making predictions about others' future behavior. However, errors in these inferences can have negative effects on family relationships, especially when an individual attributes another's actions to negative characteristics (e.g., malicious intent) or misjudges how others will react to his or her own actions. Assumptions commonly are adaptive when they are realistic representations of people and relationships, and many standards that individuals hold, such as moral standards about avoiding abuse of others, contribute to the quality of family relationships. Nevertheless, inaccurate or extreme assumptions and standards can lead individuals to interact inappropriately with others, as when a parent holds a standard that children's and adolescents' opinions and feelings are not to be taken into account as long as they live in the parents' home.

Beck and his associates (e.g., A. T. Beck, Rush, Shaw, & Emery, 1979; J. Beck, 1995) refer to moment-to-moment stream of consciousness ideas, beliefs, or images as automatic thoughts; for example, "My husband left his clothes on the floor again. He doesn't care about my feelings" or "My parents are saying 'no' again because they just like giving me a hard time." CB therapists have noted how individuals commonly accept automatic thoughts at face value, as opposed to examining their validity. Although all five of the types of cognition identified by Baucom et al. (1989) can be reflected in an individual's automatic thoughts, CB therapists have emphasized the moment-to-moment selective perceptions and the inferences involved in attributions and expectancies as the most likely to be within a person's awareness. Assumptions and standards are thought to be broader underlying aspects of an individual's worldview, considered to be schemas in Beck's cognitive model (A. T. Beck, Rush, Shaw, & Emery, 1979; J. S. Beck, 1995; Leahy, 1996).

The cognitive model proposes that the content of an individual's perceptions and inferences is shaped by relatively stable underlying schemas, or cognitive structures such as the personal constructs described by Kelly (1955). Schemas include basic beliefs about the nature of human beings and their relationships, and they are assumed to be relatively stable and may become inflexible. Many schemas about relationships and the nature of couples and family interaction are learned early in life from primary sources such as family of origin, cultural traditions and mores, the mass media, and early dating and other relationship experiences. The "models" of self in relation to other that have been described by attachment theorists appear to be forms of schemas that affect individuals' automatic thoughts and emotional responses to significant others (Johnson & Denton, 2002). In addition to the schemas that partners or family members bring to a relationship, each member develops schemas specific to the current relationship.

As a result of years of interaction among family members, the individuals often develop jointly held beliefs that constitute the family schema (Dattilio, 1994). To the extent that the family schema involves cognitive distortions, it may result in dysfunctional interaction. An example of this might be family members who jointly view another member as being unreliable. Consequently, they unknowingly may be enabling unreliable behavior, which facilitates its continuation.

Schemas about relationships are often not articulated clearly in an individual's mind but do exist as vague concepts of what is or should be (Beck, 1988; Epstein & Baucom, 2002). Those that have been previously developed influence how an individual subsequently processes information in new situations, for example, influencing what the person selectively perceives, the inferences he or she makes about causes of others' behavior, and whether the person is pleased or displeased with the family relationships. Existing schemas may be difficult to modify, but repeated new experiences with significant others have the potential to change them (Epstein & Baucom, 2002; Johnson & Denton, 2002).

In addition to automatic thoughts and schemas, Beck et al. (1979) identified cognitive distortions or information-processing errors that contribute to cognitions becoming sources of distress and conflict in individuals' lives. In terms of Baucom et al.'s (1989) typology, they result in distorted or inappropriate perceptions, attributions, expectancies, assumptions, and standards. Exhibit 1 includes descriptions of these cognitive distortions, with examples of how they may occur in family interactions. (See Exhibit 1, after the reference section in this chapter.)

There has been much more research on attributions and standards than on the other forms of cognition in Baucom et al.'s (1989) typology (see Epstein & Baucom, 2002, for a review of findings). A sizable amount of research on couples' attributions has indicated that members of distressed couples are more likely than are members of nondistressed couples to attribute their partner's negative behavior to global, stable traits; negative intent; selfish motivation; and a lack of love (see Bradbury & Fincham, 1990, and Epstein & Baucom, 2002, for reviews). In addition, members of distressed relationships are less likely to attribute positive partner behaviors to global, stable causes. These biased inferences can contribute to family members' pessimism about improvement in their relationships and to negative communication and lack of problem solving. One area of research on schemas has focused on potentially unrealistic beliefs that individuals may hold about marriage (Epstein & Eidelson, 1981). Baucom, Epstein, Rankin, and Burnett (1996) assessed one major type of relationship beliefs, the relationship standards that individuals hold about boundaries between partners, distribution of control/power, and the degree of investment one should have in the relationship. They found that individuals who were less satisfied with the manner in which their standards were met in their couple relationships were more distressed in the relationships and communicated more negatively with their partners.

*Deficits in Communication and Problem-Solving Skills*

There is considerable empirical evidence that members of distressed couples and families exhibit a variety of negative and ineffective patterns of communication involving their expression of thoughts and emotions, listening skills, and problem-solving skills (Epstein & Baucom, 2002; Walsh, 1998). Expression of thoughts and emotions involves self-awareness, appropriate vocabulary to describe one's experiences, freedom from inhibiting factors such as fear of rejection by the listener, and a degree of self-control (e.g., not succumbing to an urge to retaliate against a person who upset you). Effective problem solving involves the abilities to define the characteristics of a problem clearly, generate alternative potential solutions, collaborate with other family members in evaluating advantages and disadvantages of each solution, reach consensus about the best solution, and devise a specific plan to implement the solution. Thus, effective couple or family problem solving requires both good skills and goodwill.

Deficits in communication and problem solving may develop as a result of various processes, such as maladaptive patterns of learning during socialization in the family of origin, deficits in cognitive functioning, forms of psychopathology such as depression, and past traumatic experiences in relationships that have left an individual vulnerable to disruptive cognitive, emotional, and behavior responses (e.g., rage, panic) during interactions with significant others. Research has indicated that individuals who communicate negatively in their couple relationships may exhibit constructive communication skills in relatively neutral outside relationships, suggesting that chronic issues in the intimate relationship are interfering with positive communication (Baucom & Epstein, 1990).

*Excesses of Negative Behavior and Deficits in Positive Behavior Between Partners or Among Family Members*

Negative and ineffective communication and problem-solving skills are not the only forms of problematic behavioral interaction in distressed couples and families. Member of close relationships commonly direct a variety of types of "noncommunication behavior" toward each other (Baucom & Epstein, 1990; Epstein & Baucom, 2002). These are positive and negative acts that are instrumental (perform a task to achieve a goal, such as completing household chores) or are intended to affect the other person's feelings (for example, giving him or her a gift). Although there typically are implicit messages conveyed by noncommunication behavior, it does not involve explicit expression of thoughts and emotions. Research has demonstrated that members of distressed relationships direct more negative acts and fewer positive ones toward each other than do members of nondistressed relationships (Epstein & Baucom, 2002). Furthermore, members of distressed couples are more likely to reciprocate negative behaviors, resulting in an escalation of conflict and distress. Consequently, a basic premise of CBT is that the frequency of negative behavior must be reduced and the frequency of positive acts must be increased. Because negative behaviors tend to have a greater impact on relationship satisfaction than do positive behaviors (Gottman, 1994; Weiss & Heyman, 1997), they have received more attention from therapists. However, an absence of negatives leaves many clients less distressed but longing for more rewarding relationships (Epstein & Baucom, 2002).

Although couple and family theorists and researchers have focused on microlevel positive and negative acts, Epstein and Baucom (2002) propose that in many instances an individual's relationship satisfaction is based on more macrolevel behavioral patterns that have significant meaning for him or her. Some core macrolevel patterns involve boundaries between and around a couple or a family (e.g., less or more sharing of communication, activities, and time), distribution of power/control (e.g., across situations and time, how the parties attempt to influence each other, and how decisions are made), and the level of investment of time and energy that each person puts into the relationship. As we noted earlier, individuals' relationship standards concerning these dimensions are associated with relationship satisfaction and communication, and the couple and family therapy literature suggests that these behavior patterns are core aspects of family interaction (Epstein & Baucom, 2002; Walsh, 1998).

Epstein and Baucom (2002) have also described negative interaction patterns between members of couples that commonly interfere with the partners' fulfillment of their needs within the relationship. These patterns include mutual (reciprocal) attack, demand–withdrawal (one person pursues and the other withdraws), and mutual avoidance and withdrawal. Epstein and Baucom propose that therapists often must help clients reduce these patterns before they will be able to work together collaboratively as a couple to resolve issues such as different preferences for togetherness versus autonomy.

## Deficits and Excesses in Experiencing and Expressing Emotions

Although the title "CB" does not refer to family members' emotions, assessment and modification of problematic affective responses are core components of this therapeutic approach. Epstein and Baucom (2002) provide a detailed description of problems that involve either deficits or excesses in individuals' experiencing of emotions within the context of their intimate relationships, as well as in their expression of those feelings to their significant others. The following is a brief summary of those emotional factors in couple and family problems.

Some individuals pay little attention to their emotional states, and this can result in their feelings being overlooked in their close relationships. Alternatively, in some cases an individual who fails to monitor his or her emotions may suddenly express them in a destructive way, such as abusive behavior toward others. The reasons vary as to why an individual might be unaware of emotions but may include learning in the family of origin that expressing feelings is inappropriate or dangerous, the individual's current fear that expressing even mild emotion will lead to losing control of one's equilibrium (perhaps associated with post-traumatic stress disorder or another type of anxiety disorder), or holding an expectancy that one's family members simply do not care how one feels (Epstein & Baucom, 2002).

In contrast, some individuals have difficulty regulating their emotions, and they experience strong levels of emotion in response to even relatively minor life events. Unregulated experience of emotions such as anxiety, anger, and sadness can decrease the individual's satisfaction with couple and family relationships, and it can contribute to the person interacting with family members in ways that increase conflict. Factors contributing to unregulated emotional experience may include past personal trauma (e.g., abuse, abandonment), growing up in a family in which others failed to regulate emotional expression, and forms of psychopathology such as borderline personality disorder (Linehan, 1993).

In addition to the degree to which an individual experiences emotions, the degree and manner in which he or she expresses emotions to significant others can affect the quality of couple and family relationships. Whereas some individuals inhibit their expression, some others express feelings in an uncensored manner. Possible factors in unregulated emotional expression include past experiences in which strong emotional displays were the only means of effectively gaining the attention of significant others, temporary relief from intense emotional tension, and limited skills for self-soothing.

The inhibited individual's family members may find it convenient not having to deal with the person's feelings, but in other cases family members are frustrated by the lack of communication, and they may pursue the person, resulting in a circular demand–withdraw pattern. In contrast, family members who receive unregulated emotional expression commonly find it distressing and either respond aggressively or withdraw from the individual. If an individual's unbridled emotional expression is intended to engage others to meet his or her needs, the pattern actually often backfires (Epstein & Baucom, 2002; Johnson & Denton, 2002).

*Difficulty Adapting to Life Demands Involving the Individuals, Relationship Issues, or the Environment*

Epstein and Baucom's (2002) enhanced CB approach integrates aspects of family stress and coping theory (e.g., McCubbin & McCubbin, 1989) with traditional CB principles. A couple or a family is faced with a variety of demands to which it must adapt, and the quality of its coping efforts is likely to affect the satisfaction and stability of its relationships. Demands on the couple or the family may derive from three major sources: (a) characteristics of the individual members (e.g., a family has to cope with a member's clinical depression), (b) relationship dynamics (e.g., members of a couple have to resolve or adapt to differences in the two partners' needs, as when one is achievement- and career-oriented and the other focuses on togetherness and intimacy), and (c) characteristics of the interpersonal environment (e.g., needy relatives, a demanding boss) and physical environment (e.g., neighborhood violence that threatens the well-being of one's children). CB therapists assess the number, severity, and cumulative impact of various demands that a couple or a family is experiencing, as well as its available resources and skills for coping with those demands. Consistent with a stress and coping model, the risk of couple or family dysfunction increases with the degree of demands and deficits in resources. Given that the family members' perceptions of demands and their ability to cope also play a prominent role in the stress and coping model, CB therapists skills in assessing and modifying distorted or inappropriate cognition can be very helpful in improving families' coping.

## METHODS OF CLINICAL ASSESSMENT

Individual and joint interviews with the members of a couple or a family, self-report questionnaires, and the therapist's behavioral observation of family interactions are the three main modes of clinical assessment (Epstein & Baucom, 2002; Snyder, Cavell, Heffer, & Mangrum, 1995). Consistent with the concepts that we described previously, the goals of assessment are to (a) identify strengths and problematic characteristics of the individuals, the couple or the family, and the environment; (b) place current individual and family functioning in the context of its developmental stages and changes; and (c) identify cognitive, affective, and behavioral aspects of family interaction that could be targeted for intervention. Our description of assessment methods necessarily is brief in this chapter, but readers can find extensive coverage of procedures in sources such as Baucom and Epstein (1990), Epstein and Baucom (2002), and Rathus and Sanderson (1999).

## Initial Joint Interview(s)

One or more joint interviews with the couple or the family are an important source of information about past and current functioning. Not only are they a source of information about the members' memories and opinions concerning characteristics and events in their family, interviews also give the therapist an opportunity to observe the family interactions firsthand. Although a family may alter its usual behavior in front of an outsider who is a stranger, even during the first interview it is common for members to exhibit some aspects of their typical pattern, expecially when the therapist engages them in describing issues that have brought them to therapy. CB therapists approach assessment in an empirical manner, using initial impressions to form hypotheses that must be tested by gathering additional information in subsequent sessions.

CB therapists generally begin the assessment process by convening as many of the family members who are likely to be involved with the presenting concerns as possible. Rather than insisting on everyone's attendance in order to begin therapy, the therapist focuses on engaging those members who are motivated to attend and then working with them in engaging absent members. Similar to therapists with other systems-oriented models, CB therapists assume that difficulties that a family presents in ensuring all members' attendance may be a sample of a broader problematic family process. Thus, from the initial

contacts the therapist is observing the family process and forming hypotheses about patterns that may be contributing to the problems that brought the family to therapy.

During the initial joint interview, the therapist asks the family as a group about its reasons for seeking assistance at this time, about each person's perspective on those concerns, and about any changes that each member thinks would make family life more satisfying. The therapist also asks about the family's history (e.g., how and when the couple met, what initially attracted the partners to each other, when they married (if relevant), when any children were born, and any events that they believe have influenced them as a family over the years. Applying a stress and coping model to assessment, the therapist systematically explores demands that the couple or the family has experienced, based on characteristics of individual members (e.g., a spouse's residual effects from childhood abuse), relationship dynamics (e.g., unresolved differences in partners' desires for intimacy and autonomy), and their environment (e.g., heavy job demands on a parent's/spouse's time and energy). The therapist also inquires about resources that the family has had available to cope with those demands and any factors that influenced its use of the resources; for example, a belief in self-sufficiency that blocks some people from seeking or accepting help from outsiders (Epstein & Baucom, 2002). Throughout the interview, the therapist gathers information about family members' cognitions, emotional responses, and behavior toward each other. For example, if a husband becomes withdrawn after his wife criticizes his parenting, the therapist may draw this to his attention and ask what thoughts and emotions he just felt after hearing his wife's comments. He might reveal automatic thoughts such as, "She doesn't respect me. This is hopeless," and feelings of both anger and deep sadness.

## Questionnaires

CB therapists commonly use standardized questionnaires to gather information on family members' views of themselves and their relationships. Often therapists ask family members to complete questionnaires before the joint and individual interviews, so that the therapist can ask for additional information about questionnaire responses during the interviews. As with interviews, individuals' reports on questionnaires are subject to biases, such as blaming others for family problems and presenting oneself in a socially desirable way (Snyder et al., 1995). Nevertheless, judicious use of questionnaires can be an efficient means of quickly surveying family members' perceptions of a wide range of issues that might otherwise be overlooked during interviews. Then, issues that are noted on questionnaires can be explored in greater depth through subsequent interviews and behavioral observation. The following are some representative questionnaires that may be useful for assessment within a CB model, even though many were not developed specifically from that perspective. Resources for reviews of a variety of other relevant measures include Touliatos, Perlmutter, and Straus (1990); Jacob and Tennenbaum (1988); Grotevant and Carlson (1989); and Fredman and Sherman (1987).

A variety of measures has been developed to provide an overview of key areas of couple and family functioning, such as overall satisfaction, cohesion, communication quality, decision making, values, and level of conflict. Examples include the Dyadic Adjustment Scale (Spanier, 1976), the Marital Satisfaction Inventory—Revised (Snyder & Aikman, 1999), the Family Environment Scale (Moos & Moos, 1981), the Family Assessment Measure—III (Skinner, Steinhauer, & Santa-Barbara, 1983), and the Self-Report Family Inventory (Beavers, Hampson, & Hulgus, 1985). Because the items on such scales do not provide specific information about each family member's cognitions, emotions, and behavioral responses regarding a relationship problem, the therapist must inquire about these during interviews. For example, if scores on a questionnaire indicate limited cohesion among family members, a CB therapist may ask the members about (a) their personal standards for types and degrees of cohesive behavior, (b) specific instances of behavior among them that did or did not feel cohesive, and (c) positive or negative emotional responses they experience concerning those actions. Thus, questionnaires can be helpful to a CB therapist in identifying areas of strength and concern, but a more fine-grained analysis is needed to understand specific types of positive and negative interaction and the factors affecting them.

An advantage of general couple and family functioning inventories is that their subscales provide a profile (through formally calculated norms or informal perusal by the assessor) of areas of strength and problems within a family. Also, some family members are likely to report concerns on questionnaires that they would not mention during joint family interviews. As with interviews, this raises important ethical issues about setting clear guidelines regarding confidentiality of information that individual family members share with the therapist. On the other hand, many inventories are long, and therapists must decide whether they can gather comparable information more efficiently through interviews.

A number of questionnaires developed specifically from a CB perspective can also be helpful in assessment of a couple or a family. For example, Eidelson and Epstein's (1982) Relationship Belief Inventory assesses five common unrealistic beliefs that have been found to be associated with relationship distress and communication problems in couples:

(a) disagreement is destructive, (b) partners should be able to mind-read each other's thoughts and feelings, (c) partners cannot change their relationship, (d) innate gender differences influence relationship problems, and (e) one should be a perfect sexual partner. Baucom, Epstein, Rankin, and Burnett's (1996) Inventory of Specific Relationship Standards assesses the degrees to which individuals hold standards for their couple relationships regarding boundaries (degree of autonomy versus sharing), distribution and exercise of power/control, and investment of time and energy into the relationship. Roehling and Robin's (1986) Family Beliefs Inventory assesses unrealistic beliefs that adolescents and their parents may hold concerning each other. The parents' form assesses beliefs that (a) if adolescents are given too much freedom, they will behave in ways that will ruin their future; (b) parents deserve absolute obedience from their children; (c) adolescents' behavior should be perfect; (d) adolescents intentionally behave in malicious ways toward their parents; (e) parents are blameworthy for problems in their children's behavior; and (f) parents must gain the approval of their children for their child-rearing methods. In turn, the adolescents' form includes subscales assessing the beliefs that (a) parents' rules and demands will ruin the adolescent's life; (b) parents' rules are unfair; (c) adolescents should have as much autonomy as they desire; and (d) parents should have to earn their children's approval for their child-rearing methods. In addition, a number of instruments have been developed to assess partners' attributions concerning causes of events in their couple relationships (e.g., Baucom, Epstein, Daiuto, Carels, Rankin, & Burnett, 1996; Pretzer, Epstein, & Fleming, 1991).

There are few self-report questionnaires that provide information about specific types of behavior that partners perceive occurring in their relationship. Christensen's (1988) Communication Patterns Questionnaire is most relevant for a systemic view of couple interaction, because the items ask about the occurrence of dyadic patterns regarding areas of conflict, including mutual attack, demand–withdrawal, and mutual avoidance. In addition, the revised Conflict Tactics Scale (CTS2; Straus, Hamby, Boney-McCoy, & Sugarman, 1996) provides information about a range of verbal and nonverbal forms of abusive behavior in couple relationships that many individuals choose not to reveal during interviews. We typically administer the CTS2 in conjunction with our interview with each partner and discuss any problematic behavior that is revealed. To date, no questionnaires are available to assess family members' moment-to-moment or typical emotional responses to each other (except overall level of distress), so we rely on interviews to track the emotional components of family interaction.

As noted earlier, even though all of these cognitive and behavioral measures are individuals' subjective reports of their experiences in their relationships, they can provide useful information about aspects of couple and family interaction that are not otherwise observable to the therapist. We do not use any of them routinely in clinical practice but believe they can be helpful as an adjunct to careful interviewing.

## Individual Interviews

An individual interview with each member of a couple or a family is often conducted next, to gather information about past and current functioning, including life stresses, psychopathology, overall health, coping strengths, and so on. Often family members are more open about describing personal difficulties such as depression, abandonment in a past relationship, and so forth, without other members present. Individual interviews give the clinician an opportunity to assess possible psychopathology that may be influenced by problems in the person's couple or family relationships (and in turn may be affecting family interactions adversely). Given the high co-occurrence of individual psychopathology and relationship problems (L'Abate, 1998), it is crucial that couple and family therapists be skilled in assessing individual functioning or make referrals to colleagues who can assist in this task. The therapist can then determine whether joint therapy should be supplemented with individual therapy. As noted earlier, therapists must set clear guidelines for confidentiality during individual interviews. Keeping secrets, such as a spouse's ongoing infidelity, places the therapist in an ethical bind and undermines the work in joint sessions; consequently, we tell couples and family members that we will not keep such secrets that are affecting the well-being of other family members. On the other hand, when the therapist learns that an individual is being physically abused and appears to be in danger, the focus shifts toward working with that person to develop plans to maintain safety and steps to exit the home when the risk of abuse increases and to seek shelter elsewhere.

## Behavioral Observation

We have already described how the therapist has opportunities to observe couple and family interaction patterns during the initial joint interview; for example, the style and degree to which members express their thoughts and emotions to each other, who interrupts whom, and who speaks for whom. In a CB approach, assessment is ongoing throughout therapy, and the therapist observes family process during each session. These relatively unstructured behavioral observations are often supple-

mented by a structured communication task during the initial joint interview (Baucom & Epstein, 1990; Epstein & Baucom, 2002). Based on information that the couple or the family provides, the therapist may select a topic that all of the family members consider an unresolved issue in their relationship and asks them to spend 10 minutes or so discussing it while the therapist videotapes them. The family members might be asked merely to express their feelings about the issue and respond to each other's expression in any way they see appropriate, or they might be asked to try to resolve the issue in the allotted time. Typically, the therapist leaves the room, to minimize influencing their interactions. Such taped problem-solving discussions are used routinely in couple and family interaction research (Weiss & Heyman, 1997), and even though family members often behave somewhat differently under these conditions than they do at home, they commonly become engaged enough in the discussion that aspects of their usual interaction emerge. This is another source of information about family members' emotional responses to each other, as when an individual rapidly exhibits anger whenever others disagree with him or her. Therapists can use behavioral coding systems that were developed for research purposes, such as the Marital Interaction Coding System (MICS-IV; Heyman, Eddy, Weiss, & Vivian, 1995), as guides for identifying frequencies and sequences of family members' positive and negative verbal and nonverbal behaviors (e.g., approve, accept responsibility, positive physical contact, complain, put-down, cross-complaining). As with observations of family interaction during interviews, the CB therapist considers these data to be interaction samples that might be typical of the family process but that require verification through repeated observations and reports from the family members about interactions that occur at home.

*Identification of Macrolevel Patterns and
Core Relationship Issues*

The therapist collects information over the course of joint and individual interviews, plus family members' responses to questionnaires, and looks for broad "macrolevel" patterns and themes that may reflect core relationship issues. Thus, the CB therapist takes an empirical approach to assessment, using initial observations to form hypotheses but waiting until repetitive patterns emerge before drawing conclusions about a family's central problems and strengths. For example, during the first joint family session, parents may describe setting firm limits on an adolescent daughter's behavior, and the therapist may hypothesize that there is a clear power hierarchy in the family. However, in an individual interview the daughter may reveal that she can easily bend the rules and talk her parents out of punishments, and in other joint family sessions the parents may fail to respond when the daughter repeatedly interrupts them. Evidence has accumulated that the parents have relatively little power.

*Assessment Feedback to the Couple
or the Family*

CBT is a collaborative approach, in which the therapist continually shares his or her thinking with the clients and develops interventions designed to address their concerns. After collecting information from interviews, questionnaires, and behavioral observations, the therapist meets with the family and provides a concise summary of the patterns that have emerged, including (a) their strengths, (b) their major presenting concerns, (c) life demands or stressors that have produced adjustment problems for the family, and (d) constructive and problematic macrolevel patterns in their interactions that seem to be influencing their presenting problems. The therapist and the family then identify the family's top priorities for change, as well as some interventions that have potential to alleviate the problems. This is also an important time for the therapist to explore potential barriers to couple or family therapy, such as members' fears of changes that they anticipate will be stressful and difficult for them, and to problem solve with the family regarding steps that could be taken to reduce the stress.

## CLINICAL CHANGE MECHANISMS AND SPECIFIC THERAPEUTIC INTERVENTIONS

*Educating Couples and Families
About the Cognitive-Behavioral Model*

It is extremely important to educate couples and families about the CB model of treatment. The structure and collaborative nature of the approach necessitate that the couple or the family members clearly understand the principles and methods involved. The therapist initially provides a brief didactic overview of the model and periodically refers to specific concepts during therapy. In addition to presenting such "mini-lectures" (Baucom & Epstein, 1990), the therapist often asks the clients to read portions of relevant popular books such as Beck's (1988) *Love Is Never Enough* and Markman, Stanley, and Blumberg's (1994) *Fighting for Your Marriage*. It is also important to explain to couples and family members that homework assignments will be an essential part of treatment and that bibliotherapy is one type of homework assignment that helps orient them to the model of treatment. Knowing the model keeps all parties attuned to the process of treatment and reinforces the notion of taking responsibility for their own thoughts and actions.

The therapist informs the clients that he or

she will structure the sessions in order to keep the therapy focused on achieving the goals that they have agreed to pursue during the assessment process (Epstein & Baucom, 2002; Dattilio, 1994, 1997). Part of the structuring process involves the therapist and the couple or the family setting an explicit agenda at the beginning of each session. Another aspect of structuring sessions involves establishing ground rules for client behavior within and outside sessions; for example, individuals should not tell the therapist secrets that cannot be shared with other family members, all family members should attend each session unless the therapist and the family decide otherwise, and abusive verbal and physical behavior is unacceptable.

## Interventions to Modify Distorted and Extreme Cognitions

### TEACH MEMBERS TO IDENTIFY AUTOMATIC THOUGHTS AND ASSOCIATED EMOTIONS AND BEHAVIOR

A crucial prerequisite to modifying family members' distorted or extreme cognitions about themselves and each other is increasing their ability to identify their automatic thoughts. After introducing the concept of automatic thoughts that spontaneously flash through one's mind, the therapist coaches couples and family members in observing their patterns of thought during sessions that are associated with their negative emotional and behavioral responses to each other. In the CB model, monitoring one's subjective experiences is a skill that can be developed further if necessary. In order to improve the skill of identifying one's automatic thoughts, clients are typically asked to keep a small notebook handy between sessions and to jot down a brief description of the circumstances in which they

feel distressed about the relationship or are engaged in conflict. This log should also include a description of the automatic thoughts that came to mind, as well as the resulting emotion response and any behavioral responses toward other family members. We typically use a modified version of the Daily Record of Dysfunctional Thoughts (Beck et al., 1979), initially developed for the identification and modification of automatic thoughts in individual cognitive therapy. Through this type of record keeping, the therapist is able to demonstrate to couples and families how their automatic thoughts are linked to emotional and behavioral responses and to help them understand the specific macrolevel themes (e.g., boundary issues) that upset them in their relationships. This procedure also increases family members' awareness that their negative emotional and behavioral responses to each other are potentially controllable through systematic examination of the cognitions associated with them. Thus, the therapist is coaching each individual in taking greater responsibility for his or her own responses. An exercise that often proves quite useful is to have couples and families review their logs and indicate the links among thoughts, emotions, and behavior. The therapist then asks each person to explore alternative cognitions that might produce different emotional and behavioral responses to a situation.

### IDENTIFYING COGNITIVE DISTORTIONS AND LABELING THEM

It is helpful for family members to become adept at identifying the types of cognitive distortions involved in their automatic thoughts. One exercise that is often effective is having each partner or family member refer to the list of distortions in Exhibit 1 and label any distortions in the automatic thoughts that he or she logged during the previous week. (See

Exhibit 1, after the reference section in this chapter.) The therapist and the client can discuss the aspects of the thoughts that were inappropriate or extreme and how the distortion contributed to any negative emotions and behavior at the time. Such in-session reviews of written logs over the course of several sessions can increase family members' skills in identifying and evaluating their ongoing thoughts about their relationships.

If the therapist believes that a family member's cognitive distortions are associated with a form of individual psychopathology, such as clinical depression, the therapist must determine whether the psychopathology can be treated within the context of couple or family therapy, or whether the individual may need a referral for individual therapy. As noted earlier, procedures for assessing the psychological functioning of individual family members are beyond the scope of this chapter, but it is important that couple and family therapists be familiar with the evaluation of psychopathology and make referrals to other professionals as needed.

## TESTING AND REINTERPRETING AUTOMATIC THOUGHTS

The process of restructuring automatic thoughts involves the individual considering alternative explanations. In order to accomplish this, the individual must examine evidence concerning the validity of a thought, its appropriateness for his or her family situation, or both. Identifying a distortion in one's thinking or an alternative way to view relationship events may contribute to different emotional and behavioral responses to other family members. Questions such as the following commonly are helpful in guiding each family member in examining his or her thoughts:

- From your past experiences or the events occurring recently in your family, what evidence exists that supports this thought? How could you get some additional information to help you judge whether your thought is accurate?
- What might be on alternative explanation for your partner's behavior? What else might have led your partner to behave that way?
- We have reviewed several types of cognitive distortions that can influence a person's views of other family members and can contribute to getting upset with them. Which cognitive distortions, if any, can you see in the automatic thoughts you had about . . . ?

For example, an adolescent who believed that his parents were being unrealistic in their restrictions on his activities reported the automatic thoughts, "They enjoy restricting me. I never get to do anything," which were associated with anger and frustration toward his parents. The therapist coached him in identifying that he was engaging in mind reading, and that it would be important to learn more about his parents' feelings. The therapist encouraged him to ask his parents to describe their feelings, and both replied that they felt sad and guilty about having to restrict their son, but that their fears for his well-being, based on his past drug involvement, were outweighing their urge to let him have more freedom. The son was able to hear that his inference may not be accurate, and the therapist noted to the family members that they probably would benefit from problem-solving discussions to address the issue of what types of restrictions were most appropriate. Similarly, the therapist coached the son in examining his thought "I never get to do anything," leading to the son's recounting several instances in which his parents did allow him some social activities. Thus, the son acknowledged that he had engaged in dichotomous thinking. The therapist discussed with the family the danger of thinking and speaking in extreme terms, because very few events occur "always" or "never."

Thus, gathering and weighing the evidence for one's thoughts are integral parts of CBT. Family members are able to provide valuable feedback that will help each other evaluate the validity or appropriateness of their cognitions, as long as they use good communication skills, which will be described later. After individuals challenge their thoughts, they should rate their belief in the alternative explanations and in their original inference or belief, perhaps on a scale from 0 to 100. Revised thoughts may not become assimilated unless they are considered credible.

## TESTING PREDICTIONS WITH BEHAVIORAL EXPERIMENTS

Although an individual may use logical analysis successfully to reduce his or her negative expectancies concerning events that will occur in couple or family interactions, often firsthand evidence is needed. CB therapists often guide family members in devising "behavioral experiments," in which they test their predictions that particular actions will lead to certain responses from other members. For example, a man who holds an expectancy that his wife and children will resist including him in their leisure activities when he gets home from work can make plans to try to engage with the family when he arrives home during the next few days and see what happens. When these plans are devised during joint family therapy sessions, the therapist can ask the other family members what they predict their responses will be during the experiment. The family members can anticipate potential obstacles to the success of the experiment, and appropriate adjustments can be made. In addition, public commitments that family members make toward cooperation with the experiment often increase the likelihood of its success.

## USING IMAGERY, RECOLLECTIONS OF PAST INTERACTIONS, AND ROLE-PLAYING TECHNIQUES

During therapy sessions, when family members attempt to identify their thoughts, emotions, and behavior that occurred in past incidents outside sessions, they may have difficulty recalling pertinent information regarding the past circumstances and each person's responses, particularly if the family interaction was emotionally charged. Imagery or role-playing techniques, or both may be extremely helpful in reviving memories regarding such situations. In addition, these techniques often rekindle family members' reactions, and what begins as a role-play may quickly become an in vivo interaction. Although recounting of past events can provide important information, the therapist's ability to assess and intervene with family members' problematic cognitive, affective, and behavioral responses to each other as they occur during sessions affords the best opportunity for changing family patterns (Epstein & Baucom, 2002).

Family members can also be coached in switching roles during role-playing exercises, in order to increase empathy for each other's experiences within the family (Epstein & Baucom, 2002). For example, spouses can be asked to play each other's role in recreating an argument that they recently had concerning finances. Focusing on the other person's frame of reference and subjective feelings provides new information that can modify one spouse's view of the other. Thus, when a husband played the role of his wife, he was able to better understand her anxiety and conservative behavior concerning spending money, based on her experiences of poverty during childhood.

Many distressed couples have developed a narrow focus on problems in their relationship by the time they seek therapy, so the therapist may ask them to report their recollections of the thoughts, emotions, and behavior that occurred between them during the period when they met, dated, and developed loving feelings toward each other. The therapist can focus on the contrast between past and present feelings and behavior as evidence that the couple was able to relate in a much more satisfying way and may be able to regenerate positive interactions with appropriate effort.

Imagery techniques should be used with caution and skill and probably should be avoided if there is a history of abuse in the relationship. Similarly, role-play techniques should not be used until the therapist feels confident that family members will be able to contain strong emotional responses and refrain from abusive behavior toward each other.

## THE "DOWNWARD ARROW"

This is a technique used by cognitive therapists (e.g., A. T. Beck et al., 1979; J. S. Beck, 1995) to track the associations among an individual's automatic thoughts, in which an apparently benign initial thought that a person reports may be upsetting because it is linked to other, more significant thoughts. For example, a child may report strong anxiety associated with the automatic thought "My dad will yell at me if I don't get mostly A grades in school." The intensity of the emotional response becomes more clear when the therapist asks a series of questions of the form, "And if that happened, what would it mean to you?" or "What might that lead to?" and the child eventually reports, "He'll get so upset with me that he'll think I'm a loser and will wish he had someone else as a son." Couples and family members can evaluate how likely the expected catastrophe is to occur. In some cases, this will lead to modification of the individual's underlying catastrophic expectancy; in other cases, it may uncover a real problem in family interaction, such as a need

for the child's father to consider changing his judgmental and rejecting behavior.

The downward arrow technique is also used to identify the underlying assumptions and standards beneath one's automatic thoughts. This is done by identifying the initial thought, having individuals ask themselves, "If so, then what?" and moving downward until the individuals identify the relevant core belief. Thus, the child in the previous example might also have developed perfectionistic standards for his performance in academics and other activities, based on his parents' belief systems, and even if his father would not reject him, the son's negative automatic thoughts may be tied to an underlying belief such as "I am a failure if I don't get high grades."

## Interventions to Modify Behavior Patterns

The major forms of interventions used to reduce negative behavior and increase positive behavior are (a) communication training regarding expressive and listening skills, (b) problem-solving training, and (c) behavior-change agreements. We describe each of these briefly further on, and readers can consult texts such as Guerney (1977), Robin and Foster (1989), Jacobson and Christensen (1996), Baucom and Epstein (1990), and Epstein and Baucom (2002) for detailed procedures.

## COMMUNICATION TRAINING

Improving couple and family skills for expressing thoughts and emotions, as well as for listening effectively to each other, is one of the most common forms of intervention across theoretical approaches to therapy. In CBT it is viewed as a cornerstone of treatment, because it can have a positive impact on problematic behavioral interactions, reduce family members' distorted cognitions about each other, and contribute to regulated experience and expression of emotion. Therapists begin by presenting instructions to couples and family members about the specific behaviors involved in each type of expressive and listening skill. Speaker guidelines include acknowledging the subjectivity of one's views (not suggesting that others' views are invalid); describing one's emotions, as well as one's thoughts; pointing out positives, as well as problems; speaking in specific, rather than global, terms; being concise so that the listener can absorb and remember one's message; and using tact and good timing (e.g., not discussing important topics when one's partner is preparing to go to sleep). The guidelines for empathic listening include exhibiting attentiveness through nonverbal acts (e.g., eye contact, nods), demonstrating acceptance of the speaker's message (the person's right to have his or her personal feelings) whether or not the listener agrees, attempting to understand or empathize with the other's perspective, and reflecting back one's understanding by paraphrasing what the speaker has said. Each family member receives handouts describing the communication guidelines that he or she can refer to these whenever needed during sessions and at home.

Therapists often model good expressive and listening skills for clients. They may use videotape examples, such as those that accompany Markman, Stanley, and Blumberg's (1994) book *Fighting for Your Marriage*. During sessions, the therapist coaches the couple or the family in following the communication guidelines, beginning with discussions of relatively benign topics so that negative emotions will not interfere with constructive skills. As the clients demonstrate good skills, they are asked to practice them more as homework, with increasingly conflictual topics. As family members practice communication skills, they receive more information about each others' motives and desires, an important source of information to disconfirm some distorted cognitions about each other. Following the guidelines also often increases each individual's perception that the others are respectful and have goodwill.

## PROBLEM-SOLVING TRAINING.

CB therapists also use verbal and written instructions, modeling, and behavioral rehearsal and coaching to facilitate effective problem solving with couples and family members. The major steps in problem solving involve achieving a clear specific definition of the problem in terms of behaviors that are or are not occurring, generating specific behavioral solutions to the problem without evaluating one's own or other family members' ideas, evaluating the advantages and disadvantages of each alternative solution and selecting a solution that appears to be feasible and attractive to all members involved, and agreeing on a trial period for implementing the selected solution and assessing its effectiveness. Homework practice of the skills is important for their acquisition (Dattilio, 2002; Epstein & Baucom, 2002).

## BEHAVIOR-CHANGE AGREEMENTS

Contracts to exchange desired behavior still have an important role in CBCT and CBFT. Therapists try to avoid making one family member's behavior change contingent on another's, so the goal is for each person to identify and enact specific behavior that would be likely to please other family members, regardless of what actions the other members take. The major challenge facing the therapist is encouraging family members to avoid "standing on ceremony" by waiting for others to behave positively first. Brief didactic presentations on negative reciprocity in distressed relationships, the fact that one can have control only over one's own actions, and the importance of making a personal commitment to improve the family atmosphere are some interventions that may reduce individuals' reluctance to "make the first positive contribution."

*Interventions for Deficits and Excesses in Emotional Responses*

Although CBT is sometimes characterized as neglecting emotions, this is not the case, and a variety of interventions is used, either to enhance the emotional experiences of inhibited individuals or to moderate extreme responses (see Epstein & Baucom, 2002, for detailed procedures). For family members who report experiencing little emotion, the therapist can set clear guidelines for behavior within and outside sessions, in which expressing oneself will not lead to recrimination by other members; use downward arrow questioning to inquire about underlying emotions, as well as cognitions; coach the person in noticing internal cues to his or her emotional states; repeat phrases that have emotional impact on the person; refocus attention on emotionally relevant topics when the individual attempts to change the subject; and engage the individual in role-plays concerning important relationship issues in order to elicit emotional responses. With individuals who experience intense emotions that affect them and significant others adversely, the therapist can help them compartmentalize emotional responses by scheduling specific times to discuss distressing topics, coach the individual in self-soothing activities such as relaxation techniques, improve people's ability to monitor and challenge upsetting automatic thoughts, encourage individuals to seek social support from family and others, develop their ability to tolerate distressing feelings, and enhance skills for expressing emotions constructively so that others will pay attention.

# EFFECTIVENESS OF COGNITIVE-BEHAVIORAL COUPLE AND FAMILY THERAPY

CBT for couples has received the most extensive evaluations in controlled outcome studies of any form of couple or family therapy, and a review of outcome studies that employed stringent criteria for efficacy indicated that cognitive-behavioral treatment is efficacious for reducing relationship distress (Baucom et al., 1998). Most studies on CBCT have been restricted to evaluations of the behavioral components of communication training, problem-solving training, and behavioral contracts, and they found that these interventions are more efficacious in reducing distress than are wait-list control and placebo conditions. A small number of studies on other approaches, such as emotionally focused and insight-oriented couple therapies (e.g., Johnson & Talitman, 1997; Snyder, Wills, & Grady-Fletcher, 1991), suggests that these have comparable or in some cases better outcomes than behaviorally oriented approaches, but there is a need for additional studies in order to draw conclusions about their efficacy. Only a few studies have examined the impact of adding cognitive restructuring interventions to behavioral protocols (e.g., Baucom, Sayers, & Sher, 1990), typically by substituting some sessions of cognitive interventions for behaviorally oriented sessions in order to keep the total number of sessions equal across the treatments that are compared. The overall results of those studies indicate that the combined CBT was equally effective as the behavioral conditions, although cognitively focused interventions tend to produce more cognitive change and behavioral interventions tend to modify behavioral interactions more (Baucom et al., 1998). Epstein (2001) has noted that there is a need for research on a truly integrated CBT that targets each couple's particular cognitive, behavioral, and affective problems in proportion to their intensity, rather than providing a fixed number of sessions of each type of intervention to all couples. Also, Whisman and Snyder (1997) argue that tests of cognitive interventions have been limited by a failure to assess the range of problematic cognitions (selective attention, expectancies, attributions, assumptions, and standards) identified by Baucom et al. (1989). Studies have also been limited to samples of predominantly White, middle-class couples, so the effectiveness with other racial and socioeconomic groups is unknown. Thus, research on the effectiveness of CBCT has been encouraging, but there are many unanswered questions.

CB approaches to family therapy have focused mostly on treatment of particular disorders in individual members, rather than on alleviating general conflict and distress within the family. For example, many studies have demonstrated the efficacy of training parents in behavioral interventions for their children's conduct disorders, based on Patterson's social learning model that was described earlier in this chapter, although an attrition rate of approximately 50% indicates limitations in the approach (Estrada & Pinsof, 1995). The Estrada and Pinsof study (1995) also shows that parent training improves noncompliant and aggressive behavior in children diagnosed with attention deficit hyperactivity disorder (ADHD), although it has much less impact on core symptoms of inattention, impulsivity, and hyperactivity. Consequently, behavioral family therapy is typically used in conjunction with other interventions (e.g., medication and self-control training) that specifically target the other ADHD symptoms (Barkley, 1998).

Psychoeducational behavioral family therapy for major mental disorders such as schizophrenia and bipolar disorder (Falloon et al., 1984; Miklowitz & Goldstein, 1997; Mueser & Glynn, 1995) includes components of (a) psychoeducation concerning the etiology, symptoms, risk factors for symptom ex-

acerbation (e.g., life stresses, including family conflict), and current effective treatments; (b) communication skill training; (c) problem-solving skills training; and (d) management of relapses and crises. Research conducted in the United States, England, Germany, and China, with families from various racial and socioeconomic groups, has demonstrated the efficacy of this approach in reducing family stress and patient relapse (Baucom et al., 1998).

The previously mentioned applications of CBFT have been tailored to the treatment of an individual member's presenting problem, rather than problems in a whole family's adaptation to developmental life-stage changes or significant areas of conflict (e.g., stepfamily issues, parent–adolescent conflicts over appropriate levels of autonomy for the child). Unfortunately, there has been an embarrassing absence of quantitative research involving CBFT for a number of reasons, some of which include lack of funding and the arduousness of involving more than two family members (Dattilio, 2003). Nevertheless, the results of the various studies indicate the effectiveness of CB interventions in improving family functioning.

## FUTURE DEVELOPMENTS/ DIRECTIONS

### Integration and Cognitive-Behavior Therapy

Therapists today are confronted with a broad range of theoretical orientations, more than at any other time in the history of family therapy, and at times proponents of different approaches have taken adversarial positions, proclaiming the superiority of their models to others (Dattilio, 1998). As noted earlier, the current empirical evidence tends to indicate that various theoretical approaches have comparable degrees of effectiveness, although most approaches have not as yet been tested or compared with others (Baucom et al., 1998). In some respect, these circumstances provide the impetus for therapists to explore integration of approaches to couple and family therapy, with the understanding that no one model fully captures the complexity of intimate human relationships.

CBT has clearly come of age as an empirically established approach that is increasingly adopted by couple and family therapists (Dattilio, 2002). Because the CB model has always been amenable to change, and because it shares with many other models of treatment an assumption that change in family relationships involves shifts in cognitive, affective, and behavioral realms, it has great potential for integration with other approaches (Dattilio, 1998).

Unfortunately, the flexibility and integrative potential of CBT for couples and families have not consistently been recognized in the family therapy field, due to what appears to be a narrow view of the model as focused on cognition and linear causal processes. This view likely derives from early CB literature that focused on simple learning processes and from assumptions that distorted cognitions routinely cause negative family interactions. Developments in CBCT and CBFT more fully capture circular processes that involve cognitive, affective, and behavioral factors, as well as influences of broader contextual factors such as the family's interpersonal and physical environment (Epstein & Baucom, 2002). Some works have underscored CBT's integrative power in the treatment of individuals (Alford & Beck, 1997) and of couples and families (Dattilio, 1998). In turn, CB therapists have increasingly integrated concepts and methods from other approaches; for example, concepts of system boundaries, hierarchy (control), and the family's ability to adapt to developmental changes emphasized in struc-

tural family therapy (Minuchin, 1974) are prominent in Epstein and Baucom's (2002) work with couples.

In general, it may not be plausible to integrate a CB approach completely with various other models, due to some incompatibilities of the approaches' concepts and methods. For example, solution-focused therapists largely eschew attention to current and historical aspects of families' presenting problems, instead emphasizing efforts toward implementing desired changes (see Nichols & Schwartz, 2001, for a review). Although CB therapists also want to build on clients' existing strengths and enhance their problem solving, they assess and intervene with cognitive, affective, and behavioral aspects of problematic patterns that are often ingrained and difficult to change. Because negative responses are often overlearned, and research has demonstrated that family members' positive and negative actions tend to have independent effects on relationship satisfaction (Epstein & Baucom, 2002), CB therapists assume that focusing on increasing positive behavior will often be insufficient to decrease negative patterns. Thus, practitioners of alternative approaches need to determine the extent to which CB concepts and methods enhance or are counter to key aspects of their models. As CB therapists continue to empirically test the effects of adding interventions derived from other models, the potential for integration in clinical practice should grow.

## REFERENCES

Adler, A. (1964). *Problems of neurosis.* New York: Harper Torch Books (original work published 1929).

Adler, A. (1978). *Cooperation between the sexes: Writings on women, love, and marriage, sexuality and its disorders.* (Translated and Edited by H. L. Ansbacher & R. R. Ansbacher). Oxford, England: Anchor Books.

Alexander, P. C. (1988). The therapeutic implications

of family cognitions and constructs. *Journal of Cognitive Psychotherapy, 2*, 219–236.

Alford, B. A., & Beck, A. T. (1997). *The integrative power of cognitive therapy*. New York: Guilford Press.

Bandura, A. (1977). *Social learning theory*. Englewood Cliffs, NJ: Prentice Hall.

Bandura, A., & Walters, R. H. (1963). *Social learning and personality development*. New York: Holt, Rinehart, and Winston.

Barkley, R. A. (1998). *Attention-deficit hyperactivity disorder: A handbook for diagnosis and treatment* (2nd ed.). New York: Guilford Press.

Baucom, D. H. (1987). Attributions in distressed relations: How can we explain them? In S. Duck & D. Perlman (Eds.), *Heterosexual relations, marriage and divorce* (pp. 177–206). London: Sage.

Baucom, D. H., & Epstein, N. (1990). *Cognitive-behavioral marital therapy*. New York: Brunner/Mazel.

Baucom, D. H., Epstein, N., Daiuto, A. D., Carels, R. A., Rankin, L. A., & Burnett, C. K. (1996). Cognitions in marriage: The relationship between standards and attributions. *Journal of Family Psychology, 10*, 209–222.

Baucom, D. H., Epstein, N., Rankin, L. A., & Burnett, C. K. (1996). Assessing relationship standards: The Inventory of Specific Relationship Standards. *Journal of Family Psychology, 10*, 72–88.

Baucom, D. H., Epstein, N., Sayers, S., & Sher, T. G. (1989). The role of cognitions in marital relationships: Definitional, methodological, and conceptual issues. *Journal of Consulting and Clinical Psychology, 57*, 31–38.

Baucom, D. H., Sayers, S. L., & Sher, T. G. (1990). Supplementing behavioral marital therapy with cognitive restructuring and emotional expressiveness training: An outcome investigation. *Journal of Consulting and Clinical Psychology, 58*, 636–645.

Baucom, D. H., Shoham, V., Mueser, K. T., Daiuto, A. D., & Stickle, T. R. (1998). Empirically supported couples and family therapies for adult problems. *Journal of Consulting and Clinical Psychology, 66*, 53–88.

Beavers, W. R., Hampson, R. B., & Hulgus, Y. F. (1985). The Beavers systems approach to family assessment. *Family Process, 24*, 398–405.

Beck, A. T. (1988). *Love is never enough*. New York: Harper & Row.

Beck, A. T., Rush, A. J., Shaw, B. F., & Emery, G. (1979). *Cognitive therapy of depression*. New York: Guilford Press.

Beck, J. S. (1995). *Cognitive therapy: Basics and beyond*. New York: Guilford Press.

Bedrosian, R. C. (1983). Cognitive therapy in the family system. In A. Freeman (Ed.), *Cognitive therapy with couples and groups* (pp. 95–106). New York: Plenum Press.

Bradbury, T. N., & Fincham, F. D. (1990). Attributions in marriage: Review and critique. *Psychological Bulletin, 107*, 3–33.

Christensen, A. (1988). Dysfunctional interaction patterns in couples. In P. Noller & M. A. Fitzpatrick (Eds.), *Perspectives on marital interaction* (pp. 31–52). Clevedon, England: Multilingual Matters.

Dattilio, F. M. (1989). A guide to cognitive marital therapy. In P. A. Keller & S. R. Heyman (Eds.), *Innovations in clinical practice: A source book* (Vol. 8, pp. 27–42). Sarasota, FL: Professional Resource Exchange.

Dattilio, F. M. (1993). Cognitive techniques with couples and families. *The Family Journal, 1*(1), 51–56.

Dattilio, F. M. (1994). Families in crisis. In F. M. Dattilio & A. Freeman (Eds.), *Cognitive-behavioral strategies in crisis intervention* (pp. 278–301). New York: Guilford Press.

Dattilio, F. M. (1997). Family therapy. In R. L. Leahy (Ed.), *Practicing cognitive therapy: A guide to interventions* (pp. 409–450). Northvale, NJ: Jason Aronson.

Dattilio, F. M. (1998). *Case studies in couples and family therapy: Systemic and cognitive perspectives*. New York: Guilford Press.

Dattilio, F. M. (2001). Cognitive behavioral family therapy: Contemporary myths and misconceptions. *Contemporary Family Therapy, 23*(1), 3–18.

Dattilio, F. M. (2002). Homework assignments in couple and family therapy. *Journal of Clinical Psychology, 58*(5), 570-583.

Dattilio, F. M. (2003). Cognitive-behavior family therapy comes of age. In R. E. Leahy (Ed.), *New advances in cognitive therapy: Festschrift for Aaron T. Beck*. New York: Guilford Press.

Dattilio, F. M., & Padesky, C. A. (1990). *Cognitive therapy with couples*. Sarasota, FL: Professional Resource Exchange.

Dicks, H. (1953). Experiences with marital tension seen in the psychological clinic in "Clinical studies in marriage and the family: A symposium on methods." *British Journal of Medical Psychology, 26*, 181–196.

Eidelson, R. J., & Epstein, N. (1982). Cognition and

relationship maladjustment: Development of a measure of dysfunctional relationship beliefs. *Journal of Consulting and Clinical Psychology, 50*, 715–720.

Ellis A. (1977). The nature of disturbed marital interactions. In A. Ellis & R. Grieger (Eds.), *Handbook of rational-emotive therapy* (pp. 170–176). New York: Springer.

Ellis, A. (1982). Rational-emotive family therapy. In A. M. Horne & M. M. Ohlsen (Eds.), *Family counseling and therapy* (pp. 302–328). Itasca, IL: Peacock.

Ellis, A., & Harper, R. A. (1961). *A guide to rational living*. Englewood Cliffs, NJ: Prentice Hall.

Ellis, A., Sichel, J. L., Yeager, R. J., DiMattia, D. J., & DiGiuseppe, R. (1989). *Rational-emotive couples therapy*. New York: Pergamon Press.

Epstein, N. (1982). Cognitive therapy with couples. *American Journal of Family Therapy, 10*, 5–16.

Epstein, N. (1992). Marital therapy. In A. Freeman & F. M. Dattilio (Eds.), *Comprehensive casebook of cognitive therapy* (pp. 267–275). New York: Plenum Press.

Epstein, N. (2001). Cognitive-behavioral therapy with couples: Empirical status. *Journal of Cognitive Psychotherapy: An International Quarterly, 15*, 299–310.

Epstein, N., & Baucom, D. H. (1989). Cognitive-behavioral marital therapy. In A. Freeman, K. M. Simon, L. E. Beutler, & H. Arkowitz (Eds.), *Comprehensive handbook of cognitive therapy* (pp. 491–513). New York: Plenum Press.

Epstein, N., & Baucom, D. H. (2002). *Enhanced cognitive-behavioral therapy for couples: A contextual approach*. Washington, DC: American Psychological Association.

Epstein, N., & Eidelson, R. J. (1981). Unrealistic beliefs of clinical couples: Their relationship to expectations, goals and satisfaction. *American Journal of Family Therapy, 9*(4), 13–22.

Epstein, N., & Schlesinger, S. E. (1996). Treatment of family problems. In M. A. Reinecke, F. M. Dattilio, & A. Freeman (Eds.), *Cognitive therapy with children and adolescents: A casebook for clinical practice* (pp. 299–326). New York: Guilford Press.

Epstein, N., Schlesinger, S. E., & Dryden, W. (1988). Concepts and methods of cognitive-behavioral family treatment. In N. Epstein, S. E. Schlesinger, & W. Dryden (Eds.), *Cognitive-behavioral therapy with families* (pp. 5–48). New York: Brunner/Mazel.

Estrada, A. U., & Pinsof, W. M. (1995). The effectiveness of family therapies for selected behavioral disorders of childhood. *Journal of Marital and Family Therapy, 21*, 403–440.

Falloon, I. R. H., Boyd, J. L., & McGill, C. W. (1984). *Family care of schizophrenia*. New York: Guilford Press.

Fincham, F. D., Beach, S. R. H., & Nelson, G. (1987). Attribution processes in distressed and nondistressed couples: 3. Causal and responsibility attributions for spouse behavior. *Cognitive Therapy and Research, 11*, 71–86.

Fincham, F. D., Garnier, P. C., Gano-Phillips, S., & Osborne, L. N. (1995). Preinteraction expectations, marital satisfaction, and accessibility: A new look at sentiment override. *Journal of Family Psychology, 9*, 3–14.

Forehand, R., & McMahon, R. (1981). *Helping the noncompliant child: A clinician's guide to parent training*. New York: Guilford Press.

Fredman, N., & Sherman, R. (1987). *Handbook of measurements for marriage and family therapy*. New York: Brunner/Mazel.

Goldenberg, I., & Goldenberg, H. (2000). *Family therapy: An overview*. Belmont, CA: Brooks/Cole.

Gottman, J. M. (1994). *What predicts divorce?* Hillsdale, NJ: Erlbaum.

Grotevant, H. D., & Carlson, C. I. (1989). *Family assessment: A guide to methods and measures*. New York: Guilford Press.

Guerney, B. G., Jr. (1977). *Relationship enhancement*. San Francisco: Jossey-Bass.

Haley, J., & Hoffman, L. (Eds.). (1968). *Techniques of family therapy*. New York: Basic Books.

Hamilton, V. (1980). An information processing analysis of environmental stress and life crisis. In I. G. Sarason & C. D. Spielberger (Ed.), *Stress and anxiety* (Vol. 7, pp. 13–30). Washington, DC: Hemisphere.

Heyman, R. E., Eddy, J. M., Weiss, R. L., & Vivian, D. (1995). Factor analysis of the Marital Interaction Coding System (MICS). *Journal of Family Psychology, 9*, 209–215.

Huber, C. H., & Baruth, L. G. (1989). *Rational-emotive family therapy: A systems perspective*. New York: Springer.

Ingram, R. E., & Kendall, P. C. (1986). Cognitive clinical psychology: Implications of an information processing perspective. In R. E. Ingram (Ed.), *Information processing approaches to clinical psychology* (pp. 3–21). London: Academic Press.

Jacob, T., & Tennenbaum, D.L. (1988). *Family assessment: Rationale, methods, and future directions*. New York: Plenum Press.

Jacobson, N. S., & Christensen, A. (1996). *Integrative couple therapy: Promoting acceptance and change*. New York: Norton.

Jacobson, N. S., & Margolin, G. (1979). *Marital therapy: Strategies based on social learning and behavior exchange principles*. New York: Brunner/Mazel.

Johnson, S. M., & Denton, W. (2002). Emotionally focused couple therapy: Creating secure connections. In A. S. Gurman & N. S. Jacobson (Eds.), *Clinical handbook of couple therapy* (3rd ed., pp. 221–250). New York: Guilford Press.

Johnson, S. M., & Talitman, E. (1997). Predictors of success in emotionally focused marital therapy. *Journal of Marital and Family Therapy, 23*, 135–152.

Kelly, G. A. (1955). *The psychology of personal constructs*. New York: Norton.

L'Abate, L. (1998). *Family psychopathology: The relational roots of dysfunctional behavior*. New York: Guilford Press.

Leahy, R. (1996). *Cognitive therapy: Basic principles and applications*. Northvale, NJ: Jason Aronson.

Liberman, R. P. (1970). Behavioral approaches to couple and family therapy. *American Journal of Orthopsychiatry, 40*, 106–118.

Linehan, M. M. (1993). *Cognitive-behavioral treatment of borderline personality disorder*. New York: Guilford Press.

Margolin, G., & Weiss, R. L. (1978). Comparative evaluation of therapeutic components associated with behavioral marital treatments. *Journal of Consulting and Clinical Psychology, 46*, 1476–1486.

Markman, H. J., Stanley, S., & Blumberg, S. L. (1994). *Fighting for your marriage*. San Francisco: Jossey-Bass.

McCubbin, M. A., & McCubbin, H. I. (1989). Theoretical orientation to family stress and coping. In C. R. Figley (Ed.), *Treating stress in families* (pp. 3–43). New York: Brunner/Mazel.

Miklowitz, D. J., & Goldstein, M. J. (1997). *Bipolar disorder: A family-focused treatment approach*. New York: Guilford Press.

Minuchin, S. (1974). *Families and family therapy*. Cambridge, MA: Harvard University Press.

Moos, R. H., & Moos, B. S. (1981). *Family Environment Scale: Manual*. Palo Alto, CA: Consulting Psychologists Press.

Mueser, K. T., & Glynn, S. M. (1995). *Behavioral family therapy for psychiatric disorders*. Boston: Allyn and Bacon.

Nicoll, W. G. (1989). Adlerian marital therapy: History, theory, and process. In R. M. Kern, E. C. Hawes, & O. C. Christensen (Eds.), *Couples therapy: An Adlerian perspective*. Minneapolis, MN: Educational Media Corporation.

Nichols, M. P., & Schwartz, R. C. (2001). *Family therapy: Concepts and methods* (5th ed.). Boston: Allyn and Bacon.

Patterson, G. R. (1971). *Families: Applications of social learning to family life*. Champaign, IL: Research Press.

Patterson, G. R., McNeal, S., Hawkins, N., & Phelps, R. (1967). Reprogramming the social environment. *Journal of Child Psychology and Psychiatry, 8*, 181–195.

Pavlov, I. P. (1927). *Conditioned reflexes*. (Translated by G. V. Anrep). London: Oxford University Press.

Piaget, J. (1960). *A child's conception of the world*. Totowa, NJ: Littlefield, Adams (originally published 1926).

Pretzer, J., Epstein, N., & Fleming, B. (1991). Marital Attitude Survey: A measure of dysfunctional attributions and expectancies. *Journal of Cognitive Psychotherapy: An International Quarterly, 5*, 131–148.

Rathus, J. H., & Sanderson, W. C. (1999). *Marital distress: Cognitive behavioral interventions for couples*. Northvale, NJ: Jason Aronson.

Robin, A. L., & Foster, S. L. (1989). *Negotiating parent–adolescent conflict: A behavioral-family systems approach*. New York: Guilford Press.

Roehling, P. V., & Robin, A. L. (1986). Development and validation of the Family Beliefs Inventory: A measure of unrealistic beliefs among parents and adolescents. *Journal of Consulting and Clinical Psychology, 54*, 693–697.

Rotter, J. B. (1954). *Social learning and clinical psychology*. Englewood Cliffs, NJ: Prentice-Hall.

Satir, V. (1967). *Conjoint family therapy*. Palo Alto, CA: Science & Behavioral Books.

Schwebel, A. I., & Fine, M. A. (1994). *Understanding and helping families: A cognitive-behavioral approach*. Hillsdale, NJ: Erlbaum.

Skinner, B. F. (1953). *Science and human behavior*. New York: Macmillan.

Skinner, H. A., Steinhauer, P. D., & Santa-Barbara, J. (1983). The family assessment measure. *Canadian Journal of Community Mental Health, 2*, 91–105.

Snyder, D. K., & Aikman, G. G. (1999). The Marital Satisfaction Inventory—Revised. In M. E. Maruish (Ed.), *Use of psychological testing for treatment planning and outcomes assessment* (pp. 1173–1210). Mahwah, NJ: Erlbaum.

Snyder, D. K., Cavell, T. A., Heffer, R. W., & Mangrum, L. F. (1995). Marital and family assessment: A multifaceted, multilevel approach. In R. H. Mikesell, D. D. Lusterman, & S. H. McDaniel (Eds.), *Integrating family therapy: Handbook of family psychology and systems theory* (pp. 163–182). Washington, DC: American Psychological Association.

Snyder, D. K., & Wills, R. M., & Grady-Fletcher, A. (1991). Long-term effectiveness of behavioral versus insight-oriented marital therapy: A 4-year follow-up study. *Journal of Consulting and Clinical Psychology, 59,* 138–141.

Spanier, G. B. (1976). Measuring dyadic adjustment: New scales for assessing the quality of marriage and similar dyads. *Journal of Marriage and the Family, 38,* 15–30.

Straus, M. A., Hamby, S. L., Boney-McCoy, S., & Sugarman, D. B. (1996). The Revised Conflict Tactics Scales (CTS2): Development and preliminary psychometric data. *Journal of Family Issues, 17,* 283–316.

Stuart, R. B. (1969). Operant-interpersonal treatment for marital discord. *Journal of Consulting and Clinical Psychology, 33,* 675–682.

Stuart, R. B. (1980). *Helping couples change: A social learning approach to marital therapy.* New York: Guilford Press.

Teichman, Y. (1981). Family therapy with adolescents. *Journal of Adolescence, 4,* 87–92.

Teichman, Y. (1992). Family treatment with an acting-out adolescent. In A. Freeman & F. M. Dattilio (Eds.), *Comprehensive casebook of cognitive therapy* (pp. 331–346). New York: Plenum Press.

Thibaut J. W., & Kelley, H. H. (1959). *The social psychology of groups.* New York: Wiley.

Touliatos, J., Perlmutter, B. F., & Straus, M. A. (Eds.). (1990). *Handbook of family measurement techniques.* Newbury Park, CA: Sage.

Walsh, F. (1998). *Strengthening family resilience.* New York: Guilford Press.

Watson, J.B. (1925). *Behaviorism.* New York: Norton.

Webster-Stratton, C., & Herbert, M. (1994). *Troubled families—problem children.* Chichester, England: Wiley.

Weiss, R. L. (1984). Cognitive and strategic interventions in behavioral marital therapy. In K. Hahlweg & N. S. Jacobson (Eds.), *Marital interaction: Analysis and modification* (pp. 309–324). New York: Guilford Press.

Weiss, R. L., & Heyman, R. E. (1997). A clinical-research overview of couples interactions. In W. K. Halford & H. J. Markman (Eds.), *Clinical handbook of marriage and couples interventions* (pp. 13–41). Chichester, England: Wiley.

Weiss, R. L., Hops, H., & Patterson, G. R. (1973). A framework for conceptualizing marital conflict, a technology for altering it, some data for evaluating it. In L. A. Hamerlynck, L. C. Handy, & E. J. Mash, (Eds.), *Behavior change: Methodology, concepts, and practice* (pp. 309–342). Champaign, IL: Research Press.

Whisman, M. A., & Snyder, D. K. (1997). Evaluating and improving the efficacy of conjoint couple therapy. In W. K. Halford & H. J. Markman (Eds.), *Clinical handbook of marriage and couples interventions* (pp. 679–693). Chichester, England: Wiley.

Wolpe, J. (1958). *Psychotherapy by reciprocal inhibition.* Palo Alto, CA: Stanford University Press.

EXHIBIT 1

*Common Cognitive Distortions*

### ARBITRARY INFERENCE

Conclusions that are made in the absence of supporting substantiating evidence; often involved in invalid attributions and expectancies. For example, a man whose wife arrives home a half-hour late from work concludes, "She must be doing something behind my back." Distressed spouses and family members often make negative attributions about the causes of each other's positive actions. For example, if a teenager starts to improve his or her behavior, parents may wonder about an ulterior motive.

### MIND READING

This is a type of arbitrary inference in which an individual believes he or she knows what another person is thinking or feeling without communicating directly with the person. For example, a husband noticed that his wife had been especially quiet and concluded, "She's unhappy with our marriage and must be thinking about leaving me."

### SELECTIVE ABSTRACTION

Information is taken out of context and certain details are highlighted, whereas other important information is ignored; involved in selective attention to family interaction. For example, a woman whose son fails to answer her greeting in the morning concludes, "He is ignoring me," even though the son cleared a place for her at the breakfast table when she entered the room. An individual's schema concerning another family member may produce "tunnel vision," in which he or she notices only the aspects of the other's behavior that are consistent with the global conception of the other person. For example, the previously mentioned mother may notice only the instances of her son's failing to engage with her, if she believes that the son has a trait of "self-centeredness."

### OVERGENERALIZATION

An isolated incident is considered to be a representation of similar situations in other contexts, related or unrelated; often contributes to selective attention. For example, after being told that she cannot go out Saturday night, an adolescent girl concludes, "My parents won't let me have any social life."

### MAGNIFICATION AND MINIMIZATION

A case or circumstance is judged as having greater or lesser importance than is appropriate; often leading to distress when the evaluation violates the person's standards for the ways family members "should" be. For example, an angry father becomes anxious and enraged when he discovers that his son has been given detention at school for fighting in the schoolyard, as he thinks, "He's turning into a juvenile delinquent."

### PERSONALIZATION

External events are attributed to oneself when insufficient evidence exists to render a conclusion; a special case of arbitrary inference commonly involved in misattributions. For example, a mother finds her family not eating as much of the meal at dinner as she had anticipated and concludes, "They hate my cooking."

## DICHOTOMOUS THINKING

Also labeled "polarized thinking," experiences are classified into mutually exclusive, extreme categories, such as complete success or total failure; commonly contributing to selective attention, as well as violation of personal standards. For example, a husband has spent several hours working on cleaning the couple's cluttered basement and has removed a considerable number of items for inclusion in a yard sale. However, when the wife enters the basement, she looks around and exclaims, "What a mess! When are you going to make some progress?" and the husband becomes angry that his efforts have not been appreciated.

## LABELING

The tendency to portray oneself or another person in terms of stable, global traits, on the basis of past actions; negative labels are involved in attributions that family members make about causes of each other's actions. For example, after a wife has made several errors in family budgeting and in balancing their checkbook, the husband concludes that "She is a careless person," and he does not consider situational conditions that may have led to those errors.

CHAPTER 9

# Structural-Strategic Approaches to Couple and Family Therapy

VICTORIA BEHAR MITRANI, PhD
MARIA ALEJANDRA PEREZ, BA

*University of Miami*

## INTRODUCTION

Other textbooks on family and couple therapy have had separate chapters for the structural and strategic approaches. In this volume, the two models, structural family therapy, as developed by Salvador Minuchin, and strategic family therapy, as developed by Jay Haley, are presented together because of their common emphasis on systems and structure. Both approaches aim to realign family organization to produce change in the entire system, and both are focused on the hierarchical organization of the family. We have chosen to highlight the branch of strategic family therapy developed by Jay Haley because of its structural framework. Other strategically oriented approaches are no less influential than Haley's and have, in fact, been precursors to many of the dominant movements in modern family therapy approaches.

There are key points of divergence between Minuchin's and Haley's approaches, however. The structural approach emphasizes family organizations composed of subsystems and focuses on boundaries between subsystems. The strategic approach focuses on repeating sequences of behavior, particularly those that break hierarchical rules through cross-generational coalitions. Structural therapists focus on resolving structural problems in the family, whereas strategic therapists focus on the presenting symptom. Although both therapeutic approaches are action- and present-oriented, structuralists utilize interpretation and tasks in the form of enactment, whereas strategists shun interpretation and utilize both straightforward and paradoxical directives. Minuchin and Fishman (1981) highlight another key difference: "The strategic therapist sees the symptom as a protective solution: the symptom bearer sacrifices himself to defend the family homeostasis. The structuralist, regarding the family as an organism, sees this

177

protection not as a purposeful, 'helpful' response, but as a reaction of an 'organism under stress'" (p. 68).

Each section of the chapter presents elements that are common across approaches, as well as elements that are unique to each. This chapter draws heavily from seminal writings, including Minuchin's *Families and Family Therapy* (1974), Minuchin and Fishman's *Family Therapy Techniques* (1981), Haley's *Problem-Solving Therapy* (1987), and Madanes's *Strategic Family Therapy* (1981). Other publications were also influential and are cited when appropriate.

## HISTORY AND BACKGROUND OF THE STRUCTURAL AND STRATEGIC APPROACHES

*Common Elements*

Both structural and strategic approaches stem from communication theory as advanced by Bateson and colleagues—most notably, Don Jackson, John Weakland, and Gregory Bateson, in Palo Alto (Bateson & Jackson, 1968; Bateson, Jackson, Haley, & Weakland, 1956). This group began its work in the area of schizophrenia but laid the groundwork for family therapy with all types of symptoms. Communication theory incorporates Wiener's (1948) theory of cybernetics, to emphasize relationships as homeostatic systems with self-correcting feedback processes, positing that human relationships are defined by the interchange of messages. Behavior is viewed in the context of a unit of at least two people, a sender and a receiver. Bateson proposed that communication can be described in terms of levels, describing how these levels can conflict in paradoxical ways. By 1962, the Palo Alto group had made the shift from describing mental illness as individual phenomena to

describing it as communicative behavior between people. They identified processes that became the building blocks of the structural/strategic approaches: the double bind, the focus on dyadic interactions, family homeostasis, and complementarity versus symmetry. Subsequent therapies developing out of this view emphasized changing families by influencing family members to communicate in new ways.

Don Jackson was the first to apply communications theory to family treatment. Jackson recognized that family relationships consist of repetitive patterns of interactions. He outlined three types of patterns that exist in all families: (1) covert norms, (2) overt family values, and (3) metarules for enforcing norms and values. Jackson planted the seeds for the strategic concepts of the function of the symptom and the importance of hierarchical structures and "quid pro quo" arrangements in marriage (Jackson, 1965). He established the Mental Research Institute (MRI) in 1959 and, together with Haley, Watzlawick, Weakland, Virginia Satir, Jules Riskin, and other colleagues, started one of the first family therapy training programs (cf., Satir, 1964; Watzlawick, Beavin, & Jackson, 1967).

The MRI group in Palo Alto has had a tremendous impact on the family therapy field. In addition to being the birthplace of Haley's approach, it directly and indirectly influenced a host of strategically oriented models and therapists. Most prominent are the *MRI model* (cf. Fisch, Weakland, & Segal, 1982; Watzlawick, Weakland, & Fish, 1974), the *Milan model* (cf. Selvini Palazzoli, Boscolo, Cecchin, & Prata, 1978) and *solution-focused therapy* (cf. de Shazer, 1988). The strategically oriented models are based on communications theory and the work of Milton Erickson. The model most closely related to Haley's strategic family therapy is the MRI model. They share a belief that symptoms are caused by repetitive sequences of behaviors that represent the family's faulty attempts to solve problems, resulting in the escalation of problems through positive feedback loops. They are both brief, pragmatic, and directive, focusing on identifying and resolving the presenting problem, rather than on offering interpretations or providing insight. Both use paradoxical directives and make strategic use of the family's resistance to bring about change, placing responsibility on the therapist for making change happen in the family. Haley's approach differs from that of MRI, in that it focuses on triadic and moderate-length sequences, rather than on dyadic and immediate sequences of behavior, and theorizes about the function of the symptom. However, the most fundamental difference between the approaches is that despite focusing on the presenting symptom, the ultimate goal in Haley's model is to change family structure. It is this structural framework, particularly with regard to hierarchy, that links Haley's strategic family therapy to the structural approach. In the sections that follow, we highlight the critical influence of Minuchin and Haley and include other important figures who have played a role in the refinement of these approaches. Most notable are Braulio Montalvo, on the structural side, and Cloe Madanes, the codeveloper of strategic family therapy.

## Structural Family Therapy

Minuchin came to family therapy in the 1950s, from a background in child psychiatry. While working with juvenile delinquents at the Wiltwyck School for Boys, Minuchin and colleagues (Auerswald, King, Montalvo, and Rabinowitz) were confronted by the impotence of the individual approach, given the social context to which the children would return. They were influenced by Jackson's emphasis on interpersonal connections and rec-

ognized that the behavior of their patients was not only an action, but also a reaction. They started to conduct conjoint sessions, built a therapy room with a one-way mirror, and taught themselves family therapy by trial and error. Minuchin's work is quite unique because, from the very beginning, he has primarily worked with poor, ethnic minority families (cf. Minuchin, Montalvo, Guerney, Rosman, & Schumer, *Families of the Slums*, 1967).

In 1965, Minuchin became professor of psychiatry at the University of Pennsylvania and director of both the Philadelphia Child Guidance Clinic and the Children's Hospital of Philadelphia's Department of Psychiatry. Upon his arrival, Minuchin began to rebel against the psychiatric establishment and was deemed "dangerous" for zealously insisting that child psychiatry was family psychiatry, even for middle-class families. At about this time, Minuchin also started to treat the families of diabetic children who had been unsuccessfully treated with individual therapy. He discovered that all of the families had a common view of themselves as normal families who would be happy except for the diabetes, and that parents detoured their conflict through the diabetic child. Minuchin conducted clinical research with families of diabetic, anorectic, and asthmatic children, as well as those with other psychosomatic complaints, demonstrating the effectiveness of family therapy for psychosomatic children (cf., Minuchin, Rosman, Baker, Liebman, Milman, & Todd, 1975; Minuchin, Rosman, & Baker, 1978).

In the 1970s Minuchin and colleagues at the Philadelphia Child Guidance Clinic (Aponte, Fishman, Greenstein, Haley, Madanes, Montalvo, Rosman, Umberger, and Walters) shaped the structural approach into the most influential family therapy approach and, due in large part to this work, family therapy was accepted in the mainstream of child psychiatry.

## Strategic Family Therapy

Jay Haley worked closely with and was influenced by the Palo Alto group, Milton Erickson, and Minuchin. Consequently, strategic family therapy is an integration of several seminal streams of family theory. From the Palo Alto/MRI group, Haley acquired the communication theorists' understanding of the nature of analogical and digital communication (Bateson & Jackson, 1968) and the belief that giving families insight into the roots of their problems was not helpful. From Minuchin, he developed the structural view of family organization as a holding framework for his strategic techniques. Perhaps most important, from Erickson he borrowed many of the cornerstones of the strategic approach: the focus on symptoms, the use of paradox, the brevity of treatment, and the stance that the therapist should take responsibility for treatment failures. Haley added a focus on the functional quality of symptoms. Later, he adopted structural concepts and widened the lens on problematic communication to include longer sequences with three (triangles) or more people. Haley and Madanes worked together at Palo Alto/MRI and the Philadelphia Child Guidance Clinic and established the Family Therapy Institute in Washington, DC.

# MAJOR THEORETICAL CONSTRUCTS

## Common Elements

The structural and strategic approaches share many fundamental principles. The first is that human behavior, including psychopathology, must be understood within the *context* in which it occurs. Human contexts are *systems* with rules that regulate behavior and *reciprocal* processes, such that the behavior of one part of the system influences the behavior of

other parts. The most influential human context is the family system. Over time, the family develops *structures*, that is, consistent, repetitive, organized, and predictable patterns of family behavior. The family is a *self-correcting, homeostatic* system, in which deviance from the normative pattern of interaction activates a governing process. If a person deviates from the repeating behavior and so defines a different interaction, the others react against that deviation and shape the behavior back into the habitual pattern. Thus family structures are self-perpetuating and resistant to change, but they are changeable. The goal of therapy is to increase the flexibility and complexity of these structures.

## Structural Family Therapy

One of the goals of the structural approach is to help individuals to experience themselves, including their problems, as belonging to part of a larger whole. When the individual is seen as part of a larger entity, his or her behavior can be understood as *complementary* or reciprocal to another's behavior. Complementarity is the defining principle of every relationship, in that one person's behavior is codetermined by another's behavior. For example, one parent's leniency is balanced by the other parent's strictness; a wife's vulnerability helps her husband feel protective; an adolescent is kept young by his parents, and his immature behavior makes the parents treat him as a young child. The family organizes itself into smaller groups, or *subsystems*. Each individual belongs to various subsystems, requiring flexibility of roles. The most prominent subsystems are the couple, the parents, and the siblings.

### THE COUPLE SUBSYSTEM

The most important task for the couple is the creation of boundaries to protect this subsystem from intrusions from other subsystems (e.g., children, in-laws). This is vital to the health of the family. Problems in this subsystem spill over to the rest of the family. This subsystem is a model for the children on adult intimate relationships.

## THE PARENTAL SUBSYSTEM

This subsystem can vary in composition (particularly in minority and poor families) and may include a grandparent, an aunt, or a parental child. The therapist has to learn who comprises the parental subsystem. Parents have the responsibility to care for, protect, and socialize the children and the right to privacy and to make decisions related to the total system. The role of the parental subsystem changes as the children grow. Children must be given more opportunities for decision making and self-determination as they develop.

## THE SIBLING SUBSYSTEM

Siblings are the child's first peer group with whom he or she learns to socialize; therefore, intrusions from adults are best kept at a minimum. Large families may have a variety of sibling groups, according to developmental stages. Although family therapists underutilize siblings, this subsystem can be very useful for changing family structures.

## BOUNDARIES

These protect the autonomy of the family and subsystems by regulating proximity and hierarchy. Families or groups within the family may have boundaries that are too diffused, resulting in *enmeshment,* or too rigid, resulting in *disengagement.* Boundary patterns within a family tend to be reciprocal, such that, for example, there could be an enmeshed mother-child dyad and a disengaged father. Problems stem from these two extreme boundary patterns. Although enmeshed relationships offer the benefit of cohesiveness and support, symptoms may emerge from the extreme closeness and overprotection between family members. Enmeshed relationships tend to stifle individual growth because it is against the rules of the relationship for members to seek affiliation outside of the family. Disengaged relationships, in contrast, offer great opportunity for individual growth and autonomy. However, they do not provide the protective functions that are a crucial aspect of family affiliation, as family members are unlikely to be aware when one of their own is experiencing distress. Much of structural family therapy is focused on defining boundaries within enmeshed dyads.

## Strategic Family Therapy

Any behavior can be conceived in units of individuals, dyads, triads, or larger groups. The size of the *conceptual unit* leads to different ideas regarding what might be done to change a behavior. A therapist who thinks in terms of dyads can consider a person's behavior as a response to another person who is eliciting the behavior. A therapist who thinks in terms of triads can seek out the triangle involved in the behavior and the interactional sequence that requires the behavior. This level of conceptualization allows treatment flexibility because the therapist can demonstrate more variety in therapeutic interventions and can consider the *coalitions* involved. Therapists must also consider themselves members of the social unit that contains the problem. Therefore, therapists must consider the coalitions in which they are involved when they act.

A distinction should be made between coalitions, which involve a joint action of two persons against a third person, and alliances, which involve two or more persons with a shared interest that is not shared by a third person. Coalitions are particularly problematic because they are typically used to detour conflict between two people. For example, say Persons A and B have a conflict that they cannot manage directly; Person C enters into the conflict by allying with Person A against Person B; consequently, A and B do not resolve their problem directly and their relationship does not develop. The preceding *sequence* of interaction is an example of a *triangle.*

All organizations have *hierarchies,* which are maintained by all participants. The simplest hierarchy involves the generation line. At most moments, there are three generations in a family therapy situation: the parents, where power often resides; the grandparents, who are usually moved to an advisory, if not superfluous, position; and the children. The most common hierarchy in poor and ethnic minority families is grandmother, mother, and child; or mother, parental child, and child. Therapists must be aware of their own position, so that they do not inadvertently form a coalition with members low in the hierarchy against those who are higher, unless it is done for strategic purposes.

## PROPOSED ETIOLOGY OF CLINICAL PROBLEMS

### Common Elements

The structural and strategic approaches view problems as stemming from rigid and repetitive patterns of interaction that restrict the repertoire of available behaviors. Both see pathology as a failure of the family to *adapt* to changed circumstances as the family proceeds through *developmental stages* and when outside forces impinge to require adjustment. In pathological families, instead of adjusting by expanding their range of behaviors, the family more rigidly adheres to its habitual patterns.

Both approaches also emphasize the importance of problems in the family hierarchy, particularly cross-generational alliances or coalitions in families presenting with a symptomatic child. Minuchin focuses on the horizontal aspects of hierarchies, that is, the importance of defining subsystems in the family with clear generational boundaries (thus reducing cross-generational alliances). Haley focuses more on the vertical aspects of hierarchy, describing pathology in a child as involving a coalition across generational lines. Madanes adds a nuance to Haley's view by stating that the child's symptom reflects an *incongruous* hierarchical organization, in that the symptom serves the function of protecting the parents (by distracting the parents from their own individual or marital problems).

### Structural Family Therapy

Pathology may be inside the patient, in his or her social context, or in the feedback between them. Certain symptoms are a clear indication of certain family structural arrangements. Therefore, presenting problems trigger an initial set of hypotheses with which the therapist will approach the family. For example, when parents are unable to control a young child, it is very likely that a parent is facilitating the child's behavior problems, either by undermining the other parental figure or by abdicating authority. When a child is functioning in a manner that is not commensurate with his or her age, it is likely that the child has an enmeshed relationship with one of the parents that keeps the child young.

Some family structures are inherently problematic. One such structure, as mentioned previously, is the cross-generation coalition. Other areas of dysfunction in a family frequently involve either enmeshment or disengagement. Therapy is thus, to a great extent, a process of monitoring proximity and distance.

Symptoms arise in enmeshed families because the family overreacts to a stressor and, in disengaged families, because the family is unaware of a problem.

Some family structures are problematic because they represent a failure to adjust to circumstances. Families use only a small fraction of the full range of behaviors and often get stuck in patterns of behavior that are either limited or obsolete. When faced with stress, healthy families adjust their structures, whereas pathological families become more rigid. Problems arise when inflexible family structures cannot adjust to maturational or situational challenges. Failure to adjust may be due to inherent flaws in structure or merely a lack of flexibility.

## Developmental Transitions

New functions must appear as the family goes through developmental stages, that is, couple formation, young children, school age and adolescent children, grown children, and non-normative transitional incidents (such as illness, loss of a job). Minuchin and Fishman (1981) have outlined several stages and the corresponding tasks that must be accomplished. An excellent resource for further understanding of family developmental stages is Carter and McGoldrick's *The Changing Family Life Cycle* (1989).

## Strategic Family Therapy

In the strategic approach, symptoms are viewed as having a *function* within the family. It is assumed that a symptom metaphorically expresses a problem. Symptomatic behavior is in some way an adaptive, albeit unsatisfactory, solution, in that a person must behave in abnormal ways when responding to abnormal social structures.

Problems in the family's hierarchical organization are at the root of symptomatic behavior. Typically, the hierarchical arrangement is confused. It may be confused by being ambiguous or because a member at one level consistently forms a coalition against a peer with a member at another level, thus violating the basic rules of organization. This type of coalition is particularly troublesome when it is secret.

Strategists define a symptom as a type of behavior that is part of a sequence of acts among several persons. In a repetitive sequence, all participants behave in a way that keeps the sequence going. Because the sequence repeats in a circle, there is a series of steps, each leading to the next and so back to the beginning again. Sequences are problematic when they either simultaneously define two opposite hierarchies or when they reflect an inconsistent (unstable) hierarchy—for example, if the parents at one point take charge of a child and at another point accept the child as the authority. For instance, a family has dual incongruous hierarchies when (1) the parents are in charge of their child by the fact of being parents, but (2) the child is also in charge of the parents because of the power of symptomatic behavior or because of the power given by coalitions with family members of high status.

### MARITAL PROBLEMS

In the strategic conceptualization of behavior as determined by units of at least three persons, a marriage does not exist as an independent entity. Marital problems can present in therapy through (1) a symptom of an individual member of the couple, (2) a child problem, or (3) a direct request for marital counseling.

Whenever a married person has a severe symptom, the symptom serves some function in the marriage, and there will be consequences in the marriage when the symptom is cured. Madanes describes a marriage with a symptomatic spouse in terms of a hierarchical incongruity in the marriage. The symptomatic spouse attempts to change the hierarchical arrangement and to balance the power in the couple through the use of a symptom. The symptomatic person is in an inferior position to the other spouse, who tries to help, yet the symptomatic spouse is also in a superior position, in that she or he refuses to be helped. The couple becomes restricted to a situation where one behavior defines both an inferior and a superior position of each spouse in relation to the other. The symptom is a solution to the couple's difficulties, in that it equalizes the power of the spouses, providing a focus of interaction that stabilizes the marriage. The job of the therapist is to organize the couple so that power and weakness are not centered on symptomatic behavior.

According to Haley, couples who cannot deal with their marital problems directly, communicate their problem through their child. The child becomes the communication intermediary and so stabilizes the marriage. Adolescent or young adult problems sometimes present because the young person has reached the age of leaving home, requiring parents to enter into a new phase of their marriage. Madanes departs subtly from this presentation. She views the triangulation of the child in the marital problem as a protective act by the child, in that the child's symptom keeps the parents involved in attempting to help the child or change the child's behavior. Parents have to put aside their own problems and hold themselves together to aid the child. In this sense the child's behavior is helpful in providing a respite from, and a reason to overcome, their own problems. This view is different from Haley's, in which, although the protective function of the symptom is understood, the child is typically thought of as involved in a coalition with one parental figure against the other.

When a couple presents a marital problem by seeking couples' therapy (as opposed to presenting as a problem in one of the marital partners or their child), it usually indicates an attempt to stay together. Presenting marital problems are the result of habitual rules of behavior, and the problem is at the level of those rules. One way to think about marital difficulties is in terms of flexibility. One of the functions of marital therapy is to enlarge the possibilities of the two partners so that they have wider range of behavior. Just as one way to see the goal of all therapy is to introduce complexity, so in marital therapy, the opportunities of the partners are greater if their relationship has more complex possibilities.

## METHODS OF CLINICAL ASSESSMENT

### Common Elements

For structural and strategic therapists, family interactions are the primary focus of treatment. The key to effective intervention thus begins with an accurate assessment and clinical formulation of family interactions that are related to the presenting problem. Assessment and clinical formulation always consider the general nature of family functioning, as well as the specific relationship between the presenting problem and general family functioning.

Assessment and clinical formulation involve identifying strengths and weaknesses within the family. Weaknesses (i.e., problematic interactions) may include parental conflict, parent–child relationship, triangulation, and a lack of subsystem differentiation and may all be related to behavior problems in a child. In contrast, strengths refer to adaptive family interactions, as well as to the particular capabilities of individual family members. This focus on strengths is not merely "lip service" or a reaction to "pathology-based" intervention models. Because structural and strategic interventions are brief and problem-focused, therapists must utilize the family's resources to maximize their impact on the family.

At a microlevel (moment by moment) in treatment, the therapist looks for intrapersonal and interpersonal strengths. Some examples of intrapersonal strengths include positive features such as love, commitment, and a desire to make things better. Interpersonal strengths include open and direct communication between family members, positive expressions of support, and the healthy expression of differences of opinion. *Intra*personal weaknesses at this level include hopelessness, anger (at worst, hate or contempt), and negative attributions about self or other. *Inter*personal weaknesses include the expression of contempt (as opposed to appropriate disagreements), intense and escalating levels of negativity, vague and indirect communication, and developmentally inappropriate parent or child behavior.

At a molar (e.g., refers to global patterns) level, the strengths and weaknesses of complex patterns of interaction are considered. Some examples of strengths at this level include the family's flexibility to respond to changing conditions and its ability to negotiate and resolve its differences of opinion. Weaknesses at the molar level include a lack of parental cooperation in setting and enforcing rules, overly connected or disconnected interpersonal boundaries, and the consistent denial, avoidance, or diffusion of family conflict.

Structural and strategic family therapists gather information about family interactions by asking directive questions about family responses to presenting problems and by encouraging family members to interact in the treatment context (enactment). The process of assessment and clinical formulation, however, varies across these approaches.

## Structural Family Therapy

The core of assessment and *diagnosis* in the structural approach involves identifying repetitive interactional patterns within the family. Diagnosis of the family system is based on observing interactions that occur in the session. It is important to do this early in the therapy before the therapist is inducted into the family culture and thereafter fails to see structures because he or she has become a part of them. The focus is on process, not content. From these observations, the therapist can map the family system. For example, *mapping* (Minuchin & Fishman, 1981) is used to identify the position of family members in relation to one another. Family maps show who is aligned with whom, who is in conflict, who are nurturers or scapegoats, and who is in the family groupings for resolving conflict. The family map also shows the delineation of boundaries between subsystems.

Minuchin and colleagues (Minuchin, 1974; Minuchin & Fishman, 1981) were the first to emphasize the importance of *enactments* in assessment of the family systems. Through enactment, the therapist gathers information about family functioning directly, by facilitating family interactions in therapy, and does not have to rely on stories about what typically happens when the therapist is not present. Enactments reflect the family's overlearned behaviors that are present in most situations. Thus, by observing enactments, the therapist can directly assess strengths and weaknesses within the family, identify circular/systemic processes, and assess changes in family interaction that occur as therapy progresses.

## Strategic Family Therapy

The most important aspect of clinical assessment in the strategic approach is to have a clear and operationalized treatment goal related to the family's presenting symptom and the sequences of interaction that are related to the symptom. This formulation is conducted in the first interview. Haley (1987) maps out five stages for the interview. These stages are as follows.

1. In the *social* stage, family members are greeted and made comfortable. The therapist respects the hierarchy in the family in order to gain cooperation and is most respectful toward the one person in the family who can bring the family back. The adult who seems less involved with the problem should be spoken to first. Usually, the most concerned person is the one most burdened with the problem. The most typical arrangement is a very concerned mother and a peripheral father.
2. In the *problem* stage, the therapist inquires about the presenting problem. Everyone is given a turn to present his or her view of the symptom. The therapist observes, but does not comment on, family process.
3. In the *interaction* stage, family members are asked to talk with each other (enact) to allow the therapist to identify problematic hierarchies. Every dyad is asked to communicate directly; subsequently, these interactions are expanded into triadic communications. The therapist brings the problem behavior into the room (e.g., asking a child to have a tantrum, if that is a symptomatic behavior) and observes the family process and organization in response to the behavior.
4. In the *goal-setting* stage, the family members are asked to specify the changes they would like to see occur in therapy. The therapist assists family members to concretely define these changes to make the problems solvable. A specific and detailed statement of the problem and the desired outcome is necessary for monitoring progress and outcome.
5. In the *task-setting* stage, the family is given a simple directive in order to keep it involved with the therapist between sessions.

## A Combined Structural/Strategic Approach to Clinical Assessment

Szapocznik and colleagues have combined structural and strategic approaches to develop and validate a family approach for behavior-problem adolescents (Hervis, Szapocznik, Mitrani, Rio, & Kurtines, 1991; Szapocznik et al., 1991). In this combined approach, family interactions are identified along five interrelated dimensions: Structure, Resonance, Developmental Stage, Identified Patienthood, and Conflict Resolution.

1. *Structure* refers to the organizational aspects of the repetitive patterns of interaction within the family. Three specific categories of family organization are examined: leadership, subsystem organization, and communication flow.
   a. *Leadership* assesses the distribution of authority and responsibility within the family. This category includes *Hierarchy* (Who takes charge of the family's directorship? Is leadership in the appropriate hands?); *Behavior Control* (Who keeps order?); and *Guidance* (Who provides advice and suggestions?).
   b. *Subsystem Organization* is concerned with the formal and informal organization of the family system, including *Alliances* (Who supports whom? Are alliances appropriate?); *Triangulations*, defined as an involvement of Family Member C in a conflict between Family Members A and B across generational lines; and *Subsystem Membership* (Who is a member of which subsystem? Are subsystems appropriate?).

c. *Communication Flow* is concerned with pathways of communication within the family, including *Directness of Communication* (Does every dyad communicate directly?); *Gatekeepers* (Is there a gatekeeper who channels communication?); and *Spokesperson* (Is there a family member who speaks for others in the family?).

2. *Resonance* is a measure of subsystem differentiation. At one extreme, boundaries can be either extremely rigid or impermeable (disengagement). At the opposite extreme, they can be too permeable (enmeshment).

3. *Developmental Stage* refers to the appropriateness of family members' interactions with respect to roles and tasks assigned to various family members, taking into consideration their age and position within the family. The following sets of roles and tasks are considered in examining this dimension:

   a. *Parenting Roles and Tasks* (Are parents parenting at a level consistent with the age of the children?).

   b. *Spousal Roles and Tasks* (Are spouses parenting at cooperative and equal levels of development?).

   c. *Child/Sibling Roles and Tasks* (Do the children function competently for their age and have appropriate rights and responsibilities?).

   d. *Extended Family Member Roles and Tasks* (Are parents able to assume proper parental position relative to their children in light of the role of their own parents and other relatives?).

4. *Identified Patienthood* (IPhood) refers to the extent to which the family is convinced that its primary problem is *all* the fault of the person exhibiting the symptom and uses that IPhood as a means of maintaining family homeostasis. There are five signs indicative of strong IPhood:

a. *Negativity about the IP* (Is the IP seen as the cause of family pain and unhappiness?).

b. *IP centrality* (Is the IP frequently the center of attention?).

c. *Overprotection of the IP* (Does the family avoid confronting the IP's dysfunction?).

d. *Nurturance of IPhood* (Do family members support or abet the IP's dysfunction?).

e. *Denial of other problems* (Does the family imply that the IP is the sole cause of problems and pain?).

5. *Conflict Resolution* is a measure of the family's style in managing disagreements. There are five conflict-resolution styles identified:

   a. *Denial*. Disagreements are not allowed to emerge.

   b. *Avoidance*. Disagreement begins to emerge but is inhibited.

   c. *Diffusion*. Moving from one disagreement to another without letting any emerge fully or making personal attacks that are not part of the conflict issue.

   d. *Emergence without resolution*. Separate accounts and opinions regarding one disagreement are clearly expressed, but no solution is reached.

   e. *Emergence with resolution*. Separate accounts and opinions regarding a single disagreement are clearly expressed and a single solution acceptable to all family members is negotiated.

## Formal Assessment Methods

In contrast to the rich clinical history of structural and strategic approaches, very little work has been done to develop and test methods of assessment that specifically target strategic or structural constructs. As such, only a few formal measures specific to these approaches are available. It should be noted that literally hundreds of family assessment measures include structural and strategic components; however, most of these measures are not based on principles of structural or strategic family therapy. Thus, these measures are not reviewed in this chapter. Table 9.1 presents a brief review of five measures that are specific to structural and strategic therapy.

## CLINICAL CHANGE MECHANISMS/ CURATIVE FACTORS

### Common Elements

Structural and strategic approaches share the tenet that symptom change and enhanced family functioning are inextricably linked. Because symptoms are caused by rigidly repeating patterns of interaction, it follows that the curative factor of therapy is to expand the family's range of available responses and its ability to use these responses to resolve its problems. Moreover, both approaches share an emphasis on the creation of an effective hierarchical structure that helps parents function as a cohesive executive subsystem. Although both approaches hold that changing a pattern of interaction (or a sequence of behavior) causes family members to undergo change, there is an important difference regarding the position of the presenting problem in this equation. That is, the structural school views symptom resolution as a byproduct of structural change, whereas the strategic school focuses on symptom resolution to bring about structural change.

### Structural Family Therapy

Structuralists believe that the most effective way to change symptoms is to change the fam-

ily patterns that maintain them. The goal of the structural approach is to facilitate the growth of the system to resolve symptoms and encourage growth in individuals, while also preserving the mutual support of the family. Therapy is therefore directed toward changing the organization of the family, unfreezing families from rigid habits, and thus creating opportunities for new structures. The goal is to activate latent adaptive structures that already exist in the family's repertoire. The underlying assumption is that families are inherently competent.

### Strategic Family Therapy

Change occurs in strategic family therapy by requiring new behavior aimed at solving the presenting symptom. The presenting problem serves as a lever to change family structure. The therapist joins the ongoing system and changes sequences by shifting the ways people respond to each other because of the ways they must respond to the therapist. The therapeutic task is to change the problematic sequence by intervening in such a way that it cannot continue.

Strategists do not subscribe to the structuralist notion that changing one part of a sequence can initiate a lasting change in an entire pattern of interactions. It is necessary to have a change in the behavior of at least two persons. Also in contrast to Structural therapy, Strategic therapy does not aim to make the family aware of the sequence, as this only causes resistance. Asking families to express feelings does not help either (unless they are expressing feelings in a different way—e.g., communicating directly, instead of needing a symptom). The way to bring about change in a sequence is to set up the situation so that people will change in order to avoid the ordeals inherent in being a client.

TABLE 9.1

Methods of Clinical Assessment: Observational and Self-Report Coding Systems

| Coding System | Construct(s) | Coding Categories | Study Citations |
|---|---|---|---|
| Structural Family Systems Ratings *(Observational)* | Family Functioning | Structure *(Leadership, Subsystem Organization, Communication Flow)* Resonance *(Differentiation, Disengagement, Enmeshment)* Developmental Stage Identified Patienthood Conflict Resolution | Santisteban et al., 1996 Szapocznik & Kurtines, 1989 Szapocznik, Kurtines, Foote, Perez-Vidal, & Hervis, 1983, 1986 Szapocznik, Kurtines, Santisteban, & Rio, 1990 Szapocznik, Rio, et al., 1989 Szapocznik, Rio, et al., 1991 Szapocznik, Santisteban, et al., 1989 |
| Wood's "Family Interaction Clinical Rating Scale" *(Observational)* | Family Behavior/ Interaction | Family Reactivity, Proximity Generational Hierarchy Enmeshment, Rigidity Overprotection Conflict Avoidance, Poor Conflict Resolution, Triangulation, Quality of Marital Relationship, | Wood, 1985 Wood, 1993 Wood, Watkins, Boyle, Nogueria, Zimand, & Carroll, 1989 |
| System for Coding Interactions and Family Functioning *(Observational)* | Family Functioning of Subsystems/ Dyads | Family (6): *Structure, Organization, Flexibility–Rigidity, Negative Conflict, Positive Affect, Focus of Problem* Marital Communication (1): *Decision Making* Parent (5): *Rejection/ Invalidation, Coerciveness, Triangulation, Withdrawal, Emotional Support* Child (2): *Affect* (Anger, Frustration) *and Behavior* (Withdrawal, Defiance) | Lindahl & Malik, 1999a Lindahl & Malik, 1999b Lindahl & Malik, 1996 Kerig & Lindahl, 2001 |
| Family Coding System *(Observational)* | Effects of Marital Conflict on Parent–Child Interaction | Interparental Affect Parent–Child Affect and Communication Child Behavior Cross-Generational Alliance | Margolin & Gordis, 1992 Margolin, John, Ghosh, & Gordis, 1996 |
| Structural Family Interaction Scale *(Self-Report)* | Family Functioning | Enmeshment, Disengagement, Flexibility, and Rigidity, Conflict Avoidance, Conflict Resolution, Conflict Without Resolution, Overprotection, Neglect, Generational Hierarchy, Patterns of Parent Coalition, Triangulation, Parent–Child Coalition, Detouring | Perosa & Perosa, 1982 Perosa & Perosa, 1990 Perosa & Perosa, 1993 Perosa, Perosa, & Tam, 1993 |

## SPECIFIC THERAPEUTIC INTERVENTIONS

In addition to the seminal works noted throughout this chapter, literally hundreds of books, chapters, and articles have been written to describe structural and strategic intervention strategies. Two of the earliest and most influential are Watzlawick, Weakland, and Fisch's *Change: Principles of Problem Formation and Problem Resolution* (1974) and Minuchin and Fishman's *Family Therapy Techniques* (1981).

### Common Elements

Both structural and strategic family therapy are directive, present, and action-oriented. They stress the importance of *joining* the family before changes in family structures can occur. Both rely on *enactment* of interactions within the therapy session for the purposes of diagnosing and transforming interactions, assign homework tasks, and prescribe *"unbalancing"* the system as a lever for changing family relationships.

### Structural Family Therapy

Structural family therapy is not a set of techniques, but rather a way of looking at families. Structuralists aim to promote growth in the family by expanding the family's repertoire of interactions. The assumption is that the family contains the ingredients for better functioning, and it is the therapist's job to unearth these underutilized resources.

The therapist establishes himself or herself as leader of the therapeutic system, watches the family in action, identifies overly rigid family structures, and plans an intervention to loosen the old and establish new structures. To change the family's usual way of interact-

ing, it is not sufficient for the therapist to be merely an observer. The therapist must enter the system to transform it. Therapists join the family and establish leadership by showing that they understand and are working to help family members, and by activating those aspects of themselves that are congruent with the family. Therapists adjust their position to accomplish therapy goals. When therapists validate, encourage, identify affect, or ally with family members, they are in a position of close proximity. In a median position, therapists listen, elicit information, and observe the family. This process is known as *tracking*. When therapists take a stance as an expert, impart information, or direct the family in a task, they are joining from a disengaged position.

Based upon their observations and experience, therapists form an initial hypothesis regarding the nature of the structural problem in the family. Every family structure, no matter how viable in some cases, has areas of possible difficulty. When therapists are familiar with the areas of potential weakness in a family shape, they can probe and plan therapy accordingly. The following are two common family configurations, the problems that tend to be associated with them, and therapist interventions.

### PAS DE DEUX (2-PERSON) FAMILIES

A family consisting of only two people tends to have an intense style of relating that may foster mutual, almost symbiotic, dependence and resentment. The therapist in such cases can plan interventions to delineate the boundary between the dyad, while opening up the boundaries between the family and the outside world.

### THREE-GENERATION FAMILIES

This configuration is common in ethnic minority and poor families. It has the strength of support and cooperation that allows for flexibility in family roles. However, because the boundaries between the top two generations do not conform to the more typically middle-class nuclear family, therapists tend to want to make delineations where these are not needed. Problems in such families occur when subsystem membership and hierarchy are unclear or inconsistent. The therapist can help clarify these boundaries, differentiate functions, and facilitate cooperation.

When families are undergoing a transitional crisis, the therapist can be helpful by imparting the normative stance that families are undergoing problems that are normal under the circumstances and can help them make the necessary adjustments. For example, therapists may assist in facilitating integration in stepfamilies, reassigning family tasks after the death of a family member, and connecting highly mobile families to extrafamilial resources.

To *restructure* interactions and thus expand the family's repertoire, the therapist must challenge the symptom, the family structure, and the family reality. The therapist challenges the family's view of the presenting problem to encourage it to search for alternative responses. The therapist maps out the family system, with special attention to boundary dysfunctions in subsystems, and corrects these dysfunctions by challenging family members' own definition of their roles and functions.

Structural family therapists use a variety of techniques to apply these strategies. Some of the most prominent techniques are described as follows.

In *focusing,* the therapist organizes the data provided by the family into a structural schema. This includes screening out some elements and emphasizing others, particularly process over content. Focusing helps the therapist make sense of the vast amounts of information to diagnose the family system and plan the therapy. It is also a strategy for shifting the family's frame of reality in a manner that facilitates change.

*Enactment* is asking the family to interact in the presence of the therapist, bringing problem sequences into the therapy room so that the therapist can observe and change these. Enactment allows for the gathering of information that is outside of the family's awareness and therefore cannot be gathered by asking questions. Enactment can also facilitate joining and helps therapists disengage if they have been inducted into the family's way of thinking or behaving.

Very frequently, family members will spontaneously enact in their typical way when they fight, interrupt, or criticize one another. However, because of the nature of therapy, it is not uncommon for family members to centralize therapists, in which case, the therapist will need to be more active in facilitating direct communication between family members. To facilitate enactments, the therapist systematically redirects communications to encourage interactions between family members.

There are three steps in enactment. The therapist (1) recognizes a problematic sequence, (2) directs an enactment, and (3) guides the family to modify the enactment. In enactment, the family members first experience their reality as they define it, and then the therapist introduces other elements and suggests alternative ways of transacting, thus challenging their reality and roles.

The therapist uses affect, repetition, duration, tone, and choice of words (clarity, not hedging) to get the message across to the family. In *achieving intensity,* the therapist heightens the impact of the therapeutic message. Intensity can also involve the family members's interactions with each other, for example, by extending an enactment beyond where the family members would have it end.

The therapist *realigns boundaries* by regulating the distance or proximity between family members. The therapist may comment on boundary violations he or she has observed, with statements such as, "You serve as your son's memory bank," or "Are you his alarm clock?". Boundaries can also be regulated by manipulating space in the session or by excluding persons from a session. Greater proximity can be achieved by directing disengaged family members to do an activity together.

In *unbalancing,* the therapist uses himself or herself to destabilize the family hierarchy by temporarily taking sides. This can be achieved by allying with a family member, ignoring a family member, or entering into a coalition with one family member against another. Unbalancing requires the therapist to assume a position of close proximity and is a difficult technique for an inexperienced therapist.

## Strategic Family Therapy

Strategic family therapy is a pragmatic approach, in which the therapist is expected to clearly define a presenting symptom and design a specific therapeutic plan for resolving it. The therapist keeps close track of therapeutic progress, and, if after a few weeks this plan is not successful, a new strategy is formulated. The therapist may borrow techniques from other models of therapy that are useful in solving a presenting problem. If the presenting problem is not resolved, the therapy is a failure (no matter what other changes have taken place), and it is the therapist who must accept responsibility for this failure.

To resolve the presenting symptom, it is not necessary to convince the family members that they have family problems, but they do need to be persuaded to cooperate in doing what the therapist asks. Persuasion and power in the family–therapist relationship are important elements in strategic family therapy. The therapist must join the family so that it will accept his or her leadership. Joining is achieved by

focusing on the presenting problem, accepting the family member's definition of the problem, and not confronting them with what they are doing wrong.

The structural goal in all cases is to draw a generational line and to prevent consistent coalitions across it. The therapist may induce change by temporarily siding with one person in the family against another (unbalancing). The therapist might present analogies and metaphors to shift behavior, a method adopted from Erickson. However, the signature technique in strategic family therapy is the use of *directives.*

The therapist assigns clear and simple directives, both within the session and as homework, to change sequences of interaction in the family. Directives introduce action into the therapy and allow family members to have a different experience with one another. As such, directives can be used to bring disengaged family members closer, increase positive interactions, help the family establish rules, define generational boundaries, or set individual goals and plans to achieve those goals. Directives are also used for joining (by intensifying the family's relationship with the therapist) and for diagnosis of family functioning (by demonstrating how the family responds to the directive).

The best directives respect and use the content that the family considers important, the presenting problem, to bring about a change in family process. This is a creative endeavor, in which the therapist thinks about the presenting problem in terms of the problematic sequence in the family and designs a directive that changes both the presenting problem and the sequence. For example, if the goal is to have a mother and her fire-setting child (identified patient) be more involved with each other, and a parental child excluded, the therapist can ask the mother to teach the identified patient how to set a safe fire.

This type of *straightforward directive* can

be given when the therapist expects family members to comply. It is essential that the therapist know how to motivate the family and assign tasks so that these are carried out. Motivational techniques involve finding some gain for each person involved and heightening the sense of urgency. Compliance is also enhanced by first getting the family to perform small tasks in the session (e.g., changing the seating arrangement or changing pathways of communication by asking the father and the mother to talk together without including their daughter). It also helps to involve the entire family, as long as hierarchy is not confused by involving children in adult aspects of the task. For example, if the directive is for the mother and the father to have a quiet dinner together, older children can be asked to help their younger siblings with homework, and younger children can be asked to help set the table. Finally, the directive must fit the family's style, and instructions must be precise and clear. The therapist asks the family members to report on the task at the next session and does not take lightly their failure to complete the task.

When the content of the intended behavior change is best not addressed directly, the therapist can use a *metaphorical directive.* For example, in the case of an adopted boy who is afraid of dogs, it might not be appropriate to talk about adoption directly. The therapist might ask the family to "adopt" a dog for the boy and thus work on both the presenting symptom (fear of dogs) and family processes related to adoption. A technique borrowed from Erickson for working with couples who are uncomfortable discussing their sexual problems directly is to assign the partners the task of enjoying a meal together, with an emphasis on doing it together, making it pleasant for all the senses, and satisfying each other.

Strategic family therapy is perhaps best known for its use of *paradoxical directives,* a technique borrowed from Erickson. When families are in a stable state, rather than in crisis, they are likely to resist attempts to directly change the system. Paradoxical directives allow the therapist to use the family's resistance to bring about the desired change. Paradoxical directives always include two contrary messages: "Change" and "Don't change." The therapist tells the family that he or she wants to help them change but at the same time asks them not to change.

One paradoxical technique is to ask the patient to produce more of the behavior that the patient wants to reduce. Regardless of whether the patient complies or resists, the nature of the symptom is transformed from involuntary to voluntary. Another paradoxical technique is for the therapist to tell a family that he or she is not sure the family is ready to accept the consequences of change. If the family accepts the directive at face value, then this opens the door to addressing the resistance directly. If family members do not accept the directive, they will change to prove the therapist wrong. A third type of paradoxical intervention involves exaggerating the symptom or rendering it absurd, especially in a manner that makes maintaining the symptom an ordeal for the family. For example, a father who is in a coalition with his small daughter against his wife can be directed to wash the daughter's sheets when she wets her bed.

To use paradox, the therapist must be able to think about problems in a game-like manner. The therapist must be able to tolerate the emotional reaction of the family, and accept the family's "spontaneous" change. The therapist must avoid taking credit for the change and must seem puzzled by the improvement. If the therapist wants to ensure that the change will continue, he or she can suggest a relapse. Erickson would say, "I want you to go back to that time when you felt miserable, feel as you did then, and see whether there is anything from that experience you wish to salvage" (Haley, 1987, p. 78).

A creative variation on paradoxical directives is offered by Madanes (1981) in the form of *pretend techniques*. In this type of intervention, the therapist asks the identified patient to pretend to have his symptom and the family members to pretend to respond in their typical manner. When a sequence is labeled "This is pretend," it is difficult for the participants to go back to the framework of "This is real." Also, when someone is pretending to have a symptom, he or she cannot really have it, or else it would not be pretending. Thus, the symptom is brought into the therapy room in a manner that allows family members to change their usual process.

Strategic therapy uses a *planned, step-by-step approach* to eliminate the symptom. A typical chain of interventions moves the family from its presenting structure to a different dysfunctional structure, which in turn is shifted to a functional one. This intermediate abnormality can take many forms. One is to redefine or reframe the problem, such as relabeling a symptom from "mental illness" to "misbehaving." Another way to induce an intermediate dysfunctional structure is to request the family to exaggerate the presenting dysfunctional structure. Likewise, there are many ways to approach any problematic structure. For example, take the most common structure in cases of symptomatic children, a two-generation triangle. The therapist has at least three options to change a sequence: (1) direct the peripheral parent to take charge of the child's problem and the intensely involved parent to stay out of it; (2) direct the intensely involved parent to become even more involved, while the peripheral parent remains peripheral; or (3) ask parents to agree on what is to be done and to carry it out.

Madanes (1981) offers a simple protocol for dealing with adolescent delinquency and drug abuse, viewing these cases as situations in which a cross-generational coalition or an incongruous hierarchy has solidified and become, in effect, a reversed hierarchy—with the parents subordinate and the adolescent in a superior position. Parents in such cases typically attempt to disqualify themselves or each other and appeal to others (the therapist, another authority, or even the adolescent) to make decisions regarding the adolescent. Therapy is aimed at redistributing power so that the parents are in charge. The therapist must elicit competent responses from the parents and discourage messages that denote their weakness.

When conducting marital therapy, it is often difficult to formulate specific treatment goals, which require negotiation between the spouses. Therapists are warned to avoid entering into a consistent coalition with one of the spouses. Such coalitions should be used only strategically (and by skilled therapists), for the purpose of destabilizing a marriage to produce change. Strategic therapists also utilize marital therapy to resolve individual symptoms in one of the spouses. The therapist does not offer any interpretation regarding the function of the symptom but helps the couple resolve the marital problems that make the symptom functional as improvement occurs.

## EFFECTIVENESS OF THE APPROACH

The efficacy and effectiveness of structural/strategic approaches have been carefully evaluated over the past 3 decades. For example, Minuchin and associates examined clinical outcomes in structural family therapy for children and adolescents with behavior problems, eating disorders, and diabetes. *Families of the Slums* (Minuchin et al., 1967) reports clinical improvement in child behavior problems in 7 of 11 families treated, noting that disengaged family-types did not respond positively to treatment. Likewise, *Psychosomatic Families* (Minuchin, Rosman,

& Baker, 1978) presents substantial improvement in eating disorders for 45 of 53 families treated. Minuchin's uncontrolled studies provided a foundation on which the evaluation of structural/strategic approaches has been built. However, Stanton and associates' groundbreaking studies with drug addicts (1982) launched an era of controlled, rigorous empirical studies of structural and strategic approaches.

## ALCOHOL, DRUGS, AND ANTISOCIAL BEHAVIOR

A substantial base of research findings supports the efficacy and effectiveness of structural and strategic approaches with adolescent and adults presenting with drug and alcohol problems and antisocial behaviors (cf. Alexander, Holtzworth-Munroe, & Jameson, 1994; Sexton, Alexander, & Mease, in press). This base is supported by Stanton & Shadish's (1997) meta-analysis, which concluded that couple and family therapy is, overall, as effective or more effective than alternative interventions in treating families with drug-abusing adolescents. Stanton and Shadish (1997) further point out that the "preponderance of family-couples therapy outcome research on this population has been performed with some version or expansion of structural, strategic, or structural-strategic family therapy" (p. 183). Thus, this area encompasses one of the most widely researched areas in the entire field of family therapy.

### FAMILY THERAPY WITH ADULT ADDICTS

The classic book *The Family Therapy of Drug Abuse and Addiction* (Stanton, Todd, & Associates, 1982) was the first formal documentation of empirically designed outcome studies focusing on the structural approach. These pioneer studies with young adult heroin addicts compared the effectiveness of family therapy combined with methadone, to non–family therapy combined with methadone. Results indicated that participants who received structural family therapy demonstrated greater rates of improvement than did those who had been in the non-family therapy conditions. Similar results were reported in a follow-up study (Stanton, Steier, Cook, & Todd, 1984) comparing structural family techniques plus methadone treatment to individual counseling and methadone treatment for detoxification cases.

### ADOLESCENTS WITH ALCOHOL, DRUG, AND OTHER DISRUPTIVE BEHAVIOR PROBLEMS

Outcome research with adolescent alcohol and drug users has exploded in the last 2 decades. Stanton and Todd's structural/strategic principles proved to be enormously influential in the development of family therapy approaches for adolescent drug abuse that emerged in the 1980s. For example, Joanning, Quinn, and Mullen (1992) and Lewis, Piercy, Sprenkle, and Trepper (1990) demonstrated the effectiveness of family-based interventions that integrated both structural and strategic techniques with drug-abusing adolescents, and as described further on, Szapocznik and colleagues' program of research has evaluated the efficacy of a combined structural/strategic approach with minority youths. It should be noted that many other empirically validated approaches have drawn heavily from structural/strategic principles. Some of these models are presented in Chapters 14, 15, and 18.

### BRIEF STRATEGIC FAMILY THERAPY

For 3 decades, Szapocznik and colleagues have evaluated the efficacy and effectiveness of brief strategic family therapy (BSFT) with Hispanic adolescents and their families at the

University of Miami (Florida) School of Medicine. Based on both structural and strategic principles, BSFT has been shown to reduce child and adolescent behavior problems and to improve family interactions (cf., Szapocznik, Robbins, et al., 2002). Perhaps the most significant findings on BSFT are in the area of engaging and retaining adolescents and their families in treatment. For example, Szapocznik, Perez-Vidal, et al. (1988) demonstrated that specialized engagement procedures substantially increased engagement into family therapy (92% versus 42%) and facilitated the completion of treatment (77% versus 25%). Santisteban et al. (1996) replicated these findings and further demonstrated that BSFT is also more effective in engaging youth and families with more severe behavior problems.

## Couples' Therapy

Though the large part of structural/strategic outcome research developed over the last 2 decades has addressed a huge umbrella of family compositions, only very few outcome studies have focused specifically on marital and couples' therapy. Of the few in existence, Goldman and Greenberg (1992) demonstrated that a combined structural and strategic approach was as effective in helping couples improve their functioning as was an emotionally focused experiential approach (emotionally focused therapy). Moreover, the couples in the integrated systemic therapy group maintained and actually improved at follow-up, whereas the emotionally focused therapy couples did not. Extending the work of Goldman and Greenberg, Davidson and Horvath (1997) examined more specifically the efficacy of paradoxical and homework components of strategic time-limited couples' therapy. They found that couples who received three sessions of immediate strategic intervention improved significantly more than those in the waiting-list control condition, in both marital satisfaction and conflict-resolution skills.

## Process Research

Despite rich outcome research findings, process research into the change mechanisms of structural and strategic family therapy is limited. The lack of research in this area is surprising because early writings included rich descriptions of process research methods, coding procedures, and clinically relevant results (e.g., Watzlawick & Weakland, 1977, pp. 71–127), whereas the establishment of the *Journal of Strategic and Systemic Therapy* in 1981 provided an excellent platform for disseminating research on structural and strategic clinical practices, systematic research failed to proliferate with the same intensity as structural and strategic theory and clinical practice. Perhaps the only exception is the rich base of research and case studies investigating the impact of paradoxical directives and reframing techniques (cf. Weeks, 1985, 1991; Weeks & L'Abate, 1982). Further on, we review process research in the following areas: (1) therapeutic relationship, (2) dropout, (3) linking process to outcome, and 4) paradoxical interventions.

### THERAPEUTIC RELATIONSHIP

Since the mid-1970s family theorists have focused on exploring the therapist–family member relationship, primarily addressing the importance of techniques such as joining with the family (Minuchin & Fishman, 1981) or attending to the coalitionary process (Sluzki, 1975). With respect to structural and strategic methods, Friedlander and colleagues (1985, 1987) explored Don Jackson's and Minuchin's in-session behaviors. Though focusing on each theorists' specific process strategies, the team concluded that Minuchin's method was characterized by (1) an active approach; (2) a focus on current or in-session behavior; (3) an emphasis on providing information, guidance, interpretation, or a course of action; and (4) less time seeking information. These structural sessions were further typified by the therapist's attempts at highlighting the parental executive subsystem, at confronting and using combined direct/indirect statements (addressing other than the target person), and at activating the system by explicitly requesting change. With respect to Jackson, Friedlander and Highlen (1984) found that he employed more strategic methods. As the forerunner of strategic family therapy, Jackson's sessions were characterized by a call for structure and management and a close alignment with the subsystem under the most stress.

## DROPOUT

Taking an in-depth look at processes associated with treatment dosage and participant dropout, Shields, Sprenkle, and Constantine (1991) showed that noncompleter cases were more likely to make frequent attempts to structure the therapist and would engage in more within-family disagreements. On the other hand, the completer cases were more likely to let the therapist do the structuring in response to family disagreements and be engaged in more family dialogues about problems.

### Linking process to outcome

The most recent available finding in the area of structural and strategic process research attempts to link process to outcome. Robbins et al. (2002) demonstated that for families who showed improvement on measures of conduct disorder, regardless of pretreatment family functioning, positive changes in family interaction were observed over the course of treat-

ment. In contrast, for those families who showed no improvement, family functioning did not change, or worsened, over the course of treatment.

## PARADOXICAL INTERVENTIONS

Excellent analyses of paradoxical intervention theory and techniques and research findings are included in reviews by Weeks and L'Abate (1982) and Weeks (1991). In fact, in the latter book, Kim, Poling, and Ascher (pp. 216–250) provide an outstanding synthesis of available research on the effectiveness of paradoxical techniques for patients presenting with insomnia, agoraphobia, obsessive-compulsive disorder, disorders of elimination, and other clinical conditions. It is important to note that much of the research on paradoxical interventions is not specific to structural and strategic approaches because paradoxical directives have been adopted by many individual, couple, and family approaches.

## FUTURE DEVELOPMENTS AND DIRECTIONS

### Ecosystemic Models

Perhaps because structural family therapy was developed for and has always been used with poor families, it is natural that it has been applied with a focus not only on the family but on other systems that have an impact on the family. Minuchin has addressed the structural problems inherent in social and mental health institutions which can exacerbate the very problems these institutions aim to solve (Elizur & Minuchin, 1989).

Others have used structural principles to transform the family's transactions with larger systems that play an important role in the lives of poor families. Fishman (1993) has developed an intensive structural therapy model that details assessment and intervention strategies for working with extrafamilial systems and has paired family therapists with community resource specialists to intervene in the family's broader social context (Fishman, Andes, & Knowlton, 2001). Likewise, Szpocznik and colleagues have integrated Bronfenbrenner's (1979) ecosystemic model with structural family therapy to form structural ecosystems therapy, which has been applied to substance-abusing adolescents (Szapocznik et al., 1997), HIV-seropostive women (Mitrani, Szapocznik, & Robinson-Batista, 2000) and family caregivers of persons with Alzheimer's-related dementias (Mitrani & Czaja, 2000).

*Research to Practice*

Although the structural/strategic approach has been empirically validated as efficacious for a variety of presenting symptoms, there is a need to transfer this research out of university-based laboratory settings and into community-based service centers. A recent effort by the National Institutes on Drug Abuse is providing an opportunity to conduct a large-scale test of brief strategic family therapy in such settings. NIDA's Clinical Trials Network is a major initiative to enhance the delivery of scientifically based treatments to drug-abuse patients by coordinating the efforts of researchers and community-based service providers to develop, validate, refine, and deliver laboratory-validated treatments at the community practice level.

## REFERENCES

Alexander, J., Holtzworth-Munroe, A., & Jameson, P. (1994). The process and outcome of marital and family therapy: Research review and evaluation. In A. Bergin & S. Garfield (Eds.), *Handbook of psychotherapy and behavior change* (4th ed., pp. 595–630). Oxford, England: Wiley.

Bateson, G., & Jackson, D. D. (1968). Some varieties of pathogenic organization. In D. D. Jackson (Ed.), *Communication, family and marriage* (Vol 1). Palo Alto, CA: Science and Behavior Book.

Bateson, G. Jackson, D. D., Haley, J., & Weakland, J. (1956). Toward a theroy of schizophrenia. *Behavioral Science, 1*(4), 251–264.

Bronfenbrenner, U. (1979). *The ecology of human development.* Cambridge, MA: Harvard University Press.

Carter. B., & McGoldrick, M., (Eds.). (1989). *The changing family life cycle: A framework for family therapy* (2nd ed.). Boston: Allyn and Bacon.

Davidson, G., & Horvath, A. (1997). Three sessions of brief couples therapy: A clinical trial. *Journal of Family Psychology, 11*(4), 422–435.

de Shazer, S. (1988). *Clues: Investigating solutions in brief therapy.* New York: W. W. Norton.

Elizur, J., & Minuchin, S. (1989). *Institutionalizing madness.* New York: Basic Books.

Fisch, R., Weakland, J., & Segal, L. (1982). *The tactics of change.* San Francisco: Jossey-Bass.

Fishman, H. C. (1993). *Intensive structural therapy: Treating families in their social context.* New York: Basic Books.

Fishman, H. C., Andes, F., & Knowlton, R. (2001). Enhancing family therapy: The addition of a community resource specialist. *Journal of Marital and Family Therapy, 27*(1), 111–116.

Friedlander, M., Ellis, M., Raymond, L., Siegel, S., & Milford, D. (1987). Convergence and divergence in the process of interviewing families. *Psychotherapy, 24,* 570–583.

Friedlander, M., & Highlen, P. (1984). A spatial view of the interpersonal structure of family interviews: Similarities and differences across counselors. *Journal of Counseling Psychology, 31,* 477–487.

Friedlander, M., Highlen, P., & Lassiter, W. (1985). Content analytic comparison of four expert counselors' approaches to family treatment: Ackerman, Bowen, Jackson, and Whitaker. *Journal of Counseling Psychology, 32,* 171–180.

Goldman, A., & Greenberg, L. (1992). Comparison of integrated systemic and emotionally focused approaches to couples therapy. *Journal of Consulting and Clinical Psychology, 60,* 962–969.

Haley, J. (1987). *Problem solving therapy* (2nd ed.). San Francisco: Jossey-Bass/ Pfeiffer.

Hervis, O., Szapocznik, J., Mitrani, V., Rio, A., & Kurtines, W. (1991). *Structural family systems ratings: A revised manual* (Tech Rep). Miami, FL: University of Miami School of Medicine, Department of Psychiatry, Spanish Family Guidance Center.

Jackson, D. D. (1965). Family rules: Marital quid pro quo. *Archives of General Psychiatry, 12,* 589–594.

Joanning, H., Quinn, T., & Mullen, R. (1992). Treating adolescent drug abuse: A comparison of family systems therapy, group therapy, and family drug education. *Journal of Marital and Family Therapy, 18*, 345–356.

Kim, R. S., Polling, J., & Ascher, L. M. (1991). An introduction to research on the clinical efficacy of paradoxical intention. In G. Weeks (Ed.), *Promoting change through paradoxical therapy* (rev. ed.) (pp. 216–250). Philadelphia: Brunner/Mazel.

Kerig, P., & Lindahl, K. (2001). *Family observational coding systems: Resources for systemic research.* Mahwah, NJ: Erlbaum.

Lewis, R., Piercy, F., Sprenkle, D., & Trepper, T. (1990). Family-based interventions and community networking for helping drug abusing adolescents: The impact of near and far environments. *Journal of Adolescent Research, 5*, 82–95.

Lindahl, K., & Malik, N. (1996). *System for coding interactions and family functioning (SCIFF).* Unpublished manual. University of Miami, Miami, Florida.

Lindahl, K., & Malik, N. (1999a). Marital conflict, family processes, and boys' externalizing behavior in Hispanic American and European American families. *Journal of Clinical Child Psychology, 28*, 12–24.

Lindahl, K., & Malik, N. (1999b). Observations of marital conflict and power: Relations with parenting in the triad. *Journal of Marriage and the Family, 61*, 320–330.

Madanes, C. (1981). *Strategic family therapy.* San Francisco: Jossey-Bass.

Margolin, G., & Gordis, E. (1992). *The family coding system.* Unpublished manual, University of Southern California, Los Angeles, California.

Margolin, G., John, R., Ghosh, C., & Gordis, E. (1996). Family interaction process: An essential tool for exploring abusive relations. In D. Cahn & S. Lloyd (Eds.), *Family violence: A communication perspective* (pp. 37–58). Newbury Park, CA: Sage.

Minuchin, S. (1974). *Families and family therapy.* Cambridge, MA: Harvard University Press.

Minuchin, S., & Fischman, S. (1981). *Family therapy techniques.* Cambridge, MA: Harvard University Press.

Minuchin, S., Montalvo, B., Guerney, B., Rosman, B., & Schumer, F. (1967). *Families of the slums: An exploration of their structure and treatment.* New York: Basic Books.

Minuchin, S., Rosman, B. L., & Baker, L. (1978). *Psychosomatic families: Anorexia nervosa in context.* Cambridge, MA: Harvard University Press.

Minuchin, S., Rosman, B. L., Baker, L., Liebman, R., Milman, L., & Todd, T. (1975). A conceptual model of psychosomatic illness in children: Family organization and family therapy. *Archives of General Psychiatry, 32*(8), 1031–1038.

Mitrani, V. B., & Czaja, S.,J. (2000). Family-based therapy for dementia caregivers: Clinical observations. *Aging and Mental Health, 3*, 200–209.

Mitrani, V. B., Szapocznik, J., & Robinson, C. (2000). Structural ecosystems therapy with HIV+ African American women. In W. Pequegnat & J. Szapocznik (Eds.), *Inside families: The role of families in preventing and adapting to HIV/AIDS.* Rockville, MD: National Institute of Mental Health.

Perosa, L., & Perosa, S. (1982). Structural interaction patterns in families with a learning disabled child. *Family Therapy, 9*, 175–187.

Perosa, L., & Perosa, S. (1990). Convergent and discriminant validity for family self-report measures. *Educational and Psychological Measurement, 50*, 855–868.

Perosa, L., Perosa, S., & Tam, H. (1996). The contribution of family structure and differentiation to identity development in females. *Journal of Youth and Adolescence, 25*(6), 817–837.

Perosa, S., & Perosa, L. (1993). Relationships among Minuchin's structural family model, identity achievement, and coping style. *Journal of Counseling Psychology, 40*(4), 479–489.

Robbins, M., Mitrani, V., Zarate, M., Perez, G. A., Coatsworth, D., & Szapocznik, J. (2002). Change processes in family therapy with Hispanic adolescents. *Hispanic Journal of Behavioral Sciences, 24*(4), 505–519.

Santisteban, D., Szapocznik, J., Perez-Vidal, A., Kurtines, W., Murray, E., & LaPerriere, A. (1996). Efficacy of interventions for engaging youth/families into treatment and some variables that may contribute to differential effectiveness. *Journal of Family Psychology, 10*, 35–44.

Satir, V. (1964). *Conjoint family therapy.* Palo Alto, CA: Science and Behavior Books.

Selvini Palazzoli, M., Boscolo, L., Cecchin, G., & Prata, G. (1978). *Paradox and counterparadox.* New York: Jason Aronson.

Sexton, T. L., Alexander, J. F., & Mease, A. L. (in press). Levels of evidence for the models and mechanism of therapeutic change in family and couple therapy. In M. Lambert (Ed.), *Handbook of psychotherapy and behavior change.* New York: Wiley.

Shields, C. G., Sprenkle, D. H., & Constantine, J.A. (1991). Anatomy of an initial interview: The importance of joining and structuring skills. *American Journal of Family Therapy, 19*(1), 3–18.

Sluzki, C. (1975). The coalitionary process in initiating family therapy. *Family Process, 14*, 67–77.

Stanton, M. (1981). An integrated structural/strategic
approach to family therapy. *Journal of Marital and
Family Therapy*, 7, 427–439.

Stanton, M., & Shadish, W. (1997). Outcome, attrition and family-couples treatment for drug abuse:
A meta-analysis and review of the controlled and
comparative studies. *Psychological Bulletin, 122*,
170–191.

Stanton, M., Steier, F., Cook, L., & Todd, T. (1984).
*Narcotic detoxification in a family and home con-
text: Final report—1980–1983.* Rockville, MD:
National Institute on Drug Abuse, Treatment Research Branch.

Stanton, M., Todd, T. C., & Associates. (1982). *The
family therapy of drug abuse and addiction.* New
York: Guilford Press.

Szapocznik, J., & Kurtines, W. (1989). *Breakthroughs in family therapy with drug-abusing and
problem youth.* New York: Springer.

Szapocznik, J., Kurtines, W., Foote, F., Perez-Vidal,
A., & Hervis, O. (1983). Conjoint versus one person family therapy: Some evidence for the effectiveness of conducting family therapy through one
person. *Journal of Consulting and Clinical Psychology, 51*, 889–899.

Szapocznik, J., Kurtines, W., Foote, F., Perez-Vidal,
A., & Hervis, O. (1986). Conjoint versus one person family therapy: Further evidence for the effectiveness of conducting family therapy through
one person with drug-abusing adolescents. *Journal of Consulting and Clinical Psychology, 54*,
395–397.

Szapocznik, J., Kurtines, W. M., Santisteban, D. A.,
Pantin, H., Scopetta, M., Mancilla, Y., Aisenberg,
S., McIntosh, S., & Coatsworth, J. D. (1997). The
evolution of a structural ecosystemic theory for
working with Latino families. In J. Garcia & M.C.
Zea (Eds.), *Psychological interventions and re-
search with Latino populations.* Boston: Allyn &
Bacon.

Szapocznik, J., Kurtines, W., Santisteban, D., & Rio,
A. (1990). The interplay of advances among
theory, research, and application in treatment interventions aimed at behavior problem children
and adolescents. *Journal of Consulting and Clinical Psychology [Special series Research on Therapies for Children and Adolescents], 58*(6), 696–
703.

Szapocznik, J., Perez-Vidal, A., Brickman, A., Foote,
F., Santisteban, D., Hervis, O., & Kurtines, W.
(1988). Engaging adolescent drug abusers and
their families into treatment: A strategic structural
systems approach. *Journal of Consulting and

Clinical Psychology, 56*, 552–557.

Szapocznik, J., Rio, A., Hervis, O., Mitrani, V.,
Kurtines, W., & Faraci, A. (1991). Assessing
change in family functioning as a result of treatment: The Structural Family Systems Rating Scale
(SFSR). *Journal of Marital and Family Therapy,
17*, 295–310.

Szapocznik, J., Rio, A., Murray, E., Cohen, R.,
Scopetta, M., Rivas-Vasquez, A., Hervis, O.,
Posada, V., & Kurtines, W. (1989). Structural fam-
ily versus psychodynamic child therapy for prob-
lematic Hispanic boys. *Journal of Consulting and
Clinical Psychology, 57*, 571–578.

Szapocznik, J., Robbins, M. S., Mitrani, V. B.,
Santisteban, D., Hervis, O., & Williams, R. A.
(2002). Brief strategic family therapy with behavior problem Hispanic youth. In J. Lebow (Ed.),
*Integrative and eclectic psychotherapies* (Vol. 4)
In F. Kaslow (Ed.), *Comprehensive handbook of
psychotherapy* (pp. 83–109). New York: Wiley.

Szapocznik, J., Santisteban, D., Rio, A., Perez-Vidal,
A., Santisteban, D., & Kurtines, W. (1989). Family effectiveness training: An intervention to prevent drug abuse and problem behaviors in Hispanic adolescents. *Hispanic Journal of Behavioral
Sciences, 11*(1), 4–27.

Watzlawick, P., Beavin, J., & Jackson, D. D. (1967).
*Pragmatics of human communication.* New York:
W. W. Norton.

Watzlawick, P., & Weakland., J. (1977). *The interactional view: Studies at the Mental Research Institute, Palo Alto, 1965–1974.* New York: Norton.

Watzlawick, P., Weakland, J., & Fish, R. (1974).
*Change: Principles of problem formation and
problem resolution.* New York: W. W. Norton.

Weeks, G. (1985). *Promoting change through paradoxical therapy.* New York: Brunner/Mazel.

Weeks, G. (1991). *Promoting change through paradoxical therapy* (Rev. ed.). New York: Brunner/
Mazel.

Weeks, G., & L'Abate, L. (1982). *Paradoxical psychotherapy: Theory and practice with individuals, couples, and families.* New York: Brunner/
Mazel.

Wiener, N. (1948). *Cybernetics.* New York: Wiley.

Wood, B. (1985). Proximity and hierarchy: Orthogo-
nal dimensions of family interconnectedness.
*Family Process, 24*, 487–507.

Wood, B. (1993). Beyond the "psychosomatic family": A biobehavioral family model of pediatric
illness. *Family Process, 32*, 261-278.

Wood, B., Watkins, J., Boyle, J., Nogueria, J.,
Zimand, E., & Carroll, L. (1989). The "psychosomatic family" model: An empirical and theoretical analysis. *Family Process, 28*, 399–417.

CHAPTER 10

# Integrative Approaches to Couple and Family Therapy

JAY L. LEBOW, PhD, ABPP

*Family Institute at Northwestern*

## INTRODUCTION

Writing a chapter on integrative methods in couple and family therapy presents a significant challenge. At the beginning of the 21st century, the practice of family therapy has substantially come to be synonymous with the practice of integrative methods. Just as Alan Gurman has pointed out that family therapy is almost intrinsically short-term therapy (Gurman, 1992), the development of family therapy has naturally led to the dominance of integrative practice. Although there continue to be notable developments in the first-generation schools of family therapy (see, for example, the chapters in this volume by Scharff and Scharff, Datillio, and Mitrani) and the generation of some new models over the last decade (see the chapter on narrative approaches by Anderson), even the approaches

that retain a core of school-based underpinnings now often include a great deal of what is termed assimilative integration (Goldfried & Norcross, 1995; Lebow, 1987a, 1987b) that is, the inclusion of methods drawn from other approaches around the foundation of a host approach. Indeed, most of the methods catalogued in this volume are integrative approaches; remarkably, almost all the methods in Part III of this volume, dealing with evidence-based approaches, and Part IV, dealing with special applications, speak to what essentially are integrative or eclectic approaches. Sometimes integrative approaches are labeled empirically supported treatments, sometimes treatments for specific disorders, sometimes ways of intervening with specific populations, and sometimes integrative and eclectic treatments, but these methods are now everywhere. Both the methods presented by the leaders in the field and the practice of most couple and family therapists are now primarily integrative or eclectic.

## HISTORY AND BACKGROUND OF INTEGRATIVE FAMILY THERAPY

In a sense it is ironic that family therapy has only recently emerged as primarily an integrative method of practice; ironic because the original roots of family therapy lay much more in shared understandings about family process than in specific theoretical formulations. The great discovery of the first generation of family therapists was that ongoing family process mattered a great deal in the lives of individuals and that individuals needed to be considered in the context of their lives. Witnessing Salvador Minuchin, Carl Whitaker, Murrey Bowen, Virginia Satir, and their contemporaries discuss families was much more about hearing about common ground than about difference.

Nonetheless, the natural processes of development of the field resulted in the creation of several very distinct and narrow schools of practice. Several reasons can be cited for the move away from the early integrative spirit of the field. First, family therapy began as a challenge to the then prevailing orthodoxy, individual psychoanalytic psychotherapy. In building the case for the importance of the family, the predominate discourse quickly moved away from any consideration of the individual. Second, the early charismatic leaders in the field sought to create their own brands of treatment. Third, in order to grow, the field needed models and training centers around which to create structures for acceptance. Such models and training centers inevitably narrowed the scope of ideas and methods. Another irony in the development of family therapy was the growth of the field around the creation of post-

graduate training centers; the field may have thrown out psychoanalytic ideas but gravitated to structures much like those in the world of psychoanalysis. These academies were structured around specific local methods, vying for popularity, much as in psychoanalysis. Finally, the consignment of behavioral approaches to academia, and away from the postgraduate centers, meant that there was almost no contact between mainstream and behavioral family methods over the first 25 years of the field's development. All of these factors caused family therapy to come to be primarily practiced in distinct schools for a considerable time.

Integrative approaches to family therapy have moved into ascendance through gradual evolution rather than sudden change. In contrast to the revolutionary way family therapy came into prominence through questioning of fundamental assumptions of what was then current practice, integrative approaches have emerged in a slow, evolving process. No one integrative method predominates. Indeed, several integrative methods are often not even typically labeled "integrative." Sometimes they have arisen through evolutionary changes within approaches, such as in Jacobson and Christenson's wrestling with the limits of behavioral couple therapy (see Chapter 13 on "Behavioral Couples' Therapy" in this volume), sometimes through lenses that focused on entities such as gender and culture (and therefore away from school of practice: see the chapter by Falicov in this volume); and sometimes through efforts to develop empirically supported approaches (see Chapters 14 and 15, in this volume).

### What Constitutes Integration?

The terms *integration* and *eclecticism* are sometimes used interchangeably, yet have come to have distinct meanings. Integration and eclecticism both involve the application of concepts and interventions that cross scholastic boundaries. The term *eclectic* has been used to describe pragmatic case-based approaches, in which the ingredients of different approaches are employed without trying to build a unifying conceptual theory. The term *integration* suggests a more extensive melding of approaches into a metalevel theory that struggles with and works through the juxtaposition of the meanings of different concepts or intervention strategies entailed.

Nonetheless, the distinction between integration and eclecticism can easily become murky. Psychotherapy is organized on a number of levels: theory, strategy, and intervention (Goldfried & Padawer, 1978). An approach may utilize one school's theoretical framework (for example, behavioral family therapy) but may be quite eclectic in employing strategies and interventions in the context of that theory. Such an approach would involve no integration at the theoretical level, yet would involve considerable crossing of scholastic boundaries at the level of strategy and intervention. As an example, integrative behavioral couples' therapy, described in a chapter in this volume, clearly remains a behavioral approach, yet extensively integrates ways of working with acceptance that typically lie in more experiential and humanistic approaches.

Most discussions of integrative and eclectic practice describe three threads of practice. One thread centers on the generation of super-ordinate integrative theories that subsume scholastic theories. Some of these approaches center on stating principles of practice that transcend client characteristics: among these models are Pinsof's (1995) problem-centered therapy and Breunlin, MacKune-Karrer, and Schwartz's meta-frameworks model (Breunlin, Schwartz, & MacKune-Karrer, 1997). Other approaches within this thread center more specifically on the treatment of specific

syndromes and problems; among these models are several methods for treating adolescent substance abuse, delinquency, and externalizing disorders, including Alexander and Sexton's functional family therapy (Alexander, Waldon, Newberry, & Liddle, 1990), Liddle and colleagues' multidimensional family therapy for adolescent substance abuse (Liddle et al., 2001), Szapocznik and colleagues' brief strategic therapy for adolescent externalizing disorders (Szapocznik & Williams, 2000), and Henggeler and colleagues' multisystemic therapy (Henggeler, Schoenwald, Borduin, Rowland, & Cunningham, 1998), as well as Goldner's treatment for spousal violence (Goldner, 1998).

The second thread of integration/eclecticism, often referred to as technical eclecticism, regards theory as less important and looks to create algorithms at the levels of strategy and intervention. Prominent methods within this thread include Barrett and Trepper's family therapy for child sexual abuse (Barrett, Duffy, Dadds, & Rapee, 2001), Kaslow's biopsychosocial therapy for child and adolescent depression (Kaslow & Racusin, 1994), and Stith and colleagues' treatment for spousal abuse (Stith & Rosen, 1990). The third thread emphasizes building treatment on the common factors that transcend particular orientation to treatment and aims primarily to promote these factors and increase the shared understanding of their potency. In the family field, this work is best represented by the approach of Miller, Duncan, and Hubble (Duncan, Hubble, & Miller, 1997), described in Chapter 6 of this volume.

Although there are some ways in which these threads represent competing visions of how to bring methods from different approaches together, these threads are best thought of as three overlapping vantage points. Most integrative/eclectic approaches show some aspect of each thread; that is, containing some effort at theoretical integration, some pragmatic efforts to bring together strategies and techniques, and some attention to common factors.

Integration in family therapy also typically extends across session formats: family, couple, parent–child, individual, and, at times, group. It is a basic tenet of most integrative family therapy that session formats are selected in relation to what will be most useful in helping improve the presenting problem. Although some integrative therapies utilize only one format (for example, couple therapy in emotion-focused therapy for marital difficulties [Johnson, 2000]), many of these therapies continually move from one session format to another, even within a specific case (as in, for example, Liddle's multidimensional family therapy [Liddle et al., 2001]).

*Integration* and *eclecticism* refer both to the process of bridging the concepts and interventions of schools of therapy and to the product that results from this process (Goldfreid & Padawer, 1978; Lebow, 1984, 1987b; Wachtel, 1977). The terms are best reserved for methods that cross some clear boundary of treatment philosophy. Simply importing one intervention into an approach in which that concept is not employed (e.g., relaxation training in the context of experiential therapy) is more appropriately labeled "assimilation" (Lebow, 1987b). The blending of approaches that are very similar (e.g., two methods of object-relations therapy or two methods of conceptualizing narratives) also does not constitute "integration." It should be noted as well that what is regarded as integrative or eclectic changes over time. For example, cognitive and behavioral therapies represent two quite different traditions that assign prime importance to thought and behavior, yet principally they are now regarded as unified in the cognitive-behavioral approach that few would view today as integrative or eclectic.

# THE STRENGTHS AND LIABILITIES OF INTEGRATION AND ECLECTICISM

Integration and eclecticism have a number of striking strengths, as well as a number of potential difficulties that need to be addressed (Johnson & Lebow, 2000; Lebow, 1984, 1987a, 1987b, 1997).

## Strengths of Integrative/Eclectic Approaches

*Advantage #1: Integrative and eclectic approaches draw from a broad theoretical base; as such, they can explain human experience in a more sophisticated manner than can simpler theories and can better account for the range of human behavior.* Theories are almost always slanted to a single framing of the human condition, but human experience is the product of a multiplicity of factors. Considerable evidence points to the importance of biological influences, intrapsychic dynamics, cognitions, behavioral contingencies, and interpersonal influences in the genesis of behavior. Theoretical conceptualizations based in only one dimension of experience are therefore limited conceptions. Integrative family therapists are able to consider a broader range of etiological constructs than are their more narrowly trained counterparts and are less likely to fall victim to inappropriately extending a theory to an area or example for which it does not fit.

*Advantage #2: Integrative and eclectic approaches allow greater flexibility in the treatment of any given individual or family and thus offer the opportunity for increased efficacy and acceptability of the care.* The open-minded stance of integrative and eclectic therapists permits the shaping of conceptualizations of problem formation and resolution to the specific case under consideration, and the vast array of techniques these therapists have available allow for the generation of a wide variety of treatment options. The integrative/eclectic clinician can move to alternative interventions and thereby increase the chances of impacting on presenting problems.

*Advantage #3: Integrative and eclectic approaches are applicable to a broader client population than are more narrowly focused approaches.* Techniques and goals can be adapted to the type of clients presenting, the treatment setting, and the time available for therapy.

*Advantage #4: Integrative/eclectic therapists are better able to match the treatment they offer to their own personal conception of problem development and change and to their own personality characteristics.* The person of the therapist clearly has a key role in therapy. Integrative approaches allow for the possibility of therapy having a best fit with the therapist who delivers the treatment. This enables the development of an organic fit between practitioner and practice, rather than an artificial graft of practice to provider. Given such a choice, therapists are more likely to offer interventions for which they are best suited, resulting in greater skill in treatment and increased efficacy. This is also likely to produce greater belief in the treatment by the therapist and the communication of this belief to the client, factors that have been demonstrated to be important to treatment efficacy (Frank, 1973).

*Advantage #5: Integrative and eclectic therapists can combine the major benefits of the specific approaches.* Each approach to psychotherapy has specific strengths. Integrative and eclectic therapists can draw freely on these strengths.

*Advantage #6: Integrative and eclectic therapists can bring greater objectivity to the selection of strategies for change.* Because

they have less of an investment in the adequacy of a particular method of practice, integrative and eclectic practitioners are freer to experiment and explore the literature relevant to the adequacy of specific techniques.

*Advantage #7: An integrative and eclectic approach can he readily adapted to include new techniques that have been demonstrated to be efficacious.* Psychotherapy is a developing field, in which new approaches and techniques are constantly emerging. In integrative and eclectic approaches, therapy is an evolving art and science.

*Advantage #8: Integrative/eclectic approaches offer several advantages in training.* Training in an integrative/eclectic approach offers a broader range of experience than does school-specific training. Integrative/eclectic training also promotes an open attitude on the part of the therapist and furthers the development of therapists' critical faculties.

## Potential Problems to Be Addressed

*Criticism #1: It has been suggested that integrative and eclectic approaches lack a theoretical basis, a rigor of definition of concepts, and a connection between a conceptualization of the human condition and practice.* At times, this is a just criticism. However, most integrative and eclectic therapies vary enormously from this caricature, being very carefully constructed around either a theoretical integration or a clear algorithm for intervention.

*Criticism #2: It is also suggested that integrative and eclectic approaches lack the consistency found in the various schools of psychotherapy.* Although there may be some validity in this criticism, this concern is greatly exaggerated. Present-day integrative and eclectic therapies offer tight frameworks leading to consistency in approach.

*Criticism #3: Integrative/eclectic treat-*

*ments have been criticized for manifesting utopian views and setting grandiose goals of resolving all levels of difficulty.* Given a giant tool kit, it can become easy to have too many goals and a perfectionistic view of treatment process and outcome. However, most integrative and eclectic therapies remain straightforward, often accenting the simplest intervention possible toward producing the desired result.

*Criticism #4: Integrative and eclectic approaches have been criticized for being too complex and too difficult to master.* Integrative and eclectic approaches do involve treatment choices that are more complex than those with a more limited perspective and require a clinician who is comfortable intervening on multiple levels. However, therapists typically not only tolerate the commitment involved in learning more complex approaches and choosing among interventions but welcome this opportunity. Integrative and eclectic training programs have begun to create smooth routes to learning and becoming skillful in the practice of these therapies.

## MAJOR THEORETICAL CONSTRUCTS

Integrative family therapies vary enormously in content and in the specific theoretical constructs about the nature of families and about strategies for intervention. There is not one integrative/eclectic family therapy, but many integrative and eclectic family therapies. Nonetheless, integrative approaches share a number of core tenets that emerge from the nature of integrative/eclectic practice, and an emerging consensus exists among most integrative approaches about several core understandings, including:

- *The presence of an underlying template: Either a theory of change that is an amal-*

*gamation of earlier theories or an algorithm for which therapeutic techniques should be used under particular conditions.*

Modern integrative and eclectic approaches present a crisp and clear formula for combining the ingredients utilized. Those that accentuate theory present bridges between the concepts of the theories represented. For example, Liddle and colleagues in multidimensional family therapy describe how the concepts of individual development in adolescents are integrated with structural concepts and concepts from traditional substance-use treatment (Liddle et al., 2001). Those approaches at the eclectic end of the spectrum similarly describe how and when to bridge intervention strategies.

- *Attention to multiple levels of human experience, including behavior, emotion, cognition, biology, family, and extra-familial interaction.*

Integrative approaches typically assume a biopsychosocial model of human functioning. Rather than focusing on which aspect of human beings represents *the* crucial causal determinant of psychological health or difficulty, integrative approaches feature both/and inclusiveness. The crucial question becomes not which is the "right" conceptualization, but which level of explanation is most helpful to the treatment of the individual case.

- *At least some, and in most cases much, attention is given to the powerful set of common factors found across psychotherapies.*

Although the majority of written works and presentations about psychotherapy focuses on the special qualities of the unique approach involved, considerable research shows that to be a set of common factors at work in most successful psychotherapy (Norcross, 2002; Orlinsky, Grawe, & Parks, 1994). Factors such as the therapeutic alliance, therapist empathy, therapist congruence, and homework have been shown to be crucial to therapy outcomes across therapist orientation. Some research has suggested that technique accounts for as little as 15% of the variance in outcome across clients (Hubble, Duncan, & Miller, 1999). One major subgroup of integrative approaches is devoted to the delineation of common factors, and almost all integrative approaches focus at least to some extent on these aspects of treatment (Goldfried, 1995).

- *An important role assigned to a systemic understanding of the presenting difficulty and to the family system as a vehicle for enabling change.*

Integrative family therapies share some variant of systems theory as a core set of assumptions. However, almost universally, integrative family therapies do not feature a radical systemic viewpoint suggesting that families are invariably involved in the cause of individual difficulties or that families inevitably move toward homeostasis (Watzlawick, Weakland, & Fisch, 1974). Instead, these approaches emphasize the broad systemic principles of the importance of feedback, the context of problems, and circular processes as one important set of considerations in the evolution and maintenance of problems. Almost invariably, integrative family approaches draw upon family members to at least some degree in helping to resolve problems.

- *The incorporation of psychoeducation and skill development as part of treatment.*

Almost all integrative and eclectic family approaches include some efforts to help families understand problems and to build family and individual competencies. Most prominently, the family psychoeducational approaches for treating schizophrenia and bipo-

lar disorder feature the sharing of information as a crucial intervention (McFarlane et al., 1995). These methods have also become commonplace in other integrative and eclectic approaches, be they focused on adolescent drug use (Liddle et al., 2001), the emotional life of couples (Christenson & Jacobson, 2000; Johnson, 2000), or child sexual abuse (Barrett, Trepper, & Fish, 1990).

- *The utilization of language for describing intervention and the change process that are simple to understand and that transcends therapeutic orientation.*

As Hubble, Duncan, and Miller (1999) have emphasized, psychotherapy readily becomes a Tower of Babel, in which the same concept can be described by innumerable varieties of jargon. Most integrative approaches find simple language to describe theory and intervention. Such language in turn readily acts as a bridge across differences in orientation and helps families better understand treatment.

- *The tailoring of intervention strategy in relation to specific populations.*

Integrative and eclectic therapies move beyond the one-size-fits-all philosophy to tailor specific intervention strategies to the kind of problem under consideration and the specific case at hand. Some of these therapies feature general methods adapted to the population in focus, as Pinsof does, for example, in the couples' therapy version of integrative problem-centered therapy (Pinsof, 1995). Other methods, such as Liddle and colleagues' (Liddle et al., 2001) multidimensional family therapy for adolescent substance abuse, are built from the ground up around the treatment of specific disorders.

- *The utilization of research findings as an important determinant of what is included within the model and how interventions are structured, and conducting research to assess and better understand the integrative/ eclectic model.*

Although it is not a prerequisite for integrative/eclectic approaches to be anchored in research data (some stellar approaches are not; consider, for example, Goldner's [1998] therapy for couple violence), most of these approaches assign a powerful role to research. Most engage in a cycle of building the theory involved and the intervention strategy employed on the findings of research, then testing the impact of the resultant therapy, and finally employing the results of the studies in refining the treatment. In part, the frequent presence of research in method development is a by-product of the fact that many of the most prominent developers of integrative family approaches are also researchers (for example, Bill Pinsof, Sue Johnson, Jim Alexander, Howard Liddle, and Betsy Wood); in part, this linkage stems from the intrinsic relationship between integrative practice and the evaluation of therapy progress.

• *The tracking of change throughout therapy, often through the use of instruments.*

Empirical data do not assume importance in integrative therapies only at the level of establishing the effectiveness of the treatment; progress data are often essential ingredients in determining changes in intervention strategy. For example, in Pinsof's (Pinsof, 1995) integrative problem-centered therapy, data assessing therapy progress are used as an essential tool in the determination of whether an intervention strategy should be continued to be employed or altered.

• *An ultimate pragmatism, centered on what works, that moves beyond broad insights.*

Although the authors of some integrative approaches can elaborate at length on the theoretical underpinnings of their approaches (see, for example, Liddle et al., 1992, on the place of developmental psychology in their approach), the content of these approaches tends to build from examining and developing what works with clients, instead of from armchair musings. Most integrative approaches, even those that accentuate theory, search for the most practical approach to presenting problems.

• *An ongoing dialectic between theory, strategy, and intervention, in which discoveries about each provide feedback to and interact with what emerges at the other levels.*

Goldfried (Goldfried & Norcross, 1995) has suggested that approaches to psychotherapy include three distinct levels: theory (an understanding of the essential elements of human functioning and the change process), strategy (the overall plan for a treatment), and interventions (the specific techniques utilized). In integrative approaches, theory, strategy, and technique reciprocally influence each other.

• *A focus on enabling change through the simplest intervention strategy available.*

Integrative and eclectic therapies intrinsically must wrestle with the problem of complexity. It clearly makes sense to be able to see the process of change from more than one perspective, but how does a therapist hold such a viewpoint while retaining focus and clarity about the direction of treatment? Most integrative and eclectic family therapies opt for parsimony in intervention, looking to the simplest path that can produce change. Pinsof (1995), for example, establishes choosing the most direct intervention possible as a basic tenet of his approach.

- *A focus on client strengths.*

Integrative family therapies are substantially strength-based. In part a by-product of the substantial roots of modern family therapies in the traditions of seeing people as typically healthy and of seeing strength in connection (F. Walsh, 1996, 1998; W. M. Walsh, 2001), integrative family therapies typically assume an underlying health that can be unleashed by drawing on the powerful healing factors in family process (see, for example, Duncan, Hubble, & Miller, 1998).

- *Building empirically supported therapies.*

Many of the newer integrative and eclectic therapies have developed in the tradition of creating therapies targeted to specific populations, building an armamentarium of empirically supported therapies for specific conditions. Such therapies as Alexander and Sexton's functional family therapy for adolescent delinquency (Alexander et al., 1990), Liddle and colleagues' multidimensional family therapy for adolescent substance abuse (Liddle et al., 2001), and Jacobson and Christenson's integrative behavioral couples' therapy (Jacobson, Christensen, Prince, Cordova, & Eldridge, 2000) have all followed this model of development.

- *Utilizing relational diagnosis.*

Integrative family approaches assume that an important aspect of treatment lies in understanding the relational processes and the generation of strategies of intervention aimed at relational difficulties that impact on the problem. Therefore, relational difficulties often move into the center of attention when present. As examples, functional family therapy accentuates an understanding of the relational value of dysfunctional behaviors in the family sys-

tem (Alexander et al., 1990), and Pinsof (1995) looks to establish and ameliorate the family's role in the problem-maintenance system.

## PROMINENT APPROACHES: BROADLY TARGETED APPROACHES

There have been several widely disseminated integrative and eclectic approaches in family therapy. Some have been broadly targeted and some have been targeted at specific populations.

### Integrative Problem-Centered Therapy

Integrative problem-centered therapy (IPCT), developed by William Pinsof (Pinsof, 1983, 1994, 1995), offers both a generic system for organizing integration across treatment methods and a specific set of principles for intervention. Ultimately, IPCT centers on the resolution of presenting problems, as delineated by the patients' definition of the problems for which they are seeking help, which become the center of the therapeutic contract. Assessment in this approach involves an ongoing process of hypothesizing about what Pinsof calls the "problem maintenance cycle" and intervening based on that hypothesis. Assessment is augmented based on the way clients respond to these interventions. Intervention begins with the simplest and most direct interventions: behavioral and biological interventions are employed first. If these fail to produce change, the therapy moves to a second level, in which cognitive and emotion-based interventions are invoked. If these interventions also fail to produce change, the intervention shifts to address issues that remain from the family of origin and, ultimately, to object relations and self-psychological exploration. Family, couple, and individual treatment formats are all utilized as needed, ideally proceeding from the most inclusive (family) to the least inclusive (individual) format. A basic premise is that clients are presumed healthy until found to be otherwise. The problem-maintenance structure is likewise assumed to be simple and easy to address until proven otherwise. A major emphasis of the approach centers on the building of a strong therapeutic alliance as the vehicle for enabling change (Pinsof, 1988). Assessing the ongoing progress of treatment through the use of instruments and augmenting or altering the treatment based on this data are also core aspects of this approach (Pinsof & Wynne, 2000).

## Metaframeworks

Metaframeworks, developed by Doug Breunlin, Betty Karrer, and Richard Schwartz (Breunlin et al., 1997), provides more of a general framework than a specific roadmap to guide intervention. Drawing from systems theory, metaframeworks emphasizes a theory of constraints; the notion that people do what they do, think what they think, or feel what they feel because they are prevented from doing, thinking, or feeling something else (Breunlin, 1999). Metaframeworks looks to identify and remove those constraints. Metaframeworks identifies and works with constraints as they appear across a number of levels, ranging from the most broad, culture and gender, to most the narrow, internal process. Interventions are targeted by the level where constraints are most evident and by sequences that indicate the presence of constraints. Interventions in this model range from ones targeted at the larger system, to others targeted at the family, to yet others targeted inside individuals.

## Client-Directed Outcome-Informed Clinical Work

The approach developed by Mark Hubble, Scott Miller, and Barry Duncan (Duncan et al., 1997; Hubble et al., 1999; Miller et al., 1997) is often classified as a solution-focused approach because of the use of positive framing as a crucial aspect of treatment, but this approach extends well beyond more typical solution-focused approaches (Adams, Piercy, & Jurich, 1991; de Shazer, 1979, 1986, 1988). Most especially, the heart of this approach lies in maximizing the so-called common factors in psychotherapy, especially the generation of hope, positive expectancy, and a strong client–therapist alliance. Central aspects of the approach include becoming change-focused, potentiating change that does occur, and tapping the client's world outside of therapy to support change processes. The therapeutic alliance is seen as a crucial ingredient in creating the context for change. Therapists in this approach accommodate to the client's view of the therapeutic alliance and the client's level of involvement and work actively to build placebo, hope, and expectancy factors through establishing a focus on possibility and creating healing rituals. In each case, the specific techniques employed are tailored to the individual client. Therapy largely consists of learning the client's theory of change and building on it. Duncan, Miller, and Hubble use progress data extensively in the course of treatment, utilizing the results both in the generation of hope and positive expectancy and in shaping treatment in relation to treatment progress.

## Internal Systems Therapy

This approach, developed by Richard Schwartz (Nichols & Schwartz, 1998), integrates structural family therapy and experiential methods, especially gestalt therapy. The mind is seen as consisting of a number of parts that parallel parts in the family-of-origin system. Some parts, termed *managers,* are viewed as working to prevent the occurrence of unpleasant thoughts and feelings; other parts, called *exiles,* are viewed as activating bad feelings; and yet others, called *firefighters,* are viewed as working to control exiled feelings. Therapy consists of working to establish the nature of self to part feelings, freeing the exiles, and unburdening the powerful feeling of the exiles. Much of this work is internally focused within individuals but is conducted in the context of spouses, other family members, or both.

## Walsh's Resilience Approach

Froma Walsh (Walsh, 1998, 2001) has pioneered an approach centered on the power of family resilience. Incorporating aspects of the Bowen approach, feminist approaches, and narrative approaches, Walsh's approach emphasizes the healing potential of families for the resolution of individual and collective difficulties. Overcoming legacies that may result from loss assumes an important place in this approach.

## Emotion-Focused Therapy

Emotion-focused therapy (EFT) has at its center a focus on emotion but moves beyond experiential methods to include treatment techniques and methods from a number of specific schools of therapy. Developed by Les Greenberg in the context of individual therapy (Greenberg & Bolger, 2001), it has been adapted and elaborated to couple therapy and more recently to family therapy by Sue Johnson and her colleagues (Johnson, 2000; Johnson & Greenberg 1992, 1994, 1995). In the context of couple and family therapies, emotion-focused therapy primarily merges knowledge about emotion, experiential family therapy, and attachment theory (Johnson, Maddeaux, & Blouin, 1998; Whiffen, Kallos-Lilly, & MacDonald, 2001), also incorporating an emphasis on promoting the common factors in therapy, especially the building of the therapeutic relationship. The essence of the work with emotion lies in establishing a collaborative focus, evoking and exploring feelings, and emotion restructuring, in which the maladaptive emotional schema is accessed, these schemas are challenged, support is provided for the emergence of a more self-affirming stance, and new meaning is created. In the couple context, partners' feelings are accessed, responded to, and ultimately accepted, as partners work though attachment injuries, which results in a greater sense of connection. In the family context, the same kind of emotional sharing is encouraged as the bridge to family connection; these family attachments are seen as invaluable in resolving individual difficulties.

# PROMINENT APPROACHES: APPROACHES TAILORED TO SPECIFIC PROBLEMS

## Multidimensional Family Therapy for Adolescent Substance Abuse

Howard Liddle and colleagues' multidimensional family therapy (MDFT) for adolescent substance abuse (Liddle, 1999) combines ingredients drawn from structural and strategic family therapy, individual developmental psychology, cognitive-behavior therapy, and traditional education-oriented substance-abuse counseling (see the chapter in this volume by Liddle and colleagues, for a more detailed description of this approach). The assumption in this approach is in that adolescent drug abuse is a multidimensional phenomenon, and change is multidetermined and multifaceted. Motivation is viewed as a malleable aspect of treatment, and the working relationship between therapist and family is seen as crucial in helping build this motivation. Interventions are individualized, presented in stages with a clear plan for each case, augmented with options for flexibility. Some of the intervention package is delivered with the individual teenagers alone, helping them to communicate more effectively, solve interpersonal problems, manage their anger and impulses, and enhance their social competence (Liddle, 1994; Liddle et al., 1992). A second set of interventions is focused on parents, looking to enhance the connection between parents and children and to improve parenting strategies. Meetings involving both parents and children are utilized to directly aim at changing interaction patterns. Other interventions are directed to other family members and other relevant social systems outside the family. Special adaptations have been made in the approach in relation to the specific culture of the families involved, most especially African American inner-city clients (Jackson-Gilfort, Liddle, Tejeda, & Dakof, 2001). Several outcome studies have demonstrated the efficacy of MDFT with this population (Liddle et al., 2001).

### Functional Family Therapy for Adolescent Delinquency and Substance Abuse

Functional family therapy (FFT) is the oldest integrative approach to family therapy developed to impact a specific population (see the chapter in this volume by Sexton and Alexander for a more detailed description of this approach). FFT was developed in relation to adolescent delinquency and has been extended to treat adolescent substance abuse (Alexander et al., 1990; Alexander, Robbins, & Sexton, 2000; Haas, Alexander, & Mas, 1988; Morris, Alexander, & Waldron, 1988). FFT focuses primarily on developing positive family functioning but also intervenes with other relevant systems and focuses on the in-

dividuals involved. FFT is structured in terms of phases of treatment. In the engagement and motivation phase, the focus is on creating a positive therapy alliance, reducing negativity and blame, and creating hope. The primary interventions in this phase center on reframing, in order to build a positive relational focus for the treatment. During the phase of behavior change, individualized positive changes are targeted with direct teaching of skills such as communication, parenting, and problem solving. During the third phase, generalization, the positive change developed within the family is extended to the context of other systems. FFT has been demonstrated to be effective for treating adolescent acting-out behavior in a number of studies (Alexander, 1967; Alexander, Holtzworth-Munroe, & Jameson, 1994; Mas, Alexander, & Turner, 1991; Morris, Alexander, & Turner 1991; Parsons & Alexander, 1973). Culture and gender are also regarded as important factors in FFT in shaping intervention strategies (Newberry, Alexander, & Turner, 1991).

### Multisystemic Therapy

Multisystemic therapy (MST) is another integrative family therapy aimed at adolescent delinquency and substance abuse (Becker et al., 1995; Borduin & Henggeler, 1990; Borduin, Henggeler, Blaske, & Stein, 1990; Brown et al., 1997; Brown, Henggeler, Schoenwald, Brondino, & Pickrel, 1999; Henggeler et al., 1998; Henggeler & Borduin, 1995). This approach integrates a perspective on individual development with concepts from structural and behavioral family therapy, with a strong emphasis on the importance of the key systems in the lives of the adolescents. MST views family as one of several systems that needs to be addressed in treatment. Peers, school, and community also receive considerable attention, as does individual skill building in the adolescent. Therapy is intensive; therapists trained in this model have small case loads, working with each of the relevant systems in which the adolescent is involved and remaining available to manage crises as these unfold. MST has acquired a great deal of empirical support for its efficacy (Brunk, Henggeler, & Whelan, 1987; Huey, Henggeler, Brondino, & Pickrel, 2000; Lebow & Gurman, 1995).

## Brief Strategic Family Therapy for Adolescent Substance Abuse

José Szapocznik and colleagues' brief strategic family therapy (BSFT) is another empirically supported therapy for adolescent delinquency and substance abuse (Achenbach & Weisz, 1976; Szapocznik et al., 1997; Szapocznik & Williams, 2000). BSFT is based on three central constructs: system, structure, and strategy. Key interventions include proactive efforts at joining, diagnosis of family interactional patterns, restructuring, working in the present, reframing, and working with boundaries and alliances. Much of the work with substance-abusing adolescents is done in client homes. BSFT also has extensive research demonstrating its effectiveness. Szapocznik and his colleagues developed BSFT in Latino communities and have developed versions of the approach to serve in other cultural contexts (Santisteban, Szapocznik, & Rio, 1993).

## Psychoeducational Family Therapies for Schizophrenia and Bipolar Disorder

Psychoeducational treatments for schizophrenia (Falloon, 2001; Falloon, McGill, Boyd, & Pederson, 1987; Liberman et al., 1987;

McFarlane et al., 1995) and bipolar disorder (Miklowitz, 1997) number among the integrative family approaches with the strongest empirical support. Although these approaches differ somewhat in the specific interventions chosen, each follows a similar form. Each includes the provision of appropriate psychopharmacology for the specific illness involved, psychoeducation for family members to help them understand typical patterns in the illness and typical family reactions to it, skill training for the person with the disorder, crisis intervention when needed, and family sessions to help families share their experiences and learn skills for coping with the illness. In each method, a common goal is reducing expressed emotion in the family. In the treatments directed at schizophrenia, the content focuses on schizophrenia; in bipolar disorder, on that illness. The efficacy of these approaches has been demonstrated in a number of multisite clinical trials (Falloon et al., 1987; Lebow & Gurman, 1995).

## Biopsychosocial Treatment for Depressed Children and Adolescents

Nadine Kaslow and colleagues have developed a biopsychosocial treatment for treating depression in children and adolescents (Kaslow, Baskin, & Wyckoff, 2002). This approach divides attention among the biological, psychological, and social factors that affect depression. Treatment is delivered by interdisciplinary teams, with a special emphasis on therapists having cultural competence to best help the family involved. Considerable attention is focused on building therapeutic alliances with both children and their families. The specific interventions employed include psychopharmacology, cognitive-behavioral techniques, interpersonal therapy techniques, multifamily psychoeducational presentations and discussions, and problem-solving family therapy.

### Treatments for Child Sexual Abuse

Barrett and Trepper (Barrett, Trepper, & Fish, 1991; Trepper & Barrett, 1986, 1989) and Sheinberg and Fraenkel (Sheinberg & Fraenkel 2001; Sheinberg, True, & Fraenkel, 1994) offer feminist-informed family systems treatments for child sexual abuse. These approaches each include intensive work with the perpetrators to help them accept responsibility for their behavior, intensive work with the victims to help them cope with their trauma, and, ultimately, conjoint work with the family to work to alter dysfunctional family sequences. In Barrett and Trepper's approach, group therapies are organized for perpetrators, victims, and nonabusing parents to help process what has occurred, and individual sessions are also employed to address specific goals.

### Biopsychosocial Therapy for Health Problems

Several integrative family approaches address families who present with issues surrounding physical health. Wood offers a biopsychosocial approach to intervening in families with child health problems (Wood, 1993, 1995, 2000, 2001; Wood, Klebba, & Miller, 2000), whereas Rolland (Rolland, 1988, 1993, 1994a, 1994b, 1998) and McDaniel and colleagues (Botelho, McDaniel, & Jones, 1990; McDaniel, Campbell, & Seaburn, 1995; McDaniel, Campbell, Wynne, & Weber, 1988; McDaniel, Harkness, & Epstein, 2001; McDaniel, Hepworth, & Doherty, 1995) offer approaches primarily directed at adult health issues. Although differing in specifics, each of these approaches includes an emphasis on understanding the biology of the illness in-

volved, involving the family in treatment, exploring individual and family belief systems in relation to the illness, attending to the health-provider system and its interface with the patient and the family, and providing individual intervention with the patient. The approaches principally vary in greater attention to parent–child attachment in Wood's treatment, to belief systems and family resilience in Rolland's, and to family-provider consultation in McDaniel and her colleagues' approach.

### Integrative Couple Therapy

Alan Gurman merged behavioral, object-relations, and systems theory in integrative couple therapy (Gurman, 1992). Gurman's approach calls for the utilization of behavioral action oriented techniques to intervene, but he views these interventions in the context of an understanding of the object relations that occur between partners in the couple. Therapy in Gurman's approach is focused and short-term.

### Integrative Behavioral Couples Therapy

Jacobson and Christensen developed integrative behavioral couples therapy (IBCT) in relation to what they perceived as limitations of behavioral couple therapy to produce clinically significant and lasting change in the majority of couples (Christensen & Jacobson, 2000; Christensen, Jacobson, & Babcock, 1995; Jacobson & Christensen, 1996; Jacobson, Christensen, Prince, Cordova, & Eldridge, 2000). IBCT adds an emphasis on acceptance derived from humanistic therapies to the typical skill building and contracting of behavioral couple therapy. IBCT builds on a functional analysis of the relationship designed to assess the core themes in the couple's interaction. The therapist utilizes this analysis to understand and alter the polarization process between the partners. The functional analysis is developed through both conjoint and individual sessions with the partners, which leads to a case formulation and feedback session with the couple in which specific goals for the treatment are suggested. Although efforts are directed at helping the couple build marital skills, the most important interventions focus on helping the partners find a unified detachment in order to help them understand their destructive patterns, to empathically join with each other, to increase tolerance of the aversive problem, and to increase self-care. IBCT has been demonstrated to be efficacious in two clinical trials (Christensen et al., 1995; Christensen & Heavey, 1999).

## Couple Therapy for Domestic Violence

Goldner and colleagues have developed a feminist family systems approach to treating domestic violence in couples (Goldner, 1998; Goldner, Penn, Sheinberg, & Walker, 1990). To understand the origins and meaning of the violence, this treatment brings together a feminist understanding of domestic violence and work with the couple. Although the approach was specifically constructed from a feminist stance toward domestic violence, the pragmatic observation that women tend to remain in these relationships, regardless of the stance of the therapist, prompted intense efforts to find ways to break the cycle of violence. The approach builds on feminist, systemic, psychodynamic, and narrative family therapy models.

## Multicouple Group Therapy for Domestic Violence

This therapy developed by Sandra Stith, Eric McCollum, and Karen Rosen (Stith, McCollum, Rosen, & Locke, 2002) utilizes a multicouple group format to deliver treatment. This approach, targeted to less-severe domestic violence, incorporates solution-oriented, narrative, and cognitive-behavioral skill-building interventions to reduce the risk of further abuse. Men and women first meet separately, then in conjoint meetings. The first stage of therapy centers on building the common factors of alliance and hope, as well as a vision of a violence-free relationship; this is followed by broader efforts to build the violence-free relationship.

## Postmodern Sex Therapy

Sex therapy in its present incarnation almost invariably involves an integrative or eclectic approach or both. As LoPiccolo (2002) describes, because of the widespread availability of information about sexuality in our society, sexual problems typically require much more than the simple sharing of educational information. Postmodern sex therapy no longer speaks of a dichotomy between physical and psychological problems, but of a continuum of physical, psychological, and relational issues to be addressed in each case. Thus, therapy becomes in part, assessment and intervention with biology; in part, individual psychology; and in part, relational dynamics. LoPiccolo (2002) describes the typical indicators of physical, psychological, and relational emphases and specific techniques that can help ameliorate each disorder across the range of sexual difficulties.

## Other Couples' Therapies

There have been several other integrative and eclectic therapies directed at couples. Clifford Sager's marriage contracts approach for couples' therapy has been extremely influential (Sager, 1976a, 1976b). This approach centers on explicating and working with an articulation of the marriage contract that includes both behavioral and psychodynamic levels of exchange. Gerald Weeks (Weeks & Hof, 1994; Weeks et al., 1995) and colleagues developed the intersystem model, integrating interactional, intergenerational, and individual perspectives. Larry Feldman (Feldman, 1985, 1992; Feldman & Pinsof, 1982) developed multilevel marital therapy, an approach in which intervention oscillated between behavioral, systems, and psychodynamic levels, and in which the therapist moved back and forth between individual and conjoint meetings. Fred Sander developed an approach that also merged psychoanalytic and behavioral levels. Don-David Lusterman (Lusterman, 1998) and Frank Pittman (1990) have each developed approaches for dealing with the crisis of infidelity.

*Therapies Tailored to Specific Cultures*

Boyd-Franklin (1989) and Falicov (Falicov, 1995, 1996, 1998) offer examples of integrative family therapies tailored to specific cultures. Boyd-Franklin describes understandings and intervention strategies that are particularly useful in African American families, whereas Falicov does the same for Latino families. These approaches offer a different vantage point for specific approaches, being rooted in the culture of the family, rather than in the area of the presenting problem.

*Coda*

The previous section describes the most widely disseminated integrative couple and family therapies at the time of publication of this volume. However, there remain many other integrative and eclectic couple and family therapies. Innumerable family therapists

have constructed their own personal integrations; many of these have been described in publications, workshops, or both and have had at least some influence.

## FUTURE DEVELOPMENTS AND DIRECTIONS

Integrative and eclectic couple and family therapies are blossoming. These methods are becoming widely disseminated in practice, and considerable evidence is accruing for their effectiveness. Specific integrative and eclectic therapies are being developed for a wider and wider range of difficulties. Most therapists doing couple and family therapy utilize integrative or eclectic methods in their treatments.

With such popular acceptance, what are the most important directions for the future development of integrative and eclectic couple and family therapies?

*Common Factors, Technical Eclecticism, or Theoretical Integration?*

As noted earlier, three major threads have been described within integrative and eclectic therapies: theoretical integration, technical eclecticism, and common factors. Theoretical integration creates super-ordinate integrative theories of practice that subsume scholastic theories. Technical eclecticism regards theory as less important and looks to create algorithms at the levels of strategy and intervention. Common factors approaches stress the exposition and augmentation of the shared factors underlying specific intervention strategies. However, these threads are converging. It is becoming the norm for integrative and eclectic family approaches to maximize common factors, state algorithms for intervention strategy, and build unifying theory.

## Numerous Specific Treatments or Principles of Change?

Much of the recent creative edge in integrative and eclectic family therapy has been concerned with the development of specific treatments for specific populations. In choosing a smaller band to speak to, these approaches have been extremely useful and become widely disseminated. The limitation of these approaches, however, also lies in their delimited scope, which easily could lead to a highly segmented view of treatment and too many treatments for clinicians to learn. Comorbidity and multiproblem families make this issue even more vexing: Will the best treatment for a family consist of receiving five different "treatments" for specific conditions? The resolution of this dilemma lies in work that integrates the various integrative/eclectic approaches. There is a need for dialogue among those promoting the various delimited models of change, as well as between those who are proponents of such models and those promoting broader models. The dialectic between general principles and specific methods can help us recognize what is special to a problem area versus that which represents a more global process.

## How to Combine Family, Couple, and Individual Session Formats

Among the thorniest problems that requires further exploration is how and when to combine different session formats in integrative couple and family therapy. Although it is easy enough to articulate the problems that occur in certain problematic configurations (for example, therapists in conjoint sessions dealing with secrets shared in individual sessions), research or discussions about methods have not shed much light on the relative merits of different ways of combining session formats.

In fact, we as yet have no useful data about the extent to which combining formats helps or hinders treatment (Lebow & Gurman, 1995). More information and discussion about how and under what circumstances session formats combine would be quite helpful.

## When to Do What?

Just as with regard to whom to include in various sessions, surprisingly little discussion or research has been devoted to the vital question of when to do what in treatment. It has probably been inevitable in the developmental process of integrative and eclectic family therapies that concern would focus first on what to include and only later on how to order intervention strategies. There does seem to be consensus between several integrative/eclectic approaches that the building of the therapeutic alliance should be the first goal of treatment, but beyond this, there is little consensus about how to structure this aspect of therapist decision making. Pinsof's (1995) concept in IPCT, which offers the principle of beginning with the most direct intervention first, would be a good launching point for discussion and examination of questions about how to sequence interventions.

## Adding Culture and Gender

In the last decade, culture and gender have begun to receive more attention as important factors in psychotherapy and, more specifically, in integrative/eclectic family therapies. The feminist and cultural perspectives have also helped elucidate underlying assumptions about gender and culture within treatment models, leading to more informed discussion of these issues (Falicov, 1995, 1996, 1998; Goldner, 1989, 1991a, 1991b). Several integrative and eclectic family therapy models are built explicitly around a consideration of gender and culture and are tailored to specific cultural groups, and numerous others now attend to these factors. It is hoped that in the future, all models of integrative and eclectic family therapy will attend to these factors.

### Toward a List of Generic Concepts

Integrative and eclectic approaches have begun to identify a number of generic interventions and dimensions of therapeutic experience, such as assessment, therapeutic alliance, enactment, contract, reinforcement, insight, and reframing. Further work building a generic list of concepts, strategies, and interventions and creating a common language to describe these concepts, strategies, and interventions will help therapists better recognize commonalities across methods, make treatment planning more efficient, and simplify the task of learning therapy skills.

### Recognizing the Importance of the Person of the Therapist

Integrative and eclectic approaches vary considerably in the extent to which the person of the therapist is emphasized in the treatment. Although most integrative/eclectic approaches do pay some attention to the therapist, particularly to his or her ability to build alliances, most models relegate the person of the therapist to a secondary position. It is hoped that more attention will focus on the therapist. Psychotherapies can only be delivered through a person, and therapists vary enormously.

### Prescriptive Versus Therapist-Centered Models

The role of the therapist within integrative and eclectic models falls along a continuum,

bounded on one end by work that accents each therapist's building of a personal method (Lebow, 1987a, 1987b), and on the other end by work that offers a highly prescriptive delineation of a preassembled combination of therapeutic ingredients and a specific map for when to do what. Prescriptive manuals stress the need for replicable methods of practice, whereas the notion of therapists' building their personal methods emphasizes the unique qualities of each therapist. Both kinds of models serve important purposes. For some, a well-organized set of directives on how to practice is most helpful, whereas others will want to build their own approaches. Often, the former type of model is most helpful early in the career of a therapist, when rules governing action are typically experienced with relief, whereas the latter type is more helpful later, when improvisation becomes the norm. We need to see more work on the development of both paradigms and specifically of the kinds of models we have begun to see, which provide a manual but also allow for considerable improvisation.

### Self-Examination by the Therapist

Much of the clinical decision making in integrative/eclectic family therapy lies outside the conscious awareness of the practitioner, emanating from a level of clinical "intuition" at a preconscious level. Integrative/eclectic practice is greatly enhanced by bringing the principles behind practice into consciousness. As an example, Grunebaum (1988) offers a very instructive example of a clinician working to understand the implicit theories, strategies, and interventions operating in the context of a specific case. Grunebaum deconstructs his own integrative/eclectic method, moving from his plan, to observations about his own behavior, uncovering the theories and precepts that guide him, which were initially out of conscious awareness. He then considers the impact of these interventions within the specific treatment and for his broader model of practice. Such self-examination would be helpful for all integrative and eclectic therapists.

## Considering Treatment Setting

Factors such as the setting, the funding of care, and the acceptability of the treatment clearly affect therapeutic decision making. To have an appropriate treatment that is inaccessible, unacceptable, or not affordable is of little use. Integrative and eclectic frameworks provide a range of options for treatment and offer the distinct possibility of setting goals in a manner consistent with resources available. We need to see more consideration of treatment setting and possible financial constraints for the therapy in our treatment models.

## Considering Values and Ethics

Integrative and eclectic family therapies move concepts and interventions anchored in contextual meanings into new contexts, creating the possibility that aspects of approaches will be incorporated without the values lying at the core of those approaches or even that two conflicting ideologies will be combined. Not only does this invoke possible confusion about the value system around which the approach is anchored (e.g., in attitudes about gender), but also, as Messer (1986) has emphasized, it creates possibilities for mixed messages about core visions of the human condition. Messer suggests that some approaches to psychotherapy are comedic, highlighting optimism and the creation of happy endings with hard work (e.g., behavioral approaches), whereas others are tragic or ironic in worldview (e.g., psychodynamic approaches). It is crucial for integrative and eclectic family therapists to

remain able to articulate their underlying belief systems.

Integrative/eclectic family therapy also calls for innumerable ethical decisions that do not arise nearly as often in more narrowly focused school-based approaches. For example: If more than one family member is included in the treatment, who is the client? How does the therapist choose among the many intervention goals that can be generated? Should these goals focus most on symptom alleviation, problem resolution, or other kinds of goals? When is a therapist practicing outside of his or her realm of expertise? How many specific kinds of intervention can therapists competently deliver and what efforts should therapists make to stay current with the state of the art in those methods? When is it appropriate to refer clients? We must have a great deal more discussion of such ethical dilemmas in integrative and eclectic family therapists' practice.

## How Do We Judge the Success of a Treatment Model?

How do we judge integrative models? Does success lie in having the highest degree of consistency and theoretical integrity, the highest level of acceptability to clients, the strongest empirical support for its efficacy in clinical trial research, the greatest ease of dissemination, or the greatest popularity? We are only beginning to evaluate integrative and eclectic models in family therapy. We need a great deal more testing of various methods, as well as a metalevel consideration of how to evaluate these models.

## Toward an All Encompassing Model?

Integrative and eclectic family approaches can help us practice more effectively. They can provide blueprints to direct efficacious intervention and allow for better tailoring of treatment to specific cases. However, we should not see the movement in integrative and eclectic family therapy as heading toward one all-encompassing model that explains all and directs all intervention. Such a model would in its comprehensiveness lose vitality and immediacy for the practitioner, would require a level of certainty about the impact of specific interventions beyond our scope, and would invoke a great deal of therapist reactivity and resistance. Models for therapeutic decision making will never fully replace clinical judgment in the art/science of psychotherapy. It is better to set our sights on attainable goals, such as developing our understanding of treatment processes and how interventions fit together, and building comprehensive models in delimited areas. It is hoped that the structure of the models and the science they invoke can serve as a springboard for the best practice of the art of couple and family therapy.

# REFERENCES

Achenbach, T. M., & Weisz, J. R. (1976). A longitudinal study of developmental synchrony between conceptual identity, seriation, and transitivity of color, number, and length. *Child Development, 46*(4), 840–848.

Adams, J. F., Piercy, F. P., & Jurich, J. A. (1991). Effects of solution focused therapy's "formula first session task" on compliance and outcome in family therapy. *Journal of Marital & Family Therapy, 17*(3), 277–290.

Alexander, J. (1967). Time and the meta-psychological concept of adaptation. *Psyche: Zeitschrift Fuer Psychoanalyse und Ihre Anwendungen, 21*(9), 693–698.

Alexander, J., Waldon, H. B., Newberry, A. M., & Liddle, N. (1990). The functional family therapy model. In A. S. Friedman & S. Granick (Eds.), *Family therapy for adolescent drug abuse* (pp. 183–199). Lexington, MA: Lexington Books/D. C. Heath.

Alexander, J. F., Holtzworth-Munroe, A., & Jameson, P. B. (1994). The process and outcome of marital and family therapy: Research review and evaluation. In A. E. Bergin & S. L. Garfield (Eds.), *Handbook of psychotherapy and behavior change* (4th ed., pp. 595–630). New York: Wiley.

Alexander, J. F., Robbins, M. S., & Sexton, T. L. (2000). Family-based interventions with older, at-risk youth: From promise to proof to practice. *Journal of Primary Prevention, 21*(2), 185–205.

Barrett, M. J., Trepper, T. S., & Fish, L. S. (1990, December). Feminist-informed family therapy for the treatment of intrafamily child sexual abuse. *Journal of Family Psychology, 4*(2), 151–165.

Barrett, M. J., Trepper, T. S., & Fish, L. S. (1991). "Feminist-informed family therapy for the treatment of intrafamily child sexual abuse": Response. *Journal of Family Psychology, 4*(4), 513–514.

Barrett, P. M., Duffy, A. L., Dadds, M. R., & Rapee, R. M. (2001). Cognitive-behavioral treatment of anxiety disorders in children: Long-term (6-year) follow-up. *Journal of Consulting & Clinical Psychology, 69*(1), 135–141.

Becker, J. V., Alpert, J. L., BigFoot, D. S., Bonner, B. L., Geddie, L. F., Henggeler, S. W., et al. (1995). Empirical research on child abuse treatment: Report by the Child Abuse and Neglect Treatment Working Group, American Psychological Association. *Journal of Clinical Child Psychology, 24* (Suppl), 23–46.

Borduin, C. M., & Henggeler, S. W. (1990). A multisystemic approach to the treatment of serious delinquent behavior. In R. J. McMahon & R. DeV. Peters (Eds.), *Behavior disorders of adolescence: Research, intervention, and policy in clinical and school settings* (pp. 63–80). New York: Plenum Press.

Borduin, C. M., Henggeler, S. W., Blaske, D. M., & Stein, R. J. (1990). Multisystemic treatment of adolescent sexual offenders. *International Journal of Offender Therapy & Comparative Criminology, 34*(2), 105–113.

Botelho, R. J., McDaniel, S. H., & Jones, J. E. (1990). A Family Systems Balint Group: A case report from a C.M.E. course. *Family Systems Medicine, 8*(3), 265–271.

Boyd-Franklin, N. (1989). *Black families in family therapy: A multi-systems approach*. New York: Guilford.

Breunlin, D. C. (1999). Toward a theory of constraints. *Journal of Marital & Family Therapy, 25*(3), 365–382.

Breunlin, D. C., Schwartz, R. C., & MacKune-Karrer, B. (1997). *Metaframeworks: Transcending the models of family therapy* (rev. & upd.). San Francisco: Jossey-Bass.

Brown, T. L., Henggeler, S. W., Schoenwald, S. K., Brondino, M. J., & Pickrel, S. G. (1999). Multisystemic treatment of substance abusing and dependent juvenile delinquents: Effects on school attendance at posttreatment and 6-month follow-up. *Children's Services: Social Policy, Research, & Practice, 2*, 81–93.

Brown, T. L., Swenson, C. C., Cunningham, P. B., Henggeler, S. W., Schoenwald, S. K., & Rowland, M. D. (1997). Multisystemic treatment of violent and chronic juvenile offenders: Bridging the gap between research and practice. *Administration & Policy in Mental Health, 25*(2), 221–238.

Brunk, M. A., Henggeler, S. W., & Whelan, J. P. (1987). Comparison of multisystemic therapy and parent training in the brief treatment of child abuse and neglect. *Journal of Consulting & Clinical Psychology, 55,* 171–178.

Christensen, A., & Heavey, C. L. (1999). Interventions for couples. *Annual Review of Psychology, 50,* 165–190.

Christensen, A., & Jacobson, N. S. (2000). *Reconcilable differences.* New York: Guilford Press.

Christensen, A., Jacobson, N. S., & Babcock, J. C. (1995). Integrative behavioral couple therapy. In N. S. Jacobson & A. S. Gurman (Eds.), *Clinical handbook of couple therapy* (pp. 31–64). New York: Guilford Press.

de Shazer, S. (1979, Summer). Brief therapy with families. *American Journal of Family Therapy, 7*(2).

de Shazer, S. (1986). *An indirect approach to brief therapy* (Family Therapy Collections, Vol. 19, pp. 48–55, Aspen Systems). Milwaukee, WI: Brief Family Therapy Center.

de Shazer, S. (1988). *Clues: Investigating solutions in brief therapy:* New York: W. W. Norton.

Duncan, B. L., Hubble, M. A., & Miller, S. D. (1997). *Psychotherapy with "impossible" cases: The efficient treatment of therapy veterans.* New York: W. W. Norton.

Falicov, C. J. (1995). Training to think culturally: A multidimensional comparative framework. *Family Process, 34*(4), 373–388.

Falicov, C. J. (1996). Mexican families. In M. McGoldrick, J. Giordano, et al. (Eds.), *Ethnicity and family therapy* (2nd ed., pp. 169–182). New York: Guilford Press.

Falicov, C. J. (1998). *Latino families in therapy: A guide to multicultural practice.* New York: Guilford Press.

Falloon, I. R., McGill, C. W., Boyd, J. L., & Pederson, J. (1987). Family management in the prevention of morbidity of schizophrenia: Social outcome of a two-year longitudinal study. *Psychological Medicine, 17*(1), 59–66.

Falloon, I. R. H. (2001). Stress management and schizophrenia. *British Journal of Psychiatry, 179,* 76–77.

Feldman, L. B. (1985). Integrative multi-level therapy: A comprehensive interpersonal and intrapsychic approach. *Journal of Marital & Family Therapy, 11*(4), 357–372.

Feldman, L. B. (1992). *Integrating individual and family therapy:* Philadelphia: Brunner/Mazel.

Feldman, L. B., & Pinsof, W. M. (1982). Problem maintenance in family systems: An integrative model. *Journal of Marital & Family Therapy, 8*(3), 285–294.

Frank, J. D. (1973) *Persuasion and healing.* Balitomore, MD: Johns Hopkins University Press.

Goldfried, M. R. (1995). Toward a common language for case formulation. *Journal of Psychotherapy Integration, 5*(3).

Goldfried, M. R., & Norcross, J. C. (1995). Integrative and eclectic therapies in historical perspective. In B. M. Bongar & L. E. Beutler (Eds.), *Comprehensive textbook of psychotherapy: Theory and practice. Oxford textbooks in clinical psychology,* (Vol. 1., pp. 254–273). New York: Oxford University Press.

Goldfreid, M. R., & Padawer, W. (1978). Current status and future directions in psychotherapy. In M. R. Goldfreid (Ed.), *Converging themes in psychotherapy.* New York: Springer.

Goldner, V. (1989). Sex, power, and gender: The politics of passion. In D. Kantor & B. F. Okun (Eds.), *Intimate environments: Sex, intimacy, and gender in families* (pp. 28–53). New York: Guilford Press.

Goldner, V. (1991a). Feminism and systemic practice: Two critical traditions in transition. *Journal of Strategic & Systemic Therapies, 10*(3–4), 118–126.

Goldner, V. (1991b). Toward a critical relational theory of gender. *Psychoanalytic Dialogues, 1*(3), 249–272.

Goldner, V. (1998). The treatment of violence and victimization in intimate relationships. *Family Process, 37*(3), 263–286.

Goldner, V., Penn, P., Sheinberg, M., & Walker, G. (1990). Love and violence: Gender paradoxes in volatile attachments. *Family Process, 29*(4), 343–364.

Greenberg, L. S., & Bolger, E. (2001). An emotion-focused approach to the overregulation of emotion and emotional pain. *Journal of Clinical Psychology, 57*(2), 197–211.

Grunebaum, H. (1988). The relationship of family theory to family therapy. *Journal of Marital & Family Therapy, 14,* 1–14.

Gurman, A. S. (1992). Integrative marital therapy: A time-sensitive model for working with couples. In S. H. Budman M. F. Hoyt, et al. (Eds.), *The first session in brief therapy* (pp. 186–203). New York: Guilford Press.

Haas, L. J., Alexander, J. F., & Mas, C. H. (1988). Functional Family Therapy: Basic concepts and training program. In H. A. Liddle, D. C. Breunlin, et al. (Eds.), *Handbook of family therapy training and supervision. The Guilford family therapy series* (pp. 128–147). New York: Guilford Press.

Henggeler, S. W., & Borduin, C. M. (1995). Multisystemic treatment of serious juvenile offenders and their families. In I. M. Schwartz & P. AuClaire (Eds.), *Home-based services for troubled children. Child, youth, and family services series* (pp. 113–130). Lincoln: University of Nebraska Press.

Henggeler, S. W., Schoenwald, S. K., Borduin, C. M., Rowland, M. D., & Cunningham, P. B. (1998). *Multisystemic treatment of antisocial behavior in children and adolescents*: New York: Guilford Press.

Hubble, M. A., Duncan, B. L., & Miller, S. D. (Eds.). (1999). *The heart and soul of change: What works in therapy*: Washington, DC: American Psychological Association.

Huey, S. J., Jr., Henggeler, S. W., Brondino, M. J., & Pickrel, S. G. (2000). Mechanisms of change in multisystemic therapy: Reducing delinquent behavior through therapist adherence and improved family and peer functioning. *Journal of Consulting & Clinical Psychology, 68*(3), 451–467.

Jackson-Gilfort, A., Liddle, H. A., Tejeda, M. J., & Dakof, G. A. (2001). Facilitating engagement of African American male adolescents in family therapy: A cultural theme process study. *Journal of Black Psychology, 27*(3), 321–340.

Jacobson, N. S., & Christensen, A. (1996). *Integrative couple therapy: Promoting acceptance and change*: New York: W. W. Norton.

Jacobson, N. S., Christensen, A., Prince, S. E., Cordova, J., & Eldridge, K. (2000). Integrative behavioral couple therapy: An acceptance-based, promising new treatment for couple discord. *Journal of Consulting & Clinical Psychology, 68,* 351–355.

Johnson, S. (2000). Emotionally focused couples therapy. In F. M. Dattilio & L. J. Bevilacqua (Eds.), *Comparative treatments for relationship dysfunction. Springer series on comparative treatments for psychological disorders* (pp. 163–185). New York: Springer.

Johnson, S., & Lebow, J. (2000). The "coming of age" of couple therapy: A decade review. *Journal of Marital & Family Therapy, 26*(1), 23–38.

Johnson, S. M., & Greenberg, L. S. (1992). Emotionally focused therapy: Restructuring attachment. In S. H. Budman, M. F. Hoyt, et al. (Eds.), *The first session in brief therapy* (pp. 204–224). New York: Guilford Press.

Johnson, S. M., & Greenberg, L. S. (1994). Emotion in intimate relationships: Theory and implications for therapy. In S. M. Johnson & L. S. Greenberg (Eds.), *The heart of the matter: Perspectives on emotion in marital therapy* (pp. 3–22). Philadelphia: Brunner/Mazel.

Johnson, S. M., & Greenberg, L. S. (1995). The emotionally focused approach to problems in adult attachment. In N. S. Jacobson & A. S. Gurman (Eds.), *Clinical handbook of couple therapy.* (pp. 121–141). New York: Guilford Press.

Johnson, S. M., Maddeaux, C., & Blouin, J. (1998). Emotionally focused family therapy for bulimia: Changing attachment patterns. *Psychotherapy, 35*(2), 238–247.

Kaslow, N. J., Baskin, M. L., & Wyckoff, S. C. (2002). A biopsychosoical treatment approach for depressed children and adolescents. In J. L. Lebow (Vol. Ed.) & F. W. Kaslow (Series Ed.), *Comprehensive handbook of psychotherapy: Vol. 4. Integrative/eclectic* (pp. 31–58). New York: Wiley.

Kaslow, N. J., & Racusin, G. R. (1994). Family therapy for depression in young people. In W. M. Reynolds & H. F. Johnston (Eds.), *Handbook of depression in children and adolescents. Issues in clinical child psychology* (pp. 345–363). New York: Plenum Press.

Lebow, J. (1997). The integrative revolution in couple and family therapy. *Family Process, 36*(1), 1–17.

Lebow, J. L. (1984). On the value of integrating approaches to family therapy. *Journal of Marital & Family Therapy, 10*(2), 127–138.

Lebow, J. L. (1987a). Developing a personal integration in family therapy: Principles for model construction and practice. *Journal of Marital & Family Therapy, 13*(1), 1–14.

Lebow, J. L. (1987b, Fall). Integrative family therapy: An overview of major issues. *Psychotherapy, 24*(3s), 584–594.

Lebow, J. L., & Gurman, A. S. (1995). Research assessing couple and family therapy. *Annual Review of Psychology, 46,* 27–57.

Liberman, R. P., Cardin, V., McGill, C. W., Falloon, I. R., et al. (1987). Behavioral family management of schizophrenia: Clinical outcome and costs. *Psychiatric Annals, 17*(9), 610–619.

Liddle, H. A. (1994, January). The anatomy of emotions in family therapy with adolescents. *Journal of Adolescent Research, 9*(1).

Liddle, H. A. (1999). Theory development in a family-based therapy for adolescent drug abuse. *Journal of Clinical Child Psychology, 28,* 521–532..

Liddle, H. A., Dakof, G., Diamond, G., Holt, M., Aroyo, J., & Watson, M. (1992). The adolescent module in multidimensional family therapy. In G. W. Lawson & A. W. Lawson (Eds.), *Adolescent substance abuse: Etiology, treatment, and prevention* (pp. 165–186). Gaithersburg, MD: Aspen.

Liddle, H. A., Dakof, G. A., Parker, K., Diamond, G. S., Barrett, K., & Tejeda, M. (2001). Multidimiensional family therapy for adolescent drug abuse: Results of a randomized clinical trial. *American Journal of Drug & Alcohol Abuse, 27*(4), 651–688.

LoPiccolo, J. (2002). Postmodern sex therapy. In J. L. Lebow (Vol. Ed.) & F. W. Kaslow (Series ed.), *Comprehensive handbook of psychotherapy: Vol. 4. Integrative/eclectic* (pp. 31–58). New York: Wiley.

Lusterman, D. D. (1998) *Infidelity: A survival guide.* New York: New Harbinger.

Mas, C. H., Alexander, J. F., & Turner, C. W. (1991). Dispositional attributions and defensive behavior in high- and low-conflict delinquent families. *Journal of Family Psychology, 5*(2), 176–191.

McDaniel, S. H., Campbell, T. L., & Seaburn, D. B. (1995). Principles for collaboration between health and mental health providers in primary care. *Family Systems Medicine, 13*(3–4), 283–298.

McDaniel, S. H., Campbell, T., Wynne, L. C., & Weber, T. (1988). Family systems consultation: Opportunities for teaching in family medicine. *Family Systems Medicine, 6*(4), 391–403.

McDaniel, S. H., Harkness, J. L., & Epstein, R. M. (2001). Medical family therapy for a woman with end-stage Crohn's disease. *American Journal of Family Therapy, 29*(5).

McDaniel, S. H., Hepworth, J., & Doherty, W. J. (1995). Medical family therapy with somatizing patients: The co-creation of therapeutic stories. In R. H. Mikesell, D.-D. Lusterman, et al. (Eds.), *Integrating family therapy: Handbook of family*

*psychology and systems theory* (pp. 377–388). Washington, DC: American Psychological Association.

McFarlane, W. R., Lukens, E., Link, B., Dushay, R., et al. (1995). Multiple-family groups and psychoeducation in the treatment of schizophrenia. *Archives of General Psychiatry, 52*(8), 679–687.

Messer, S. B. (1986). Eclecticism in psychotherapy: Underlying assumptions, problems, and tradeoffs. In J. C. Norcross (Ed.), *Handbook of eclectic psychotherapy* (pp. 379–397). New York: Brunner/Mazel.

Miklowitz, D. J., & Goldstein, M. J. (1997). *Bipolar disorder.* New York: Guilford Press.

Miller, S. D., Duncan, B. L., & Hubble, M. A. (1997). *Escape from Babel: Toward a unifying language for psychotherapy practice:* New York: W. W. Norton.

Morris, S. B., Alexander, J. F., & Turner, C. W. (1991). Do reattributions of delinquent behavior reduce blame? *Journal of Family Psychology, 5*(2).

Morris, S. B., Alexander, J. F., & Waldron, H. (1988). Functional family therapy. In I. R. H. Falloon (Ed.), *Handbook of behavioral family therapy* (pp. 107–127). New York: Guilford Press.

Newberry, A. M., Alexander, J. F., & Turner, C. W. (1991, December). Gender as a process variable in family therapy. *Journal of Family Psychology, 5*(2), 158–175.

Nichols, M. P., & Schwartz, R. C. (1998). *Family therapy: Concepts and methods* (4th ed.). Needham Heights, MA: Allyn and Bacon.

Norcross, J. (Ed.). (2002). *Psychotherapy relationships that work.* New York: Oxford Press.

Orlinsky, D. E., Grawe, K., & Parks, B. K. (1994). Process and outcome in psychotherapy: Noch einmal. In A. E. Bergin & S. L. Garfield (Eds.), *Handbook of psychotherapy and behavior change* (4th ed., pp. 270–376). New York: Wiley.

Parsons, B. V., & Alexander, J. F. (1973, October). Short-term family intervention: A therapy outcome study. *Journal of Consulting & Clinical Psychology, 41*(2), 195–201.

Pinsof, W. M. (1983). Integrative problem-centered therapy: Toward the synthesis of family and individual psychotherapies. *Journal of Marital & Family Therapy, 9*(1), 19–35.

Pinsof, W. M. (1988). The therapist–client relationship: An integrative systems perspective. *International Journal of Eclectic Psychotherapy, 7*(3), 303–313.

Pinsof, W. M. (1994, Feburary). An overview of

Integrative Problem Centered Therapy: A synthesis of family and individual psychotherapies. *Journal of Family Therapy, 16*(1).

Pinsof, W. M. (1995). *Integrative problem-centered therapy: A synthesis of family, individual, and biological therapies.* New York: Basic Books.

Pinsof, W. M., & Wynne, L. C. (2000). Toward progress research: Closing the gap between family therapy practice and research. *Journal of Marital & Family Therapy, 26*(1), 1–8.

Pittman, F. (1990). *Private lies.* New York: Norton.

Rolland, J. S. (1988). A conceptual model of chronic and life-threatening illness and its impact on families. In C. S. Chilman, E. W. Nunnally, et al. (Eds.), *Chronic illness and disability. Families in trouble series* (Vol. 2, pp. 17–68). Thousand Oaks, CA: Sage.

Rolland, J. S. (1993). Mastering family challenges in serious illness and disability. In F. Walsh (Ed.), *Normal family processes* (2nd ed.). Guilford Family Therapy Series (pp. 444–473). New York: Guilford Press.

Rolland, J. S. (1994a). *Families, illness, and disability: An integrative treatment model*: New York: Basic Books.

Rolland, J. S. (1994b). In sickness and in health: The impact of illness on couples' relationships. *Journal of Marital & Family Therapy, 20*(4), 327–347.

Rolland, J. S. (1998). Beliefs and collaboration in illness: Evolution over time. *Families, Systems & Health, 16*(1–2), 7–25.

Sager, C. J. (1976a). *Marriage contracts and couple therapy: Hidden forces in intimate relationships*: New York: Brunner/Mazel.

Sager, C. J. (1976b). The role of sex therapy in marital therapy. *American Journal of Psychiatry, 133*(5), 555–558.

Santisteban, D. A., Szapocznik, J., & Rio, A. T. (1993). Family therapy for Hispanic substance abusing youth. In R. S. Mayers, B. L. Kail, et al. (Eds.), *Hispanic substance abuse* (pp. 157–173). Springfield, MO: Charles C. Thomas.

Sheinberg, M., & Fraenkel, P. (2001). *The relational trauma of incest: A family-based approach to treatment*: New York: Guilford Press.

Sheinberg, M., True, F., & Fraenkel, P. (1994). Treating the sexually abused child: A recursive, multimodal program. *Family Process, 33*(3), 263–276.

Stith, S. M., McCollum, E. E., Rosen, K. H., & Locke, L. (2002). Multicouple group therapy for domestic violence. In J. L. Lebow (Vol. Ed.) & F. W. Kaslow (Series Ed.), *Comprehensive handbook of psychotherapy: Vol. 4. Integrative/eclectic* (pp. 31–58). New York: Wiley.

Stith, S. M., & Rosen, K. H. (1990). Family therapy for spouse abuse. In S. M. Stith, M. B. Williams, et al. (Eds.), *Violence hits home: Comprehensive treatment approaches to domestic violence. Springer series on social work* (Vol. 19, pp. 83–101). New York: Springer.

Szapocznik, J., Kurtines, W., Santisteban, D. A., Pantin, H., et al. (1997). The evolution of structural ecosystemic theory for working with Latino families. In H. G. Garcia & M. C. Zea (Ed.), *Psychological interventions and research with Latino populations* (pp. 166–190). Needham Heights, MA: Allyn and Bacon.

Szapocznik, J., & Williams, R. A. (2000, June). Brief Strategic Family Therapy: Twenty-five years of interplay among theory, research and practice in adolescent behavior problems and drug abuse. *Clinical Child & Family Psychology Review, 3*(2), 117–135.

Trepper, T. S., & Barrett, M. J. (1986, Summer). Treating incest: A multimodal systems perspective: Introduction. *Journal of Psychotherapy & the Family, 2*(2), 96–101.

Trepper, T. S., & Barrett, M. J. (1989). *Systemic treatment of incest: A therapeutic handbook*: Philadelphia: Brunner/Mazel.

Wachtel, P. (1977). *Psychoanalysis and behavior therapy*. New York: Basic Books.

Walsh, F. (1996). The concept of family resilience: Crisis and challenge. *Family Process, 35*(3), 261–281.

Walsh, F. (1998). *Strengthening family resilience*: New York: Guilford Press.

Walsh, W. M. (2001). Integrative family therapy for couples. In L. Sperry (Ed.), *Integrative and biopsychosocial therapy: Maximizing treatment outcomes with individuals and couples.* The Family Psychology and Counseling Series (pp. 17–41). Alexandria, VA: American Counseling Association.

Watzlawick, P., Weakland, J. H., & Fisch, R. (1974). *Change: Principles of problem formation and problem resolution*: New York: W. W. Norton.

Weeks, G. R., & Hof, L. (Eds.). (1994). *The marital-relationship therapy casebook: Theory and application of the Intersystem Model.* Philadelphia: Brunner/Mazel.

Weeks, G. R., Hof, L., Howard, B., Turner, M., Westfall, A., & Sachs, P. R. (1995). *Integrative solutions: Treating common problems in couples therapy.* Philadelphia: Brunner/Mazel.

Whiffen, V. E., Kallos-Lilly, A. V., & MacDonald, B. J. (2001). Depression and attachment in couples. *Cognitive Therapy & Research, 25*(5), 577–590.

Wood, B. L. (1993). Beyond the "psychosomatic family": A biobehavioral family model of pediatric illness. *Family Process, 32*(3), 261–278.

Wood, B. L. (1995). A developmental biopsychosocial approach to the treatment of chronic illness in children and adolescents. In R. H. Mikesell, D.-D. Lusterman, Don-David, et al. (Eds.), *Integrating family therapy: Handbook of family psychology and systems theory* (pp. 437–455). Washington, DC: American Psychological Association.

Wood, B. L. (2000). Disentangling pathways of effect in family intervention for chronic illness. *Families, Systems & Health, 18*(4), 419–422.

Wood, B. L. (2001). Physically manifested illness in children and adolescents: A biobehavioral family approach. *Child & Adolescent Psychiatric Clinics of North America, 10*(3), 543–562.

Wood, B. L., Klebba, K. B., & Miller, B. D. (2000). Evolving the biobehavioral family model: The fit of attachment. *Family Process, 39*(3), 319–344.

# PART III

# Evidence-Based Couple and Family Intervention Programs

## INTRODUCTION

Over the last 2 decades family therapy (FT) developed a rich research foundation built on ecologically valid, clinically relevant process and outcome research. The early focus on "schools" of therapy has given way to specific, systematic, and well-articulated clinical models that are research-based yet clinically responsive. This shift is in part due to the fact that our early research found little evidence of efficacy for "theoretical" approaches," leading many to suggest that global therapeutic orientations do not represent the important and distinguishing characteristics that differentiate effective and ineffective interventions (Alexander et al., 1994; Sexton et al., in press). The shift is also due to the growth in clinically valid and reliable research that can inform practice. In fact, family and couple therapy research now leads the way in systematic, research-based clinical intervention models. Liddle (1999) notes that although the traditional approaches to FT still have an impact on the field, the new family therapy models extend beyond traditional theoretical boundaries, are more comprehensive, and include the role of ecological factors outside the

family in understanding the etiology of problems. These models have successfully blended theory and research into systematic treatment intervention programs that have permitted us to successfully implement clinical change mechanisms.

It seems that we are now at a point where we can begin to provide specific evidence for specific application, of specific approaches for specific problems. Although different in theoretical principles and therapeutic process, the emerging models share a common focus: they are well-articulated systematic approaches to treatment, in which (a) clinically meaningful problems are targeted; (b) there is a coherent conceptual framework underlying the clinical interventions; (c) there are specific interventions described in detail, with an articulation of the therapist qualities necessary to follow them; (d) process research identifies how the change mechanisms work; and (e) outcome research that demonstrates how it will work.

This section of the handbook provides a comprehensive review of the outcome and process research in the family and couple therapy fields. In this chapter, Sexton and colleagues use a "levels of evidence" approach aimed at matching specificity of research evidence with the type of policy or clinical process question, with the aim of helping make research more relevant. The four chapters that follow focus on two couple (Atkins and colleagues; Johnson) and two family (Sexton & Alexander; Sheidow, Henggeler, & Schoenwald) approaches that are the best current examples of the ways in which systematic research and theory come together to produce systematic yet clinically responsive approaches to practice. The systematic, comprehensive models presented in this section not only inform current practice but also provide a model for future research-based interventions. Although these are not the only research-based approaches, they do represent empirically based clinical models with the best long-term incorporation of research and practice.

CHAPTER 11

# Efficacy, Effectiveness, and Change Mechanisms in Couple and Family Therapy

THOMAS L. SEXTON, PhD

*Indiana University*

MICHAEL S. ROBBINS, PhD

*University of Miami School of Medicine*

AMY S. HOLLIMON, MS, NCC
ALYSON L. MEASE, MA

*Indiana University*

CARLA C. MAYORGA, BA

*University of Miami School of Medicine*

## INTRODUCTION

Couple and family therapy (CFT) research has grown dramatically during the last 2 decades. What began as a need to demonstrate efficacy and justify the existence of CFT has evolved into a rich knowledge base involving complex and innovative research strategies for investigating change processes and clinical outcomes that mirror the unique clinical challenges of CFT. In this evolution, the research lens has been broadened from simple questions of outcome (does it work?) to examine specific applications of CFT with specific clinical problems in specific settings (effectiveness). The growth in complexity of outcome research has been accompanied by efforts to identify the change mechanisms that underlie positive clinical outcomes (process research). The result of the last 2 decades of research is a strong scientific evidence base for the practice of CFT (Sexton, Alexander, & Mease, in press). These research findings have spawned the development of numerous approaches to couple and family therapy (CFT) that are based on integrated theory and systematic research. Consequently, CFT practitioners have at their disposal systematically developed guidance for their general and specific approaches to treatment of both couples and families.

Despite these advances, research into the outcomes and process of CFT remains a significant challenge. The traditional methods of outcome and process research, developed primarily in individually focused psychotherapy research, are not always applicable in CFT because of the relational and systemic nature of problems, pathology, interventions, and change. For example, the interventions of primary study are multidimensional, focusing on problems with etiologies and outcomes that are not solely within a person but also within patterns of marital or family interaction. However, because there is no unified theory of "healthy" marital/family functioning, it is difficult to identify a specific reference point representing the attainment of successful change. Thus, different and at times divergent perceptions of relational patterns and expectations for change make the study of family and marital therapy quite challenging.

A number of specific methodological challenges also make CFT clinical research difficult (Bray, 2002). Unlike individual psychotherapy research, there is no "gold standard" set of measurement tools in CFT. Thus, each research study uses different self-reports, interviews, and behavior observations. Beyond issues of measurement, CFT research findings have been limited by the fact that the statistical methods necessary to study and model the systemic, nonlinear, and reciprocal process of family relationship are only recently emerging (Bray, 2002).

The challenges of conducting rigorous studies of CFT are partially responsible for creating a complex, unique, and varied array of CFT psychotherapy research studies. For example, the current standard in clinical research trials is to design studies that include the evaluation of outcome goals, process studies to identify presumed mechanisms of change, and moderators that may help identify differential features to identify which treatment applies to which client (Greenberg & Pinsof, 1986; Liddle et al., 2002; Rohrbaugh & Shoham, 2002). Large-scale studies are also part of systematic research agendas that follow increasingly specific and complex questions of outcome and change process within different clinical problems (Sexton, Alexander, & Mease, in press). The focus of CFT research has moved beyond "horse race" comparisons of intervention outcomes, to identifying the clinical change mechanisms that are critical for successful clinical work (Friedlander & Heatherington, 1998; Jacobson & Addis, 1993; Sexton et al., in press).

One outcome of the increasing quality of psychotherapy research is the development of evidence-based clinical models in CFT. These models are built on systematic research that guides and supports the theoretical notions of clinical practice. As such, these models have emerged through a systematic interplay between theory, research, and practice (Szapocznik, Kurtines, & Santisteban, 1994). This volume, and particularly this section, illustrates the systematic, phasic, and clinically responsive nature of current intervention programs in marital and family therapy. The integrated theoretical models presented in this section are principle-based and tailored to fit the context in which they operate. As such, these interventions have been specified in great detail, most often in comprehensive treatment manuals.

As the research knowledge base has increased, it has become increasingly clear that if these models are to become valuable clinical tools, we need to better understand the outcomes and process of CFT in new ways.

Outcomes beyond those representing broad, nonspecific treatments with nonspecific problems and with heterogeneous populations of clients are now required. Similarly, the mechanisms that promote successful clinical outcomes as they exist both within (specific change mechanisms) and between (common change mechanisms) clinical models are now important. Furthermore, as practitioners increasingly implement manualized and specific treatment approaches, there will be a further need for developing detailed operations manuals and adherence protocols, as well as specific procedures for monitoring and assessing clinical activities. Thus, new efforts in developing methods for disseminating these models into the practice community and systematically studying the dissemination process become critical.

Although the recent research efforts represent expansions of the traditional gold standard of randomized clinical trial criteria and thus offer new links between research and clinical practice, this work continues to have little impact on actual CFT practice (Pinsoff & Wynne, 2000; Sexton et al., in press). The reasons for the gap between research and practice have been lamented many times. Although there are numerous reasons, including relevance, openness to new ideas, and problems with dissemination, the general failure of integrating CFT research and practice is also compounded by the fundamental differences in the practices of each. Practice is a decision-making process about a myriad of immediate and very individual issues, including which treatment to use in what setting, what approach to apply to which client, and how to integrate the personality and strengths of the therapist into clinical work, or how to respond to the most immediate needs of the client. Thus, the primary concern of the practitioner is an *ideographic* one: the application of interventions for an individual client in a specific situation. The focus of the researcher is a *nomothetic*

one, seeking general trends that apply to many. The questions of research are not always practice-related but instead are driven by the last finding and the drive for future discoveries (Gurman et al., 1991). Unfortunately, these differences have become part of the gap that divides research and practice.

The purpose of this review is to identify the major research-based trends in CFT that have the potential to inform practice and guide the development of future research efforts by identifying holes and gaps in the current literature. To accomplish this task, we relied on all of the published reviews (both qualitative and meta-analytic) of CFT published during the last 15 years. These reviews served as the evidence for our conclusions, implications, and recommendations. Our review begins with a consideration of three levels of outcome research evidence regarding the broad efficacy of CFT (does it work?), the specific clinical problems for which there is evidence to have confidence that it will be successful (what does it work for?), and the specific intervention model/programs successful in specific contexts with specific client populations (what works, with what client, in what context?). Next, we focus on the common change mechanisms that produce the outcome results. Finally, we make recommendations for future research and the integration of research into practice.

## LEVELS OF EVIDENCE AND CLINICAL CHANGE MECHANISM IN CFT

CFT has evolved into a complex domain, involving thousands of research studies asking a myriad of questions and producing results that can be difficult to understand. Organizing this information in such a way that it is useful is overwhelming for practicing clinicians. In fact, this difficulty in matching clinical questions with the appropriate research findings might be one of the main reasons for the dramatic gap between research and practice in CFT (Sexton et al., in press).

Our review is based upon three assumptions. First, we think the knowledge base of CFT can be a useful source of policy decisions, treatment choices, and the identification of specific clinical change mechanisms to be used with specific clients in immediate situations. Second, we believe that one of the fundamental reasons for the research practice gap is that the range of questions asked (policy, clinical, and research) requires different types of research evidence. For example, policy questions require efficacy evidence regarding broad categories of action. Questions regarding the choice of treatments may require more specific and well-defined effectiveness evidence, including the clear identification of specific treatments and specific problems and a clear delineation of the treatment context. Specific moment-to-moment clinical decisions that must be made by the CFT practitioner require an even more specific process-outcome type of study. We suggest that when the specific question is not matched with the appropriate research strategy/finding, research becomes difficult to use and the gap between research and practice grows. Finally, we suggest that the basis of successful CFT practice is in understanding the specific mechanisms of change that are part of the systematic change mechanism that have demonstrated efficacy. From our perspective, change mechanisms do not represent "common factors" but instead are evidence-based mechanisms whereby clinical change occurs. Change mechanisms cannot be understood outside of the context of the systematic intervention model within which they are hypothesized to occur. Figure 11.1 represents our "levels of evidence" model that will be the basis of this review.

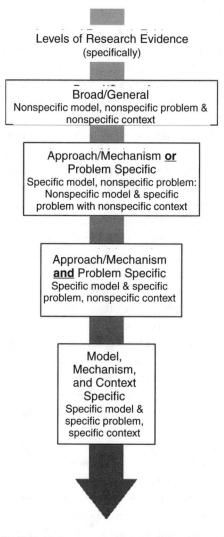

FIGURE 11.1. Levels of Evidence in Couple and Family Therapy Research and Practice

## THE GENERAL OUTCOMES OF COUPLE AND FAMILY THERAPY: DOES IT WORK?

The most fundamental question is whether or not CFT works to help families and couples. This broad question does not examine specific models of CFT or specific problems or outcomes for which CFT is particularly useful. Instead, this level of evidence focuses on general trends in the field of CFT. As such, this nonspecific level of evidence is inherently less informative for the clinician choosing a therapeutic domain or program in which to practice. Its utility lies in the broad-based information lent to educators, administrators, policy makers, and other macrolevel interventionists who train, hire, and develop professional standards of practice. (Sexton et al., in press). In this section we explore this broadest level of evidence by highlighting historical and current reviews and meta-analyses of CFT and of FT and CT taken separately.

The broad outcomes of CFT have been studied for quite sometime. The earliest reviews of CFT (Beck, 1975; Gurman, 1971, 1973, 1975; Gurman & Kniskern 1981; 1991; Gurman, Kniskern, & Pinsof, 1975) concluded, albeit with cautious optimism, that couple and family interventions were efficacious. Gurman and Kniskern (1981) identified over 200 relevant studies involving couple or family therapy in which the explicit focus was on altering the interaction between family members. Their results clearly established the efficacy of CFT. Furthermore, family therapy was often either as effective or more effective than many individual treatments for problems attributed to family conflict. Also, behavioral and nonbehavioral couple and family treatments produced beneficial outcomes that were superior to no-treatment controls in about two-thirds of the cases.

In a later review of qualitative review articles, Pinsof and Wynne (1995) suggested that for a range of problems, CFT is more effective in both statistically and clinically significant ways than no treatment. In addition, they surmised that CFT has demonstrated greater efficacy than standard or individual treatments for some problems. Furthermore, within the broad category of CFT interventions, it was difficult to identify the superiority of any specific treatment. Also, for clients with schizo-

phrenia and conduct disorder, FT approaches are more cost-effective than other treatment modalities. Despite such conclusions, these authors remained somewhat cautious in their assertions, noting that within the substantial body of evidence that has accumulated, "many methodological problems still plague the research and hinder the accumulation of a coherent and clear body of knowledge about the efficacy and effectiveness of MFT" (p. 603). Thus, at the broadest level of examination, CFT interventions have fared well in general and in comparison to other treatment modalities across different presenting problems and divergent schools of CFT approaches. However, in part due to methodological flaws in CFT research, conclusions regarding the effectiveness of these approaches must be drawn with caution. It is helpful to separate family from couple therapy, to speak more specifically about the efficacy of each separate modality in terms of broad-level efficacy and effectiveness (Sexton et al., in press). Table 11.1 is a summary of all the meta-analyses for both family and couple therapy.

*Family Therapy*

Recent qualitative reviews (see Table 11.3) conclude that FT treatments are efficacious in the broadest sense, they are efficacious for a wide range of problems, they produce positive results with different types of families, and the positive results endure over long periods of time (Alexander & Barton, 1996; Carr, 2000a; Lebow & Gurman, 1995; Pinsof & Wynne, 1995; Sexton et al., in press). In their review, using the criteria of "efficacious" as an intervention having at least two controlled studies with positive results and no studies with negative results, Pinsof and Wynne (1995, 2000) found that FT produced positive results for a wide variety of specific clinical problems

TABLE 11.1

Marital and Family Therapy Meta-Analyses

| Study | MT, FT or MFT | # Studies Included | Model/ Intervention/ Approach | Client Problem | Contexts | Primary Findings |
|---|---|---|---|---|---|---|
| Butler & Wampler (1999) | MT | 16 | CCP in group setting | Communication skills in relationships | Social setting (church, university) | Attitude composite/observed behavior: CCP only (pre-post) = .57, 1.06; CCP vs. control (post only) = .32, .95; CCP vs. comparison (post only) = .16, .28 |
| Cuijpers (1999) | FT | 16 | Family interventions | Major mental illness (schizophrenia) | NS | Overall (vs. control): improvement = .46, psychological improvement = .32, family relationship with patient improvement = .22, distress improvement = .39 |
| Dunn & Schwebel (1995) | MT | 15 | BMT, CBMT, IOMT | Broad outcomes: behavior, cognitions, affect, and assessment | NS | Post-treatment (overall—BMT, CBMT & IOMT): behavioral = .76, cognitive = .61, affective = .52, assessment = .90; of relationship BMT vs. CBMT vs. IOMT (post-treatment assessment of relationship) = .78 vs. .71 vs. 1.37 |
| Edwards & Steinglass (1995) | MT | 21 | FIT, CRA | Alcoholism | Inpatient and outpatient | FIT—family systems vs. control = .75; FIT—behavioral treatment & rehabilitation = .86 (without CRA studies = .58); FIT—aftercare = .94 |
| Giblin, Sprenkle, & Sheehan (1985) | MFT | 85 | Premarital, marital, and family enrichment programs | Distressed and nondistressed couples and families | NS | Premarital = .53; marital = .42; family programs = .55 |

| Study | Type | N | Treatments | Population | Setting | Findings |
|---|---|---|---|---|---|---|
| Hahlweg & Markman (1988) | MT | 17, 7 | BMT (17), BPI (7) | General marital distress | U.S. and European couples | BMT vs. control = .95 (U.S. = 1.05, Europe = .81); BPI vs. control = .79; BMT vs. nonspecific control = .63; BPI vs. no-treatment control = .55 |
| Hazelrigg, Cooper, & Borduin (1987) | FT | 20 | FT | Child, adolescent, and adult behavior problems | Inpatient and outpatient | FT vs. no-treatment: family interactions = .45, behavior ratings = .50; FT vs. alternative treatment: family interactions = .65, behavior ratings = .23; recidivism at follow-up: outpatient = .43, inpatient = .41 |
| Mari & Streiner (1994) | FT | 6 | Family therapy (crisis-oriented FT, home-based FT, general family counseling) and family-assisted educational treatments | Relapse rates of schizophrenic clients | Conjoint settings | (Probability, rather than effect size outcome); relapse probabilities increased (a decreased effect) as the follow-up rates increased; risk of relapse among those treated in FBT were between 6% and 41% at 9 months & 14% and 33% at 2 years |
| Markus, Lange, & Pettigrew (1990) | FT | 19 | FFT, BFT | Youth behavior problems | NS | Overall = .70; FFT = .80; BFT = 1.05 |
| Stanton & Shadish (1997) | FT | 15 | MFT + medication: contextual FT, drug family psychoeducational, CBT, BMT, paid FT, unpaid FT, SFT, FFT, MST, MDFT, peer group treatment | Adolescent and adult abuse | Individual therapy, group, varying ethnicities | Overall: MFT vs. alternative interventions (including MFT alternatives) = .48, (including non-MFT alternatives) = .55; FT vs. IT = .55; FT vs. peer group therapy = .51; MFT vs. TAU = .38 |

*(Continued)*

235

TABLE 11.1
Continued

| Study | MT, FT or MFT | # Studies Included | Model/ Intervention/ Approach | Client Problem | Contexts | Primary Findings |
|---|---|---|---|---|---|---|
| Shadish, Montgomery, Wilson, Wilson, Bright, & Okwumabua (1993) | MFT | 163 | MFT: behavioral and psychoeducational, systemic, humanistic, psychodynamic, and eclectic | Marital dissatisfaction, communication, conduct disorders, phobias, schizophrenic symptoms | NS | MFT vs. control: posttest = .51; behavioral & psychoeducational = .56, systemic = .28, humanistic = .23, psychodynamic = .63, eclectic = .58, unclassified = .79; MT vs. FT = .60 vs. .47; MFT vs. IT & conjoint: overall = -.05; FT vs. IT = -9; MT vs. IT = .05 |
| Wampler (1982) | MT | 20 | CCP | Couple communication skills | NS | CCP (attitudes) post = .46, follow-up = .40; CCP (behavior) post = .91, follow-up = .94; CCP vs. control: (attitudes) post = .43, follow-up = .34, (behavior) post = 1.01, follow-up = .20 |

FT = family therapy, MT = marital therapy, MFT = marital and family therapy, IT = individual therapy, CCP = couples' communication program, BMT = behavioral marital therapy; CBMT = cognitive-behavioral marital therapy, IOMT = insight-oriented marital therapy, FIT = family involved treatment, CRA = community reinforcement approach, BPI = premarital intervention studies, FFT = functional family therapy, BFT = behavioral family therapy, CBT = cognitive-behavioral therapy, SFT = structural family therapy, MST = multisystemic family therapy, MDFT = multidimensional family therapy, NS = not specified.

when compared to no-treatment controls, and some FT interventions are more effective than are individual or standard treatments for a number of disorders. These conclusions are supported by a recent systematic review of all the published efficacy, effectiveness, and process research (7 meta-analyses and 82 studies) of couple and family therapy across the last decade (1993–2002) (Sexton et al., in press). With specific regard to family interventions, Sexton and colleagues (in press) concluded that FT had been implemented for a wide range of client problems and was found to have particularly extensive research and positive results for schizophrenia and adolescent conduct disorders. However, only a few types of FT have undergone substantial research regarding their outcomes and mechanisms of change. Overall, FT demonstrates better results than treatment-as-usual groups, but few studies compare the relative effectiveness of different types of FT.

The meta-analyses support the claims of qualitative reviews in the area of family therapy. Shadish and colleagues (1993, 1995) found that a weighted mean effect size was .47, somewhat lower but not significantly different than the effect size for CT (.60). That is, those receiving family-based interventions fared better than those receiving no treatment at all. With regard to the different effect sizes of FT and CT, these authors report a number of important differences between the two treatment modalities. First, FT research included more types of presenting problems that were considered to be more difficult to treat than those addressed in CT studies. In addition, measures of clinical significance were unavailable for FT. As noted previously, most of the studies included were efficacy studies conducted in highly controlled laboratory settings. Fortunately, new recent meta-analyses have focused on the systematic evidence-based models presented later in this chapter.

*Couple Therapy*

The qualitative reviews (see Table 11.2), as identified here, unequivocally conclude that couple therapy (CT) is an efficacious treatment, particularly for the broad areas of relationship dissatisfaction and to a lesser extent for specific presenting problems. Successful outcomes are most apparent when CT treatments are compared to no treatment groups and to a lesser extent to other comparison groups (Alexander, Holtzworth-Monroe, & Jameson, 1994, Sexton et al., in press). For example, Sexton et al. (in press) found that improvements in marital satisfaction and distress are experienced by about 40% of couples in treatment. Although several types of CT treatment have not yet provided evidence of their effectiveness, those varieties that are researched tend to demonstrate similar degrees of client improvement to other types of treatment modalities. Though much further research is needed, these authors concluded that CT might be effective in treating depression in women. In addition, CT may improve the outcomes for substance-using adults when supplementing other forms of treatment. Although these results provide some positive evidence for the effectiveness of CT, many outcomes found in this review were not sustained at longer-term follow-up data collection periods. Similar findings were demonstrated in meta-analyses in the field of CT (Dunn & Schwebel, 1995; Hahlweg & Markman, 1988; Shadish, Montgomery, Wilson, Wilson, Bright, & Okwumabua, 1993).

In addition to the qualitative reviews, two meta-analyses evaluated the broad outcomes of CT. Dunn and Schwebel (1995) found that CT was more effective than no treatment in fostering changes in various areas of couple relationships at post-treatment ($d = .79$) and follow-up ($d = .52$). These results were apparent for a variety of outcomes, including

TABLE 11.2
Couples' Therapy Qualitative Reviews

| Study | Model/Area of Interest | Couples' Problems | Context |
|---|---|---|---|
| Bakely (1996) | General MT, BMT compared to psychodynamic MTs | Marital distress | NS |
| Baucom, Shoham, Mueser, Daiuto, & Stickle (1998) | BMT, CMT, CBMT, IOMT, EFT, PAE, PACBT, PAE+CC, IPT, SST, CRA, CALM, BFT | Marital distress and individual, adult d/o: depression, anxiety, alcoholism, sexual dysfunction, schizophrenia | NS |
| Beach, Fincham, & Katz (1998) | General MT, IPT, BMT | Major depressive disorder | NS |
| Boddington & Lavender (1995) | BMT, CMT, IOMT, EFT, SCT, BSCT | NS | NS |
| Bray & Jouriles (1995) | BMT, PREP | Marital distress | NS |
| Craske & Zoellner (1995) | CBMT | Anxiety disorders | NS |
| Christensen & Heavey (1999) | BMT, CBMT, EFMT, CCP, RE, PREP | Depression, anxiety disorders, sexual disorders, alcohol abuse | NS |
| Huggins (1997) | MFT | Depression, schizophrenia, youth-behavior disorders, alcohol/substance abuse (youths and adults) | Multidisciplinary settings |
| Jacobson & Addis (1993) | BCT, EFT, IOMT, prevention programs | General MT problems | NS |
| Johnson & Lebow (2000) | BMT, EFT, IOMT, PREP, RE | Individual disorders, domestic violence | NS |
| Lebow & Gurman (1995) | BCT, BFT, CMT, CBMT, EFT, IOMT, SFT, strategic FT, systemic FT, FFT, MDFT, MST, psychoeducational, (education, medication, interpersonal skills) | Adolescent drug abuse, depression, alcoholism, delinquency, parent training, schizophrenia, agoraphobia | NS |
| Pinsof & Wynne (1995) | Broadly defined MFT | Schizophrenia, affective d/o developmental d/o of childhood, CD, marital distress, alcoholism, drug abuse, physical d/o | NS |
| Prince & Jacobson (1995) | BMT, ICT, combined BMT-ICT | Affective disorders, conjoint IPT, individual IPT, IFI | Outpatient, inpatient |
| Wesley & Waring (1996) | BMT, CBMT, EFMT, IOMT | General distress in couples | NS |

NS = not specified, BMT = behavioral marital therapy, CMT = cognitive marital therapy, CBMT = cognitive-behavioral marital therapy, IOMT = insight-oriented marital therapy, EFT = emotionally focused therapy, PAE = partner-assisted exposure, PACBT = partner-assisted cognitive-behavioral treatment, SST = sexual skills training, CRA = community reinforcement approach, CALM = counseling for alcoholic marriages, BFT = behavioral family therapy, IPT = interpersonal psychotherapy, SCT = systemic couples therapy, BSCT = behavioral-systems couples therapy, PREP = premarital relationship enhancement program, EFMT = emotionally focused couples' therapy, CCP = couples' communication program, RE = relationship enhancement, BFT = behavior family therapy, SFT = structural family therapy, FFT = functional family therapy, MDFT = multidimensional family therapy, MST = multisystemic family therapy, ICT = individual cognitive therapy, IFI =inpatient family intervention

238

cognition, affect, and general attitudes toward relationship quality. Shadish et al. (1993, 1995) found CT to be moderately more effective than no treatment ($d = .60$). More specifically, these authors identified two outcome domains in which the effect of marital therapy was significant: global marital satisfaction ($n = 16$, $d = .71$) and communication/problem solving ($n = 7$, $d = .52$). There were too few studies to determine effect sizes for CT in the treatment of specific mental health problems. Given these results, the authors stated that the literature supporting these conclusions is at least as strong as it is for other forms of psychotherapy.

Despite the apparent large effect sizes in these analyses of CT effectiveness, the clinical significance of couple therapy remains in question. As reported in the most recent review in the field (Sexton et al., in press), clinically significant changes for couples in therapy are reported for less than half of couples treated. Wesley and Waring (1996) remarked that this finding was consistent across studies and types of couple therapy. For example, in an analysis of their meta-analytic results Shadish et al. (1995) examined clinical significance as the percentage of couples that, following treatment, was no long considered to be "distressed" and found that 41% of couples in treatment groups experienced significant clinical improvement. Christenson and Heavey (1999) echoed this conclusion in their review by stating, "We can say with confidence that fewer than half of couples treated in therapy will move from distressed to non-distressed status" (p. 169). In those studies where longer-term follow-up is present, it seems that the effects of CT deteriorate significantly at follow-up periods beyond 6 months (Christenson & Heavey, 1999). An explanation for these results may lie in the rather narrow contexts in which CT studies tend to be conducted. Controlled investigations of CT in natural settings may be critical

for drawing conclusions about the effectiveness of CT and FT, the differences between orientations, and the application of these treatments for specific problems. Sexton et al. (in press) concluded that in CFT as a whole, the trend toward research in actual clinical settings has begun. Currently, evidence is increasing regarding the effectiveness of CT outside the laboratory setting.

## WITH SPECIFIC CLINICAL PROBLEMS: WHAT DOES IT WORK FOR?

The next important clinical question is, what are the presenting client problems for which there is evidence of success when couple and family therapy is applied? This more specific level of evidence is useful for both policy makers and clinicians. The preponderance of evidence suggests that both couple and family therapy are efficacious with specific clinical problems.

### Family Therapy

Qualitative research reviews (Alexander & Barton, 1996; Friedlander & Tuason, 2000) conclude that both the broad category of approaches and specific family-based intervention models are potentially successful with a variety of clinical problems. Current trends suggest that FT treatments or family-based treatments (that involve family members) are effective for the treatment of adult schizophrenia, alcoholism, and drug abuse, and for the treatment of adolescent conduct/oppositional defiant disorders and drug abuse (Alexander et al., 1994; Estrada & Pinsof, 1995; Pinsof & Wynne, 1995, 2000; Sexton et al., in press). Table 11.3 is a summary of the qualitative reviews of family therapy.

TABLE 11.3

Family Therapy Qualitative Reviews

| Study | Model/Area of Interest<sub>a</sub> | Families' Problems | Context |
|---|---|---|---|
| Alexander & Barton (1995) | FFT, SFT, SLBPMT, BMT, BFT | Child and adolescent behavior problems, schizophrenia, depression, alcohol/substance abuse, marital problems | NS |
| Alexander, Holtzworth-Munroe, & Jameson (1994) | BMT, CMT, CBMT, EFT, IOMT, SLBPMT, FFT, SFT | Aggressiveness, alcohol/substance-abusing youths and adults, delinquency | NS |
| Carr (2000a) | MST, BPT, FFT, TFC, BFT, CFT | Child abuse and neglect, conduct problems, emotional problems, and psychosomatic problems | Outpatient and inpatient |
| Carr (2000b) | BMT, CMT, CBMT, IOMT, EFCT, M&J ST, psychoeducation FT, P-AE, ERP, CIT, SCT, family focused treatment, IFT, CRA, family psychoeducational groups, CT or FT + medication | Adult: Marital distress, psychosexual problems, anxiety d/o, mood d/o, psychotic d/o, alcohol abuse, chronic pain, family management of neurologically impaired adults | Outpatient, inpatient, groups |
| Chamberlain & Rosicky (1995) | SLFT, SFT, MET | Adolescent conduct disorders (CD) and delinquency | Caucasian and Hispanic families in outpatient, family preservation, or treatment foster care |
| Diamond, Serrano, Dickey, & Sonis (1996) | CBT, PMT, FFT, MST | Schizophrenia, depression, anxiety, eating disorders, attention deficit, CD, and substance abuse | Inpatient, outpatient, groups |
| Dixon & Lehman (1995) | BFT, education components, BFM, PEMFG, PESFT, FDMFG | Schizophrenia | Inpatient, outpatient, clinics home-based, multifamily groups |
| Estrada & Pinsof (1995) | PMT (primary or as adjunct) | Child CD, autism, ADHD, fears, and anxieties | Homes, school settings |
| Goldstein & Miklowitz (1995) | Psychoeducational family-oriented intervention | Acute schizophrenia | VA hospitals, medical centers |

240

| Author (year) | Therapies | Disorders | Setting/Population |
|---|---|---|---|
| Henggeler, Borduin, & Mann (1993) | Social learning approaches, FFT, MST, BSFT, PBFT, MDFT | Antisocial behavior, substance abuse, child maltreatment, schizophrenia | Clinics and home-based |
| Kazdin (1997) | PMT, FFT, MST | CD | NS |
| Liddle & Dakof (1995) | CFT, OPFT, SSSE, FFT, MST, MDFT, AFP | Adolescent and adult drug abuse | Cuban Hispanic families, European American middle-class, Hard drug users, peer groups |
| Lipps (1999) | BFT, BMT, FST | Alcoholism | NS |
| Sexton & Alexander (2002) | FFT, MDFT, MST, SFT | Adolescent behavior problems, antisocial behavior, schizophrenia, CD, alcohol/drug use (parents and youths), communication | Community settings |
| Sexton, Alexander, & Mease (in press) | FT: FFT, MDFT, MST, SFT; CT: BMT, CBMT, IOMT, EFCT, IBCT | FT: (CD, drug abuse, schizophrenia, adolescent depression, eating d/o) CT: (Depression, sexual d/o, alcohol/drug use) | NS |
| Waldron (1997) | FFT, MST, SSBFT | Adolescent substance abuse | NS |

NS = not specified, FFT = functional family therapy, SFT = structural family therapy, SLBPMT = social-learning–based parent management training, BMT = behavioral marital therapy, BFT = behavioral family therapy, CFT = conjoint family therapy, CMT = cognitive marital therapy, FST = family systems therapy, TFC = treatment foster care, MET = multitarget ecological treatment, EFCT = emotionally focused couple therapy, M&J ST = Masters and Johnson sex therapy, P-AE = partner-assisted exposure, ERP = exposure & response prevention, CIT = conjoint interpersonal therapy, SCT = systemic couples' therapy, IFT = inpatient family therapy, CRA = community reinforcement approach, SLFT=social learning family therapy, MET = multitarget ecological treatment, CBT = cognitive behavioral treatment, PMT = parent management training, MST = multisystemic therapy, BFM = behavioral family management, PEMFG = psychoeducational family intervention delivered in multiple family group, PESFT = psychoeducational and single family therapy, FDMFG = family dynamic multiple family group, BSFT = brief structural family therapy, PBFT = parent management family therapy, MDFT= multidimensional family therapy, OPFT = one-person family therapy, SSSE = structural strategic systems engagement, AFP = addicts and families project, CBMT = cognitive-behavioral marital therapy, IOMT = insight-oriented marital therapy, IBCT = integrated behavioral couple therapy, SSBFT = strategic structural behavioral family therapy.

241

### Conduct Disorder/Oppositional Defiant Problems

Behavior problems are one of the most frequent clinical referrals for children and adolescents (Kazdin, 1997). Because of the comorbid nature of the problems (e.g., behavior, drug, delinquency), many systems (e.g., child, parent, family, and context) and therefore many seemingly distinct populations of clients are often involved. Despite the complex clinical nature of conduct and behavior problems, the outcome evidence is clear; FT is effective, and specific models of FT are more successful than others (Alexander et al., 1994; Sexton et al., in press).

Two systematic qualitative reviews from outside the traditional research settings also shed light on the extent of the evidence for FBT with conduct disorders. Elliott (1998) conducted a systematic search of existing intervention programs for youth violence for the Center for the Study and Prevention of Violence (CSPV), which was the basis for the "Blueprint" program. This collaborative venture between the CSPV, the Centers for Disease Control, and the Office of Juvenile Justice and Delinquency Prevention (OJJDP) was undertaken to identify the best practices in the treatment of adolescent behavior problems. Only 10 (now 11) of 1,000 interventions met their strict standards, and 3 of these approaches were family-based interventions: functional family therapy (FFT) (Alexander et al., 2000; Alexander & Sexton, 2002; Sexton & Alexander, 2002); multisystemic therapy (MST; Chapter 14, this volume), and Oregon Therapeutic Foster Care (OTFC) (Chamberlain & Rosicky, 1995). The second review was conducted by the Surgeon General (U.S. Public Health Service, 2001). Based on stringent standards of evidence, four intervention programs were identified as "Level 1" programs, effective for use with the range of clinical problems labeled conduct disorder and violent youth (FFT, MST, and OTFC).

In a rather unique study using cost savings as an outcome, the Public Policy Institute of the State of Washington completed an economic analysis of the outcome and cost-effectiveness of various approaches to reduce delinquency (Aos & Barnoski, 1998). Two family-based intervention programs, functional family therapy and multisystemic therapy, had the strongest effectiveness ratings and highest cost savings when compared to other juvenile offender programs. The cost savings (including taxpayer and crime victim cost) for MST and FFT ranged from $13,908 to $21,863 (per adolescent treated), respectively.

### Drug Abuse

Adolescent and adult drug abuse is a serious public health problem, with consequences that extend beyond the drug users to their families and communities. Family therapy approaches have long been considered one of the viable treatment interventions for this category of problems. Drug abuse is difficult to single out as a sole clinical problem because it often occurs as a complex profile of externalizing behavior disorders (e.g., drug use, delinquency, risky sexual behaviors) and related family and individual psychological problems. Particularly in the areas of adolescent drug problems, many of the programs with proven efficacy for conduct disorders are also useful for the specific issues of adolescent drug use/abuse.

Two systematic literature reviews have considered the efficacy of FT with adolescent and adult drug abuse. Liddle and Dakof (1995) identified random assignment clinical trial and quasi-experimental studies of adolescent and adult drug abuse that employed well-articulated therapy models conducted since

1979. The 10 studies of adolescent drug abuse treatment suggest that family therapy is successful in engaging and retaining youths and their families in drug treatment when compared to peer-group and individual therapy. When compared to treatment as usual and other treatments (e.g., peer-group therapy, individual therapy, and other family-based treatments), FTs were successful in reducing drug use with abstinence rates ranging from 73% (White middle-class youths using marijuana) to 44% (for hard drug users), and these reductions were maintained at follow-up periods up to 1 year. The five studies identified by Liddle and Dakof (1995) that evaluated the outcomes of family therapy treatment for adult alcohol and drug use were less encouraging.

Waldron (1997) reviewed 13 random assignment clinical trial studies investigating the outcomes of family-based treatment for adolescent drug use. She identified three categories of effective family-based intervention models: family systems models (structural-strategic models and FFT), behavioral family models, and ecological family-based intervention models (MST). Waldron notes, "Taken together, the results of randomized clinical trials provide ample evidence that family therapy is an effective treatment for adolescent substance abusers," and "The consistency of support for family therapy interventions is remarkable, given the problems, limitations, and widely varying theoretical models, design, approaches to measurement, and other methodological issues" (p. 224).

Stanton and Shadish (1997) conducted a comprehensive analysis of family-based interventions in the treatment of adolescent and adult drug abuse, including 1,571 cases involving 3,500 clients and family members. FT approaches were found to be more effective than were individual counseling, peer therapy, and family psychoeducational interventions for both adults ($d = .48$, $p < .01$) and adolescents ($d = .39$, $p < .01$) immediately follow-ing treatment and at follow-ups as long as 4 years. Though not clear cut, evidence suggested that family-based interventions were more cost-effective than were other approaches to drug-abuse treatment. One of the most pertinent findings was that substantially more family therapy clients stayed in treatment as compared to those in non–family treatment.

## Schizophrenia

The role of family relational interactions in the development and maintenance of schizophrenia has long been of interest to family systems researchers and theorists. In the late 1970s, there was a renewed interest in the role of family-oriented interventions with schizophrenic clients. This new wave of family intervention programs was primarily psychoeducational and was intended to be an adjunct to pharmacotherapy. Currently, there is strong evidence to suggest that these psychoeducational interventions that involve the whole family provide a significant improvement to traditional treatments for schizophrenia relapse prevention (Sexton et al., in press).

The two major reviews of the family-oriented intervention programs for schizophrenia both concluded that there is consistent and robust evidence demonstrating the positive impact of family interventions in delaying and possibly preventing relapse (Dixon & Lehman, 1995; Goldstein & Miklowitz, 1995). The long-term maintenance of the treatment effects is both questioned (Dixon & Lehman, 1995) and supported at 2-year follow-up (Goldstein & Miklowitz, 1995). Also, evidence from a subset of these studies suggests that family interventions may actually improve patients' functioning and help improve family well-being. The evidence does not support one model over another.

Two meta-analyses studied the impact of various family-assisted and family therapy interventions with families in which one member suffered from a major mental illness (most often, schizophrenia). Mari and Streiner (1994) studied the impact of family interventions on the relapse rates of schizophrenic clients. Family interventions proved to reduce the probability that a schizophrenic family member would relapse. Cuijpers (1999) studied the effects of family interventions on the symptoms of relatives with family members suffering from major mental illness (e.g., schizophrenia). Cuijpers found that family interventions (largely, family assisted/involved treatments vs. direct family therapy) had a positive effect on the relatives' psychological distress, on the relationship between family members, and on the overall family functioning. These effects decreased significantly at follow-up.

## Couple Therapy

CT has been used to treat a variety of relationship and individual adult and child problems. CT has been used as both a direct intervention and an adjunct to individually oriented interventions. Clinical problems treated range from general categories of concern, like relationship distress, to specific clinical problems, such as depression. When applied to specific clinical problems, CT is most frequently used as part of multicomponent treatment intervention package for specific disorders. When used in this way, CT is often an adjunct to the primary individual treatment that does not assume relationship difficulties are part of the problem or require attention in the treatment of the individual problem. Table 11.2 is a summary of the qualitative reviews of couple therapy outcomes. What is surprising is that CT is the "least" commonly used format for the treatment of specific clinical problems

(outside of relational adjustment and distress). In their comprehensive review, Baucom, Shoham, Mueser, Daiuto, and Stickle (1998) found that CT was the primary treatment for only one specific problem, depression. Our analysis of other qualitative literature reviews, meta-analyses, and the current clinical trial studies confirms this observation. The literature suggests that even when there is no reported relationship distress, both partner-assisted and disorder-specific interventions are helpful. In an analysis of CT for specific clinical problems, Shadish et al. (1995) were unable to find effects of CT that clearly exceeded the control conditions for major affective disorders, divorce problems, sexual dysfunction, and coping with medical illness.

## Depression

Individual depression creates the potential to generate interpersonal stress. Depressed individuals' seeking (negative feedback or reassurance) and withdrawing behaviors (Joiner, 2000) and partners' or spouses' responses and interactions can also serve as a catalyst or a buffer against stress (Lakey & Lutz, 1996). A growing body of literature suggests that not attending to marital and family issues in the treatment for depression can interfere with the recovery process and can increase risk of relapse (Hooley & Gotlib, 2000).

Beach, Fincham, and Katz (1998) conducted a comprehensive review of the treatment of depression with CT. They identified a second generation of research, focusing on well-specified marital therapy, comparing CT to control groups, and suggested that CT is better and more effective than no treatment, and CT is an alternative approach for distressed married couples with a depressed member. These data provide strong support that well-specified, manualized forms of marital therapy can alleviate symptoms for clients with major depression. In the four studies reviewed by Beach et al. (1998), the mechanism of change appears to be improved marital satisfaction. However, no significant differences between individual and couple therapy were found at post treatment in any of these studies. Baucom et al. (1998) suggest that BMT is a useful treatment for alleviating depression in maritally distressed couples. In fact, marital therapy might be preferable to individual psychotherapy among distressed couples with a wife who is depressed because it leads to both an improvement in depression and marital adjustment. Similarly, Prince and Jacobson (1995) argued that outpatient marital therapy appears to be as effective as individual treatment for depressed women in distressed marriages, and it is more effective in alleviating marital distress.

### Alcohol and Drug Problems

Alcohol and drug abuse and dependence are not only difficult individual problems, but they can have a major impact on the relationships of couples (Edwards & Steinglass, 1995). For example, abuse and dependence are associated with higher rates of physical and psychological problems among nondrinking spouses, marital dissatisfaction, and violence within couple relationships (Baucom et al., 1998). Recent reviews (Baucom et al., 1998: Sexton et al., in press) found that CT was effective for these problems only when specific intervention programs were used. Two CT approaches from over 30 studies met the criteria of efficacious treatments: Community Reinforcement Approach (CRA; Azrin, 1976) and Counseling for Alcoholic Marriages (CALM)—O'Farrell and colleagues' adaptation of BMT for male alcoholics. The CRA model appears to be significantly different in treatment engagement, drinking reduction, subsequent hospitalizations, and improve-

ments in social, employment, and marital adjustment. The results of CRA were maintained (at a rate of 90% abstinent days) through a 2-year follow-up and attrition rates were less than 10%. The CALM treatment resulted in BMT clients having 100% abstinent days. In addition, O'Farrell et al. (1985) were able to demonstrate that the CALM treatment resulted in a significant decrease in the negative consequences usually associated with drinking, a low client attrition rate (between 3% and 12%), and decreased relapse.

Edwards and Steinglass (1995) conducted a meta-analysis of 21 studies of what they call family-involved therapy for alcoholism. Almost all of these studies investigated the outcome of partner-assisted and partner-involved CT interventions. The results of their investigation suggest that it is quite useful to involve family, mostly spouses, in all phases of alcohol treatment. CT as a primary treatment modality was less clear-cut. When compared to individual treatment, two approaches to CT demonstrated results superior to individual treatment, but after 1 year, CT was no longer superior. More encouraging is that CT treatments have the additional benefit of improving marital functioning.

## EVIDENCE-BASED APPROACHES IN COUPLE AND FAMILY THERAPY: "WHAT SPECIFIC MODELS WORK FOR WHICH SPECIFIC PROBLEMS?"

The most specific level of outcome evidence informs clinicians and researchers about which specific clinical models of couple and family therapy are effective for specific clinical problems when applied in specific contexts (e.g., with specific clients in a specific community/culture). This level of evidence is the most useful outcome information for clinicians in that it allows a matching of intervention programs with the clinical problem and the setting and researchers in known areas of needed research (Sexton et al., in press). The good news is that in some areas of couple and family therapy, we can now identify this useful level of clinical evidence.

Early attempts to identify what works with whom under what conditions focused on understanding the efficacy of various "schools" of CFT (Gurman et al., 1986). These schools were nonspecific theoretical models of practice. Early reviews found little evidence for the efficacy of these "theoretical approaches" for specific clinical problems. The approaches that did have some degree of research support were active or highly directive in nature (Hazelrigg, Cooper, & Borduin, 1987). These findings led later researchers to suggest that global therapeutic orientations do not represent the important and distinguishing characteristics that differentiated effective and ineffective interventions (Alexander et al., 1994; Sexton et al., in press). Over the last number of years the "schools" of therapy have given way to specific, systematic, and well-articulated clinical models. Seemingly, we are now at a point where we can begin to provide specific evidence for specific applications of specific approaches for specific problems.

Although different in theoretical principles and therapeutic process, the emerging models share a common focus: they are well-articulated systematic approaches to treatment, in which (a) clinically meaningful problems are targeted; (b) a coherent conceptual framework underlies the clinical interventions; (c) specific interventions are described in detail, with an articulation of the therapist qualities necessary to follow them; (d) process research identifies how the change mechanisms work; and (e) outcome research demonstrates how it will work. What follows is a review of the outcome research for the models of couple and family therapy that fit this emerging criteria.

*Systematic Family Therapy Models*

A number of family therapy and family-based intervention models have enough evidence to suggest they are effective with specific client problems and populations. Each of these programs is systematic and manual-based, with a strong emphasis on outcome and process mechanism articulation. Kazdin's (1997) review identified three promising treatment approaches in the area of adolescent externalizing-behavior disorders: parent management training (PMT), functional family therapy (FFT), and multisystemic therapy (MST). In a review of the literature on adolescent drug use/abuse problems, Sexton and Alexander (2002) suggest that four programs met the criteria of research-based: multidimensional family therapy (MDFT); brief strategic family therapy (BSFT); functional family therapy (FFT); and multisystemic therapy (MST). Interestingly, these family models address clinical problems often considered to be very difficult to treat (adolescent conduct disorders, drug abuse, and schizophrenia). Furthermore, the consistent positive outcomes of these models seem to hold true with a variety of client cultural, ethnic, gender, and problem classification characteristics (Alexander & Barton, 1995; Gurman et al., 1986; Sexton & Alexander, 2002; Sexton et al., in press).

*Functional family therapy* (FFT) (Alexander & Sexton, 2002; Sexton & Alexander, 2002) is a multisystemic family therapy intervention that assumes that clinical "symptoms" are both mediated by and embedded in complex relational sequences involving all other family members and that it has come to serve some legitimate relational outcome (closeness, distance, hierarchy). From an FFT perspective, treatment is considered to be phasic, and each phase of intervention (engagement/motivation, behavior change, and generalization) has a set of therapeutic goals, related change mechanisms that help accomplish those goals, and therapist interventions most likely to activate those change mechanisms. FFT is short-term (12–16 sessions over 3 to 6 months) and targets youths aged 11–18, although younger siblings of referred adolescents may also be seen. See Chapter 15 in this volume for more specific information. A number of the reviews noted previously have found FFT to be an effective program with at-risk youths, from preadolescents who are at-risk to older youths with very serious problems, such as conduct disorder, drug involvement, risky sexual behaviors, truancy, and the like. FFT is effective with multiethnic, multicultural populations living in diverse communities (Elliott, 1998; Kazdin, 1997; Sexton et al., in press; Surgeon General, 2000).

*Multisystemic therapy* (MST) is systematic, manual-driven, family-based intervention for youths and families facing problems of juvenile delinquency, adolescent conduct disorder, and substance abuse (Henggeler, et al., 1999). MST is an approach derived from social-ecological models of behavior, family systems, and social learning theories (Henggeler, et al., 1993, 1998). Targets of change in MST include individual- and family-level behaviors, as well as outside system dynamics and resources like the adolescent's social network. Treatment interventions are on an "as needed" basis, focusing on whatever it takes to alter individual, family, and systems issues that contribute to the problem behavior. The typical treatment course for MST implementation ranges from 2 to 4 months. Multiple-level assessments of family and social systems functioning are embedded within the treatment protocol. Like FFT, MST has demonstrated outcomes with a wide range of adolescent externalizing disorders (conduct disorders, adolescent drug abuse, adolescent mental health issues), with families that represent diverse cultural and ethnic groups, in a number of contexts (Kazdin, 1997; Sexton et al. in press). See

Chapter 14 in this volume for more information.

*Brief strategic family therapy* (BSFT) was developed by Szapocznik and his colleagues at the University of Miami as a family therapy intervention for adolescent drug use (Szapocznik & Kurtines, 1989). The approach was an elaboration of the early structural family therapy approaches. Though somewhat limited in its outcome findings, BSFT does seem successful in reducing adolescent drug use (reported changes in abstinence rates from 7% at admission to 80% at termination). These results were maintained up to the 12-month follow-up. The model is also effective in engaging youths and families in treatment (Santisteban et al., 1996).

*Multidimensional family therapy* (MDFT) is a treatment designed specifically for adolescent substance abuse (Liddle, 1992, 1999). MDFT is rooted in integrative structural and strategic family therapy, but it is also a specialized model that integrates the current thinking of drug abuse and delinquency, and individual attachment and development, with the notions of structural and strategic family therapy. As such, it adopts a multidimensional focus that considers individual, family, and community factors in the development and change of drug-abuse problems. Although research is somewhat limited, evidence suggests that MDFT is successful in reducing adolescent drug use. MDFT is impressive in the diverse contexts in which it has been applied (Philadelphia, Miami, San Francisco), with ethnically diverse and multiproblem adolescents.

*Parent management training* (PMT) for conduct-disordered youth is one of the most extensively researched interventions available (Kazdin, 1997). Studies have included a range of ages (young to adolescent), with varying degrees of severity (oppositional, conduct disorder, delinquent) (Chamberlain & Rosicky, 1995; Kazdin, 1997). Currently, PMT is represented in a number of specific research programs (Chamberlain & Reid, 1991; Patterson, 1997; Webster-Stratton, 1991). PMT is based on the social learning principles and is designed to help parents develop skills to alter their child's behavior in the home. The primary goal of PMT is to alter these interchanges between parent and child, promoting prosocial, rather than coercive, behavior through developing different parenting behavior. Treatment is primarily conducted with parents, who are taught to identify and define problem behaviors in new ways and to develop new prosocial ways of using positive reinforcement, mild punishment, guided practice, and so on. The accumulated evidence for PMT led Kazdin (1997) to conclude that it was one of the most promising programs for the treatment of children with conduct disorder. In his review of PMT, Kazdin identified several features of the program that influence outcome. Shorter treatments (less than 10 sessions) are not as effective as longer treatments (more than 50–60 hours). In-depth knowledge of social learning principles and specific time-out procedures for reinforcement in the home enhance treatment. More skilled therapists seem to produce more durable and lasting effects. Families characterized by multiple risk factors tend to show fewer gains than do families with fewer risk factors.

*Successful Systematic Approaches to Couple Therapy*

Three couple therapy models meet the criteria for successful intervention programs described previously: behavior couple (marital) therapy (BCT), emotionally focused couple therapy (EFCT), and the Prevention and Relationship Enhancement Program (PREP).

*Behavioral marital therapy* (now behavioral couple therapy) is probably the most studied

approach in couples' therapy. The concepts of BMT (BCT), first articulated by Jacobson and Margolin (1979), are based on a social learning theory of human behavior. BMT targets increasing the levels of reinforcing behavior exchanges through teaching communication and problem-solving skills. A goal is to enable couples to cope with their differences in ways that increase reinforcement and decrease punishment within the couple interactions (Chernen & Friedman, 1993). BMT is typically short-term, ranging from 10 to 26 sessions. Early meta-analyses reported effect sizes from BMT to be 0.95, when compared to waiting-list controls, and 0.55 when compared to nonspecific treatments (Hahlweg & Markman, 1988; Shadish et al., 1993). Later meta-analyses confirmed these results, finding a weighted mean effect size of 0.78 at post and 0.54 at follow-up (Dunn & Schwebel, 1995). When translated into measure of clinical significance (noticeable changes in psychological functioning), between 33% and 66% of couples are likely to be nondistressed at the end of treatment (Dunn & Schwebel, 1995). Unfortunately, up to 50% of couples relapse at (Jacobson, et al., 1987). Three qualitative reviews systematically evaluated the outcomes of BCT (Baucum et al., 1998; Sexton et al., in press; Wesley & Waring, 1996). All found that BCT is more effective than no-treatment controls and some nonspecific treatments in regard to changes in marital adjustment, negative communication, improvement on measures of presenting problems, some aspects of communication, and marital satisfaction (additional review of this model can be found in Chapter 13 of this volume).

*Emotionally focused couple therapy* (EFCT), developed by Greenberg and Johnson (1988) and Johnson and Greenberg (1996), is based on attachment theory (Bowlby, 1969). From this perspective, relationship distress results from a failure of the relationship to provide a secure base for one or both partners. The goal of therapy is to uncover unresolved emotions that affect and maintain negative interaction patterns between couples by (a) accessing and reprocessing the emotional experience of partners and (b) restructuring the interactional patterns (Johnson & Greenberg, 1994).

Meta-analysis suggests that the weighted effect size for marital behavior was 0.87 at post-treatment and 0.69 at follow-up. Effect sizes for relationship quality outcomes were 1.37 at post-treatment and 1.04 at follow-up. The average follow-up time was 12.4 months (Dunn & Schwebel, 1995). Trends from the qualitative reviews suggest that EFCT is a significant benefit to distressed couples in comparison to no treatment and that these improvements remain unchanged at follow-up. When clinical significance is the criteria, between 75% and 90% of couples were improved, and between 35% and 75% were no longer distressed at post-treatment (Baucom et al., 1998; Sexton et al. in press).

Most couple prevention programs use psychoeducational approaches aimed at building relationship skills as a method to improve relationship functioning, thereby preventing marital distress. Two decades of research suggest that prevention programs can change the behavior of couples such that they have moderate-term increases in relationship adjustment and stability (Christensen & Heavey, 1999). Unfortunately, evidence from controlled outcome studies for the efficacy of most prevention programs is lacking (Bray & Jouriles, 1995), and few of these programs have long-term follow-up measures. Of those that do exist, it seems that like marital therapy, the positive impact of prevention programs dissipate over time. Of the available prevention programs, the Prevention and Relationship Enhancement Program (PREP), developed by Markman and colleagues, has demonstrated significant changes in both relationship satisfaction and adjustment. Markman, Renick, Floyd, Stanley, & Clements (1993) found that PREP proved effective in preventing relationship dissolution prior to marriage, and positive results were maintained up to 5 years following the intervention (Sexton et al., in press).

## COMMON CHANGE MECHANISMS IN EFFECTIVE COUPLE AND FAMILY THERAPY

One interesting and important question in clinical practice is "What makes therapy effective?" This is the most specific level of evidence and the most useful for increasing practitioners' understanding of the immediate interactions between clients and therapists. Unfortunately, in contrast to the solid base of evidence supporting the efficacy of CFT, few studies have examined the presumed mechanisms of action responsible for the impressive outcome data. As such, change mechanisms research, with few exceptions (see Chapters 13, 14, and 15), has had little impact on the evolution of couple and family therapy (CFT). A remedy is needed because "process" research into the clinical interior of couple and family approaches has the potential for identifying intervention strategies, specific techniques, and interpersonal processes that contribute to effectiveness and—as such—has the potential for further developing, improving, and disseminating effective treatments.

### A Review of Reviews

Starting with Greenberg and Pinsof's (1986) comprehensive overview of process research in psychotherapy, several excellent reviews have documented extant process research findings (Alexander, Holtzworth-Munroe, & Jameson, 1994; Diamond & Diamond, 2002; Friedlander, Wildman, Heatherington, & Skowron, 1994; Robbins, Szapocznik, Alexander, & Miller, 1998; Sexton et al., in press). Numerous authors have also proposed strategies for capturing change processes in CFT, including developing frameworks for conducting process studies and organizing process research findings (Alexander, Newell, Robbins, & Turner, 1995); articulating a theoretical and research framework for capturing the change process at multiple levels and across multiple perspectives (Heatherington, 1989); and highlighting the critical role of process research in treatment manual development (Gaston & Gagnon, 1996). Also, clinical researchers have articulated strategies for linking process and outcome, as well as elucidating the dynamic relationship between treatment processes (Greenberg, 1986; Greenberg & Pinsof, 1986). A central theme in these prescriptions is the recommendation of the need for a programmatic approach to research that cycles between discovery and verification (Greenberg, 1991; Greenberg & Newman, 1996).

Most recently, critical evaluations of the status of process research have suggested that such research has had only a marginal impact on actual clinical practices. For example, Kazdin (2001) noted many gaps between research and practice and provided specific recommendations for bridging this gap by increasing our understanding of the underpinnings of treatment and the change process. Also, Pinsof and Wynne (2000) critically evaluated factors that limit the relevance of process and outcome research findings to practicing clinicians and outlined a "progress" research framework that integrates process and outcome perspectives into a unified methodology that feeds research data back into therapy. Feedback in this framework is idiographic; that is, it is specific to the case in question. As such, findings are immediately relevant to both clients and therapists.

## A Focus on Core Processes in Change Mechanism Research

A major concern that has been raised in the psychotherapy research literature is the debate about the movement toward identifying empirically supported/validated treatments (Henry, 1998). Of particular relevance for this section on change mechanism research is the concern that controlled clinical trial studies (the "gold standard" in the validation process) restrict the range of client and therapist variables and therefore may not the best means for identifying process-outcome links (Garfield, 1990; Henry, 1998). Thus, it is recommended that research utilize a process analysis on the basis of comparisons of two or more forms of psychotherapy (Garfield, 1990, p. 278). For this reason, we have attempted to present research support for "common/core" change mechanism constructs that have been identified from research across intervention models.

In presenting "common/core" constructs, we are sensitive to the existing tension in the psychotherapy research literature regarding research focusing on intervention-specific process-outcome links versus core/common change processes. This debate has become increasingly polarized and intensified as theorists and researchers have forced all relevant variables onto a single continuum, ranging from intervention-specific to core process. On the one hand, our view is that there are common ingredients that contribute to the efficacy/effectiveness of CFT. However, on the other hand, we also believe that how these "core" processes operate and contribute to effectiveness may vary across intervention models. For example, Sexton et al. (in press) suggest that there were common change mechanisms in effective therapies but that these mechanisms could not be understood outside the systematic change models from which and within which they took place. Moreover, we also believe that "intervention-specific" processes may be critically related to outcome, and that specific intervention processes may be particularly effective with specific couples/families (Rohrbaugh, Shoham, Trost, Muramoto, Cate, & Leischow, 2001). Thus, the constructs presented further on represent ideas that transcend models but that may operate uniquely across interventions.

In this review, we focus on existing empirical research rather than on theoretical articulations. Unfortunately, only a handful of studies have identified critical processes that are essential in CFT. Much of the process research that has been conducted falls within three domains: (1) establishing a therapeutic alliance with couples and family members; (2) managing conflicted couple/family interactions; and (3) changing couple and family interactions.

## Alliances in CFT

Perhaps the most studied variable in individual, group, couple, and family therapy is the therapeutic alliance. Although most conceptualizations of common factors in psychotherapy suggest that the therapeutic alliance is important in all psychotherapies (Orlinsky, Grawe, & Parks, 1994), most of the research on alliance has focused on individual therapy. Nonetheless, as early as 1978, Gurman and Kniskern concluded that "the ability of the therapist to establish a positive relationship . . . receives the most consistent support as an important outcome-related therapist factor in marital and family therapy" (p.

875). Also, in their review, Friedlander et al. (1994) assert that components of alliance in family therapy have been predictive of session effectiveness, continuation in treatment, and therapeutic outcome. Although these reviews assert that the therapeutic alliance is critical in family therapy, few studies have been specifically designed to examine the alliance in family therapy.

One reason why research on alliances has not flourished is that very little work has been done to develop measures of the alliance in CFT. This is quite surprising, given that excellent theory-based measures of alliances in CFT have been developed and disseminated over the last 3 decades. Most prominent among these measures is the Integrative Psychotherapy Alliance Scale developed by Pinsof & Catherall (1986). Unfortunately, in contrast to individual psychotherapy research, where single measures have been used by various investigators across models, alliance scales in family therapy have not been widely embraced.

## A Review of Selected Studies

In social learning-based behavioral marital therapy, client involvement and compliance, which may be conceptualized as therapeutic alliance (Frieswyk, 1986), have been shown to be largely responsible for successful treatment outcomes (Holtzworth-Munroe, Jacobsen, DeKlyen, & Whisman, 1989). For example, in this study, the couples that made the most gains in therapy are those who believe that they are actively and collaboratively participating in therapy and who are complying with assignments. Similarly, deKemp and Van Acker (1997) demonstrated that establishing a positive working relationship between the therapist and the mother promotes therapeutic progress in family therapy.

Attempts to change family interactions are often met with considerable resistance. For example, therapists encounter the most "resistance" during the phase of treatment in which they attempt to change family interactions (Chamberlain, Patterson, Reid, Kavanagh, & Forgatch, 1984). In CFT, the concept of resistance can be conceptualized as a family characteristic or as a family response to an interaction with the therapist, and, as such, therapists can intervene to prevent or manage resistance (Szapocznik & Kurtines, 1989; Szapocznik et al., 1989). This theoretical work and the empirical research of Patterson and colleagues, Alexander and colleagues, and Szapocznik and colleagues clearly demonstrate that so-called family resistant behaviors appear to be elicited in interactions with the therapist and as a result can be modified by altering the therapist's behaviors. For example, Patterson and Forgatch (1985) examined the immediate impact of therapist interventions on client noncompliance in families with a conduct-disordered youth. The results of this study demonstrated that therapists' teaching and confronting were associated with increased noncompliance, whereas therapists' facilitating and supporting were associated with decreased noncompliance.

Taken together, these results provide specific recommendations for handling "resistant" behaviors in family therapy. In particular, resistant behaviors must first be reconceptualized as part of an interaction with the therapist. Adopting this view permits therapists to examine their own contribution to resistance and opens up possibilities for strategically altering their own behavior to influence family members. Therapist facilitative, supportive, and reframing interventions may be particularly useful when "working through" so-called resistant interactions. Likewise, therapist interventions that block negative affect, promote constructive dialogue, or both, appear to decrease resistant interactions in family therapy.

## "The Whole 'Is' and 'Is More Than' the Sum of Its Parts"

The evolution of advanced statistical procedures for modeling the clinical interior of CFT in a manner that is sensitive to multilevel and multidimensional processes, such as hierarchical linear modeling, has clearly facilitated a new wave of CFT psychotherapy research. These statistical methods provide clinical researchers with valuable tools for capturing systemic aspects of therapy. Unfortunately, researchers are just beginning to use the procedures to focus on these systemic processes. Thus, most of the studies that have been conducted to date have examined linear relationships between variables, have focused solely on individual family members, subgroups, or aggregated family scores, or have tested for some combination of these.

To capture systemic aspects of therapy process, researchers must grapple with measuring individual and family processes, as well as determining the most appropriate methods for aggregating "individual" data at the "family" level. One of the simplest methods for aggregating data involves constructing a "sum" score that is a composite of each family member's score on an important dimension. For example, outcome (e.g., retention/dropout) may be predicted by the presence of sufficient "sum" alliance provided by the family members. However, this aggregate sum may or may not represent the interior of the therapeutic system (Dakof, 1996). For example, a family therapy session where the parent has a very high alliance and the adolescent has a very low alliance is not the same phenomenon as a session where a parent and an adolescent both experience an average alliance. Studies have found that a "split alliance" such as this may be a common occurrence (Heatherington & Friedlander, 1990; Pinsof & Catherall, 1986). Thus, within-family "discrepancy" scores represent another useful strategy for aggregating individual data at the family-level. That is, parent minus adolescent differences in alliances may represent an "unbalanced alliance," and this unbalance may predict dropout.

Initial findings from an ongoing study suggest that both types of aggregation strategies appear to be important for understanding the link between alliance and dropout (Robbins, Alexander, Turner, & Perez, in press). In this study, alliances were captured by independent raters using the Vanderbilt Therapeutic Alliance Scale–Revised, and differences in patterns of alliance between families that dropped out of treatment and families that stayed in treatment were examined at the individual (parent, adolescent) and family level (within-family differences).

An interesting aspect of this study is that it utilizes two different family-based interventions for adolescents with severe behavior problems and that the two interventions differed in how sessions were delivered. In one intervention, sessions were conducted individually with adolescents and parents, whereas in the other intervention, the majority of sessions was delivered conjointly. In the mixed (individual and conjoint sessions) approach, results demonstrated that adolescents and parents in families that dropped out of therapy had statistically significant lower alliance scores than did adolescents and parents who completed treatment. In the conjoint approach, results demonstrated that the level of individual parent and adolescent alliances did not predict retention. Rather, it was unbalanced alliances that differentiated dropouts from completers in the conjoint approach. For ex-

ample, dropout cases had significantly higher unbalanced alliances (parent minus adolescent) than did completer cases.

The findings suggest that the therapeutic alliance may be a core mechanism that predicts dropout, but that how the alliance operates may be unique to a treatment approach or a mode of delivery. Interestingly, these patterns of findings indicate that "The whole is and is more than the sum of its parts."

*Managing Conflicted Couple/Family Interactions*

Specific aspects of negativity and high levels of conflict have been shown to predict individual, couple, and family problems in both marital (Gottman & Levenson, 1992; Margolin, Burman, & John, 1989) and family research (Alexander, Waldron, Barton, & Mas, 1989). As such, it is not surprising that conflicted interactions are a primary target of both couple and family approaches.

Conflict/negativity appears to play a similar role in the process of therapy itself, with numerous examples linking negativity in the therapy session to poor therapy outcome. Alexander, Barton, Schiavo, and Parsons (1976), for example, found that the ratio of negative to supportive statements was significantly higher in cases that dropped out of therapy than among cases that completed treatment. In turn, premature termination predicted recidivism in adolescents. In the same study, among the families that completed therapy, a reduction in family member negative behaviors during treatment was associated with positive outcome. Greater rates of within-family disagreements have also been shown to be characteristic of noncompleters in structural-strategic family therapy (Shields, Sprenkle, & Constantine, 1991). Finally, a comprehensive review of the process of family therapy concluded that, in general, negativity may be predictive of premature termination (Friedlander, Wildman, Heatherington, & Skowron, 1994).

Research findings suggest that conflict/negativity is malleable in treatment. For example, Melidonis & Bry (1995) demonstrated that therapists could reduce family members' blaming statements and increase their positive statements by asking questions about exceptions and by selectively attending to positive statements. Similarly, reframing interventions has been shown to reduce the likelihood of family members' defensive communications in family therapy (Robbins, Alexander, Newell, & Turner, 1996; Robbins, Alexander, & Turner, 2000). Finally, Diamond and Liddle (1996) demonstrated that in successful resolutions of therapy impasses, therapists were able to create an emotional treaty among family members by blocking and working through negative affect and by amplifying thoughts and feelings that promoted constructive dialogue.

Results of process studies demonstrate that highly negative and conflicted family interactions may be modified by therapist interventions. In particular, interventions that are positive and nonblaming appear to have a powerful effect on negative family interactions. Future research must attempt to link these changes in in-session conflict and negativity to other therapeutic changes and to the ultimate outcome of therapy.

## Changing Couple and Family Interactions

A core feature of couple and family treatment is a focus on identifying and improving couple and family interactions. Although approaches differ in the specific interactions identified and therapeutic strategies recommended for changing interactions (from highly directive to nondirective), all of them provide a ratio-nale for helping couples and families learn to interact in new ways. Most intervention theories are well-informed by research implicating couple and family factors in the evolution of specific problems (e.g., lack of parental monitoring associated with adolescent behavior problems, personal attacks of spouse that predict marital dissolution). Moreover, process studies have begun to demonstrate a link between in-session improvements on key variables and treatment outcomes. For example, Schmidt, Liddle, and Dakof (1996) demonstrated significant decreases in negative parenting practices and significant increases in positive parenting features over the course of family therapy, and they linked these improvements in parenting to improvements in adolescent drug use and behavior problems. Likewise, to account for marital dissolution, Gottman and Levenson (1992) supported a balance theory requiring regulation of interactive behavior at a ratio of positive to negative codes of approximately 5.0 to 1.0 for marital stability. In another study, Gottman, Coan, Carrere, and Swanson (1998) linked contempt, belligerence, and defensiveness to destructive outcomes during conflict resolution. Furthermore, negative start-up by the wife, refusal of the husband to accept influence from his wife, the wife's reciprocation of low-intensity negativity in kind, and the absence of de-escalation of low-intensity negativity by the husband was the pattern shown to predict divorce. The amount of positive affect in the conflict predicted both marital stability and marital happiness among stable couples (Gottman et al., 1998, p. 17).

Unfortunately, process research has failed in general to provide information to therapists about the mechanisms by which therapists achieve these gains. That is, it is not clear what therapist interventions, family processes, or therapist-family processes predicted these improvements. Thus, there is a major need for process research (1) to move beyond analyses of early session processes, (2) to include therapist and family variables as targets of study, and (3) to link in-session changes to out-of-session outcomes.

## CONCLUSIONS

The shifting focus from efficacy to effectiveness of CFT research has changed the nature of the questions of outcome to examine specific application of CFT with specific clinical problems in specific clinical settings. After reviewing the current intervention programs in CFT, the impressive findings of the studies that tap into a broad range of clinical populations are encouraging. Specifically, this review addressed three levels of outcome research: the broad efficacy of CFT, the specific clinical problems for which there is evidence, and the specific intervention model/programs successful in specific contexts with specific client populations. Useful to educators, administrators, policy makers, and other macrolevel interventionists who train, hire, and develop professional standards of practice, the broadest level of evidence shows that CFT interventions have been successful in general and in comparison to other treatment modalities across different presenting problems and divergent schools of approaches. Useful for both policy makers and clinicians, the second, more specific, question of evidence suggests that family therapy is efficacious with specific clinical problems, including adult schizophrenia, alcoholism and drug abuse, and adolescent conduct/oppositional defiant disorders and drug abuse. In addition, the efficacy of couple therapy has also been reported when used to treat a variety of relationship and individual adult and child problems, ranging from general categories of concern, like relationship distress, to specific clinical problems, such as depression. The third and most specific level of outcome evidence provides help to clinicians in matching intervention programs to clinical problems and settings, as well as to researchers in known areas of needed research. Remarkably, various family therapy and family-based intervention models have enough evidence to suggest they are effective with specific client problems and populations. With consistent positive outcomes, these family models (FFT, MST, BSFT, MDFT, and PMT) address clinical problems often considered very difficult to treat, and, as reported, they hold true with a variety of client cultural, ethnic, gender, and problem classification characteristics. Similarly, successful systematic approaches to couple therapy include BCT, EFCT, and PREP.

One positive aspect of CFT research is that findings are frequently immediately transferable to real-world settings with real-world clients. That is, although much of the existing research has been conducted using rigorous empirical procedures in efficacy and effectiveness trials, the therapists and participants who have been included were frequently housed within community-based clinics. Moreover, in many studies, the therapy that was carried out used treatment manuals that were flexible to the range of problems that clients, even those within a relatively circumscribed condition such as drug abuse, present in treatment. Likewise, change mechanisms research has also had an impact on CFT research and practice. Guided by a central recommendation by clinical researchers to utilize a programmatic approach to research that cycles between discovery and verification, CFT process research has begun to demonstrate a link between in-session improvements on key variables and treatment outcomes. To further develop, improve, and disseminate effective treatments, this review calls for the identification of process mechanisms by which therapists achieve these gains to become a priority.

A major trend that will continue to gain momentum in the coming years will be research identifying processes involved in the successful dissemination of empirically based interventions into practice settings. Major initiatives in this area are already underway, and literally hundreds of clinics and thousands of therapists are being trained in the implementation of research-proven interventions. Unfortunately, the research infrastructure for tracking these massive dissemination efforts has lagged behind this latest trend in training and practice. Thus, the context is rich with opportunities for examining training, supervision, implementation, interventions process, and global treatment outcomes in an entirely new context. The next wave of CFT research must rise to meet this challenge to ensure that decades of research on outcomes and the interior of treatment are translated in the most efficient and effective way for community practitioners.

## REFERENCES

Alexander, J. F., & Barton, C. (1995). Family therapy research. In R. H. Mikesell, D. D. Lusterman et al. (Ed.), *Integrating family therapy: Handbook of family psychology and systems theory* (pp. 199–215). Washington, DC: American Psychological Association.

Alexander, J. F., Barton C., Schiavo, R. S., & Parsons, B. V. (1976). Behavioral intervention with families of delinquents: Therapist characteristics and outcome. *Journal of Consulting and Clinical Psychology, 44*, 656–664.

Alexander, J. F., Pugh, C., & Sexton, T. L. (2000). Functional family therapy. (2nd Edition.) In D. S. Elliott (Series Ed.), *Blueprints for violence prevention* (Book 3). Boulder, CO: Center for the Study and Prevention of Violence, Institute of Behavioral Science, University of Colorado.

Alexander, J. F., Holtzworth-Munroe, A., & Jameson, P. (1994). The process and outcome of marital and family therapy: Research review and evaluation. In A. E. Bergin & S. L. Garfield (Eds.), *Handbook of psychotherapy and behavior change* (4th ed., pp. 595–630). Oxford, England: Wiley.

Alexander, J. F., Newell, R. M., Robbins, M. S., & Turner, C. W. (1995). Observational coding in family therapy process research. *Journal of Family Psychology, 9*(4), 355–365.

Alexander, J. F., & Sexton, T. L. (2002). Functional family therapy: A model for treating high-risk, acting-out youth. In J. Lebow (Ed.), Wiley series in couples and family dynamics treatment, *Comprehensive handbook of psychotherapy (Vol. IV). Integrative/eclectic*. New York: Wiley.

Alexander, J. F., Waldron, H. B., Barton, C., Mas, C., & Haydee. (1989). The minimizing of blaming attributions and behaviors in delinquent families. *Journal of Consulting and Clinical Psychology, 57*(1), 19–24.

Aos, S., & Barnoski, R. (1998). *Watching the bottom line: Cost-effective interventions for reducing crime in Washington*. Washington State Institute for Public Policy: RCW 13.40.500.

Azrin, N. H. (1976). Improvements in the community-reinforcement approach to alcoholism. *Behavior Research & Therapy 14*(5), 339–348.

Bakely, J. (1996). Couples therapy outcome research: A review. *Journal of Couples Therapy 6*(1/2). 83–94.

Baucom, D. H., Shoham, V., Mueser, K. T., Daiuto, A. D., & Stickle, T. R. (1998). Empirically supported couple and family interventions for marital distress and adult mental health problems. *Journal of Consulting and Clinical Psychology, 66*(1), 53–88.

Beach, S. R. H., Fincham, F. D., & Katz, J. (1998). Marital therapy in the treatment of depression: Toward a third generation of therapy and research. *Clinical Psychology Review, 18*(6), 635–661.

Beck, D. F. (1975). Research findings on the outcomes of marital counseling. *Social Casework, 56*, 153–181.

Boddington, S. J. A., & Lavender, A. (1995). Treatment models for couples in therapy: A review of the outcome literature in the dodo's verdict. *Sexual and Marital Therapy, 10*(1), 69–81.

Bowlby, J. (1969). *Attachment and loss: Vol. 1. Attachment*. New York: Basic Books.

Bray, J. H. (2002). Methodological issues and innovations in family psychology intervention research. In H. A. Liddle, D. A. Santisteban, R. F. Levant, & J. H. Bray (Eds.), *Family psychology: Science-based interventions* (pp. 89–101). Washington, DC: American Psychological Association.

Bray, J. H., & Jouriles, E. N. (1995). Treatment of marital conflict and prevention of divorce. *Journal of Marital and Family Therapy, 21*(4), 461–473.

Butler, M. H., & Wampler, K. S. (1999). A meta-

analytic update of research on the couple communication program. *American Journal of Family Therapy, 27*, 223–237.

Carr, A. (2000a). Evidence-based practice in family
therapy and systemic consultation. I: Child-focused problems. *Journal of Family Therapy, 22*,
29–60.

Carr, A. (2000b). Evidence-based practice in family
therapy and systemic consultation. II: Adult-fo-
cused problems. *Journal of Family Therapy, 22*,
273–295.

Chamberlain, P., Patterson, G., Reid, J., Kavanagh,
K., & Forgatch, M. (1984). Observation of client
resistance. *Behavior Therapy, 15*(2), 144–155.

Chamberlain, P., & Reid, J. B. (1991). Using a specialized foster care community treatment model
for children and adolescents leaving the state mental hospital. *Journal of Community Psychology,
19*, 266–276.

Chamberlain, P., & Rosicky, J. G. (1995). The effectiveness of family therapy in the treatment of adolescents with conduct disorders and delinquency.
*Journal of Marital and Family Therapy, 21*(4),
441–459.

Chernen, L., & Friedman, S. (1993). Treating the
personality disordered agoraphobic patient with
individual and marital therapy: A multiple replication study. *Journal of Anxiety Disorders, 7*(2),
163–177.

Christensen, A., & Heavey, C. L. (1999). Interventions for couples. *Annual Review of Psychology,
50*, 165–190.

Craske, M. G., & Zoelliner, L. A. (1995). Anxiety
disorders: The role of marital therapy. In N. S.
Jacobsen & A. S. Gurman (Eds.), *Clinical handbook of couple therapy* (pp. 394–410). New York:
Guilford Press.

Cuijpers, P. (1999). The effects of family interventions of relatives' burden: A meta-analysis. *Journal of Mental Health, 8*(3), 275–285.

Dakof, G. A. (1996). Meaning and measurement of
family: Comment on Gorman-Smith et al. *Journal of Family Psychology, 10*(2), 142–146.

de Kemp, R. A. T., & Van Acker, J. C. A. (1997).
Therapist–parent interaction patterns in home-
based treatments: Exploring family therapy process. *Family Process, 36*(3), 281–295.

Diamond, G., & Liddle, H. A. (1996). Resolving a
therapeutic impasse between parents and adolescents in multidimensional family therapy. *Journal of Consulting and Clinical Psychology, 64*(3),
481–488.

Diamond, G. S., & Diamond, G. M. (2002). Studying a matrix of change mechanisms: An agenda
for family-based process research. In H. A. Liddle,
D. A. Santisteban, et al. (Eds.), *Family psychology: science-based interventions* (pp. 41–66).
Washington, DC: American Psychological Association.

Diamond, G. S., Serrano, A. C., Dickey, M., & Sonis,
W. A. (1996). Current status of family-based outcome and process research. *Journal of the American Academy of Child and Adolescent Psychiatry, 35*(1), 6–16.

Dixon, L. B., & Lehman, A. F. (1995). Family interventions for schizophrenia. *Schizophrenia Bulletin, 21*(4), 631–643.

Dunn, R. L., & Schwebel, A. I. (1995). Meta-analytic review of marital therapy outcome research.
*Journal of Family Psychology, 9*(1), 58–68.

Edwards, M. E., & Steinglass, P. (1995). Family
therapy treatment outcomes for alcoholism. *Journal of Marital and Family Therapy, 21*(4), 475–
509.

Elliott, D. S. (Series Ed.). (1998). *Blueprints for violence prevention*. University of Colorado, Center
for the Study and Prevention of Violence. Boulder CO: Blueprints Publications.

Estrada, A. U., & Pinsof, W. M. (1995). The effectiveness of family therapies for selected behavioral disorders of childhood. *Journal of Marital
and Family Therapy, 21*(4), 403–440.

Friedlander, M. L., & Heatherington, L. (1998). Assessing clients' constructions of their problems in
family therapy discourse. *Journal of Marital and
Family Therapy, 24*(3), 289–303.

Friedlander, M. L., & Tuason, M. T. (2000). Processes and outcomes in couples and family
therapy. In S. D. Brown & R. W. Lent (Eds.),
*Handbook of counseling therapy* (3rd ed., pp. 797–
824). New York: Guilford Press.

Friedlander, M. L., Wildman, J., Heatherington, L.,
& Skowron, E. A. (1994). What we do and don't
know about the process of family therapy. *Journal of Family Psychology, 8*(4), 390–416.

Frieswyk, S. H. (1986). Therapeutic alliance: Its
place as a process and outcome variable in dynamic psychotherapy research. *Journal of Consulting and Clinical Psychology, 54*(1), 32–38.

Garfield, S. L. (1990). Issues and methods in psychotherapy process research. *Journal of Consulting and Clinical Psychology, 58*(3), 273–280.

Gaston, L., & Gagnon, R. (1996). The role of process research in manual development. *Clinical
Psychology: Science and Practice, 3*(1), 13–24.

Giblin, P., Sprenkle, D. H., & Sheehan, R. (1985).

Enrichment outcome research: A meta-analysis of premarital, marital and family interventions. *Journal of Marital & Family Therapy, 11*(3), 257–271.

Goldstein, M. J., & Miklowitz, D. J. (1995). The effectiveness of psychoeducational family therapy in the treatment of schizophrenic disorders. *Journal of Marital and Family Therapy, 21*(4), 361–376.

Gottman, J. M., Coan, J., Carrere, S., & Swanson, C. (1998). Predicting marital happiness and stability from newlywed interactions. *Journal of Marriage and the Family, 60*(1), 5–22.

Gottman, J. M., & Levenson, R. W. (1992). Marital processes predictive of later dissolution: Behavior, physiology, and health. *Journal of Personality and Social Psychology, 63*(2), 221–233.

Greenberg, L. S. (1986). Change process research. *Journal of Consulting and Clinical Psychology, Special Issue: Psychotherapy Research, 54*(1), 4–9.

Greenberg, L. S. (1991). Research on the process of change. *Psychotherapy Research, 1*(1), 3–16.

Greenberg, L. S., & Johnson, S. M. (1988). *Emotionally focused couples therapy.* New York: Guilford Press.

Greenberg, L. S., Newman, F. L., & Frederick, L. (1996). An approach to psychotherapy change process research: Introduction to the special section. *Journal of Consulting and Clinical Psychology 64*(3), 435–438.

Greenberg, L. S., & Pinsof, W. M. (1986). Process research: Current trends and future perspectives. In L. S. Greensberg & W. M. Pinsof (Eds.), *The psychotherapeutic process: A research handbook.* Guilford clinic psychology & psychotherapy series (pp. 3–20). New York: Guilford Press.

Gurman, A. S. (1991). Back to the future, ahead to the past: Is marital therapy going in circles? *Journal of Family Psychology, 4*(4), 402–406.

Gurman, A. S. (1975) Couples' facilitative communication skill as a dimension of marital therapy outcome. *Journal of Marriage and Family Counseling, 1,* 163–174.

Gurman, A. S. (1973). The effects and effectiveness of marital therapy: A review of outcome research. *Family Process, 12,* 45–54.

Gurman, A. S. (1971). Group marital therapy: Clinical and empirical implications for outcome research. *International Journal of Psychotherapy, 21,* 174–189.

Gurman, A. S., & Kniskern, D. P. (1978). Research on marital and family therapy: Progress, perspective, and prospect. In S. L. Garfield & A. E. Bergin (Eds.), *Handbook of psychotherapy and behavior change: An empirical analysis* (2nd ed., pp. 817–901). New York: Wiley.

Gurman, A. S., & Kniskern, D. P. (Eds.). (1981). *Handbook of family therapy.* New York: Brunner/Mazel.

Gurman, A. S., & Kniskern, D. P. (Eds.). (1981). *Handbook of family therapy, Vol. 2.* Philadelphia: Brunner/Mazel.

Gurman, A. S., Kniskern, D. P., & Pinsof, W. M.. (1986). Research on marital and family therapies. In S. L. Garfield & A. E. Bergin (Eds.), *Handbook of psychotherapy and behavior change* (3rd ed., pp. 565–624). New York: Wiley.

Hahlweg, K., & Markman, H. J. (1988). Effectiveness of behavioral marital therapy: Empirical status of behavior preventing and alleviating marital distress. *Journal of Consulting and Clinical Psychology, 56*(3).

Hazelrigg, M. D., Cooper, H. M., & Borduin, C. M. (1987). Evaluating the effectiveness of family therapies: An integrative review and analysis. *Psychological Bulletin, 101*(3), 428–442.

Heatherington, L. (1989). Toward more meaningful clinical research: Taking context into account in coding psychotherapy interaction. *Psychotherapy: Theory, Research, Practice, Training, 26*(4), 436–447.

Heatherington, L., & Friedlander M. L. (1990). Couple and family alliance scales: Empirical considerations. *Journal of Marital and Family Therapy, 16*(3), 299–306.

Henggeler, S. W., Borduin, C. M., & Mann, B. J. (1993). Advances in family therapy: Empirical foundations. *Advances in Clinical Child Psychology, 15,* 207–241.

Henggeler, S. W., Mihalic, S. F., Rone, L., Thomas, C., & Timmons-Mitchell, J. (1998). *Blueprints for violence prevention, book six: Multisystemic Therapy.* Boulder, CO: Center for the Study and Prevention of Violence.

Henry, W. (1998). Science, politics, and the politics of science: The use and misuse of empirically validated treatment research. *Psychotherapy Research, 8*(2), 126–140.

Holtzworth-Munroe, A., Jacobsen, N. S., DeKlyen, M., & Whisman, M. A. (1989). Relationship between behavioral marital therapy outcome and process variables. *Journal of Consulting and Clinical Psychology, 57*(5), 658–662.

Hooley, J. M., & Gotlib, I. H. (2000). A diathesis-stress conceptualization of expressed emotion and clinical outcome. *Applied & Preventive Psychology, 9*(3), 135–151.

Huggins, D. (1997). Marital and family therapy research: Outcomes and implications for practice. *Family Journal, 5*(4), 212.

Jacobson, N. S., & Addis, M. E. (1993). Research on couples and couple therapy: What do we know? Where are we going? *Journal of Consulting and Clinical Psychology, 6*(1), 85–93.

Jacobson, N. S., & Margolin, G. (1979). *Marital therapy: Strategies based on social learning and behavior exchange principles.* New York: Brunner/Mazel.

Jacobson, N. S., Schmaling, K. B., & Holtzworth-Monroe, A. (1987). Component analysis of behavioral marital therapy: 2 year follow-up and prediction of relapse. *Journal of Marital and Family Therapy, 13,* 187–195.

Johnson, S. M., & Greenberg, L. S. (1995). The emotionally focused approach to problems in adult attachment. In N. S. Jabobson & A. S. Gurman (Eds.), *Clinical handbook of couple therapy* (pp. 121–141). New York: Guilford Press.

Johnson, S. M., & Greenberg, L. S. (1994). *The heart of the matter: Perspectives on emotion in marital therapy.* New York: Brunner/Mazel.

Johnson, S., & Lebow, J. (2000). The "coming of age" of couple therapy: A decade review. *Journal of Marital and Family Therapy, 26*(1), 23–38.

Joiner, T. E., Jr. (2000). Viscious scree: Self-propogation an erosive process in depression chronicity. *Clinical Psychology: Science & Practice, 7*(2), 203–218.

Kazdin, A. E. (1997). Practitioner review: Psychosocial treatments for conduct disorder in children. *Journal of Child Psychology & Psychiatry & Allied Disciplines 38*(2), 161–178.

Kazdin, A. E. (2001). Progression of therapy research and clinical application of treatment require better understanding of the change process. *Clinical Psychology: Science and Practice, 8*(2), 143–151.

Kniskern, D. P. (1975). *Research prospects and perspectives in family therapy.* Paper presented at the Society for Psychotherapy Research, Boston, June, 1975.

Lakey, B, & Lutz, C. J. (1996). Social support and preventative and therapeutic interventions. In G. R. Pierce & B. R. Sarason et al. (Eds.), *Handbook of social support and the family: Plenum series on stress and coping* (pp. 435–465). New York: Plenum.

Lebow, J. L., & Gurman, A. S. (1995). Research assessing couple and family therapy. *Annual Review of Psychology, 46,* 27–57.

Liddle, H. A., & Dakof, G. A. (1995). Efficacy of family therapy for drug abuse: Promising but not definite. *Journal of Marital and Family Therapy, 21*(4), 511–543.

Liddle, H. A., Bray, J. H., Levant, R. F., & Santisteban, D. A. (2002). Family psychology intervention science: An emerging area of science and practice. In H. A. Liddle, D. A. Santisteban, R. F. Levant, & J. H. Bray (Eds.), *Family psychology: Science-based interventions* (pp. 3–15). Washington, DC: Psychological Association.

Liddle, H. A., Bray, J. H., Levant, R. F., & Santisteban, D. A. (2002). *Family psychology: Science-based interventions.* Washington, DC: Psychological Association.

Lipps, A. J. (1999). Family therapy in the treatment of alcohol related problems: A review of behavioral family therapy, family systems therapy and treatment matching research. *Alcoholism Treatment Quarterly, 17*(3), 13–23.

Margolin, G., Burman, B., & R. S. John (1989). Home observations of married couples reenacting naturalistic conflicts. *Behavioral Assessment, 11*(1), 101–118.

Mari, J., & Streiner, D. L. (1994). An overview of family interventions and relapse on schizophrenia: Meta-analysis of research findings. *Psychological Medicine, 24*(3), 565–578.

Markman, H. J., Renick, M. J., Floyd, F. J., Stanley, S. M., & Clements, M. (1993). Preventing marital distress through communication and conflict management training: A 4- and 5-year follow-up. *Journal of Consulting and Clinical Psychology, 61,* 70–77.

Markus, E., Lange, A., & Pettigrew, T. F. (1990). Effectiveness of family therapy: A meta-analysis. *Journal of Family Therapy, 12*(3), 205–221

Melidonis, G. G., & Bry, B. H. (1995). Effects of therapist exceptions questions on blaming and positive statements in families with adolescent behavior problems. *Journal of Family Psychology, 9*(4), 451–457.

O'Farrell, T. J., Cutter, H. S., & Floyd, F. J. (1985). Evaluating behavioral marital therapy for male alcoholics: Effects on marital adjustment and communication from before to after treatment. *Behavior Therapy, 16*(2), 147–167.

Orlinsky, D. E., Grawe, K., & Parks, B. K. (1994). Process and outcome in psychotherapy: Noch einmal. In A. E. Bergin & S. L. Garfield (Eds.), *Handbook of psychotherapy and behavior change* (4th ed., pp. 270–376). Oxford, England: Wiley.

Patterson, G. R. (1997). Performance models for parenting: A social interactional perspective. In J.

E. Grusec & L. Kuczynski (Eds.), *Parenting and children's internalization of values: A handbook of contemporary theory* (pp. 193–226). New York: Wiley.

Patterson, G. R., & Forgatch, M. S. (1985). Therapist behavior as a determinant for client noncompliance: A paradox for the behavior modifier. *Journal of Consulting and Clinical Psychology, 53*(6), 846–851.

Pinsof, W. M., & Wynne, L. C. (1995). The efficacy of marital and family therapy: An empirical overview, conclusions and recommendations. *Journal of Marital and Family Therapy, 21*(4), 585–613.

Pinsof, W. M., & Wynne, L. C. (2000). Toward progress research: Closing the gap between family therapy practice and research. *Journal of Family and Marital Therapy, 26*, 1–8.

Pinsof, W. M., & Catherall, D. R. (1986). The integrative psychotherapy alliance: Family, couple, and individual therapy scales. *Journal of Marital and Family Therapy, 12*(2), 137–151.

Prince, S. E., & Jacobson, N. S. (1995). A review and evaluation of marital and family therapies for affective disorders. *Journal of Marital and Family Therapy, 21*(4), 377–401.

Robbins, M. S., Alexander J. F., Newell, R. M., & Turner, C. W. (1996). The immediate effect of reframing on client attitude in family therapy. *Journal of Family Psychology, 10*(1), 28–34.

Robbins, M. S., Alexander J. F., & Turner, C. W. (2000). Disrupting defensive family interactions in family therapy with delinquent adolescents. *Journal of Family Psychology, 14*(2), 769–998.

Robbins, M. S., Szapocznik, J., Alexander, J. F., & Miller, J. R. (1998). Family systems therapy with children and adolescents. In M. Hersen & A. S. Bellack (Series Eds.) & T. H. Ollendick (Vol. Ed.), *Comprehensive clinical psychology* (Vol. 5), *Children and adolescents: Clinical formulation and treatment*. Oxford: Pergamon.

Robbins, M. S., Turner, C. W., Alexander, J. F., & Perez, G. A. (in press). Alliance and dropout in family therapy with drug using adolescents: Individual and systemic effects.

Rohrbaugh, M. J., Shoham, V. (2002). Couple treatment for alcohol abuse: A systemic family-consultation model. In S. G. Hofmann & M. C. Tompson (Eds.), *Treating chronic and severe mental disorders: A handbook of empirically supported interventions* (pp. 277–295). New York: Guilford.

Rohrbaugh, M. J., Shoham, V., Trost, S.; Muramoto, M., Cate, R., & Leischow, S. (2001). Couple-dynamics of change resistant smokers: Toward a family-consultation model. *Family Process, 40*, 15–31.

Santisteban, D. A., Szapocznik, J., Perez-Vidal, A., Kurtines, W. M., Murray, E. J., & La Pierre, A. (1996). Efficacy of intervention for engaging youth and families into treatment and some variables that may contribute to differential effectiveness. *Journal of Family Psychology, 10,* 35–44.

Schmidt, S. E., Liddle, H. A., & Dakof, G. A. (1996). Changes in parenting practices and adolescent drug abuse during multidimensional family therapy. *Journal of Family Psychology, 10*(1), 12–27.

Sexton, T. L., & Alexander, J. F. (2002). Family-based empirically supported interventions. *The Counseling Psychologist, 30*(2), 238–261.

Sexton, T. S., Alexander, J. F., & Mease, A. L. (in press). Levels of evidence for the models and mechanisms of therapeutic change in couple and family therapy. In M. Lambert (Ed). *Handbook of psychotherapy and behavior change*. New York: Wiley.

Shadish, W. R., Montgomery, L. M., Wilson, P., Wilson, M. R., Bright, I. & Okwumabua, T. (1993). Effects of family and marital psychotherapies: A meta-analysis. *Journal of Consulting and Clinical Psychology, 61*(6), 992–1002.

Shadish, W. R., Ragsdale, K., Glaser, R., & Montgomery, L. M. (1995). The efficacy and effectiveness of marital and family therapy: A perspective from meta-analysis. *Journal of Marital and Family Therapy. Special Issue: The effectiveness of marital and family therapy, 21*(4), 345–360.

Shields, C. G., Sprenkle, D. H., & Constantine, J. A. (1991). Anatomy of an initial interview: The importance of joining and structuring skills. *American Journal of Family Therapy, 19*(1), 3–18.

Stanton, M. D., & Shadish, W. R. (1997). Outcome, attrition, and family-couples treatment of drug abuse: A meta-analysis and review of the controlled, comparative studies. *Psychological Bulletin, 122*(2), 170–191.

Szapocznik, J., & Kurtines, W. M. (1989). *Breakthroughs in family therapy with drug abusing and problem youth*. New York: Springer.

Szapocznik, J., Rio, A., Murray, E., Cohen, R., et al. (1989). Structural family versus psychodynamic child therapy for problematic Hispanic boys. *Journal of Consulting and Clinical Psychology, 57*(5), 571–578.

U.S. Public Health Service. (2001). *Youth violence: A report of the Surgeon General*. Rockville, MD:

Department of Health and Human Services, National Institutes of Health, National Institute of Mental Health.

Waldron, H. B. (1997). Adolescent substance abuse and family therapy outcome. In T. H. Ollendick & R. J. Prinz (Eds.), *Advances in clinical child psychology* (Vol. 19, pp. 199–232). New York: Plenum Press.

Wampler, K. S. (1982). Bringing the review of literature into the age of quantification: Meta-analysis as a strategy for integrating research findings in family studies. *Journal of Marriage and the Family, 44*(4), 1009–1023

Wesley, S., & Waring, E. M. (1996). A critical review of marital therapy outcome research. *Canadian Journal of Psychiatry, 41*, 421–428.

CHAPTER 12

# Emotionally Focused Couples Therapy

## *Empiricism and Art*

SUSAN M. JOHNSON, EdD

*University of Ottawa, Canada*

## INTRODUCTION

Emotionally focused couples therapy is a brief, integrative approach that focuses on helping partners in close relationships create secure attachment bonds. In practice, EFT combines a focus on how people in close relationships construct their emotional experience and the patterns of interaction that define the quality of their relationships. The EFT therapist is a process consultant, helping partners expand constricted and constricting inner emotional realities and interactional responses.

The EFT model, first tested in the early 1980s (Johnson & Greenberg, 1985), has many strengths. They may be listed as the following:

• The EFT model fits very well with recent research on the nature of marital distress and satisfaction, which focuses on the qual-ity of emotional engagement, the power of negative interaction patterns, and the need for soothing responsiveness in close relationships. There is an empirical basis to the belief that EFT interventions are "on target." At the moment, EFT appears to achieve the most positive outcomes of any marital interventions, in terms of both helping clients reach recovery from marital distress and maintaining these results over time (Johnson, Hunsley, Greenberg, & Schindler, 1999). Research into the process of change also aids the therapist in the construction of key change events (Johnson & Greenberg, 1988).

• EFT has a clear and empirically validated theory of adult relatedness in the form of attachment theory, which has, in the last decade, generated a plethora of creative research on adult love relationships (Cassidy & Shaver, 1999; Johnson & Whiffen, 2003).

There is nothing so practical as a good theory.

- EFT has been applied in many different settings and with many different kinds of clients—for example, gay and low SES couples and couples where partners suffer from depression and post-traumatic stress disorder.
- EFT is consonant with important recent developments in the field of couple and family therapy (Johnson & Lebow, 2000). It is integrative, combining an experiential focus on self with a systemic focus on interaction. It is collaborative and respectful of clients, as are all humanistic interventions, focusing as they do on growth, rather than on pathology, and it is consonant with feminist approaches.

If we were able to take a snapshot of EFT, what would we see the therapist doing? At any given moment we might see the therapist reflecting the pattern of interactions occurring between the partners in a couple, then systematically unfolding one partner's key emotional response and helping this partner access marginalized emotion or piece his or her experience together in a new or more complete way. The therapist would then help the partner to express and enact this newly formulated experience and support the other partner to hear and respond, thus creating a new level and kind of dialogue. The goals of the EFT therapist are to restructure the key attachment emotions that organize interactions and so shift and restructure interactional cycles. This shift is specifically toward key prototypical bonding interactions that are a natural antidote to the negative patterns that characterize marital distress.

## THE HISTORY OF EFT

Much has happened in the field of couples' therapy since the early 1980s, when Les Greenberg and I first wrote a manual for EFT. At that time, the only theory of close relationships that was being systematically used as the basis for intervention was exchange theory, which focuses on profit and loss in close relationships and best characterizes business relationships. Behavioral interventions, which used exchange theory as a basis for intervention, offered the only clearly structured and tested treatment for relationship distress. Emotion was seen as part of the problem of distress, rather than as part of the solution. Interventions tended to focus on skill acquisition, negotiated behavior change, or, in more psychodynamic models, insight into past relationships. The application of attachment theory was limited to the relationship between parent and child, and emotion, if discussed at all, was seen mostly in terms of ventilation and catharsis and was generally avoided in couple therapy sessions (Mahoney, 1991). Unless the therapist adopted a behavioral perspective, there was very little specific guidance in the literature on how to conduct couples' therapy. Even though clinicians such as Satir (Satir & Baldwin, 1983) had formulated a number of interventions, there was no articulated model of couple therapy that combined a focus on inner realities and systemic interaction patterns. We began then to watch videotapes of our attempts to change distressed relationships, in the hopes that clients could teach us how to help them, and indeed they did just that. However, a particular theoretical framework guided our observation.

This perspective was the humanistic experiential approach put forward by Carl Rogers and Fritz Perls (Cain & Seeman, 2002); it focuses on the proactive processing of experience as it occurs and on how meaning is constructed (Neimeyer, 1993). Rogers, in particular, modeled active empathic collaboration with the client in the processing of experience and emphasized the power of emotion to organize meaning making and behavior (Rogers, 1951). However, as Bateson pointed out (1972, p. 493), "When you separate mind from the structure in which it is immanent, such as human relationships . . . you embark on a fundamental error," so to this general experiential perspective, it was necessary to add a systemic orientation, epitomized by Minuchin and other structural family therapists (Minuchin & Fishman, 1981). In both systems theory and experiential approaches, problems are seen in terms of process, rather than being inherent in the person; that is, it is how the inner processing of experience or how interactions in key relationships are organized that cues and maintains dysfunction or distress.

It was also not very long before clinical observation began to evoke Bowlby's attachment theory as a natural explanatory framework for how relationships became troubled and how they could be repaired (Johnson, 1986). Partners spoke of disconnection and isolation as traumatizing, and the power of safe emotional engagement and responsiveness became obvious as we watched how partners repaired their relationship. Attachment theory, which has been extensively applied to adult relationships in the last decade, now offers the EFT couple and family therapist a clearly articulated theory of adult love and close relationships to guide goal setting and intervention (Johnson & Whiffen, 1999, 2003). It is important to note that attachment theory integrates a focus on self and system and views individuals' construction of self in the context of their closest relationships. It is then easily integrated with systems perspectives (Johnson & Best, 2002).

Since the 1980s, there has also been an appreciation of the role emotion plays in individual functioning and health (Goleman, 1995; Salovey, Rothman, Detweiler, & Steward, 2000) and relationship functioning. As Zajonc notes (1980, p. 152), "Affect dominates social interaction and it is the major currency in which social interaction is transacted." The role of emotion in creating change in therapy has also gradually become more explicit and refined (Fosha, 2000; Greenberg & Paivio, 1997). For example, core emotions have been identified and are present across all cultures; these are anger, fear, sadness/despair, shame/disgust, hurt/anguish, and positive emotions such as surprise and joy (Izard, 1977; Plutchik, 2000). Therapists have also identified different kinds of emotion, such as secondary reactive emotion and more primary emotion that is often avoided or left unarticulated, but that can be used to create change in therapy. This literature focuses on how emotion, which comes from the Latin word "to move," can move people toward change, and how emotional communication defines the nature of relationships (Johnson & Greenberg, 1994). As a new technology of working with emotion emerges, systemic therapists are beginning to incorporate a focus on emotion in their work (Johnson, 1998b; Schwartz & Johnson, 2000).

At the beginning of the new millennium, EFT appears to have begun to fulfill the potential suggested by the powerful treatment effects of the first outcome study (Johnson & Greenberg, 1985) and is being refined and applied to new populations and problems. For example, the study of impasses in EFT that block recovery from distress is progressing (Johnson, Makinen, & Millikin, 2001), interventions that shape key change events are being delineated (Bradley & Furrow, in press), and EFT is being used to address individual problems that co-occur with relationship distress; for example, it is used with partners suffering from post-traumatic stress disorders (Johnson, 2002).

## THE THEORETICAL PERSPECTIVE OF EFT ON MARITAL DISTRESS AND ADULT INTIMACY

### What Is the Essential Nature of Marital Distress?

The EFT perspective focuses on the power of absorbing states of negative affect and negative interaction patterns, such as criticize/

demand followed by defend/distance, and how they generate and maintain each other. Negative affect, in this model, is potentiated by the fact that this affect is attachment-related and attachment is associated with primal needs for comfort and closeness in the face of threat, danger, and uncertainty. This focus on the power of negative affect and interaction patterns echoes recent empirical findings on the nature of relationship distress and satisfaction (Gottman, 1994; Gottman, Coan, Carrere, & Swanson, 1998; Pasch & Bradbury, 1998), and researchers such as Gottman view EFT as consonant with these findings. Some of the specific commonalities between these findings and the EFT approach can be summarized as

- Both emphasize the power of negative affect, as expressed in facial expression, for example, to predict long-term stability and satisfaction in relationships.
- Both focus on the importance of emotional engagement and how partners communicate, rather than on the content or the frequency of arguments.
- Both view cycles such as demand–withdraw as potentially fatal for close relationships.
- Both look beyond conflict resolution or the use of communication skills to the necessity for soothing, comforting interactional cycles and stress the importance of such soothing in satisfaction and relationship stability.
- Both stress the power of positive affect to define relationships, whether this is called, as in the behavioral literature, positive sentiment override or, as in the EFT literature, secure attachment.

There is, however, also a key difference between the EFT perspective and the research noted previously. Theory is the explanation of pattern, and the EFT therapist places the data on distress in an attachment framework. This framework helps to explain and give meaning to such findings. For example, there is some controversy (Stanley, Bradbury, & Markman, 2000) as to how to label the response of husbands in satisfying relationships to their wives' complaints. Gottman reports that wives in happier relationships start their complaints in a softer, less confrontational manner and husbands "accept their influence." Others have questioned this interpretation and suggest that a more accurate description is that these husbands are able to tolerate their spouses' negative emotion and stay engaged. An attachment view of such data would support this latter conclusion and would refine the meaning of this behavior, seeing this as an example of a more securely attached husband remaining accessible and responsive to the attachment "protest" behavior of his spouse and perceiving the implicit bid for contact in such behavior.

Attachment theory also offers an explanation of why the "stonewalling" response has been found to be so corrosive in close relationships. In attachment relationships such a response, much like the still face experiments where mothers show no response to children's attempts at connection, shatters assumptions of responsiveness and induces overwhelming distress. The research data on distress also focus on computations such as ratios; for example, one finding is that to have a satisfying relationship, it is necessary to have five times more positive than negative affect. As a clinician, it is difficult to grasp the meaning of this kind of ratio. Attachment theory suggests, more specifically, that when one partner fails to respond at times when the other partner's attachment needs become urgent, these events will have a momentous and disproportional negative impact on the affective tone of the relationship and its level of satisfaction (Simpson & Rholes, 1994). Conversely, when partners are able to respond at such times, this will potentiate the connection between them. The previously mentioned research findings also tend to view marital relationships as friendships, which does not seem to account for the intensity of affect and the impact of distressed marital relationships in people's lives. From the EFT viewpoint, then, the attachment perspective on adult love can elucidate and refine the research findings on marital distress, thus making them more pertinent for the clinician.

## What Is the Essential Nature of Adult Love?

Attachment theory, based on the work of John Bowlby (1969, 1973, 1980, 1988), has become "one of the broadest, more profound, and most creative lines of research in 20th century psychology" (Cassidy & Shaver, preface, 1999). This theory offers the couples' therapist a coherent conceptualization of adult love and relatedness to specify treatment goals and guide intervention. From the attachment perspective, the therapist can foster many changes, but the creation of emotional accessibility and responsiveness is the essential ingredient that defines the viability of a bond and predicts the quality of a marital relationship. What are the essential tenets of attachment theory? They can be summarized as follows:

1. The need for a predictable emotional connection or a tie with a few significant others is an innate, primary motivating principle in human beings. More specifically, this connection is our "primary protection against helplessness and meaninglessness" (McFarlane & van der Kolk, 1996, p. 24). A sense of "felt security" with a loved one offers us a *safe haven* in a dangerous world. The need for this emotional connection with one's attachment figures, and for most adults their key attachment figure is their spouse, is a compelling issue, and one that becomes particularly poignant at times of transition, stress, uncertainty, or danger.

2. A sense of "felt security," that we can turn to and depend on another, fosters autonomy and self-confidence. A secure interdependence in an adult relationship allows partners to be separate and different without anxiety and encourages them to explore their world. In contrast to the pathologization of dependency that has been common in Western cultures, this perspective views a secure emotional tie as offering a *secure base* that provides people with the optimal environment in which to learn and grow. Sensitive caring connections with others enable autonomy. There is no such thing as self-sufficiency or overdependence; there is only effective or ineffective dependency.

3. The essential elements in a secure connection are emotional accessibility and responsiveness. Emotional engagement is crucial. From this perspective any response, even an angry one, is better than none. If there is no emotional engagement, the message is read as "Your signals do not impact me. They do not matter and there is no connection between us." From this perspective, the frustration of this innate need for accessibility and responsiveness would spark and maintain significant conflict in an attachment relationship. However, a sense of felt security is not an all-or-nothing proposition. It is more like a channel one may have trouble tuning into (Karen, 1998) or may need more at times of stress.

4. Adult attachment integrates caregiving (which is associated with parenting in adult–child attachment), attachment needs, and sexuality. The elements of sexuality, such as touching, emotional connection and soothing, are highlighted here (Hazan & Zeifman, 1994), as opposed to a focus on sexual release. Adult attachment, in contrast to parent–child attachment, is mutual and reciprocal. It is worth noting that relationships characterized by mutuality,

intimacy, reciprocity, and interdependence are similar to the kinds of relationships promoted by gender-sensitive therapists (Haddock et al., 2000). This attachment is also representational, so that adults do not always need the concrete presence of an attachment figure. It is part of secure attachment that we experience attachment figures as keeping and holding us in their mind (Fonagy & Target, 1997).

5. If an attachment figure is not perceived as accessible and responsive, then a predictable drama that is the process of separation distress ensues. This involves angry protest, clinging and seeking, depression and despair, and finally detachment. Bowlby distinguishes between the anger of hope and the anger of despair. It is the latter that most often leads to the destructive coercive patterns that couples' therapists are only too familiar with. Bowlby saw emotion as conveying to the self and to others crucial information about the motives and needs of the individual. In separation distress, intense emotions such as fear, anger, and sadness will arise and take control over all other cues (Tronick, 1989). Emotion may be considered the music of the attachment dance.

6. An attachment bond involves a set of behaviors that elicits contact with the loved one. In secure attachment these involve the sending of clear, congruent messages that pull the loved one closer. Secure attachment is associated with the ability to self-disclose, with assertiveness and openness (Kobak, Ruckdeschel, & Hazan, 1994; Kobak & Sceery, 1988). In less secure relationships, people rely on forms of engagement with their partner that tend to maintain or exacerbate the lack of safe emotional connection. That is, they send the message that you cannot depend on your partner, that he or she is inaccessible and is unlikely to respond to you, or any

combination of these. There appear to be two basic strategies in less secure relationships. The first strategy involves an overactivation of the attachment system and is characterized by high anxiety and intense pursuing behaviors. Attachment needs are focused on and their expression *maximized*. People are fearful of losing their loved ones and are vigilant for any sign of distance. The second strategy involves an underactivation of the attachment system. People are inhibited emotionally and are avoidant. In this way, attachment needs are *minimized*. Engagement is limited, especially when vulnerability is experienced or expressed by the other partner, and there is a strong focus on activities and tasks. These patterns were first formulated from observing mothers and children in separation and reunion events (Ainsworth, Blehar, Waters, & Wall, 1978). Children who were classified as secure were able to modulate their distress when separated, ask for and accept comfort when the mother returned, and, confidant of her responsiveness, return to exploration and play. Secure adults can better acknowledge their needs, can give and ask for support, and are less likely to be verbally aggressive or withdrawn during problem solving (Senchak & Leonard, 1992; Simpson, Rholes, & Phillips, 1996). In the child literature, different habitual forms of engagement have often been viewed as styles that characterize the individual and may be brought forward into adulthood. In the adult attachment literature, however, they are viewed more as strategies or habitual forms of engagement that exist on a continuum and characterize a particular relationship, and that are formed in response to and confirmed by the partner's responses in that relationship. They are seen as more fluid and transactional (Kobak, 1999; Shaver & Hazan, 1993). The insecure strategies mentioned previously are not problematic in themselves. They become so when they become so habitual and self-reinforcing that they are difficult to modify, refine or update in response to new situations. Such inflexibility constrains interactions in close relationships. It is important to note, however, that these individual differences in attachment relations are now being viewed dimensionally, rather than categorically, in terms of variations in anxiety and avoidance.

7. Attachment theory is systemic in its understanding of how constrained patterns of interaction tend to narrow down the construction of inner realities (Johnson & Best, 2002). Bowlby believed that working models of self and other were constructed by interactions with key attachment figures. This is consonant with recent perspectives on the relational construction of the self (Fishbane, 2001). Specifically, Bowlby stressed that models concerning the dependability of others and the worthiness of the self are formed and maintained in the emotional communication with attachment figures. In recent research, more secure attachment has been found to be associated with a sense of self-efficacy and a more coherent and positive sense of self (Mikulincer, 1995). These working models may change in new relationships (Davila, Karney, & Bradbury, 1999), and to be useful they must be open to revision and adjustment in different contexts.

Without such a theory, how do we know which differences or changes will really make a difference? Individual therapists need a model of individual personality and growth, and couple therapists need a model, a map to the territory of love and close relationships (Roberts, 1992). There is now a large and growing body of literature addressing adult love from an attachment perspective (Bartholomew & Perlman, 1994; Cassidy & Shaver, 1999; Shaver & Hazan, 1993). Secure attachment has been found to be associated with effective affect regulation, information processing and communication, and relationship satisfaction (Johnson & Whiffen, 1999). Based on these empirical and theoretical viewpoints, the goals of EFT are to help couples restructure both their emotional experience and their interactions in the direction of increased attachment security.

## RESEARCH ON EFT

If EFT is consonant with research data that describe relationship distress and subscribes to a theory of relatedness that has a considerable research base, is there also empirical support for the effectiveness of EFT? EFT is accepted as empirically validated by the American Psychological Association, and there is also research on predictors of success in EFT and on the process of change. There is even one preliminary study of emotionally focused family therapy with bulimic adolescents (Johnson, Maddeaux, & Blouin, 1998) and a number of outcome studies of experiential interventions in the context of individual therapy (Elliott, 2002; Paivio & Nieuwenhuis, 2001). Research on EFT for couples has been summarized elsewhere (Johnson, Hunsley, Greenberg, & Schindler, 1999). Generally, a meta-analysis of the four most rigorous studies of EFT found an impressive effect size of 1.3. This translates into a 90% significant improvement over controls and a 70–73% rate for recovery from distress by the end of treatment. This is an improvement over the 0.79 effect size recently found for behavioral interventions (Dunn & Schwebel, 1995). All EFT outcome studies have included treatment integrity checks and, except for one where extremely novice therapists were used (Denton, Burleson, Clark, Roderiguez, &

Hobbs, 2000), have shown a very low attrition rate. In addition, EFT results appear to be stable even in stressed populations at risk for marital distress (Clothier, Manion, Walker, & Johnson, 2002), and often appear to continue to improve after treatment. This may reflect the power of the bonding interactions that constitute change events in EFT and continue after termination. There is evidence that EFT impacts depression in distressed partners and increases intimacy (Dandeneau & Johnson, 1994). In a study on the impact of EFT on low sexual desire, the sexual dysfunction that appears to be most resistant to intervention, there was significant improvement on some measures, but, generally, results failed to reach significance (MacPhee, Johnson, & van der Veer, 1995). The usual number of the sessions in these studies was 10; however, the effect of clinical supervision on outcome must be taken into account, and in general practice EFT is commonly implemented in 10 to 20 sessions.

In terms of predictors of success in EFT (Johnson & Talitman, 1997), one of the most interesting results so far is that whereas in BMT the initial distress level was found to account for 46% of the variance in outcome, this factor was found to account for only 4% of the outcome variance in couples treated with EFT. This finding is consonant with clinical experience, in that EFT therapists report that it is client engagement in the therapy process in sessions that seems to determine clinical outcome. The theory of EFT suggests that if key bonding events that constitute corrective emotional experiences can occur in therapy sessions, these events have the power to create significant shifts even in exceedingly distressed relationships. Also, in this study, EFT was found to work better with partners over 35 and with husbands described as "inexpressive" by their spouses. Traditionality did not seem to affect outcome. A recent study (Denton et al., 2000) also found EFT to be particularly effective with low socioeconomic

status partners. The most powerful predictors of outcome were, first, a particular aspect of the therapeutic alliance that reflects how relevant partners found the tasks of therapy, and by implication, their level of engagement in them and, second, the faith of the female partner—that is, her level of trust that her spouse still cared for her. Presumably, once this faith has been lost, the emotional investment necessary for change is difficult to come by. These results appear to fit with the general conclusion that "the quality of the client's participation in therapy stands out as the most important determinant of outcome" (Orlinsky, Grawe, & Parks, 1994).

There are also several process studies of EFT (summarized in Johnson et al., 1999). Perhaps the most interesting results are that depth of experiencing and moves toward affiliative responses are associated with change events in EFT and that specific change events have been identified that predict positive outcome. Two change events are fostered in Stage 2 of EFT, the reengagement of the more withdrawn partner and the "softening" of the more critical or pursuing partner. The latter event has been empirically linked to positive outcome.

Recent research has delineated the key therapist interventions that predict the successful completion of such softening events (Bradley & Furrow, in press). These were consistent with the theory of EFT. A current study is also examining the steps in the change process where couples resolve particular impasses in treatment that block recovery from distress. These impasses are termed *attachment injuries* (Johnson, Makinen, & Millikin, 2001). Future studies will examine the therapist interventions associated with the resolution of these impasses. A preliminary outcome study is also planned to examine outcomes and the process of change in EFT with trauma survivors suffering from complex PTSD as a result of childhood sexual abuse.

## THE PRACTICE OF EFT

EFT is a relatively brief intervention that is implemented in three phases. These phases are the de-escalation of negative interaction patterns, the structuring of new interactions that shape attachment security, and, finally, consolidation and integration. Violence in the relationship is a contraindication for EFT and the creation and maintenance of a positive alliance with the therapist that offers a safe haven and a secure base for exploration are considered essential. The process of change is outlined in nine steps, which are as follows:

*Stage One: Cycle De-Escalation*

Step 1: Assessment. Creating an alliance and clarifying the core issues in the couple's conflict, using an attachment perspective.

Step 2: Identifying the problematic interactional cycle that maintains attachment insecurity and relationship distress.

Step 3: Accessing the unacknowledged emotions underlying interactional positions.

Step 4: Reframing the problem in terms of the cycle, the underlying emotions, and attachment needs.

The goal, by the end of Step 4, is for the partners to have a metaperspective on their interactions. They are framed as unwittingly creating, but also being victimized by, the narrow patterns of interaction that characterize their relationship. At this point, partners' responses tend to be less reactive and more flexible, but the organization of the dance between them has not changed. As a client remarked, "We are nicer to each other and things are easier, but nothing has really changed. I still chase and he still dodges me." If therapy stops here, the couple will likely relapse.

*Stage Two: Restructuring Interactional Positions/Patterns*

Step 5: Promoting identification with disowned attachment needs and fears (such as the need for reassurance and comfort) and aspects of the self (such as a sense of shame and unworthiness) and integrating these emotional responses into relationship interactions.

Step 6: Promoting acceptance of each partner's new construction of experience and new responses by the other spouse.

Step 7: Facilitating the expression of specific needs and wants and creating emotional engagement.

Partners usually move through the steps of Stage One together. Stage Two is more intense, and, unless the couple is experiencing relatively low distress, the therapist invites one spouse to precede the other. Because a more critical distressed spouse will not take risks with a partner who remains withdrawn, the more withdrawn partner is invited to navigate Steps 5–7 before the more blaming, critical spouse actively engages in Step 5. The goal here is to have withdrawn partners reengaged in the relationship and actively stating the terms of this reengagement. For example, a spouse might state, " I am opening up. I can do that. But I want some respect from you. You don't have to be so sharp—you are all edges sometimes. I want to learn to be close and I want you to make it a little easier for me to get there." Once this partner is more accessible and responsive, the goal is then to have the more blaming partner complete Steps 5–7 and "soften," that is, to ask for his or her attachment needs to be met from a position of vulnerability. This is a position that pulls for responsiveness from the partner. As stated previously, this latter event has been found to be associated with recovery from relationship distress in EFT (Johnson & Greenberg, 1988). When both partners have completed Step 7, a new form of safe emotional engagement is possible and prototypical bonding events of reciprocal confiding, connection, and comforting can occur. These events are carefully shaped by the therapist in the session, but also occur at home. Transcripts of both key change events, withdrawer reengagement and blamer softening, can be found in texts and other chapters on EFT (Johnson, 1996, 1998a, 1998b, 2000, 2002), and snapshots of the process can be found near the end of this chapter.

*Stage Three: Consolidation and Integration*

Step 8:  Facilitating the emergence of new solutions to old problematic relationship issues.
Step 9:  Consolidating new positions and cycles of attachment behavior.

The goal here is to consolidate new responses and cycles of interaction by, for example, reviewing the accomplishments of the partners in therapy and helping the couple create a narrative of its journey into and out of distress. The therapist also supports the couple to solve concrete problems that have been destructive to the relationship. This is now relatively easy because dialogues about these problems are no longer infused with overwhelming negative affect and issues of relationship definition. The partners are supported to actively plan how to retain the connection the partners have forged in therapy.

## INTERVENTIONS IN EFT

EFT interventions are described in detail in the literature (Johnson, 1996, 1999; Johnson

& Denton, 2002). The therapist moves recursively between three tasks, monitoring and actively fostering a positive alliance, expanding and restructuring key emotional experiences, and structuring enactments that either clarify present patterns of interaction or, step by step, shape new, more positive patterns. In general terms, the EFT therapist is always tracking and reflecting the process by which both inner emotional realities and interactions are created. The therapist also validates each partner's realities and habitual responses so that partners feel safe to explore and own these. Internal experience is expanded by evocative questions that develop the outline of such experience into a sharply focused and detailed portrait. Emotion may be heightened by images or repetition, or the therapist may go one step beyond how clients construct their experience by adding an element, such as asking if someone is not, as they say, only "uncomfortable" but even a little anxious. The therapist also reframes interactional responses in terms of underlying emotions and attachment needs and fears and choreographs enactments. The therapist follows and leads but is most active in Stage Two, particularly when structuring the change events mentioned previously.

At this point, the person of the therapist and how the interventions above are operationalized and shaped to client needs are crucial (Palmer & Johnson, 2002). EFT promotes emotional engagement and so requires this of the therapist. It is hard to do at a distance. It requires that the therapist be, as Rogers articulated, genuine and transparent. Sometimes this involves being willing to be confused and lost and actively learning with one's clients how a relationship drama or an inner dilemma evolves. The therapist has to develop a certain comfort with powerful emotion and learns, for example, that emotions come into focus when the pace of dialogue is slow and somewhat repetitious (emotion takes more time to process), when the therapist is using a low evocative voice, and when images are conjured up to capture the experience. There is now empirical evidence for such stylistic traditions common to experiential therapies; for example, there is evidence that imagery elicits physiological responses that abstract words do not (Borkovec, Roemer, & Kinyon, 1995). The therapist also finely tunes levels of enactment by moving to the level a client can tolerate at any given moment. That is, if a client cannot turn and state an emotional response, clarified in the dialogue with the therapist, to his or her spouse, the therapist will ask the client to express how hard it is to share this and explore this reluctance to engage the partner. If this is not possible, the therapist will help the clients share their blocks and even their refusal to share. The EFT therapist, however, even when caught up in the multileveled drama that is a distressed relationship, always returns to the core emotions of fear, anger, sadness, and shame, the attachment perspective as a meaning frame, and the structuring of new enactments with the partner. The focus of EFT is always the couple's habitual ways of regulating and expressing affect and how these constitute habitual forms of engagement with attachment figures.

If readers examine one of the many transcripts of the process of EFT in the literature (e.g., Johnson, 1998a, 1998b), they will notice that in the task of expanding how key relational experiences are processed when attachment insecurity and defensiveness constrict such processing, the therapist moves between all the interventions mentioned previously in a manner that fosters the unfolding of key emotional experiences and defining relational moments. The developmental concept of scaffolding is useful here. A scaffold is an external structure that allows children to acquire abilities just beyond their reach (Wood, Bruner, & Ross, 1976), in their zone of "proximal development" (Vygotsky, 1978). The

therapist then goes to the edge of a client's formulated experience and focuses on "bottom up" details to give this experience shape, form, and color, integrating all the interventions listed previously. For example, a therapist might say the following:

"So, what happened when he turned away from you in that moment, in the moment before you ran from the house, before, as you put it, you 'shut down for good'?" (Reflection, evocation responding focused on a key moment, image of relational stance).

"So, you felt sick?—'Nauseated,' as you put it—And said to yourself, I am invisible to him, he isn't there for me—is that it? It was like you didn't matter, your pain didn't matter to him? And that moved you into—'I must protect myself? I must shut down—not let myself need?' Is that it?" (Evocative responding, heightening, inference into meaning of incident for attachment security).

"How do you feel as you talk about this now? You say you are angry, but I notice that you also weep. There is grief as well? You felt like you lost him that day—your trust—your sense of being able to count on him?" (Heightening, interpretation, reflection).

"Can you tell him—right now—'In that moment I lost my faith in you—in us—so I shut down—shut you out'?" (Structuring of enactment).

The number of questions here is significant, in that the unfolding of this experience is done in partnership with the client, who constantly corrects and refines the therapist's empathic construction of a response, an event, and it's interactional consequences. The therapist acts as a surrogate processor of experience and structures engagement tasks for the couple. In change events, such as successful softenings, EFT therapists particularly use evocative questions, heightening, and reframing in terms of attachment significance (Bradley, 2001). This research, however, also found interventions that were not formally written up in the EFT manual (Johnson, 1996). In successful softenings, therapists also offered images of "just out of reach" attachment responses that would constitute a step toward more secure attachment for a partner. The therapist might say, "So you could never turn to him and say, 'How could you stay so cool and separate, when I needed you? And now, I am so far away—I can't listen to my longings—can't ask you to comfort me.' You could never say 'I need your reassurance—your closeness, to know you see me and I am not invisible to you'?" This, then, offers the client a model of what a disclosing interaction that makes a bid for responsiveness from the partner might look like, invites the client to struggle with this possibility, and addresses blocks to this kind of risk taking. This is an example of how accountability and empirical research that allows us to know what we do and when it works, spurs on innovation and the refinement of the art of therapy.

*Snapshots of Client's Change Process in EFT*

The case of "Now you see me—now you don't."

If we were to take snapshots of key moments in change events, a withdrawer's reengagement and a blamer's softening, what would they look like?

Mark and Cora, a successful professional couple with two children who had been married for 20 years, had come to the end of the line. Cora had asked for a divorce. Cora's whole body radiated rage. She described the relationship as a "charade." She was critical but from a detached standpoint. She had already given up pursuing Mark, stating that she had "no hope" and that "It was too late to save this marriage." Mark was on the defensive. "She explodes, she blames," he said. "So what can I do? I try to stay calm and use logic."

Cora described Mark as a loving father and as doing chores in the house but as offering no closeness. However, they were not a typical extremely distressed couple, in that they described brief periods of close connection and sexuality all through their marriage. This had now become part of the problem, however. Cora described Mark as "Jekyll and Hyde," by which she meant, close and available and then gone for weeks. As she stated it, "He can pick me up and then put me down—so now I don't initiate. I'd rather be alone, than this now you see me, now you don't." Once this couple's cycle had been clarified and the partner's began to see the cycle, rather than each other, as the enemy, they began to spend more time together. Cora became less enraged and acknowledged that she and Mark were "friends," and Mark began to talk about his "guilt" about failing as a husband and how he froze in the face of Cora's rage and "unpredictability." De-escalation had occurred. Let us now look at snapshots of this couples' journey thorough Stage Two of EFT. These comments, distilled from the ongoing dialogue and heightened by the therapist, would also be used as the basis of enactments to generate new forms of engagement between Mark and Cora.

*Key Statements in Mark's Journey to Reengagement*

- *I am a mathematician—I like logic. When she gets hysterical—I am so lost—so I withdraw. I stay out of the way. I feel so helpless—totally out of my depth. It's not safe enough to initiate any connection.*
- *I get terrified—I was alone in my family—she is the only one I have ever felt connected to—if it disappears! So I just go oblivious—frozen in despair.*
- *(To Cora) I get overwhelmed—the message that I disappoint you—stops me dead. I*

*can't meet your expectations—I want more safety—maybe then I can show you my emotions. I do need you—I do want to be close.*

- *I disappear when her rage gets too much. (To Cora) I want you to stop the bombardment—then I can come out of the foxhole—no more name calling. You go too far. No more defining me.*
- *(To Cora) I do long for closeness—I think of it every day, but then—it's like pressure—I've done my repertoire—nothing to give then—can't please you—can't pass the test. But I don't want to go paralyzed any more—I want your reassurance—no more "on test" stuff.*
- *I can tell you now when I go paralyzed. Can I ask to be comforted? It feels strange. I think we can make it—put your armor away now—I want you to hope with me—risk it.*

*Key Statements in Cora's Journey to Softening and Bonding*

- *We make love—get close—and then—the big disconnect. I can't rely on the closeness—so I wait and hope he will come back—I feel this deep disappointment—better to be alone. I get so absorbed in my feelings—I can't even see him.*
- *I guess I am more sad than anything—hurt—that he can just put me down. Can't bear the uncertainty—even when we are close—I can't count on it. It hurts too much to need this.*
- *I see him risking—but. What do I want? Too scared to count on him—I'll risk it and then suddenly be alone—betrayed. So I rebuff him—even now when he does risk.*
- *(to Mark) I have a huge barrier—a wall. I won't let you hurt—abandon me anymore.*
- *I am too scared to respond—see him reaching—I go on guard. I make you walk through fire—keep my armor on. Don't know how to let you in. It's too hard.*

- *Do I really matter so much to you? Maybe . . . It scary to let those barriers down—I think I need to cry for a long time—but you can help me take them down—will you hold me now?*

The bonding interactions that occur at this point in EFT redefine the nature of the relationship and create new patterns of safe emotional engagement.

## NEW DIRECTIONS IN THE PRACTICE OF EFT

Three major areas of growth are apparent in the present practice of EFT. First, interventions continue to be refined and elaborated. Second, as mentioned earlier, the nature of impasses continues to be conceptually clarified and the process of resolving them understood. Third, the application of EFT to partners struggling with post-traumatic stress disorders and associated depression is being elaborated.

One example of how interventions become refined was just given. When key tasks and change events are identified and systematically studied, it is possible to identify the interventions that help clients to complete such tasks and events successfully. Other interventions become elaborated simply through the process of observation and the supervision of sessions. For example, in Stage Three, the fostering of coherent narratives of how rifts occurred in a relationship and how partners repaired such rifts has become more deliberate and thorough. This has evolved through observation, through input from narrative models of therapy and from the influence of attachment theory, which stresses the association of the ability to form coherent attachment narratives and secure attachment (Hesse, 1999).

A second area of growth is in the study of impasses that block the completion of change events in Stage Two of EFT—namely, with-drawer reengagement and blamer softening. One form of impasse has recently been termed an *attachment injury* (Johnson, Makinen, & Millikin, 2001; Johnson & Whiffen, 1999). This is a relationship trauma in the form of an abandonment or a betrayal at a time of intense need that shatters assumptions of safe depen-dency. These traumas are re-evoked when a therapist suggests that one partner put him-self or herself in the hands of the other in Stage Two change events. Such incidents were then observed, recognized as blocking recovery from distress, clarified by reference to attach-ment theory, and then the process of resolu-tion studied in a series of case studies. These incidents typically occur after loss, after ill-ness diagnosis, after miscarriages, as part of infidelity, or in transitions, such as immigra-tion. A sequence of steps has been identified in the resolution process, and this sequence is now being tested to determine if it differenti-ates couples who resolve these injuries from those who do not. This sequence involves steps such as the injuring spouse explicitly validat-ing the other's pain and expressing sorrow and offering comfort for this pain. In a broader context, this can also be viewed as the EFT contribution to the recent growing literature on forgiveness and reconciliation (Enright & Fitzgibbons, 2000).

The third area of growth is the use of EFT for trauma survivors and their partners (Johnson, 2002; Johnson & Makinen, in press). This evolved because EFT was used in the context of a hospital clinic that routinely was asked to treat severely distressed trauma survivors, such as the victims of violent crime or severe childhood sexual abuse. A secure attachment relationship is the natural healing arena for such trauma. However, just as trauma increases the need for protective attachments, it also undermines the ability to trust and cre-ate such bonds. When EFT is used with this population, components are added, such as an

educational component on trauma and its im-pact on attachment, and interventions are re-fined. For example, emotions are contained more, the pace of treatment is slower and so takes longer, and "safety rules" are established to contain behavior such as self-harm. The alliance must be monitored more intensely and affect, such as shame, dealt with more actively. This work is a prime example, together with the work of others using couple therapy to address depression (Jacobson, Dobson, Fruzetti, Schmaling, & Salusky, 1991), of couple therapy being used to address indi-vidual symptomatology. Depression and PTSD are the two such problems found most often to co-occur with marital distress (Whisman, 1999).

## CONCLUSION

A number of critical goals have been identi-fied for the field of couples' therapy (Johnson & Lebow, 2000; Pinsof & Wynne, 1995). These are, first, that the field become more empirically based; second, that research into the process of change increase and so be used to bridge the gap between research and prac-tice and to refine the art of intervention; and third, that we strive toward conceptual coher-ence, where there are clear links between models of adult love and relatedness and prag-matic "if this . . . then that" interventions.

The field of couples' therapy is becoming more empirically based on many different lev-els; on the level of the description of the na-ture of relationship distress and satisfaction that can be used to focus intervention, on the level of predictions concerning who can re-spond to models of intervention and what out-comes we can expect, and on the delineation of theories of relationship that can be empiri-cally investigated and tested (Johnson, 2002b). The growth of EFT as a model addresses this first goal of addressing description, prediction, and explanation. EFT has and continues to use process research to refine interventions and, as an experiential model, to return to and learn from the clinical reality of sessions where partners fight to define their relationships and themselves. It also has a growing conceptual coherence, based as it is on the most articulated and tested theory of adult love. This coherence offers a map of the terrain of distress that can help the couples' therapist to chart what is universal and common in distressed couples and in their change process and also to recognize and respect what is unique and particular to each individual couple. Many years ago, a study of health in families (Lewis, Beavers, Gossett, & Phillips, 1976) suggested that couple relationships are the primary context for individual health and well-being and the basis of healthy families. Intervention with couples then offered the therapist a uniquely powerful way into self and system that could maximize therapeutic impact and promote health on many different levels and in many different ways. It is hoped that EFT will continue to contribute to the growth of the couple therapy field and EFT therapists will continue to learn from the moment-to-moment magic that is the redefinition and growth of that most precious of gifts, an intimate partnership.

## REFERENCES

Ainsworth, M. D. S., Blehar, M., Waters, E., & Wall, S. (1978). *Patterns of attachment*. Hillsdale, NJ: Erlbaum.

Bartholomew, K., & Perlman, D. (1994). *Attachment processes in adulthood: Advances in personal relationships* (Vol. 5). London: Jessica Kingsley.

Bateson, G. (1972). *Steps to an ecology of mind*. New York: Chandler.

Borkovec, T., Roemer, L., & Kinyon, J. (1995). Disclosure and worry: Opposite sides of the emotional processing coin. In J. Pennebaker (Ed.), *Emotion, disclosure and health* (pp. 47–70). Washington, DC: American Psychiatric Press.

Bowlby, J. (1969). *Attachment and loss: Vol. 1, Attachment*. New York: Basic Books.

Bowlby, J. (1973). *Attachment and loss: Vol. II, Separation*. New York: Basic Books.

Bowlby, J. (1980). *Attachment and loss: Vol. III, Loss*. New York: Basic Books.

Bowlby, J. (1988). *A secure base*. New York: Basic Books.

Bradley, B. (2001). *Toward a mini-theory of therapist behaviors facilitating a softening*. Unpublished dissertation. School of Psychology–Fuller Seminary, California.

Bradley, B., & Furrow, J. (in press). EFT therapist behaviors facilitating a softening. *Journal of Marital and Family Therapy*.

Cain, D. J., & Seeman, J. (2002). *Humanistic psychotherapies: Handbook of research and practice*. Washington, DC: APA Press.

Cassidy, J., & Shaver, P. (1999). *Clinical handbook of attachment: Theory, research and clinical applications*. New York: Guilford Press.

Clothier, P. F., Manion, I. G., Walker, J. G., & Johnson, S. M. (in press). Emotionally focused interventions for couples with chronically ill children: A two year follow-up. *Journal of Marital and Family Therapy, 28*, 391–399.

Dandeneau, M., & Johnson, S. M. (1994). Facilitating intimacy: A comparative outcome study of emotionally focused and cognitive interventions. *Journal of Marital and Family Therapy, 20*, 17–33.

Davilla, J., Karney, B., & Bradbury, T. N. (1999). Attachment change processes in the early years of marriage. *Journal of Personality and Social Psychology, 76*, 783–802.

Denton, W. H., Burleson, B. R., Clark, T. E., Roderiguez, C. R., & Hobbs, B. V. (2000). A randomized trial of emotionally focused therapy for couples in a training clinic. *Journal of Marital and Family Therapy, 26*, 65–78.

Dunn, R., & Schwebel, A. (1995). Meta-analytic review of marital therapy outcome research. *Journal of Family Psychology, 9*, 58–68.

Elliott, R. (2002). The effectiveness of humanistic therapies: A meta-analysis. In D. Cain & J. Seeman (Eds.), *Humanistic psychotherapies: Handbook of research and practice* (pp. 57–81). Washington, DC: APA Press.

Enright, R. D., & Fitzgibbons, R. P. (2000) *Helping clients forgive*. Washington, DC: APA Press.

Fishbane, M. D. (2001). Relational narratives of the self. *Family Process, 40*, 273–291.

Fonagy, P., & Target, M. (1997) Attachment and reflective function: Their role in self-organization. *Development and Psychopathology, 9*, 679–700.

Fosha, D. (2000) *The transforming power of affect.* New York: Basic Books.

Goleman, D. (1995). *Emotional intelligence.* New York: Bantam Books.

Gottman, J. (1994). *What predicts divorce?* Hillsdale, NJ: Erlbaum.

Gottman, J., Coan, J., Carrere, S., & Swanson, C. (1998). Predicting marital happiness and stability from newlywed interactions. *Journal of Marriage and the Family, 60,* 5–22.

Greenberg, L. S., & Paivio, S. C. (1997). *Working with emotions in psychotherapy.* New York: Guilford Press.

Haddock, S., Schindler-Zimmerman, T., & MacPhee, D. (2000). The power equity guide: Attending to gender in therapy. *Journal of Marital and Family Therapy, 26,* 153–170.

Hazan, C., Zeifman, D. (1994). Sex and the psychological tether. In K. Bartholomew & D. Perlman (Eds.), *Attachment processes in adulthood: Advances in personal relationships* (Vol 5, pp. 151–177). London: Jessica Kingsley.

Hesse, E. (1999). The adult attachment interview: Historical and current perspectives. In J. Cassidy & P. Shaver (Eds.), *Handbook of attachment: Theory, research and clinical applications* (pp. 395–433). New York: Guilford Press.

Izard, C. E. (1977). *Human emotions.* New York: Plenum Press.

Jacobson, N. S., Dobson, K., Fruzzetti, A. E., Schmaling, D. B., & Salusky, S. (1991). Marital therapy as a treatment for depression. *Journal of Consulting & Clinical Psychology, 59,* 547–557.

Johnson, S. M. (1986). Bonds or bargains: Relational paradigms and their significance for marital therapy. *Journal of Marital and Family Therapy, 12,* 259–267.

Johnson, S. M. (1996). *Creating connection: The practice of emotionally focused marital therapy.* New York: Brunner/Mazel.

Johnson, S. M. (1998a). Emotionally focused interventions: Using the power of emotion. In F. D'Attilio (Ed.), *Case studies in couple and family therapy: Systemic and cognitive perspectives,* (pp. 450–472). New York: Guilford Press.

Johnson, S. M. (1998b). Listening to the music: Emotion as a natural part of systems theory. *The Journal of Systemic Therapies, 17,* 1–17. New York: Guilford Press.

Johnson, S. M. (1999). Emotionally focused therapy: Straight to the heart. In J. Donovan (Ed.), *Short term couple therapy* (pp. 11–42). New York: Guilford Press.

Johnson, S. M. (2002a). *Emotionally focused couple therapy with trauma survivors: Strengthening attachment bonds.* New York: Guilford Press.

Johnson, S. M. (2002b). Marital problems. In D. Sprenkle (Ed.), *Effectiveness research in marriage and family therapy* (pp. 163–190). Washington, DC: AAMFT.

Johnson, S. M., & Best, M. (2002). A systematic approach to restructuring adult attachment: The EFT model of couples therapy. In P. Erdman & T. Caffery (Eds.), *Attachment and family systems: Conceptual, empirical and therapeutic relatedness* (pp. 165–192). New York: Brunner-Routledge.

Johnson, S. M., & Denton, W. (2002). Emotionally focused couples therapy: Creating connection. In A. S. Gurman (Ed.), *The clinical handbook of couple therapy* (3rd ed., pp. 221–250). New York: Guilford Press.

Johnson, S. M., & Greenberg, L. S. (1988). Relating process to outcome in marital therapy. *Journal of Marital and Family Therapy, 14,* 175–183.

Johnson, S. M., & Greenberg, L. S. (Eds.). (1994). *The heart of the matter: Emotion in marital therapy.* New York: Brunner/Mazel.

Johnson, S. M., & Greenberg, L. S. (1985). The differential effects of experiential and problem solving interventions in resolving marital conflicts. *Journal of Consulting & Clinical Psychology, 53,* 175–184.

Johnson, S. M., Hunsley, J., Greenberg, L., & Schindler, D. (1999). Emotionally focused couples therapy: Status & Challenges. *Clinical Psychology: Science & Practice, 6,* 67–79.

Johnson, S. M., & Lebow, J. (2000). The coming of age of couple therapy: A decade review. *Journal of Marital & Family Therapy, 26,* 9–24.

Johnson, S. M., Maddeaux, C., & Blouin, J. (1998). Emotionally focused family therapy for bulimia: Changing attachment patterns. *Psychotherapy: Theory, Research and Practice, 35,* 238–247.

Johnson, S. M., & Makinen, J. (in press). Creating a safe haven and a secure base: Couples therapy as a vital element in the treatment of post-traumatic stress disorder. In D. Snyder & M. Whisman (Eds.), *Treating difficult couples.* New York: Guilford Press.

Johnson, S. M., Makinen, J., & Millikin, J. (2001). Attachment injuries in couple relationships: A new perspective on impasses in couples therapy. *Journal of Marital & Family Therapy, 27,* 145–155.

Johnson, S. M., & Talitman, E. (1997). Predictors of success in emotionally focused marital therapy. *Journal of Marital & Family Therapy, 23,* 135–152.

Johnson, S. M., & Whiffen, V. (Eds.). (in press). *At-tachment theory: A perspective for couple and family therapy.* New York: Guilford Press.

Johnson, S. M., & Whiffen, V. (Eds.). (2003). *Attachment processes in couple & family therapy.* New York: Guilford Press.

Johnson, S. M., & Whiffen, V. (1999). Made to measure: Attachment styles in couples therapy. *Clinical Psychology: Science & Practice, Special Edition on Individual Differences and Couples Therapy, 6,* 366–381.

Karen, R. (1998). *Becoming attached.* New York: Oxford University Press.

Kobak, R. (1999). The emotional dynamic of disruptions in attachment relationships. In J. Cassidy & P. Shaver (Eds.), *Handbook of attachment: Theory, research and clinical applications* (pp. 21–43). New York: Guilford Press.

Kobak, R., & Sceery, A. (1988). Attachment in late adolescence: Working models, affect regulation and representations of self and others. *Child Development, 59,* 135–146.

Kobak, R., Ruckdeschel, K., & Hazan, C. (1994). From symptom to signal: An attachment view of emotion in marital therapy. In S Johnson & L. Greenberg (Eds.), *The heart of the matter: Perspectives on emotion in marital therapy* (pp. 46–71). New York: Brunner/Mazel.

Lewis, J. M., Beavers, W. R., Gossett, J. T., & Phillips, V. A. (1976). *No single thread: Psychological health in family systems.* New York: Brunner/Mazel.

MacPhee, D., Johnson, S. M., & van der Veer, M. C. (1995). Low sexual desire in women: The effects of marital therapy. *Journal of Sex & Marital Therapy, 21,* 159–182.

McFarlane, A. C., & van der Kolk, B. A. (1996). Trauma and its challenge to society. In B. A. Van der Kolk, A. C. McFarlane, & L. Weisaeth (Eds.), *Traumatic stress* (pp. 24–45). New York: Guilford Press.

Mahoney, M., (1991). *Human change processes.* New York: Basic Books.

Mikulincer, M. (1995). Attachment style and the mental representation of self. *Journal of Personality and Social Psychology, 69,* 1203–1215.

Minuchin, S., & Fishman, H. C. (1981). *Techniques of family therapy.* Cambridge, MA: Harvard University Press.

Neimeyer, R. (1993). An appraisal of constructivist psychotherapies. *Journal of Consulting & Clinical Psychology, 61,* 221–234.

Orlinsky, D. E., Grawe, K., & Parks, B. K. (1994).

Process and outcome in psychotherapy—noch einmal. In A. E. Bergin & S. L. Garfield (Eds.), *Handbook of psychotherapy and behavior change* (pp 257–310). New York: Wiley.

Paivio, S., & Nieuwenhuis, J. A. (2001). Efficacy of emotionally focused therapy for survivors of child abuse: A preliminary study. *Journal of Traumatic Stress, 14,* 109–127.

Palmer, G., & Johnson, S. M. (2002). Becoming an emotionally focused couples therapist. *Journal of Couple and Relationship Therapy, 3,* 1–20.

Pasch, L. A., & Bradbury, T. N. (1998). Social support, conflict and the development of marital dysfunction. *Journal of Consulting & Clinical Psychology, 66,* 219–230.

Plutchik, R. (2000). *Emotions in the practice of psychotherapy.* Washington, DC: APA Press.

Roberts, T. W. (1992). Sexual attraction and romantic love: Forgotten variables in marital therapy. *Journal of Marital and Family Therapy, 18,* 357–364.

Rogers, C. R. (1951). *Client centered therapy.* Boston: Houghton-Mifflin.

Salovey, P., Rothman, A. J., Detweiler, J. B., & Stewart, W. T. (2000). Emotional states and physical health. *American Psychologist, 55,* 110–1421.

Satir, V. M., & Baldwin, M. (1983). *Satir step by step: A guide to creating change in families.* Palo Alto, CA: Science & Behavior Books.

Schwartz, R., & Johnson, S. M. (2000). Does family therapy have emotional intelligence? *Family Process, 39,* 29–34.

Senchak, M., & Leonard, K. E. (1992). Attachment styles and marital adjustment among newlywed couples. *Journal of Personal and Social Relationships, 9,* 51–64.

Shaver, P., & Hazan, C. (1993). Adult romantic attachment: Theory and evidence. In D. Perlman & W. Jones (Eds.), *Advances in personal relationships* (Vol. 4, pp. 29–70). London: Jessica Kingsley.

Simpson, J., & Rholes, W. (1994). Stress and secure base relationships in adulthood. In K Bartholomew & D. Perlman (Eds.), *Attachment processes in adulthood* (pp. 181–204). London: Jessica Kingsley Publications.

Simpson, J. A., Rholes, W. S., & Phillips, D. (1996). Conflict in close relationships: An attachment perspective. *Journal of Personality and Social Psychology, 71,* 899–914.

Stanley, S. M., Bradbury, T. N., & Markman, H. J. (2000). Structural flaws in the bridge from basic research on marriage to interventions for couples. *Journal of Marriage and the Family, 62*, 256–264.

Tronick, E. Z. (1989). Emotions and emotional communication in infants. *American Psychologist, 44*, 112–119.

Vygotsky, L. S. (1978). *Mind in society: The development of higher psychological processes.* Cambridge, MA: Harvard University Press.

Whisman, M. A., (1999). Marital dissatisfaction and psychiatric disorders: Results from the national co-morbidity study. *Journal of Abnormal Psychology, 108*, 701–706.

Wood, D., Bruner, J. S., & Ross, G. (1976). The role of tutoring in problem solving. *Journal of Child Psychology & Psychiatry, 17*, 89–100.

Zajonc, R. B. (1980). Feeling and thinking: Preferences need no inferences. *American Psychologist, 35*, 151–175.

CHAPTER 13

# Behavioral Couple Therapy

## *Past, Present, and Future*

DAVID C. ATKINS, PhD

SONA DIMIDJIAN, MSW

*University of Washington*

ANDREW CHRISTENSEN, PhD

*University of California, Los Angeles*

## INTRODUCTION

In Gurman and Kniskern's *Handbook of Family Therapy* (1981), our late friend, colleague, and mentor Neil Jacobson commented, "What distinguishes [Behavioral Couple Therapy] from other approaches to treating couples is its single-minded commitment to empirical investigation as the optimal road to development" (p. 557, Jacobson, 1981). We believe that this statement is as true today as it was then. To be clear, other couple therapies have demonstrated empirical support (see Christensen & Heavey, 1999, for a review), but behavioral couple therapy (BCT) is unique in both the quantity of empirical support it has

received and the role that research plays in its ongoing evolution. Far from being a static treatment, BCT faces constant scrutiny and revision as researchers and clinicians try to develop an ever more potent therapy.

This chapter presents both the research support for and the clinical application of BCT. We will focus primarily on two versions of BCT. The first is the "classic" BCT of Jacobson and Margolin (1979) that focuses on skills and behavior change. We refer to this as traditional behavioral couple therapy (TBCT). The second version of BCT, and perhaps the most radical revision to date, is integrative behavioral couple therapy (IBCT), which emphasizes emotional acceptance and tolerating partner differences, in addition to behavior change (Christensen & Jacobson, 2000; Jacobson & Christensen, 1996).*

## HISTORY AND BACKGROUND OF BCT

Most BCT researchers point to Stuart's (1969) report as the first published example of the application of behavioral psychology principles of reinforcement with couples. At that time behaviorism had shown great success with certain clinical issues such as phobias, mental retardation, and behavior problems on inpatient psychiatric wards (Masters, Burish, Hollon, & Rimm, 1987). Behavioral researchers, buoyed by their successes, were rapidly targeting new disorders and problems. In addition to Stuart's work, a group of researchers at the University of Oregon was studying problem behaviors in children and developing behavioral interventions for parents (Patterson, 1982). In the course of their research, they observed that some couples needed parenting skills; however, other couples needed relationship skills in addition to parenting skills. The research group began to study relationship problems in their own right and published a series of case studies applying behavioral principles to relationship distress (Patterson, Hops, & Weiss, 1975; Weiss, Hops, & Patterson, 1973).

Research and clinical work on BCT gained momentum at the end of the 1970s and the beginning of the 1980s, as several books were published that described behavioral approaches to couple therapy (Jacobson & Margolin, 1979; Stuart, 1980). Research evidence (reviewed in the section "Research Evidence That Supports the Model") rapidly accumulated, showing that BCT was an effective approach to increasing relationship satisfaction and stability, yet there was also evidence that not all couples were being helped (Jacobson, Follette, Revenstorf, Baucom, Hahlweg, & Margolin, 1984; Jacobson, Schmaling, & Holtzworth-Munroe, 1987). In fact, the accumulating evidence suggested that not all couples benefited in therapy and that some couples relapsed shortly after finishing therapy. These findings led BCT researchers to explore various ways to extend the basic model of couple therapy and gave rise to cognitive-behavioral couple therapy (CBCT; Baucom & Epstein, 1990; Halford, Sanders, & Behrens, 1993) and integrative behavioral couple therapy (IBCT; Jacobson & Christensen, 1996). Research into the efficacy of these "post-TBCT" therapies is ongoing, including the recent completion of the largest trial of couple therapy to date, comparing TBCT and IBCT (Christensen, Atkins, Berns, Wheeler, Baucom, & Simpson, 2003).

## MAJOR THEORETICAL AND RESEARCH-BASED CONSTRUCTS

BCT is a behavioral therapy and, as such, was developed from the basic principles of learning and conditioning. For many clinicians, behavior therapy connotes a mechanistic therapy, in which there is little regard for the person and the focus of therapy is on specific, prescribed interventions. Although this stereotype may be appropriate for particular instances where behavior therapy has been applied, we believe that nothing in the theory mandates such a mechanistic focus and that much in the theory, particularly its emphasis on context and unique individual histories, would promote regard for the complex, whole individual human being. Although it is beyond the scope of this chapter to provide a thorough

---

*We will use the overarching term BCT when referring to behavioral couple therapy in general and TBCT and IBCT when we are referring to the specific versions covered in this chapter.

review of behavior therapy (see Goldfried & Davison, 1994, or Masters et al., 1987), in this section we introduce some of the key theoretical constructs of BCT; we hope to do this in a way that minimizes jargon and that conveys BCT for what it is: a flexible, clinically sophisticated therapy constructed from the solid science of behavioral theory.

## Model of Relationships and Distress

Any coherent model of couple therapy must contain an understanding of why partners form relationships, and consequently, what goes wrong in relationships. This framework guides the process of assessment and the direction of treatment. From a behavioral point of view, people form relationships because they find their partner and the relationship rewarding. We use the term *reward* not in a generic sense but in the specific sense of operant conditioning (Skinner, 1974); that is, a reward or a reinforcer is something that increases the frequency of the behavior in question. Thus, in the case of intimate relationships, being with one's partner is a reinforcing experience, to the extent that it increases one's wanting to be with one's partner in the future. Simultaneously, there must be relatively fewer aversive qualities in the partner. Thus, there is a positive ratio of reinforcing to punishing qualities. In fact, work by Gottman and Levenson (1999) has shown that there are different ratios of positive to negative behaviors among happy couples, as compared with distressed couples. However, it is crucial to keep in mind that reinforcers are not generically "good" behaviors; reinforcers are defined by their function, not by their normative value. Thus, it is impossible to form a general list of reinforcers that works with couples because reinforcers are specific to each individual within a couple.

In fact, reinforcers do not have to be "good"

at all; if something serves to increase the rate of a given behavior, it is by definition a "reinforcer." For example, attention from a partner, even if that attention consists of criticism and complaints that would be widely viewed as "negative," may function as a reinforcer in some relationships. Conversely, just because a given behavior is positive or pleasurable does not imply that it will be an effective reinforcer for a given behavior. For example, most people find backrubs enjoyable. However, this does not necessarily mean that a backrub will be an effective reinforcer for washing dishes. This idiographic and functional nature of reinforcers is essential to behavior therapy and lies at the heart of a core element of behavior therapy: functional analysis.

Very simply put, a functional analysis is an analysis that reveals the immediate, proximal contingencies of a given behavior. Said another way, a functional analysis answers the question: What controls a given behavior? In conducting a functional analysis, the therapist focuses on the antecedents and consequences of behavior: What came before and what was the effect? For example, in understanding why one partner is critical of the other, the therapist may observe what occurs just before the criticism. This analysis may reveal the "triggers" of the criticism (e.g., the partner is sarcastic), which can then be targeted for intervention. In addition, the functional analysis may focus on the consequences of the criticism (e.g., the criticized partner refuses to communicate).

Behavioral research has also demonstrated that reinforcers are not static. We can habituate to reinforcers over time, so that the jokes and funny faces that used to elicit laughter and affection from our partner now bring forth eye rolling and exasperation. This process has been coined *reinforcement erosion* (Jacobson & Margolin, 1979). The changing value of reinforcers highlights the dynamic nature of relationships; the skills that were necessary for a happy relationship at the start are likely to be different from those that are necessary for a happy relationship 10 years into the marriage.

The behavioral theory of relationships is quite simple, in that it rests on the functional analysis; however, the simplicity of the theory does not translate into "easy" therapy. A functional analysis is a very powerful tool, yet it can be exceedingly difficult to understand the contingencies of a given behavior! In fact, how to address the inherent challenges and difficulties of conducting a functional analysis represents one of the key differences between TBCT and IBCT.

### Theoretical Differences Between TBCT and IBCT

The two styles of BCT presented in this chapter have much in common, theoretically. Nonetheless, a few key theoretical differences undergird and explain the divergence in therapeutic interventions between the two approaches. In this section, we discuss four primary differences between TBCT and IBCT: the unit of analysis, how the functional analysis is used, the issue of rule-governed versus contingency-shaped behavior, and the target of treatment. In discussing the differences, we focus mainly on the theory in this section. How the theoretical differences are translated into practice is described in the intervention section.

The first difference between the two therapies is that TBCT tends to focus on small, specific behaviors, whereas IBCT tends to focus on larger "themes." TBCT places great emphasis on identifying discrete and specific behaviors that can be targeted for intervention. Indeed, this is the main focus of assessment in TBCT, something we return to later in greater depth. IBCT also acknowledges the importance of identifying specific behaviors for intervention, but it takes a wider view than

does TBCT. Different behaviors can serve the same function, and in IBCT, the therapist works to identify classes of behavior based on shared function. These themes are common patterns that may appear in several spheres of couples' lives but serve the same function.

A second difference has to do with the functional analysis. Conducting a functional analysis is much like conducting an experiment; ideally, all sources of influence are held constant while a single antecedent influence is manipulated. Because TBCT focuses on such small events, there are a bewildering number of behaviors to subject to a functional analysis. Imagine two partners discussing something important about their relationship for 5 minutes; there are innumerable antecedents and consequences to explore. In describing TBCT, Jacobson (1981) put it this way:

> In a marital dyad, behavior exchanges are continuous, and the behavior of each member serves as both antecedent and consequence for the behavior of the partner. As a result, any attempt to establish functional relationships between behavior and the environment by applying a unidirectional cause–effect model was unsatisfactory. . . . The solution to this dilemma has been to emphasize the skills which couples need to sustain a satisfying relationship over a long period of time. (pp. 557–558)

The traditional approach to BCT contends that in most instances, it is simply too difficult to conduct functional analyses of problematic partner behavior. Thus, although TBCT acknowledges the utility of functional analysis, it steers away from an idiographic approach and assumes that a set of core skills exists that is useful in most relationships. Following from this basic assumption, the primary interventions in TBCT are a prescribed set of skills thought to have general use. In contrast to TBCT, IBCT attempts to remain true to a functional analytic approach. This is accomplished by broadening the targets of the functional analysis. As we noted earlier, IBCT focuses on patterns and themes, as opposed to small, discrete behaviors. These patterns and themes become the focus of the functional analysis in IBCT.

The third significant difference between the two therapies relates to relative emphasis of the treatments on rule-governed versus contingency-shaped behavior (Skinner, 1966). Up to this point, our description of the behavioral theory of relationships has focused on contingency-shaped behavior, behavior that is controlled via the rewards and punishments that it "naturally" elicits. Behaviorists have noted, however, that some behavior is controlled by rules (Kohlenberg & Tsai, 1991). A rule is a statement of relationship, "If you do X, then Y will occur." From an early age, we are reinforced for following rules, and parenting involves many rules: "If you have a snack late in the day, you'll ruin your appetite for dinner." For the behaviorist, the important point is that rules specify contingencies, and people often behave according to those contingencies because of the rules. For example, a child's behavior may be elicited by a rule ("I need to eat my vegetables before I get dessert") and reinforced because it meets the requirements of the rule ("Now I get dessert because I have finished my vegetables"). If someone behaves in a certain manner because of a rule, behaviorists refer to this as "rule-governed" behavior. Rules are neither good nor bad; they are essential in learning many tasks in life. However, natural contingencies also come into play that may be consistent or inconsistent with the rule. For example, the parent in our example may prepare vegetables in an attractive way that appeals to the child (e.g., the "ants on a log" for celery) so that the child eats the vegetables, not because of the rule, but because of the reinforcement that comes from observing, discussing, and eating the attractive vegetables. In contrast, the vegetables may be unappealing, the interaction around their eating may be negative, so that repeated appeals

to the rule and strict application of the reinforcers specified by the rule are necessary to ensure any vegetable consumption. Rules are instituted because desired behavior does not occur naturally. If children typically liked broccoli as much as they do ice cream, there would never need to be rules like the previously mentioned one. However, one ideally structures the environment to "naturally" promote "good" behavior, either in addition to or instead of a rule. Otherwise, continued vigilance about the relevant behavior and regular applications of the reinforcers set forth by the rule are necessary.

From this vantage point, TBCT is largely a rule-governed therapeutic approach. In introducing the skills, the therapist is teaching the couple a rule, "If you learn these skills, your relationship will improve." For example, one of the components of TBCT is communication training, including training in "I statements" and paraphrasing (described in depth in the section "Treatment Protocols for TBCT and IBCT"). Couples vary in their assimilation of these new communication skills. Some couples are able to assimilate the skills into their relationships; the couple's experience benefit from the skills (the skills achieve reinforcing effects), and the skills subsequently become contingency-based, rather than rule-governed. Thus, they use "I statements," no longer because the therapist said that was the right way to talk, but because they have experienced more rewarding interactions as a result. In contrast, other couples are not able to assimilate the skills in the same manner. For these couples, the skills remain rule-governed, under the control of the therapist's instruction and guidance. While the couple is in therapy, the therapist may serve to reinforce the rule (i.e., "You should use these skills"), but when the couple ends therapy, the partners are unlikely to sustain the therapeutic behaviors. These couples are at high risk of relapse. The rule-governed nature of the TBCT interventions was a primary motivation in the development of IBCT. Unlike TBCT, IBCT uses a functional analysis to identify and target the specific contingencies of behavior in a given relationship. Ideally, the change that occurs in IBCT should all be contingency-shaped, as opposed to rule-governed. Thus, couples in IBCT should be able to maintain their therapeutic gains after therapy ends, as the reinforcers that were used were specific to their relationship. This is one of the primary hypotheses of our recent clinical trial (Christensen et al., 2003).

The final difference between the two therapies involves the target of treatment. In TBCT, there is an exclusive focus on actions and lack of actions: Which behaviors need to be increased and which decreased? In contrast, IBCT places great importance on *reactions* in addition to actions; in particular, the functional analysis often reveals how reactions maintain negative behavior and interfere with positive behavior. For example, Jim's strong negative reaction when Sue is not interested in sex with him actually reduces Sue's own sexual interest, which is a major reinforcer for him. Feedback loops such as the one just described are quite common in couple interactions. TBCT, with its emphasis on actions, may miss the dynamic interplay of couple's behavior, whereas IBCT focuses on the wider patterns of action and reaction. Thus, IBCT focuses on negative reactions and works toward having partners accept one another's behaviors. This acceptance counters the negative reactions that serve to maintain cycles of punishing exchanges.

## RESEARCH EVIDENCE THAT SUPPORTS THE MODEL

TBCT is, by far, the most commonly studied couple therapy. Over two dozen controlled studies have empirically tested the efficacy of TBCT (for reviews, see Baucom, Shoham, Mueser, Daiuto, & Stickle, 1998, and Christensen & Heavey, 1999). Moreover, using the criteria established by Chambless and Hollon (1998) for delineating empirically supported treatments, TBCT was the only couple therapy noted as an "efficacious and specific treatment." IBCT has not yet received similar empirical scrutiny, though there is some preliminary support for its efficacy (Jacobson, Christensen, Prince, Cordova, & Eldridge, 2000). In addition, IBCT is currently being tested in the largest trial of couple therapy to date (Christensen et al., 2003). The results of that study will provide important information regarding its efficacy. In this section, we will review the empirical support for both TBCT and IBCT.

## TBCT

Early research on TBCT included reports of case studies by Weiss et al. (1973) and Patterson et al. (1975). Jacobson (1977) conducted the first randomized clinical trial of TBCT with a modest sample size of 5 couples in active treatment and 5 couples in a wait-list control group. TBCT led to impressive gains in marital satisfaction with a very large effect size ($d > 2$). Several additional clinical trials rapidly expanded the evidence that TBCT could affect significant improvements in relationship satisfaction. Moreover, Hahlweg and Markman (1988) conducted the first meta-analysis of couple therapy, in which they examined 17 studies of TBCT. They found that TBCT produced a large amount of change compared with control groups ($d = 0.95$) and that most couples maintained their improvements over the year following therapy.

Unfortunately, not all of the findings were so encouraging. Virtually all outcome studies use inferential statistics to determine whether a statistically significant difference exists between change that occurs in couples during therapy, compared to change in control couples who did not receive therapy. However, as Jacobson, Follette, and Revenstorf (1984) noted, statistically significant change does not imply that a distressed couple would be considered nondistressed at the end of therapy. To address the issue of how individuals (or couples) change in therapy, Jacobson et al. proposed a method of clinical significance. Clinical significance classifies individuals (or couples) at the end of therapy into one of four categories: Deteriorated, Unchanged, Improved, or Recovered.

When TBCT was evaluated in terms of clinical significance and long-term outcome, the picture was not so optimistic. Approximately one third of couples received no benefit from TBCT, and one third of those couples who were classified as Recovered at the end of treatment relapsed during the 1–2 years following therapy (Jacobson et al., 1984; Jacobson et al., 1987). Moreover, two additional studies have shown poor long-term outcomes of TBCT at longer post-therapy assessments. Snyder, Wills, and Grady-Fletcher (1991) found that 38% of couples who had received TBCT divorced within 4 years following therapy, compared to only 3% who had received insight-oriented couple therapy. More recently, Halford, Sanders, and Behrens (2001) found that low-distress couples who had received a premarital intervention based on TBCT were more distressed than a no-treatment control group at 4 years post-intervention. Thus, although TBCT has proven its efficacy to improve relationship satisfaction in a number of studies, there are ongoing concerns about the post-therapy adjustment of couples who improve with TBCT and those couples who never respond to TBCT.

## Post-TBCT Behavioral Couple Therapies

The research findings reviewed here have led researchers to try to improve upon the basic TBCT intervention model. Several researchers have explored the possibility of enhancing TBCT by including interventions focused on the cognitions of the partners and emotional expressiveness (Baucom & Lester, 1986; Baucom, Sayers, & Sher, 1990; Halford, Sanders, & Behrens, 1993). Each of these studies compared TBCT to an "enhanced" version of TBCT that included cognitive interventions. However, in each instance, TBCT performed just as well as the enhanced version. Thus, the addition of cognitive strategies was not effective in increasing the percentage of couples that responded to TBCT nor did those strategies lead to reduced relapse among those couples who did respond. Recently, Epstein and Baucom (2002) have published a description of an enhanced cognitive-behavioral couple therapy model, which broadens the context of this approach by paying greater attention to the environment in which the couple functions, factors within the individual partners themselves, and developmental change in the relationship. However, there is no research as yet on this important revision of the cognitive behavioral approach.

Integrative behavioral couple therapy is an extensive revision of TBCT that has received empirical support. Two unpublished studies (cited in Christensen & Heavey, 1999) and a small clinical trial (Jacobson et al., 2000) suggest that IBCT is better than no treatment and possibly more effective than TBCT. However, the most convincing evidence for IBCT comes from a recent large randomized clinical trial ($N = 134$ couples) that compared IBCT to TBCT (Christensen et al., 2003). There are several interesting findings from this study. First, therapeutic interventions from over 200 sessions of therapy were coded by raters who were uninformed about the treatments involved. These ratings showed that the two therapies were quite different. Greater than three times the number of "acceptance-oriented" interventions occurred in IBCT as compared to TBCT, and over three times the number of "change-oriented" interventions occurred in TBCT as compared to IBCT. The adherence coding shows that TBCT and IBCT have little overlap in their interventions and can be considered distinct therapies.

Second, consistent with previous studies, TBCT and IBCT demonstrated similar and large levels of change in marital satisfaction from pretreatment to post-treatment. However, there were some notable differences in how this change occurred. Change in TBCT occurred rapidly during the initial phases of therapy but then slowed later in therapy. In IBCT, change occurred at a constant rate over the entire course of therapy. Moreover, the most highly distressed couples in both therapies showed early gains that slowed later in therapy. Thus, in highly distressed couples in TBCT, their improvement in therapy not only slowed down but reversed direction such that at the end of therapy, these couples were beginning to deteriorate (Christensen et al., 2003). We believe that these differences in the course of therapy will have implications for couples' relationship satisfaction following therapy. In particular, we predict that couples who received IBCT will have lower levels of relapse relative to couples who received TBCT. At the present time, however, these are only hypotheses, as the study is ongoing.

## TREATMENT PROTOCOLS
## FOR TBCT AND IBCT

### Assessment and Case Formulation

The structure of the assessment portion of therapy is identical for TBCT and IBCT; how-

ever, the focus and goals are quite different. A hallmark of behavior therapy is a thorough assessment that includes both subjective and objective measures. In research studies, the first four sessions are typically set aside for assessment, including an initial conjoint session, an individual session with each partner, and a conjoint feedback session. In community settings, the two individual sessions are sometimes condensed into a single session, with half of the session spent with each partner.

As in all couple therapies, the BCT therapist wants to hear the couple's story and each partner's views on how their problems developed. In addition to this verbal report, it is equally important to use objective assessment measures, most often questionnaires. This is important for several reasons. First, questionnaires are often more comprehensive than an interview alone, covering more relationship areas. Second, they also allow comparisons and feedback about a given couple's problems relative to couples in general, via normative data for the questionnaires. Third, for sensitive topics (e.g., domestic violence and extramarital affairs), research has shown that individuals are more likely to endorse these issues on questionnaires than in interviews (O'Leary, Vivian, & Malone, 1992).

Listed as follows is a summary of the primary questionnaires that were used in our recent study comparing TBCT and IBCT (Christensen et al., 2003), which we believe are most relevant for clinical purposes.

• Dyadic Adjustment Scale (DAS; Spanier, 1976): The most widely used global measure of relationship satisfaction. There is normative data on the DAS that is useful for gauging the couple's level of distress.
• Frequency and Acceptability Partner Behavior (FAPB; Christensen & Jacobson, 1997): The FAPB has each partner rate both the frequency and the acceptability of a number of positive and negative behaviors.

- Marital Satisfaction Inventory—Revised (MSI-R; Snyder, 1997): A multiscale measure of relationship functioning that provides a profile of couple distress.
- Marital Status Inventory (MSI; Weiss & Cerreto, 1980): The MSI measures the steps taken toward divorce. It is a useful gauge of commitment.
- Conflict Tactics Scale (CTS; Straus, Hamby, Boney-McCoy, & Sugarman, 1996): The CTS is a widely used measure of domestic violence.

In research studies, couples will complete the questionnaires at a pre-therapy assessment. In the community, couples are typically given the questionnaires at the first session and instructed to bring the completed questionnaires to their individual session; however, therapists could also mail the packet of questionnaires to couples prior to the first appointment. Couples often expect that "therapy" (i.e., intervention) will begin immediately, and it is essential to orient the couple that the first few sessions will be assessment and that therapy will not begin until the assessment is completed. In our experience, couples respond positively to the notion of an extended assessment; it conveys to the partners that their problems are serious and that the therapist wants to have a thorough understanding before proceeding with therapy.

The first session is a mixture of hearing about the presenting problems and about the history of the relationship. Therapists in both TBCT and IBCT are interested in hearing a thorough description of the present problems from each partner's point of view. However, it is also essential to gather some information about the relationship history. In particular, it is useful to hear about the early stages of the relationship: What initially attracted the partners to one another? In the early phases of the relationship, what were the strong points of the relationship? When did things begin to change? It is also helpful to look at the couple's experience of stressful events, transitions or both, such as changing jobs, having children, moving, and so forth. Throughout the first session, it is important for the therapist to listen attentively to both partners, making sure that they feel that they are being heard and understood.

The individual sessions are a crucial part of the assessment process. Oftentimes, important information about the relationship is revealed during the individual sessions that would not have been revealed were the other partner present. Before the therapist begins the individual interview, it is crucial to clarify confidentiality, and we typically begin by noting, "Unless you tell me otherwise, I will assume that everything you say today will be okay to share in our conjoint sessions." The primary focus of the individual sessions is to hear each partner's view on the relationship, which can be notably different from what was shared in the initial, conjoint interview! In addition, it is useful to hear about the individual's family of origin, which provides the model of relationships that each partner learned growing up. Finally, issues of individual pathology, such as depression, can be explored in the individual interview.

In addition to these overarching guidelines, several specific topics should be covered in the individual session. First, the therapist should assess each partner's level of commitment to the relationship. If the partners completed the MSI (Weiss & Cerreto, 1980), the therapist can discuss their responses to the questionnaire. Second, the therapist should assess to what extent the individual feels that he or she contributes to the relationship problems. If the individual asserts that the problems are wholly due to the partner, therapy will likely need to begin by looking at the ways in which both partners are involved in and contribute to the problems.

Third, the individual sessions afford an

opportunity to assess several sensitive topics. Domestic violence is not uncommon in relationships, particularly in distressed relationships (Holtzworth-Munroe, Meehan, Rehman, & Marshall, 2002). We believe it is crucial—especially in the individual session with the wife—to assess for domestic violence. If the couples completed the CTS (Straus et al., 1996), the therapist can use their responses to guide the assessment by following up on specific behaviors that they endorsed. Use of measures such as the CTS is strongly recommended, given that research suggests that significantly more individuals will disclose violence on such measures, when compared to general intake forms or clinical interviews (O'Leary et al., 1992). If, however, the CTS was not used, it is important to ask verbally about specific behaviors (e.g., "Has your partner ever slapped or pushed you?"), as opposed to asking generally about abuse or violence (e.g., "Have you ever been abused by your partner?"). Some experts also suggest using statements such as "Describe your worst argument" as a method of assessing domestic violence (e.g., Holtzworth-Munroe et al., 2002). Whether the CTS is used or not, we believe it is important to inquire about the frequency of violence, the extent of injury, and the worst case of violence. When there is evidence of violence, it is crucial to assess certain safety issues, such as whether weapons were involved or available and whether children were involved or present during violent episodes. We also try to assess whether or not the violence constitutes battering. By battering, we mean "the use of violence to control, intimidate, or subjugate another human being" (Jacobson & Gottman, 1998). In assessing for battering, we look for a history of injury and fear. If there is evidence of battering, we believe that couple therapy is contraindicated (Bograd & Mederos, 1999) and that individual therapy for the perpetrator of the violence is the preferred therapy modality. Holtzworth-

Munroe et al. (2002) provide further details about handling domestic violence in couple therapy.

Extramarital relationships should also be assessed during the individual interviews. Like domestic violence, affairs are quite common and are not likely to be mentioned if not directly assessed. Therapists should inquire about sexual or significant emotional relationships or both outside of the primary relationship. In general, we believe that couple therapy when there is an undisclosed affair is counterproductive, at best. When a spouse reveals an affair that is unknown to the partner, we encourage the spouse to either tell the partner or end the affair with the other person. If the individual is not willing to take either of these courses of action, then we believe the therapist should indicate that couple therapy is inappropriate at this time and should refer for individual therapy. For further discussion of affairs and couple therapy, see Glass (2002) and Gordon and Baucom (2000).

Before turning to the feedback session, we would like to comment briefly on differences between TBCT and IBCT during the assessment phase. As we noted earlier, the structure is identical, but there are important differences in what the therapist attends to during the assessment, how the information is gathered, and how it contributes to the case formulation. In TBCT, therapists use the assessment period to identify discrete behaviors that can then be targeted during the intervention phase of therapy. For example, if partners mention that they have trouble communicating and cannot agree about finances, the therapist will note these areas as targets for communication and problem-solving training interventions. At the feedback session, the therapist will present the couple with his or her understanding of the couple's problems and also describe how the skills of TBCT can target each of these problems. In addition, the therapist will present an overview for how therapy will progress.

In IBCT, the therapist looks for themes and patterns among the specific problems that couples mention. The problems that the couple notes may represent a single instance of a broader underlying problem. Focusing on the particular instances as separate and distinct may miss the "true, important controlling variables in marital interaction" (Christensen, Jacobson, & Babcock, 1995, p. 35). As noted previously, IBCT takes as its aim a functional analysis of the couple's problems. For example, imagine a couple in which the wife feels ignored by her husband. There are likely a number of ways that the husband may act that will lead to his wife feeling ignored: deciding to spend time with friends, spending time alone, not showing any interest in his wife's activities, and so forth. In TBCT, these specific behaviors would become the target list for skills, whereas in IBCT, the therapist would look for the pattern or underlying theme (i.e., feeling ignored) that gives rise to the various problems.

In accordance with this emphasis on larger patterns, the case formulation plays an important role in IBCT and consists of three important pieces: the theme, polarization process, and mutual trap. As noted earlier, the theme is a fundamental difference between partners that runs throughout the couple's various problems and complaints. Oftentimes, the theme can be seen in the partners' initial attractions to one another. The qualities that once seemed novel and interesting have become grating and hurtful. The wife who naturally connects to and depends upon other people was initially attracted to her husband because of his independence and autonomy. Now, the couple's problems revolve around a theme of "closeness–distance," in which the wife wants greater contact and connection, and the husband wants to maintain his autonomy. Often, the differences between partners are made emotionally volatile by the emotional vulnerabilities that they touch. For example, if the previously mentioned wife is afraid of being abandoned or the husband is fearful of being suffocated in the relationship, then the differences in closeness and distance will be especially problematic. As the partners struggle with their differences, they will often engage in a pattern of interaction that attempts to solve the problem but usually makes it worse. In the previous example, the husband may withdraw to achieve his desired distance and the wife may push to achieve her desired closeness. A reciprocal, escalating pattern of interaction, which we call the "polarization process," may then ensue, in which each partner's attempts to solve the problem serve to make it worse. The more he withdraws, the more she pursues, and vice versa. This polarization process only serves to alienate the partners from each other, as they demand change and stake out their own positions. Finally, the "mutual trap" refers to the natural endpoint of the polarization process. It is the point at which the partners feel despairing, discouraged, and trapped.

In IBCT, the therapist focuses on identifying the theme, polarization process, and mutual trap during the assessment phase. In the feedback session, the therapist presents this information as a model of the couple's distress and invites the couple's response. It is important that the feedback session be a collaborative process between the therapist and the couple, not one in which the therapist hands out a prescription for the couple's problems. In addition, the therapist also presents an overview of therapy, which serves to transition the therapy from assessment to intervention.

## TBCT Interventions

### BEHAVIORAL EXCHANGE

TBCT therapists often begin the treatment phase of therapy with behavior exchange (BE). By the time that couples enter therapy, their relationships have ceased to be an enjoyable and rewarding aspect of their lives. Instead, they find their partners irritating and difficult to be around. Behavior exchange seeks to increase the positive behaviors in the relationship. For many couples, it quickly increases relationship satisfaction and provides momentum in the early phase of therapy.

Couples entering therapy are working very hard to change their relationship; however, almost all of the partners' efforts are aimed at changing the other person! Behavior exchange takes the opposite tactic. The fundamental principle underlying BE is that individuals are better (and more successful) at changing themselves than at changing their partners. The basic task in BE is for each partner to perform pleasing behaviors for each other, thereby increasing the overall positivity in the relationship. There are several different formats for conducting BE (Jacobson & Margolin, 1979), but all contain the same basic elements. The following description is the typical format used in our treatment outcome research (Christensen et al., 2003; Jacobson et al., 2000).

At the end of the feedback session, partners are given a homework assignment: both are asked to make a list of behaviors that they believe their partner would enjoy. They are asked to do this separately and not to share their lists. At the following therapy session, each list is read aloud, and the "receiving" partner has a chance to rate how pleasing each behavior would be. It is important that each partner generate his or her own list, as opposed to simply asking the partner, "What would you like me to do?" Sometimes, partners will feel cared for even through the simple act of hearing the lists of things that their partners have created. After the lists are read, the therapist works with the couple to ensure that each list contains items that would be truly pleasurable, avoiding any "off-target" items. As part of this process, the therapist may ask each partner to add pleasing behaviors to the list that the other person created. Finally, each partner is instructed to perform several of the items from his or her list in the upcoming week. Specific days are sometimes set aside for the positive behaviors, called caring days (Stuart, 1980). An important aspect of BE is that partners do not commit to performing specific behaviors, only that they will do one or more behaviors from the list. At the following therapy session, the therapist has each person describe his or her experience of both performing pleasing behaviors for the partner and also being the recipient of pleasing behaviors.

BE directly targets the problem of reinforcement erosion. It teaches couples to monitor their own behavior more closely and to evaluate the impact of their behavior on their partners. Moreover, BE provides a means for spouses to get feedback from one another on what they each enjoy and do not enjoy. At times, partners are very mistaken about what the other really likes! Finally, as we have noted, couples change, and the events and behaviors that used to be pleasing may no longer be so. BE can highlight this state of affairs and provide a framework for learning new behaviors.

## COMMUNICATION/PROBLEM-SOLVING TRAINING

Following BE, TBCT generally progresses to communication training, consisting of didactic teaching, practice, and reading. The communication/problem-solving training interventions deal with two of the most common presenting problems in couple therapy: difficulty in communicating and intractable problems that couples have been unable to solve on their own. In our research work, therapists use the Gottman, Notarius, Gonso, and Markman (1976) book as a guide to teaching communication skills.

One of the initial (and most difficult) skills

is the speaker/listener task. Couples are instructed that at any given time in their discussion, one partner is designated as the speaker and the other partner is designated as the listener. Speakers are encouraged to "level" with their feelings and edit overly negative comments (Gottman et al., 1976). They should be open and honest about their feelings and avoid overly critical statements. In addition, they should be specific, rather than global, in their concern and take responsibility for their concerns through the use of "I" statements (e.g., "I get irritated when you repeatedly ask me to take out the garbage"; as opposed to, "You always nag me."). Listeners are instructed to closely follow what their spouses are saying and to paraphrase what was said after the speakers finish. Finally, listeners verify with the speakers that the message they received is the message that was intended (for a thorough treatment of communication training, see Gottman et al., 1976).

In discussing difficult topics, partners often interrupt one another and dispute the claims of the other person. Communication training, with its emphasis on speaker and listener, provides needed structure so that partners can express their point of view and be assured that their spouses will hear them out. Couples are instructed to start using the skills with smaller, less conflictual problems, as it is extremely difficult to learn and practice communication skills with highly volatile topics. In the first few sessions of teaching the skills, the therapist acts as both coach and referee. As the partners learn the skills, they are encouraged to use the format for increasingly difficult problems.

Oftentimes, there is a natural progression with communication skills. Initially, the couple finds the new skills difficult and unnatural. Once these are learned, the couple can see the benefit of using the structured communication skills. However, there comes a point when partners may become frustrated that even after communicating effectively, they are still stuck at an impasse with a particular problem. Problem-solving training (PST) picks up where communication training ends. PST defines a clear set of procedures for addressing problems, emphasizing a collaborative approach. It should be noted, however, that the skills learned in communication training are also used throughout PST.

In addressing problems, couples are encouraged to see the ways in which each partner plays a role in the problem. Some partners are very resistant to the idea that they contribute to the problem, focusing entirely on how their partner is the cause of the problem. However, as much as possible, partners are encouraged to have a collaborative approach to problem solving. The first step in PST is arriving at a clear definition of the problem. Distressed couples often have a difficult time defining a single problem; their arguments move from one source of disagreement to another. Nonetheless, it is essential that both partners agree upon a clearly defined problem. Once the problem is defined, partners brainstorm a number of possible solutions, with the help of the therapist. Yet again, this can be very challenging for couples. They have seen the problem in a single light for so long that it can be excruciating for them to see it any other way. One strategy that can be effective in such a situation is for the therapist to suggest extreme (and often ridiculous) solutions to jar the partners free from their entrenched views.

After a number of possible solutions have been generated, they discuss the various options. The therapist serves as instructor and coach throughout the process, encouraging them to consider all the possibilities and to use their communication skills. Finally, when a single solution has been reached, the couple works out a "contract" specifying the exact terms of the agreement—who will do what, when, and for how long. The couple then implements its plan and debriefs its success or failure with the therapist at the following session. If the solution was not successful, the couple can then discuss and negotiate a better solution.

## IBCT Interventions

IBCT interventions are broken down into two broad classes, acceptance interventions and change interventions. The primary acceptance strategies include empathic joining and unified detachment; these interventions help the partners to discuss their problems in a nonjudgmental fashion. The goal of these acceptance interventions is to create intimacy between the partners, as they are able to experience and see their problems in a new way. The second class of IBCT acceptance interventions, called tolerance interventions, is unlikely to promote greater intimacy by itself. However, as the name suggests, tolerance interventions can promote tolerance of aversive behaviors. Tolerance interventions include positive aspects of negative behavior, practicing negative behavior in session, faking negative behavior at home, and self-care. These strategies tend to be used after the primary acceptance interventions. Change interventions are the interventions described previously under TBCT. However, they are typically only employed when acceptance interventions have not achieved the desired results. Also, they tend to be applied in a less structured fashion than in TBCT, and the therapist moves easily back and forth between acceptance and change interventions. Because we described change interventions earlier, we will describe only acceptance interventions in the following pages.

## Primary Acceptance Interventions

*Empathic Joining.* Couples in therapy are in a lot of pain. Yet they are so frustrated and angry that this pain is most often expressed through accusation and blame, which serves only to increase their distress. In empathic joining, the goal is to get past the anger and accusation to the original hurt. However, expressing the pain behind the accusation is a vulnerable thing to do, and typically, the last thing partners want to do in therapy is be vulnerable with one another.

The primary technique in empathic joining is for the therapist to help each partner express his or her strong emotions in ways that will lead to closeness and understanding through empathy. The formulation in the feedback session takes the first step toward empathic joining by reformulating the couple's problems in light of their theme. As an example, Mary and Jim were in therapy following a brief affair by Jim. Following the revelation of the affair, the theme that ran through many of their arguments was control versus trust. Mary felt like she needed to have complete control in the relationship, virtually dictating everything Jim could and could not do, whereas Jim was very remorseful of his affair and wanted her to begin to trust him again. During the course of therapy, the therapist reformulated Mary's controlling behavior, which was very aversive to Jim, as coming from her hurt and humiliation from the affair, as opposed to her desire to punish him or because of a "personality flaw" (e.g., "That's just the way she is!"). The goal of empathic joining is to give both partners a different emotional view of their problems; ideally, they will experience the problem through their partner's eyes.

Another useful approach in empathic joining is for the therapist to elicit the "soft" emotions underlying the "hard" emotions. As we noted, partners typically express their anger and frustration about problems. However, many times there is hurt or vulnerability at the root of the anger. Therapists may ask a partner directly whether there is an underlying, softer emotion, or they may suggest it (e.g., "If I were in your place, I might feel sad that your partner did what he did. Do you feel that way at all?"). An important aspect of a soft disclosure is that the primary "target" of the intervention is the partner *hearing* the soft disclosure and not necessarily the partner making the soft disclosure. Certainly, the intervention teaches partners to be vulnerable with one another, but a primary goal is that hearing the partner's pain will provide a radically different view of the problem to the other partner. When one partner sees and hears the other's sadness, it will cause the first partner to change his or her own perspective and behavior around the problem.

There is one final point to be made about "soft" and "hard" emotions. More often than not, couples in therapy express anger rather than hurt or express hurt in an angry way. Generally, a shift toward the expression of hurt without anger leads to a less adversarial, more constructive relationship. However, a different pattern may exist. For example, Aaron was threatening to leave Heidi. When he made his threats, Heidi would become very sad and cry, which served to infuriate Aaron and shut down any discussion of their problems. When the therapist helped Heidi to express some of her anger, Aaron experienced her not as pathetic but as strong. His view of her changed, and they were able to seriously discuss their relationship problems, as partners. Thus, although there are certainly common themes and patterns across couples, we never take behavior at face value; the function of the behavior always needs to be taken into account in fashioning interventions.

*Unified Detachment.* When couples arrive for therapy, there are typically several "lightning rod" topics. Often, partners are unable to discuss these issues because mere mention of the topics elicits extreme emotion. From a behavioral perspective, the topic has been repeatedly paired with an intense emotion, such that it is now classically conditioned. The mere presentation of the topic elicits the emotion

without any intervening thought or discussion. As therapists, we would like to interrupt this sequence so that the couple can once again discuss the topic. One avenue for this is unified detachment.

The goal of unified detachment is for the partners to get some distance from the problem so that they are able to discuss the problem in an intellectual, nonemotional manner. One strategy to seek unified detachment is to discuss the problem as something beyond the two partners, as a kind of "third party"; this intervention is sometimes called "treating the problem as an 'it.'" The therapist walks the couple through the sequence of events in a typical argument about the issue and may highlight when the problem "takes over." For example, the therapist might note, "So that's the point at which the problem gets the two of you. You go into this frustrating routine that neither of you feels able to stop." Another strategy is to name the couple's difficult interaction or the partners' roles in it. This also serves to highlight the problem as an "it," as opposed to a "you," and can also inject some humor. For example, a couple in a pattern of criticism and defensiveness might label themselves the "district attorney" and the "hostile witness," as a way of distancing themselves from the intense emotion involved in their pattern. In other strategies of unified detachment, the therapist engages the partners in an analytic effort to compare and contrast different incidents of their problematic interactions or to rate their responses in a particular problematic incident. All of the strategies help the partners to step back, get "out of the ring," and view their problems together with some intellectual detachment.

When unified detachment is successful, several changes take place. First, the couple's experience of the problem changes from one in which the partners feel swept away by the problem to one in which they see the problem coming and have choices about how to proceed. Second, the couple is able to discuss the issue in a less emotional manner. Whereas previously intense emotion was always intertwined with the problem, now the couple is able to discuss it in a rational fashion. Finally, sometimes the process of identifying the problem as a third party gives the partners enough distance that they are able to completely stop the negative sequence. They see it coming and say, "Wait. Here comes the problem to get us. Let's just side-step it."

### TOLERANCE INTERVENTIONS

As an adjunct to our primary acceptance strategies, we include tolerance interventions. IBCT therapists typically start off therapy with the primary acceptance interventions, but if those interventions do not prove effective, tolerance interventions are used. They can make difficult interactions less offensive, and when successful, they can provide an occasion for primary acceptance interventions.

*Positive Aspects of Negative Behavior.* The goal in this intervention is to highlight how issues and behaviors that the couple identifies as problems actually have certain positive characteristics. However, we need to raise a point of caution about this intervention. This is not a "silver lining" intervention, in which the therapist asserts, "There must be something positive in here." For many problems that couples face, nothing is positive about them, and therapists should use this intervention only when they truly feel there is a positive component to the problem.

Oftentimes, the qualities that initially attracted the partners to one another now are a source of annoyance. These types of problems can be effectively targeted with positive aspects of negative behaviors. In these cases, the therapist may remind the partners of the aspect of the behavior that was once a source of attraction. For instance, the therapist can point out how the partners are very different in a

certain way, and that this difference can be perceived in *both* a positive and a negative light. Whereas Kari once found Terence's spontaneity fun and exciting, she now sees him as irresponsible. When the therapist presented the "two sides" of Terence's behavior, Kari was able to recall that she valued this quality of Terence's when they first met and to admit that there were things about Terence's spontaneity that she continued to find enjoyable. It is important to keep in mind that tolerance interventions do not aim to create greater intimacy, though sometimes they can lead to that. The message is not that "Everything will be better" but that "This is the way things are, and there are some positive components to it."

We have also used this intervention with affair couples. After the initial turmoil of the discovery has passed, many couples in which there has been an affair want to "just move on" or get back to the relationship they had before the affair. We often note that they will never be the couple to whom the affair didn't happen. However, for couples who have made progress in therapy, we also may highlight the things they have learned about themselves and their relationship—the unanticipated, positive sequelae of a negative event. For instance, Beth and Mark worked very hard in therapy for a year after Mark disclosed his affair. Although it was painful for both to realize the ways in which they would never be able to recapture elements of their pre-affair relationship, both acknowledged the value of what they had learned in the past year. Beth acknowledged a deeper understanding of Mark's need for closeness and physical intimacy, which he often had difficulty expressing, and Mark acknowledged a more thorough understanding of Beth's strong professional ambitions and goals, which previously he had tended to minimize or ignore.

*Practicing Negative Behavior in Session.* Another tolerance intervention is to have the partners "practice" their negative behavior during a therapy session. This intervention is somewhat similar to paradoxical interventions used in strategic therapy, in which the partners are instructed to engage in precisely the behaviors that they want to stop. The two interventions are similar, in that sometimes couples find it difficult to be negative "on demand," though the intended effect is different. In IBCT, the primary purpose of practicing negative behavior in IBCT is to alter the context in which these negative behaviors occur and thus give the couples a different experience of the negative behaviors. This experience may desensitize couples to areas of significant distress; also, the exercise gives the therapist a firsthand experience of their problems. The therapist can intervene as needed if an argument escalates. In addition, this intervention affords an opportunity to move directly to empathic joining or unified detachment. If one or both members of the couple react emotionally to the negative behavior, then the therapist might use the occasion to promote empathic joining. If the couple reacts humorously to the enactment or is able to see it at a distance, then the therapist might use the occasion to foster unified detachment.

Emily would often criticize Jason, which would lead him to feel overwhelmed and not know how to respond. In these times, he would simply stare back at Emily, without saying anything. This would infuriate her all the more. The therapist asked the two of them to enact one of these interactions during session. Upon seeing their reenactment, the therapist was able to use empathic joining to expose the strong and vulnerable feelings that each experienced in these difficult interactions.

*Faking Negative Behavior at Home.* A similar tolerance strategy is to have the couple "fake" negative behavior at home. One partner is instructed to perform some negative behavior at home when he or she would *not* normally do so. It is crucial that this be done when the individual truly does not feel like engaging in the behavior. The person is instructed to "act out" the behavior for just a few minutes and then inform the partner that he or she was faking. Then, the two of them should debrief the experience together; specifically, the partner who faked the behavior can share with the partner what it was like to see that individual's reaction. The intervention is designed so that, ideally, the person faking the behavior is not emotionally involved in the interaction and thus should be able to observe the partner from a detached position.

The primary goal of the intervention is to interrupt the couple's negative interaction around the problematic issue, and this is accomplished in several ways. First, the instructions are given in front of both partners. As a result, the "receiving" partner knows that the other one will fake behavior at some point during the week and often will be wondering when this will happen. This alone can serve to interrupt the negative behavior in some instances. Similarly, the partner who is planning to fake the argument will tend to monitor his or her own behavior more closely. If an actual argument does occur, it will likely be less emotional and less damaging. As we noted in our description of unified detachment, couples often experience their problems as being out of control—once the volatile topic is breached, they are on a roller coaster not of their own choosing. Through interrupting the typical progression of the argument, faking negative behavior can lead to a greater experience of control in heated exchanges. Whereas previously, the couple felt helpless to stop the interactions and the emotions that went along with it, now couples are able to see the argument coming and choose to stop it or at least discuss the topic in a much less heated fashion.

*Self-Care.* Partners provide many physical and emotional needs for one another. With some couples, one person may be particularly demanding that he or she *needs* the partner to perform some specific behavior. When these demands stall therapy or do not seem amenable to other interventions, we sometimes work with the individual to get his or her needs met in ways that do not involve the partner. When these needs are met from a different source, therapy can move forward again.

For example, Charleen was a very extraverted person and felt that she and James should talk much more frequently than they did. This was very difficult for James, as he was quite introverted and felt uncomfortable with frequent demands for verbal expression. The therapist affirmed that the two of them had different personalities and that neither one was right or wrong to want more or less conversation. In addition, the therapist encouraged Charleen to talk with her friends and family, while working to make conversation between James and Charleen more comfortable. With other outlets for her need for conversation, Charleen made fewer demands on James. With less demands, James was able to engage in discussion more easily with Charleen.

## METHODS OF MODEL EVALUATION

As we noted earlier, the efficacy of BCT is no longer in question. Numerous clinical trials point to the ability of BCT to improve couples' relationship satisfaction over the course of therapy. However, the question of how the therapy effects this change is largely unanswered, as research on the process of change in BCT is still in its nascent phase. In this section, we briefly review the existing process literature and mention areas for further research.

A number of studies have looked at possible mediators of the treatment effect in BCT.

Whisman and Snyder (1997) define mediators in couple therapy as "those characteristics of the individual or couple that are changed by the treatment and which in turn produce change in outcome (e.g., relationship satisfaction)" (p. 683). A number of studies have shown that BCT changes couples' behavior, including relationship-related behaviors (Baucom & Mehlman, 1984; Halford et al., 1993; Jacobson, 1984; Snyder & Wills, 1989) and communication patterns (Baucom & Mehlman, 1984; Hahlweg, Revenstorf, & Schindler, 1984; Kelly & Halford, 1995; Snyder & Wills, 1989). Yet these changes in couple functioning have not, in turn, been shown to be related to relationship satisfaction in most instances. When changes in a mediator variable have been shown to be related to relationship satisfaction, the results have been difficult to interpret. For example, two studies have found an association between acquisition of positive communication skills and relationship satisfaction (Emmelkamp, van Linden, van den Heuvell, Sanderman, & Scholoing, 1988; Sayers, Baucom, Sher, Weiss, & Heyman, 1991), yet other studies have found negative relationships between communication and outcome (Baucom & Mehlman, 1984; Hahlweg et al., 1984)! Thus, at the present date, the literature on mediators of change in BCT remains ambiguous.

There is a single study that directly assessed the differences between TBCT and IBCT with respect to therapy process. Cordova, Jacobson, and Christensen (1998) examined the impact of TBCT and IBCT on couples' in-session behavior over the course of therapy. Six sessions (2 early, 2 middle, and 2 late) were rated, using a coding system developed to measure theoretically relevant couple behavior in 12 different couples. Cordova et al. found that couples who received IBCT showed greater expression of "soft" emotions at the end of therapy, relative to couples who had received TBCT. In addition, IBCT couples showed greater detachment in discussing their problems compared to TBCT couples. Finally, there was some modest evidence that increases in these couple behaviors were related to increases in relationship satisfaction. However, there is a possible confound in this study, in that the IBCT couples had greater overall gains in relationship satisfaction (Jacobson et al., 2001). It is possible that the differences in mediators between the two treatments reflect the difference in treatment gains, as opposed to different mechanisms of action.

There is a clear and pressing need for greater research on the process of change in BCT. As we understand how the therapy creates change, it will help us to know which aspects of the therapy are most crucial for that change. In addition, elucidating the process of change in BCT may help create more specific and effective goals in therapy for couples.

## IMPLEMENTATION OF THE MODEL IN COMMUNITY/PRACTICE SETTINGS

Another active area of research with BCT is testing its effectiveness in community settings. There is significant anecdotal evidence of the effectiveness of BCT from researchers and research therapists involved in clinical trials, who also use BCT in their private practices. However, we are not aware of any research studies that show that BCT can successfully be transported from the research lab to the community. Although there is no specific research on the effectiveness of BCT in community settings, there are several research studies relevant to this issue.

Fals-Stewart and Birchler (2002) conducted a study examining whether bachelor's-level counselors could be trained and could achieve similar results with BCT, as compared to master's-level counselors. The authors found that bachelor's-level counselors achieved simi-

lar ratings of treatment adherence to those of master's-level counselors but were rated lower in terms of competence in treatment delivery. However, couples seen by the two groups of counselors showed similar strong gains in relationship satisfaction. Although this was a research study with inclusion and exclusion criteria, the findings hold out optimism that the skills required to effectively deliver BCT can be learned by counselors with little formal training in psychotherapy.

Though not focusing specifically on BCT, we think it is worth briefly mentioning the single, significant study of marital therapy in community settings. Hahlweg and Klann (1997) examined the outcomes of couples receiving marital therapy in Germany. Therapy was in no way limited to BCT, and, in fact, only 17% of the therapists identified themselves as behavior therapists. The marital therapy outcomes achieved in this community-based sample were far below what is typically found in research studies. The overall effect size was small ($d = 0.28$), compared to that found for efficacy studies of marital therapy in general ($d = 0.60$; Shadish et al., 1993) and efficacy studies of BCT in particular ($d = 0.95$; Hahlweg & Markman, 1988). However, the Hahlweg and Klann study did not specifically look at BCT, and there are many alternative explanations for the small effects. Nonetheless, it is a discouraging finding regarding the effectiveness of marital therapy in the community.

One final obstacle to the effective dissemination of BCT to the community is the lack of research on diversity. It is true that BCT has been shown to be effective in several countries outside the United States, including Germany, Australia, and the Netherlands. However, these countries all share a similar Western worldview, and the research samples have been largely Caucasian. Thus far, there have been no studies specifically focusing on the efficacy of BCT with ethnic minorities, either within the United States or elsewhere. Like much clinical research, samples have been largely Caucasian and middle class. There is a pressing need for greater diversity in research samples.

## CONCLUSIONS

At this point in its evolution, BCT has arrayed an impressive body of research support, and basic questions regarding its efficacy to help distressed couples have been answered. Ongoing research explores extensions to the basic TBCT model, and IBCT is one post-TBCT therapy that has shown some promising initial results. Despite this impressive track record, there are still numerous pursuits for researchers and clinicians interested in the ongoing development of BCT. In particular, further research and study are needed to understand how the therapy achieves its results and whether BCT can be as effective in the community as it is in the lab. Furthermore, greater attention needs to be paid to the issue of diversity, particularly with respect to race and socioeconomic status.

## REFERENCES

Baucom, D. H., & Epstein, N. (1990). *Cognitive-behavioral marital therapy*. New York: Brunner/Mazel.

Baucom, D. H., & Lester, G. W. (1986). The usefulness of cognitive restructuring as an adjunct to behavioral marital therapy. *Behavior Therapy, 17*, 385–403.

Baucom, D. H., & Mehlman, S. K. (1984). Predicting marital status following behavioral marital therapy: A comparison of models of marital relationships. *Marital interaction: Analysis and modification* (pp. 89–104). New York: Guilford Press.

Baucom, D. H., Sayers, S., & Sher, T. (1990). Supplementing behavioral marital therapy with cognitive restructuring and emotional expressiveness training: An outcome investigation. *Journal of Consulting and Clinical Psychology, 58,* 636–645.

Baucom, D. H., Shoham, V., Mueser, K. T., Daiuto, A. D., & Stickle, T. R. (1998). Empirically supported couple and family interventions for marital distress and adult mental health problems. *Journal of Consulting and Clinical Psychology, 66,* 53–88.

Bograd, M., & Mederos, F. (1999). Battering and couples therapy: Universal screening and selection of treatment modality. *Journal of Marital and Family Therapy, 25,* 291–312.

Chambless, D. L., & Hollon, S. D. (1998). Defining empirically supported therapies. *Journal of Consulting and Clinical Psychology, 66,* 7–18.

Christensen, A., Atkins, D. C., Berns, S. B., Wheeler, J., Baucom, D. H., & Simpson, L. (2003). *Integrative versus traditional behavioral couple therapy for moderately and severely distressed married couples*. Manuscript submitted for publication.

Christensen, A., & Heavey, C. L. (1999). Interventions for couples. *Annual Review of Psychology, 50,* 165–190.

Christensen, A., & Jacobson, N. S. (1997). *Frequency and acceptability of partner behavior.* Unpublished questionnaire.

Christensen, A., & Jacobson, N. S. (2000). *Reconcilable differences.* New York: Guilford Press.

Chistensen, A., Jacobson, N., & Babcock, J. (1995). Integrative behavioral couple therapy. In N. S. Jacobson & A. S. Gurman (Eds.), *Clinical handbook of couple therapy.* New York: Guilford Press.

Cordova, J. V., Jacobson, N. S., & Christensen, A. (1998). Acceptance versus change interventions in behavioral couples therapy: Impact on couples' in-session communication. *Journal of Marital and Family Therapy, 24,* 437–455.

Emmelkamp, P. M., van Linden, van den Heuvell, C., Sanderman, R., & Scholoing, A. (1988). Cognitive marital therapy: The process of change. *Journal of Family Psychology, 1,* 385–389.

Epstein, N. B., & Baucom, D. H. (2002). *Enhanced cognitive-behavioral therapy for couples: A contextual approach.* Washington, DC: American Psychological Association.

Fals-Stewart, W., & Birchler, G. R. (2002). Behavioral couples therapy with alcoholic men and their intimate partners: The comparative effectiveness of bachelor's- and master's-level counselors. *Behavior Therapy, 33,* 123–147.

Glass, S. P. (2002). Extramarital relationships. In N. S. Jacobson & A. S. Gurman (Eds.), *Clinical handbook of couple therapy.* New York: Guilford Press.

Goldfried, M. R., & Davison, G. C. (1994). *Clinical behavior therapy.* New York: Wiley.

Gordon, K. C., & Baucom, D. H. (2000). A multitheoretical intervention for promoting recovery from extramarital affairs. *Clinical Psychology: Science and Practice, 6,* 382–399.

Gottman, J. M., & Levenson, R. W. (1999). What predicts change in marital interaction over time? A study of alternative medicine. *Family Process, 38,* 143–158.

Gottman, J. M., Notarius, C., Gonso, J., & Markman, H. (1976). *A couple's guide to communication.* Champaign, IL: Research Press.

Hahlweg, K., & Klann, N. (1997). The effectiveness of marital counseling in Germany: A contribution to health services research. *Journal of Family Psychology, 11,* 410–421.

Hahlweg, K., & Markman, H. J. (1988). Effectiveness of behavioral marital therapy: empirical status of behavioral techniques in preventing and alleviating marital distress. *Journal of Consulting and Clinical Psychology, 56,* 440–447.

Hahlweg, K., Revenstorf, D., & Schindler, L. (1984). Effects of behavioral marital therapy on couples' communication and problem-solving skills. *Journal of Consulting and Clinical Psychology, 52,* 553–566.

Halford, K., Sanders, M., & Behrens, B. (1993). A comparison of the generalization of behavioral marital therapy and enhanced behavioral marital therapy. *Journal of Consulting and Clinical Psychology, 61,* 51–60.

Halford, K., Sanders, M., & Behrens, B. (2001). Can skills training prevent relationship problems in at-risk couples? Four-year effects of a behavioral relationship education program. *Journal of Family Psychology, 15,* 750–768.

Holtzworth-Munroe, A., Meehan, J. C., Rehman, U., & Marshall, A. D. (2002). Intimate partner violence: An introduction for couple therapists. In N. S. Jacobson & A. S. Gurman (Eds.), *Clinical handbook of couple therapy.* New York: Guilford Press.

Jacobson, N. S. (1977). Problem solving and contingency contracting in the treatment of marital discord. *Journal of Consulting and Clinical Psychology, 45,* 92–100.

Jacobson, N. S. (1981). Behavioral marital therapy. In A. S. Gurman & D. P. Kniskern (Eds.), *Handbook of family therapy.* New York: Brunner/Mazel.

Jacobson, N. S. (1984). A component analysis of behavioral marital therapy: The relative effectiveness of behavior exchange and communication/problem-solving training. *Journal of Consulting and Clinical Psychology, 52,* 295–305.

Jacobson, N. S., & Christensen, A. (1996). *Integrative couple therapy: Promoting acceptance and change.* New York: Norton.

Jacobson, N. S., Christensen, A., Prince, S. E., Cordova, J., & Eldridge, K. (2000). Integrative behavioral couple therapy: An acceptance-based, promising new treatment for couple discord. *Journal of Consulting and Clinical Psychology, 68,* 351–355.

Jacobson, N. S., Follette, W. C., & Revenstorf, D. (1984). Psychotherapy outcome research: Methods for reporting variability and evaluating clinical significance. *Behavior Therapy, 15,* 336–352.

Jacobson, N. S., Follette, W. C., Revenstorf, D., Baucom, D. H., Hahlweg, K., & Margolin, G. (1984). Variability in outcome and clinical significance of behavioral marital therapy: A reanalysis of outcome data. *Journal of Consulting and Clinical Psychology, 52,* 497–504.

Jacobson, N. S., & Gottman, J. M. (1998). *When men batter women: New insights into ending abusive relationships.* New York: Simon & Schuster.

Jacobson, N. S., & Margolin, G. (1979). *Marital therapy: Strategies based on social-learning and behavior exchange principles.* New York: Brunner/Mazel.

Jacobson, N. S., Schmaling, K. B., & Holtzworth-Munroe, A. (1987). Component analysis of behavioral marital therapy: 2-year follow-up and prediction of relapse. *Journal of Marital and Family Therapy, 13,* 187–195.

Kelly, A. B., & Halford, W. K. (1995). The generalisation of cognitive behavioural marital therapy in behavioural, cognitive, and physiological domains. *Behavioural & Cognitive Psychotherapy, 23,* 381–398.

Kohlenberg, R. J., & Tsai, M. (1991). *Functional analytic psychotherapy: Creating intense and curative therapeutic relationships.* New York: Plenum Press.

Masters, J. C., Burish, T. G., Hollon, S. D., & Rimm, D. C. (1987). *Behavior therapy: Techniques and empirical findings* (3rd ed.). New York: Harcourt Brace.

O'Leary, K. D., Vivian, D., & Malone, J. (1992). Assessment of physical aggression against women in marriage: The need for multimodal assessment. *Behavioral Assessment, 14,* 5–14.

Patterson, G. R. (1982). *Coercive family process.* Eugene, OR: Castalia.

Patterson, G. R., Hops, H., & Weiss, R. L. (1973).

Interpersonal skills training for couples in early stages of conflict. *Journal of Marriage and Family, 37,* 295–303.

Sayers, S. L., Baucom, D. H., Sher, T. G., Weiss, R. L., & Heyman, R. E. (1991). Constructive engagement, behavioral marital therapy, and changes in marital satisfaction. *Behavioral Assessment, 13,* 25–49.

Shadish, W. R., Montgomery, L. M., Wilson, P., Wilson, M. R., Bright, I., & Okwumabua, T. (1993). Effects of family and marital psychotherapies: A meta-analysis. *Journal of Consulting and Clinical Psychology, 61,* 992–1002.

Skinner, B. F. (1966). An operant analysis of problem solving. In B. Kleinmuntz (Ed.), *Problem solving: Research method teaching* (pp. 225–257). New York: Wiley.

Skinner, B. F. (1974). *About behaviorism.* New York: Knopf.

Snyder, D. K. (1997). *Marital Satisfaction Inventory, Revised (MSI-R).* Los Angeles: Western Psychological Services.

Snyder, D. K., & Wills, R. M. (1989). Behavioral versus insight-oriented marital therapy: Effects on individual and interspousal functioning. *Journal of Consulting and Clinical Psychology, 57,* 39–46.

Snyder, D. K., Wills, R. M., & Grady-Fletcher, A. (1991). Long-term effectiveness of behavioral versus insight-oriented marital therapy: A 4-year follow-up study. *Journal of Consulting and Clinical Psychology, 59,* 138–141.

Spanier, G. B. (1976). Measuring dyadic adjustment: New scales for assessing the quality of marriage and similar dyads. *Journal of Marriage and the Family, 38,* 15–28.

Straus, M. A., Hamby, S. L., Boney-McCoy, S., & Sugarman, D. B. (1996). The Revised Conflict Tactics Scales: Development and preliminary psychometric data. *Journal of Family Issues, 17*(3), 283–316.

Stuart, R. B. (1969). Operant-interpersonal treatment for marital discord. *Journal of Consulting and Clinical Psychology, 33,* 675–682.

Stuart, R. B. (1980). *Helping couples change: A social-learning approach to marital therapy.* New York: Guilford Press.

Weiss, R. L., & Cerreto, M (1980). The marital status inventory: Development of a measure of dissolution potential. *The American Journal of Family Therapy, 8,* 80–86.

Weiss, R. L., Hops, H., & Patterson, G. R. (1973). A framework for conceptualizing marital conflict, a technology for altering it, some data for evaluating it. In L. A. Hamerlynck, L. C. Handy, E. J. Mash (Eds.), *Behavioral change: Methodology, concepts, and practice.* Champaign, IL: Research Press.

Whisman, M. A., & Snyder, D. K. (1997). Evaluating and improving the efficacy of conjoint couple therapy. In W. K. Halford and H. J. Markman (Eds.), *Clinical handbook of marriage and couples interventions* (pp. 679–693). New York: Wiley.

# CHAPTER 14

# Multisystemic Therapy

ASHLI J. SHEIDOW, PhD

SCOTT W. HENGGELER, PhD

SONJA K. SCHOENWALD, PhD

*Family Services Research Center*
*Department of Psychiatry and Behavioral Sciences*
*Medical University of South Carolina*

## INTRODUCTION

Multisystemic therapy is a family-based treatment with empirical support for effectively treating chronic behavior problems and serious emotional disturbances in adolescents. The multisystemic therapy treatment model also has research support for treating juvenile sex offending and child maltreatment. Utilizing an ecological conceptualization of youth problems, individualized assessment and treatment planning, and integration of evidence-based techniques, multisystemic therapy addresses risk and protective factors comprehensively, using strong quality-assurance mechanisms. This chapter presents the history and origins of multisystemic therapy, the theoretical and empirical bases of the treatment model, a summary of the clinical treatment model, and a synopsis of research outcomes.

## HISTORY AND ORIGINS

The clinical procedures that have come to define multisystemic therapy (MST) were first used by Scott Henggeler and a cadre of talented doctoral students in clinical psychology at Memphis State University (now the University of Memphis) in the late 1970s. Henggeler had obtained a modest amount of extramural funding to develop a treatment program for juvenile offenders, diverted from the juvenile justice system. The funding was used to pay the stipends of doctoral students who served as therapists, and graduate and undergraduate students were recruited as research assistants. In a quasi-experimental design, the project was conducted for several years, and the findings of the first MST outcome study were published in 1986 (Henggeler et al., 1986).

The designs of the early MST treatment protocols were based largely on the integration of state-of-the-art theory and intervention models that were being developed in the early 1970s—approaches to which Henggeler had gravitated while in graduate school at the University of Virginia. Particularly influential were works of Jay Haley, Salvador Minuchin, Gerald Patterson, and James Alexander. Haley and Minuchin had developed pragmatic family therapy approaches that were well suited to the types of problems experienced by juvenile offenders and their families. Patterson was developing and testing a potentially powerful intervention technology, based on social learning theory, that aimed to change the ways that parents interacted with young children presenting behavior problems. Alexander had recently published a well-designed randomized trial using functional family therapy, a blend of family systems and behavioral approaches, with juvenile status offenders (Alexander & Parsons, 1973). The emerging conceptual and methodological emphases of these pioneers, combined with the experimental rigor emphasized in the Psychology Department at the University of Virginia, provided much of the basis for the development and evaluations of MST.

In addition, however, the then robust field of community psychology had a major influence on the development of the MST model. Community psychology emphasizes the role that influences outside the individual play in the development of behavior. Although the aforementioned pioneers were expanding the field of child mental health services to focus on the broader family system, it was becoming clear that youth and family functioning is linked with many other environmental influences. It is important to remember that a portion of these could be modified to change problem behavior. For example, subsequent research demonstrated that association with deviant peers is the single most powerful predictor of antisocial behavior in adolescents. Similarly, researchers have demonstrated the significance of extrafamilial systems, such as the school, the family support network, and social service agencies, in the functioning of children and their families. Thus, MST expanded the intervention playing field to include other systems in which youths and their families are embedded. Such expansion was highly consistent with social ecological conceptualizations of behavior articulated by Urie Bronfenbrenner in 1979.

Several former doctoral students at Memphis State University were also influential in the refinement and validation of MST, but the most significant contributions were made by Molly Brunk, now a senior MST consultant, and Charles Borduin, now at the University of Missouri. Brunk directed one of the first randomized trials in the field of child maltreatment (Brunk, Henggeler, & Whelan, 1987), and this work is the basis of a larger National Institute of Mental Health (NIMH) funded trial with maltreating families currently being conducted by Cynthia Swenson. Upon taking a faculty position at the University of Missouri in 1982, Borduin began and has continued the longest continuous research project on MST. In 1990, he collaborated with Henggeler in the first extensive clinical specification of MST (Henggeler & Borduin, 1990), and that same year he published the first randomized trial in the field of juvenile sexual offending (Borduin, Henggeler, Blaske, & Stein, 1990). Subsequently, Borduin published a highly influential outcome study of MST with chronic juvenile offenders that included a 4-year follow-up (Borduin et al., 1995), and his many contributions to the development and validation of the model have continued. For example, Henggeler and Borduin are currently collaborating on a National Institute of Mental Health (NIMH) funded randomized trial of MST with adolescent sex offenders, conducted in a large urban setting.

As discussed later in this chapter, the findings from these early MST outcome studies were very promising. Nevertheless, significant funding for MST research was not forthcoming during the 1980s, in spite of considerable effort to procure such. It was not until the end of that decade that, with the support of Gary Melton (now at Clemson University, then at the University of Nebraska) and the South Carolina Department of Mental Health, significant research funding for MST was obtained from the National Institutes of Health (NIH). Their collaboration with Henggeler produced two influential MST randomized trials with violent juvenile offenders (Henggeler, Melton, Brondino, Scherer, & Hanley, 1997; Henggeler, Melton, & Smith, 1992) that in combination with earlier work, clearly demonstrated the potential viability of the model.

In 1992 Henggeler moved to the Medical University of South Carolina (MUSC), where, in the Department of Psychiatry and Behavioral Sciences, he founded the Family Services Research Center (FSRC). Since then, investigators in the FSRC have been awarded more than $25,000,000 in research support, the vast majority from NIH (NIMH, National Institute on Drug Abuse, National Institute on Alcohol Abuse and Alcoholism). The FSRC currently includes 10 full-time faculty members and approximately 30 staff members who have the explicit mission of improving the nation's mental health and substance-abuse services by developing, validating, and studying the transport of clinically effective and cost-effective services for youths presenting serious clinical problems and their families.

In the mid-1990s, as evidence of MST effectiveness became more widely known, stakeholders in communities across the nation began to request the development of MST programs. Initially, FSRC faculty, following training and quality assurance protocols used in MST clinical trials, provided program development and ongoing support to new and distal MST sites. This arrangement, however, resulted in decreased research productivity for the faculty and less than optimal consultation services for the distal MST sites. Under the leadership of Sonja Schoenwald, associate director of the FSRC, quality assurance protocols were specified to support the development of high quality MST programs in other states. Equally as important, in consultation with university officials, a new organization, MST Services, was formed in 1996 with the mission of supporting the effective transport and dissemination of MST programs for serious juvenile offenders. MST Services has the exclusive license through MUSC for the transport of MST technology and intellectual property. As of August 2002, this organization provides ongoing support and technical assistance to licensed MST programs in 27 states and 7 nations. Moreover, consistent with the mission of the FSRC and also under the leadership of Schoenwald, considerable research resources are being devoted to determining the conditions needed for the effective transport of evidence-based practices to community settings.

## THEORETICAL AND RESEARCH-BASED CONSTRUCTS

The MST theoretical model was based largely on general systems theory (von Bertalanffy, 1968), which had a major influence on the field of family therapy; and Bronfenbrenner's (1979) theory of social ecology, which has become the preeminent model of behavioral development. Major tenets in these models have been supported by considerable research on the etiology of behavior problems and have lent themselves to the development of corresponding intervention strategies.

*Theoretical Bases of MST*

Briefly, general systems theory (von Bertalanffy, 1968) prescribes a circular causality conceptualization of a phenomenon. Systems theorists view phenomena as interrelated (e.g., parental monitoring affects youth behavior, but youth behavior could, in turn, affect monitoring), contrasting with reductionist thinking, in which phenomena are viewed as occurring in a linear fashion (e.g., poor parental monitoring directly results in youth antisocial behavior). Furthermore, systems theorists would regard youth behavior as being part of a larger system of interrelated phenomena, such as other family, peer, and community relationships. Thus, rather than being a direct result of a single phenomenon, adolescent mental health and behavior problems may be both a result of and a contributing factor to many systemic factors, such as low parental control, reduced family cohesion, or marital conflict.

The social ecological theory of Bronfenbrenner (1979) also conceptualizes human behavior within a contextual framework. Unlike most systems theorists in the area of human behavior, social ecological theorists emphasize systems beyond the family context. Specifically, Bronfenbrenner describes a set of concentric circles in which the individual's behavior is the innermost circle, and outer circles represent contexts such as the family, peer, school, community, and culture in which the individual is embedded. Like systems theorists, ecological theorists also hypothesize dynamic relationships, with contexts having reciprocal effects upon one another. For example, youth behavior would be perceived by the social ecological theorist as simultaneously being affected by, and having an effect upon, a wide variety of characteristics within the individual context (e.g., biological factors, cognitive deficits), family context (e.g., marital discord, parenting practices), peer context (e.g., antisocial peers, poor socialization skills),

neighborhood context (e.g., few prosocial activities, criminal activity), and so forth.

*Empirical Bases of MST*

Much research during the past few decades has focused on understanding the correlates and causes of adolescent problems. Such research has identified individual level factors that contribute to youth problems, such as biological processes (e.g., adrenal hormones, serotonin levels, teratogenic effects) and cognitive functioning (e.g., social information processing, problem solving, verbal ability). However, this research has consistently demonstrated that youth problems are not determined solely by individual characteristics, but has found extensive support for multidetermined conceptualizations of adolescent problems. Indeed, several recent reviews have summarized the associations found between youth problems and individual, family, peer, school, and community constructs (e.g., Hann & Borek, 2001; Hawkins et al., 1998; Lipsey & Derzon, 1998; Reid, Patterson, & Snyder, 2002).

Family factors that contribute to the development of youth problems include both caregiver characteristics, such as drug use, maternal age, and caregiver psychopathology, as well as family-level characteristics, such as deficient conflict management, poor monitoring, and ineffective discipline. Because such factors can be directly addressed within the family unit, they are frequently the main focus for change among family-based treatments. However, factors that have been found to be more proximal determinants of youth behavior problems are seen at the school and peer level. Peer influences include association with deviant peers, lack of association with prosocial peers, and poor socialization skills, whereas school-related predictors of adolescent problems include low academic achievement, dropout, and low commitment to education. Finally, community constructs, such as violence exposure, neighborhood criminal activity, neighborhood supports, and mobility, have been predictive of youth problems.

Thus, developmental research has significantly elucidated correlates and causes of adolescent mental health problems, and these problems clearly are multidetermined. It is important to note that these research findings are consistent with both general systems theory (von Bertalanffy, 1968) and social ecological theory (Bronfenbrenner, 1979). Moreover, the ecological, systemic focus of the MST treatment approach based on these theories and on research has been supported by clinical research. Huey, Henggeler, Brondino, and Pickrel (2000) used data from two separate randomized trials (Henggeler et al., 1997; Henggeler, Pickrel, & Brondino, 1999) to demonstrate the mediation of treatment outcomes by family functioning and peer-relationship variables. Results showed that observed MST treatment effects on antisocial behavior were mediated by improved family cohesion and monitoring and by decreased affiliation with deviant peers. In another investigation using MST to treat delinquent adolescents, improvements in youth symptomatology were related to improvement in the marital relationship (Mann, Borduin, Henggeler, & Blaske, 1990). Thus, the theoretical underpinnings of the MST theory of change are consistent with the observed data.

## OUTCOMES FROM CLINICAL TRIALS

MST is widely regarded as one of the best validated mental health and substance-abuse interventions in the field. For example, federal entities such as the Surgeon General (U.S. Public Health Service, 1999, 2001), National Institute on Drug Abuse (1999), and Center for Substance Abuse Prevention (2001), as well as leading reviewers (e.g., Burns, Hoagwood, & Mrazek, 1999; Elliott, 1998; Farrington & Welsh, 1999; Kazdin & Weisz, 1998; Mihalic, Irwin, Elliott, Fagan, & Hansen, 2001; Stanton & Shadish, 1997) have identified MST as demonstrating effectiveness or showing considerable promise in the treatment of youth criminal behavior, substance abuse, and emotional disturbance. These conclusions are based on the findings from eight published outcome studies (seven randomized, one quasi-experimental) with youths presenting serious clinical problems and their families. This section summarizes the results from these trials, as well as current MST outcome research.

### Youth Violence and Criminal Behavior

As noted previously, in the first MST outcome study, Henggeler et al. (1986) used a quasi-experimental design (i.e., MST youths were matched with control youths on key characteristics) to evaluate the short-term effectiveness of MST with juvenile offenders. MST was more effective than usual diversion services at improving both self-reported and observed family relations, as well as decreasing youth behavior problems and youth association with deviant peers.

These favorable findings led to three randomized trials of MST with chronic and violent juvenile offenders that were published in the 1990s. Henggeler, Melton, and Smith (1992) evaluated the capacity of MST to serve as an effective community-based alternative to incarceration for a sample ($N = 84$) of serious juvenile offenders. MST services were delivered by real-world clinicians (not gradate students) working in a community-based setting. At post-treatment, MST was more effective than usual juvenile justice services at improving family relations and peer relations. It is important to note that MST reduced recidivism by 43% and out-of-home placement by 64% at the 59-week follow-up. Moreover, a 2.4-year follow-up (Henggeler, Melton, Smith, Schoenwald, & Hanley, 1993) showed that MST doubled the survival rate (i.e., the percentage of youths not rearrested) of these serious offenders. Similarly, in a randomized trial that included 176 chronic juvenile offenders, Borduin and colleagues (Borduin et al., 1995) demonstrated improved family functioning and decreased psychiatric symptomatology at post-treatment and a 69% decrease in recidivism at a 4-year follow-up, compared to those in individual counseling. Borduin is currently preparing a manuscript describing favorable outcomes from a 10-year follow-up with this sample. Finally, in a randomized trial of MST with 155 violent and chronic juvenile offenders conducted at two community sites, Henggeler, Melton, Brondino, Scherer, and Hanley (1997) found that MST was more effective than usual juvenile justice services at decreasing youth psychiatric symptomatology at post-treatment and produced a 50% reduction in incarceration at a 1.7-year follow-up. Although recidivism was reduced by only 26%, analyses showed significant associations between therapist adherence to MST treatment principles, which was allowed to vary considerably by design, and long-term outcomes.

Together, findings from these studies demonstrated the capacity of MST to change key determinants of antisocial behavior (e.g., family relations, peer relations) and to produce significant reductions in rearrest and out-of-home placement for youths presenting very serious antisocial behavior. Such success has led the Washington State Institute for Public Policy (Aos, Phipps, Barnoski, & Lieb, 2001) to conclude that the average net economic gain for MST was more than $130,000 per youth served in reduced placement costs, criminal justice costs, and crime victim benefits.

*Alcohol and Drug Abuse*

Henggeler et al. (1991) summarized alcohol and drug-related finding based on data from Henggeler et al. (1992) and Borduin et al. (1995). The former study showed MST treatment effects at post-treatment for self-report alcohol and drug use, whereas the latter found MST effects for alcohol and drug-related rearrests at 3 years post-treatment. These favorable outcomes served as the foundation of a randomized trial of MST versus usual community services in the treatment of 118 juvenile offenders meeting diagnostic criteria for substance abuse or dependence (Henggeler, Pickrel, et al., 1999). Findings showed decreased drug use at post-treatment, a 50% reduction in days in out-of-home placement at 1-year follow-up, and a 26% reduction in recidivism (statistically nonsignificant) at 1-year follow-up. Pertaining to this same study, the incremental cost of MST was offset by the reduced placement of youths in the MST condition (Schoenwald, Ward, Henggeler, Pickrel, & Patel, 1996), and MST increased attendance in regular school settings at 6-month follow-up (Brown, Henggeler, Schoenwald, Brondino, & Pickrel, 1999). It is important to note that 4-year follow-up data (Henggeler, Clingempeel, Brondino, & Pickrel, 2002) showed that MST significantly reduced violent criminal activity and increased drug use abstinence.

*Serious Emotional Disturbance*

With the success of MST in treating serious antisocial behavior in adolescents, research was funded in the mid-1990s to adapt the MST model to treat youths with serious emotional disturbance (Henggeler, Schoenwald, Rowland, & Cunningham, 2002). In a randomized trial, MST was evaluated as an alternative to emergency psychiatric hospitalization in a sample of 156 youths in psychiatric crisis because they were suicidal, homicidal, or psychotic. If at all possible, youths in the MST condition were stabilized outside the hospital, and a full course of MST was subsequently provided. Youths in the comparison condition were admitted to a child psychiatry inpatient unit and provided with community services following release. Analysis of short-term outcomes (Henggeler, Rowland, et al., 1999) showed that MST was more effective than hospitalization at improving family relations, increasing school attendance, decreasing externalizing problems, and improving consumer satisfaction. In addition, at 4 months post-referral, MST produced a 75% reduction in days hospitalized and a 50% reduction in days in other out-of-home placements (Schoenwald, Ward, Henggeler, & Rowland, 2000). Analyses of outcomes through 2.5 years post-referral are currently in progress.

## Juvenile Sex Offending

To date, the only published randomized trial in the field of juvenile sexual offender treatment was an MST study directed by Borduin (1990). Although the sample was small ($N = 16$), MST demonstrated significantly lower recidivism for both sexual offending, and criminal offending in comparison with individual counseling.

## Child Maltreatment

As noted earlier in this chapter, Brunk et al. (1987) conducted one of the first randomized trials that focused on maltreating families ($N = 33$). Based on observational family interaction measures, MST was more effective than behavioral parent training at improving aspects of parent–child interactions that have been associated with child abuse.

## Replications and Extensions

The strongest evidence for MST effectiveness has been developed for youths presenting serious antisocial behavior, such as criminal activity, violence, and substance abuse. As such, MST programs for treating such behavior are being developed and transported through MST Services. MST programs focusing on serious emotional disturbance, sex offending, and child maltreatment, however, will not be ready for transport until sufficient refinement of intervention protocols and replication of results have been achieved. Considerable research is focusing on this refinement and replication.

### YOUTH VIOLENCE AND CRIMINAL BEHAVIOR

Several large randomized trials are being conducted in practice settings in the United States, Canada, and Norway. Findings from these trials will provide important information regarding the challenges and successes of the strategies used to transport MST programs to real-world settings.

### ALCOHOL AND DRUG ABUSE

Henggeler is directing a large randomized trial with substance-abusing juvenile offenders in Charleston, South Carolina. This study is examining the effectiveness of integrating evidence-based treatment into juvenile drug court (Randall, Henggeler, Cunningham, Rowland, & Swenson, 2001). In addition, procedures are being evaluated that aim to enhance the effectiveness of MST with this population.

### SERIOUS EMOTIONAL DISTURBANCE

A small randomized trial directed by Rowland has recently been completed for youths with serious emotional disturbance in Hawaii, and the results of this study are under review. In addition, Schoenwald is currently directing a randomized trial of juvenile offenders with serious emotional disturbance in Philadelphia.

### JUVENILE SEX OFFENDING

Borduin has recently completed a second and larger randomized trial with juvenile sexual offenders. Manuscripts describing these findings are being prepared for publication. In addition, Henggeler, Letourneau, and Borduin have recently been funded to conduct a large randomized trial of MST with juvenile sex offenders in Chicago.

### CHILD MALTREATMENT

Cynthia Swenson is conducting a major randomized trial of MST with families in Charleston, South Carolina, that have physically abused their children.

*Extensions to New Populations*

Investigators at several universities are currently conducting randomized trials that aim to extend key aspects of MST (e.g., commitment to overcome barriers to service access, strong quality assurance, use of evidence-based intervention techniques, view that caregivers are the key to achieving outcomes) to new clinical populations. Michael Epstein, at the University of Nebraska, is adapting MST for young children with serious behavior problems. Deborah Ellis and her colleagues (Ellis, Narr-King, Frey, Rowland, & Greger, in press) at Wayne State University are studying the adaptation of MST to treat inner-city adolescents with Type I diabetes who are under poor metabolic control. Bahr Weiss, at Vanderbilt

University, is examining the use of MST for children in classrooms for the emotionally disturbed. Each of these studies is being supported by faculty members at the FSRC who are assisting in clinical adaptations and helping to assure treatment fidelity.

*Research-Based Treatment Protocol*

MST clinical procedures for adolescent antisocial behavior are described in a clinical volume (Henggeler, Schoenwald, Borduin, Rowland, & Cunningham, 1998), and a recent volume describes MST adaptations for treating youth with serious emotional disturbance and their families (Henggeler, Schoenwald, Rowland, et al., 2002). Furthermore, the MST supervision protocol has been manualized (Henggeler & Schoenwald, 1998). The MST manuals delineate the process by which youth and family problems are prioritized and targeted for change. Guided by ecological and systems theory, the assessment process and specific interventions focus on the individual, family, peer, school, and social network variables that are linked with identified problems, as well as on the interface of these systems. Clinical procedures are briefly outlined here.

*Treatment Provision*

MST employs a home-based model of service delivery that aims to decrease barriers to service access and increase engagement in treatment (e.g., Henggeler, Pickrel, Brondino, & Crouch, 1996). MST is provided by full-time master's-level therapists who carry caseloads of four to six families. Three to four therapists work within a team, supervised by an advanced master's-level or doctoral-level supervisor, to provide 24-hour/7 day-a-week availability so that therapists can react quickly to crises that may threaten goal attainment (i.e., prevent out-of-home placement). Services are provided in the natural ecology of the family (i.e., in their home, school, and community) and at a time that is convenient for the families. Services are time-limited, typically lasting 4 to 6 months.

## Treatment Engagement

MST is particularly effective at engaging and retaining families in treatment. For example, in two recent trials of MST (Henggeler et al., 1996; Henggeler, Rowland, et al., 1999), 98% of the youths and the families randomly assigned to the MST conditions completed treatment. The success of MST in minimizing dropout is most likely due to the comprehensive use of multiple strategies that have been linked with treatment retention by previous investigators (McKay, 2000; Stark, 1992). These strategies include: (1) The philosophy that the most effective and ethical route to helping youths is through helping their families. MST therapists identify caregivers as valuable resources, even when caregivers have serious and multiple needs. (2) Services are individualized and strength-focused, and the family and the MST therapist set goals collaboratively. This promotes therapeutic alliance and buy-in and increases the relevance of treatment to the family. (3) Weekly supervision by an MST expert reduces therapist drift from MST principles, as do additional quality assurance mechanisms (e.g., monthly reports from families on treatment adherence; see the succeeding section). (4) The MST therapist and the supervisor assume responsibility for treatment engagement and outcome, and considerable resources are devoted to achieving these goals.

## Treatment Goals

The fundamental goal of MST is to empower families to effectively resolve and manage the serious clinical problems presented by their youths, as well as the potential problems that are likely to occur during the youths' adolescence. Thus, therapists aim to help youths and their families develop the capacity to cope with problems that have a multisystemic set of causal and sustaining factors, utilizing resources within the families' ecologies to develop this capacity.

At the family level, therapists often aim to reduce conflict and ineffective communication patterns, while improving cohesion, discipline, and monitoring. Furthermore, treatment may target parental or marital functioning, if it is identified as a contributor to youth problems. Regardless of the specific goal, caregivers are seen as the key to treatment generalization and maintenance. However, caregivers often need significant resources and support from their ecologies to achieve desired goals. For instance, the caregiver might engage other trustworthy adults (e.g., neighbors, relatives, teachers, etc.) throughout the youth's ecology to assist in providing adequate monitoring of the youth while the caregiver is at work.

Given the proximal nature of peer associations to problem behavior, MST therapists also typically target peer-level factors, such as association with deviant peers, lack of association with prosocial peers, and poor socialization skills. However, because MST therapists view caregivers as the key to reaching treatment goals, much attention is focused on improving caregivers' ability to manage youths' ecologies without continued therapist intervention. For example, an aim of treatment might be to devise a system for a parent to use for rewarding engagement in prosocial activities (e.g., providing transportation, attending performances, increasing privileges) and discouraging negative peer associations (e.g., monitoring peer activities, limiting activities, removing privileges).

Similarly, MST aims to empower caregivers to intervene on their youths' behalf within the school setting. The parents of youths with severe problems often have a history of negative interactions with school personnel, making the first goal within this aim to improve the communication between caregivers and school personnel. This foundation of positive communication is then used to empower caregivers in collaborating with school personnel on specific interventions aimed to improve their youths' problems. Besides fostering effective communication between parents and school personnel, specific targets for intervention within the school setting also might include implementing a behavioral monitoring plan, connecting in-school behavior with consequences at home, reducing in-school interactions with negative peers, or assessing for possible learning disabilities.

*Integration of Evidence-Based Interventions*

MST provides a comprehensive framework that can efficiently integrate specific interventions into a unified, methodical strategy. Interventions are integrated on an as-needed basis and selected interventions are typically pragmatic and problem-focused. MST clinicians and supervisors also rely heavily on the empirical literature when deciding what approach to integrate into treatment. Family-based interventions often incorporated into assessment and treatment include the structural (Minuchin, 1974) and strategic (Haley, 1987) models of family therapy. Behavioral techniques and cognitive behavioral interventions are also frequently employed when indicated. In addition, psychopharmacological treatment is integrated when such treatment

has empirical support for treating an identified problem.

*Treatment Principles*

Because each youth and each family have very different needs and strengths, treatment should utilize the strengths while addressing the needs of each family. Rather than providing a rigid manualized plan for treatment, the MST manual provides a framework in which treatment occurs. Specifically, MST interventions should follow a set of nine core principles that guide all assessment practices and the integration of evidence-based interventions within the MST framework (Henggeler, Schoenwald, et al., 1998). These nine principles are used to design interventions to meet the goals of treatment:

1. **Finding the Fit.** The primary purpose of assessment is to understand the "fit" between the identified problems and their broader systemic context. Utilizing what we know about the correlates and causes of youth problems, MST providers conceptualize youth and family symptoms from an ecological, systemic perspective. Thus, clinicians investigate and target for treatment "fit factors," or characteristics of the youth's ecology that are maintaining the problem behavior. The implementation of this principle within assessment is described further in the succeeding section. Notably, the assessment process is dynamic throughout treatment, with regular monitoring of progress and updating of newly identified or appropriately resolved fit factors.

2. **Positive and Strength-Focused.** Therapeutic contacts emphasize the positive and use systemic strengths as levers for change. Clinicians maintain an optimistic perspective that is clearly communicated to the

family throughout the assessment and treatment process. This optimism is overtly supported through supervision and peer consultation. Providers look for potential strengths within the various ecological contexts, investigating child factors (e.g., competencies, attractiveness, altruism), caregiver factors (e.g., resources, affective bonds, social support), peer factors (e.g., competencies, prosocial activities), school factors (e.g., management practices, concern, prosocial activities), and neighborhood or community factors (e.g., law enforcement, business involvement, health care, neighbor concern). Identified strengths are then utilized in interventions. For instance, if low monitoring during afterschool hours is contributing to the adolescent's involvement in antisocial behavior, then monitoring may be partially addressed by empowering the caregiver to engage the youth in organized prosocial activities available at the school or in the community. It is important to note that clinicians be trained to incorporate this strength-based approach throughout their work. For instance, supervisors assist clinicians in identifying "barriers" to treatment success, rather than perceiving clients as being resistant to change.

3. **Increasing Responsibility.** Interventions are designed to promote responsible behavior and decrease irresponsible behavior among family members. Providers view parents as a primary lever for change. Rather than providing individual treatment for the youth, providers empower caregivers to bring about changes in the youth's behavior and within the youth's ecology. For example, caregivers may be instructed in basic behavioral techniques such as spelling out rules and contingencies and appropriately enforcing the contingency plan. Furthermore, youths are di-

rected to take responsibility for their behavior through this process by having input into the contingency plan.

4. **Present-Focused, Action-Oriented, and Well-Defined.** Interventions are present-focused and action-oriented, targeting specific and well-defined problems. This principle is closely tied with assessment, in that treatment goals are determined through a collaborative effort among the provider, caregivers, youth, and other key players in the youth's ecology (e.g., teacher, probation officer). These clearly stated goals are then translated into an explicit treatment plan, in which the MST treatment team integrates pragmatic, ecologically minded interventions. This plan is closely monitored to ensure that treatment is making quantifiable progress in improving identified problems. As a result, treatment is highly focused and geared toward swift improvement in and resolution of symptoms.

5. **Targeting Sequences.** Interventions target sequences of behavior within or between multiple systems that maintain the identified problems. This principle is also closely tied to assessment, in that identified problems are conceptualized from a social ecological perspective, and this conceptualization guides treatment decisions. For example, an identified problem behavior within the school may be maintained, in part, because the behavior is not being consequented in a timely and systematic manner at home. If the clinician discovers that this lack of consequenting is due to a pattern of hostile or derogatory interactions between the caregiver and the school that has reduced the effectiveness of communication, the clinician might aim to alter communication between the caregiver and the school as a means of improving behavioral contingencies and resultant youth behavior.

6. **Developmentally Appropriate.** Interventions are developmentally appropriate and fit the developmental needs of the youth. MST individualizes treatment to the developmental stage of a youth and a family. For instance, cognitive interventions may be more suited to an older adolescent who has the ability to monitor and process cognitions, rather than to a preteen who may not have the capacity for such tasks. Another example of tailoring treatment to the developmental needs of the youth is in peer interventions. An adolescent has increased need for independence and autonomy from the family and should be allowed and encouraged to maintain peer relationships. However, this peer interaction should be monitored and directed by caregivers to prevent interaction with negative peers and to promote interaction with prosocial peers.

7. **Continuous Effort.** Interventions are designed to require daily or weekly effort by family members. After adequately engaging families, MST clinicians provide treatment in a manner that is meant to bring about rapid change. Because clinicians collaborate with the caregivers, the youth, and other key players in the youth's ecology to identify and define treatment goals, these participants are expected, and supported, to share the responsibility in achieving these goals. This participation must be intensive (i.e., daily or weekly) to bring about rapid and acute change in youth problems, with families learning that they are the "change agents" (i.e., they become empowered to bring about change).

8. **Evaluation and Accountability.** Intervention effectiveness is evaluated continuously from multiple perspectives, with providers assuming accountability for overcoming barriers to successful outcomes. As mentioned earlier, assessment within MST is a dynamic process that circularly in-

forms treatment. Because goals are well-defined, measurable outcomes can be monitored. As detailed in the succeeding section, the supervisory process works to provide frequent checks of treatment progress, as well as to assist clinicians in identifying and targeting barriers to treatment success. MST clinicians are trained to hold themselves accountable for treatment progress, rather than deeming a family or a youth at fault for a lack of success. Clinicians are taught to "never give up" on a youth or a family, but instead to identify the barriers to success and to develop means to overcome those barriers.

9. **Generalization.** Interventions are designed to promote treatment generalization and long-term maintenance of therapeutic change by empowering caregivers to address family members' needs across multiple systemic contexts. Caregivers are viewed as the key to maintaining treatment successes, and much effort is spent helping caregivers to develop the skills necessary for continuing the progress made during treatment. For example, caregiver interaction with the school system may be targeted for a specific problem, but general communication skills are developed so that the caregiver can continue to have effective interactions as the youth progresses to other classrooms or schools. Within the family system, behavioral techniques are practiced for a variety of circumstances so that the parent is competent to employ them without the guidance of the clinician. Likewise, a caregiver may be instructed on the use of simple cognitive-behavioral or problem-solving techniques so that he or she may help guide the youth through such exercises without the presence of the clinician. Thus, the interventions that occur within MST are integrated in a way that will support long-term maintenance of treatment progress.

## METHODS OF MODEL EVALUATION

The purpose of treatment model evaluation should be twofold. First, efforts to ensure client outcomes require careful initial evaluation to clearly identify and specify goals of treatment, as well as continuous monitoring throughout treatment. Second, adherence to the treatment model should be monitored to ensure integrity of treatment. This section highlights the analytical procedure used within MST to assess client outcomes, as well as the system for assessing and maintaining treatment integrity.

### Assessment Procedures

As previously stated, the role of assessment within MST is to identify "fit factors," or characteristics of the youth's ecology that are maintaining the problem behavior, so that they may be targeted for change. MST therapists begin by identifying all key players in a youth's ecology and setting treatment goals based on the needs and desired outcomes of the youth and these key players (after achieving suitable alignment and engagement, that is). Goals are always set in very specific, well-defined, and directly measurable terms (e.g., elimination of physical aggression at school, as evidenced by no more fighting at school as reported by teachers). Once these "overarching goals" are set, MST therapists work to identify the ecological-fit factors that directly contribute to (i.e., directly cause or actively sustain) the targeted behavior. Through consultation and supervision, these factors are prioritized and targeted for treatment, with more proximal and powerful factors receiving higher priority.

The conceptualization of the "fit" begins the continuously evolving portion of the assessment process of MST (see Figure 14.1), informally called the "Do Loop." Short-term "in-termediary goals" are developed to focus on treatment of prioritized fit factors, and specific interventions are selected to achieve these intermediary goals. The outcome of an intervention is assessed through weekly supervision, with the treatment team identifying factors that contributed to or barriers that prevented the success of the intervention. Barriers to success may include such factors as inadequate engagement, flawed conceptualization of fit factors for a problem, inappropriate intermediary goals, or ineffective application of intervention strategies. The treatment plan is then revised to build on that success in planning interventions for succeeding intermediary goals or to develop strategies for overcoming barriers to successful intervention. Regardless of the barriers identified, the treatment team takes responsibility for achieving the goals of treatment, constantly striving for ways to overcome barriers to successful intervention.

### Quality Assurance System

As is standard in clinical research trials, initial MST outcome studies maintained tight control over clinical implementation. As trials began to expand to multiple sites and as the MST treatment protocol was disseminated into community provider organizations across the country, specification of quality assurance mechanisms became necessary to maintain the internal validity of the treatment model. The goal of the MST quality assurance system is to help treatment teams achieve positive clinical outcomes for youths and families by supporting adherence to the MST treatment model. As discussed next, several empirical studies have supported linkages between adherence to MST treatment principles and clinical outcomes (Henggeler et al., 1997; Henggeler, Pickrel, et al., 1999; Huey et al., 2000; Schoenwald, Henggeler, Brondino, &

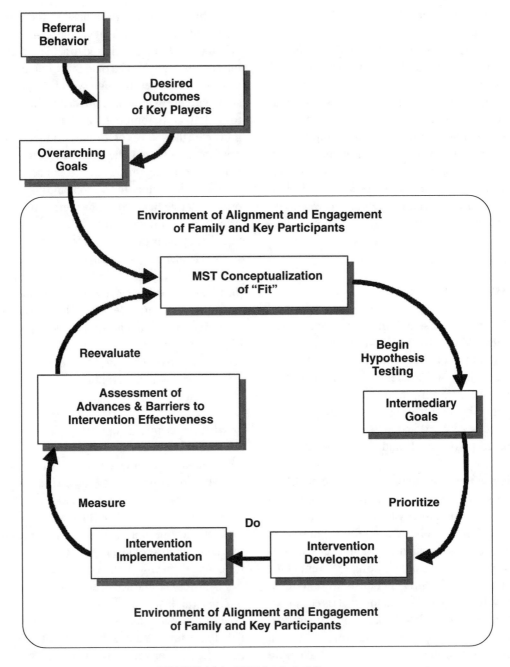

FIGURE 14.1. MST Analytical Process

Rowland, 2000; Schoenwald, Sheidow, & Letourneau, 2002; Schoenwald, Sheidow, Letourneau, & Liao, in press).

The MST model includes a comprehensive quality assurance system, with multiple lay-ers of clinical and programmatic support. Spe-cifically, the protocol begins with a pretraining site assessment by MST consultants to evalu-ate and address contextual factors that have been anecdotally identified and recently empirically supported (Schoenwald et al., in press), as predictive of successful program performance and clinical outcomes. During program start-up, provider organizations receive extensive technical assistance to assure the provision of necessary resources and to overcome barriers to implementation (see the next section for more detail). An intensive 5-day orientation to MST theory and practice includes didactic and experiential training for all MST staff and is followed by quarterly 1½-day booster training designed to meet observed gaps in performance. The quality assurance protocol maintains treatment integrity through weekly team supervision to therapists by an on-site supervisor trained in the manualized MST supervisory protocol (Henggeler & Schoenwald, 1998) and weekly phone consultation with an MST expert who follows a specified consultation protocol (Schoenwald, 1998). Supervision and consultation include feedback from measures of treatment integrity, including monthly caregiver-reported ratings of therapist adherence (Henggeler & Borduin, 1992) and therapist- and supervisor-reported ratings of supervisor and consultant adherence to the MST treatment model (Henggeler, Schoenwald, Liao, Letourneau, & Edwards, 2002; Schoenwald et al., in press). Thus, adherence to the treatment model is monitored and fostered continuously.

Several studies have supported a link between therapist adherence to MST treatment principles and short- and long-term clinical outcomes (Henggeler et al., 1997; Henggeler, Pickrel, et al., 1999; Huey et al., 2000; Schoenwald, Henggeler, et al., 2000). Ongoing research is also examining the influence of clinician, organizational, and service system variables on treatment fidelity and youth outcomes in 41 communities (Schoenwald et al., in press). Findings indicate that both therapist adherence and organizational climate predict parent-reported child outcomes immediately post-treatment. Six- and 12-month

follow-up data, including recidivism, are currently being collected on the 2,000 youths and families participating in this 5-year study. In addition, examination of a previously untested linkage in the quality assurance system—ongoing consultation from an MST expert—indicates that therapist reports of MST consultation predict both therapist adherence and post-treatment child outcomes reported by caregivers (Schoenwald, Sheidow, & Letourneau, 2002). Additional research focusing on quality assurance methods and their relationship to treatment fidelity and child outcomes in community settings is sorely needed, and several grant proposals examining these issues in relation to MST and other evidence-based practices are currently under review at several federal funding agencies.

## IMPLEMENTATION IN COMMUNITY SETTINGS

Demand for MST increased considerably following the publication of the short- term, long-term, and cost-effectiveness findings described previously. Numerous state and county juvenile justice and mental health authorities, state legislators, and executives of large service provider organizations contacted MUSC (Medical University of South Carolina) with the hope of establishing MST programs in their communities. To meet that demand, the multilevel approach to quality assurance described previously was designed to duplicate at remote sites the clinical training, supervision, and fidelity monitoring procedures used in previous randomized trials of MST. Detailed descriptions of this multilevel approach to supporting community implementation of MST can be found in Henggeler and Schoenwald (1999) and in Edwards, Schoenwald, Henggeler, and Strother (2001). The following summary highlights aspects of the community context that are assessed and addressed prior to the establishment of an MST program and monitored by the MST consultant, MST program, and community stakeholders as the program is being implemented.

The first step toward the establishment of a community-based MST program is the MST Site Assessment process. This process is designed to facilitate the assessment of the mutual compatibility of MST with the goals, needs, and capacities of the community as represented by pertinent community stakeholders. The objectives of the process are to (a) assess the philosophical compatibility of MST with community agency and consumer groups; (b) identify referral and funding incentives and disincentives that could impact long-term sustainability of the program; (c) establish the interagency collaboration necessary for the MST program and client families to take the lead in clinical decision making; and (d) align the structure, procedures, and culture of the organization hosting the MST program to support therapist adherence to MST and provider accountability for family engagement and outcomes. These objectives are met through discussions designed to prompt key community stakeholders to identify major political, economic, and social drivers of interest in MST and to articulate how these and other (i.e., organizational, clinical) factors could impact the implementation of an MST program. If, for example, the political mandate of a state's juvenile justice system is more consistent with punishment than with a rehabilitative stance, officials from that agency may prohibit youths with serious criminal offenses from participation in MST. In such a scenario, the referral base will most likely be insufficient for sustaining an MST program for serious offenders. Key stakeholders typically include representatives from juvenile justice, mental health, education, family court, social welfare agencies, and other entities (i.e., third party payers) who may fund services.

MST programs are funded through a variety of mechanisms, including fee-for-service, case rate, and program-level funding. Through the site assessment process, the sources and mechanisms of funding for MST program start-up and continued operations are identified and negotiated. Such negotiation can be challenging, because most states follow traditional guidelines for reimbursement for mental health services that focus on the provision of a predetermined quantity of services (i.e., reimbursement based on number of hours of face-to-face contact), rather than on the attainment of treatment goals as in MST. Reimbursement based on face-to-face contact with the referred youth causes problems for the delivery of MST, which requires substantial contact with family members and others in the youth's ecology, titration of contact frequency and intensity, and at least 3 hours weekly of clinical supervision and consultation. Funding problems also occur when public agencies face financial disincentives if they prescribe community-based services versus institution-based services. For example, referral sources might be required to pay for a community-based treatment like MST but not for incarceration; or, the margin a provider makes on a higher reimbursement rate for a restrictive service (i.e., a residential bed) may be greater than the margin associated with a home-based service. Similarly, changes in funding (e.g., funds diverted toward building a county juvenile detention center) or in public attitudes (e.g., increased desire to have gang-related youth incarcerated) might lead to a significant decrease in referrals to an MST program and a resultant loss of funding.

When such disincentives are identified during the Site Assessment, they are proactively addressed. Generally, the strategy has been to demonstrate to key stakeholders how each disincentive leads to program failure and to facilitate the identification or development of reimbursement mechanisms and incentives to promote the utilization of community-based services like MST. Restructuring elements of the service system to support MST can be challenging. Cultivating an unwavering focus among stakeholders on outcomes to youths and families served, rather than on the provision of quantities of traditional service delivery packages (e.g., residential beds, clinic hours) is critical to the restructuring process. Sustaining the outcomes focus of stakeholder discussions is among the responsibilities of the MST Services representative facilitating the site assessment. The MST facilitator must also be sufficiently knowledgeable about the funding and regulatory mechanisms that characterize a particular community to assess with stakeholders the extent to which existing and alternative mechanisms are compatible with the requirements of MST, and vice versa.

A third objective of the Site Assessment process is to cultivate sufficient collaboration and trust among the prospective MST service provider organization and key stakeholders to allow MST therapists to take the lead in clinical decisions that affect youths and families served by the program. MST programs emphasize accountability for youth and family outcomes, but a program cannot be accountable if it does not have clinical decision-making authority. Examples of decisions to be negotiated by MST therapists and professionals in other sectors of the local service system (i.e., judges, probation officers, caseworkers, court administrators) are discussed, as are scenarios that capture acceptable procedures for negotiating the capacity of the MST team to "take the clinical lead." Although some stakeholder groups forge formal memoranda of agreement between agencies, such agreements are not required, nor do they guarantee that control over clinical decision making will reside with the MST team and the family on a case-by-case basis. Instead, the MST provider organization, with ongoing assistance from MST Services, is responsible for maintaining interagency relations that support effective

case-by-case problem solving. Strategies used to accomplish this goal include the establishment of information-sharing parameters (e.g., the frequency and types of information about clients to be shared, with client consent, among MST and other agencies); maintenance of community-liaison functions by the MST supervisor, program administrator, or both; and using MST consultation to identify and address barriers to retention of the clinical lead in specific cases.

Finally, the site assessment process focuses on developing the staff, structure, policies, procedures, climate, and culture conducive to implementing MST with the fidelity needed to achieve favorable child outcomes. For example, policies such as flextime and resources such as cell phones and pagers are needed to enable therapists to meet the 24/7 availability guaranteed in the home-based MST model. Establishing salaries that are competitive and attractive, when compared with salaries received by clinicians providing traditional office-based outpatient therapy, may be necessary to attract a viable applicant pool. It is important to ensure that the MST clinical supervisor has both clinical and administrative responsibility for the team (i.e., can make hire-and-fire decisions). Numerous administrative and clinical details, including procedures for opening, closing, and reporting on clinical cases, are negotiated. Within these details is a subset of program elements that experience suggests are necessary conditions for program success (see Henggeler, Mihalic, Rone, Thomas, & Timmons-Mitchell, 1998). These include specifications regarding team size, caseload, and frequency of supervision and consultation.

The Site Assessment process concludes with the development of a document that establishes individualized MST goals and guidelines for each MST provider. This document specifies the resolution of numerous administrative and clinical details, including the definition of the target population, participant inclusion and exclusion criteria, program goals, referral criteria, termination criteria (outcomes-based), program elements, and documentation details. A semiannual assessment of MST program implementation and the clinical, organizational, community and MST Services–related variables that appear pertinent to performance is conducted. This assessment involves pertinent stakeholders and is designed to facilitate the capacity of the provider organization and stakeholders to sustain or improve (or both) positive performance.

## ACKNOWLEDGMENTS

This manuscript was supported by grants DA10079 and DA99008 from the National Institute on Drug Abuse; MH59138, MH51852, and MH60663 from the National Institute of Mental Health; AA122202 from the National Institute on Alcoholism and Alcohol Abuse and the Center for Substance Abuse Treatment; and the Annie E. Casey Foundation.

## REFERENCES

Alexander, J. F., & Parsons, B. V. (1973). Short-term behavioral intervention with delinquent families: Impact on family process and recidivism. *Journal of Abnormal Psychology, 81*(3), 219–225.

Aos, S., Phipps, P., Barnoski, R., & Lieb, R. (2001). *The comparative costs and benefits of programs to reduce crime* (Document 01-05-1201). Olympia: Washington State Institute for Public Policy.

Borduin, C. M., Henggeler, S. W., Blaske, D. M., & Stein, R. J. (1990). Multisystemic treatment of adolescent sexual offenders. *International Journal of Offender Therapy & Comparative Criminology, 34*(2), 105–113.

Borduin, C. M., Mann, B. J., Cone, L. T., Henggeler, S. W., Fucci, B. R., Blaske, D. M., & Williams, R. A. (1995). Multisystemic treatment of serious juvenile offenders: Long-term prevention of criminality and violence. *Journal of Consulting & Clinical Psychology, 63*(4), 569–578.

Bronfenbrenner, U. (1979). *The ecology of human development: Experiments by nature and design.* Cambridge, MA: Harvard University Press.

Brown, T. L., Henggeler, S. W., Schoenwald, S. K., Brondino, M. J., & Pickrel, S. G. (1999). Multisystemic treatment of substance abusing and dependent juvenile delinquents: Effects on school attendance at posttreatment and 6-month follow-up. *Children's Services: Social Policy, Research, & Practice, 2*(2), 81–93.

Brunk, M. A., Henggeler, S. W., & Whelan, J. P. (1987). Comparison of multisystemic therapy and parent training in the brief treatment of child abuse and neglect. *Journal of Consulting & Clinical Psychology, 55*(2), 171–178.

Burns, B. J., Hoagwood, K., & Mrazek, P. J. (1999). Effective treatment for mental disorders in children and adolescents. *Clinical Child & Family Psychology Review, 2*(4), 199-254.

Center for Substance Abuse Prevention. (2001). *Exemplary substance abuse prevention programs award ceremony.* Washington, DC: Substance Abuse and Mental Health Services Administration, Author.

Edwards, D. L., Schoenwald, S. K., Henggeler, S. W., & Strother, K. B. (2001). A multi-level perspective on the implementation of multisystemic therapy (MST): Attempting dissemination with fidelity. In G. A. Bernfield, D. P. Farrington, & A. W. Leschied (Eds.), *Offender rehabilitation in practice: Implementing and evaluating effective programs* (pp. 97–120). London: Wiley.

Elliott, D. S. (Ed.). (1998). *Blueprints for violence prevention.* Boulder: University of Colorado, Center for the Study and Prevention of Violence, Blueprints Publications.

Ellis, D. A., Narr-King, S. N., Frey, M. A., Rowland, M. D., & Greger, N. (in press). Case study: feasibility of multisystemic therapy as a treatment for urban adolescents with poorly controlled Type 1 diabetes. *Journal of Pediatric Psychology.*

Farrington, D. P., & Welsh, B. C. (1999). Delinquency prevention using family-based interventions. *Children & Society, 13*(4), 287–303.

Haley, J. (1987). *Problem-solving therapy* (2nd ed.). San Francisco, CA: Jossey-Bass.

Hann, D. M., & Borek, N. (2001). *Taking stock of risk factors for child/youth externalizing behavior problems* (NIH Publication No. 02-4938). Washington, DC: Department of Health and Human Services, Public Health Service, National Institutes of Health, National Institute of Mental Health.

Hawkins, J. D., Herrenkohl, T., Farrington, D. P., Brewer, D., Catalano, R. F., & Harachi, T. W. (1998). A review of predictors of youth violence.

In R. Loeber & D. P. Farrington (Eds.), *Serious & violent juvenile offenders: Risk factors and successful interventions* (pp. 106–146). Thousand Oaks, CA: Sage.

Henggeler, S. W., & Borduin, C. M. (1990). *Family therapy and beyond: A multisystemic approach to treating the behavior problems of children and adolescents.* Pacific Grove, CA: Brooks/Cole.

Henggeler, S. W., & Borduin, C. M. (1992). *Multisystemic Therapy Adherence Scales.* Charleston: Medical University of South Carolina, Department of Psychiatry and Behavioral Science.

Henggeler, S. W., Borduin, C. M., Melton, G. B., Mann, B. J., Smith, L., Hall, J. A., Cone, L., & Fucci, B. R. (1991). Effects of multisystemic therapy on drug use and abuse in serious juvenile offenders: A progress report from two outcome studies. *Family Dynamics of Addiction Quarterly, 1*(3), 40–51.

Henggeler, S. W., Clingempeel, W. G., Brondino, M. J., & Pickrel, S. G. (2002). Four-year follow-up of multisystemic therapy with substance abusing and dependent juvenile offenders. *Journal of the American Academy of Child & Adolescent Psychiatry, 41*(7), 868–874.

Henggeler, S. W., Melton, G. B., Brondino, M. J., Scherer, D. G., & Hanley, J. H. (1997). Multisystemic therapy with violent and chronic juvenile offenders and their families: The role of treatment fidelity in successful dissemination. *Journal of Consulting & Clinical Psychology, 65*(5), 821–833.

Henggeler, S. W., Melton, G. B., & Smith, L. A. (1992). Family preservation using multisystemic therapy: An effective alternative to incarcerating serious juvenile offenders. *Journal of Consulting & Clinical Psychology, 60*(6), 953–961.

Henggeler, S. W., Melton, G. B., Smith, L. A., Schoenwald, S. K., & Hanley, J. H. (1993). Family preservation using multisystemic treatment: Long-term follow-up to a clinical trial with serious juvenile offenders. *Journal of Child & Family Studies, 2*(4), 283–293.

Henggeler, S. W., Mihalic, S. F., Rone, L., Thomas, C., & Timmons-Mitchell, J. (1998). *Blueprints for violence prevention, book six: Multisystemic therapy.* Boulder, CO: Center for the Study and Prevention of Violence.

Henggeler, S. W., Pickrel, S. G., & Brondino, M. J. (1999). Multisystemic treatment of substance abusing and dependent delinquents: Outcomes, treatment fidelity, and transportability. *Mental Health Services Research, 1*(3), 171-184.

Henggeler, S. W., Pickrel, S. G., Brondino, M. J., & Crouch, J. L. (1996). Eliminating (almost) treatment dropout of substance abusing or dependent delinquents through home-based multisystemic therapy. *American Journal of Psychiatry, 153*(3), 427–428.

Henggeler, S. W., Rodick, J. D., Borduin, C. M., Hanson, C. L., Watson, S. M., & Urey, J. R. (1986). Multisystemic treatment of juvenile offenders: Effects on adolescent behavior and family interaction. *Developmental Psychology, 22*(1), 132–141.

Henggeler, S. W., Rowland, M. D., Randall, J., Ward, D. M., Pickrel, S. G., Cunningham, P. B., Miller, S. L., Edwards, J., Zealberg, J. J., Hand, L. D., & Santos, A. B. (1999). Home-based multisystemic therapy as an alternative to the hospitalization of youths in psychiatric crisis: Clinical outcomes. *Journal of the American Academy of Child & Adolescent Psychiatry, 38*(11), 1331–1339.

Henggeler, S. W., & Schoenwald, S. K. (1998). *The MST supervisory manual: Promoting quality assurance at the clinical level.* Charleston, SC: MST Services.

Henggeler, S. W., & Schoenwald, S. K. (1999). The role of quality assurance in achieving outcomes in MST programs. *Journal of Juvenile Justice and Detention Services, 14*, 1–17.

Henggeler, S. W., Schoenwald, S. K., Borduin, C. M., Rowland, M. D., & Cunningham, P. B. (1998). *Multisystemic treatment of antisocial behavior in children and adolescents.* New York: Guilford Press.

Henggeler, S. W., Schoenwald, S. K., Liao, J. G., Letourneau, E. J., & Edwards, D. L. (2002). Transporting efficacious treatments to field settings: The link between supervisory practices and therapist fidelity in MST programs. *Journal of Clinical Child & Adolescent Psychology, 31*(2), 155–167.

Henggeler, S. W., Schoenwald, S. K., Rowland, M. D., & Cunningham, P. B. (2002). *Serious emotional disturbance in children and adolescents: Multisystemic therapy.* New York: Guilford Press.

Huey, S. J., Jr., Henggeler, S. W., Brondino, M. J., & Pickrel, S. G. (2000). Mechanisms of change in multisystemic therapy: Reducing delinquent behavior through therapist adherence and improved family and peer functioning. *Journal of Consulting & Clinical Psychology, 68*(3), 451–467.

Kazdin, A. E., & Weisz, J. R. (1998). Identifying and developing empirically supported child and adolescent treatments. *Journal of Consulting & Clinical Psychology, 66*(1), 19–36.

Lipsey, M. W., & Derzon, J. H. (1998). Predictors of violent or serious delinquency in adolescence and early adulthood: A synthesis of longitudinal research. In R. Loeber & D. P. Farrington (Eds.), *Serious & violent juvenile offenders: Risk factors and successful interventions* (pp. 86–105). Thousand Oaks, CA: Sage.

Mann, B. J., Borduin, C. M., Henggeler, S. W., & Blaske, D. M. (1990). An investigation of systemic conceptualizations of parent–child coalitions and symptom change. *Journal of Consulting & Clinical Psychology, 58*(3), 336–344.

McKay, M. M. (2000). What we can do to increase involvement of urban children and families in mental health services and prevention programs. *Emotional and Behavioral Disorders in Youth, 1*(1), 11–12.

Mihalic, S., Irwin, K., Elliott, D., Fagan, A., & Hansen, D. (2001). *Blueprints for violence prevention*. Boulder, CO: Center for the Study of Violence Prevention.

Minuchin, S. (1974). *Families & family therapy*. Cambridge, MA: Harvard University Press.

National Institute on Drug Abuse. (1999). *Principles of drug addiction treatment: A research-based guide* (NIH Publication No. 99-4180). Rockville, MD: U.S. Department of Health and Human Services, National Institutes of Health, Author.

Randall, J., Henggeler, S. W., Cunningham, P. B., Rowland, M. D., & Swenson, C. C. (2001). Adapting multisystemic therapy to treat adolescent substance abuse more effectively. *Cognitive & Behavioral Practice, 8*(4), 359–366.

Reid, J. R., Patterson, G. R., & Snyder, J. (2002). *Antisocial behavior in children and adolescents: A development analysis and model for intervention*. Washington, DC: American Psychological Association.

Schoenwald, S. K. (1998). *Multisystemic therapy consultation guidelines*. Charleston, SC: MST Institute.

Schoenwald, S. K., Henggeler, S. W., Brondino, M. J., & Rowland, M. D. (2000). Multisystemic therapy: Monitoring treatment fidelity. *Family Process, 39*(1), 83–103.

Schoenwald, S. K., Sheidow, A. J., & Letourneau, E. J. (2002). *Toward effective quality assurance in evidence-based practice: Links between expert consultation, therapist fidelity, and child outcomes*. Manuscript submitted for publication.

Schoenwald, S. K., Sheidow, A. J., Letourneau, E. J., & Liao, J. G. (in press). *Transportability of multisystemic therapy: Evidence for multilevel influences*. Mental Health Services Research.

Schoenwald, S. K., Ward, D. M., Henggeler, S. W., Pickrel, S. G., & Patel, H. (1996). Multisystemic therapy treatment of substance abusing or dependent adolescent offenders: Costs of reducing incarceration, inpatient, and residential placement. *Journal of Child & Family Studies, 5*(4), 431–444.

Schoenwald, S. K., Ward, D. M., Henggeler, S. W., & Rowland, M. D. (2000). Multisystemic therapy versus hospitalization for crisis stabilization of youth: Placement outcomes 4 months postreferral. *Mental Health Services Research, 2*(1), 3–12.

Stanton, M. D., & Shadish, W. R. (1997). Outcome, attrition, and family-couples treatment for drug abuse: A meta-analysis and review of the controlled, comparative studies. *Psychological Bulletin, 122*(2), 170–191.

Stark, M. J. (1992). Dropping out of substance abuse treatment: A clinically oriented review. *Clinical Psychology Review, 12*(1), 93–116.

U.S. Public Health Service. (1999). *Mental health: A report of the Surgeon General*. Rockville, MD: U.S. Department of Health and Human Services, National Institutes of Health, National Institute of Mental Health.

U.S. Public Health Service. (2001). *Youth violence: A report of the Surgeon General*. Washington, DC: Author.

von Bertalanffy, L. (1968). *General system theory: Foundations, development, applications*. New York: Braziller.

CHAPTER 15

# Functional Family Therapy

## A Mature Clinical Model for Working with At-Risk Adolescents and Their Families

THOMAS L. SEXTON, PhD

*Indiana University*

JAMES F. ALEXANDER, PhD

*University of Utah*

## INTRODUCTION

Since its emergence over 30 years ago, functional family therapy (FFT) has evolved from a set of theoretically integrated and clinically based principles to a well-articulated model of clinical intervention firmly rooted in science, theory, and clinical practice. FFT has emerged from its history as one of the best examples of the new generation of evidence-based clinical models, primarily used in the treatment of at-risk adolescents and their families (Alexander, Sexton, & Robbins, 2002; Sexton & Alexander, 2002a). FFT is a "true" family-based approach that focuses on the multiple domains of client experience (cognition, emotion, and behavior) across the mul-

tiple perspectives within and around a family system (individual, family, and contextual/multisystemic). In order to understand and intervene successfully across these domains, FFT has remained grounded in *relational context*. This has allowed FFT to embrace the inherent dialectic tension in family therapy—that is, the tension between clinical practice, foundational theory (systems, developmental psychopathology, epidemiology, the sociology of culture, etc.), and rigorous science. FFT has adopted both a client focus based in sound clinical experience (ideographic), while at the same time attending to the common research and theory and change mechanisms (nomothetic) underlying a range of good therapeutic interventions. FFT also represents what

323

Alexander and colleagues defined as a "mature clinical model" (Alexander et al., 2002). FFT is a "mature" model because it has evolved beyond a set of theoretical principles to become a comprehensive intervention program that includes: a *clinical core*, consisting of an integrated set of guiding theoretical principles; a *systematic therapeutic program that relies upon phasically based change mechanisms*; well-developed *multi-domain clinical assessment and intervention* techniques; an *ongoing research* program; and, finally, *systematic training, supervision, and implementation* protocols.

The integrative and systematic nature of the FFT clinical model, along with its repeated demonstrations of successful outcomes with at-risk adolescents and their families, has led to widespread community-based application in many settings with a wide range of clients (Alexander, Holtzworth-Munroe, & Jameson, 1994; Sexton & Alexander, 2002; Sexton, Alexander, & Mease, in press). As a treatment program, FFT is successful with a wide range of problem youths (from early-entry first offenders to serious and high-end offender youths) and their families and in various contexts (Alexander & Sexton, 2002a; Alexander, Sexton, & Robbins, 2002). As a prevention program, FFT is effective in diverting the trajectory of at-risk adolescents away from entering the mental health and justice systems (Alexander, Robbins, & Sexton, 2000). In both applications, FFT is a short-term family therapy intervention for adolescents and their families that generally ranges from, on average, 8 to 12 one-hour sessions for mild cases and up to 30 hours of direct service for more difficult situations. In most programs, sessions are spread over a 3- to 6-month period. Target populations are youths between the ages of 11 and 18, although younger siblings of referred adolescents are also often involved. The youths represent multi-ethnic, multicultural populations, ranging from at-risk preadoles-

cents to youths with very serious problems, such as severe conduct disorder (Alexander, Pugh, Parsons, & Sexton, 2000).

In this chapter, we present an overview of FFT. The chapter is written to focus on core theoretical constructs, clinical change mechanisms, and therapist interventions that have led to the positive outcomes reported across outcome studies (for additional information, see, Alexander & Sexton, 2002; Sexton & Alexander, 2002b). We first focus on the dynamic evolution of FFT from an early set of core beliefs to a mature and comprehensive clinical model. Our primary focus will be on the core constructs of how FFT views therapy and understands families and the clinical problems they present, the relational systems of family, and the fundamental change mechanisms that produce positive change. An overview of the outcome research that supports FFT as an effective program and the process research that has uncovered the foundation of the change mechanisms of FFT will follow. We end the chapter with a discussion of the mechanisms of supervision and dissemination and the critical procedures used to measure model fidelity in the various community contexts in which FFT currently "lives."

## THE DYNAMIC EVOLUTION OF FUNCTIONAL FAMILY THERAPY

FFT can't be adequately described by any single theoretical label (e.g., behavioral, systemic). Instead, FFT is a systematic clinical model that evolved along a path best described as a dynamic process of model integration (Alexander, Sexton, & Robbins, 2002). FFT's developmental path has been both systematic (through careful consideration of the choice points) and responsive (through necessary adaptation to its changing clinical and epistemological context). As an "open" dynamic system (Katz & Kahn, 1966), it has been adaptable (viable) with respect to input from various contexts in which it has developed, while at the same time retaining its coherence of underlying core principles. Using a rather appropriate metaphor, FFT developed much like any child. Its early "core" identity is open to input from the outside. Over time, the child becomes increasingly viable and responsive to the outside environment, as it incorporates and assimilates, in systematic ways, input from its various experiences. With development of a core self, the child adds competencies and abilities, becoming well rounded and competent in various arenas. The child enters maturity with a rich set of experiences that is much more than the mere "sum" of events but instead represents a dynamic integration of experiences.

Early on (the late 1960s and early 1970s), FFT grew out of a *clinical* need to serve a population of at-risk adolescents and families who were underserved, had few resources, and were difficult to treat. These families typically entered the system resistant, fearful, hopeless, disrespectful, and angry, and many had already failed at several of their change attempts. Traditional treatment providers often required individuals and families to be "motivated" as a prerequisite for change; thus, the helping professions tended to view these families as treatment-resistant, and they were notoriously unsuccessful in addressing the needs of this population. When clinical outcomes were poor, the usual conclusions were that the youths and their families were the source of failure. Families were often called "unmotivated," "defensive," and "irresponsible." The "reasons" for treatment failure included such factors as single parenting, "dysfunctional family," "cultural factors" (e.g., poverty and racism), or any combination of these.

As an alternative, FFT focused on understanding why the resistance occurred and on providing the type of intervention that would motivate family members, reduce their nega-

tivity, and give them hope. Clinical experience made it clear that interventions could not begin with a primary focus on stopping the maladaptive behavior patterns. Instead, interventions had to develop the unique strengths of the family in a culturally sensitive way, while enhancing family members' efficacy and ability to make positive future changes. When this was accomplished, lasting changes in behavioral (including emotional and attitudinal) patterns could be attained. Thus, FFT has been based on the premise that our job is to take responsibility for motivating families and to accept families "on their own terms," rather than to apply a treatment goal that was based on someone else's version of what a family "should be," what a culture "should be," and what a particular spiritual belief, sexual orientation, or economic system "should be," and we needed to give all family members hope, and engage and motivate them very quickly and effectively.

The emphasis on understanding, defining, describing, and researching the process of intervention began early in the FFT evolution. This emphasis emerged because it became clear that *theoretical development* was necessary if this population were to be well served. Clinical interventions of the time provided no vehicle for understanding the relational elements of family functioning or clinical change, clinical accountability, model replication, or understanding the change process. In that early context it was critical that FFT develop a clinical "model" that could guide practice. Early articulations of FFT (Barton & Alexander, 1981) relied heavily on work of early communication theorists (e.g., Watzlawick, Beavin, & Jackson, 1967) and incorporated the notion that behavior serves to define and create interpersonal relationships, and that behavior has meaning only in its relational context. At this time the model also relied on the use of specific behavioral technologies such as communication training (Parsons &

Alexander, 1973). This led to the classification of FFT as a behavioral approach, whereas others characterized FFT as a systems-behavioral approach in some early family therapy texts. As the model evolved, cognitive theory, particularly attribution and information-processing theories, helped explain some of the mechanisms of meaning and emotion often manifested as blaming and negativity in family interactional patterns (Jones & Nisbett, 1972; Kelley, 1973; Taylor & Fiske, 1978). More recently, social constructionist ideas have informed FFT through a focus on meaning and its role in the constructed nature of problems, in interrupting family negativity, and in organizing therapeutic themes (Friedlander & Heatherington, 1998; Gergen, 1985). Throughout the integration of various theoretical constructs, FFT has retained its primary core of being relationally focused.

FFT has also held a core belief in the value and necessity of rigorous evaluation and clinical accountability. As a result, FFT has always been informed by the findings of *scientific inquiry*. The early clinical trial studies (Alexander & Parsons, 1973; Klein, Alexander & Parsons, 1977) focused on questions of efficacy, with pragmatic outcome measures that had both clinical and social relevance (recidivism). These early studies established FFT as an effective approach with a variety of offending adolescents. Process studies attempted to identify the mechanisms by which FFT was successful. These studies informed clinical practice by indicating that family negativity significantly impacted engagement and motivation (Alexander, Barton, Schiaroe, & Parsons, 1976) and that the gender of the therapist was differentially related to both the rate and the quantity of speech by family members (Mas, Alexander, & Barton, 198; Mas, Alexander, & Turner, 1991; Newberry, Alexander, & Turner, 1991). These early process studies raised additional questions that were answered by a second wave of clinical

trials focusing on the effectiveness of FFT in different settings with different populations (Barton, Alexander, Waldron, Turner, & Warburton, 1985; Lanz, 1982; Gordon, Arbuthnot, Gustafson, & McGreen, 1988; 1995; Hansson, 1998; Sexton, Ostrom, Bonomo, & Alexander, 2000). More recent studies have focused on the role of therapist model adherence as a primary mediating variable in successful outcomes (Sexton, Hollimon, Mease, & Alexander, 2002; Barnoski, 2002a). The outcome of these studies suggested that FFT was applicable across an even wider client population over diverse settings, with real therapists in local communities.

## MAJOR THEORETICAL, CLINICAL, AND RESEARCH-BASED CONSTRUCTS

As a clinical model, FFT is composed of *both* a set of theoretically integrated guiding principles and a clearly defined clinical "map," based on specific within-session process goals, linked together in a phasic model. The guiding principles provide the parameters for understanding family functioning, the etiology of clinical problems, the driving forces and motivations behind successful change, and the principles of how to deal with individual and unique families in a way that fits them. The clinical map guides the therapeutic process by using specifically defined change mechanisms that lead to successful therapy. In the next section we present the theoretical principles that form the foundation of FFT. In the section that follows, we detail the treatment protocol.

As a "true" family therapy, FFT views the "family" as the primary source from which it understands the clinical meaning of the behaviors of each family member. FFT defines the family as the primary psychosocial system in which adolescents may spend most of their "family" time. FFT works with "families" characterized by a wide variety of structural arrangements, such as two parents ("natural," adoptive, step, foster) and an adolescent, an adolescent and his or her uncle or aunt (grandparent, etc.) caretaker, and single parent with adolescent families. What is most important is that in FFT, *the family is the client*—FFT focuses on the primary psychosocial unit of the adolescent as our major source of information to understand regularities in interpersonal behavior that explain the existence of various risk or protective factors (or both) that characterize the daily life of our families.

Three major constructs form the foundation of FFT: (1) the nature of clinical problems, (2) the relational functioning of the family system, and (3) the core mechanisms of successful therapeutic change.

*The Nature of Clinical Problems:*
*Risk and Protective Factors*
*Within Relational Contexts*

FFT views clinical problems multisystemically, both within the systems of the family relational units and between the family and its environmental and social context. This principle is based on the growing evidence that the problems of these youths are best understood by looking at their individual behavior, nested within the family, which is part of a broad community system (Hawkins, Catalano, & Miller, 1992; Robbins, Mayorga, & Szapocznik, Chapter 2, this volume; Szapocznik & Kurtines, 1989). Thinking beyond specific behaviors of a youth with a clearly articulated model of the etiology of clinical problems is critical because it becomes the basis upon which change targets are identified and change mechanisms are utilized. What becomes complex with acting-out youths is that the serious behaviors they

present at referral represent a multitude of clinical syndromes that must ultimately change. However, in FFT these behaviors are not the immediate focus of therapeutic intervention. Instead, FFT focuses on the relational patterns that are represented by these behaviors as the basis of therapeutic intervention.

A central element in FFT is the well-articulated, theoretically integrated, and multisystemic principles that guide our understanding of the "presenting clinical problems" of families. These principles help target points of change and identify appropriate therapeutic mechanisms to change both specific problem behavior and the family relational patterns that support those behaviors. FFT views specific presenting clinical problems (clinical syndromes) as relational problems—as specific behaviors embedded within enduring patterns of behaviors that are the foundation for stable and enduring relational "functions" within family relationships (Alexander & Sexton, 2002; Sexton & Alexander, 2002a). Figure 15.1 illustrates FFT's views of clinical problems. *Specific problem behaviors* are manifestations of the relational system of the family. FFT looks beyond these specific behaviors, viewing them as manifestations of enduring *family behavioral patterns*. Though not as easily apparent, family behavior patterns are relational sequences of behaviors, central to the "character" of the family, that form the basis of the family's daily life. Some of these patterns are quite effective in accomplishing the tasks of the family (e.g., parenting, communicating, supporting) and may protect the family and its members from specific behavior problems manifesting. Other patterns put an individual or the family as a whole at risk for individual symptoms of mental health, drug abuse/use, relational conflict, and externalizing behavior disorders. Finally, FFT views even these family risk/protective patterns as maintained and supported by the ways in which relationships "*function*" within the

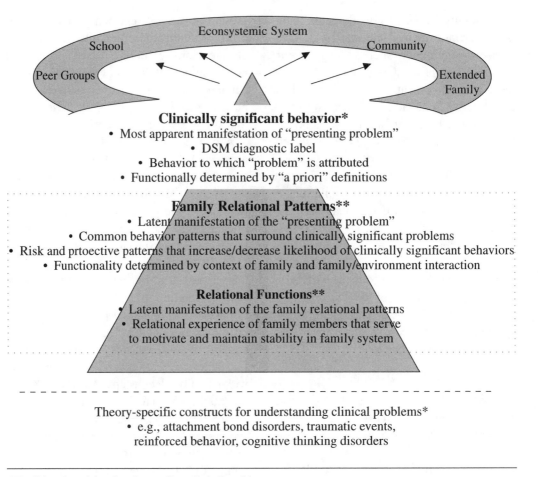

**Clinically significant behavior***
- Most apparent manifestation of "presenting problem"
- DSM diagnostic label
- Behavior to which "problem" is attributed
- Functionally determined by "a priori" definitions

**Family Relational Patterns****
- Latent manifestation of the "presenting problem"
- Common behavior patterns that surround clinically significant problems
- Risk and prtoective patterns that increase/decrease likelihood of clinically significant behaviors
- Functionality determined by context of family and family/environment interaction

**Relational Functions****
- Latent manifestation of the family relational patterns
- Relational experience of family members that serve to motivate and maintain stability in family system

Theory-specific constructs for understanding clinical problems*
- e.g., attachment bond disorders, traumatic events, reinforced behavior, cognitive thinking disorders

*Traditional models of understanding clinical problems
**FFT unique features of understanding clinical problems

FIGURE 15.1. Multisystemic View of Clinical Problems: Specific Problematic Behavior, Family Behavior Patterns, and Relational Functions

family and for individuals. The notions of relational functions are covered in the next section.

FFT's construct of family risk and protective patterns is a particularly useful way of looking at adolescents with externalizing behavior disorders. Adolescents represent complex clinical profiles of behavior problems, including drug use and abuse, antisocial conduct disorder behavior, as well as many other mental health problems. Using risk and protective *patterns* as an approach to understanding "clinical" problems is useful because it

describes patterns of alterable behavior, rather than "labeling" the youth or the family with characteristics that become stable and enduring. In addition, this way of thinking about problems is useful because it describes a probability (the likelihood of problems), rather than causal relationships. The notions of risk and protective factors as a basis for understanding clinical problems suggest that the "problem" behavior is not the source of family difficulty; rather, the way in which the problem behavior is managed within the family relational system creates the difficulty. The ultimate functionality of family behavioral patterns is contextual, depending upon the unique elements of the family history, individual temperaments/personalities, and environmental situations. Thinking of clinical problems as based in risk and protective factors allows the FFT therapist to focus on relational patterns between family members, where the patterns are judged on how they "function" in the unique context of the family, in a way that allows for descriptions and thus interventions aimed at family systems.

## Relational Dynamics As the Organizing Focus of Change

Like most other models of clinical change, FFT attempts to understand and systematically address, in the various stages of change, the factors that "drive" or "motivate and reinforce" behavior. In order to do so, FFT is no different than most (if not all) change models. Behavior happens for a reason. Where models differ is with respect to what those reasons are and how to address them.

FFT assumes that all individuals develop on the basis of a combination of initial capacities, or diatheses (e.g., level of intelligence, emotionality, physical ability), which then interact with experience (learning histories, culture, "role models," as well as various physiological and neurological stressors, etc.) in an emergent process involving cognitive, emotional, and behavioral domains. By adolescence, these domains represent cognitive and emotional processes of appraisal and reaction, which are coupled with behavioral response tendencies. In turn, these tendencies interact with the environment (parents, other members of the youth's microsystem) on a moment-by-moment basis, in which each participant influences (constrains, reinforces, punishes, etc.) the other.

Families are the first and perhaps the most powerful learning context for children. Among the primary domains of this learning are the meaning of relationships and strategies for developing and maintaining them. After their initial development in the context of the family, the patterns are then carried into new contexts, such as schools and peer relationships, and often even into adulthood. Unfortunately, for many of the youths referred to FFT, the only interpersonal strategies that their environment (especially their family) supports are dysfunctional. Some families reinforce gaining a sense of control via drugs or violence, some allow youths to gain attention only via coercion, and some youths are able to achieve a sense of belonging only by gang membership. The patterns carried to the world end up in "problem behaviors" that come to be labeled according to various clinical syndromes (e.g., oppositional defiant disorder, conduct disorder, drug/use and abuse). According to diverse theoretical perspectives (e.g., as diverse as Freud, Sullivan, Skinner, and Bandura, and even biblical [i.e., "as the twig is bent . . . "]), these strategies, even when they can be modified as a basis of experience, become stable and difficult to change. Explaining the phenomena in a different way, the early interactionists (Watzlawick, Weakland, & Fisch, 1974) suggested that the patterns of relational interaction become stable and enduring and even come to define the relationship between people.

In the language of FFT, these stable patterns of interaction between the youth and the family, are represented by the internal experiences of the individual in those relationships and are referred to as *relational functions* (Alexander & Parsons, 1982, Alexander et al., 2000; Alexander & Sexton, 2002a). From the perspective of individuals, the relationship patterns of which they are a part "drift" into the background. It is the "experience" of these stable patterns (e.g., how they feel, what they mean, and the symbolic interpretation) that is most predominant, or in the foreground. A useful metaphor may be the old saying by Bateson, "it is only the fish [that] don't know it is water in which they swim." Thought of in this way, we don't see the relational patterns that bind us to others—but we have internal representations and "experiences" of these patterns that we come to expect, that we tend to reproduce, and that become the standard by which we judge the stability of the relationship.

Thus, from this perspective, "relational functions" represent the *outcomes* of patterned behavioral sequences, not specific behaviors in and of themselves. There are two main dimensions of relational functions in FFT that are used to understand the internalized experience, or functional outcomes of the redundant and common relational patterns within the family (or "relational space"): relational connection (or "interdependency") and relationship hierarchy (Alexander & Parsons, 1982, Alexander et al., 2000; Claiborn & Lichtenberg, 1989; Waltzalawick et al., 1974).

*Relational connection* (or "interdependency") refers to the characteristic pattern that describes a relationship in terms of the degree to which high rates of mutual and emotionally vulnerable contact are necessary to maintain the relationship. High degrees of relatedness (relational interdependency) are experienced not only as a sense of interconnectedness, but as psychological intensity in regard to frequency of contact in the relationship, emotional contact, enmeshment, or any combination of these. Low degrees of relatedness are characterized by feelings of autonomy, distance, independence, and a low degree of psychological intensity and prolonged contact. Note that low degrees of relatedness are not necessarily associated with "not loving" someone: One can "love" someone very much but not require a high rate of contact and ongoing "in vivo" communication to maintain the relationship.

In addition, from the FFT perspective, high and low degrees of relatedness are not different ends of a continuum. Instead, they represent two dimensions, both of which are evident to some degree in the experience of a relationship. Midpointing is an experience of a relationship represented by both high connectedness (autonomy) and distance (independence). This balance can be one that manifests itself as an acceptable relational pattern or can be maladaptive (as we see often in such phenomena as "borderline" or "ambivalent" parenting patterns).

*Relational hierarchy* is a measure of relational control and influence based on structure and resources. Hierarchical control also ranges from high to low, with relational symmetry being an experience of balanced structure and shared resources in the relationship. So-called one-up and one-down relationships ("complementary," according to Haley, 1964) are those in which one member of a relationship possesses resources (economic, physical, positional, or role power supported by external systems) that are less available to the other member(s) in the relationship. According to FFT, relational hierarchy, as a means of control in relationships, represents a more primitive and utilitarian approach to interpersonal influence; one that is characteristic of large segments of the animal kingdom (e.g., "the alpha male" ensures continuity of the species). In contrast, relational connection tends to represent a more mutually enhancing approach to control in relationships—that is, when people influence each other through affection or "commitment to the relationship" or both, rather than through hierarchical power. Although relational connection is seen occasionally in the animal kingdom, affection or commitment-based connectedness does not characterize the majority of relationships in species other than human.

Identifying relational functions is more than a trivial matter. Based upon the concept of equifinality, proposed by the early communication and systemic theorists (Watzlawick et al., 1974) and clinical experience, FFT learned that very different family relational patterns (e.g., constant bickering vs. warmth and cooperation) could produce the same relational experience (e.g., a high degree of interconnectedness). In contrast, very similar interactional sequences (warm communication and intimacy behaviors) can produce entirely different relational outcomes (e.g., they will enhance contact in one relationship and can increase distance in another relationship). From the FFT perspective, there is nothing wrong (or to be changed) with respect to any of these "experiences" (e.g., having a sense of control, receiving attention, or having a sense of belonging). Each has its strengths and its weaknesses. *Consequently, FFT therapists do not attempt to change the core relational experiences of the family members any more than they would consider changing such major factors as culture, parental gender identity, or spiritual beliefs.* In fact, FFT argues that different cultures, family configurations, and learning histories produce and value a wide range of relational patterns, and each of these patterns can produce both positive and negative behavioral expressions.

FFT does, however, insist on changing the *means* by which they are attained (drugs, violence, coercion, gang membership); that is, FFT changes the expression of these components when they damage others. For example, parents who control via violence learn to control via nurturance and guidance. A so-called one-up pattern of parenting is unacceptable if it involves physical and emotional abuse, but it is generally applauded when it involves authoritative parenting, child-sensitive resource allocation, and nurturing. In other words, FFT does not attempt to change the hierarchy of abusive parents, only the patterns of behavior that serve the relational function ("one-up"). In a similar manner, FFT does not attempt to

force an "enmeshed" parent to change the relational function of contact/closeness, instead, FFT helps that parent replace "enabling" behaviors with appropriate nurturance that is contingent upon prosocial (not dysfunctional) youth behavior.

FFT also prioritizes the order in which these dimensions of relational function are addressed. Unfortunately, hierarchy—that is, "control" based on a position of authority—has emerged as the predominant focus in many treatment programs dealing with youth behavior disorders. The field often seems to presume that these youths must be "controlled" by institutions and parents, primarily through clear expectations, behavioral management, and consequences. Although FFT agrees that this dimension of relational functioning is important, as an empowerment model FFT places the first treatment emphasis on relationship connection/interdependency, rather than on relationship hierarchy, as a means to influence behavior. For example, FFT would rather empower youths to not use drugs because they wouldn't want to hurt their mothers (i.e., damage the relationship), versus because they fear their mother would "hurt" (punish, give consequences) them if they did use. Similarly, FFT would aim for a spouse or a parent to stop physical violence because the spouse or parent wouldn't "want" to hurt the other. In other words, for FFT both relational connection and hierarchy are important treatment foci, but enhancing positive relational patterns represents the first priority. As noted elsewhere, this is why the first phase of FFT, engagement and motivation, emphasizes the affective component of family relationships (reducing blame and negativity, creating hope and positive alliance) as the necessary *first* step in the change process.

Relational functions can be difficult to identify because they must be inferred by an observer from what is produced by the interaction process of the family, rather than being phenomena that can be observed directly. In other words, functional outcomes must be understood as an end result (an outcome) of varying and often arbitrarily punctuated relational sequences. It is important to note that FFT views these outcomes as the state of the relationship "when the dust settles." In order to get a sense of this state, the therapist must understand how the behaviors characterize the family over time and across situations.

The focus on the outcomes of relational patterns and relational functions, rather than on individual behaviors, has helped FFT develop an ideographic and relationally focused approach to understanding families. Regardless of their form, the common, repetitive, and highly entrenched behavioral sequences apparent in families lead to consistent relational outcomes (functions) that can be understood only from an ideographic perspective. Relationship functions are reflected in patterns of behavior that maintain, albeit often in painful ways, the relationships between family members. A so-called enabling parent does so not out of "stupidity" but because this represents the relational function of maintaining a level of contact ("connectedness") with the drug-involved youth. In the same manner, a "rejecting parent" does so in order to maintain a high level of separation ("autonomy") from a youth, whereas the youth at the same time may be acting out in order to maintain more connection with that parent. In other words, so-called maladaptive behavior patterns represent people meeting their relational functions in ways that their learning histories, their capacities, and their environment will allow, but doing so in ways that are maladaptive and often destructive to others. This is the reason that FFT targets for change both the individual youth and the particular environment (first the family, then others) in which the youth is embedded. Positive changes in a youth's cognitive appraisal, emotional, and behavioral patterns will be maintained only if the youth's environment supports those changes; and in turn, positive changes in parenting will be maintained only if others, including the youth, support the changes.

### Principles of Change in Functional Family Therapy

FFT is built upon four clearly articulated and theoretically integrated principles that guide the process of change: (1) change is predicated upon alliance-based motivation; (2) behavior change first requires meaning change, primarily through techniques such as reframing; (3) behavioral change goals are obtainable and appropriate for the families' culture, abilities, and living context; and (4) intervention strategies match and respect the unique characteristics of the family.

#### ALLIANCE-BASED MOTIVATION

Motivation is a construct that is frequently studied and often a central feature in most theoretical approaches. The dictionary definition of *motivation* is an "incentive to action." In the context of therapy, motivation is often viewed as a static construct—that is, a condition (incentive) that exists within that client that moves him or her to change. In fact, a number of change models (e.g., Prochaska, 1999) suggest that the focus of early assessment should be on assessing clients' readiness or stage of change; this often leads community practitioners to choose or at least prefer clients who are "ready" for change. However, in the 30-year history of FFT the majority of our families contains one or more members who are not motivated to change—in fact, many at first present as unwilling to even begin the change process. As a result, FFT has developed strategies and techniques to create the motivation to change, leading to high success rates even in populations characterized as "unmotivated to change."

Accomplishing this has required that FFT follow an "empowerment," rather than a "management," philosophy and strategy of change (Alexander & Sexton, 2002; Sexton & Alexander, 2002a). According to FFT, a change process that is maintained is one in which the therapist is successful in developing an atmosphere, which is shared by the family, of hope, expectation of change, a sense of responsibility (internal locus of control), and a positive sense of alliance. This sense of alliance is not only between each family member and the therapist, but among family members as well. When they come to us, family members often have very little sense of alliance with one another; thus our first goal is to begin to develop that within-family alliance as part of the platform of change.

To be clear, it is perhaps misleading to suggest that our youths and families are "not motivated." FFT views most clients coming to therapy as motivated to some sort of action. Unfortunately, they are motivated to maintain or engage in actions that do not produce successful resolution of the concern. From the FFT perspective, therapeutic motivation occurs when the incentive to action results in new and adaptive patterns. Furthermore, FFT defines therapeutic motivation (an incentive to change or to act) as a relational process (alliance) that is an early therapeutic goal that is based on the alliance (a relational process). In FFT, motivation has an intrapersonal (within the client), a family interpersonal (between family members), and a therapeutic (between the therapist and each family member) component. When activated in a therapeutic way, each of these components contributes to producing an incentive to action and a push to change that is critical for successful family therapy.

Alliance is a well-defined construct in psychotherapy literature, which is usually defined as agreement on the tasks and goals within the context of an emotional bond (Horvath, 2001). *Within-family alliance* is demonstrated by family members overcoming their negativity and working together to the same end, with agreement on how to get there within an emotional bond. As noted further on, that bond might exist in various forms (connected or autonomous), both of which are different representations of a bond. *Family to therapist alliance* is a similar working together between family members and the therapist. It is increasingly clear from process research that alliance is critical and, in addition, that this alliance needs to be balanced. Balanced alliance occurs when the therapist has the same level of working alliance with the parents and the youth, regardless of the overall level (Robbins, Jimenez, Alexander, & Turner, 2001). The *intrapersonal (within client)* component of motivation is usually the result of the development of relational motivation. The *cognitive* aspect of internal motivation is related to the way in which clients understand the problems and emotions they experience—what they "think" about the problem. "Problem definitions" are attributional constructions that describe who, why, and what is the cause of the problematic experience—they provide a context for the problem, giving it meaning. The *affective* or emotional element of internal motivation is related to the way in which a person feels about the problem or concerns. At the point that family members enter therapy, the cognitive and affective/emotional components of their attributions about the "problem," and about each other, generally reflect considerable blame and negativity. Successful motivation (for positive action) occurs when the therapist helps family members to view the "presenting concern" as one to which all members contribute but for which none are to be blamed. In addition, motivation is enhanced when the FFT therapist, through interpersonal processes such as reframing, helps all family members experience reductions in negativity and blaming and instead provides them with reasons to feel hope and an expectation of potential success.

### MEANING CHANGE THROUGH REFRAMING

Reframing has a particularly important place in FFT because it is an essential activity in each phase of FFT. More important, it represents a relationally based way of changing the cognitive and perceptual basis for negative interaction, painful emotions, and unsuccessful change strategies. Reframing was initially made popular by the early communication theorists (Watzlawick et al., 1974) and strategic therapies (Selvini-Palazzoli, Boscolo, Cecchin, & Prata, 1978) and has become one of the most universal therapeutic techniques across all family therapies. Regardless of the specific name (positive connotation, finding positive intent, interpretation), reframing is most often classified as a technique: an event or events in which the therapist delivers an alternative frame of reference to the clients, in hopes that the clients will "buy" or accept the new interpretation and ultimately change.

In FFT, reframing is a relational and therapeutic process that involves a series of ongoing interchanges between the therapist and the clients over the course of therapy. Successful reframing creates alternative cognitive and attributional perspectives that help redefine meaning events and thus reduce the negativity and redirect the emotionality surrounding the events. Reframes then challenge clients (implicitly at first, then explicitly later in therapy) to identify new directions for future change, and they link family members to one another, such that each shares in the responsibility for the family struggles. This view of reframing is rooted in attributional and information processing constructs of cognitive psychology (Jones & Nisbett, 1972; Kelley, 1973;

Taylor & Fiske, 1978), social influence process of social psychology (Heppner & Claiborn, 1988), and the more recent systemic (Claiborn & Lichtenberg, 1989) and social *constructionist* ideas regarding the meaning basis of problem definitions (Friedlander & Heatherington, 1998; Gergen, 1985; Sexton & Griffin, 1997).

Figure 15.2 illustrates reframing as a multistage ongoing relational process, involving (1) validation of the client-presented perspective, (2) a reattribution, and (3) a reformation of the next reframing response that incorporates client feedback. The process of reframing begins when a family member discusses some aspect of the presenting concern (content) that is negative and that usually contains blaming. This "content" presentation has an attributional component (who/what did it), an emotional reaction to the attribution (anger, fear, hurt), and related, usually negative, behavioral interchanges that have become common. These client statements offer the therapist a reframing opportunity because they generally set off a process of defensive responding and "counterblaming," into which the therapist contingently intrudes. Reframing begins with the therapist first *validating* the position, statement, emotion, or primary meaning of the speaker. The validation response supports and engages the client. The validation demonstrates support, understanding, and respect for the client. To be successful, the validation avoids broad generalizations ("all parents feel this way") and instead focuses on personal, individual, and insightful statements, such that the client believes the therapist to be working hard to understand his or her unique perspective.

Validation is followed by a *reattribution statement*, which presents an alternative theme that targets the attributional scheme embedded in the client presentation (see figure 15.2). The reattribution statement can take many forms, including offering an alternative expla-

## Validation
Demonstrated
support and
understanding for
emotion/values/position
in a personal way

## Reframe/Reattribution
Change meaning of emotion,
motivation, intent of
behavior/situation

### Meaning Change
• Emotion of self / another
• Behavior of another
• Intention of another
*Leads to negativity/blame
reduction & family
focus*

### Change
• "Where you go from here . . . "
• "Your challenge is . . . "
• "Therefore . . . the thing to
change is . . . "
*Leads to behavior change goal
identification*

### Linking
• "So . . . you and he are much
alike in . . . "
• Therefore, both of you . . . "
• "It seems that between you . . . "
*Leads to a family focus of the
presenting problem*

## Check for
## Fit/Adjust/Reformulate
Assess degree to which reframe fits family—add
family response—reformulate change reframe

## Outcome of Reframing
Explanation of the event, behavior, person, intention of family
problem/situation that is mutually constructed by the therapist and
family, and mutually accepted or "real" for the family and therapist

FIGURE 15.2. Reframing As a Relational Therapeutic Process

nation for the "cause" of the problem behavior, providing a metaphor that implies an alternative construction of the problem, or even using humor to imply that "all is not what it seems." The alternative meaning or theme must be plausible and believable to the client, such that it fits him or her. Among many possibilities, there are three general directions for the reattribution statement. *Meaning change* helps reattribute an emotion, a behavior, or the intent of another to a more benign attribution. For example, it is possible to reframe anger as the hurt that the individual feels in response to the trouble in the family, with the angry person being "willing to be the emotional barometer for the sake of the whole family." The reattribution is helpful because it changes the focus of the behavior from being directed to another person to inside the speaker. Thus, the blame inherent in anger is now redefined as hurt and even sacrifice, which removes negative emotions, while retaining behavioral responsibility. The cognitive sets, or problem definitions, are the meanings that contribute to the emotional intensity that is often behind the anger, blaming, and negativity seen in the interpersonal interactions between family members. Focusing on meaning change often achieves the goal of negativity reduction.

During the second and third phases of therapy (behavior change, generalization), it can be useful to expand reframing by *challenging* the client/family to move toward a new solution attempt (see Figure 15.2). For example, it is possible to reframe the anger and frustration of parents to the challenge of needing to manage one's own emotions so that parents can help teach their child new ways of negotiating alternative behaviors. In this way the reframe moves the focus of attention from the child (being irresponsible) to the parents (managing emotions and teaching), in a way that builds individual responsibility and leads toward behavior change.

Reframing can also *link* family members together and develop a joint family definition of the struggles experienced (see Figure 15.2). A joint or family-focused definition of the "presenting problem" is essential in the early phases of FFT. It is only natural that all family members come to therapy with well-defined explanations for the problems they experience. These definitions may exist in emotional ("It hurts and I am angry"), behavioral ("Stay away from me," "You don't deserve a break"), or cognitive terms ("You are just trying to hurt me," "Why does he (or she)

intentionally do this?"). A family-focused problem definition is one in which everyone in the family has some responsibility and thus some part in the problem. However, no family member receives blame for the state of affairs in the family. The difficult goal is the reduction of blame, while having each family member retain a sense of responsibility for his or her own actions.

Note in Figure 15.2 that reframing does not end with a therapist intervention. Instead, the validation and reframing statements of the therapist are followed by an assessment of the "fit," by listening to the client response and incorporating changes or alternative ideas into the next validation and reframing statement by the therapist. In this way, reframing is a constant feedback loop between therapist and client interactions that builds toward the therapeutic goal. As a process, the therapist and the client are actually constructing a mutually agreed-upon and jointly acceptable alternative explanation for an emotional set of events or series of behaviors. Because it is jointly constructed, it is "real" and relevant to both client and therapist. Over time, the small individual "reframes" become thematic, involving many family members, a series of events, and a complex alternative explanation for the "problem." In this way, the reframing process helps organize and provide a therapeutic thread to the engagement and motivation phase. In fact, the constructed, family-focused problem definition helps organize therapy and becomes the major theme that explains the problems of the family and thus organizes behavior change efforts. Without this redefinition to include all family members, it is almost impossible to get everyone in the family involved in the behavior change phase.

## OBTAINABLE CHANGE GOALS

One of the great strengths of FFT is that in the multiproblem families with whom we work, we are able to find ways to make changes that become meaningful *for the family*. FFT accomplishes this by focusing on significant yet obtainable behavioral changes that will have a lasting impact on the family. In that regard, FFT seeks to pursue obtainable outcomes that "fit" the values, capability, and style of the family, rather than to mold families into someone's version of "healthy" or to reconstruct the "personality" of the family or individuals therein. The goal is to focus on obtainable behavioral changes that are individualized and tailored for each family, with the resources family members have, with the values that they hold, and in the circumstances in which they live. These specific and obtainable behavior changes have a major impact on family functioning because they are targeted to alter the underlying risk and protective patterns (see Figure 15.1) that support and maintain other problematic behaviors. Thus, what can seem to be small behavior changes in family process (positive monitoring; affirmation of prosocial steps, rather than emotionally abusive criticisms) are ones that are lasting because they enhance the relevant protective factors and decrease the important risk factors in the individual family in treatment. In this way the obtainable changes that occur in these families not only have an immediate effect of changing a specific "problem" but also have an additional impact of actually empowering a family to continue applying changes to future circumstances. Thus, what currently seems like a small change becomes, over time, a significant and lasting alteration in the functioning of the family that is reflected in major changes in the behavioral outcomes, such as cessation of drug use and within-family violence.

## MATCHING

"Matching to" in FFT is a way to negotiate the dialectic between the theoretical and clinical goals of a model and the individual differences of specific clients. Matching to the *phase* guides therapists to consider the goals of the change phase in determining which direction to go, how to respond, and where to focus intervention or assessment activities. Matching to the *client* directs the therapist to achieve the phase goals in a way that fits with the clients' relational needs, problem definitions, or abilities of the family. Matching to the client allows FFT to respect, value, and work within the important cultural, racial, religious, and gender based values of the client. Matching to *sample* suggests that the therapist target outcomes and changes that fit this particular client, in this situation, acknowledging that individual's specific abilities and unique values. Match to sample allows the therapist to target obtainable and therefore lasting change. It also helps therapists to avoid imposing their own value systems, social agenda, and interpersonal needs on the youth and the family. Contingent clinical decisions are guided by the principle of matching therapeutic activities to the phase, the client, and the "sample."

The matching principle allows FFT therapists to negotiate the dialectic of structure through an a priori change process, while at the same time being respectful of the unique features of individual families. It is a respectful position that asserts that although families are different and may not fit one or another societal stereotype, they have the potential to function in a positive and adaptive manner. The match to principle also allows therapists to view "resistance" as a situation that exists when the offered activity, intervention, or belief does not feel as if it will be in the best interest of the receiver. Thus, resistance occurs when therapy does not "fit" the clients or their perceived circumstances.

Finally, FFT therapists support and sometimes initiate the reframing process with a "theme hint." Theme hints represent comments, many of which are not even explained, that suggest that very problematic patterns of interaction may be "hiding" deep and very human emotions. Typical examples are found in sessions where a single parent and a child begin to escalate their criticism and name calling. In response, the FFT therapist might simply start shaking her head and say, "Wow—you two are sure working hard to hide your real feelings." This theme hint implies that rather than the obvious anger and maladaptive behavior on both the mom's and the daughter's parts, the therapist is instead interested in examining the underlying feelings (pain, abandonment) that in fact they may both share.

Techniques such as reframing point out relational processes from a strength perspective, and theme hints represent a dramatic departure from the great majority of intervention programs with youths and parents who are "highly dysfunctional." By adopting the tone of respect and working hard to uncover the underlying strength and more benign motives behind problematic and often even destructive behaviors, FFT can quickly create a sense of hope and alliance that simply cannot be attained in confrontational models and or even in "therapeutic" models that imply that these people are deficient, maladaptive, or destructive.

## THE FFT TREATMENT PROTOCOL: A SYSTEMATIC, INTENTIONAL, AND PHASIC APPROACH TO CHANGE

FFT is a phasic clinical change model consisting of three specific and distinct phases of clinical intervention: (1) engagement and motivation, (2) behavior change, and (3) generalization (see Figure 15.3). Each phase has specific therapeutic goals and specific therapist skills that, when used, increase the likelihood of successful accomplishment of these goals. Each phase of the model involves clini-

cally rich assessment and intervention components that are organized in a coherent manner and that build on the core principles noted previously.

It is important to note that FFT "savors the dialectic" by embracing two seemingly incompatible forces: being systematic and structured, while being relational and clinically responsive. The clinical model and accompanying treatment manual (Alexander et al., 2000) is a "map" that details the specific goals and strategies of each phase of change. FFT clinicians use the powerful clinical processes that emerge when working with a troubled family by being clinically responsive to the family, while at the same time relying on phase-specific change mechanisms in a systematic approach to change. However, the clinical model applies these strategies and approaches these goals in ways that are unique to each family. FFT is therefore both a responsive process of discovery and a verification that is directional and focused (Alexander & Sexton, 2002).

An appropriate metaphor is that of a family vacation. Upon setting off, the vacationers orient themselves by relying on the general knowledge of the terrain, the location of appropriate highways, and the most efficient way to arrive at a destination. Along the way, the map serves as a marker of proximal success, providing guideposts that indicate progress, thus verifying the expected route in the journey and allowing the travelers to remain on the directional path. The map serves to provide guidance when unexpected events (e.g., road construction) appear. Without the map, the journey can be frustrating and inefficient and can lead to an experience filled with so many discouraging detours that the potential experiences and subsequent learning are missed. Yet the map does not provide any indication of what the traveler will encounter on the journey. There is nothing to suggest the nature of the experiences along the way, the

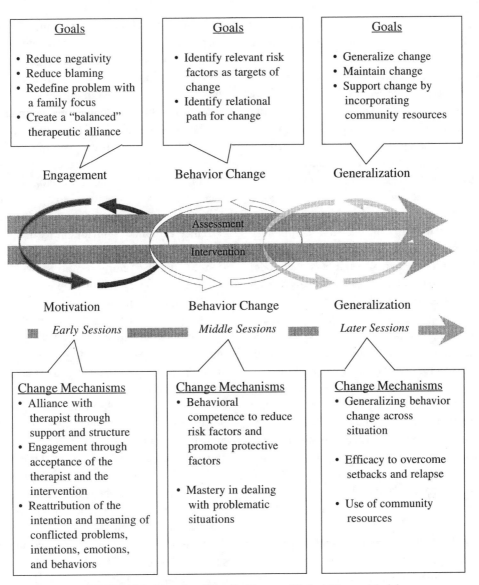

FIGURE 15.3. Functional Family Therapy Clinical Change Model

quality of the relationships one might make in stops, the experiences and sights while traveling. Thus, the travelers remain open to discovery of new and unexpected experiences. FFT views clinical process much the same way, a structured, purposeful, and directional process that is open to wonderful and unique experiences to be found on the journey.

Although the implementation of FFT takes place according to the map—the stages of FFT take place in order—the relative emphasis and importance within each phase may differ, depending on the unique features of the family that are encountered in this seemingly ordered process. For example, in one family the negativity and blaming may be so intense that the therapist spends a significant amount of time (three to five sessions) during the early phase realizing that without the requisite level of motivation, any move into behavior change would likely produce noncompliance and would not allow the family to accomplish change. In another family, the initial motivation level, family focus on the problem, and negativity may take very little time to address. In this case the therapist may move more quickly to the behavior change phase, where it may be the development of competencies and the building of skills that take significant time (four to five sessions). In yet another family, both of the early phases may be accomplished relatively quickly, but maintaining change in the difficult peer and community environment of the family may take the most energy. In each of these examples, the model has retained its direction and the goals of each phase were accomplished; however, the distribution of these efforts was contingent on the needs of the family.

Accomplishment of the phase goals, though while structured and directional, is not linear. As such, the conversations between therapist and client may actually revolve around similar content areas as the therapist takes the opportunities that occur to accomplish the goals of the phase. In early phases, therapists take the opportunities to respond in ways that promote engagement and motivation. In the second phase, the therapists respond to client issues by focusing on specific behavior changes. In the third phase, therapists seek opportunities to support, generalize, and maintain the changes already made by clients. The clinical model becomes the primary source of guidance in how to respond within a context of the "real" events of the family and its relational context. Within this contingent process, each action of the therapist is viewed as having therapeutic potential.

The *engagement and motivation phase* has three primary goals: alliance building, negativity reduction, blame reduction, and developing a shared family focus to the presenting problems (see Figure 15.3). Engagement and motivation begin with the first contact between the therapist and the family, as the therapist purposefully attempts to involve the family members in the immediate activities (of the session or of an initial phone call), such that they become interested in taking part in and accepting of therapy (engagement). In an active and engaging way FFT therapists immediately focus on the process goals of the phase: reducing between–family member negativity and blame, while trying to develop a family focus to the problems presented by the family by actively reframing and creating a sense of "balanced alliance" with all family members. The desired outcome of these early interactions is that the family develops motivation by experiencing a sense of support in its position, emotions, and concerns; a sense of hope that the problem can change; and a belief that the therapist and therapy can help promote those changes. When negativity and blaming are reduced, hope can emerge and therapists can demonstrate that they are capable and competent to be a helpful influence. Reduction of blaming and negativity also creates more positive interactions among family members, which contribute to a sense of hope. The outcome is an alliance that develops where each family member believes that the therapist supports and understands his or her position, beliefs, and values.

The engagement and motivation phase is successful when the family members begin to believe that although everyone in the family has a different and unique contribution to the primary concerns, everyone shares in the emotional struggle that is occurring. The family comes to trust in the therapist; its members believe that the therapist has an understanding of their unique position, albeit they may not agree, and the therapist has the ability to help. They come to know that regardless of what they may have done, the therapist will protect and help them as much as anyone else. They become engaged in the process and come to believe that it will benefit them personally and the family as a whole and that the solution will require changes from each of them. In a sense they will each be more hopeful that a solution is possible and will feel motivated to take the responsibility to try new behaviors and techniques in search of this solution (see Figure 15.2).

The primary goal of the *behavior change phase* is to target and change specific behavioral skills of family members, thereby increasing their ability to more competently perform the myriad of tasks (e.g., communication, parenting, supervision, problem solving) that contribute to successful family functioning (see Figure 15.3). Successful behavior change is accomplished by identifying the risk factors that contribute to the specific problem behavior for which the family was referred and helping to change these in a way that matches the relational functions of the individual family. The emphasis in this phase is on building protective family skills that will improve the factors that put the family and adolescent at risk. The desired outcomes of this phase are the competent performance of the primary activities associated with risk factors: parenting, giving rewards and punishments, communicating between adolescent and parent, negotiating limits and rules, problem solving, and managing conflict in a way that matches the relational capabilities of the particular family, that is developmentally appropriate, and that is possible for this family with these abilities in this context.

Although the targets of a behavior change plan are the risk factors common in many families (e.g., communication, parenting, problem solving) in the population of at-risk adolescents, the way in which those changes are made must be uniquely crafted to fit the relational functioning of the individual family in treatment. Thus, the goal is to increase competent performance of, for example, communication, but in a way that matches the relational functions of that particular parent and

that adolescent. In one family the implementation of communication change might take the form of close and connected negotiation of changes so that both parents feel connected and part of a collaborative relationship with one another. In another family, with a different relational profile, the same communication changes would look more disconnected and distanced, with information exchanged via notes instead of conversation. Therefore, the goal of our behavioral intervention is not to change the relational functions of behaviors but instead to change the manifestation of these functions. By focusing on the expression of functional outcomes, not on the outcomes themselves, FFT individualizes the changes of behavior to fit the existing relational functioning of the family. Making behavioral technologies "fit" the family relational system allows the family therapist to take the path of least resistance.

In the *generalization phase*, the therapeutic goals are generalizing, maintaining, and supporting the changes the family has made earlier. The focus of attention changes from within-family changes to the ways in which the family will respond to other similar and future struggles, and how the family interacts with the systems around it (e.g., schools, community, extended family). Generalization takes place both within the family and between the family and its environment. As the generalization phase begins, the therapist helps the family generalize changes that have occurred in the behavior change and engagement/motivation phases to other areas of family function that have not been specifically addressed. Then, the therapist works to help the family maintain change by overcoming the natural "roller coaster" of change. Maintenance of change occurs through using relapse-prevention techniques to normalize the typical problems that will inevitably occur in the future, while having confidence that the family's newly acquired skills will work in different situations over time. Finally, the goal of supporting change is usually accomplished by bringing the necessary community resources and support to the family. In general, long-term change is accomplished when the family is helped to use its own skills to obtain these changes with the guidance of the therapist. The desired outcomes of the generalization stage are to stabilize emotional and cognitive shifts made by the family in engagement and motivation and the specific behavior changes made to alter risk and enhance protective factors. This is done by having the family develop a sense of mastery around its ability to address future and different situations.

The three phases of the FFT represent a directional, purposeful, yet relationally based map of the therapeutic process. The dynamic nature of the FFT model is one of its most unique features. By embracing the dialectic between structure, direction, systematic intervention, and contingent, individually focused, and clinically responsive treatment, it is a model that has clinical relevance and widespread application. What the FFT model attempts to do is depict the systemic nature of the FFT change model, while understanding that any change must occur within the context of a relational process between a family and therapist.

## SCIENTIFIC FOUNDATIONS OF FUNCTIONAL FAMILY THERAPY

Functional family therapy is based on a long-term, systematic, and independently replicated series of outcome and process research studies. These results have led the Center for Substance Abuse Prevention (CSAP) and the Office of Juvenile Justice and Delinquency Prevention (OJJDP) to identify FFT as a "model" program for both substance abuse and delinquency prevention (Alvarado, Kendall, Beesley, & Lee-Cavaness, 2000). Similarly,

the Center for the Study and Prevention of Violence (CSPV) designated FFT as one of the 11 (out of over 1,000 reviewed programs) "Blueprint" programs (Elliott, 1998). The Surgeon General's Report (Surgeon General, 2001) identified FFT as one of only four Level I programs for successfully intervening with conduct disorder, violent, and multiproblem at-risk adolescents. Finally, FFT is an evidence-based intervention model that meets the current benchmarks of empirically validated treatments (Sexton & Alexander, 2001).

The results of published studies suggest that FFT is effective in reducing recidivism between 26% and 73% with status-offending, moderate, and seriously delinquent youths, as compared to both no treatment and juvenile court probation services (Alexander, et al., 2000). Of most interest is the range of community settings and client ethnicities that have composed these studies (a more complete list can be found in Alexander, et al., 2000). These positive outcomes of FFT remain relatively stable even at follow-up times as long as 5 years (Gordon, Arbuthnot, Gustafson, & McGreen, 1988) and the positive impact also affects siblings of the identified adolescent (Klein, Alexander, & Parsons, 1977). Although these studies typically used recidivism as the dependent measure, a recent community-based effectiveness study of violent and drug-abusing youths in a large urban setting with a multi-ethnic and multicultural population found that those adolescents in the FFT treatment condition not only had significantly lower recidivism rates but also committed significantly fewer crimes that were significantly less severe, even when pretreatment crime history was factored into the analysis (Sexton, Ostrom, Bonomo, & Alexander, 2000). For a complete review of the outcome studies of FFT, consult Alexander et al. (2002), Alexander and Sexton (2002a) and Sexton and Alexander (2002a).

FFT has also proven to be a cost-effective

intervention. Sexton and Alexander (2000) found FFT to be significantly more effective in reducing recidivism and $5,000 per case *less costly* than an equivalent juvenile detention intervention, and $12,000 *less expensive* than residential treatment of a similar course. In the most comprehensive investigation of the economic outcomes of family-based interventions to date, the State of Washington found that FFT had among the highest cost *savings* when compared to other juvenile offender programs. The cost of implementing the program was approximately $2,500 per family, with a cost savings (taxpayer and crime victim cost) of $13,908 (Aos & Barnoski, 1998).

A recent study investigated the role of therapist model fidelity in the outcomes of FFT (Barnoski, 2002b; Sexton, Hollimon, & Mease, 2002). What is unique about this study is that it is a true community effectiveness trial, in which FFT was tested with actual clients and with therapists trained to do the model, rather than with therapists who are part of a clinical trial research team. Over a 1-year period, FFT was implemented in 13 counties in the State of Washington. Moderate to high-risk adolescent juvenile offenders were randomly assigned to either an FFT condition (*n* = 427) or a treatment-as-usual condition (*n* = 323). Youths in the FFT and TAU group did not differ on risk level (as determined by the Washington State Risk Assessment Instrument) or on previous crime history or severity. Of the adolescents in the study, almost half (46.9%) had been expelled from school, many had comorbid disorders of alcohol/drug abuse and conduct disorder (85.4%), 27% had other identifiable mental health disorders, and more than half had been adjudicated with felony crimes (56.2%). FFT was delivered according to a treatment manual (Alexander et al., 2000). In addition, the FFT therapists received weekly supervision during which they were rated using the FFT supervisor rating form (Sexton & Alexander, 2000—see next sec-

tion), resulting in multiple ratings of therapist competence for each therapist.

The results indicated that FFT was effective in a number of ways. First, 89.8% of families who attended a first session of FFT completed the intervention program. This outcome is fairly dramatic, given the traditionally high rates of dropout (50–75%) in most treatment programs (Kazdin, 1997). FFT also resulted in a reduced felony recidivism rate 18 months after therapy (30% reduction) that was significantly different than the TAU. Cost-benefits suggest that when compared to the TAU condition, FFT saved $16, 250 per adolescent, or over $1 million across the project for the time period of the study. In addition, the results suggest that these dramatic outcomes are evident only for those therapists rated as competent in the model, based on supervisor ratings. Cases with therapists rated by supervisors as "highly competent" and "competent" had felony recidivism rates lower than the TAU group (14% and 17% vs. 22%, respectively), whereas those who were rated "borderline" and "not competent" had recidivism rates greater than those of the control group (25% and 29% vs. 22%, respectively) (Sexton, Hollimon, & Mease, 2002). The suggestion is that FFT is effective in reducing serious reoffense rates of at-risk adolescents, but that those reductions occur only when FFT is delivered as the model was intended to be delivered (e.g., in a competent fashion).

FFT also has a long history of process studies aimed at understanding therapeutic change mechanisms. What is unique about this line of research is that it has systematically verified many of the theoretically identified change mechanisms of the model and has been the source of information for improving the model. For example, Alexander, Barton, Schiavo, and Parsons (1976) found that the ratio of negative to supportive statements made by family members was significantly higher in cases that dropped out of therapy than among cases that completed treatment. In turn, premature termination predicted recidivism in adolescents. Newell, Alexander, and Turner (1996) confirmed that levels of family member negativity could successfully predict program dropouts. Newberry, Alexander, and Turner (1991) found that in the engagement and motivation phase, therapist supportiveness increased the likelihood of a positive response and thus the reduction of negativity by family members. Negativity reduction is a primary objective of the engagement and motivation phase. These process studies are critical, in that they provide evidence for the theoretical constructs and mechanisms of change proposed by FFT.

## METHODS OF MODEL EVALUATION AND ADHERENCE

It seems increasingly clear that without model fidelity and therapist model adherence, the demonstrated outcomes of evidenced-based approaches cannot be replicated in community settings (Henggeler & Schoenwald, 1999; Sexton & Alexander, 2002a; Sexton et al., 2002). Functional family therapy (FFT) has developed a comprehensive fidelity and adherence protocol (Sexton & Alexander, 2000) that is based on three assumptions: (a) model fidelity must be measured from different perspectives (therapist, client, and outside consultant); (b) fidelity and adherence information should be readily available to therapists, supervisors, and program administers for daily use; and (c) attention to fidelity and adherence should be a central part of clinical practice and supervision. In its national dissemination efforts, FFT utilizes four methods to monitor and track model fidelity: Therapist Progress Notes, Counseling Process Questionnaire, Supervisor Ratings, and Services Delivery Profiles. These instruments provide information from multiple perspectives (clients, thera-

pists, and supervisors) about different activities (therapist intentions, family behaviors, and service delivery decisions and profiles), in order to provide a comprehensive assessment of model fidelity.

Managing the multiple sources of information necessary to promote treatment fidelity is a daunting yet critical task. Sexton and colleagues (Sexton & Alexander, 2000; Sexton & Wilkenson, 1999) developed a computer-based monitoring and tracking system to serve as an additional tool to aid in the training and adherence of community practice sites. The Functional Family Therapy Clinical Services System (FFT-CSS) is an intuitive, user-friendly, web-based program used by community-based FFT therapists to record client information (e.g., contact information, demographic information, previous history), client contacts (visits, scheduled visits, phone contacts, etc.), assessment information (individual, family, and behavioral assessment), adherence measures, and outcome measurements. The goal of the CSS is to increase therapist adherence, competence, and skill by keeping therapists focused on the relevant goals, skills, and interventions necessary for each of the phases of FFT. The CSS provides immediate "real-time" feedback to therapists on model fidelity, client outcomes, and service delivery profiles. In addition, it provides site clinical supervisors with specific information to be used in helping supervise cases and maintain model fidelity.

## THE DISSEMINATION OF FUNCTIONAL FAMILY THERAPY: TRAINING, IMPLEMENTATION, AND SUPERVISION

FFT has been implemented as the primary intervention model in over 90 community sites in more than 15 states between 1998 and 2002 (Sexton & Alexander, 2002). At those sites, approximately 375 therapists helped approximately 10,000 families each year with functional family therapy. The organizations, therapists, and clients at these replication sites represent a very diverse cultural, community, and ethnic range. To date, FFT has been used in agencies that primarily serve clients who are Chinese Americans, African Americans, White-Caucasian families, and Vietnamese, among others. The agencies in which FFT has been replicated range from community not-for-profit youth development agencies, to drug and alcohol groups, to traditional mental health centers. The therapists at these sites are as diverse as the clients in regard to gender, age, and ethnic origin. At these sites FFT is delivered both as an in-home service and as a traditional outpatient program. Increasingly, FFT is being implemented in school-based settings (Mease & Sexton, in press). An increasing emphasis has been on statewide implementation of FFT in various treatment systems. For example, FFT has worked within the juvenile justice system in Washington State for over 5 years. FFT recently began a project to train all adolescent and family therapists in the New York mental health system (over 60 individual sites).

Successfully disseminating FFT has been a complex task. The technology required to transfer intervention programs from the laboratory into practice settings is only beginning to be clearly understood (Henggeler, Schoenwald, Liao, Letourneau, & Edwards, 2002). FFT has adopted the same therapeutic and scientific principles that guide the clinical model to direct the implementation process: provide FFT in a way that maximizes model fidelity, while matching to the needs of the community and the families. To accomplish the task of replication with high fidelity, FFT developed a systematic training and implementation program as well as a model-specific clinical supervision approach (Sexton & Alexander, 2002a). People in each participating site are trained and supervised using a similar protocol; each site implements the same clinical model, and thus comparative information from multiple sites can be used to improve practice. Each site engages in ongoing fidelity monitoring and outcome assessment (see previous section), and each site participates in the national network of FFT sites by using the web-based CSS system (see previous section).

In each domain of training and implementation, the primary objective is to help therapists adopt both the guiding principles and the clinical "map" of FFT as their primary sources of clinical decisions. We have described this process as one in which the therapists adopt the "lens" of FFT, using it to focus their inherent and developed strengths so that precise, high quality, and systematic clinical decisions can be made that increase the likelihood of success with families. Therapists bring their professional and personal knowledge, individual strengths and abilities, and relational qualities to the process of delivering FFT. The FFT model provides a focusing "lens" that takes individual therapist strengths and focuses them through the principle of the approach and the "map" that guides service delivery. In this way, the strengths of the therapist (professional and personal) are focused into a precise, efficient, and intense way through the model, thereby improving outcome.

## CONCLUSIONS

Functional family therapy evolved from its early clinical and scientific roots into a clinical model that attends to treatment, assessment, quality assurance, and community implementation in a systematic way, organized around consistent theoretical principles, while remaining "open" to scientific and theoretical developments. FFT is comprehensive in its attention to family process, successful outcome, and fidelity-based community replication. Throughout its evolution and in its current form, FFT is a model that moves science into practice and practice into science. This integration is so central to the development of FFT that we don't believe it is possible to ignore either clinical wisdom to produce "good science" or the important and stable principles of science, if one is to develop a clinically competent model. In fact, over the years a unifying principle of FFT has been to "savor the dialectic" (Alexander & Sexton, 2002; Sexton & Alexander, 2002a). As a result, FFT is now a model that is clinically responsive and theoretically integrated, while at the same time it meets all the recent benchmarks of evidence-based practice and empirically supported treatments (Sexton & Alexander, 2002a).

Throughout its evolution FFT has grown, changed, and yet remained the same—a family relational approach to change. The open nature of FFT's development has allowed it to become a "mature clinical model" that integrates clinical experience, scientific findings, and theoretical principles into a "whole" model that systematically guides the process of helping troubled families. We believe that this dynamic open-system evolution led FFT to being theoretically viable yet conceptually stable, clinically responsive yet directional and systematic, and integrative of the most current research. From our perspective, one must constantly move between the therapy room; the research lab; the writing desk; the multisite, multicultural implementation site; and the supervision context, in order to build a viable clinical model that truly represents the dynamic nature of family therapy.

## REFERENCES

Alexander, J. F., Barton, C., Schiaro, R. S., & Parsons, B. V. (1976). Behavioral intervention with families of delinquents: Therapist characteristics and outcome. *Journal of Consulting and Clinical Psychology, 44,* 656–664.

Alexander, J. F., Holtzworth-Monroe, A., & Jameson, P. (1994). The process and outcome of marital and family therapy: Research review and evaluation. In A. E. Bergin & S. L. Garfield (Eds.), *Handbook of psychotherapy and behavior change* (pp. 594–630). New York: Wiley.

Alexander, J. F., & Parsons, B. V. (1973). Short term behavioral intervention with delinquent families: Impact on family process and recidivism. *Journal of Abnormal Psychology, 81*(3), 219–225.

Alexander, J. F., Pugh, C., Parsons, B., & Sexton, T. L. (2000). Functional family therapy. In D. Elliott (Series Ed.), Book three: *Blueprints for violence prevention* (2nd ed.). Golden, CO: Venture.

Alexander, J. F., Robbins, M. S., & Sexton, T. L., (2000). Family-based interventions with older, at-risk youth: From promise to proof to practice. *The Journal of Primary Prevention, 42,* 185–205.

Alexander, J. F., & Sexton, T. L. (2002). Functional family therapy: A model for treating high-risk, acting-out youth. In J. Lebow (Ed.), Wiley series in couples and family dynamics and treatment, *Comprehensive handbook of psychotherapy, vol. IV: Integrative/eclectic.* New York: Wiley.

Alexander, J. F., Sexton, T. L., & Robbins, M. S. (2002). The developmental status of family therapy in family psychology intervention science. In H. S. Liddle, D. Santsiteban, R. Levant, & J. Bray (Eds.), *Family psychology intervention science.* Washington, DC: American Psychological Association.

Alvarado, R., Kendall, K, Beesley, S., & Lee-Cavaness, C. (2000). *Strengthening America's families: Model family program for substance abuse and delinquency prevention.* Washington, DC: Office of Juvenile Justice and Delinquency Prevention.

Aos, S., & Barnoski, R. (1998). *Watching the bottom line: Cost-effective interventions for reducing crime in Washington.* Washington State Institute for Public Policy: RCW 13.40.500.

Barnoski, R. (2002a). Monitoring vital signs: Integrating a standardized assessment into Washington State's juvenile justice system. In R. R. Corrado et al. (Eds.), *Multi-problem violent youth: A foundation for comparative research on needs, interventions and outcomes.* Series I: Life and behavioural sciences (Vol. 324, pp. 219–231). Amsterdam, Netherlands Antilles: IOS Press.

Barnoski, R. (2002b). Washington state's implementation of functional family therapy for juvenile offenders: Preliminary findings. *Washington State*

*Institute for Public Policy,* www.wsipp.wa.gov

Barton, C., & Alexander, J. F. (1981). Functional family therapy. In A. Gurman & D. Kniskern (Eds.), *Handbook of family therapy* (pp. 403–443). New York: Brunner/Mazel.

Barton, C., & Alexander, J. F., Waldron, H., Turner, C. W., & Warburton, J. (1985). Generalizing treatment effects of functional family therapy: Three replications. *The American Journal of Family Therapy, 13*(3), 16–26.

Claiborn, C. D., & Lichtenberg, J. W. (1989). Interactional counseling. *Counseling Psychologist, 17*(3), 355–453.

Elliott, D. S (1998). Editor's introduction. In D. Elliott (Series Ed.), Book Three: *Blueprints for violence prevention.* Golden, CO: Venture/Denver, CO: C & M Press.

Friedlander, M. L., & Heatherington, L. (1998). Assessing client's constructions of their problems in family therapy discourse. *Journal of Marital and Family Therapy, 24,* 289–303.

Gergen, K. (1985). The social constructionist movement in modern psychology. *American Psychologist, 40,* 266–273.

Gordon, D. A., Arbuthnot, J., Gustafson, K., & McGreen, P. (1988). Home-based behavioral systems family therapy with disadvantaged juvenile delinquents. *American Journal of Family Therapy, 16,* 243–255.

Haley, J. (1964). Research on family patterns: An instrument measurement. *Family Process, 3*(1), 41–76.

Hansson, K. (1998, January). *Functional Family Therapy replication in Sweden: Treatment outcome with juvenile delinquents.* Paper presented to the Eighth Conference on Treating Addictive Behaviors, Santa Fe, NM.

Hawkins, J. D., Catalano, R. F., & Miller, J. Y. (1992). Risk and protective factors for alcohol and other drug problems in adolescence and early adulthood: Implications for substance abuse preventions. *Psychological Bulletin, 112,* 64–105.

Henggeler, S. W., & Schoenwald, S. K. (1999). The role of quality assurance in achieving outcomes in MST programs. *Journal of Juvenile Justice and Detention Services, 14,* 1–17.

Henggeler, S. W., Schoenwald, S. K., Liao, J. G., Letourneau, E. J., & Edwards, D. L. (2002). Transporting efficacious treatment to field settings: The link between supervisory practices and therapist fidelity in MST programs. *Journal of Child Clinical Psychology, 31,* 155–167.

Henggeler, S. W., Schoenwald, S. K., & Pickrel, S. (1995). Multisystemic therapy: Bridging the gap

between university and community-based treatment. *Journal of Consulting and Clinical Psychology, 5,* 709–717.

Heppner, P. P., & Claiborn, C. D. (1988). Social influence research in counseling: A review and critique. *Journal of Counseling Psychology, 36*(3), 365–387.

Horvath, A. O. (2001). The alliance. *Psychotherapy: Theory, Research, Practice, Training, 38*(4), 365–372.

Horvath, A. O., & Symonds, B. D. (1991). Relation between working alliance and outcome in psychotherapy: A meta-analysis. *Journal of Counseling Psychology, 38*(2), 139–149.

Jones, E. E., & Nisbett. R. E. (1972). The actor and the observer: Divergent perceptions of the causes of behavior. In E. E. Jones, D. E. Kanouse, H. H. Kelley, R. E. Nisbett, S. Valins, & B. Weiner (Eds.), *Attribution: Perceiving the causes of behavior* (pp. 79–94). Morristown, NJ: General Learning Process.

Katz, D., & Kahn, R. L. (1966). *The social psychology of organizations.* Oxford, England: Wiley.

Kazdin, A. E. (1997). Practitioner review: Psychosocial treatments for conduct disorder in children. *Journal of Child Psychology and Psychiatry, 38*(2), 161–178.

Kelley, H. H. (1973). The process of causal attribution. *American Psychologist, 28,* 107–128.

Klein, N., Alexander, J., & Parsons, B. (1977). Impact of family systems interventions on recidivism and sibling delinquency: A model of primary prevention and program evaluation. *Journal of Consulting and Clinical Psychology, 45,* 469–474.

Lanz, B. (1982). Preventing adolescent placement through Functional Family Therapy and tracking. Utah Department of Social Services, West Valley Social Services, District 2K, Kearns, UT 84118. Grant #CDP 1070 UT 83-0128020 87-6000-545-W.

Mas, C. H., Alexander, J. F., Barton, C. (1985). Modes of expression in family therapy: A process study of roles and gender. *Journal of Marital & Family Therapy, 11*(4), 411-415.

Mas, C. H.; Alexander, J. F.; Turner, C. W. (1991). Dispositional attributions and defensive behavior in high- and low-conflict delinquent families. *Journal of Family Psychology, 5*(2), 176–191.

Mease, A. L., & Sexton, T. L. (in press). Functional family therapy as school-based intervention program. In K. Robinson (Ed.), *Advances in School Based Mental Health: Best Practices and Program Models.* Kingston, NJ: Civic Research Institute.

Newberry, A. M., Alexander, J. F., & Turner, C. W. (1991). Gender as a process variable in family therapy. *Journal of Family Psychology, 5,* 158–175.

Newell, R. M., Alexander, J. F., & Turner, C. W. (1996, June). *The effects of therapist divert and interrupt on family members' reciprocity of negativity in delinquent families.* Poster session presented at the Annual Convention of the American Family Therapy Academy, San Francisco.

Parsons, B., & Alexander, J. (1973). Short-term family intervention: A therapy outcome study. *Journal of Consulting and Clinical Psychology, 48,* 195–201.

Prochaska, J. O. (1999). How do people change, and how can we change to help many more people? In M. A. Hubble, B. L. Duncan, et al. (Eds.), *The heart and soul of change: What works in therapy* (pp. 227–255). Washington, DC: American Psychological Association.

Robbins, M. S., Jimenez, D., Alexander, J. F., & Turner, C. W. (November, 2001). *Discriminating adolescent and parent alliances with therapists in families that complete or dropout of family therapy for adolescent drug abuse.* Paper presented at the Society for Psychotherapy Research: North American Region/Conference. Puerta Vallarta, Mexico.

Robbins, M. S., Turner, C. W., Alexander, J. F., & Perez, G. A. (in press). Alliance and dropout in family therapy with drug using adolescents: Individual and systemic effects. *Journal of Family Psychology.*

Selvini-Palazzoli, M. Boscolo, L., Cecchin, G., & Prata, G. *(1978). Paradox and counterparadox.* New York: Jason Aronson.

Sexton, T. L., & Alexander, J. F. (December, 2000). Functional Family Therapy. *Juvenile Justice Bulletin,* Office of Juvenile Justice and Delinquency Prevention. Washington DC: Department of Justice.

Sexton, T. L., & Alexander, J. F. (2002a). Functional family therapy: For at risk adolescents and their families. In T. Patterson (Ed.), Wiley series in couples and family dynamics and treatment, *Comprehensive handbook of psychotherapy, vol II: Cognitive-behavioral approaches.* New York: Wiley.

Sexton, T. L., & Alexander, J. F. (2002b). Family-based empirically supported interventions. *The Counseling Psychologist, 30*(2), 238–261.

Sexton, T. L., Alexander, J. F., & Mease, A. L. (in press). Levels of evidence for the models and mechanisms of change for couple and family therapy. In M. Lambert (Ed.), *Handbook of psychotherapy and behavior change* (5th ed.). New York: Wiley.

Sexton, T. L., & Griffin, B. L. (Eds). (1997). *Constructivist thinking in counseling practice, research, and training. Counseling and development series,* New York: Teachers College Press.

Sexton, T. L., Hollimon, A. S., & Mease, A. L. (2002). *Family-based interventions in community settings.* Presented at American Association of Marriage and Family Therapy's annual convention, Cincinnati, OH.

Sexton, T. L., Hollimon, A. S., Mease, A. L., & Alexander, J. F. (2002, August). *Implementing Evidence-based Family Interventions: Results of a National Dissemination Project.* Symposium conducted at the American Psychological Association annual convention, Chicago, IL.

Sexton, T. L., Ostrom, N., Bonomo, J., & Alexander, J. F. (2000). *Functional family therapy in a multicultural, multiethnic urban setting.* Paper presented at the annual conference of the American Association of Marriage and Family Therapy, Denver, CO.

Sexton, T. L., & Wilkenson, J. (1999). *The functional family therapy clinical services system.* RCH Henderson, NV: Enterprises.

Szapocznik, J., & Kurtines, W. (1989). *Breakthroughs in family therapy with drug abusing problem youth.* New York: Springer.

Taylor, S. E., & Fiske, S. T. (1978). Salience, attention, and attribution: Top of the head phenomena. In L. Berkowitz (Ed.), *Advances in experimental social psychology* (Vol. 11, pp. 250–288). New York: Academic Press.

U.S. Public Health Service. (2001). *Youth violence: A report of the Surgeon General.* Washington, DC.

Watzlawick, P., Beavin, J. H., & Jackson, D. D. (1967). *Pragmatics of human communication: A study of interactional patterns, pathologies, and paradoxes.* New York: Norton.

Watzlawick, P., Weakland, J., & Fisch, R. (1974). *Change: Principles of problem formation and problem resolution.* New York: Norton.

# PART IV

# Special Applications and Special Populations in Couple and Family Therapy

## INTRODUCTION

The three previous sections of this handbook covered the issues of the history and foundations of family therapy, the main theoretical models of couple and family therapy, and empirically supported interventions. However, the handbook would not be complete, if that is ever possible, without covering some other common issues in this field that do not neatly fit under the first three sections.

The topics in this section represent new applications of family therapy. They are important because they break new ground in practice, theory, and research. Sex therapy is often viewed as a field unto itself. It has its own professional organizations, credentialing, and primary body of knowledge and research. Most all sexual problems are treated in the context of the couple and often involve an exploration of the messages from the family of origin. Thus, it is pragmatically and theoretically impossible to divorce sex therapy from the larger fields of couple and family therapy.

Medical family therapy, the treatment of adolescent conduct disorder and drug abuse,

and psychoeducational approaches are relatively recent and highly specialized applications of the systems approach. The medical family therapist helps the family and its various subcomponents deal with life-threatening or chronic illnesses and death. Research in this field is showing the connections between mental and physical health. The treatment of drug abuse was once viewed as an individual problem, requiring individual treatment. As younger people have become involved in drug and alcohol use, family therapists found that they could reduce substance abuse by understanding the function the drug abuse served in the family. Psychoeducational intervention is a movement that has gained substantial momentum in the last few years and is the application of the systems approach to "normal" couples and families, with the intent of improving functioning and preventing future problems. A wide array of programs has been developed, varying in the degree of structure and specificity.

The use of writing to facilitate treatment is a new and controversial topic in our field. Technology has become part of every field of endeavor and raises many opportunities and dilemmas for the family therapist. At this point, the only issue that is certain is that technology will become part of family therapy. Is it possible that in the future, all therapy will be technologically mediated and the long-cherished role of the person of the therapist isn't as important as once believed? The applications of this technology are only beginning to be discovered.

Finally, family therapy is a profession that is still searching for the best ways to organize curricula and help professors teach a large body of knowledge that will lead to licensure and effective practice. As therapy is a profession that is based on an apprenticeship or mentor model, supervision is of vital importance. Supervision is the core experience of any clinical training program. A number of modalities of supervision have been explored and will continue to be explored. Supervision is a transtheoretical concept that cuts across all the major models of family therapy.

CHAPTER 16

# Evaluation and Treatment of Sexual Dysfunction

S. MICHAEL PLAUT, PhD

*University of Maryland*

KAREN M. DONAHEY, PhD

*Northwestern University*

## INTRODUCTION

We sometimes like to think that we have come of age in the sexual arena. Sex is more openly discussed than ever, information about sexuality is more readily available via self-help books and the Internet, and it is even more acceptable to admit that one may have a sexual dysfunction. However, although the spectrum of values and the comfort level may have shifted to the more open, liberal end of the spectrum, there are still many among us for whom sex is a very difficult topic. Sexuality is still not discussed with a sense of comfort in many homes, if it is discussed at all. Sex education in school is still a controversial topic. Although we are addressing various forms of sexual abuse more effectively than ever, a disturbingly large proportion of our population still experiences unwanted sex, which may have far-reaching effects on those individuals' comfort with sex as an important and meaningful part of an intimate relationship.

Those of us who are trained to help people with personal and relationship problems are generally no different than the rest of the population with regard to our own sense of comfort with sexuality. Although the topic may be more easily discussed in the abstract, it is generally considered a private matter that is not readily shared even with those closest to us. For these reasons, many therapists and physicians do not make sexual issues a part of their evaluation or consider that aspect of relationships when helping their clients (Maurice, 1999). Furthermore, the special nature of sex in our lives requires specific therapeutic techniques that many therapists are not taught. The treatment of sexual disorders is, in fact, a specialty within our field, and for good reason.

In addition to these psychosocial considerations, sexual function is increasingly understood as a truly biopsychosocial phenomenon. A healthy sexual response depends on certain functions of our nervous and endocrine systems and is subject to modification by illness, disability, and the aging process itself. For this reason, sexual problems may require treatment in a multidisciplinary context.

The appearance of new medical treatments for sexual dysfunction, such as sildenafil (Viagra), may lead some mental health professionals to be concerned about what is sometimes called the "medicalization" of sex therapy. Clearly, an overreliance on either organic or psychosocial factors in the evaluation and treatment of sexual dysfunction is not likely to fulfill the needs of the patient with a sexual dysfunction, any more than it will with any other disease or disability. However, we are optimistic that an increased openness and sophistication of both medical and mental health professionals, as well as increased patient education, can only lead to the kind of integrative approach that truly embraces the richness and complexity of our sexual lives (Althof, 1998).

The last decade has seen a number of other new developments in the sexuality area, including the publishing of the first large-scale well-designed sociological study since the Kinsey report (Laumann, Gagnon, Michael, & Michaels, 1994). An increased attention to women's issues has been reflected by new research and has been formalized by the formation of the International Society for the Study of Women's Sexual Health (ISSWSH). Finally, the Internet has provided additional sources of information for both professionals and patients, while also providing new therapeutic issues (Cooper, 2002).

This chapter will briefly review the sexual dysfunctions and their evaluation and treatment, focusing on aspects typically addressed by the mental health professional. For the sake of simplicity in discourse, couples will be assumed to be heterosexual throughout this discussion. However, gay and lesbian couples may present with similar concerns, and most of the issues and techniques described here will apply. When the therapist works with homosexual couples, however, it is especially important neither to stereotype all sexual behavior of homosexual individuals, nor to apply heterosexual stereotypes to their behavior. Rather, the therapist should be aware of issues that may be pertinent to homosexual men and women (Nichols, 2000).

## BASIC CONSIDERATIONS IN SEX THERAPY

There are two general subtypes of sexual dysfunctions, as currently classified (American Psychiatric Association, 1994). The first, consisting of six specific diagnostic categories, are dysfunctions of the three phases of the sexual response cycle—desire, arousal (or excitement), and orgasm (Kaplan, 1974). Desire disorders include hypoactive sexual desire and sexual aversion disorder. Arousal disorders include male erectile disorder, traditionally referred to as "impotence," and female sexual arousal disorder, which has been getting increased attention in recent years. Orgasm disorders include premature and retarded ejaculation in men and inhibited orgasm (or anorgasmia) in women. The second category of dysfunctions is the sexual pain disorders, dyspareunia and vaginismus.

Modern sex therapy began in the late 1960s with the pioneering work of Masters and Johnson (1966, 1970), who demonstrated the value of behavioral therapy techniques in alleviating sexual symptoms. Treatment was done in an intense, 2-week format, using male and female co-therapists. Later, Kaplan (1974) showed that the same techniques could be effective in the more traditional 1-hour-per-week therapy format, using a single therapist. Although the Masters and Johnson block format has the advantage of focusing on the sexual problem in a "protected" environment, the more spaced format has the advantage of flexibility for both patient and therapist, while also integrating the ongoing treatment into the patient's normal lifestyle.

A central precept under which the Masters and Johnson technique developed was the conviction that the sexual response is a *natural function*—that is, barring any medical disturbance to the normal cycle, sexual responses will occur under appropriate psychosocial or tactile stimulation, unless something else in the intrapsychic or interpersonal environment serves to block these responses. Kaplan (1974) referred to these factors as the *immediate causes* of sexual dysfunction. These may include such things as performance anxiety, absence of fantasy, inability to immerse oneself in a sexual situation (or "spectatoring"), or difficulties in seducing or arousing one's partner.

Although *deeper causes*, such as psychodynamic issues, relationship problems, or early conditioning, may also be very much involved in the etiology of sexual dysfunctions, a short-term behavioral approach focused on the immediate causes of the dysfunction has often proven more successful and more economical than longer-term insight-oriented therapy. In most cases, however, the therapist must approach the presenting problem at more than one level of intervention. For example, concomitant problems in the couple's relationship often demand the simultaneous attention to communication and control issues or the need to deal with a partner's fear of intimacy or fear of separation. A few authors have focused in detail on relationship dynamics as related to sexual function (e.g., Schnarch, 1991).

There is usually no direct correspondence between specific deeper causes and specific dysfunctions, which become the "final common pathway" for a number of possible precipitating factors. For example, a woman's incest history may be reflected sexually in hypoactive desire (or sexual aversion), anorgasmia, vaginismus, a combination of these, or she may show no sexual pathology at all. Her reaction will depend upon idiosyncratic factors, ranging from physiological or anatomical characteristics to the symbolic significance of the incest experience, her current partner, or the act of sex itself.

Another central premise upon which the techniques of Masters and Johnson were developed is the conviction that *the couple is the patient.* Thus, although one person may present with a sexual symptom, it is important that the treatment not support the blaming of one partner for the problem, that it elicit the cooperation and support of the asymptomatic partner, and that the sexual problem be evaluated and treated with the couple present. Indeed, the originally asymptomatic partner may display sexual symptoms (e.g., absence of desire) in the course of treating the presenting problem, especially if the original symptom was in some way functional for the partner.

Of course, there may be times when the person who presents with a sexual symptom has no partner, or the partner may refuse to participate in treatment. It is usually best in such instances to do what one can with the individual patient, while explaining clearly the therapist's conviction that treatment done in the relationship context is more likely to be effective. Some sexual dysfunctions, such as a global anorgasmia, premature ejaculation, or vaginismus, can at least initially be treated through the use of individual therapy, masturbation exercises, or both.

*Levels of Intervention—
The PLISSIT Model*

Annon and Robinson (1978) proposed the

PLISSIT Model to characterize the step-wise approach to counseling a person with a sexual problem. The first level of intervention is the giving of *permission*—for example, to discuss sex openly, to use the language of sex without guilt, or to engage in certain sexual behaviors that are generally considered normal. In providing such permission, however, the therapist must take care not to insist that the patient violate any strongly held values. The therapist may also provide *limited information* about sexual development, male–female differences, genital anatomy, and so on. *Specific suggestions* may be provided that will enhance sexual pleasure or function, such as varying the time or the location of sexual activity, using certain sexual techniques, approaching a partner more effectively, or rejecting a partner in a supportive way. In many cases, suggestions may take the form of assigned reading, which some therapists call "bibliotherapy." A few books often found useful for this purpose include those by Barbach (1984, 1985), Heiman, LoPiccolo, and Pallidini (1988), Kennedy and Dean (1986), Kroll and Klein (1992), Laken and Laken (2002), Nelson (1978), Penner and Penner (1981), Valins (1992), and Zilbergeld (1999).

A number of websites may also be helpful to patients seeking information, support, or sex aids. The Sexual Information and Education Council of the United States (www.siecus.org) is an excellent source of information on various topics related to sexuality. Those experiencing sexual problems related to physical disability may find help at www.sexualhealth.com. Sex therapists may be found through the American Association of Sex Educators, Counselors, and Therapists (www.aasect.org) or the Society for Sex Therapy and Research (www.sstarnet.org). Books, videotapes, sex aids, and information about various sexual topics may be found through the Sinclair Intimacy Institute (www.intimacyinstitute.com). Yahoo.com and America Online, among other

general resources, sponsor closed chat rooms and listservs for people suffering from certain sexual dysfunctions.

Many times, a sexual concern can be dealt with by utilizing only the first three levels of counseling. However, if a dysfunction is clearly present, *intensive therapy* should be undertaken by someone who is skilled in the techniques of sex therapy, in which case all four levels of intervention are usually involved. Referral to qualified medical professionals or sex therapists can be extremely helpful in alleviating the patient's sexual concerns.

The American Association of Sex Educators, Counselors, and Therapists (AASECT) certifies sex therapists and has developed standards of training and practice that therapists are expected to meet, as well as continuing education standards. Because certification is rarely, if ever, a legal standard for the practice of sex therapy, many qualified sex therapists are not certified but have sought training and supervision in recognized training centers.

## EVALUATION OF SEXUAL PROBLEMS

The evaluation of a presenting sexual problem is aimed at identifying both the immediate and the deeper causes of the problem and at developing an initial treatment plan. In keeping with the central idea that "the couple is the patient," equivalent histories are taken from both members of the couple. Detailed descriptions of evaluation procedures are beyond the scope of this discussion. However, it may be of value to highlight some of the key issues that should be addressed in conducting the initial interviews. With the exception of the first section on tests and questionnaires, the format followed will basically be that proposed by Kaplan (1983).

Some therapists like to get some background information from the patient, in the form of either pencil-and-paper tests or questionnaires. Formal testing may include general assessments (e.g., MMPI, SCL-90), assessments of sexual function (e.g., LoPiccolo's Sexual Interaction Inventory, Derogatis's Sexual Function Inventory), or inventories of relationship status (e.g., Dyadic Adjustment Inventory). Questionnaires may gather pertinent data such as ages and number of children, household occupants, religious background, names of physicians and time of last physical examination, illnesses, surgeries and present medications, a brief description of the presenting problem, and the patient's expectations for therapy.

The first two parts of the interview are the *description of the chief complaint* and what Kaplan (1983) calls the *sexual status examination*. These are the most important aspects of the psychosexual evaluation, as they help determine the extent to which the problem may be medical versus psychosocial in origin and in that they enable the therapist to identify the immediate causes of the sexual problem.

This phase of the evaluation should include a description of the problem, its history, and why the patient sought help at the present time. It is here that clear communication and definitions of terms need to be established. What does the patient mean by "having sex," "making love," "partial erection," or "pain during intercourse?" Does "having sex" mean (only) vaginal intercourse? Is the "partial erection" sufficient for penetration? Is the pain experienced during intercourse deep in the vagina or at the entrance? And so on. It is here that a reluctance to communicate in detail may prevent an adequate definition of the problem. The therapist should take care not to assume that patients mean one thing when they may mean something quite different. As a supervisor of one of the authors used to say, "Don't connect the dots for the patient!"

A critical aspect of the description of the chief complaint is the determination of

whether the symptoms are global or situational—that is, under what conditions the symptoms occur. This will help the therapist to determine (a) whether a medical examination might aid in a complete diagnosis and (b) the extent to which the symptoms are relationship-related. For example, if a patient presents with an erectile problem, the therapist should attempt to determine whether the patient experiences erections in masturbation or upon awakening, and whether the onset of symptoms was sudden or gradual. The more global the symptoms and the more gradual the onset, the more likely it is that the problem has a medical etiology. If the erectile problem occurs primarily in the context of the patient's current relationship, it is important to know whether the problem began at the beginning of the relationship or whether it was related to a specific event or situation that occurred since the relationship began (e.g., moving in together, marriage). Does the problem occur with all partners, or perhaps with certain kinds of partners, such as those for whom the patient has strong feelings?

## Sexual Status Examination

The sexual status examination is the patient's complete account of a recent or typical sexual encounter. The patient may be uncomfortable doing this at first, but the therapist can play an important role in helping the patient to feel more comfortable discussing his or her sexual activity in detail, pointing out its importance to the therapist's understanding of the problem. This is the therapist's way of determining the often-subtle immediate causes of symptoms, and it should be done during each session in order to elucidate both progress and problems. The sexual status examination should assess all three phases of the sexual response cycle—desire, arousal, and orgasm. The therapist should determine under what conditions the sexual encounter took place (e.g., time of day, location, ambience); who initiated it; what took place; what problems occurred, if any; how each partner responded to the problems; and how the encounter ended. The therapist should also attempt to determine what thoughts or feelings accompanied any problems experienced during the encounter, and this may be reassessed during individual interviews, as necessary.

It is often useful to know under what conditions the woman is orgasmic. Many women do not experience orgasm during intercourse without specific clitoral stimulation. This knowledge may have implications for the therapy if, for example, either partner is uncomfortable with oral or manual stimulation of the genitals or if a complaint of premature ejaculation is based solely on the relative occurrence of male and female orgasm.

When appropriate, it may be useful to do a detailed account of masturbatory practices, dreams, or fantasies, as these may provide keys to the immediate causes of sexual symptoms, while also aiding in the development of suitable behavioral assignments.

### Medical and Psychiatric Histories

The medical history should concentrate on illnesses, surgeries, and medications that are likely to cause or exacerbate sexual dysfunction, such as diabetes, vaginal infections, or circulatory problems. Assessment of drug use should include smoking, alcohol, illicit drugs, and over-the-counter medications, as well as prescription medications. A comprehensive description of the effects of many pharmacological agents on various aspects of sexual function has been provided by Crenshaw and Goldberg (1996). For example, over-the-counter antihistamines will often inhibit vaginal lubrication. If appropriate, the couple should be asked about menstrual cycling, the

couple's sexual practices during menstruation, contraceptive use, and plans for having children. At times, a couple will have stopped using contraception, because "we're not having sex, anyway." Unless the couple is trying to get pregnant, the therapist should encourage the partners to begin or resume whatever contraceptive practices they may wish to use. This will minimize another possible source of anxiety regarding sexual "success," while helping the partners learn how to comfortably integrate contraceptive use into their sexual encounters. In doing the medical history, the therapist may also find it helpful to ask about any alternative practitioners, such as homeopaths or acupuncturists, being seen by the patient; why they are seeing these practitioners; and how helpful they have been.

The psychiatric history focuses on previous or existing emotional problems and treatment, as well as on a brief family history of psychiatric problems. In most cases, existing psychiatric problems, such as substance abuse or psychosis, should be stabilized before sex therapy is attempted. If a patient is in ongoing individual therapy, the sex therapist should establish consent and communication with the other therapist. Financial considerations may require that the other therapy be suspended while sex therapy is in progress.

### Family and Sexual Histories

The family history concentrates on relationships in the home during childhood and adolescence, with special attention to the patient's perception of the intimate relationships of parents or other caregivers. This is followed by the sexual history, which includes a description of sexual learning and modeling, as well as accounts of sexual experiences, both with and without partners. Patients should specifically be asked about any unwanted sexual experiences, including, but not limited to, rape, incest, or other traumatic sexual experiences. Both the patient's and the family's responses to these experiences should be assessed, as well as any treatment related to these events and the patient's current feelings about them. These questions should be asked of men as well as women, as it is not unusual for men to have experienced an event that they may not have previously identified as a sexual trauma. Such incidents may include incest, pedophilia, overexposure to nudity or sexuality in the home, threats of castration by older boys during adolescence, and so on.

### Relationship History and Status

This is usually assessed gradually throughout the evaluation, although specific questions may remain at the end. Depending on the nature and age of the relationship, the therapist should determine how the relationship began, how the partners feel about each other (both positive and negative feelings are important), how the relationship may be different from previous relationships, any problems with intimacy, existence of communication and control issues, and plans for cohabitation, children, marriage, and so on.

### Individual Sessions

Each member of the couple should be seen alone for at least part of a session, with the invitation for further individual sessions, as needed, and the agreement that any information presented as confidential will be maintained as such. The therapist may introduce these sessions with the assurance that any well-functioning couple has "secrets" that the partners may not feel comfortable sharing with each other, but that such information may be useful to the therapy. Both partners are asked, individually, whether there is anything about

the relationship or about their own development that they were not comfortable disclosing in the other partner's presence but that may be important for the therapist to know. The therapist may ask about the nature of each person's fantasies and how comfortable he or she is with fantasy. It is also important to ask at this session about any other ongoing sexual relationships. The therapist may point out that such other relationships, though the patient's business, will not serve the therapy, and that it is best that these be discontinued for the duration of therapy. It is in response to this question that a patient experiencing erectile or desire problems may admit good performance with another partner, signifying problems in the primary relationship that need to be addressed in therapy. Alternatively, such relationships may become a separate issue requiring treatment.

The tendency of the patient to seek alternative forms of sexual stimulation from other sources, whether videos, print media, or the Internet, can be just as much an inhibition to a primary relationship and thus to therapy as can a relationship with a real person. As Shaw (1997) has written, the real issue is the diversion of sexual energy from the primary relationship, whatever form it may take.

### Considerations in Overall Assessment

In evaluating the presenting problem, it often becomes clear that the presenting symptom is secondary to a more primary sexual problem, and the therapy must take both into account. For example, lack of desire in a male may be secondary to an erectile problem. Vaginismus is frequently secondary to an underlying hypoactive desire or sexual aversion. A good understanding of the conditions under which symptoms present themselves, as well as of the history of the presenting problem, will clarify the real nature of the problem and enable the therapist to develop an appropriate treatment plan.

When it appears that there may be a medical etiology to a sexual dysfunction, the patient should be referred to a physician who is knowledgeable of current diagnostic and treatment techniques, respectful of the psychosocial aspects of sexual dysfunction, and comfortable dealing with sexual issues. It is of utmost importance that the various professionals involved in a case communicate clearly about the patient's status. As physicians become increasingly comfortable and sophisticated in the treatment of sexual dysfunctions, referrals are often likely to come from them. For example, it is not unusual for a woman to speak to her gynecologist about her husband's erectile dysfunction, for which he has declined to seek professional help on his own. Even if a sexual dysfunction is related exclusively to a chronic illness, disability, or medication, a mental health therapist can often be helpful in helping the couple address changes in self-image or in relationship dynamics, as well as experimenting with new, more effective sexual techniques (Sipski & Alexander, 1997).

## TREATMENT TECHNIQUES

As indicated earlier, modern sex therapy often involves the combined use of a number of therapeutic techniques, customized to the needs of particular patients. These may include behavioral, cognitive, individual, couples', or medical approaches, as appropriate. Because the behavioral and cognitive techniques are most characteristic of sex therapy, the rest of this discussion will focus on those. Even though the importance of these techniques has sometimes been downplayed in recent years, they still often represent the most effective and most conservative approach to the treatment of sexual dysfunctions. In addition, because of their apparent simplicity, the classic behav-

ioral techniques are often used in a somewhat rigid "textbook" style by therapists who are not well skilled in their proper use. This often results in unsatisfactory outcomes, which either remain uncorrected or which result in searches for more effective therapy. The subtleties emphasized earlier as important to the determination of sexual status are equally important in the prescription and follow-up of behavioral assignments.

### Education and Reassurance—Reframing One's Concept of Sexuality

Another extremely important aspect of sex therapy is the need to educate the patients about various aspects of sexuality, or to help restructure or *reframe* their conception of what sexuality is or what it can be. This does not mean that a therapist imposes his or her ideas of what sex should be upon the patient. If both members of a couple are satisfied with their level of activity or with their sexual repertoire, it is not for the therapist to "sell" the value of what he or she believes to be "enhanced" sexual practices. However, when two partners are incompatible in their approach to sex, or if one partner experiences a disability or an illness that precludes certain kinds of sexual activity, a broader approach to sex can have a "freeing" effect, thus allowing the partners to relate to each other in a more satisfying way (Schover & Jensen, 1988). For example, if sex is seen primarily as a reproductive act, which focuses on vaginal intercourse, the therapist can help the patients to understand that sex can also serve other functions. It can be seen as a recreational activity—as fun! It can be seen as the expression of caring and affection. It can be seen simply as a release of sexual energy. It can be any combination of these four things at different times for the same couple.

The reproductive focus of sexuality in our culture also often leads to an excessive focus on genitals, genital contact, and orgasm as goals of a fulfilling sexual response. Excessive focus on genitals, intercourse, orgasm, and performance only tend to heighten the level of anxiety in the man who experiences erectile problems or the woman who suffers from vaginismus or hypoactive desire. One of the major accomplishments of sex therapy can be a broadening of the couples' approach, so that sexual practices become more varied and creative, anxiety about specific practices diminishes, and the needs of both members of the couple are met.

A third aspect of reframing is helping the partners to become more "immersed" in a sexual experience—leaving their daily cares outside the bedroom, being comfortable with a variety of sexual fantasies, and being involved in *experiencing* sex, rather than watching themselves perform (or what Masters and Johnson called "spectatoring"). Fantasy is an especially difficult thing for many people to experience, as they may have paraphilic fantasies or fantasies about partners other than the one to whom they are making love at the moment, or they may feel pressure from their partner to disclose their fantasies. People often need to be assured that in most cases, sexual fantasies—even unusual ones—are natural, and that they can be kept private.

## Sensate Focus

The cornerstone of behavioral sex therapy is the sensate focus technique developed by Masters and Johnson (1970). It is often applied, with appropriate variations, in the treatment of all sexual dysfunctions because of its ability to help partners broaden their approach to sexuality, while reducing the frequently threatening focus on mutuality, performance, genital stimulation, and orgasm.

The typical first stage of sensate focus involves two 1-hour sessions per week, in which the partners stimulate each other in turn, one being the active partner, the other passive. Depending on the nature of the presenting problem, one or both partners may be instructed to take the initiative in planning the sessions. At this stage, genitals and breasts are off limits to both partners, not only during the exercises but at all other times prior to the next therapy session. Individuals are asked to touch, not specifically to pleasure their partner, but *for their own interest*. They are also asked to be prepared to give a complete account of their experience to the therapist at the following session.

At the next session, the therapist will assess the experiences and perceptions of the two partners, with particular emphasis on what they learned about themselves and about their partners, and how they communicated about the exercises. In subsequent assignments, restrictions are lifted as appropriate, addressing any blocks to compliance or performance as necessary.

Even at the basic first stage of sensate focus, the therapist needs to be flexible in defining the assignment so that it meets the specific needs of the couple. This need may be easily overlooked, because nongenital contact would seem to represent the most elemental form of physical intimacy. However, if one or both members of the couple are uncomfortable with nudity or with the environment that typically represents a sexual encounter (e.g., bed and bedroom), it may be necessary to begin the exercises at a less threatening level. For example, taking a shower together is more easily perceived as a functional activity but can also help promote a basic level of physical intimacy. If nudity is a problem, it can be suggested that the couple wear agreed-upon articles of clothing during initial exercises. In some cases, it may be necessary to recommend anatomical restrictions in addition to breasts and genitals, as areas adjacent to genital areas, such as inner thighs, may be initially problematic for some patients.

In summary, the use of behavioral exercises should be creative, flexible, and combined appropriately with other therapeutic modalities, so that the specific needs of the patient are met. The need for patience, support, and attention to detail on the part of the therapist cannot be overemphasized in developing and maintaining an effective treatment plan. It is hoped that the patient will learn that taking time, being willing to take risks, and maintaining a sense of humor are indispensable elements to creative sex, especially when one is required to readjust one's approach after an illness or injury.

## TREATMENT OF SPECIFIC DYSFUNCTIONS

The rest of this discussion will highlight new developments in the evaluation and treatment of specific sexual dysfunctions. The reader is referred to other sources for more complete discussions regarding each dysfunction (e.g., Kaplan, 1974, 1979, 1987; Leiblum & Rosen, 2000; Masters & Johnson, 1970). In the last 15 years, major changes have taken place in the treatment of sexual disorders. Increasingly, research has focused on the role of organic factors that may play a role in hypoactive sexual desire, erectile dysfunction, and female sexual arousal. Although sex therapists continue to address psychogenic and interpersonal factors in treating sexual disorders, no discussion of sexual dysfunction would be complete without a review of new pharmacological and mechanical devices developed to treat desire and arousal problems.

In 1998, with the advent of sildenafil citrate (Viagra), the first approved drug to treat erectile disorder, the approach to sexual dysfunction has changed dramatically. In particular, there was, and continues to be, a new focus on the integration of medical and psychological treatments of sexual dysfunc-

tion and on combining pharmacological with educational and counseling interventions (Leiblum & Rosen, 2000, p. 4). In addition, a new openness about sexual problems emerged. Both men and women began speaking up about the difficulties they were experiencing. Women started to question when research would focus on them. Whereas for many years the emphasis had been on the similarities between men and women regarding sexual response, now the focus has shifted to how women and men may be different from one another.

There has been a flurry of activity from the pharmaceutical companies to discover and market pills, creams, and therapeutic devices to stimulate or increase desire or arousal (or both) for hypoactive sexual desire disorder, male erectile disorder, and female sexual arousal disorder. There are medications that act on the nervous system to impede ejaculation for those men suffering from premature ejaculation. For example, it was discovered, by accident, that SSRI (selective serotonin reuptake inhibitors) antidepressants have a noticeable effect on ejaculatory latency. Researchers were intrigued by this, and several studies were undertaken to see whether this could be a helpful treatment for premature ejaculation. Results indicated that ejaculatory latency was increased. Consequently, this is now considered a treatment option for premature ejaculation. Though no drugs have been FDA-approved for women, there are numerous clinical drug Phase I and II trials, using both vasoactive and androgenically active drugs (Leiblum & Rosen, 2000). The use of testosterone therapy has also become popular in treating hypoactive sexual desire in both men and women. Studies have shown some success in increasing desire and arousal for women, although some of the data are conflicting and require further study (Davis, 2000).

Currently, there is only one FDA-approved

method of treating female sexual dysfunction. The EROS-CTD, a clitoral therapy device, is a small suction device that fits over the clitoris to increase blood flow to the clitoris. It is similar to the vacuum pump that was devised for men to increase blood flow to the penis. It is intended as a treatment for female sexual arousal disorder and produces a vacuum-like sucking sensation when the device is turned on. Reports regarding the EROS-CTD have been mixed. Some women have found that it helps with arousal and orgasm, whereas others feel that it exerts too much pressure and prefer using a vibrator (Leiblum & Sachs, 2002).

In discussing vaginismus and dyspareunia, current thinking is that these should be reconceptualized as pain disorders rather than as sexual disorders. Up until very recently, both of these disorders were conceptualized as sexual disorders because of the pain experienced with sexual intercourse. However, Binik, Bergeron, and Khalife (2000) have proposed that vaginismus and dyspareunia be considered a type of genital pain disorder, as it has been demonstrated in the majority of cases that the same pain experienced during intercourse can usually be elicited in non-sexual situations, such as gynecological examinations, tampon insertion, urination, manual or oral stimulation, and so on. They suggest that the failure to distinguish between genital pain and the primary activity with which it interferes, sexual intercourse, has not been helpful to the patient. Instead, treatments that focus on reducing or eliminating the pain and that attend to the attitudes and feelings about the pain are necessary. This necessitates working with urologists, gynecologists, physical therapists, pain specialists, or any combination of these.

Another syndrome, the exact opposite of female sexual arousal disorder, is persistent sexual arousal syndrome (PSAS), which is described by Leiblum and Nathan (2001) as an excessive and often unremitting arousal,

rather than deficient or absent arousal. This phenomenon has not been previously reported. It is to be differentiated from hypersexuality, in that "hypersexuality denotes hypertrophied or excessive desire with or without persistent genital arousal; PSAS refers to physiological arousal in the absence of desire" (Leiblum & Nathan, 2001, p. 366). Leiblum and Nathan note that very little is known yet about the etiology, course, or treatment for PSAS, but that it is important to consider it an aspect of female sexual response.

As mentioned earlier, there is a concern that the field of sex therapy will become too "medicalized" as new pharmacological and medical treatments are introduced, leading some to believe that a simple medical solution exists for any number of sexual disorders. However, rather than seeing this as a threat, sex therapists are challenged to learn how they can utilize or integrate (or both) medical treatments with traditional psychotherapeutic and sex therapy in a way that ultimately benefits the patient. This also means a willingness and an openness to work with other professionals, such as physicians, physical therapists, or those working in alternative medicine (e.g., acupuncture), when deemed appropriate. The increase in medical and drug treatments also encourages and requires controlled outcome studies for sex therapy; something that had been declining in this field since the mid-1980s (Heiman & Meston, 1999). Comparisons of psychological, pharmacological, and combined treatments for sexual disorders have not been adequately researched and, with the increasing number of treatment options becoming available, will become more necessary if we are to determine the efficacy of sex therapy.

## CONCLUSION

This chapter has provided an overview of the current status of modern sex therapy, including the philosophical basis for sex therapy, a discussion of general issues in sex therapy, qualifications of sex therapists, stages of the psychosexual evaluation, and evaluation and treatment considerations related to specific sexual dysfunctions. As indicated earlier, more detailed information about most of these issues may be found in the cited references.

Whatever techniques may be used in treating these dysfunctions, there can be no substitute for the therapists' comfort level, skill, creativity, flexibility, humor, sensitivity, patience, and warmth in making this process work. The couple presenting with a sexual problem should be able to leave therapy feeling good about sex, however the partners may define it, and they need to feel good about themselves as sexual people. In this frequently uncomfortable area, often with little of the right kind of help and support, the sensitive, prepared professional can both provide relief and facilitate growth. This is one of the things that makes sex therapy so rewarding as a clinical specialty.

# REFERENCES

Althof, S. E. (1998). New roles for mental health clinicians in the treatment of erectile dysfunction. *Journal of Sex Education and Therapy, 23,* 229–231.

American Psychiatric Association. (1994). *Diagnostic and statistical manual of mental disorders* (3rd ed., Rev.). *(DSM-IV).* Washington, DC: Author.

Annon, J. S., & Robinson, C. H. (1978). The use of vicarious learning in the treatment of sexual concerns. In J. LoPiccolo & L. LoPiccolo (Eds.), *Handbook of sex therapy.* New York: Plenum Press.

Barbach, L. (1984). *For each other: Sharing sexual intimacy.* New York: Signet.

Barbach, L. (1985). *Pleasures: Women write erotica.* New York: Harper and Row.

Binik, Y., Bergeron, S., & Khalife, S. (2000). Dyspareunia. In S. Leiblum & R. Rosen (Eds.), *Principles and practice of sex therapy* (3rd ed.). New York: Guilford Press.

Cooper, A. (Ed.). (2002). *Sex and the Internet: A guidebook for clinicians.* New York: Brunner-Routledge.

Crenshaw, T. L., & Goldberg, J. P. (1996). *Sexual pharmacology: Drugs that affect sexual function.* New York: W. W. Norton.

Davis, S. (2002). Testosterone and sexual desire in women. *Journal of Sex Education and Therapy, 25,* 25–32.

Derogatis, L. R. (1997). The Derogatis Interview for Sexual Functioning (DISF/DISF-SR): An introductory report. *Journal of Sex & Marital Therapy, 23*(4), 291–304.

Heiman, J. R., LoPiccolo, J., & Pallidini, D. (1988). *Becoming orgasmic: A sexual and personal growth program for women.* Paramus, NJ: Prentice Hall.

Heiman, J. R., & Meston, C. M. (1999). Empirically validated treatment for sexual dysfunction. *Annual Review of Sex Research, 6,* 148–194.

Kaplan, H. S. (1974). *The new sex therapy.* New York: Brunner/Mazel.

Kaplan, H. S. (1979). *Disorders of sexual desire.* New York: Brunner/Mazel.

Kaplan, H. S. (1983). *The evaluation of sexual disorders.* New York: Brunner/Mazel.

Kaplan, H. S. (1987). *Sexual aversion, sexual phobias, and panic disorder.* New York: Brunner/Mazel.

Kennedy, A. P., & Dean, S. (1986). *Touching for pleasure.* Chatsworth, CA: Chatsworth Press.

Kroll, K., & Klein, E. L. (1992). *Enabling romance: A guide to love, sex, and relationships for the disabled (and the people who care about them).* New York: Harmony Books.

Laken, V., & Laken, K. (2002). *Making love again: Hope for couples facing loss of sexual intimacy.* East Sandwich, MA: Ant Hill Press.

Laumann, E. O., Gagnon, J. H., Michael, R. T., & Michaels, S. (1994). *The social organization of sexuality: Sexual practices in the United States.* Chicago: The University of Chicago Press.

Leiblum, S. R., & Nathan, S. G. (2001). Persistent sexual arousal syndrome: A newly discovered pattern of female sexuality. *Journal of Sex & Marital Therapy, 27,* 365–380.

Leiblum, S. R., & Rosen, R. C. (Eds.). (1988). *Sexual desire disorders.* New York: Guilford Press.

Leiblum, S. R., & Rosen R. C. (Eds.). (2000). *Principles and practice of sex therapy* (3rd ed.). New York: Guilford Press.

Leiblum, S. R., & Sachs, J. (2002). *Getting the sex you want: A women's guide to becoming proud, passionate, and pleased in bed.* New York: Crown.

Masters, W., & Johnson, V. (1966). *Human sexual response*. Boston: Little, Brown.

Masters, W., & Johnson, V. (1970). *Human sexual inadequacy*. Boston: Little, Brown.

Maurice, W. L. (1999). *Sexual medicine in primary care*. St. Louis: Mosby.

Nelson, J. B. (1978). *Embodiment: An approach to sexuality and Christian theology*. Minneapolis, MN: Augsburg.

Nichols, M. (2000). Therapy with sexual minorities. In S. R. Leiblum & R. C. Rosen (Eds.), *Principles and practice of sex therapy* (3rd ed., pp. 335–367). New York: Guilford Press.

Penner, C., & Penner, J. (1981). *The gift of sex: A Christian guide to sexual fulfillment*. Dallas: Word Publishing.

Schnarch, D. M. (1991). *Constructing the sexual crucible: An integration of sexual and marital therapy*. New York: W.W. Norton.

Schover, L. R., & Jensen, S. B. (1988). *Sexuality and chronic illness: A comprehensive approach*. New York: Guilford Press.

Shaw, J. (1997). Treatment rationale for Internet infidelity. *Journal of Sex Education and Therapy, 22*, 29–34.

Sipski, M. L., & Alexander, C. J. (1997). *Sexual function in people with disability and chronic illness: A health professional's guide*. Frederick, MD: Aspen.

Valins, L. (1992). *When a woman's body says no to sex: Understanding and overcoming vaginismus*. New York: Penguin.

Zilbergeld, B. (1999). *The new male sexuality, revised edition*. New York: Bantam.

CHAPTER 17

# Medical Family Therapy

NANCY BREEN RUDDY, PhD

*Hunterdon Family Practice Residency Program*

SUSAN H. MCDANIEL, PhD

*University of Rochester School of Medicine and Dentistry*

## INTRODUCTION

Illness creates loss, necessitates role changes, and siphons financial and emotional resources. Experiencing illness is a major stressor, in and of itself. Therefore, it is not difficult to imagine how illness sets the stage for psychological and interpersonal difficulties.

Most physicians now recognize the importance of the interplay between biological, psychological, and social factors in illness. The "biopsychosocial model" (Engel, 1977) has become increasingly integrated into modern medicine. However, many medical providers feel overwhelmed by the tasks of monitoring and treating their patients at all levels. Frequently, medical providers find they need assistance in helping patients who have serious mental health or relational difficulties, whose medical and psychosocial issues are intertwined, or who are struggling to cope with their own or a family member's illness.

The field of medical family therapy has developed in order to meet the needs of these patients (McDaniel, Hepworth & Doherty, 1992). Although medical family therapy utilizes many theories and techniques from other types of family therapy, it is a metaframework that draws attention to the biopsychosocial nature of human experience. Medical family therapists must be familiar with illness and its effects on individuals and families; they must understand the medical system and how to work collaboratively with medical providers; and they must be familiar with techniques that assist families in coping with the unique stress illness places on them. This chapter will review these areas, beginning with the various settings in which medical family therapy is likely to be practiced. We will then discuss the approaches and techniques used in medical family therapy, and the literature regarding the utility of these approaches and techniques.

## CONTEXT AND MEDICAL FAMILY THERAPY

Many mental health professionals are surprised when they learn that most patients with mental health issues are not treated in a mental health setting. Primary care medicine has been called the "de facto mental health system" (Regier, Goldberg, & Taube, 1978) because such a large proportion of significant mental health issues is treated in this setting. Other statistics support the contention that primary care providers are central to mental health care delivered in the United States. Ormel and others (1994) found that approximately 25–30% of patients in primary care present with depression, anxiety, substance abuse, and somatoform disorders. Primary care clinicians prescribe 70% of the psychotropic medications (Miranda, Hohnmann, & Attkisson, 1994) that are prescribed each year. Seventy-eight percent of patients with a diagnosable mental health condition will seek care from a primary care physician, as opposed to 28% who will seek care from a specialty provider (Miranda et al., 1994).

Although many primary care visits have a psychosocial component, patients often present in this context with somatic, rather than psychological, issues. Thus, the provider must deftly balance the need for an appropriate biomedical work-up to rule out serious, treatable biomedical illness, and the need to go beyond the "somatic ticket in the door" to understand underlying psychological issues. Medical family therapists who work in primary care settings can serve a unique role in helping medical providers find this middle ground. First, they can educate their medical colleagues regarding the importance of conducting an interview that intersperses and integrates both the biomedical and the psychosocial issues from the beginning of the diagnostic process (Doherty & Baird, 1983; McDaniel, Campbell, & Seaburn, 1990). Sec-

ond, they can serve as a resource for medical providers, both by providing information regarding psychosocial issues and by providing clinical services to patients whose needs exceed the medical provider's capabilities. This sense of shared care and appropriate back-up helps medical providers delve into psychosocial issues without fearing that they will not know how to manage what they discover.

Tertiary care settings also serve patients with psychotherapeutic needs. In specialty care, there has been an increasing recognition of the need to treat patients holistically, rather than each organ system individually. With this enlarged systems view has come a greater recognition of the impact of illness on individuals and their families. Tertiary care settings, particularly clinics that focus on chronic and terminal illnesses, have expanded their services to include individual and family support groups and psychoeducation. Data suggest that these services help patients cope better and may improve health outcomes (Kazak et al., 1999; Langelier & Gallagher, 1989).

Chronic illness presents unique challenges and opportunities for medical family therapists. Patients with chronic disorders, such as diabetes, coronary artery disease, high blood pressure, and cystic fibrosis, present with rates of depression and anxiety significantly higher than those of the general population (Frasure-Smith et al., 1993; Mann, 1999; Rozanski, Blumenthal, & Kaplan, 1999). Thus, families often have to cope not only with the impact of the illness, but also with the psychological sequalae. The challenges of adapting to a family member's chronic illness alone can be daunting. Chronic illness is like an uninvited guest who will not leave—it disrupts normal routines, creates uncertainty, and increases tension.

There are a number of adaptations the family must make to cope with chronic illness (see Table 17.1). First, family roles often need to change, as the ill person cannot fulfill old

**TABLE 17.1**

Continuation of Family Adaptations Necessary to Cope with Chronic Illness

- Family role changes to care for the illness—flexible vs. rigid.
- Caregiver burden—shared vs. individual.
- Financial hardship due to loss of employment and health-care costs—light vs. heavy.
- Family members' accomodation to treatment regimens—willing vs. resentful.
- Communication about the illness—open vs. secretive.

roles, and caregivers may find much of their time devoted to caring for the ill person. These necessary changes range from reassigning child-care arrangements and domestic tasks, to reworking who oversees the emotional health of the family.

Second, caregivers often feel stressed and overburdened, while experiencing guilt about these feelings in the context of their own relative health. Caregivers may have difficulty asking others for assistance. In addition, some families have very limited resources available to assist the caregiver.

Third, chronically ill people often see a decrease in their earning power, even a complete inability to work at the same time that medical bills can be very taxing. The financial ramifications can be devastating, particularly if the ill person has been the primary wage earner or is at the height of his or her earning potential.

Fourth, everyone in the family must make accommodations for treatment regimens. These accommodations may be relatively simple dietary changes or may be much more complicated. For example, the family members may need to integrate time-consuming treatment regimens into their everyday routines. The varying levels of willingness and ability to make such changes among family members can create enormous tension (McDaniel & Cole-Kelly, in press). Well family members may feel resentment as they make difficult changes to assist the ill member of the family. Some family members may willingly embrace necessary changes, whereas

others struggle. It is not uncommon for family members to interpret the attitudes toward and success with such changes as an indication of loyalty to the ill family member, to the family itself, or both.

Fifth, families often struggle to maintain communication about the illness, while protecting each other from painful realities. Family members often have different ideas about how much and what type of information should be shared and with whom. This can be complicated if the illness has a shroud of shame or secrecy (e.g., HIV, chronic mental illnesses) (Landau-Stanton, Clements, & Associates, 1992), or if the prognosis is particularly poor or unclear.

Finally, the family must cope with and grieve multiple losses. These might include the loss of the "old normal lifestyle," loss of function, loss of intimacy, and perhaps the anticipated death of a loved one.

Characteristics of the illness itself also affect the ways the family is challenged and its options for coping. In his book *Families, Illness and Disability*, John Rolland (1994) describes a psychosocial typology of illness, identifying the elements of different illnesses that stress families in different ways (see Table 17.2).

Rolland notes that different illness courses challenge the family in different ways. Illnesses can have a gradual or a sudden onset and can have a progressive (always getting worse), constant (staying at about the same level), or relapsing (alternating periods of function and dysfunction) course. The course

**TABLE 17. 2**

Elements of Chronic Illness That Stress Families Differently

- Onset—gradual or sudden
- Course—progressive, constant, or relapsing
- Outcome—nonfatal, shortened life span, imminently fatal, or sudden death
- Disability–mild to severe
- Predictability of the course—very predictable to very uncertain
- Genetic component—none, multifactorial, to single gene dominant disorder with high penetrance

of the illness affects the family in terms of how much uncertainty it must cope with day in and day out, how much time it has to make necessary changes and learn to cope with the effects of the illness, and how much hope it has for the future of the ill person. In addition, families often struggle with how to communicate about the illness course. For example, families coping with a relapsing illness may find that the definition of "relapse" or "health crisis" changes over time, as family members cycle through health and illness, time and time again.

A second illness characteristic that Rolland noted was the anticipated outcome. Outcomes of a chronic illness can be nonfatal, a shortened life span, imminently fatal, or sudden death. When the anticipated outcome is nonfatal, the family does not have to engage in anticipatory grieving but must determine how to cope with the illness over the long haul. The other anticipated outcomes involve various levels of anticipatory grieving and coping with the uncertain life span of their loved one.

Finally, the illness can result in varying levels of incapacitation. Clearly, when the ill family member is largely incapacitated, physically or mentally, the illness places greater stress on caregivers and necessitates more role shifts and resource reallocation. In addition, greater incapacitation often places greater financial and social pressures on the family. Financially, the family loses income from the ill person and others who stop working or has to pay for professional assistance. Socially, greater in-

capacitation generally results in greater social isolation.

Rolland notes that all illnesses also have a degree of uncertainty/predictability that affects the challenges the family faces. Other variables, such as visibility of symptoms, incidence and severity of health crises, and the extent to which the illness has a genetic component create different trials for families.

Obviously, the family's own characteristics affect adaptation to illness. The stress of an illness can serve to pull a somewhat disengaged family together or to heighten tensions in an already struggling family. Pre-existing patterns of communication and roles often become more rigid when the family is stressed by illness. The pre-illness role of the ill family member impacts how stressed the family is by the potential loss of function, and how able family members are to replace the functions that person is no longer able to perform.

All families have some patterns of behavior and scripts about illness management before they are stressed by a major illness. These patterns can facilitate or complicate healthy adaptation. Destructive scripts include a negative history with the particular illness, a pessimistic view of one's ability to impact particular health outcomes, or a negative history with health-care professionals.

Finally, illness creates different challenges for families who are in different stages of development. Caring for both children and an ill adult may overwhelm a family with young children. Illness that strikes young people is inconsistent with the normal life cycle and carries a particularly sad burden. Illness that strikes just as children are planning to leave-home greatly complicates the leaving-home process. Families that have recently suffered a loss may find it overwhelming to cope with the losses associated with chronic illness. Even illness that is within the normal life cycle can be extremely difficult, as adults are "sand-wiched" between the needs of their elderly failing parents and the needs of their spouse and children (McDaniel, Hepworth, & Doherty, 1997).

## SPECIAL NEEDS IN MEDICAL FAMILY THERAPY

The primary theoretical underpinning of medical family therapy is systems theory and the biopsychosocial model (Engel, 1977) (see Figure 17.1). The biopsychosocial model emphasizes the interelatedness of biological, psychological, interelational, and community factors on health and disease. It applies systems theory to human functioning by recognizing how all of these levels simultaneously affect one another, and how health-care intervention affects many levels of human experience.

The concept of collaboration is also essential to medical family therapy. Medical family therapists must be willing to bridge the largely separate worlds of mental health care and medical care. They must be willing to be "a stranger in a strange land" and learn about medical culture, to constructively work in a different set of mores and traditions. Medical family therapists must familiarize themselves with the illnesses of patients, to predict how the characteristics of the illness might differentially stress the family. Medical family therapists must also find a productive means of communicating with medical providers and increasing awareness of parallel process between the family, family therapist, and medi-

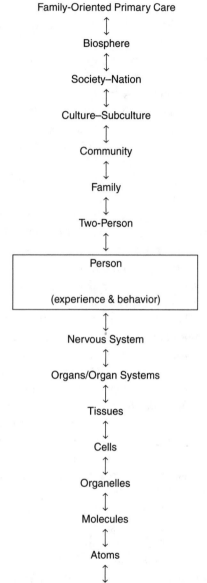

**FIGURE 17.1.** Systems Hierarchy. Source: G. L. Engel (1980), The clinical application of the biopsychosocial model. *American Journal of Psychiatry, 137,* 535–544. Copyright © May, 1980. The American Psychiatric Association. Reprinted by permission.

cal team. Creating an environment of collaboration and shared care facilitates each of these goals. Family therapists' joining and systems consultation skills assist in creating such an atmosphere. Often, it takes time and the sharing of difficult cases to create an environment of mutual respect and trust.

Before embarking on medical family therapy work, therapists need to examine some of their own biases and beliefs about illness, the medical system, and the interplay of the mental health and medical systems. Most people have experience with illness and loss in their own family, which can facilitate or complicate working with families experiencing illness. Familiarity with one's own "illness scripts" is essential (McDaniel, Hepworth, & Doherty, 1997; Ruddy, 1997). It is very helpful to feel comfortable working with families at multiple levels (individual, couples', and family work), as families often need multiple types of intervention. Ascribing to the belief that all levels of functioning are important, from the interplay of cells to the impact of larger systems on the administration of health care, helps family therapists avoid an overly rigid view that only their contribution to the intrapsychic and relational functioning of the person and family is important. Family therapists beginning to work in a medical setting should be aware of their own feelings about the medical system as a whole and their role in it. Clearly, negative feelings about the medical culture or a sense of being treated as a second-class citizen will make it difficult for a family therapist to be productive in this setting.

Medical family therapists also benefit from a collaborative approach with the families themselves. Families facing illness have lost so much control and sense of power that they need their therapist to support them and treat them as equals, rather than judge them or behave in a hierarchical "one-up" manner. Therapists who are able to discern and join with the family's chosen "family health expert" have an ally in facilitating growth and change in the family (Landau, 1981).

## SPECIAL APPROACHES THAT WORK

### Psychoeducation

Family therapists who are familiar with the impact of illness on families can help by educating families about what they can expect, in terms of both the illness itself and how families tend to react to such a situation. This helps the family plan for the future and normalizes a range of reactions. Information gives the family a sense of agency, as family members learn that there are things they can do to help themselves cope and to enhance their quality of life (McDaniel et al., 1992). Psychoeducation can be provided through support groups, bibliotherapy, including medical providers in sessions to answer family questions, and multifamily educational groups (Gonzalez & Steinglass, 2002). In addition, family members can learn from their own experiences as they discuss the unique challenges they've experienced in the context of illness.

Two examples of psychoeducational groups come from our work at the University of Rochester. The first we termed a "Wellness Group." This psychoeducational group was part of the treatment in a study of collaborative care (medical family therapists and family physicians) for distressed high utilizers of primary care services (Campbell & McDaniel, 1997). This is an underserved population, in that these patients define their problems as "medical," though they have multiple psychological/interpersonal problems in addition to their medical problems. To reach these patients, we developed a 6-week multifamily group run by a medical family therapist, which included a medical question-and-answer period with a physician, relaxation techniques with a nurse practitioner, and a psychoeducational support group, with topics such as communicating with your physician, dealing with stress and understanding how it impacts your health, dealing with chronic problems, and the role of the family in coping with chronic illness.

A second psychoeducational group was for women who tested positive or uncertain to the BrCa 1 or 2 breast cancer mutation genes. The impetus for this group came from a geneticist who had enrolled these women in a study of genetic testing for breast cancer. A year after the study was over, the research team noticed that about half of the women who tested positive or uncertain for the mutation remained distressed. The geneticist asked that we develop some service for these women. We constructed a family-sensitive psychoeducational group for patients who label themselves as having a physical, rather than a psychological, problem (McDaniel & Speice, 2001; Speice, McDaniel, Rowley, & Loader, in press). We used the same format as with the primary care high-utilizing patients. A medical family therapist facilitated the 6-week group, which began with a medical question-and-answer period with the geneticist and genetics counselor. This was followed by a psychoeducational support group with topics developed by the women themselves, including family reactions to testing; disclosure—who in the family is also at risk, who to tell and when; confidentiality with insurers and the workplace; their own emotional reactions

and coping strategies; body image; and relationships with physicians and other health professionals.

## Promoting Adaptation to the Illness

As mentioned earlier, families have to make many adaptations to manage illness (see Table 17.3). First, family members' roles and the accompanying patterns of behavior, from daily routines to emotional/interactional patterns, must shift. Such shifts may involve negotiating the redistribution of various concrete daily tasks (e.g., who will pick up the children?) or may involve more subtle changes in roles, such as the management of the emotional life of the family or the management of communication in the family (e.g., "switchboard" role). Medical family therapists can help the family redistribute daily tasks by facilitating conversation and planning of tasks and by normalizing that even everyday things become more difficult for families facing illness. The more subtle role shifts can be facilitated by making them overt and facilitating discussion of both what shifts need to be made and how these shifts affect the family. It is important to highlight how the ill person can still contribute to the family in meaningful ways. In addition,

### TABLE 17. 3
#### Techniques to Promote Family Adaptation to Illness

- Heighten awareness of shifting family roles—pragmatic and emotional
- Facilitate major family lifestyle changes—smoking cessation, dietary changes, and so on.
- Increase communication within and outside the family, regarding the illness
- Help family members to accept what they cannot control, focus energies on what they can
- Find meaning in the illness
- Facilitate their grieving inevitable losses—of function, of dreams, of life
- Increase productive collaboration among patients, families, and the health-care team
- Trace prior family experience with the illness through constructing a genogram
- Set individual and family goals related to illness and to non-illness developmental events

Table constructed from a psychosocial typology of illness presented by John Rolland, *Families, Illness and Disability* (New York: Basic Books, 1994).

the focus on roles can include how the ill person has or has not adopted an "illness role" and how this impacts the rest of the family. Sometimes, the ill person will not accept new limitations, resulting in a great deal of frustration for other family members. Other times, the ill person all too willingly takes on a role of reduced responsibility and then, upon recovery or during periods of remission, does not function or take responsibilities that are appropriate to his or her actual ability. A very rigid "illness role" can be just as problematic as a rigid "well role."

Gender and the role gender plays in a particular family also affect the family's ability to adapt (McDaniel & Cole-Kelly, in press). Rigid traditional gender roles may be problematic in different ways, depending upon who is sick. If the woman becomes ill, the man may feel ill-equipped to take on a caregiver role. If the man becomes ill, the woman may take on a rigid caregiver role and may have difficulty asking for or accepting assistance. In addition, the traditional female coping mode of "emoting" and the traditional male coping model of "action" may clash, particularly when the illness interferes with communication or taking action. Nontraditional gender roles also can be problematic, in that the medical system tends to assume more traditional roles and may not recognize how an illness differentially challenges a father who is a househusband or a mother who is the primary breadwinner. Finally, gender roles can affect how ill individuals cope with the limits placed on them by the illness. Men often have been socialized to "be strong" and "suck it up," making it difficult for them to ask for or accept assistance or even to acknowledge the illness and its effects. Women's socialization may be more consistent with accepting a passive sick role, making it more difficult for them to take an active role in their medical treatment or in adjusting to renewed health upon cure or improved management. Medical family therapists can heighten awareness of these issues, possibly enlarging the family's repertoire of role options.

Second, the family may need to make major lifestyle changes. Medical family therapists can give family members a sense of agency by assisting them to help their ill loved one make changes. Without assistance, lifestyle modifications such as dietary changes or smoking cessation can become a battleground between family members, and between the family and medical providers. Family discussions of the pros and cons of making changes, as well of as the barriers to change, can help family members understand and accept change that is less than optimal. In addition, these discussions can motivate the patient or other family members to make changes, as they become aware of the impact of not changing on other family members and possibly on the course of the illness itself. Normalizing the difficulty of such changes and helping the family discuss means of making such changes will improve overall coping (Doherty, 1988; Harkaway, 1983).

Third, the medical family therapist must help the family communicate about the stresses of the illness and find support both within and outside the family. This sense of "communion" (McDaniel, Hepworth & Doherty, 1992) can reduce conflict and increase emotional closeness. Facilitating open discussion of how the illness is affecting each individual within the family creates opportunities for family members to better understand each other's experiences and to support family members who are struggling. This process can maximize the amount of support available among family members and highlight how much they need to work together to cope. In addition, reaching out to people outside the family who have experienced similar challenges reduces the isolation that tends to accompany illness, normalizes experiences, and helps families identify means of coping that have worked for others.

Fourth, the medical family therapist can help families recognize what they can and cannot control about the situation. Feeling unable to control aspects of an illness can generalize into an incapacitating sense of helplessness. It is important for family members to identify and understand elements of the illness they cannot control and to begin to accept these issues as reality. Family members with realistic beliefs about what they can control typically cope much better than do family members with unrealistic or inaccurate beliefs (McDaniel et al., 1992).

Fifth, finding meaning in the illness can give the family a sense of peace and acceptance (McDaniel et al., 1992; Rolland, 1994). Medical family therapists can help families move beyond "Why us?" and find meaning in the illness. In therapy sessions, the family members can be encouraged to reflect on how the illness has changed their lives for the better. This discussion often helps families recognize a purpose for the illness. For example, family members often note that the illness has created greater closeness and made them appreciate each other more. The illness can be a crisis that leads to growth for the family and puts old grievances in perspective.

Sixth, the medical family therapist can help the family grieve. Losses associated with illness range from the anticipated loss of life associated with terminal illness to the simple loss of the sense that we can predict life from day to day (McDaniel & Cole-Kelly, in press; Rolland, 1994). Discussing death can be particularly difficult, because family members often want to protect themselves and one another from mortality. However, these discussions may help family members make critical decisions at the end of life and cope better after the death of their loved one.

Seventh, the medical family therapist can help families develop collaborative, productive relationships with their medical providers. This can be achieved by helping the family members recognize any biases they may have toward the medical community, coaching the family members on how to get their needs met and questions answered, and helping them recognize any parallel process between themselves and their interactions with the medical community. Often family members find that their modes of interaction, which are functional between themselves are not functional with the medical system. In other cases, the family's struggles are reenacted with the medical team. In addition, the therapist should work collaboratively with the medical team, to improve communication and collaboration between the family and medical team. This may be accomplished by having joint meetings with the family and medical team or by consulting with the medical providers to better understand both sides of the issues.

Many techniques are widely used in multiple models of family therapy, which find an alternate or complementary use in the context of a medical illness. Many of the previous goals can be achieved by giving the family the opportunity to share its illness experience through narratives. Some families are able to simply allow each person to tell the story of the illness from his or her own perspective, while other families benefit more from the structure of creating an illness timeline together. Genograms are a fantastic tool for eliciting the family's history with illness, experiences with the medical community, management of loss and grief, and pre-illness functioning and structure (Daly et al., 1999; McGoldrick, Gerson, & Shellenberger, 1999). In addition, mapping the family in this way can help make old and new roles more overt. Structured goal setting gives each family member an opportunity to share his or her hopes and fears for the future and to gauge how realistic the family is about the future.

### Managing Problematic Patterns Related to Illness

As noted earlier, the stress of illness often results in the development of maladaptive patterns. Caregiver burnout and depression are common problems (Schultz, O'Brien, Bookwala, & Fleissner, 1995). In many families, caregivers do not feel supported, either because they do not ask for help directly or other family members are unable or unwilling to help. This type of perceived lack of support can reflect the exacerbation of old issues. Communication difficulties, old resentments, over/under functioning patterns, and other problems can become entrenched or intensified just when adaptability and support are most needed.

Unfortunately, just as the family most needs support, the members may be less able to access it. It can be difficult to find time and energy for a social life when the ill person often doesn't feel well enough to socialize, and the caregiver feels overwhelmed with responsibilities. In addition, friends and family may withdraw because they do not know how to support the couple or are overwhelmed by their own emotional reactions to the illness. Even within the family, the illness can increase emotional distance, by creating "an elephant in the living room." For example, family members may avoid discussion of the illness to protect other family members, as well as themselves. Finally, couples may experience greater emotional distance if the illness disrupts sexual intimacy.

Other problematic patterns can result from differing coping mechanisms among family members. One family member may withdraw in an attempt to shield self and others from his or her own pain, whereas others may seek comfort and support from other family members. Differences in coping styles may negatively influence individual and family functioning. Differing levels of denial often cause conflict. Some denial is almost necessary to allow the family to continue functioning, whereas too much denial—for example, denial that interferes with appropriate treatment—can be problematic. Family members often disagree on what constitutes a "crisis," when medical personnel should be involved, when family members should be notified of a health event, or how much information should be shared with various people. Some family members may feel that others are making too much of a small issue, whereas others feel that very real issues are not being dealt with. This tension is particularly challenging for families who are facing illness with an unclear prognosis or treatment plan.

Similar problems can occur when family members are at differing levels of acceptance and understanding of the illness. Differing levels of acceptance can result in mismatched expectations, coping behaviors, and readiness to make decisions and take action. This discrepancy can create conflict, particularly when family members need to make treatment or end-of-life decisions collectively. Such discrepancies can be exacerbated by illness characteristics. For example, an illness that remits and returns may force the family to endure the acceptance process many times over. An illness that does not coincide with the course and prognosis predicted by health-care providers may also confound the family.

Simply heightening awareness of and communication about problematic patterns is often enough to help families make the needed changes. Sometimes families need a mediator to help them negotiate the new caregiving tasks, to ensure that no one person is overburdened. In these situations, it can be helpful to create a schedule outlining each person's caregiving responsibilities and ensuring that the primary caregiver gets breaks. Clearly, there are times when family members simply are unable or unwilling to help. In these instances, it is useful to help the family procure outside help. Families often need encouragement to continue a social life and to revive old traditions and routines. Some families find it helpful to create an "illness-free" zone in their home, where no one is allowed to discuss the illness and life is to be as close to the "old normal" as possible. At the same time, it is important that the family doesn't sentimentalize the "old normal," such that any "new normal" will always be worse. Families need to incorporate as much of the positive from the "old normal," while accepting the "new normal" as a reality. In this vein, families often need to determine how their larger social network can be part of the "new normal." Identifying the barriers to continuing a social life and creating solutions to these problems are essential. Sometimes, it is just a matter of recognizing the importance of maintaining connection with the family's social support and making this a priority. Sometimes this is complicated when the family had little social interaction before the illness and has few resources to turn to.

Family therapists working with families facing illness also need to get a history beyond the onset of the illness. Often, difficult patterns predate the illness or reflect issues unrelated to or simply exacerbated by the illness. Illness can be reframed as an opportunity to discuss and bring closure to old hurts, to improve communication, and to improve family functioning in general. This is one common way that families find a sense of meaning and purpose in the illness.

In summary, family therapists can provide psychoeducation about illness and its effects on families, help families adapt to the challenges that illness brings, and recognize and change problematic patterns that arise in the context of illness. Illness can be the crisis that creates an opportunity for healing and growth, thus giving the family members a sense that the illness brought them closer together, rather than drove them apart.

## EVALUATION/RESEARCH EFFICACY RESEARCH IN MEDICAL FAMILY THERAPY

Medical family therapy is a young field. Although clinicians have been practicing in medical settings for some time, only in the last 10 to 15 years did medical family therapy emerge as a separate area, with a structure for communication and collaboration among medically centered therapists. Also, because the field has grown largely out of clinical need, only recently have researchers started to use systematic methods to evaluate its efficacy.

Most of the research on psychotherapeutic intervention in medical settings has focused on group and individual interventions. Few of these studies have included family members in interventions or have measured the impact of the interventions on family functioning or even the functional level of family members. Weihs, Fisher, Baird, and the Working Group on Family Interventions with Chronic Illness (2002) reviewed the literature as part of an Institute of Medicine, Health, and Behavior report. This review reported beginning evidence that psychoeducational and family-focused interventions can improve adherence to a treatment regimen and even health outcomes, such as metabolic control for insulin-dependent diabetes. The group recommends family interventions to mobilize the patient's natural support system, to help families cope with and manage the continuing stresses of chronic illness, and to minimize intrafamilial conflict and criticism, in order to reduce disease-related stress on everyday family life. Some of the child-focused interventions are the most elaborated on and researched.

In 1995, Campbell and Patterson reviewed the literature on family interventions in the context of medical illness. They found a paucity of studies that examined the effects of systemically based family therapy on physical health. The few studies that did investigate the effects of family therapy had methodological problems, such as an extremely small number of subjects or no control group. Despite these issues, they reported the results of family intervention studies with pediatric disorders, adult disorders, caregiver stress, and health promotion and disease prevention. They concluded that family interventions improved outcomes for children with diabetes, asthma, or recurrent abdominal pain. Although there is evidence that family variables such as level of family support and conflict are predictive of adult health outcomes, there is no evidence that family interventions are more effective than is usual care. However, interventions for caregivers of dementia and stroke patients appear to reduce caregiver stress and depression and may delay institutionalization of the patient. Finally, there is some evidence that dietary change programs are enhanced by including family members, but including family members in smoking cessation programs does not affect success rates.

Some research has examined the correlation of family variables with health outcomes for patients with chronic illness. Helgeson (1994) reviewed the research on the goals of agency and communion and the association of these constructs with illness coping. She found that unmitigated agency, or unmitigated communion, is associated with increased symptomatology and decreased coping. In other words, balancing an individual sense of efficacy and a relational sense of connection facilitates good physical and mental health outcomes in the context of chronic and serious illness. Medical family therapy works to increase and achieve a balance of agency and communion for the patient and the family.

In addition to the few articles that provide outcome data, a number of articles describe family-oriented treatment models, usually in the context of a specific illness. Baider (1995) reviewed the ways couples are challenged post-mastectomy and presented a rationale for treatment and a time-limited thematic group for couples after mastectomy. Invernizzi, Brioch, Bressi, Guggeri, Caparelli, and Deliliers (1999) described a counseling service based in a bone marrow transplant unit. They reviewed common family responses to the stress of a bone marrow transplant, particularly focusing on expressed emotion and anticipatory grieving. Although they reviewed elements of the family therapy they provide, they did not provide outcome data. Gonzalez, Steinglass, and Reiss (1989) gave a detailed description of their multiple family discussion group for families facing chronic illness. However, they did not present any outcome data on the impact of the group. A number of articles described groups to facilitate the grieving process for families (Goldstein, Alter, & Axelrod, 1996; Hopmeyer & Werk, 1994; Kissane, Bloch, McKenzie, McDowall, & Nitzan, 1998). However, none of them presented outcome data, beyond general feedback from group participants about their experience of the group.

Another research area that focuses on the impact of mental health work with medically ill patients examines the efficacy of collaborative care models in primary care. Evidence suggests that collaborative care can improve acute illness recovery (Mumford, Schlesinger, & Glass, 1982), depression treatment (Katon & Gonzalez, 1994; Katon et al., 1995; Schulberg, Block, & Madonia, 1996), and enhance disease prevention and health promotion (Doherty & Campbell, 1988). There is also evidence that collaborative care can reduce overall health-care costs (Finney, Riley, & Cataldo, 1991; Jones & Vischi, 1979, Mumford, Schlesinger,

Glass, Patrick, & Cuerdon, 1984; Sloan & Chamel, 1991).

## FUTURE DEVELOPMENTS AND DIRECTION IN MEDICAL FAMILY THERAPY

From the scant data discussed previously, it is obvious that the most pressing need in medical family therapy at this time is outcome research. Does medical family therapy help families cope better? Do patients who undergo medical family therapy have better health outcomes secondary to reduced stress and better family support and functioning? Does medical family therapy save health-care dollars? Do physicians note improvements in their interactions with families who have undergone medical family therapy? Do families who undergo medical family therapy have an easier time making health care decisions, particularly the difficult decisions families encounter at the end of life? These are but a few of the many important questions yet to be answered.

In addition to "simple" outcome research, medical family therapy must adapt to developments in medical care. Genetic testing is likely to become more central in medicine, with the potential to create myriad family issues. Families must struggle with decisions about who should undergo genetic testing and how the results for one person affect others in the family. Some couples must decide if they will undergo genetic testing before starting a family, and how they will proceed if the results of the genetic testing indicate potential problems for future children. Medical technology has already blurred the boundary between life and death, complicating already almost impossible decisions families must make at the end of life. Medical family therapists must stand ready to help families confront these new challenges in a productive manner with innovative approaches.

Health-care delivery systems have been in flux for over a decade, with no end in sight. Though a source of much frustration for many medical and mental health providers, this chaos may serve as an opportunity for medical family therapy. Some medical systems have started to experiment with integrating medical and mental health services (Stauffer & Perez, 1996), and, as noted previously there is some evidence that these arrangements can save health-care dollars while improving care.

Changes in demographics guarantee that there will be work for medical family therapists for a long time to come. As our population ages, families will encounter more and more difficult decisions and situations that could well come under the purview of medical family therapists. This seems even more likely, given that "baby boomers" are more open to mental health intervention than their parents' generation was. In addition, beyond the sheer numbers of people who will face their elder years at the same time, the baby boomer generation has been noted to change the concepts and expectations connected to various life stages. Baby boomers may not be as accepting of mental and physical decline, and may thus look for a variety of ways to minimize the impact of illness and age-related ailments on everyday functioning. Medical family therapists can assist in this regard.

Changes in disease patterns have created opportunities for medical family therapists. Health threats have shifted from sudden illnesses, such as influenza, to chronic illnesses often arising from lifestyle variables, such as diet, smoking, exercise, and stress. Because families are most stressed by chronic illness and often play a significant role in lifestyle changes necessary to prevent and treat such illnesses medical family therapists have a large potential role in the provision of health care in the future.

# REFERENCES

Baider, L. (1995). Psychological intervention with couples after mastectomy. *Support Care Cancer, 3,* 239–243.

Belar, C. D., & Deardorff, W. W. (1995). *Clinical health psychology in medical settings: A practitioners guidebook.* Washington DC: American Psychological Association.

Campbell, T. L., & McDaniel, S. H. (1997, Winter). Branching out: A randomized trial of collaborative family healthcare for distressed high utilizers of the medical system. *American Family Therapy Academy Newsletter, 19.*

Campbell, T. L., & Patterson, J. M. (1995). The effectiveness of family interventions in the treatment of physical illness. *Journal of Marital & Family Therapy, 21*(4), 545–584.

Daly, M., Farmer, J., Harrop-Stein, C., Montgomery, S., Itzen, M., Costalas, J. W., Rogatko, A., Miler, S., Balsham, A., & Gillespie, D. (1999). Exploring family relationships in cancer risk counseling using the genogram. *Cancer Epidemiology, Biomarkers, and Prevention, 8,* 393–398.

Doherty, W. J. (1988). Implications of chronic illness for family treatment. In C. Childman, E. Nunnally, & F. Cox (Eds.), *Chronic illness and disability.* Newbury Park, CA: Sage.

Doherty W. J., & Baird, M. (1983). *Family therapy and family medicine.* New York: Guilford Press.

Doherty, W. J., & Campbell, T. L. (1988). *Families and health.* Newbury Park, CA: Sage.

Engel, G. L. (1977). The need for a new medical model: A challenge for biomedicine. *Science, 196,* 129–136.

Engel, G. L. (1980). The clinical application of the biopsychosocial model. *American Journal of Psychiatry, 137,* 535–544.

Finney, J., Riley, A., & Cataldo, N. (1991). Psychology in primary health care: Effects of brief targeted therapy on children's medical care utilization. *Journal of Pediatric Psychology, 16,* 447–461.

Frasure-Smith, N., & Lesperance, F. (1993). Depression and myocardial infarction. *Journal of the American Medical Association, 270*(15), 1819–1825.

Goldstein, J., Alter, C., Axelrod, R. (1996). A psychoeducational bereavement-suppport groups for families provided in an outpatient cancer center. *Journal of Cancer Education, 11,* 233–237.

Gonzalez, S., & Steinglass, P. (2002). Application of multi-family groups in chronic medical disorders. In W. R. McFarlane (Ed.), *Multifamily groups in the treatment of severe psychiatric disorders* (pp. 315–349). New York: Guilford Press,

Gonzalez, S., Steinglass, P., Reiss, D. (1989). Putting the illness in its place: Discussion groups for families with chronic medical illnesses. *Family Process, 28,* 69–87.

Harkaway, J. (1983). Obesity: Reducing the larger system. *Journal of Strategic and Systemic Therapy, 2,* 2–16.

Helgeson, V. (1994). Relation of agency and communion to well-being: Evidence and potential explanations. *Psychological Bulletin, 116,* 412–428.

Hopmeyer, E., & Werk, A. (1994). A comparative study of family bereavement groups. *Death Studies, 18,* 243–256.

Invernizzi, G., Brioch, G., Bressi, C., Caparelli, S., & Deliliers, G. L. (1999). The organization of a counseling service for the families of patients undergoing bone marrow transplant. *Anticancer Research, 19*(3B), 2293–2297.

Jones, K., & Vischi, T. (1979). Impact of alcohol, drug abuse, and mental health treatment on medical care utilization. *Medical Care, 17,* 1–82.

Katon, W., & Gonzales, J. (1994). A review of randomized trials of psychiatric consultation-liaison studies in primary care. *Psychosomatics, 35,* 268–278.

Katon W., VonKorff, M., Lin, E., Walker, E., Simon, G., Simon, G. E., Bush, T., Robinson, P., & Russo, J. (1995). Collaborative management to achieve treatment guidelines: Impact on depression in primary care. *Journal of the American Medical Association, 273,* 1026–1031.

Kazak, A. E., Simms, S., Baraket, L., Hobbie, W., Foley, B., Golomb, V., & Best, M. (1999). Surviving cancer competently intervention program (SCCIP): A cognitive-behavioral and family therapy intervention for adolescent survivors of childhood cancer and their families. *Family Process, 38,* 175–191.

Kissane, D. W., Bloch, S., McKenzie, M., McDowall, A. C., & Nitzan, R. (1998). Family grief therapy: A preliminary account of a new model to promote healthy family functioning during palliative care and bereavement. *Psycho-Oncology, 7,* 14–25.

Landau, J. (1981). Link therapy as a family therapy technique for transitional extended families. *Psychotherapia, 7*(4), 1–15.

Landau-Stanton, J., Clements, C., & Associates. (1992). *AIDS, health, and mental health: A primary sourcebook.* New York: Brunner/Mazel.

Langelier, R. P., & Gallagher, R. M. (1989). Outpatient treatment of chronic pain groups for couples.

*The Clinical Journal of Pain, 5*, 227–231.

Mann, S. J. (1999). Severe paroxysmal hypertension: Understanding the cause and treatment. *Archives of Internal Medicine, 159*, 670–674.

McDaniel, S. H., & Campbell, T. L. (2000). Consumers and collaborative family healthcare. *Families, Systems and Health, 18*, 133–136.

McDaniel, S. H., Campbell, T. L., & Seaburn, D. B. (1990). *Family-oriented primary care.* New York: Springer Verlag.

McDaniel, S. H., & Cole-Kelly, K. (in press). Gender, couples and illness: A feminist analysis of medical family therapy. In T. J. Goodrich & L. Silverstein (Eds.), *Feminist family therapy.* Washington DC: American Psychological Association Books.

McDaniel, S. H., Hepworth, J., & Doherty, W. J. (1992). *Medical family therapy: A biopsychosocial approach to families with health problems.* New York: Basic Books.

McDaniel, S. H., Hepworth, J., & Doherty, W. J. (1997). *The shared experience of illness.* New York: Basic Books.

McDaniel, S. H., & Speice, J. (2001). What family psychology has to offer women's health: The examples of conversion, somatization, infertility treatment, and genetic testing. *Professional Psychology, 32*, 44–51.

McGoldrick, M., Gerson, M., & Shellenberger, R. (1999). *Genograms: Assessment, and intervention.* New York: W. W. Norton.

Miranda, J., Hohnmann, A. A., & Attkisson, C. A. (1994). *Epidemiology of mental health disorders in primary care.* San Francisco, CA: Jossey-Bass.

Mumford, E., Schlensinger, H., & Glass, G., (1982). The effects of psychological intervention on recovery from surgery and heart attacks: An analysis of the literature. *American Journal of Public Health, 72*, 141–151.

Mumford, E., Schlesinger, H., Glass, G., Patrick, C., & Cuerdon, T. (1984). A new look at evidence about reduced cost of medical utilization following mental health treatment. *American Journal of Psychiatry, 141*, 1145–1158.

Ormel, L., VoKorff, M., Ustin, T., Pini, S., Korton, A., & Oldehinkel, T. (1994). Common mental disorders and disability across cultures: Results from the WHO collaborative study on psychological problems in general health care. *Journal of the American Medical Association, 272*, 1741–1748.

Regier, D. A., Goldberg, I. D., & Taube, C. A. (1978). The de facto U.S. mental health services system:

A public health perspective. *Archives of General Psychiatry, 35*, 685–693.

Rinaldi, R. (1985). Positive effects of psychosocial interventions on total health care: A review of the literature. *Family Systems Medicine, 3*, 417–426.

Rolland, J. (1994). *Families, illness and disability: An integrative treatment model.* New York: Basic Books.

Roy, R. (1989). Couple therapy and chronic headache: A preliminary outcome study. *Headache, 29*, 455–457.

Rozanski, A., Blumenthal, J. A., & Kaplan, J. (1999). Impact of psychological factors on the pathogenesis of cardiovascular disease and implications for therapy. *Circulation, 99*, 2192–2217.

Ruddy, N. B. (1997). Mothers aren't supposed to get sick: A case of chronic obstructive pulmonary disorder. In S. H. McDaniel, J. Hepworth, & W. J. Doherty (Eds.), *The shared experience of illness.* New York: Basic Books.

Schulberg, H. C., Block, M. R., & Madonia, M. J. (1996). Treating major depression in primary care practice: Eight-month clinical outcomes. *Archives of General Psychiatry, 53*, 913–919.

Schultz, R., O'Brien, T., Bookwala, J., & Fleissner, K. (1995). Psychiatric and physical morbidity effects of Alzheimer's disease caregiving: Prevalence, correlates and causes. *The Gerontologist, 35*, 771–791.

Seaburn, D. B., Lorenz, A., Gawinski, B. A., & Gunn, W. (1996). *Models of collaboration: A guide for family therapists practicing with health care professionals.* New York: Basic Books.

Sloan, D., & Chamel, M. (1991). *The quality revolution and health care: A primer for purchasers and providers.* New York: American Society for Quality Control.

Speice, J., McDaniel, S. H., Rowley, P., & Loader, S. (in press). Family issues in a psychoeducational group for women with BRCA mutation. *Clinical Genetics.*

Stauffer, M., & Perez, S. (1996). Integrating mental health and primary care: Solution or problem? *Behavioral Healthcare Tomorrow, 5*, 77–79.

Weihs, K., Fisher, L., & Baird, M. (2002). Families, health, and behavior: A section by the commissioned report by the Committee on Health and Behavior: Research, Practice, and Policies, Division of Neuroscience and Behavioral Health and Division of Health Promotion and Disease Prevention; Institute of Medicine, National Academy of Sciences, *Families, Systems, and Health, 20*, 7–46.

CHAPTER 18

# The Treatment of Adolescent Conduct Disorders and Drug Abuse

Timothy J. Ozechowski, PhD

Charles W. Turner, PhD

Holly B. Waldron, PhD

*Oregon Research Institute*

## INTRODUCTION

During the early and mid-1990s, the field of family therapy faced criticism for its inattention to the scientific study of its theories and methods (e.g., Henggeler, Borduin, & Mann, 1993). In fact, the field's empirical values were called into question, and fears arose that family therapy would marginalize itself among psychotherapy professions thereby jeopardizing its very survival (Liddle, 1991; Shields, Wynne, McDaniel, & Gawinski, 1994). Amid a climate of increasing accountability and quality assurance requirements, family therapy faced the challenge of aligning itself more closely with developmental trends and scientific standards emerging within mainstream mental health disciplines (e.g., Kazdin, 1994).

A decade or so later, the empirical foundation of family therapy has been greatly solidi-

fied (see Alexander, Sexton, & Robbins, 2002; Sexton & Alexander, 2002). Arguably, in no area is family therapy's maturation as a scientific discipline and a clinical specialty more pronounced than in the treatment of adolescent conduct disorder and drug abuse. The breadth and depth of science-based treatment research in this area is unprecedented in the family therapy field. Formal experimental studies in this area date back to the 1970s (e.g., Alexander & Parsons, 1973; Patterson & Reid, 1973) and were among the first controlled trials ever conducted in family therapy. By the early 1990s, an actual base of scientific knowledge had accumulated and was articulated in a landmark issue of the *Journal of Marital and Family Therapy* (*JMFT*) (Pinsof & Wynne, 1995). The empirical reviews of family therapy for conduct disorder (Chamberlain & Rosicky, 1995) and drug abuse (Liddle &

Dakof, 1995) in that special issue of *JMFT* were evolutionary milestones that helped stimulate further research and development in this area. Subsequently, Stanton and Shadish's (1997) meta-analysis of family therapy for adolescent drug abuse helped solidify a growing conviction that family therapy is at least as efficacious (possibly more so, in some respects) as other established treatments for adolescent behavioral problems. More recent empirical reviews of the family therapy literature further attest to the efficacy and legitimacy of family therapy for adolescent conduct disorder and drug abuse (Alexander, Robbins, & Sexton, 2000; Ozechowski & Liddle, 2000; Sexton & Alexander, 2002; Waldron, 1997).

Although still in a fairly formative stage of empirical development, family therapy stands as a model of science-based treatment for adolescents. Models of family therapy are among the most rigorously developed and tested clinical approaches in the adolescent treatment field (see Brestan & Eyberg, 1998; Kazdin, 2002; Williams & Chang, 2000). The leading research-based family therapy models for adolescent conduct disorder and drug abuse include the following (in alphabetical order): brief strategic family therapy (BSFT; see Szapocznik & Kurtines, 1989; Szapocznik, Robbins, Mitrani, Santisteban, & Williams, in press), family behavior therapy (FBT; Azrin et al., 2001; Donohue & Azrin, 2001), functional family therapy (FFT; Sexton & Alexander, Chapter 15, this volume), multidimensional family therapy (MDFT; Liddle, 1999, 2002a; Liddle & Hogue, 2001), multidimensional treatment foster care (MTFC; Chamberlain, 1994; Chamberlain, Fisher, & Moore, 2002), multisystemic therapy (MST; Sheidow, Henggeler, & Schoenwald, Chapter 14, this volume), and parent management training (PMT; Forgatch & Patterson, 1989; Patterson & Forgatch, 1987).

This chapter is not intended to describe the facets of each treatment model listed here. This chapter instead highlights cross-cutting clinical elements and summarizes empirical evidence of the effectiveness of family therapy for adolescent behavioral problems. Finally, priorities for ongoing treatment research and development are presented.

## CROSS-CUTTING CLINICAL ELEMENTS

As made apparent in the reviews by Chamberlain and Rosicky (1995) and Liddle and Dakof (1995), early family-based approaches to the treatment of adolescent conduct and drug problems were primarily derived from structural-strategic and behavioral models of family therapy (e.g., Lewis, Piercy, Sprenkle, & Trepper, 1989; Szapocznik & Kurtines, 1989). Since the 1980s and early 1990s, the theoretical and conceptual bases of family therapy have evolved considerably. Contemporary family therapy models integrate family systems theory (Stanton, Todd, & Associates, 1982), cognitive-behavior theory (Waldron, Brody, & Slesnick, 2001), attachment theory (Liddle & Schwartz, 2002), and social ecology theory (Sheidow et al., Chapter 14, this volume). The range, foci, and methods of family therapy interventions have evolved as well. Cross-cutting clinical features are highlighted further on.

### Focus on Engagement

Crafting a strong therapist–family alliance has always been a central focus in family therapy. The classic structural family therapy technique of *joining* is a core element of engagement in family therapy for conduct-disordered and drug-abusing adolescents (Minuchin, 1974; Minuchin & Fishman, 1981). The most salient aspect of joining, as conceptualized by Minuchin, is the therapist operating from an accommodating position in the early stages of treatment to convey acceptance and respect for the family's idiosyncratic culture and structure. Joining behaviors such as warmth, friendliness, acknowledgment, and affirmation of each family member are keys to gaining entry and leverage within the families of drug-abusing and delinquent adolescents (Cunningham & Henggeler, 1999).

Alexander and colleagues have extensively studied and developed the engagement stage of FFT (Sexton & Alexander, Chapter 15, this volume). Engaging families in FFT hinges on diffusing hostile exchanges and minimizing blaming attributions among family members during initial treatment sessions (Alexander, Waldron, Barton, & Mas, 1989; Robbins, Alexander, Newell, & Turner, 1996; Robbins, Alexander, & Turner, 2000). At the same time, FFT therapists strive to promote a relational or systemic view of problem behavior among family members—emphasizing strengths, resiliencies, and the potential for change inherent within family relationships.

In MDFT, the engagement process differs for parents and adolescents, and distinct engagement interventions have been developed. Briefly, the crux of engaging parents in MDFT is rekindling a commitment to the parental role and to the parent–adolescent relationship (Diamond, Diamond, & Liddle, 2000; Liddle, Rowe, Dakof, & Lyke, 1998). On the other hand, engaging adolescents hinges on establishing a therapeutic alliance with the adolescent clearly distinct from that with the parents and developing a set of treatment goals meaningful to the adolescent (Diamond, Liddle, Hogue, & Dakof, 1999). Much engagement activity in MDFT takes place in separate meetings with parents and adolescents, using individual sessions to lay the groundwork for pivotal family meetings.

Szapocznik and colleagues have developed and tested pretreatment procedures for engaging resistant families (Santisteban et al., 1996; Szapocznik & Kurtines, 1989; Szapocznik et al., in press). These engagement procedures center around the therapist forming an alliance with a key family member deemed to have significant power in the family system. The therapist implements basic joining and restructuring techniques intended to capitalize on the influential family member's ability to mobilize the family to enter treatment. Most pretreatment engagement activity occurs over the phone but may also take place in the therapist's office or the family home.

## Reframing

The classic family therapy technique of reframing has proven to be a potent intervention in family therapy for adolescents (Robbins, Alexander, & Turner, 2000; Robbins et al., 1996). Briefly, reframing is proposing an alternative explanation or attribution for behaviors initially characterized by the family in negative or antagonistic terms (Minuchin & Fishman, 1981; Watzlawick, Weakland, & Fisch, 1974). Reframes are used for several purposes in family therapy (Alexander et al., 1989). The first is to neutralize negativity by focusing on underlying aspects of problem behavior that are benevolent, well-intentioned, or even noble. Second, reframes are used to enhance treatment engagement and motivation by drawing attention to family strengths and potential for change. Third, reframes are used to promote a systemic or relational perspective on adolescent problem behavior. The technique of reframing is particularly well developed conceptually and clinically in FFT. See Sexton and Alexander (Chapter 15, this volume) for more specific details on the use of reframes in family therapy.

## Enactment

Enactments are therapist-directed in-session activities designed to either assess or change family interaction patterns (Minuchin, 1974; Minuchin & Fishman, 1981). Family therapists take an active role in orchestrating in-session interventions with adolescents and families. For instance, parents may be directed to clearly define expectations, rules, and consequences with the adolescent (Chamberlain, 1994; Sheidow et al., Chapter 14, this volume). Likewise, therapists may utilize in-session behavioral rehearsal or role-play activities with family members (Donohue & Azrin, 2001; Waldron, Brody, & Slesnick, 2001). Enactments may also be used to restructure family boundaries (Szapocznik & Kurtines, 1989; Szapocznik et al., in press). For example, family therapists may ask disengaged family members to talk directly or else may *restrain* overly enmeshed family members from talking. Finally, family therapists may use enactments to help parents and adolescents extract themselves from conflictual impasses by shifting the focus of communication from surface behavior to underlying relationship issues (Diamond & Liddle, 1999).

## Multisystemic Interventions

A distinguishing feature of contemporary family therapy is attention to systems and influences outside the family (Sexton & Alexander, Chapter 15, this volume; Chamberlain et al., 2002; Sheidow et al., Chapter 14, this volume; Liddle & Hogue, 2001). In keeping with an ecological perspective on adolescent and family development (see Robbins et al., Chapter 2, this volume), family therapy approaches incorporate manualized interventions with extrafamilial systems, including peers, schools, juvenile justice agencies, child welfare and social service organizations, family services, and so on. Multisystemic interventions may take a variety of forms. For example, arranging meetings between school personnel and the family to discuss educational needs is a common focus. Therapists may also work closely with police officers, probation officers, and judges to address adolescent and the family legal issues. Moreover, family therapists may help the adolescent and the family access vocational services, youth development organizations, formal and informal social support networks, religious groups, and so on. Ecologically focused family therapies will undoubtedly evolve over the next decade and occupy a prominent place in the continuum of care for children and adolescents (see Henggeler & Santos, 1997; Stormshak & Dishion, 2002).

## OVERVIEW OF RESEARCH FINDINGS

Research on family therapy has accelerated substantially over the last decade, and federal support for family-based treatment research is extremely robust.[1] We know a great deal more today than a decade ago about the effects of family therapy, as well as about core components, processes, and mechanisms associated with treatment outcomes (Ozechowski & Liddle, 2000; Sexton & Alexander, 2002; Waldron, 1997). This section highlights empirical evidence of the effects of family therapy for adolescent conduct disorder and drug abuse. Because an exhaustive review of the research is beyond the scope of this chapter, we focus primarily on research conducted subsequent to the reviews by Chamberlain and Rosicky (1995) and Liddle and Dakof, (1995).

## Delinquency and Antisocial Behavior

There is overwhelming evidence that delinquent and antisocial behavior improves among adolescents receiving family therapy. Significant reductions in parent, adolescent, or teacher (or any combination of these) reports of adolescent problem behavior have been obtained for PMT (Dishion & Andrews, 1995; Dishion, Patterson, & Kavanaugh, 1992; Kazdin, Seigel, & Bass, 1992), MDFT (Liddle, 2001; Liddle, Dakof, Parker, et al., 2001), FBT (Azrin et al., 2001), and BSFT (Coatsworth, Santisteban, McBride, & Szapocznik, 2001). A number of studies indicates that improvement in reports of adolescent behavioral problems can be maintained at least 1 year beyond treatment termination (Dishion & Andrews, 1995; Kazdin et al., 1992; Liddle, 2001; Liddle et al., 2001). Superior treatment outcomes relative to non–family based treatments have been obtained for PMT (Dishion & Andrews, 1995; Dishion et al., 1992; Kazdin et al., 1992) and MDFT (Liddle, 2001).

An additional set of studies focuses on clinically and socially significant outcomes in family therapy that include recidivism, re-arrest, posttreatment incarceration, out-of-home placement, and so on (see Kazdin, 1999). In particular, Henggeler and colleagues have examined the effectiveness of MST as an alternative to incarceration for juvenile offenders (Borduin et al., 1995; Henggeler, Melton, & Smith, 1992) and to inpatient hospitalization for adolescents in psychiatric crisis (Henggeler, Rowland, Randall, et al., 1999; Schoenwald, Ward, Henggeler, & Rowland, 2000). Overall, these studies show that MST is substantially more effective than are typical juvenile justice and youth mental health services in preserving families and keeping adolescents out of juvenile detention, in-patient psychiatric hospitals, and other costly out-of-home placements (Sheidow et al., Chapter 14, this volume). Similar results have been reported by Chamberlain and Reid (1998), who found MTFC to be more effective than community-based residential treatment in reducing post-treatment criminal offenses, ar-

rests, and number of days incarcerated among a sample of adjudicated adolescent offenders. Moreover, MTFC proved to be a much more effective route toward family preservation and reunification than was residential treatment. Finally, a number of clinical trials have shown FFT (Alexander & Parsons, 1973; Barton, Alexander, Waldron, Turner, & Warburton, 1985; Klein, Alexander, & Parsons, 1977) and PMT (Bank, Marlowe, Reid, Patterson, & Winrott, 1991) to be more effective than non–family based treatments in reducing recidivism and time spent in institutional settings among chronic juvenile delinquents and offenders. The effects of FFT have been shown to endure up to 5 years beyond treatment termination (Gordon, Graves, & Arbuthnot, 1995).

*Drug Use*

Empirical evidence is equally impressive regarding the effects of family therapy on adolescent drug use. No published study has failed to show significant improvements based substantially on adolescents' reports of their own drug use (see Ozechowski & Liddle, 2000). The effects of family therapy on adolescent drug use appear to endure well beyond treatment termination (Henggeler, Glinghempeel, Brondino, & Pickrel, 2002; Henggeler, Pickrel, & Brondino, 1999; Liddle, 2001; Liddle et al., 2001; Waldron, Slesnick, Brody, Turner, & Peterson, 2001). Furthermore, recent studies suggest that family therapy may be more effective than some non–family based treatments (see Stanton & Shadish, 1997). Specifically, MDFT has been shown to produce superior reductions in adolescent drug use compared to adolescent group therapy and multifamily group education (Liddle et al., 2001), individual cognitive-behavioral therapy (Liddle, 2001), and residential treatment (Liddle & Dakof, 2002). Likewise, superior drug use outcomes have been obtained for MST compared to standard community-based outpatient treatment (Henggeler, Rowland, et al., 1999; Henggeler, Schoenwald, et al., 2002). Finally, Waldron et al. (2001) reported greater reductions in drug use for FFT compared to individual cognitive-behavioral therapy and adolescent group therapy, although, by 7 months after treatment intake, the effects of FFT and group treatment were equivalent. Preliminary analyses of the 19-month follow-up to the Waldron et al. (2001) study indicate on average that adolescents receiving FFT maintained their treatment gains, whereas those in group therapy relapsed to near pretreatment levels of drug use.

*Family Functioning*

Improvements in aspects of family functioning (e.g., reduced conflict, increased cohesion, more functional communication and parenting practices) are hypothesized to be primary mechanisms of change in family therapy. Similar to the case for behavioral problems and drug use, family functioning has been shown to improve for adolescents receiving family therapy in virtually every study in which family functioning has been assessed (see Ozechowski & Liddle, 2000). It is also evident, however, that family functioning generally improves in alternative treatments, even those not directly involving the family or addressing family functioning (e.g., Dishion & Andrews, 1995; Kazdin & Wassell, 2000; Waldron et al., 2001). Notable exceptions include Liddle et al. (2001) who reported superior improvements on observational ratings of global family health in MDFT, compared to adolescent group therapy and multifamily group education. Moreover, Henggeler and colleagues have found that parent and adolescent reports of family cohesion improve more substantially in MST compared to standard youth services (Borduin et al., 1995; Henggeler, Melton, & Smith, 1992) and psy-

chiatric hospitalization (Henggeler, Rowland, Randall, et al., 1999). Finally, Szapocznik, Rio, et al. (1989) found that family functioning improved among behaviorally troubled preadolescents receiving BSFT, whereas family functioning deteriorated among youths receiving individual psychotherapy.

Comparisons of the magnitude of change in family functioning between family therapy and alternative treatments do not directly address hypotheses about mechanisms of change. Rather, the more critical focus for investigating change mechanisms is the *linkage* between improvements in family functioning and reductions in adolescent delinquency and drug use (see Weersing & Weisz, 2002). Specifically, hypotheses about mechanisms of change in family therapy can be supported by evidence showing that improvements in family functioning predict subsequent reductions in adolescent problem behavior, with these linkages being evident in family therapy and not in alternative treatments.

Only a few studies have attempted to link changes in family functioning with improvements in adolescent behavior. One of the first experimental studies to do so was conducted by Mann, Borduin, Henggeler, and Blaske (1990), who reported that improvements in mother–father communication in MST were correlated with reductions in adolescent symptomatology. Likewise, Dishion et al. (1992) found that improvements in discipline practices among parents of delinquent adolescents in PMT were related to improvements in teacher-rated antisocial behavior in school. Similarly, Schmidt, Liddle, and Dakof (1996) found that improved parenting behavior was accompanied by reductions in adolescent drug use in 59% of treated cases in MDFT and by reductions in adolescent acting-out behavior in 50% of cases—both statistically significant associations.

Relatively more formal analyses of mechanisms of change have been conducted by Eddy and Chamberlain (2000) and Huey, Henggeler, Brondino, and Pickrel (2000). Both of these studies evaluated the extent to which improvements in family functioning *mediate* (see Holmbeck, 1997) the effects of MTFC and MST (respectively) on adolescent antisocial behavior. Eddy and Chamberlain (2000) found that a set of family functioning variables, including supervision, discipline, and adult–youth relationship quality, mediated the impact of treatment condition (MTFC vs. group treatment) on adolescent delinquency and criminal offenses, with MTFC achieving more favorable results on the adolescent outcomes and the mediators. Likewise, Huey, Henggeler, Brondino, and Pickrel (2000) found that the beneficial effects of high levels of therapist adherence in MST on adolescent delinquent behavior were partially mediated by improvements in family functioning. Collectively, these findings support the assertion that family-based treatments help reduce adolescent drug use and delinquency by promoting adaptive changes in core dimensions of family functioning.

## Peer Relationships and School Functioning

Family therapy is designed to have a broad-based impact on a range of risk and protective factors besides family functioning. In particular, family therapy aims to diminish adolescents' association with drug-using and delinquent peers and to promote stronger connections to school—both well-established correlates of adolescent problem behavior (Hawkins, Catalano, & Miller, 1992). The impact of family therapy on these risk and protective factors has been assessed in relatively few studies. Among these, Huey et al. (2000) document that parent reports of adolescents' affiliation with delinquent peers have been shown to decrease in MST from pre- to post-treatment in relation to enhanced parental monitoring and family functioning. Decreased delinquent peer association in turn predicts reduced adolescent delinquent behavior in MST. Likewise, Eddy, and Chamberlain (2000) found that interviewer impressions of adolescent deviant peer associations (based on interviews with adolescents and adult caregivers) were highly correlated with changes on measures of family management and also mediated the effects of MTFC on adolescent antisocial behavior.

Several studies have examined the impact of family therapy on adolescent behavioral and academic functioning in school. For instance, teacher ratings of in-school behavior problems have been shown to improve significantly in PMT (Dishion & Andrews, 1995; Dishion et al., 1992; Kazdin et al., 1992). Similarly, Henggeler and colleagues have reported that adolescents in MST spend fewer days out of school compared to adolescents receiving standard youth services (Brown, Henggeler, Schoenwald, Brondino, & Pickrel, 1996; Henggeler, Rowland, et al., 1999). Finally, Liddle et al. (2001) reported that adolescents in MDFT exhibited significant increases in grade point average compared to those receiving adolescent and multifamily group treatments.

## Treatment Factors Related to Outcome

### ENGAGEMENT AND RETENTION IN TREATMENT

As discussed previously, specialized pre-treatment engagement interventions have been developed and tested by Szapocznik and colleagues (Coatsworth et al., 2001; Santisteban et al., 1996) as well as by Donohue, Azrin, Lawson, et al. (1998). These interventions have been shown to substantially improve rates of engagement in family therapy among resistant adolescents and families (see Robbins et al., Chapter 2, this volume, for further details).

Retention in treatment is another factor that may contribute to the effectiveness of family therapy in reducing adolescent drug use and delinquent behavior. Historically, rates of retention in family therapy have been quite high—typically, between 70% and 90% (e.g., Coatsworth et al., 2001; Henggeler, Pickrel, Brondino, & Crouch, 1996; Waldron et al., 2001). There is some evidence that rates of retention in family therapy are generally higher than in non–family based adolescent treatments (Stanton & Shadish, 1997). This finding is not universal, however, as several studies have obtained equivalent rates of retention between family therapy and non–family based treatments (Liddle, 2001; Waldron et al., 2001).

### THERAPIST BEHAVIORS AND CLINICAL PROCESSES

Studies of in-session therapist behaviors and clinical processes associated with outcomes are an indispensable element of family therapy research and development (Alexander, Newell, Robbins, & Turner, 1995; Diamond & Diamond, 2002). A relatively small number of process studies has yielded rich information about core clinical components of family therapy for adolescent behavioral problems (Diamond et al., 1999; Diamond & Liddle, 1996, 1999; Patterson & Chamberlain, 1994; Robbins, et al., 1996, 2000). See Sexton, Robbins, Hollimon, Mease, & Mayorga (Chapter 11, this volume) for a review of these clinical process studies.

## PRIORITIES FOR FURTHER RESEARCH AND DEVELOPMENT

A major research frontier is establishing the feasibility and effectiveness of family therapy

for adolescent conduct disorder and drug abuse when administered in community settings by non–research therapists and practitioners. Efforts to transfer science-based family therapy into community service delivery systems are well underway and much has been learned about the process (Sexton & Alexander, Chapter 15, this volume; Dennis, Dawud-Noursi, Muck, & McDermeit, in press; Dennis, Titus, Diamond, et al., 2002; Sheidow et al., Chapter 14, this volume; Liddle, Rowe, Quille, et al., 2002). The few treatment-effectiveness studies conducted to date suggest that family therapy is no more effective than other types of research-based adolescent treatments and is marginally more effective than existing clinical services when administered under non-research conditions in the community (Dennis, Godley, Diamond, et al., 2002; Henggeler et al., 1999, 2002). A major reason for these modest clinical outcomes is that therapist adherence to family therapy principles and practices appears markedly lower in community settings compared to research settings (Henggeler, Rowland, Pickrel, et al., 1997, Henggeler et al., 1999; Liddle et al., 2002). Accordingly, a pivotal focus in family therapy research is developing training tools and methods for imparting family therapy skills and maintaining high levels of adherence among front-line clinicians, therapists, and supervisors (Henggeler, Schoenwald, Liao, Letourneau, & Edwards, 2002). Administrative and organizational impediments to family therapy program implementation have also been identified and addressed (Alexander et al., 2000; Liddle et al., 2002). State-of-the-art family therapy technology transfer packages have been developed and are currently being implemented in nationwide treatment dissemination studies.[2] Insights and findings from these dissemination projects will undoubtedly propel the effort to transport and integrate family therapy into existing adolescent treatment systems.

Research is needed on other factors bearing on the transportability of family therapy for adolescent conduct disorder and drug abuse. Foremost among these is treatment cost and cost-effectiveness. A few studies have examined cost issues in family therapy for adolescent drug abuse and problem behavior. Specifically, the CSAT-funded Cannabis Youth Treatment (CYT) study examined the cost of MDFT as well as five other research-based outpatient adolescent drug treatments administered in community settings (Dennis, Godley, et al., 2002; French, Roebuck, Dennis, et al., 2002). Analyses from the CYT study indicate that 12 weeks of MDFT costs about $1,968 per adolescent. Likewise, a treatment dissemination study funded by the Washington State Institute for Public Policy (Aos, Phipps, Barnosky, & Lieb, 2001) estimates that FFT costs approximately $2,161; MTFC costs $2,052; and MST costs $4,743 per adolescent. French et al. (2002) conclude that the cost figures for family therapy are generally in line with those of other outpatient adolescent treatments and appear sustainable under current funding patterns.

Other studies have focused on the *cost-effectiveness* of family therapy. Two sets of findings are particularly relevant. One is that family therapy interventions have been shown to achieve either comparable or superior treatment outcomes at a dramatically lower cost than inpatient and residential programs and other expensive out-of-home placements that are centerpieces of the current adolescent treatment system in the United States (see Sexton & Alexander, Chapter 15, this volume; Aos et al., 2001; Chamberlain & Mihalic, 1998; Sheidow et al., Chapter 14, this volume). Second, family therapy has been shown to produce substantial *cost-savings* stemming from long-term reductions in post-treatment arrests, incarcerations, hospitalizations, and other types of service utilization compared to standard clinical services for adolescents (Sexton

& Alexander, Chapter 15, this volume; Aos, et al., 2001; Sheidow et al., Chapter 14, this volume). These attractive cost-effectiveness findings are unquestionably appealing to adolescent treatment administrators and policy makers at federal, state, and local levels. Additional cost-effectiveness studies of family therapy are underway and promise to add momentum to the dissemination effort.

In addition to studies looking to expand family therapy outward into community settings, more research is needed to examine the inner workings of family therapy. In particular, very little is known about factors potentially moderating the effects of family therapy, including (a) demographic variables such as age, gender, race and ethnicity, family structure, and SES; (b) variations in the amount, type, frequency, and age of onset of adolescent conduct and drug problems; (c) the co-occurrence of conduct disorder and drug abuse, as well as other conditions such as depression and ADHD; and (d) the presence of family psychopathology, including substance abuse and addiction; mental illness; criminal activity; physical, sexual, and emotional abuse; and so on. Preliminary analyses underway by Waldron and colleagues suggest that adolescents who enter treatment with elevated levels of comorbid emotional and behavioral problems in addition to drug abuse are least likely to achieve long-term benefits from family therapy. Adapting family therapy to enhance its effectiveness with chronic multiproblem adolescents and families is a pressing need.

A great deal more research is needed on the components, mechanisms, and processes associated with outcomes in family therapy. Research designs intended for such investigations (e.g., parametric, dismantling, constructive, process-outcome [see Kazdin, 1998]) are underrepresented in the family therapy literature. Likewise, advances in clinical data analysis have yet to be realized in family therapy research. These advances include multilevel and latent growth curve modeling (Raudenbush & Bryk, 2002; Willett & Keiley, 2000), growth mixture modeling (Muthen, 2001), survival analysis (Luke & Homan, 1998), cluster analysis (Morral, Iguchi, Belding, & Lamb, 1997), and latent transition analysis (Collins, Hyatt, & Graham, 2000). Greater diversity in research design and analytic methodology is necessary for examining a broader range of questions about how, for whom, and under what conditions family therapy is effective.

This chapter provides only a brief glimpse of family therapy's status as a bona fide science-based treatment for adolescent conduct disorder and drug abuse. The exemplary track record of research discussed in this chapter has garnered the recognition and respect of the adolescent treatment and research communities at large.[3] The scientific progress realized in family therapy has played an instrumental role in what has been described as a renaissance period in adolescent treatment research (Dennis et al., 2002; Liddle, 2002b). At the very least, we hope this chapter makes apparent that the spirit of generativity and vitality characterizing the work of early family therapy pioneers (see Hoffman, 1981) continues to prevail. We believe the future holds much promise for further scientific advances and "breakthroughs" (see Szapozcnik & Kurtines, 1989) in family therapy for adolescent conduct disorder and drug abuse.

## NOTES

1. For instance, the National Institute on Drug Abuse (NIDA) sponsors a research center (1 of only 10 NIDA research centers in the United States) and a postdoctoral training program specializing in family-based treatment research (http://www.med.miami.edu/ctrada).

2. For example, the Adolescent Treatment Models program is a multisite nationwide study, funded by the Center for Substance Abuse Treatment (CSAT), that examines the effectiveness of a range of research-based inpatient, residential, and outpatient adolescent treatments, including MDFT (Dennis, Dawad-Noursi, et al., in press). In addition, a family therapy research site (Jose Szapocznik, director) is a component of the Clinical Trials Network, which is a national treatment research and development consortium funded by NIDA (www.nida.nih.gov/CTN/Index.htm). Finally, three family therapy treatment models (FFT, MST, and MTFC) are being disseminated among hundreds of community sites around the country as part of the Blueprints for Violence Prevention program funded by the Office of Juvenile Justice and Delinquency Prevention (http://www.colorado.edu/cspv/blueprints/Default.htm; see also Sexton & Alexander, Chapter 15, this volume; Sheidow et al., Chapter 14, this volume).

3. For instance, practice parameters specified by the American Academy of Child and Adolescent Psychiatry (1997), the National Institute on Drug Abuse (1999), and the Center for Substance Abuse Treatment (1999) each identify family therapy among model adolescent treatment approaches. Moreover, family therapy approaches are given favorable coverage in numerous highly regarded scientific reviews and clinical texts on effective treatments for adolescent conduct disorder and drug abuse (e.g., Brestan & Eyeberg, 1998; Crane, 1998; Hibbs & Jensen, 1996; Kazdin, 2002; Kazdin & Weisz, 1998; Williams & Chang, 2000).

## REFERENCES

Alexander, J. F., Newell, R. M., Robbins, M. R., & Turner, C. W. (1995). Observational coding in family therapy process research. *Journal of Family Psychology, 9,* 355–365.

Alexander, J. F., & Parsons, B. V. (1973). Short term behavioral interventions with delinquent families: Impact on family process and recidivism. *Journal of Abnormal Psychology, 81,* 219–225.

Alexander, J. F., Robbins, M. S., & Sexton, T. L. (2000). Family-based interventions with older, at-risk youth: From promise to proof to practice. *Journal of Primary Prevention, 21,* 185–205.

Alexander, J. F., Sexton, T. L., & Robbins, M. S. (2002). The developmental status of family therapy in family psychology intervention science. In H. A. Liddle, D. A. Santisteban, R. F. Levant, & J. H. Bray (Eds.), *Family psychology: Science-based interventions* (pp. 17–40). Washington, DC: American Psychological Association.

Alexander, J. F., Waldron, H. B., Barton, C., & Mas, C. H. (1989). Minimizing blaming attributions and behaviors in delinquent families. *Journal of Consulting and Clinical Psychology, 57,* 19–24.

American Academy of Child and Adolescent Psychiatry. (1997). Practice parameters for the assessment and treatment of children and adolescents with substance use disorders. *Journal of the American Academy of Child and Adolescent Psychiatry, 36,* 140S–156S.

Aos, S., Phipps, P., Barnoski, R., & Lieb, R. (2001). *The comparative costs and benefits of programs to reduce crime.* Washington State Institute for Public Policy. www.wa.gov/wsipp.

Azrin, N. H., Donohue, B., Teichner, G. A., Crum, T., Howell, J., & DeCato, L. H. (2001). A controlled evaluation and description of individual-cognitive problem solving and family-behavior therapies in dually diagnosed conduct–disordered and substance–dependent youth. *Journal of Child and Adolescent Substance Abuse, 11,* 1–43.

Bank, L., Marlowe, H., Reid, J. B., Patterson, G. R., & Winrott, M. R. (1991). A comparative evaluation of parent-training interventions for families of chronic delinquents. *Journal of Abnormal Child Psychology, 19,* 15–33.

Barton, C., Alexander, J. F., Waldron, H., Turner, C. W., & Warburton, J. (1985). Generalizing treatment effects of functional family therapy: Three replications. *American Journal of Family Therapy, 13,* 16–26.

Borduin, C. M., Mann, B. J., Cone, L. T., Henggeler, S. W., Fucci, B. R., Blaske, D. M., & Williams, R. A. (1995). Multisystemic treatment of serious juvenile offenders: Long-term prevention of criminality and violence. *Journal of Consulting and Clinical Psychology, 63,* 569–578.

Brestan, E. V., & Eyberg, S. M. (1998). Effective psychosocial treatments of conduct-disordered children and adolescents: 29 years, 82 studies, and 5,272 kids. *Journal of Clinical Child Psychology, 27,* 180–189.

Brown, T. L., Henggeler, S. W., Schoenwald, S. K., Brondino, M. J., & Pickrel, S. G. (1996). Multisystemic treatment of substance abusing and dependent juvenile delinquents: Effects on school attendance at post-treatment and 6-month follow-up. *Children's Services, 2,* 81–93.

Center for Substance Abuse Treatment. (1999). Treatment of adolescents with substance use disorders. *Treatment Improvement Protocol (TIP) Series 32.* Rockville, MD: Department of Health and Human Services.

Chamberlain, P. (1994). *Family connections: A treatment foster care model for adolescents with delinquency.* Eugene, OR: Castalia.

Chamberlain, P., Fisher, P. A., & Moore, K. (2002). Multidimensional treatment foster care: Applications of the OSLC intervention model to high-risk youth and their families. In J. B. Reid, G. R. Patterson, & J. Snyder (Eds.), *Antisocial behavior in children and adolescents: A developmental analysis and model for intervention.* Washington, DC: American Psychological Association.

Chamberlain, P., & Mihalic, S. F. (1998). *Blueprints for violence prevention, book eight: Multidimensional treatment foster care.* Boulder, CO: Center for the Study and Prevention of Violence.

Chamberlain P., & Reid, J. B. (1998). Comparisons of two community alternatives to incarceration for chronic juvenile offenders. *Journal of Consulting and Clinical Psychology, 66,* 624–633.

Chamberlain, P., & Rosicky, J. G. (1995). The effectiveness of family therapy in the treatment of adolescents with conduct disorders and delinquency. *Journal of Marital and Family Therapy, 21,* 441–459.

Coatsworth, J. D., Santisteban, D. A., McBride, C. K., & Szapocznik, J. (2001). Brief strategic family therapy versus community control: Engagement, retention, and an exploration of the moderating role of adolescent symptom severity. *Family Process, 40,* 313–332.

Collins, L., Hyatt, S. L., & Graham, J. W. (2000). Latent transition analysis as a way of testing models of stage-sequential change in longitudinal data. In T. D. Little & K. U. Schnabel (Eds.), *Modeling longitudinal and multilevel data: Practical issues, applied approaches, and specific examples* (pp. 147–161). Mahwah, NJ: Erlbaum.

Crane, J. (Ed.). (1998). *Social programs that work.* New York: Russell Sage.

Cunningham, P. B., & Henggeler, S. W. (1999). Engaging multiproblem families in treatment: Lessons learned throughout the development of multisystemic therapy. *Family Process, 38,* 265–281.

Dennis, M. L., Dawud-Noursi, S., Muck, R. D., & McDermeit, M. (2002). The need for developing and evaluating adolescent treatment models. In S. J. Stevens & A. R. Morrall (Eds.), *Adolescent drug abuse treatment: Theory and implementation in eleven national programs* (pp. 3–56). Binghamton, NY: Haworth Press.

Dennis, M., Godley, S. H., Diamond, G. S., Tims, F. M., Babor, T., Donaldson, J., et al. (2002, May).

*Main findings of the Cannabis Youth Treatment (CYT) randomized field experiment.* Paper presented at the American Psychiatric Association Annual Conference. Philadelphia, PA.

Dennis, M. L., Titus, J. C., Diamond, G., Donaldson, J., Godley, S. H., Tims, F., et al. (2002). The Cannabis Youth Treatment (CYT) experiment: Rationale, study design, and analysis plans. *Addiction, 97*(Supp.), 16–34.

Diamond, G. S., & Diamond, G. M. (2002). Studying a matrix of change mechanisms: An agenda for family-based process research. In H. A. Liddle, D. A. Santisteban, R. F. Levant, & J. H Bray (Eds.), *Family psychology: Science-based interventions* (pp. 41–66). Washington, DC: American Psychological Association.

Diamond, G. M., Diamond, G. S., & Liddle, H. A. (2000). The therapist–parent alliance in family-based therapy for adolescents. *Journal of Clinical Psychology, 56,* 1037–1050.

Diamond, G. M., Liddle, H. A., Hogue, A., & Dakof, G. A. (1999). Alliance-building interventions with adolescents in family therapy: A process study. *Psychotherapy, 36,* 355–368.

Diamond, G. S., & Liddle, H. A. (1996). Resolving a therapeutic impasse between parents and adolescents in Multidimensional Family Therapy. *Journal of Consulting and Clinical Psychology, 64,* 481–488.

Diamond, G. S., & Liddle, H. A. (1999). Transforming negative parent–adolescent interactions: From impasse to dialogue. *Family Process, 38,* 355–368.

Dishion, T. J., & Andrews, D. W. (1995). Preventing escalation in problem behaviors with high-risk young adolescents: Immediate and 1-year outcomes. *Journal of Consulting and Clinical Psychology, 63,* 538-548.

Dishion, T. J., Patterson, G. R., & Kavanaugh, K. A. (1992). An experimental test of the coercion model: Linking theory, measurement, and intervention. In J. McCord & R. Tremblay (Eds.), *The interaction of theory and practice: Experimental studies of intervention* (pp. 253–282). New York: Guilford Press.

Donohue, B., & Azrin, N. (2001). Family behavior therapy. In E. F. Wagner & H. B. Waldron (Eds.), *Innovations in adolescent substance abuse interventions* (pp. 205–227). New York: Pergamon.

Donohue, B., Azrin, N., Lawson, H., Friedlander, J., Teicher, G., & Rindsberg, J. (1998). Improving initial session attendance of substance abusing and conduct disordered adolescents: A controlled study. *Journal of Child and Adolescent Substance Abuse, 8,* 1–13.

Eddy, J. M., & Chamberlain, P. (2000). Family management and deviant peer association as mediators of the impact of treatment condition on youth antisocial behavior. *Journal of Consulting and Clinical Psychology, 68,* 857–863.

Forgatch, M. S., & Patterson, G. R. (1989). *Parents and adolescents living together: Vol. 2. Family problem solving.* Eugene, OR: Castalia.

French, M., Roebuck, M. C., Dennis M., Godley, S., Tims, F., et al. (2002). The economic cost of outpatient marijuana treatment for adolescents: Findings from a multisite experiment. *Addiction, 97*(Supp.), 84–97.

Gordon, D. A., Graves, K., & Arbuthnot, J. (1995). The effect of functional family therapy for delinquents on adult criminal behavior. *Criminal Justice and Behavior, 22,* 60–73.

Hawkins, J. D., Catalano, R. F., & Miller, J. Y. (1992). Risk and protective factors for alcohol and other drug problems in adolescence and early adulthood: Implications for substance abuse prevention. *Psychological Bulletin, 112,* 64–105.

Henggeler, S. W., Borduin, C. M., & Mann, B. J. (1993). Advances in family therapy: Clinical foundations. In T. H. Ollendick & R. J. Prinz (Eds.), *Advances in clinical child psychology* (Vol. 15, pp. 207–241.). New York: Plenum Press.

Henggeler, S. W., Glinghempeel, W. G., Brondino, M. J., & Pickrel, S. G. (2002). Four-year follow-up of multisystemic therapy with substance-abusing and substance-dependent juvenile offenders. *Journal of the American Academy of Child and Adolescent Psychiatry, 41,* 868–874.

Henggeler, S. W., Melton, G. B., & Smith, L. A. (1992). Family preservation using multisystemic therapy: An effective alternative to incarcerating serious delinquent juvenile offenders. *Journal of Consulting and Clinical Psychology, 60,* 953–961.

Henggeler, S. W., Pickrel, S. G., & Brondino, M. J. (1999). Multisystemic treatment of substance-abusing and dependent delinquents: Outcomes, treatment fidelity, and transportability. *Mental Health Services Research, 1,* 171–184.

Henggeler, S. W., Pickrel, S. G., Brondino, M. J., & Crouch, J. L. (1996). Eliminating (almost) treatment dropout of substance abusing or dependent delinquents through home-based multisystemic therapy. *American Journal of Psychiatry, 153,* 427–428.

Henggeler, S. W., Rowland, M. D., Pickrel, S. G.,

Miller, S. L., Cunningham, P. B., Santos, A. B., et al. (1997). Investigating family-based alternatives to institution-based mental health services for youth: Lessons learned from the pilot study of a randomized field trial. *Journal of Clinical Child Psychology, 26,* 226–233.

Henggeler, S. W., Rowland, M. D., Randall, J., Ward, D. M., Pickrel, S. G., Cunningham, P. B., et al. (1999). Home-based multisystemic therapy as an alternative to the hospitalization of youth in psychiatric crisis: Clinical outcomes. *Journal of the American Academy of Child and Adolescent Psychiatry, 38,* 1331–1339.

Henggeler, S. W., & Santos, A. B. (Eds). (1997). *Innovative approaches for difficult-to-treat populations.* Washington, DC: American Psychiatric Press.

Henggeler, S. W., Schoenwald, S. K., Liao, J., Letourneau, E. J., & Edwards, D. L. (2002). Transporting efficacious treatments to field settings: The link between supervisory practices and therapist fidelity in MST programs. *Journal of Clinical Child Psychology, 31,* 155–167.

Hibbs, E. D., & Jensen, P. S. (Eds.). (1996). *Psychosocial treatments for child and adolescent disorders: Empirically based strategies for clinical practice.* Washington, DC: American Psychological Association.

Hoffman, L. (1981). *Foundations of family therapy.* New York: Basic Books.

Holmbeck, G. N. (1997). Toward terminological, conceptual, and statistical clarity in the study of mediators and moderators: Examples from the child-clinical and pediatric psychology literatures. *Journal of Consulting and Clinical Psychology, 65,* 599–610.

Huey, S. J., Henggeler, S. W., Brondino, M. J., & Pickrel, S. G. (2000). Mechanisms of change in multisystemic therapy: Reducing delinquent behavior through therapist adherence and improved family and peer functioning. *Journal of Consulting and Clinical Psychology, 68,* 451–467.

Kazdin, A. E. (1994). Methodology, design, and evaluation in psychotherapy research. In A. E. Bergin & S. L. Garfield (Eds.), *Handbook of psychotherapy and behavior change* (4th ed., pp. 19–71). New York: Wiley.

Kazdin, A. E. (1998). *Research design in clinical psychology* (3rd ed.). Needham Heights, MA: Allyn & Bacon.

Kazdin, A. E. (1999). The meanings and measurement of clinical significance. *Journal of Consulting and Clinical Psychology, 67,* 332–339.

Kazdin, A. E. (2002). Psychosocial treatments for conduct disorder in children and adolescents. In P. E. Nathan & J. M. Gorman (Eds.), *A guide to treatments that work* (2nd ed., pp. 57–85). London: Oxford University Press.

Kazdin, A. E., Seigel, T. C., & Bass, D. (1992). Cognitive problem-solving skills training and parent management training in the treatment of antisocial behavior in children. *Journal of Consulting and Clinical Psychology, 60,* 733–747.

Kazdin, A. E., & Wassell, G. (2000). Therapeutic changes in children, parents, and families resulting from treatment of children with conduct problems. *Journal of the American Academy of Child and Adolescent Psychiatry, 39,* 414–420.

Kazdin, A. E., & Weisz, J. R. (1998). Identifying and developing empirically supported child and adolescent treatments. *Journal of Consulting and Clinical Psychology, 66,* 19–36.

Klein, N. C., Alexander, J. F., & Parsons, B. V. (1977). Impact of family systems intervention on recidivism and sibling delinquency: A model of primary prevention and program evaluation. *Journal of Consulting and Clinical Psychology, 45,* 469–474.

Lewis, R. A., Piercy, F. P., Sprenkle, D. H., & Trepper, T. S. (1989). The Purdue brief family therapy model for adolescent substance abusers. In T. Todd & M. Selekman (Eds.), *Family approaches with adolescent substance abusers.* New York: Gardner.

Liddle, H. A. (1991). Empirical values and the culture of family therapy. *Journal of Marital and Family Therapy, 17,* 327–348.

Liddle, H. A. (1999). Theory development in a family-based therapy for adolescent drug abuse. *Journal of Clinical Child Psychology, 28,* 521-532.

Liddle, H. A. (2001, June). *Advances in family-based therapies for adolescent substance abuse.* Paper presented at the Annual Meeting of the College on Problems of Drug Dependence. Scottsdale, AZ.

Liddle, H. A. (2002a). *Multidimensional family therapy for adolescent cannabis users: Cannabis Youth Treatment (CYT) Series (Vol. 5).* Rockville, MD: Center for Substance Abuse Treatment. New York: Norton Professional Books.

Liddle, H. A. (2002b, May). The research renaissance in adolescent substance abuse treatment. *Connection: A Newsletter Linking the Users and Producers of Drug Abuse Services Research.* (http://www.academyhealth.org).

Liddle, H. A., & Dakof, G. A. (1995). Efficacy of family therapy for drug abuse: Promising but not definitive. *Journal of Marital and Family Therapy, 21,* 511–543.

Liddle, H. A., & Dakof, G. (2002, June). *A randomized controlled trial of intensive outpatient, family-based therapy vs. residential drug treatment for co-morbid adolescent substance abusers.* Paper presented at the Annual Meeting of the College on Problems of Drug Dependence. Quebec City, Quebec, Canada.

Liddle, H. A., Dakof, G. A., Parker, K., Diamond, G. S., Barrett, K., & Tejeda, M. (2001). Multidimensional family therapy for adolescent drug abuse: Results of a randomized clinical trial. *American Journal of Drug and Alcohol Abuse, 27,* 651–688.

Liddle, H. A., & Hogue, A. (2001). Multidimensional family therapy for adolescent substance abuse. In E. F. Wagner & H. B. Waldron (Eds.), *Innovations in adolescent substance abuse interventions* (pp. 229–261). New York: Pergamon.

Liddle, H. A., Rowe, C., Dakof, G., & Lyke, J. (1998). Translating parenting research into clinical interventions for families of adolescents. *Clinical Child Psychology and Psychiatry, 3,* 419-443.

Liddle, H. A., Rowe, C. L., Quille, T. J., Dakof, G. A., Mills, D. S., Sakran, E., & Biaggi, H. (2002). Transporting a research-based adolescent drug treatment into practice. *Journal of Substance Abuse Treatment, 22,* 231–243.

Liddle, H. A., & Schwartz, S. I. (2002). Attachment and family therapy: Clinical utility of adolescent-family attachment. *Family Process, 41,* 455–476.

Luke, D. A., & Homan, S. M. (1998). Time and change: Using survival analysis in clinical assessment and treatment evaluation. *Psychological Assessment, 10,* 360–378.

Mann, B. J., Borduin, C. M., Henggeler, S. W., & Blaske, D. M. (1990). An investigation of systemic conceptualizations of parent–child coalitions and symptom change. *Journal of Consulting and Clinical Psychology, 58,* 336–334.

Minuchin, S. (1974). *Families and family therapy.* Cambridge, MA: Harvard University Press.

Minuchin, S., & Fishman, H. C. (1981). *Family therapy techniques.* Cambridge, MA: Harvard University Press.

Morral, A. R., Iguchi, M. Y., Belding, M. A., & Lamb, R. J. (1997). Natural classes of treatment response. *Journal of Consulting and Clinical Psychology, 4,* 673–685.

Muthen, B. (2001). Second-generation structural equation models with a combination of categorical and continuous latent variables: new opportunities for latent class/latent growth modeling. In L. M. Collins & A. G. Sayer (Eds.), *New methods for the analysis of change.* Washington, DC: American Psychological Association.

National Institute on Drug Abuse, (1999). *Principles of drug addiction treatment: A research-based guide.* Rockville, MD: National Institute on Drug Abuse.

Ozechowski, T. J., & Liddle, H. A. (2000). Family-based therapy for adolescent drug abuse: Knowns and unknowns. *Clinical Child and Family Psychology Review, 3,* 269-298.

Patterson, G. R., & Chamberlain, P. (1994) A functional analysis of resistance during parent training therapy. *Clinical Psychology Science and Practice, 1,* 53–70.

Patterson, G. R., & Forgatch, M. S. (1987). *Parents and adolescents living together: Part 1: Living together.* Eugene, OR: Castalia.

Patterson, G. R., & Reid, J. B. (1973). Intervention for families of aggressive boys: A replication study. *Behavior Research and Therapy, 11,* 383–394.

Pinsof, W. M., & Wynne, L. C. (1995). The efficacy of marital and family therapy: An empirical overview, conclusions, and recommendations. *Journal of Marital and Family Therapy, 21,* 585–613.

Raudenbush, S. W., & Bryk, A. S. (2002). *Hierarchical linear models: Applications and data analysis methods* (2nd ed.). Newbury Park, CA: Sage.

Robbins, M. S., Alexander, J. F., Newell, R. M., & Turner, C. W. (1996). The immediate effect of reframing on client attitude in family therapy. *Journal of Family Psychology, 10,* 28–34.

Robbins, M. S., Alexander, J. F., & Turner, C. W. (2000). Disrupting defensive interactions in family therapy with delinquent adolescents. *Journal of Family Psychology, 14,* 688–701.

Santisteban, D. A., Szapocznik, J., Perez-Vidal, A., Kurtines, W. M., Murray, E. J., & La Pierre, A. (1996). Efficacy of intervention for engaging youth and families into treatment and some variables that may contribute to differential effectiveness. *Journal of Family Psychology, 10,* 35–44.

Schmidt, S. E., Liddle, H. A., & Dakof, G. A. (1996). Changes in parental practices and adolescent drug abuse during multidimensional family therapy. *Journal of Family Psychology, 10,* 12–27.

Schoenwald, S. K., Ward, D. M, Henggeler, S. W., & Rowland, M. D. (2000). Multisystemic therapy versus hospitalization of youth: Placement outcomes 4 months postreferral. *Mental Health Services Research, 2,* 3–12.

Sexton, T. L., & Alexander, J. F. (2002). Family-based empirically supported interventions. *The Counseling Psychologist, 30,* 238–261.

Shields, C. G., Wynne, L. C., McDaniel, S. H., & Gawinski, B. A. (1994). The marginalization of family therapy: A historical and continuing problem. *Journal of Marital and Family Therapy, 20,* 117–138.

Stanton, M. D., & Shadish, W. R. (1997). Outcome, attrition, and family-couples treatment for drug abuse: A meta-analysis and review of controlled, comparative studies. *Psychological Bulletin, 122,* 170–191.

Stanton, M. D., Todd, T. C., & Associates (1982). *The family therapy of drug abuse and addiction.* New York: Guilford Press.

Stormshak, E. A., & Dishion, T. J. (2002). An ecological approach to child and family clinical and counseling psychology. *Clinical Child and Family Psychology Review, 5,* 197–215.

Szapocznik, J., & Kurtines, W. (1989). *Breakthroughs in family therapy with drug abusing problem youth.* New York: Springer.

Szapocznik, J., Robbins, M. S., Mitrani, V., Santisteban, D., & Williams, R. A. (in press). Brief strategic family therapy with behavior problem Hispanic youth. In F. Kaslow (Series Ed.) & J. Lebow (Vol. Ed.), *Comprehensive handbook of psychotherapy. Vol. 4: Integrative and eclectic psychotherapies.* New York: Wiley.

Szapocznik, J., Rio, A. T., Murray, E., Cohen, R., Scopetta, M. A., Rivas-Vasquez, A., et al. (1989). Structural family versus psychodynamic child therapy for problematic Hispanic boys. *Journal of Consulting and Clinical Psychology, 57,* 571–578.

Waldron, H. B. (1997). Adolescent substance abuse and family therapy outcome: A review of randomized trials. In T. H. Ollendick & R. J. Prinz (Eds.), *Advances in clinical child psychology* (Vol. 19, pp. 199–234). New York: Plenum Press.

Waldron, H. B., Brody, J. L., & Slesnick, N. (2001). Integrative behavioral and family therapy for adolescent substance abuse. In P. M. Monti, S. M. Colby, & T. A. O'Leary (Eds.), *Adolescents, alcohol, and substance abuse: Reaching teens through brief interventions.* New York: Guilford Press.

Waldron, H. B., Slesnick, N., Brody, J. L., Turner, C. W., & Peterson, T. R. (2001). Treatment outcomes for adolescent substance abuse at 4- and 7-month assessments. *Journal of Consulting and Clinical Psychology, 69,* 802-813.

Watzlawick, P., Weakland, J., & Fisch, R. (1974). *Change: Principles of problem formation and resolution.* New York: Norton.

Weersing, V. R., & Weisz, J. R. (2002). Mechanisms of action in youth psychotherapy. *Journal of Child Psychology and Psychiatry, 43,* 3–29.

Willett, J. B., & Keiley, M. K. (2000). Using covariance structure analysis to model change over time. In H. E. A. Tinsley & S. D. Brown (Eds.), *Handbook of applied multivariate statistics and mathematical modeling* (pp. 665–694). San Diego, CA: Academic Press.

Williams, R. J., & Chang, S. Y. (2000). A comprehensive and comparative review of adolescent substance abuse treatment outcomes. *Clinical Psychology: Science and Practice, 7,* 138–166.

# CHAPTER 19

# Treatment Through Writing

## A Unique New Direction

Luciano L'Abate, PhD

*Georgia State University*

## INTRODUCTION

Historically, the development of psycho-therapy can be distinguished according to three stages: (1) a passive-reactive one, as exemplified by psychoanalysis and client-centered therapy in the first half of last century; (2) an active-directive one, as exemplified by cognitive-behavioral, rational-emotive, and family therapies, in the second half of last century; and (3) an interactive stage, which began during the last quarter of the last century. In this third stage, families were encouraged to become involved and take responsibility for the treatment process by completing homework assignments.

Impetus for this approach was given by sex therapists and behavioral marital therapists (Holtzworth-Munroe & Jacobson, 1991). Among the former, Heiman, LoPiccolo, and LoPiccolo (1991), for instance, stated that "therapy structure begins via homework assignments" (p. 610). Weeks and Gambescia

(2000) adamantly declared that "One of the hallmarks of sex therapy is homework" (p. 108). Among the latter, Jacobson (1981), for instance, alluded to the same point, by concluding that "Couples tend to be more compliant with homework assignments when the task is explicitly made synonymous with therapy than when the link between these tasks and their in-session use is unclear or unspecified" (p. 573). This third stage was also coupled with the administration of written homework assignments, requiring families to come together at home to complete and discuss assignments interactively, as a condition of being accepted into a therapeutic contract. This requirement assured a much greater degree of cooperation and compliance than obtained otherwise (L'Abate, 1986; L'Abate, Ganahl, & Hansen, 1986).

According to one estimate (T. Patterson, personal communication, March 28, 2002): "90% of couple, family, and parent-child therapy practiced today incorporates either

397

homework, reading, self-monitoring, writing, or other methods." If that is the case, one could argue that these methods are usually administered ad hoc, without any systematic background, and, even more important, without evidence or theory to support them.

## BACKGROUND: RATIONALE FOR THIS APPROACH

The purpose of this chapter is to go one step further in the third stage of development of family therapy and to argue in favor of using writing as a medium of intervention for families. Rather than just unstructured, face-to-face (f2f), talk-based interventions, reviewed in previous chapters, this step requires interactive involvement of families with structured, systematically written homework assignments (L'Abate, 1986, 1990, 1992, 2001, 2002a, 2002b, in press; L'Abate & De Giacomo, 2003; L'Abate & Kern, 2002).

Systematically written homework assignments, that is, workbooks, can be administered through the mail, computers, TV, and online. *In the not too distant future, the internet will become increasingly important in the delivery of mental health services, especially in prevention* (Maheu, Whitten, & Allen, 2001). In addition, this chapter will argue that the traditional, f2f, talk-based, one family/one therapist paradigm of family therapy, if not bankrupt, needs to expand not just for shortcomings of its own, but for its failure to reach the many families who need some kind of help and not just therapy. For every family who receives f2f, talk-based family therapy, there are at least 5 to 10 families who could use some help, but who, for whatever reason, cannot accept, afford, or profit by f2f therapy.

Different media and modalities of intervention will need to be introduced. Talk is too inefficient and expensive to be used alone, without using additional media available to us,

as well as to families—namely, nonverbal and written homework assignments (L'Abate, 1999a). We need to rely on new technologies to reach as many families who need our help as possible (L'Abate & Odell, 1995). However, perhaps the most challenging obstacle in developing and implementing these new technologies is how to change the attitudes and habits of mental health professionals who still believe in the magic of personal contact and of the spoken word (L'Abate, 1997, 1999a, 1999b).

How can a therapist help as many families as possible per unit of time at the lowest possible cost without sacrificing standards and criteria of responsible practice? The most cost-effective and mass-oriented way to preventively help families *at risk* for personal, marital, or family breakdown and therapeutically *in need* of mental health services is to help them at a distance. "At risk" means that most families are vulnerable to unexpected and sudden stresses that will test their resiliency and strength. "In need" means that some families, because of their composition (children of alcoholic parents, abusive families, families of criminals, neglectful parents, children of divorce), even though they may deny wanting help, eventually will produce a breakdown in one family member, or in both parents, or between parents and children. *In crisis* means that fewer families are chronically dysfunctional or are in extreme crisis, exhibiting clinical conditions requiring professional help. Families in crisis or with chronic conditions may receive initial help through f2f, talk-based contact. However, once the crisis is reduced, they can be helped just as well though writing, via computers, and online. Writing can and should be used synergistically with talk, as well as with nonverbal interventions (medication, exercise, diet, etc.).

Writing became standard operating procedure in my past clinical practice for at least three reasons: (1) to facilitate respondents' (individuals, couples, and families) assuming greater responsibility for changes in their relationships; (2) to save my time and energy; and (3) to make psychotherapy more cost-effective. This process, starting with nonsystematic, generally ad hoc homework assignments, culminated in the creation of systematically written workbooks that required writing from families, rather than direct contact with a therapist or intermediaries (L'Abate, 1986). Programmed, systematically written homework assignments—that is, workbooks—were administered in addition to f2f psychotherapy or as an alternative to psychotherapy when dealing with families who did not need it or who, after terminating family therapy proper, could use alternative or additional interventions; resided too far away to be seen f2f; could not afford private practice fees and could be seen only on an as-needed basis, once a month or less; or still needed help when I was out of town, on vacation, or sick (L'Abate, L'Abate, & Maino, 2002).

The rest of this chapter will explain how it is possible to help families at a distance from, and without direct f2f, talk-based contact with, a therapist. Change in families at a distance can and does occur with support, supervision, and feedback by a professional; provided that a proper evaluation of the referral question has been undertaken, and an informed consent form has been signed by family caretakers beforehand.

## Contextual Background for the Use of Writing in Family Therapy

The major issue here, of course, lies in defining what does constitute "progress" in family therapy? If we are not clear, concerned, and competent to address this issue, the status quo will continue to prevail and nothing will change. Consequently, progress in therapy

means helping more families in need of help per unit of professional time in more cost-effective and mass-oriented ways than is possible through talk and f2f contact alone. Here is where two different practice paradigms collide. A public health paradigm wants to offer cost-effective, mass-oriented ways of helping families who want and need professional help. A private practice paradigm offers fee-for-service only to families who can afford it. By distinguishing among families who are at risk (primary prevention) from those who are in need (secondary prevention) and those who are in crisis (tertiary prevention), it will be possible to tailor-make specific interventions for specific needs, matching interventions with evaluation.

Apparently without any distinction, every family is treated with the same approach, defective in specificity and replicability. If we cannot distinguish what is relevant from what is irrelevant, then we are destined to continue operating in the same way, no change will take place, and no progress will occur (Keen, 2000; L'Abate, 1997, 1999a, 1999b). What is needed is greater specificity of approaches linked directly to the referral question.

## The Inefficiency of the Face-to-Face Talk-Based Paradigm in Family Therapy

Psychotherapy, as presently practiced with individuals, couples, and families, cannot deal with the number of people that need some kind of help. If the Surgeon General's Report on Mental Health (U.S. Department of Health and Human Services, 1999) is correct, there is no way that f2f psychotherapy can reach and deal with all the problems present in our communities.

There are too many weaknesses in the verbal medium for it to be effectively delivered to the population in need of services. L'Abate (1999a, 1999b) has argued that talk is expensive and cheap at the same time. Anyone can talk, but talking with a professional is expensive. Talk cannot be controlled and cannot be directed. It is infinite in its expressions and is uncontrollable as far as what professionals will say, to what their patients will say. It can be forgotten, distorted, or used abusively (Bandler & Grinder, 1975; Grinder & Bandler, 1976). As Keen (2000) has argued, psychotherapy is replete with talk that is completely irrelevant to achieving the goal of improvement. In short, talk is a very inefficient medium. It lacks specificity, and one could question whether talk is necessary to achieve improvement in respondents (individuals, couples, and families).

The infinite and incontrollable nature of talk is visible in the veritable Tower of Babel that characterizes current psychotherapeutic practices and the many kinds of family therapy presented in this handbook. How is one able to find which approach will produce which outcome if each therapist represents a uniqueness that cannot be replicated?

## CRITERIA FOR A PUBLIC HEALTH APPROACH TO FAMILY PROBLEMS

To qualify as a public health approach to deal with the myriad problems of families at risk, in need, and in crisis, any responsible and responsive intervention will need to satisfy at least five criteria:

1. *Cost-effectiveness:* The intervention will need to be cost-effective to deal with as many problems as there are today. Cost-effective will mean also relying either on intermediary paraprofessional personnel or mechanical devices to minimize the high cost of professional time (U.S. Dept. of Health and Human Services, 1999). The latter should be reserved for the most difficult cases that cannot be addressed by

less trained or experienced personnel and mechanical devices. It remains to be seen whether writing and programmed writing are as cost-effective as I claim they are (L'Abate et al., 2002).

2. *Mass-administration:* To be effective, a preventive or therapeutic approach needs to reach as many families as possible, starting from the most economical to the most expensive (L'Abate, 1990, 2002a). These successive sieves or stepped-care approaches suggest using the least expensive preventive interventions first. If these fail, the family can then be introduced to more expensive interventions, requiring f2f talk-based professional intervention. This process, of course, could be short-circuited if appropriate evaluation became a standard operating procedure in most family-oriented interventions (L'Abate, 1994). To be mass-administered, a method needs to be versatile in dealing with a variety of family problems and issues. In this regard, computers and the Internet have the potential to become the third avenue of delivery for mental health services after medication and psychotherapy. The question to answer is whether computers can fulfill some functions until now reserved for f2f psychotherapy. If they do, *how* can they be utilized in the prevention and treatment of mental disorders in families? Software for such delivery, in the form of workbooks, has already been created to deal with individual, marital, and family problems (L'Abate, 1986, 1992, 1996, 2001, 2002a).

3. *Replicability:* Subjective opinions must be verified; otherwise, the field of family therapy will continue to rely on personal, idiosyncratic beliefs and opinions unsubstantiated by objective evidence. Without replicability, the status quo will continue to reign supreme (L'Abate, 1997). Writing, instead, is replicable, specific, and

versatile in ways that allow verification from one therapist to another and from one clinical setting to another. Thus far, the evidence gathered in my Family Study Center (L'Abate, 2001, in press) with couples does suggest that homework assignments, as well as f2f, talk-based therapy, do help. Furthermore, the review by Esterling, L'Abate, Murray, and Pennebaker (1999) attests to the usefulness of expressive writing. Smyth and L'Abate (2001), in their meta-analysis of workbooks, found a moderate, mean effect size of .44 that is sufficient to justify their use as alternatives or synergistic adjuncts to f2f, talk-based therapies, both in prevention and in psychotherapy.

4. *Accountability:* Managed-care companies have been reviled for their stress on this criterion from many mental health professionals. That professionals be required to account for their results was unheard of for decades. Yet without this criterion, the field would remain open to charlatans using unprofessional or gimmicky practices. Of course, this criterion is predicated on objective, pre-post intervention evaluation, a practice that is still not present in family therapy, as some chapters in this handbook indicate. Verifiability and accountability are two independent criteria. An approach may be verifiable, but it may produce questionable or poor outcomes, whereas a difficult-to-verify approach may produce acceptable outcomes (L'Abate, 2002a, 2002b).

5. *Specificity:* How can we be specific in our interventions as long as we rely on talk? By definition, as argued earlier, talk is nonspecific. It can be forgotten or distorted to the point that therapy becomes a slow, expensive process (Bandler & Grinder, 1975; Grinder & Bandler, 1976). Lacking evaluation and relying on talk make it impossible to link interventions with referral

questions or problems. Specificity is achieved when a specific, replicable treatment matches a particular problem referral or diagnosis.

Of course, another possible criterion, by now forgotten, is whether an intervention is theory-derived. With its frenzy of empirically based approaches, on one hand, and eclecticism in practice, on the other, theory-derivation has either been completely forgotten or relegated to a tertiary place in any possible intervention (L'Abate, 2002a, 2002b; L'Abate & DeGiacomo, 2003). A recent treatise on science-based interventions in family psychology (Liddle, Santisteban, Levant, & Bray, 2002), for instance, fails to mention any theory, even though various unsystematically unconnected models were introduced.

This position is predicated on the assumption that (1) writing is the next revolution in the delivery of mental health services (Lepore & Smyth, 2002; Levy & Ransdell, 1996); (2) computers will be used in this delivery of mental health services, at least in unstructured ways that mimic online talk-based psychotherapy, as it is already happening; and (3) workbooks will permit therapists to match diagnosis or referral questions with treatment, provided that we have a sufficiently large number of workbooks to cover as many clinical conditions presented to us as possible (L'Abate, 1996, 2001, 2002a, 2002b, in press).

## EMPIRICAL SUPPORT FOR THE USE OF WRITING IN FAMILY THERAPY

Overall, there is a robust and increasingly coherent body of literature that points to the widespread use and benefits of writing as one of a growing repertoire of adjunct techniques that support the therapeutic process and improve coping abilities and perceptions of control over stressful and traumatic events.

Results from various sources (Esterling et al., 1999; L'Abate, 1992, 2001, 2002a, 2002b, in press; Smyth & L'Abate, 2001) suggest that writing could be considered a cost-effective, mass-oriented, replicable, versatile, and, when programmed, specific way to reach and help large numbers of families on parapreventive and parapsychotherapeutic bases.

## A Classification of Writing

Writing can be classified according to (1) structure, (2) content, (3) goals, and (4) levels of abstraction (L'Abate, 2001a, 2001b, 2002a, 2002b, in press; L'Abate & De Giacomo, 2003). Going from least to most structured, this continuum can be devided into four possible types: (1) *open-ended,* as in diaries or journals (Progoff, 1975), with a minimum of structure; to (2) *focused*, as in "For 15–20 minutes a day for 4 days write about all the hurts you have received in your life, including those hurts that you have never shared with anyone else" (Esterling et al., 1999; Pennebaker, 2001); to (3) *guided*, as in "I have read your diary and I have written some questions that I would like you to answer in writing," and the most structured, (4) *programmed,* as in workbooks, a series of homework assignments devoted to one single topic.

Content is classified according to whether it is general versus specific or traumatic versus trivial. Content also specifies the topic at hand—that is, arguing, temper tantrums, sibling rivalry, and so on. Goals are classified according to whether the written homework assignments are designed to be cathartic, to express feelings; prescriptive, to direct families toward performance or rehearsal of specific tasks; hortatory; or explanatory. Abstraction deals with whether the writing is abstract (high), as in "Write about the meaning of life," or concrete (low), as in "Brush your teeth every morning for 5 minutes." The rest of this chapter will be devoted to the second and fourth types of writing.

### FOCUSED WRITING

The major components of focused writing include the following: (1) setting a regular time of constant length for writing, for example, half an hour twice a week, at 9 P.M. on Tuesday and Thursday; (2) seeking out a location to write that allows open disclosure and uninterrupted writing, free from distracting sights, sounds, and smells; (3) choosing a specific topic or theme that provides a greater sense of focus and direction; (4) writing freely in any style that is natural and comfortable, without concern for sentence structure, grammar, or logic; (5) focusing on emotions and thoughts surrounding past or present events, whether they are positive or negative; (6) getting clear, unambiguous feedback from the partner, other family members, and, of course, the therapist; and (7) avoiding overreliance on ruminative writing—writing should not substitute for action.

Instructions for one type of focused writing, for instance, consist of asking families to write individually for 20 minutes a day for 4 consecutive days about all their hurts or traumas (Pennebaker, 2001). This beginning homework assignment opens up a great deal of information that is available for f2f discussion in family conferences, with written notes about what happened during the conference to be brought to the therapist (L'Abate et al., 1986). A second example of focused writing consists of asking families to list all the defeats and victories they have inflicted to, and suffered from, other family members. Once each member has completed this list, a family conference is devoted to sharing and discussing these defeats, as well as victories

I have used this approach with individuals, couples, and families from the very outset of therapy, after three evaluation sessions (where respondents are also asked to evaluate the therapist) and the signing of an informed consent form and a therapeutic contract (L'Abate et al., 2002). The focus on hurts finds its theoretical basis in a developmental, contextual theory of personality socialization in the family and other settings that makes hurt feelings the bottom line of our existence. However, one must always be alert to possible side effects, because hurt feelings, especially at the outset of therapy, are a potentially explosive topic (L'Abate, 2002a, 2002b; L'Abate & De Giacomo, 2003; Pennebaker, 2001). Nonetheless, through this medium many families reported that they confided more "secret" information in writing than they would have told f2f. These testimonials need to be validated further.

From an initially focused approach, however, I began to rely more and more on systematically written, programmed homework assignments around a specific topic, in order to match the treatment with the referral problem (L'Abate, 1986, 1990, 1996, 2001, 2002a, 2002b, in press a, in press b). This process has led eventually to the development, production, and marketing online of about 100 workbooks (L'Abate, 1996).

## PROGRAMMED WRITING: WORKBOOKS FOR INDIVIDUALS, COUPLES, AND FAMILIES

Creation of workbooks finds its historical roots in teaching machines and programmed instruction (Brown & L'Abate, 1969). Programmed writing, therefore, means workbooks, consisting of a series of assignments written around a specific topic and containing a variety of questions, exercises, and comments that need to be responded to in writing. The last decade has seen the publication, at least in the United States, of a plethora of workbooks (L'Abate, 2002, in press).

The goal of workbooks, therefore, is to de-

crease debilitating clinical conditions or symptoms. What was originally a general "focused" assignment ("Write about your hurts [or defeats] for 1 hour every other day [or once or twice a week], at *predetermined* times.") became a more specific and systematic workbook ("This is the first homework in an eight-assignment workbook to be completed this week. I will give you the next assignment once you complete this one.") that paralleled a theoretical model developed over the years (L'Abate, 1986).

Consequently, workbooks allow the addressing of individual, couple, and family issues that may be time-consuming or difficult to deal in f2f interactions. For instance, while family therapy is going on, the parental couple may follow a workbook on temper tantrums for one child or the negotiation workbook for themselves. If the wife is depressed, both partners may profit by the "Depression in Couples" workbook. If the husband is driven or shows a comorbid or subsyndromal condition, he may profit by a workbook to reduce drivenness, substance abuse, or anxiety. Hence, workbooks allow therapists to tailor-make interventions to specific needs of families, couples, and individuals. Workbooks, therefore, form the basis for software applications with computer-assisted interventions online. They are to psychological interventions what medications are for psychiatric interventions (L'Abate, in press), matching a specific condition with a specific intervention.

The functions of these workbooks are, among others, to (1) train graduate students to deal with a variety of issues in individuals, couples, and families, following written-down, structured interviews or guidelines provided for them in workbooks; (2) serve as guidelines for professionals in need of specific treatment plans for a variety of individual, couples', and family issues that arise in f2f situations, but that would be time-consuming to deal with in such a format; (3) serve as alternatives or additions to ongoing f2f professional relationships, providing verbal or written feedback after completion of such homework; (4) help family members receive feedback from each other after completion and discussion of homework assignments, and later from the therapist; and (5) perform research under controlled conditions in inexpensive ways that cannot be matched by talk, which is expensive to control, record, and code (L'Abate, 1999a, 2001).

An annotated bibliography about workbooks published within the last decade about a variety of clinically, semiclinically, and preventively relevant topics contains over 300 workbooks (L'Abate, 1996, 2001).

The main issue with most workbooks relates to their not having been subjected to empirical verification by most authors. Only very few of these workbooks have been subjected to controlled studies to evaluate their clinical usefulness (L'Abate, 2001, in press; Smyth & L'Abate, 2001). Nonetheless, they furnish the basis for applications with computer-assisted interventions, as discussed further on.

*Toward a Classification of Workbooks*

Workbooks that I have developed (L'Abate, 1986, 1992, 1996, 2002a, in press) can be classified according to the following dimensions: (1) composition of respondents, (2) theoretical orientation, (3) format, (4) derivation, (5) style, (6) level and type of functionality, and (7) content.

### 1. COMPOSITION

*Children and Adolescents.* Workbooks in this category can be used by schools and institutions, based on the referral question as well as on test results. They are distinguished from other workbooks when referral questions are related to children's behaviors under the responsibility of the family—that is, when the family, rather than a school or an institution, is referring the child. Workbooks have been developed from test scores or test profiles relating to (a) externalizations (anger, hostility, and aggression), juvenile psychopathy, school conduct problems, school social skills, unusual or troublesome behavior; and (b) internalizations, such as anxiety, depression, and fears, as well as emotional problems.

*Adults.* This category contains the largest number of workbooks and is divided according to (a) the referral question, where only an interview and no tests are used; (b) single-score tests, like the Beck and Hamilton Anxiety and Depression Inventories for internalizations; (c) adult psychopathy, anger expression, hostility, gambling, personality disorders, adult temper, and abusive talk for externalizations; (d) psychological test profile, like the Content Scales of the Minnesota Multiphasic Personality Inventory-2, the Five-Factors Model, the Personality Assessment Inventory, and the Self–Other Profile Charts; and (e) serious psychopathology, like workbooks derived from the Brief Psychiatric Rating Scale, Post-Traumatic Stress Disorder, Posttraumatic Stress Symptoms, Social Growth, and Symptoms Scale.

*Couples. Workbooks based on test profiles:* This category contains workbooks based on multiple-scores questionnaires about improving relationships, marital satisfaction, problems in relationships, and relationship conflict. *Workbooks based on the referral question:* This category contains workbooks with no direct relationship to an assessment instrument, even though there may be some available, such as arguing and fighting, depression in couples, intimacy, couple violence, negotiation, premarital preparation, and standing up for oneself.

*Families. Workbooks based on test profiles:* These workbooks were derived either from a test; from list of symptoms, like the *DSM-IV;* or from factor analyses of symptoms, such as, when parents and children argue; when parents argue, as seen from the child's viewpoint; self-report measures of family functioning; and the family profile form. *Workbooks based on the referral question:* This category includes workbooks for binge eating, divorce adjustment for children, domestic violence and child abuse, feelings in the family, foster/adoptive family care, initial family interview and feelings, lying, negativity, relationship styles, temper tantrums, shyness, sibling rivalry, stealing, time-out procedures, and verbal abuse.

## 2. THEORETICAL ORIENTATION

There are three levels of theoretical orientation:

*Theory Derived.* Certain workbooks have been derived directly from a developmental, relationally contextual theory of interpersonal competence (L'Abate, 1986, 2002a, 2002b; L'Abate & De Giacomo, 2003), as well as from other theories and models.

*Theory Related.* This means that a workbook was developed from a model of a theory, rather than from a theory itself. For instance, two workbooks on self-awareness and relational styles were developed from one theoretical model (L'Abate & De Giacomo, 2003). Having to break down or dismantle a theoretical model into its component parts allows therapists to clarify the nature of each assignment, as well as the relationship of component parts of the model to its isomorphic assignments (L'Abate, 1986, 1990, 1992, 2002a). Consequently, workbooks, when derived directly from a theory or a model, do become evaluators of that theory or model in a more dynamic fashion than are static test scores that were derived from the same theory or model or from artificial and contrived laboratory experiments (L'Abate, 1986).

*Theory Independent.* There are workbooks developed strictly on clinical bases, with no direct link to theories or models. For instance, workbooks on depression and sexual abuse were developed on the basis of clinical experience rather than theory, even though links with theories and models could be established on a post hoc basis.

## 3. FORMAT

This characteristic can be *fixed,* that is, nomothetic, the same number and sequence of assignments for everybody; or can be *flexible,* that is, idiographic by allowing respondents to rank-order descriptive items in an initial sequence that determines how the following assignments will be administered. Idiographic workbooks can also be administered in a fixed format for a predetermined number of assignments for research purposes.

## 4. DERIVATION

Certain workbooks were derived from clinical practice, theories, theoretical models, empirical findings as in factor-analyses, and items of single- and multiple-score tests, like the Beck Depression Inventory or the MMPI-2, the *DSM-IV* manual, and pop psychology books.

## 5. STYLE

Workbooks can be written in a straightforward linear style or in paradoxical, circular style, where the symptom is prescribed once a positive reframing is given, as in depression (L'Abate, 1986).

## 6. LEVEL OF FUNCTIONALITY

Some workbooks were developed for four levels of functionality: (a) normative conditions and experiences, such as the development of emotional competence and experience, self-awareness, emotional intelligence, multiple abilities, and social skills; (b) externalizations, such as anger, hostility, aggression, impulsivity, and character disorders; (c) internalizations, such as anxiety, depression, panic disorders, dependent personality, dissociative experiences, and loneliness; and (d) psychopathology, such as psychiatric symptomatology and post-traumatic stress disorders.

## 7. CONTENT

Titles of the workbooks indicate the topic to be addressed by the workbook itself, as covered by the foregoing dimensions.

### Advantages of Workbooks

Workbooks may provide at least six benefits to professionals and families that still need evaluation: (1) they are *cost-effective*, especially if each hour of face-to-face relationships is matched with 1 hour of homework assignments; (2) they can be *mass-produced* and administered to a variety of families through verbal (tape-recorded), written, and electronic media, like the Internet, TV, and PCs; (3) they are *issue-specific*—each workbook is written to match specific referral questions, conditions, test-results, and diagnoses; (4) they are *reusable* as often as necessary by approved purchasers; (5) they are *versatile*, to be used especially when treatment for a specific condition or symptom is not part of a therapist's repertoire, and (6) they can be used during or after f2f therapy, when an alternative or adjunct approach is needed, such as in structured interviews or as verbatim manuals for students, as well as for professionals who need a specific treatment plan that is not otherwise available.

### Disadvantages of Workbooks: Ethical and Professional Issues

There is no doubt that distance and written practices do and will raise a variety of ethical and professional issues (Budman, 2000; L'Abate, 2001, 2002a), as well as a great deal of resistance from many therapists. Paradoxically, the profession that claims to change people's behavior for the better is the one with the greatest degree of reservations about changing its own practices (L'Abate, 1997). A great deal of this resistance will be focused on the importance of the personal presence and verbal power of the therapist and of nonverbal clues that would not be visible online. An indication of this resistance at the organizational level is found in legislation that limits online practices to the state in which one is licensed (Budman, 2000; L'Abate, 2002a). On the other hand, potential issues will not arise until and unless these nontraditional practices will take place. At least at the present time, there are three basic issues that need confrontation: (1) confidentiality; (2) vicarious liability; and (3) fidelity. Many other issues will come to the fore once this practice is expanded and its actual limits and limitations are found.

### CONFIDENTIALITY

With the many encryption possibilities available online, it is now possible to assure maximum confidentiality to respondents who want it.

### VICARIOUS LIABILITY

This liability pertains to responsibility given to the producers of workbooks. If a workbook about arguing and fighting, for instance, is administered to partners who do not reveal the extent of abuse already present in their relationship, they could sue the producer of the workbook for increasing the abuse level. By the same token, a family with a problem child, whose aggressive behavior increases after administration of a workbook, could suit the producer of the workbook for inappropriate use. This is why it is crucial for professionals who want to use this approach to evaluate carefully the background for the referral question and to obtain a signed informed consent form before administration of any workbook (L'Abate, 2002, in press).

## FIDELITY

How does the professional know that the family he or she is working with online is the family with whom a contract was established? Of course, this issue is more much likely to occur with acting-out, character-disordered individuals than with families. Furthermore, if an objective evaluation has been completed, with a signed informed consent form from adult caretakers, it is difficult for an entire family to find someone else to take its place!

*Workbooks and Computer-Assisted Interventions (CAIs)*

One advantage of the computer over either physical or psychological f2f treatments is the possibility of administering cost-effective, mass-produced programs. If one estimates that psychotherapy in the United States is a $6 billion-plus business, without even counting the costs of psychiatric medication, alternative interventions that capitalize on writing, computers, and the Internet may substantially reduce mental health costs, shortening the process of treatment. For example, if treatment is shortened even by 5%, millions of dollars

would be saved. This possibility may mean an important reduction in existing and spiraling mental health costs. Hence, there is a strong need for evaluating whether computers and online administration of written homework assignments can shorten the length and cost of family therapy. However, a beginning must be made to perform such an assessment (L'Abate, L'Abate, & Maino, 2002).

The Internet is fast becoming an alternative source of service delivery in the mental health field (Maheu, Whitten, & Allen, 2001). With managed-care and insurance companies pressuring for cost-effective and accountable therapies, at least in the United States, CAIs can fulfill these requirements. They also fulfill a requirement of reaching families that are either not willing or unable to seek mental health facilities and interact in a f2f relationship with a mental health professional. Thus far, CAIs using written communications have been found to be helpful in the treatment of panic disorders, obesity, test anxiety, phobias, and depression (Newman, Kenardy, Herman, & Taylor, 1997). Before long, a variety of clinical conditions will be treated through CAIs, to determine which clinical condition can be treated through this medium and which clinical condition needs to be treated by a professional in a f2f relationship.

## CONCLUSION

The implications of this approach are relevant to the delivery of both preventive and therapeutic treatment approaches with families. If it can be demonstrated that workbooks, computers, and the Internet allow easy access to families who (1) would not otherwise access existing mental health facilities or (2) who may not need f2f treatment, but who can use self-administered workbooks, a new, cost-effective delivery system could be opened. This delivery system would reach more families per unit of professional time than was possible in the past. This approach would in no way decrease or diminish functions of existing family-oriented services. It would enhance their functions by empowering them to reach more families through this approach than has been possible heretofore.

If we want to intervene effectively with families, we will need to rely on as many media of intervention as are available—verbal, nonverbal, and written, as well as on new technological advances in television, computers, and conventional communication media like mail, telephone, and faxes. This change means that we need to intervene with families at a distance. This transition will be very difficult for many family therapists to undertake. Unless this change occurs, however, many families and our profession are going to be shortchanged. Ultimately, family therapists have to decide whether to stay in the last century or join the present one.

## ACKNOWLEDGMENTS

I am greatly indebted to Terence Patterson, Michael S. Robbins, George F. Ronan, Thomas L. Sexton, and Gerald R. Weeks for their helpful comments to early drafts of this chapter.

## REFERENCES

Bandler, R., & Grinder, J. (1975). *The structure of magic, I: A book about language and therapy.* Palo Alto, CA: Science and Behavior Books.

Brown, E. C., & L'Abate, L. (1969). An appraisal of teaching machines and programmed instruction. In C. M. Franks (Ed.), *Behavior therapy: Appraisal and status* (pp. 396–414). New York: McGraw-Hill.

Budman, S. H. (2000). Behavioral healthcare dot.com and beyond: Computer-mediated communications in mental health and substance abuse treatment. *American Psychologist, 55*, 1290–1300.

Esterling, B. A., L'Abate, L., Murray, E., & Pennebaker, J. M. (1999). Empirical foundations

for writing in prevention and psychotherapy: Mental and physical outcomes. *Clinical Psychology Review, 19*, 79–96.

Grinder, J., & Bandler, R. (1976). *The structure of magic, II: A book about communication and change.* Palo Alto, CA: Science and Behavior Books.

Heiman, J. R., LoPiccolo, L., & LoPiccolo, J. (1991). The treatment of sexual dysfunction. In A. S. Gurman & D. P. Kniskern (Eds.), *Handbook of family therapy* (pp. 593–627). New York: Brunner/Mazel.

Holtzworth-Munroe, A., & Jacobson, N. S. (1991). Behavioral marital therapy. In A. S. Gurman & D. P. Kniskern (Eds.), *Handbook of family therapy* (Vol. 2, pp. 96–133). New York: Brunner/Mazel.

Jacobson, N. S. (1981). Behavioral marital therapy. In A. S. Gurman & D. P. Kniskern (Eds.), *Handbook of family therapy* (pp. 557–591). New York: Brunner/Mazel.

Keen, E. (2000). *Ultimacy and triviality in psychotherapy.* Westport, CT: Praeger.

L'Abate, L. (1986). *Systematic family therapy.* New York: Brunner/Mazel.

L'Abate, L. (1990). *Building family competence: Primary and secondary prevention strategies.* Newbury Park, CA: Sage.

L'Abate, L. (1992). *Programmed writing: A self-administered approach for interventions with individuals, couples and families.* Pacific Grove, CA: Brooks/Cole.

L'Abate, L. (1994). *Family evaluation: A psychological perspective.* Thousand Oaks, CA: Sage.

L'Abate, L. (1996). Workbooks for better living. www.mentalhealthhelp.com.

L'Abate, L. (1997). The paradox of change: .etter them than us! In S. R. Sauber (Ed.), *Managed mental health care: Major diagnostic and treatment approaches* (pp. 40–66). Bristol, PA: Brunner/Mazel.

L'Abate, L. (1999a). Decisions we (mental health professionals) need to make (whether we like them or not): A reply to Cummings and Hoyt. *The Family Journal: Counseling and Therapy for Couples and Families, 7*, 227–230.

L'Abate, L. (1999b). Taking the bull by the horns: Beyond talk in psychological interventions. *The Family Journal: Counseling and Therapy for Couples and Families, 7*, 206–220.

L'Abate, L. (Ed.). (2001). *Distance writing and computer-assisted interventions in psychiatry and mental health.* Westport, CT: Ablex.

L'Abate, L. (2002a). *Beyond psychotherapy: Pro-*

*grammed writing and structured computer-assisted interventions*. Westport, CT: Greenwood.

L'Abate, L. (2002b). *Family psychology III: Theory-building, theory-testing, and psychological interventions*. Lanham, MD: University Press of America.

L'Abate, L. (in press a). *A guide to self-help workbooks for clinicians and researchers*. Binghamton, NY: Haworth.

L'Abate, L. (Ed.). (in press b). *Workbooks in prevention, psychotherapy and rehabilitation: A resource for clinicians and researchers*. Binghamton, NY: Haworth.

L'Abate, L., & De Giacomo, P. (2003). *Intimate relationships and how to improve them: Integration of theoretical models with psychological interventions*. Westport, CT: Ablex.

L'Abate, L., Ganahl, G., & Hansen, J. C. (1986). *Methods of family therapy*. Englewood Cliffs, NJ: Prentice-Hall.

L'Abate, L., & Kern, R. (2002). Workbooks: Tools for the expressive writing paradigm. In S. J. Lepore & J. Smyth (Eds.), *The writing cure: How expressive writing influences health and well-being* (pp. 239–255). Washington, DC: American Psychological Association.

L'Abate, L., L'Abate, L. B., & Maino, E. (2002). Reviewing twenty-five years of part-time professional practice. (Submitted for publication).

L'Abate, L., & Odell, M. (1995). Expanding practices and roles of family clinicians. In M. Harway (Ed.), *Treating the changing family: Handling normative and unusual events* (pp. 321–339). New York: Wiley.

Lepore, S. J., & Smyth, J. (Eds.).(2002). *The writing cure: How expressive writing influences health and well-being*. Washington, D.C.: American Psychological Association.

Levy, C. M., & Ransdell, S. (Eds.). (1996). *The science of writing: Theories, methods, individual differences, and applications*. Mahwah, N.J.: LEA.

Liddle, H. A., Santisteban, D. A., Levant, R. F., & Bray, J. H. (Eds.). (2002). *Family psychology: Science-based interventions*. Washington, DC: American Psychological Association.

Maheu, M. M., Whitten, P., & Allen, A. (2001). *E-health, telehealth, and telemedicine: A guide to start-up and success*. San Francisco, CA: Jossey-Bass.

Newman, M. G., Kenardy, J., Herman, S., & Taylor, C. B. (1997). Comparison of palm-top-computer-assisted brief cognitive-behavioral treatment for panic disorder. *Journal of Consulting and Clinical Psychology, 65*(1), 178–183.

Pennebaker, J. W. (2001). Explorations into the health benefits of disclosure: Inhibitory, cognitive, and social processes. In L. L'Abate (Ed.), *Distance writing and computer-assisted interventions in psychiatry and mental health* (pp. 33–44). Westport, CT: Ablex.

Progoff, I. (1975). *At a journal's workshop*. New York: Dialogue House Library.

Smyth, J., & L'Abate, L. (2001). A meta-analytic evaluation of workbook effectiveness in physical and mental health. In L. L'Abate (Ed.), *Distance writing and computer-assisted interventions in psychiatry and mental health* (pp. 77–90). Westport, CT: Ablex.

U.S. Department of Health and Human Services. (1999). *Mental health: A report of the Surgeon General*. Rockville, MD: National Institute of Mental Health.

Weeks, G. R., & Gambescia, N. (2000). *Erectile dysfunction: Integrating couple therapy, sex therapy, and medical treatment*. New York: Norton.

# CHAPTER 20

# Psychoeducation and Enrichment

## *Clinical Considerations for Couple and Family Therapy*

RITA DeMARIA, PhD

*Council for Relationships*

## INTRODUCTION

Contemporary marriage, couples', and family education programs are an extension of programs that go back to the earliest roots of marriage and family therapy and marriage enrichment. Although family psychoeducational programs have been used most extensively with families of patients with schizophrenia (Goldstein & Miklowitz, 1995; McFarlane, 1991), families of adolescents with conduct disorders (Chamberlain & Rosicky, 1995), parents of children with behavioral disorders (Estrada & Pinsof, 1995), and in health-related treatment programs (alcoholism, eating disorders, heart disease) (Campbell & Patterson, 1995), basic research on marriage and intimacy is being applied to marriage and relationship education programs, which is furthering yet more research, theory, program development, and debate (Gottman,

Carrere, Coan, & Swanson, 2000; Stanley, Bradbury, & Markman, 2000). The inclusion of a chapter on couples' and family education in a text on family therapy requires a discussion of clinical practice implications. Given advances in the literature describing psychoeducation for couples (Arcus, Schvaneveldt, & Moss, 1993; Berger & Hannah, 1999; Hunt, Hof, & DeMaria, 1998), this chapter will explore how marriage and couples' education, in particular, can enhance clinical work with couples. In addition, a systemically based model is proposed that clinicians can use to determine how educational and enrichment programs might be useful in their family treatment plans, especially with seriously distressed couples and families. In the proposed model, couple, marriage, and family treatment, education, and enrichment are not either/or services geared to the level of family distress and dysfunction; rather, each of the three is a distinct service modality, with overlaps among them.

## MARRIAGE AND COUPLES' EDUCATION AND ENRICHMENT: CLINICAL CONSIDERATIONS

Although there has been no meta-theory guiding the development of marital interventions, several unified theories have contributed to the understanding of marital distress and of the means for improving marital relations (see, for example, Stuart's [1980] social-learning approach, Gottman & Gottman [1999] scientific marital therapy, and Johnson's [1996] emotionally focused therapy). Many recently developed marital therapies are eclectic, in that they focus on diverse aspects of marital interaction, including behavioral, emotional, and cognitive components. Likewise, marriage/couples' education and enrichment, with its focus on multiple areas of relationship functioning such as empathy, communication skills, conflict negotiation, and bonding, represents the integration of diverse theoretical perspectives. Through this eclectic integration of diverse theories, marriage/couples' education and enrichment have become intertwined with marital/couples' treatment. An example of this is the saga of PAIRS (Practical Application of Intimate Relationship Skills), as described by Lori Gordon, whose integrated program took form during the 1960s and 1970s (Gordon, 1988).

Supported by advances in basic research on marriage (Gottman, Carrere, Swanson, & Coan, 2000; Stanley, Bradbury, & Markman, 2000), the roots of marriage/couples education and enrichment are vital and diverse, springing from family sociology, human sexuality, conflict resolution, small group dynamics, affective education, programmed instruction, social skills training, humanistic psychology, and communication theory

(Leigh, Loewen, & Lester, 1986). Although Marriage Encounter and the Maces were pioneers of what came to be called the marriage enrichment movement, marriage and relationship education has become part of what some refer to as the "marriage movement" (Gallagher, 2000; Glenn, Nock, & Waite, 2002)

Historically, marriage and couples' treatment has not been clearly separated from education and enrichment. The 1970s and 1980s, in particular, were years of expansion for marriage/couples' education and enrichment. For example, Miller, Nunnally, and Wackman (1975) laid the foundation for the Couple Communication Program (Miller, Wachman, & Nunnally, 1976; Miller, Wackman, & Nunnally, 1983). Bernard Guerney published *Relationship Enhancement* (1977). John Gottman established the early framework for his marriage lab (Gottman, 1979). David Olson and his associates (Fournier, Olson, & Druckman, 1983) developed a reliable, valid, and clinically practical premarital assessment tool (PREPARE). By 1984, the PAIRS program was refined, and a standard curriculum for professional training was established (Gordon, 1988).

During the 1970s and 1980s, only a few clinicians and researchers examined the overlap between marital enrichment programs and marital therapy. Schauble and Hill (1976), for example, called for a skills-based marriage lab to supplement traditional marriage counseling, akin to the notion of a chemistry class lecture accompanied by a chemistry lab. As opposed to viewing enrichment as a separate service, they believed that marital treatment should take a variety of forms, with the laboratory approach to communication skills training providing a valuable treatment component. Similarly, Gershenfeld (1985) emphasized the importance of a microlab (a group training model) for couples. She suggested that microlabs differed from marriage enrichment programs by professional involvement in the microlab's leadership, as opposed to the lay leadership of marriage enrichment programs.

In the mid-1980s, a new generation of marital and relationship enrichment and education programs began to gain precedence, borrowing from ongoing advances in research and practice. In contrast to earlier marriage/couples' education and enrichment programs, which had been developed primarily by and for religious denominations, social workers, psychologists, and family therapists developed the current generation of programs based on behavioral, psychodynamic, developmental, cognitive, and emotion-focused therapeutic models and practice methods. As Meadors (1991) suggested, marriage/couples' education and enrichment emerged as a specialty within the field of marriage counseling. Confirming this emergence, in 1996 the Coalition for Marriage, Couple, and Family Education held its first annual conference with presentations by over 100 representatives of programs falling along the entire spectrum of couple and family interventions. Highlighting the connections between treatment, education, and enrichment, in his plenary address to the 2002 CMFCE Annual Conference, John Gottman reaffirmed a model of marriage education that puts clinicians in charge of service delivery.

Some of the early criticisms of the enrichment movement (Smith, Shoffner, & Scott, 1979) included the observations that enrichment was being viewed as a cure-all, that there was questionable training of leaders, that participants might expect more than the programs deliver, that enrichment and education cannot prevent major social ills, that changing gender roles, lifestyles, and gender equity were not taken into account, and that participants were not making informed choices. Having attended to ethical matters, training issues, and program evaluation as they have developed, refined, updated, and evaluated their programs,

the leading program developers now have addressed many of these concerns.

Although the fields of enrichment and education have begun to diverge, both modalities use a supportive group milieu to help couples improve or enrich their relationships through the acquisition of skills and attitudes that foster marital success (Mace, 1986; Mace & Mace, 1986). Although both models emphasize companionship and peer relationship, enrichment models are characterized by mutual support, which promotes community among couples, thereby weakening the myth of naturalism (i.e., relationships are natural and do not require skill) and the breaking down of the intermarital taboo ("We don't discuss our intimate relationship issues with strangers"). Educational models, in particular, emphasize the developmental nature of family relationships and provide problem-solving skills for participants. Using a life-span developmental model, Stahman and Salts (1993) delineated five areas for educating couples: general marriage preparation, premarital counseling, enrichment programs, divorce education, and remarriage education.

## Education for Distressed Couples?

Research on marriage/couples' education and enrichment has focused on satisfaction/distress outcomes, along with the demographics of participants, but there is very little information on the clinical characteristics (like aggression, couple typology, sexuality, attachment styles) of couples that attend these programs. The marriage/couples' education and enrichment literature suggests that participants have been predominantly Caucasian, middle-class, and religiously affiliated couples. Based on their quasi-meta-analytic review of the outcome studies available in the literature, Powell and Wampler (1982) concluded that marriage/couples' education and enrichment participants are less satisfied with their marriage than are nonparticipants. These authors went on to suggest that couples who participate in marriage/couples' education and enrichment are neither as discouraged nor as distressed as couples seeking marital therapy. Similarly, in a study of participation in marriage/couples' education and enrichment among church populations, Noval, Combs, Winamake, Bufford, and Halter (1996) reported a mean Dyadic Adjustment Scale (Spanier, 1976) score of 102, which is neither above the level established neither for satisfaction nor below the cutoff for distress. However, Krug and Ahadi (1986), who examined personality characteristics of husbands and wives participating in marriage/couples' education and enrichment, found that couples who had participated in the program were more similar to couples with problem marriages than to those with well-functioning marriages Likewise, Ford, Bashford, and Dewitt (1984) conducted a study of three marriage enrichment approaches and they found that one third of the sample had seriously considered divorce, and 30% of the subjects had participated in marital therapy in the past. DeMaria (1998) conducted a survey of married couples who enrolled in the PAIRS programs. The findings indicated that the majority of married couples who enroll in the PAIRS program were seriously distressed. Almost the entire survey sample was categorized as either devitalized or conflicted (93%), according to the ENRICH couple typology (Olson & Fowers, 1993), with the majority (58.8%) being characterized as devitalized. These reports suggest that distressed couples do indeed appear to seek education for serious marital distress.

Although early proponents advocated marriage/couples' education and enrichment programs for well-functioning couples, some clinicians and researchers suggested that marriage/couples' education and enrichment were also appropriate adjuncts to conjoint

treatment for distressed couples. Cookerly (1976) found that when risk for divorce was high, group marital counseling was more effective than traditional conjoint treatment. Giblin's (1986) meta-analysis reinforced Cookerly's (1976) findings: seriously distressed couples, especially those considering divorce, appeared to benefit from marriage/couples' education and enrichment programs. Such positive findings on the use of marriage/couples' education and enrichment with distressed couples stand in contrast to prevailing marital and couples' therapy practice, which emphasizes conjoint treatment for distressed couples (Tolman & Molidor, 1994). Group marital counseling is not routinely offered for couples at risk of separation and divorce (Khesgi-Genovese & Constable, 1995), and psychoeducational methods have been primarily used with premarital couples (Tolman & Molidor, 1994). However, there is very little discussion in the literature on how clinicians can incorporate educational and enrichment programs in their clinical work with couples and families.

## TOWARD A DYNAMIC INTERSYSTEMIC MODEL OF PRACTICE

Although an educational model of marital and family treatment is a viable one from some perspectives (Accordino & Guerney, 2001; Guerney, 1977; Guerney, Brock, & Coufal, 1986; Guerney, Vogelsong, & Coufal, 1983), defining education as a viable form of treatment underscores the importance of examining psychoeducational programs in clinical practice from a dynamic systemic perspective. There is no definite reference point for the use of the term *psychoeducation* in the family therapy literature. In addition, the term is not widely used in the family therapy literature and generally has become affiliated with adjunctive educational programs for families, especially families with a member who has a biologically based psychiatric disorder, such as schizophrenia or autism. In a recent effort, Campbell and Patterson (1995) defined family psychoeducation as helping a "family cope more effectively with an illness or disorder" (p. 548). These authors distinguished between family psychoeducation and family information and support programs, suggesting that family psychoeducation emphasizes systematic assessment and planned intervention. Complicating matters further, the term *marriage and family enrichment* is used synonymously with *psychoeducation for couples* (Giblin, 1986; Guerney & Maxson, 1990) and *preventive approaches to couples' therapy* (Berger & Hannah, 1999). A further difficulty in defining psychoeducational approaches is that family psychologists have gone on to categorize marriage enrichment programs as "preventive approaches" to couples' therapy (Berger & Hannah, 1999; Silliman, Stanley, Coffin, Markman, & Jordan, 2001).

Although the prevention model can be applied to contemporary premarital and marriage education programs, it does not help the clinician who practices with a diverse range of clinical problems. Even though preventive approaches can be comprehensive, there has been a presumption that educational, skill-training programs are essentially a type of primary prevention (large-scale intervention with normal participants) or perhaps of secondary prevention (intervention with at-risk populations) but do not address the needs of disturbed couples and families. This assumption was articulated in Hof and Miller (1981) examination of marital enrichment programs, in Berger and Hannah's (1999) review of preventive approaches to couples' therapy, as well as in Arcus, Schvaneveldt, and Moss's (1993a, b) *Handbook of Family Life Education—Volumes I & II*.

Underscoring how clinicians have dismissed educational programs as a resource for their clients, Riehlmede and Willi (1993) explored clinicians' ambivalence toward enrichment programs and identified three factors that influence the use of these programs: (1) doubts about the long-term effectiveness of enrichment programs; (2) the general lack of acceptance of prevention strategies; and (3) the typical refusal by clinicians to accept pedagogic and norm-oriented interventions. Arcus (1995) suggested that such concerns could explain why marriage/couples' education and enrichment and family life education usually are not included in professional training programs. Consequently, educational programs that emphasize skills training are viewed as a service point along a continuum. For example, L'Abate and McHenry (1983) suggested that marital interventions take place along a continuum ranging in structure from preventive skill-training programs to unstructured remedial therapies. Similarly, Doherty (1995) proposed a continuum model based on five levels of involvement, which established a boundary between education and treatment. Unfortunately, such artificial distinctions are not useful to clinicians who are trying to determine the most effective interventions for couples and families.

This brief overview of the underpinnings of marriage and relationship education does not take into account all of the recent advances in family psychology and sociology. It does, however, highlight the need to clarify the distinctions between, as well as the commonalities among, the three intervention modalities: treatment, education and enrichment.

*The Need for a Dynamic Intersystemic Model of Intervention*

How can clinicians assess the extent to which psychoeducation could meet the needs of their clients? To answer this question, there must be a shift toward thinking about service modalities as distinct intervention models. In contrast to prevention and continuum models, which claim that psychoeducational programs are best suited for a less distressed population (L'Abate, 1981; McFarlane, 1991), Hoopes, Fisher, and Barlow (1984) were among the first to address the overlaps among enrichment, education, and treatment. They promoted a model called "structured family facilitation programs." Although Guerney and Maxson (1990) maintained that sharp distinctions should not be made between prevention, enrichment, and treatment, I would propose, along with Hoopes, Fisher, and Barlow, that treatment, education, and enrichment are best conceptualized as three different yet overlapping modalities. Within this model, overlaps exist between education and treatment, rather than their existing as points on a linear model. This perspective implies that marriage and family therapists ought to be informed about the unique properties of each of the three, in order to assess their usefulness for specific clients.

Although the field has tended to dichotomize these models, thus underscoring the assumption that distinct populations participate in the various programs, educational and enrichment/support programs are often components of the services offered to very distressed families suffering from a host of psychiatric, behavioral, health-related, and addictive problems. A dynamic model that views the three types of intervention—treatment, education, and enrichment—as separate yet overlapping spheres reflects this reality by allowing a client to participate in any one or any combination of two or three spheres of intervention, based on that particular client's needs. I refer to this conceptualization as the "ABC Intervention Assessment Model" (see Figure 20.1).

A Venn diagram is useful to illustrate this model for clinical practice because no one modality is one-dimensional; each is a complex sphere in its own right. Each modality can stand alone as a service, or it can incorporate aspects of the other two modalities. In the clinical literature one often finds discussions of overlaps between treatment and prevention, for example. Treatment (Area A of the Venn diagram) involves remedial methods (albeit treatment can be defined in terms of levels of prevention) characterized by individual, conjoint, or collateral sessions that aim to improve cognitive, emotional, or behavioral aspects of intimate relationships, or any combination of these, in order to ameliorate distress caused by dysfunctional relational patterns within the family. Education (Area B) includes methods that provide participants with knowledge and problem-solving skills to improve their ability to cope with personal needs or psychosocial problems within the family. Here, interventions are based on adult learning styles and educational techniques that include didactic, experiential, and participant participation exercises and lessons. Enrichment (Area C) encompasses methods that provide information and peer support. Support groups are the typical modality in marriage enrichment approaches (Hunt, Hof, & DeMaria, 1998). Similarly, family enrichment programs provide support for single family or multiple family groups and address physical and psychiatric problems, as well as life transitions such as parenting, divorce, and remarriage.

Figure 20.1 illustrates that the three intervention modalities yield eight regions: A—Treatment; B—Education; C—Enrichment; AB—Treatment/Education; AC—Treatment/Enrichment; BC—Education/Enrichment; ABC—Treatment/Education/Enrichment; and Area D (the area outside the bounds of the diagram), representing no intervention. The treatment/education region (AB) has been described in various places in the literature (Alexander, Robbins, & Sexton, 2000; Guerney, 1977; Guerney, Brock, & Coufal, 1986). Likewise, marriage enrichment during

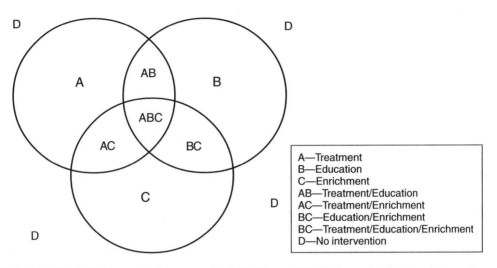

FIGURE 20.1. The ABC Intervention Assessment Model. Figure 20.1 illustrates that the three intervention modalities yield eight regions: A—Treatment; B—Education; C—Enrichment; AB—Treatment/Education; AC—Treatment/Enrichment; BC—Education/Enrichment; ABC—Treatment/Education/Enrichment; and Area D, which is the area outside the bounds of the diagram, represents no intervention.

the 1960s and 1970s had overlaps with treatment (region BC) (Hof & Miller, 1981). A variety of family and couples' programs also represents the region ABC, which incorporates all three modalities, often being delivered to very distressed families and couples. For example, couples' group therapy incorporates peer support, as do enrichment programs (Coche & Coche, 1990). Similarly, marital growth groups often use skills-based activities found in marriage education, and marriage education may include family-of-origin exploration (DeMaria & Hannah, 2003; Parrott & Parrott, 1999), which is a hallmark of many couples' therapy approaches.

Conceptualizing treatment, education, and enrichment as three separate practice modalities that intersect with one another in dynamic ways is helpful in exploring the applications of each modality. Because each has been found to be effective with couples, parents, and families affected by a wide range of presenting problems, clinicians can offer greater benefit to their clients by incorporating multiple intervention modalities, rather than by providing a one-dimensional approach.

Because the ABC Assessment Intervention model is not a continuum model, service modalities need not occur in any particular sequence, and a client who enters treatment may then participate in a psychoeducational program and may even participate in a ongoing support group. In addition, the entry point into service for one client might be through treatment, whereas another enters through education or enrichment. Some have suggested that effective educational experiences may contribute to the use of treatment services when needed, as often occurs with premarital education. For example, couples who have a positive experience with a premarital education program may be more likely to participate in enrichment programs or couples' therapy in the future (Center for Marriage and Family, 1995). Couples who participate in educational programs often bring their understanding and skills to the treatment setting, which fosters more constructive use of treatment.

In the ABC model, the area outside the three spheres of service represents the general public. Currently, several research initiatives are exploring current trends in cohabitation, marriage, divorce, and remarriage in the United States, including those headed by the following groups: Centers for Disease Control and Prevention at the National Center for Health Statistics; the Institute for American Values (www.iva.org); the National Marriage Project at Rutgers University (www.marriage.rutgers.edu); the Center for Marital and Family Studies at the University of Denver (www.prepinc); the Heritage Foundation (www. heritage.org); the Center for Law and Social Policy (www.clasp.org); and the Religion, Culture, and the Family Project at the University of Chicago (www.divinity.uchicago.edu/family/). Gottman (2002) suggests that basic research on trends in marriage, cohabitation, and remarriage will continue as a focus for our field.

## AN OVERVIEW OF PSYCHOEDUCATIONAL PROGRAMS FOR COUPLES AND FAMILIES

The following sections will provide a review of premarital programs, marriage education and enrichment programs, parent education, divorce education, and family enrichment and education. Educational programs for youths exploring relationship skills, marriage preparation, sexuality, and teenage pregnancy are beyond the scope of this chapter. (Readers who would like to learn about the vast array of educational programs for youths, couples, and families should consult the Coalition for Marriage, Couples, and Family Education, which maintains a directory of programs throughout the United States and elsewhere, at www.smartmarriages.com. Readers can also learn more about the specific models of couples/marriage education and enrichment by reviewing Preventive Approaches in Couples Therapy [Berger & Hannah, 1999] and Marriage Enrichment: Preparation, Mentoring and Outreach [Hunt, Hof, & DeMaria, 1998].)

Although an exhaustive review is beyond the scope of this chapter, a few representative programs, including Relationship Enhancement (RE), Couple Communication, PREPARE/ENRICH, and PAIRS, will be described here. These programs were selected because they are frequently referred to in the literature on marriage education and enrichment, and because in various ways each is uniquely different from other programs. In the only study of its kind, a meta-analysis by Giblin (1986) identified RE as the most effective of the programs that had published program findings at that time. RE provides highly structured training in empathic listening and responding. Couple Communication (CC) has been the most extensively researched program. PREP is an empirically based program that originally was designed as an intervention with premarital couples. In contrast, PAIRS is a practice-based model. PREPARE/ENRICH began as a premarital intervention program; however, the emphasis was on assessing couples' strengths and weaknesses. PREPARE is perhaps the most widely used intervention model for premarital couples. Generally, educational programs affiliated with universities benefit from the opportunity provided to graduate students to conduct research projects. For example, the PREP program at the University of Denver has obtained funding from the National Institute of Mental Health for conducting research on its program.

Various of educational programs are packaged as seminars, video or audio programs, or all of these, and often are based on books that were written for the public. These include Harville Hendrix's (1988) *Getting the Love You Want,* Michel Weiner-Davis's (1992) *Keeping Love Alive*, John Gottman's (1999) *Marriage Survival Kit,* and David Schnarch's (1991) *Passionate Marriage* workshop.

There is also a wide array of marriage enrichment programs, usually offered through religious organizations that provide retreats, support groups, structured mentoring and lay counseling, and other grassroots support. These programs include youth-based programs, premarital counseling/education/enrichment, ongoing marriage enrichment, and mentoring and support for distressed couples, stepfamilies, and singles. Clearly, the spheres of enrichment and education have been expanding.

## Premarital and Marriage Education and Enrichment Programs

Although skills training with premarital populations is widely accepted, most premarital programs were not designed exclusively for that population. Programmatic distinctions have blurred, whereas education and enrichment have become more defined. Educational programs, such as PREP, emphasize skills training (Area B); enrichment programs like ACME emphasize peer support and experiential learning (Area C), whereas other programs, such as PREPARE—Growing Together, incorporate both elements (Area BC). As L'Abate (1981) predicted, the entrance of the federal government into prevention has yielded funding and an expansion of educational programs in the military and in state-sponsored and federally funded initiatives (see Oklahoma Marriage Initiative, for example, at www.okmarriage.org).

ACME and Marriage Encounter led the way in the evolution of the marriage enrichment movement, which has now diversified. David Mace, who in 1943 opened the first marriage counseling clinic in Europe, spearheaded the development of ACME. After returning to the United States in 1949, Mace and his wife, Vera, became convinced that preventive services were needed to supplement remedial services for couples. Then in 1962, the Maces led their first marriage/couples' education and enrichment program for married couples.

Eventually, they formed the Association of Couples for Marriage Enrichment (Area C). Coincidentally, in 1962, Father Gabrael Calvo, a Catholic priest in Spain, began a weekend retreat that would become the Marriage Encounter movement. By the late 1970s, Marriage Encounter was reaching over 250,000 couples per year and had spread beyond the Catholic community into other religious denominations. It is currently comprised of three separate groups: National, International, and Worldwide Marriage Encounter. Along with Engaged Encounter for premarital couples, Retrovaille evolved out of the Marriage Encounter program. Retrovaille is a self-help program for highly distressed couples who are seriously considering divorce (Area AC), providing another example of the usefulness of a multidimensional model of intervention.

RE and CC are mainstays within communication skills–training programs. Both programs integrate theory, research, and practice. Developed by pioneer Bernard Guerney, RE teaches empathic communication and problem-solving skills. An integrated program that emerged from work with couples, RE incorporates psychodynamic, behavioral, humanistic, and interpersonal models in its nine specific skills: expressive skill, empathic skills, discussion and negotiation skills, facilitative (coaching) skill, problem or conflict-resolution skill, changing-self skill, helping-others-change skill, transfer and generalization skill, and maintenance skills (Calvedo & Guerney, 1999). RE has been used in a variety of settings with individuals, couples, and families. In addition to the numerous controlled studies on RE, this program has been found to be effective in improving relationships within a wide variety of clinical populations, such as psychiatric outpatients and their families, patients in a community residential rehabilitation center, alcoholics, codependents, spouse batterers, depressed clients, juvenile delinquents, drug addicts in rehabilitation, and those suffering from narcissistic personality disorder (Aradi, 1985; Avery, Ridley, Leslie, & Milholland, 1980). Recently, Brooks (1997) studied the efficacy of RE therapy in a rural southern outpatient setting with distressed couples attending marital therapy. Again, findings were encouraging. The effects of RE not only were maintained at follow-up of approximately a year (Griffin & Apostal, 1993; Waldo, 1986) but also improved over time (Griffin & Apostal, 1993; Guerney, Vogelsong, & Coufal, 1983). Special RE program materials have been designed for lower levels of literacy and lower socioeconomic populations and also offer a video-based distance-learning program that includes phone coaching. There is no doubt that RE is a strong representative of the educational modality (Area B).

Couple Communication (CC) is one of the oldest and best researched skills-based programs for couples. Initially affiliated with the University of Minnesota, CC focuses on increasing awareness, teaching skills, expanding options, and increasing satisfaction. Clinicians, clergy, EAP counselors, and lay leaders teach the program to a wide range of couples. Although the program can be used in a variety of formats and settings, most outcome research on CC has studied the effects of the 12-hour, structured-skills program. A recent review (Wampler, 1990) found strong gains in communication quality that tended to diminish over time. Gains in individual functioning and relationship quality appeared more durable, although the longest-term follow-up assessment point was less than a year.

Without a doubt, the PREPARE Inventory for premarital couples and the ENRICH Inventory for married couples are among the most comprehensive and empirically supported premarital and marriage education programs. In addition to being nationally normed and having demonstrated excellent psychometric properties (Fowers & Montel, 1996; Fowers & Olson, 1986; Fowers & Olson,

1989), these inventories have the advantage of a solid theoretical foundation, as provided by Olson's (1997) integrated Circumplex Model. In addition to doing extensive empirical examination of the inventory, Olson and his associates used it to derive a typology of couples, which also was replicated with African American couples (Allen, 1996; Fowers & Olson, 1992; Olson & Fowers, 1993). Although there is no way to establish which education programs reach the most couples, more than 1,000,000 couples have taken the PREPARE/ENRICH inventory, and there are more than 50,000 PREPARE/ENRICH counselors worldwide (Olson, 1997).

The empirically based PREP program by Markman and his associates (Markman, Stanley, & Blumberg, 1994) is clearly the most recognized effort to address the needs of couples, especially premarital couples. With over 20 years of research funded by NIMH, the PREP developers have been able to conduct numerous evaluations (Hahlweg, Baucom, & Markman, 1988; Hahlweg, Markman, 1988; Markman, Renick, Floyd, Stanley, & Clements, 1993; Stanley, Blumberg, & Markman, 1999) of their program. The PREP program, which includes essential communication and problem-solving skills, along with a focus on commitment and companionship, is widely used in the military and by clergy, as well as by clinicians.

PAIRS (Gordon, 1988, 1993), a 120-hour relationship skills–based program, is perhaps the most intensive of all the programs. Using an integrated model that incorporates treatment, education, and enrichment (Area ABC), the curriculum pays attention to communication skills, conflict-resolution processes, emotional literacy, individual differences and family-of-origin influences, sexuality and sensuality, and the development of conscious expectations (Berger & Hannah, 1999; DeMaria, 1993; DeMaria & Hannah, 2003; Gordon, 1993).

PAIRS's duration, use of different modalities, and broad range of techniques and theoretical rationales make research on this program particularly challenging. Participants attend PAIRS hoping to learn how to improve communication and conflict resolution, understand their partners, build trust, express feelings, and increase positive feelings and intimacy (DeMaria, 1998; Durana, 1994, 1995a, 1995b, 1995c; Turner, 1997). Findings have suggested that for most participants, these expectations are met; the components most highly valued include communication and conflict-resolution techniques and approaches for expressing feelings and needs. Studies on the specific change-inducing elements of PAIRS have focused primarily on the Bonding and Emotional Literacy (B.E.L.) segment and have revealed that B.E.L. is indeed a key element, in keeping with findings that support affective interventions (Johnson, 1996). Although there have been limitations to the research conducted on the PAIRS program, PAIRS exemplifies a clinically based educational model that attends to ethics, program evaluation, and ongoing training for leaders.

*Parent Education*

In their overview of parent education programs, Brock, Oertwein, and Coufal (1993) examined five major contemporary programs, including Parent Effectiveness Training (PET; Gordon, 1975), one of the first such programs; Nurturing Parent Program (Bavolek & Comstock, 1985); Systematic Training for Effective Parenting (STEP; Dinkmeyer & McKay, 1976); Active Parenting (Popkin, 1983); and Relationship Enhancement (Guerney, 1977). Although this is far from an exhaustive list of parenting and family enrichment programs, the authors concluded that there is "almost no evidence to support the effectiveness of one group parent education

program over another" (Brock, Oertwein, & Coufal, 1993, p. 108).

Childbirth education classes do not typically include parenting or relationship-skills training. Instead, these courses focus on preparation for labor and birth, place fathers in a subordinate role, and do little to prepare parents for the many life changes that will accompany the birth of a first child (Jordan, 1995, 1995a). Nevertheless, the Becoming a Family Project (Cowan & Cowan, 1992, 1995), one of the first skills-based transition-to-parenthood programs, has shown encouraging results. Using a modified version of the PREP program, Jordan (1995) explored the effects of relationship skills training on married couples who were expecting the birth of their first child. Although few differences were found between intervention and comparison couples in their transition to parenthood, findings indicated that couples expecting the birth of a first child were very open to such programs, found them useful, and evaluated them positively. To further examine the effects of relationship skills training on this population, a randomized, controlled trial of a structured, comprehensive transition-to-parenthood intervention based on PREP has been designed and is underway (Jordan, 1995a).

*Divorce Education*

Given the impact of divorce and remarriage and the needs of families experiencing these transitional crises, divorce education programs would seem to be an important form of intervention. Surprisingly, however, few programs address the special needs of this group. Although some jurisdictions mandate coparenting education for couples when they file for divorce, the available programs are limited in scope (Arbuthnot & Gordon, 1997). The Center for Divorce Education (CDE: www.divorce-education.com) provides educational videos for use with groups of divorcing/separating parents. Outcome studies suggest that CDE's "Children in the Middle" improves communication between divorcing/separating parents (Kramer, Arbuthnot, Gordon, Roussis, & Hoza, 1998; Krukowski, Gordon, & Arbuthnot, 1996).

The Stepfamily Association of America, established by the Vishers (1993), who were leaders in the field of intervention with stepfamilies, pioneered the development of community-based stepfamily enrichment groups. Furthermore, Wing and Wing (2003) described a modification of the PAIRS program for use with remarried couples. However, such services are not widespread, and unfortunately, as of this date, the field of marriage and family therapy has contributed relatively little to the education and enrichment of remarried couples or of couples who choose alternative lifestyles.

*Psychoeducation and Family Groups*

Single family and multifamily education and enrichment groups are offered by a variety of programs treating diverse problems, such as alcoholism, eating disorders, autism, and heart disease, to name a few. Many of these programs are modeled after those developed for psychiatric patients. Educating families on the impact of mental illness has long been considered crucial in the treatment of schizophrenic patients (McFarlane, 1991). With its emphasis on peer support via its Al-Anon and Alateen programs, Alcoholic Anonymous could be classified as an enrichment program for families. Community education and enrichment programs offered by numerous hospitals provide individual and family support for a host of health problems, including, for example, cancer, stroke, diabetes, and chronic illness. The prevalence of use of

these programs by clinicians has yet to be explored.

### EFFECTIVENESS OF EDUCATION AND ENRICHMENT PROGRAMS

Research on educational and enrichment programs has not advanced much since Gurman and Kniskern's (1981) *Handbook of Family Therapy.* Limited funding is available from the federal and state governments, and even less is available from foundations. However, since 1995, due to the efforts of groups like CMFCE, the National Marriage Project, the Chicago Project, and the Institute for American Values, there has been a growing interest in marriage and relationship education. Unfortunately, these projects have become politicized, being viewed by some as holding biased and antidiversity points of view (Winawer, AFTA Newsletters, Spring 1997, Winter 1999, Fall 1999). Findings on the extent to which participants derive benefit from marriage/couples' education and enrichment are conflicting (Giblin, 1996), perhaps because research has been conducted in a piecemeal fashion. Studies have examined levels of marital satisfaction (Powell & Wampler, 1982; Urbaniak, 1982), personality characteristics of husbands and wives (Krug & Ahadi, 1986), and outcomes (Emerson, 1993; Durana, 1996a, b, c; Giblin, 1986; Gurman & Kniskern, 1977). For example, Hawley and Olson (1995) used ENRICH as a pre and post measure to evaluate the effects of three newlywed enrichment programs. These programs included Growing Together (Dyer & Dyer, 1990), TIME (Dinkmeyer & Carlson, 1985), and Learning to Live Together (Bader & Remmel, 1987). In contrast, Emerson's (1993) study of the effectiveness of the Imago Couples Weekend Workshop examined levels of satisfaction, communication, conflict, understanding family-of-origin issues, and commitment. Finally, research upholds the supposition that the social support developed in a group interaction format helps couples with the awareness, development, and integration of behavioral changes (Toseland & Siporin, 1986a, 1986b); Worthington, Buston, and Hammonds (1989), for example, found that group discussion improved marital satisfaction and intimacy more than did assessment or information alone.

Although some educational and enrichment programs have been empirically evaluated for their effectiveness, many have not. Furthermore, the impact of comprehensive interventions that use all of the three ABC modalities with seriously distressed and dysfunctional families has not yet been examined. As a whole, however, research on the outcomes of skills-based interventions has appeared promising (Silliman et al., 2001). Current research on marriage/couples' education and enrichment has been focused primarily on examining distress levels recorded before and after participation in a program. Various researchers (Durana, 1996a, 1996b, 1996c; Emerson, 1993; Giblin, 1985; Gurman & Kniskern, 1977) have suggested that marriage/couples' education and enrichment programs are effective, given that participants have demonstrated improvement in marital satisfaction. Limited follow-up research has shown increases in post-test scores at follow-up points as long as 5 years postprogram (Zimpher, 1988). Gottman (1997), however, challenged the strength of these findings on methodological grounds. In contrast to Gottman's view, Giblin's (1986) meta-analysis of 85 studies on 3,866 couples or families varying widely in age, income, education, location, and nature of treatment led to the conclusion that distressed couples gain the most benefit from these programs.

Guerney and Maxson's (1990) review of the marriage/couples' education and enrichment research from 1980 to 1990 concluded that on the whole, enrichment programs work, and the field is a legitimate one. "The major questions, however, are which programs, for what populations, what makes them best, and how they may [the programs] be made more efficient, less costly, and better marketed" (p. 1133). Giblin (1996) suggested that life stage, ethnic diversity, economic status, educational background, gender differences, different family forms, and levels of distress all warranted exploration in terms of their relation to the effectiveness of particular treatments. Similarly, Sullivan and Bradbury (1997), who investigated whether couples who participated in premarital counseling were at a greater or a lesser risk for marital difficulties, concluded that premarital prevention programs do produce reliable improvements in relationship function, but that there was a need for further investigation of the characteristics of couples who participate versus those who do not participate in such programs. Clearly, the need for ongoing research to evaluate the characteristics of educational and enrichment programs, as well as their effectiveness, is needed.

## FUTURE DEVELOPMENTS AND DIRECTIONS

David Mace, a founder of the marriage/couples' education and enrichment movement, as well as of marriage and relationship therapy, repeatedly called for greater attention by the professional community to education and enrichment programs. He believed that marriage/couples' education and enrichment offered several advantages that traditional models of treatment do not provide: skill-building, greater public access and lessened stigma, group process for modeling and support, and suitability for research (Mace, 1986). What Mace did not anticipate was the potential impact of these programs for distressed couples and families.

There has been a general belief among professionals that marriage/couples' education and enrichment are for stable marriages, marriage education is for stable to moderately distressed couples, and marital therapy is for distressed couples (Hof & Miller, 1981; Powell & Wampler, 1982). However, a close examination of the literature reveals an incomplete picture and assessment of the characteristics of couples who participate in these programs, and findings suggest that distressed couples benefit from these programs. Lester and Doherty (1983) presented one of the few substantive arguments against participation by distressed couples in marriage/couples' education and enrichment programs. They argued that a weekend model of marriage/couples' education and enrichment programs could resurrect issues that distressed couples would be unable to address in the enrichment setting. Their observations emphasized the need for follow-up with couples who, while attending enrichment programs, identify problems in their marriages. The current generation of marriage education programs has incorporated improvements in design, methodology, and evaluation and draws upon an expanding base of knowledge about intimate relationships.

The literature suggests that the assumptions and professional training of practitioners affect their recommendations regarding the application of marriage education and enrichment programs to distressed couples (Fournier, Olson, & Druckman, 1983; Tolman & Molidor, 1994; Riehlmede & Willi, 1993). Eliot and Saunders (1982) noted that clinicians in their study made three assumptions about marriage/couples' education and enrichment programs: (1) Participants are generally satisfied with their relationships; (2) enrichment emphasizes strengths; and (3) enrichment is preventive. Mace (1986) affirmed these attitudes, stating that ACME discourages "clinical" couples from participating in ACME retreats. In a review article entitled, "Is Couples Therapy Obsolete? Psychoeducation Raises Questions About Traditional Clinical Approaches," Lebow (1997) underscored these prevailing beliefs about marriage/couples' education and enrichment among the clinical community. Lebow elucidated the assumptions described earlier by Elliott and Saunders (1982) and by Riehlmede and Willi (1993):

> How are these programs similar or different from couples therapy? In contrast to the highly individualized approach of most couples therapy, these brief, time-limited programs use a group format and teach generic skills. *Couples who enroll are basically satisfied with their relationship and do not, typically, describe themselves as having substantial difficulties* [italics mine]. Usually, they are seeking enrichment, education, and new skills, not immediate help with a marital crisis. (p. 88)

Lebow's observations underscored how the biases of practitioners influence their views of marriage/couples' education and enrichment programs.

Although debates over terminology, qualifications of providers, and outcome research continue, Guerney and Maxson's (1990) seminal question remains unanswered: Who should participate what program and for what reason? Echoing some of his predecessors, Gottman and Notarius (2002), who himself has developed a weekend educational program, advocates that clinicians monitor participants for signs of distress and then provide these couples with a treatment component. These questions and concerns highlight the need for an intervention model that is not one-dimensional, presenting either/or decisions for clinicians. Consequently, a systemic model, such as presented here, provides a more comprehensive perspective for clinical decision making.

## SUMMARY

Family therapy, family education, and family enrichment have dynamic and complex inter-relationships. Recent developments in marriage education and enrichment have helped distinguish these models. Clinicians can use the multimodal ABC model, which was presented in this chapter, to expand their knowledge and use of educational and enrichment programs. There is much in the literature to support the contention that the more distressed a couple or a family, the more it needs all three modalities. In contrast to the prevailing view that the most distressed couples and families require treatment, rather than education/enrichment, this model proposes that these clients might be best served by receiving all interventions or an integrated program thaat incorporates multiple modalities. As previously stated, this type of programming is more common for families with serious problems, such as schizophrenia. However, there has been greater confusion about integrating education and enrichment in clinical practice with couples. Increasingly, contemporary marriage/couples' education and enrichment programs incorporate elements of enrichment (group process), education (instruction), and treatment (cognitive, emotional, and behavioral changes). The PAIRS program is an example of an integrated educational program for couples that is appropriate for highly distressed couples (DeMaria, 1998; Durana, 1994; Turner, 1997).

If consumers are to be assisted in making informed choices regarding their treatment, clinicians must learn about education and enrichment interventions and find ways to integrate these programs into their treatment plans. Because there are opportunities for many clinicians to provide such services themselves, some may choose that option. On the other hand, networking with providers of education and enrichment programs in the community would not only yield expanded choices for clients but would also provide the field with an opportunity to explore which interventions are the most effective with the various client types. Perhaps, as a field, we could then begin to answer Guerney and Maxson's (1990) yet unanswered query: "Which programs work best for what populations, what makes them best, and how they can be made more efficient and less costly and be better marketed?" (p. 1133).

## REFERENCES

Accordino, M. P., & Guerney, B. G., Jr. (2001). The empirical validation of Relationship Enhancement® couple and family therapy. In D. J. Cain & J. Seeman (Eds.), *Humanistic psychotherapies: Handbook of research and practice* (pp. 403–442). Washington, DC: American Psychological Association.

Alexander, J. F., Robbins, M. S., & Sexton, T. L. (2000). Family-based interventions with older, at-risk youth: From promise to proof to practice. *The Journal of Primary Prevention, 21*(2), 185–205.

Allen, W. D. (1996). *Five types of African-American marriages based on ENRICH: A replication study*. A dissertation submitted to the Graduate School at the University of Minnesota.

Aradi, N. S. (1985). *The relative effectiveness of relationship enhancement therapy and strategic therapy for the treatment of distressed married couples*. Unpublished doctoral dissertation, Purdue University.

Arbuthnot, J., & Gordon, D. A. (1997). Divorce education for parents and children. In L. Vandecreek & S. Knapp (Eds.), *Innovations in clinical practice: A source book* (Vol. 15, pp. 341–364). Sarasota, FL: Professional Resource Press.

Arcus, M. (1995). Advances in family life education—past, present, and future. *Family Relations, 44,* 336–344.

Arcus, M. E., Schvaneveldt, J. D., & Moss, J. J. (1993a) *Handbook of family life education. Vol. I: Foundations of family life education*. Newbury Park, CA: Sage.

Arcus, M. E., Schvaneveldt, J. D., & Moss, J. J.(1993b) *Handbook of family life education. Vol.*

*II: The practice of family life education.* Newbury Park, CA: Sage.

Avery, A. W., Ridley, C. A., Leslie, L. A., & Milholland, T. (1980). Relationship Enhancement with premarital dyads: A six-month follow-up. *American Journal of Family Therapy, 8,* 60–66.

Bader, E., & Remmel, A. (1987). *Learning to live together.* Toronto: University of Toronto.

Bavolek, S., & Comstock, C. (1985). *Nurturing parent handbook.* Park City, UT: Family Development Resources.

Berger, R., & Hannah. M. T. (1999) *Preventive approaches in couples therapy.* Philadelphia, PA: Brunner/Mazel.

Brock, G. W., Oertwein, M., & Coufal, J. D. (1993). Parent education: Theory, research, and practice. In M. E. Arcus, J. D. Schvaneveldt, & J. J. Moss (Eds.), *Handbook of family therapy., Vol. 2: The practice of family life education* (pp. 87–114). Newbury Park, CA: Sage.

Brooks, L. W. (1997). *An investigation of Relationship Enhancement therapy in a group format with rural, southern couples.* Unpublished doctoral dissertation, Florida State University School of Social Work, Tallahassee, FL.

Calvedo, C., & Guerney, B.G. (1999). Relationship Enhancement® enrichment and problem-prevention programs: Therapy-derived, powerful, versatile. In R. Berger, & M.T. Hannah (Eds.), *Preventive approaches in couples therapy.* Philadelphia, PA: Brunner/Mazel.

Campbell, T. L., & Patterson, J. M. (1995) The effectiveness of family interventions in the treatment of physical illness. *Journal of Marital and Family Therapy, 21*(4), 545–584.

Center for Marriage and Family. (1995). Marriage preparation in the Catholic Church: Getting it right. Omaha, NE: Creighton University.

Chamberlain, P., & Gilbert Rosicky, J. (1995). The effectiveness of family therapy in the treatment of adolescents with conduct disorders and delinquency. *Journal of Marital and Family Therapy, 21*(4), 441–460.

Coche, J., & Coche, E. (1990). *Couples group psychotherapy.* New York: Brunner/Mazel.

Cookerly, J. R. (1976). Evaluating different approaches to marriage counseling. In D. Olson (Ed.), *Treating relationships.* Iowa: Graphic Press.

Coufal, J., & Brock. G. (1983). *Parent–child relationship enhancement: A 10 week program.* Menomonie: University of Wisconsin.

Cowan, C. P., & Cowan, P. A. (1992). *When partners become parents.* New York: Basic Books.

Cowan, C. P., & Cowan, P. A. (1995). Interventions to ease the transition to parenthood: Why they are needed and what they can do. *Family Relations, 44,* 412–423.

DeMaria, R. (1993). Integrating marriage enrichment and marital therapy: A case study of PAIRS, a contemporary psychoeducational marital intervention program. *Families, VI,* 42–59. (Family Institute of Philadelphia.)

DeMaria, R. (1998). *Satisfaction, couple type, divorce potential, conflict styles, attachment patterns, and romantic and sexual satisfaction of married couples who participated in PAIRS.* Unpublished doctoral dissertation, Bryn Mawr College, Bryn Mawr, PA.

DeMaria, R., & Hannah, M. T. (2003). *Building intimate relationships: Bridging treatment, education, and enrichment through the PAIRS program.* New York: Brunner-Routledge.

Dinkmeyer, D., & Carlson, J. (1985). TIME for a better marriage. *Journal of Psychotherapy and the Family, 2,* 111–125.

Dinkmeyer, D., & McKay, G. (1976). *Systematic training for effective parenting: Parents' handbook.* Circle Pines, MN. American Guidance service.

Doherty, W. J. (1995) Boundaries between parent and family education and family therapy: The levels of family involvement model. *Family Relations, 44,* 353–358.

Durana, C. (1994). The use of bonding and emotional expressiveness in the PAIRS training: Psychoeducational approach for couples. *Journal of Family Psychotherapy, 5*(2), 65–81.

Durana, C. (1996a). A longitudinal evaluation of the effectiveness of the PAIRS psychoeducational program for couples. *Family Therapy, 23*(1), 11–36.

Durana, C. (1996b). Bonding and emotional reeducation of couples in the PAIRS training: Part I. *The American Journal of Family Therapy, 24*(3), 269–280.

Durana, C. (1996c). Bonding and emotional reeducation of couples in the PAIRS training: Part II. *The American Journal of Family Therapy, 24*(4), 315–328.

Dyer, P., & Dyer, G. (1990). *Growing together.* Minneapolis, MN: PREPARE/ENRICH, Inc.

Edwards, M. E. & Steinglass, P. (1995) Family therapy treatment outcomes for alcoholism. *Journal of Marital and Family Therapy, 21*(4), 475–510.

Elliott, S. S., & Saunders, B. E. (1982). The systems marriage enrichment program: An alternative model based on systems theory. *Family Relations, 31,* 53–60.

Emerson, D. E. (1993). *Evaluating the effectiveness of "Getting the love you want" enrichment semi-*

*nars*. Dissertation presented to the faculty of the Graduate School of Psychology, Fuller Theological Seminary.

Estrada, A. O., & Pinsof, W. M. (1995). The effectiveness of family therapies for selected behavioral disorders of childhood. *Journal of Marital and Family Therapy, 21*(4), 403–440.

Ford, J. D., Bashford, M. B., & DeWitt, K. N. (1984). Three approaches to marital enrichment: Toward optimal matching of participants and interventions. *Journal of Sex and Marital Therapy, 10*(1), 41–48.

Fournier, D. G., Olson, D. H., & Druckman, J. M. (1983). Assessing marital and premarital relationships: The PREPARE-ENRICH inventories. In E. E. Filsinger (Ed.), *Marriage and family assessment* (pp. 229–250). Beverly Hills, CA: Sage.

Fowers. B. J., & Olson, D. H. (1986). Predicting marital success with PREPARE: A predictive validity study. *Journal of Marital and Family Therapy, 12*, 403–413.

Fowers, B. M., & Olson, D. H. (1989). ENRICH marital inventory: A discriminant validity and cross-validation assessment. *Journal of Marital and Family Therapy, 15*, 65-79.

Fowers, B. J., & Olson, D. H. (1992). Four types of premarital couples: An empirical typology based on PREPARE. *Journal of Family Psychology, 6*, 10–21.

Fowers, B. J., & Montel, K. H. (1996). Predicting marital success for premarital couple types based on PREPARE. *Journal of Marital and Family Therapy, 22*(1), 103–119.

Gallagher, M. (2000) *The marriage movement: A statement of principles*. New York: Institute of American Values.

Gershenfeld, M. K. (1985). A group is a group is a group: Working with couples in groups. In D. C. Goldberg (Ed.), *Contemporary marriage* (pp. 374–419). Homewood, IL: Dorsey Press.

Glenn, N., Nock, S., & Waite, L. Chairs. (2002). *Why marriage matters: Twenty-one conclusions from the social sciences.* New York: Institute for American Values.

Giblin, P. (1986). Research and assessment in marriage and family enrichment: A meta-analysis study. *Journal of Psychotherapy and the Family, 2*(1), 79–92.

Giblin, P. (1996). Marital and family enrichment: A process whose time has come (and gone). *The Family Journal, 4*, 143–151.

Goldstein, M. J., & Miklowitz, D. J., (1995). The effectiveness of marital and family therapy in the treatment of schizophrenic disorders. *Journal of*

*Marital and Family Therapy, 21*(4), 361–376.

Gordon, T. (1975). *Parent effectiveness training*. Bergenfield, NJ: Penguin.

Gordon, L. H. (1993). *Passage to intimacy.* New York: Simon & Schuster.

Gordon, L. H. (1988). *PAIRS curriculum guide and training manual.* Falls Church, VA: PAIRS Foundation.

Gottman, J. M. (1979). *Marital interaction: Experimental investigations.* New York: Academic Press.

Gottman, J. M. (1997). *From the roots up: A research based marital therapy.* Seattle, WA: Seattle Marital and Family Institute.

Gottman, J. M. (2002, July). *Update from the love lab.* Keynote address presented at the annual meeting of the Coalition for Marriage, Couples, and Family Education, Washington, DC, July 11–14.

Gottman, J., Carrere, S., Swanson, C., & Coan, J. A. (2000, February). Reply to "From Basic Research to Interventions." *Journal of Marriage and the Family, 62*, 265–273.

Gottman, J. M., & Gottman, J. S. (1999). The marriage survival kit: A research-based marital therapy, In R. Berger & M. T. Hannah (Eds.), *Preventive approaches in couple therapy* (pp. 304–330). Philadelphia, PA: Brunner/Mazel.

Gottman, J. M., & Notarius, C. I. (2002). Research in the 20th century and a research agenda for the 21st century. *Family Process, 41*(2), 159–197.

Griffin, J. M., Jr., & Apostal, R. A. (1993). The influence of Relationship Enhancement training on differentiation of self. *Journal of Marital and Family Therapy, 19*(3), 267–272.

Guerney, B. G. (1977). *Relationship enhancement.* San Francisco: Jossey-Bass.

Guerney, B. G., Brock, G., & Coufal, J. (1986). Integrating marital therapy and enrichment: The relationship enhancement approach. In N. S. Jacobson & A. S. Gurman (Eds.), *Clinical handbook of marital therapy.* New York: Guilford Press.

Guerney, B. G., & Maxson, P. (1990). Marital and family enrichment research: A decade review and look ahead. *Journal of Marriage and the Family, 52*, 1127–1135.

Guerney, B. G., Jr., Vogelsong, E., & Coufal, J. (1983). Relationship Enhancement versus a traditional treatment: Follow-up and booster effects. In D. Olson & B. Miller (Eds.), *Family studies review Yearbook* (Vol. 1, pp. 738–756). Beverly Hills, CA: Sage.

Gurman, A. S., & Kniskern, D. P. (1977). Enriching research on marital enrichment programs. *Journal of Marriage and Family Counseling, 3*(2), 3–11.

Hahlweg, K., Baucom, D. H., & Markman, H. J. (1988). Recent advances in therapy and prevention. In I. R. R. Falloon (Ed.), *Handbook of behavioral family therapy* (pp. 413–448). New York: Guilford Press.

Hahlweg, K., & Markman, H. J. (1988). Effectiveness of behavioral marital therapy: Empirical status of behavioral techniques in preventing and alleviating marital distress. *Journal of Consulting and Clinical Psychology, 56*, 440–447.

Hawley, D. R., & Olson, D. H. (1995). Enriching newlyweds: An evaluation of three enrichment programs. *The American Journal of Family Therapy, 23*(2), 129–147.

Hendrix, H. (1988). *Getting the love you want: A guide for couples.* New York: Henry Holt.

Hof, L., & Miller, W. R. (1981). *Marriage enrichment: Philosophy, process and program.* Bowie, MD: Robert J. Brady.

Hoopes, M. H., Fisher, B. L., & Barlow, S. H. (1984). *Structured family facilitation programs.* Rockville, MD: Aspen.

Hunt, R., Hof, L., & DeMaria, R. (1998). *Marriage enrichment: Preparation, mentoring and outreach.* Philadelphia, PA: Brunner/Mazel.

Johnson, S. M. (1996). *The practice of emotionally focused marital therapy: Creating connection.* New York: Brunner/Mazel (Taylor & Francis).

Jordan, P. L. (1995). The mother's role in promoting fathering behavior. In J. L. Shapiro, M. J. Diamond, & M. Greenberg (Eds.), *Becoming a father: Contemporary, social, developmental, and clinical perspectives.* New York: Springer.

Jordan, P. L. (1995a). *PREP pilot: Transition to parenthood.* Paper presented at the Association for the Advancement of Behavioral Therapy 29th Annual Convention, Washington, DC.

Khesgi-Genovese, Z., & Constable, R. (1995, November). Marital practice in social work. *Families in Society: The Journal of Contemporary Human Services,* 559–565.

Kramer, K. M., Arbuthnot, J., Gordon, D. A., Rousis, N., & Hoza, J. (1998). Effects of skill-based divorce education programs on domestic violence and parental communication. *Family and Conciliation Courts Review, 36*(1), 9–31.

Krug, S. E., & Ahadi, S. A. (1986). Personality characteristics of wives and husbands participating in marriage enrichment. *Multivariate Experimental Clinical Research, 8,* 149–159.

Kurkowski, K., Gordon, D. A., & Arbuthnot, J. (1996, October). *Current research outcomes in parent education for divorcing families.* Paper presented

at Annual Conference of Family Mediation. Canada, Winipeg, Manitoba.

L'Abate, L. (1981). Skill training programs for couples and families. In A. S. Gurman & D.P. Kniskern, *Handbook of family therapy* (pp. 631–661). New York: Brunner/Mazel.

L'Abate, L., & McHenry, S. (1983). *Handbook of marital interventions.* New York: Grune & Stratton.

Lebow, J. (1997). Is couples therapy obsolete? *Networker, 21*(5), 81–88.

Leigh, G. K., Loewen, I. R., & Lester, M. E. (1986). Caveat emptor: Values and ethics in family life education and enrichment. *Family Relations: Journal of Applied Family and Child Studies, 35*(4) 573–580.

Lester, M. E., & Doherty, W. J. (1983). Couples' long-term evaluations of their marriage encounter experience. *Journal of Marital and Family Therapy, 9*(2), 183–188.

Mace, D. R. (1986). Three ways of helping married couples. *Journal of Marital and Family Therapy, 13*(2), 179–186.

Mace, D. R., & Mace, V. C. (1986). The history and present status of the marriage and family enrichment movement. *Journal of Psychotherapy and the Family, 2*(1), 7–17.

Markman, H. J., Renick, M. J., Floyd, F. J., Stanley, S. M., & Clements, M. (1993). Preventing marital distress through communication and conflict management training: A 4- and 5-year follow-up. *Journal of Consulting and Clinical Psychology, 61*(1), 70–77.

Markman, H. J., Stanley, S. M., & Blumberg, S. L. (1994). *Fighting for your marriage.* San Francisco: Jossey-Bass.

Mattson, D. L., Christensen, O. J., & England, J. T. (1990). The effectiveness of a specific marital enrichment program: Time. *Individual Psychology, 46*(1), 88–92.

McFarlane, W. R. (1991) Family psychoeducational treatment. In A. S. Gurman & D. P.Kniskern (Eds.), *Handbook of family therapy* (Vol. II, pp. 363–395) New York: Brunner/Mazel.

Meadors, R. E. (1991). Marriage enrichment: An emerging specialty of prevention in the field of marriage counseling. *Dissertation Abstract, 51*(7-A), 1170.

Miller, S., Nunnally, E. M., & Wackman, D. B. (1975). *Alive and aware: Improving communication in relationships.* Minneapolis: Interpersonal Communications Program.

Miller, S., Wackman, D. B., & Nunnally, E. W.

(1976). A communication-training program for couples. *Social Casework, 57*(1), 9–18.

Miller, S., Wackman, D. B., & Nunnally, E. W. (1983). Couple communication: Equipping couples to be their own best problem solvers. *The Counseling Psychologist, 11*(3), 73–77.

Noval, L. S., Combs, C. W., Winamake, M., Bufford, R. K., & Halter, L. (1996). Cognitive-behavioral marital enrichment among church and non-church groups: Preliminary findings. *Journal of Psychology and Christianity, 24*(1), 47–53.

Olson, D. H. (1997). *PREPARE/ENRICH counselor's manual.* Minneapolis, MN: Life Innovations.

Olson, D. H., & Fowers, B. J. (1993). Five types of marriage: An empirical typology based on EN-RICH. *The Family Journal: Counseling and Therapy for Couples and Families, 1*(3), 196–207.

Parrott, L., & Parrott L. (1999). Preparing couples for marriage: The SYMBIS model. In R. Berger & M. T. Hannah (Eds.), *Preventive approaches in couples therapy* (pp. 237–254). Philadelphia: Brunner/Mazel.

Popkin, M. (1983). *Active parenting handbook.* Atlanta, GA: Active Parenting Publishers.

Powell, G. W., & Wampler, K. (1982, July). Marriage enrichment participants: Levels of marital satisfaction. *Family Relations,* 389–393.

Riehlmede, A., & Willi, J. (1993). Ambivalence of psychotherapists towards the prevention of marital conflicts. *System Familie-Forchung Und Therapie, 6*(2), 79–88.

Schauble, P. G., & Hill, C. G. (1976). A laboratory approach to treatment in marriage counseling: Training in communication skills. *The Family Coordinator, 25,* 277–284.

Schnarch, D. (1991). *Constructing the sexual crucible: An integration of sexual and marital therapy.* New York: W. W. Norton.

Silliman, B., Stanley. S. M., Coffin, W., Markman, H. J., & Jordan, P. L. (2001). Preventive interventions for couples. In H. Liddle, D. Santisteban, R. Levant, & J. Bray (Eds.), *Family psychology: Science-based interventions* (pp. 123–146). Washington, DC: American Psychological Association.

Smith, R. M., Shoffner, S. M., & Scott. J. P. (1979). Marriage and family enrichment: A new professional area. *The Family Coordinator, 28,* 87–93.

Spanier, G. H. (1976). Measuring dyadic adjustment: New scales for assessing the quality of marriage and similar dyads. *Journal of Marriage and the Family, 38,* 15–28.

Stahman, R. F., & Salts, C. J. (1993). Educating for marriage and intimate relationships. In M. E. Ar-

cus, J. D. Schvaneveldt, & J. J. Moss (Eds.), *Handbook of family therapy. Vol. 2: The practice of family Life education* (pp. 33–61). Newbury Park, CA: Sage.

Stanley, S. M., Blumberg, S. L., & Markman, H. J. (1999). Helping couples fight for their marriages: The PREP approach. In R. Berger & M. T. Hannah (Eds.), *Preventive approaches to couples therapy* (pp. 279–303). Philadelphia, PA: Brunner/Mazel.

Stanley, S. M., Bradbury, T. N, & Markman, H. J. (2000). Structural Flaws in the Bridge from basic research on marriage to interventions for couples. *Journal of Marriage and the Family, 62,* 256–264.

Stuart, R. (1980). *Helping couples change.* New York: Guilford Press.

Sullivan, K. T., & Bradbury, T. N. (1997). Are premarital prevention programs reaching couples at risk for marital dysfunction? *Journal of Consulting and Clinical Psychology, 65*(1), 24–30.

Tolman, R. M., & Molidor, C. E. (1994). A decade of social group work research. Trends in methodology, theory, and program development. Special issue: Empirical research on the outcomes of social work with groups. *Research on Social Work Practice, 4*(2), 142–159.

Toseland, R. W., & Siporin, M. (1986a). When to recommend group treatment: A review of the clinical and the research literature. *International Journal of Group Psychotherapy, 36*(2), 171–201.

Toseland, R. W., & Siporin, M. (1986b). Response to critiques by George Gazda and K. Roy Mackenzie. *International Journal of Group Psychotherapy, 36*(3), 483–485.

Turner, L. (1997). *The impact of a psychoeducational group intervention on marital discord, adult interaction style, projective identification and perceptive identification.* A dissertation submitted to the faculty of the School of Social Service of the Catholic University of America in partial fulfillment of the requirements for the degree Doctor of Social Work. Washington, DC.

Urbaniak, L. M. (1982). *ME: Description of part and comparison to caring relationships inventory norm group.* Doctoral dissertation, Loyola University of Chicago.

Visher, E. B., & Visher, J. S. (1993). *Stepfamilies: Myths and realities.* New York: Carol Publishing Group.

Waldo, M. (1986). Group counseling for military personnel who battered their wives. *Journal for Specialists in Group Work, 2*(3), 132–138.

Wampler, K. S. (1990). An update of research on the Couple Communication Program. *Family Sci-*

*ence Review, 3*(1), 21–40.

Weiner-Davis, M. (1992). *Divorce-busting: A step-by-step approach to making your marriage loving again.* New York: Fireside (Simon & Schuster).

Winawer, H. (1997, Spring; 1999, Winter; 1999, Fall). AFTA Newsletter.

Wing, L., & Wing, B. (2003). Stepfamilies. In R. DeMaria & M. T. Hannah (Eds.), *Building intimate relationships: Bridging treatment, education,* *and enrichment through the PAIRS program* (pp. 189–205). New York: Brunner-Routledge.

Worthington, E., Buston, B., & Hammonds, T. (1989). A component analysis of marriage enrichment: Information and treatment modality. *Journal of Counseling and Development, 67*(10), 555–560.

Zimpher, D. G. (1988). Reviews and developments; Marriage enrichment programs: A review. *Journal for Specialists in Group Work, 13,* 44–53.

CHAPTER 21

# The Metamorphosis of Training and Supervision

CHERYL L. STORM, PhD

TERESA MCDOWELL, MA

*Pacific Lutheran University, Tacoma*

JANIE K. LONG, PhD

*Purdue University*

We suggest in this chapter that couple and family therapy (CFT) trainers and supervisors are at a key juncture in time, within a rapidly changing social context, to carefully review many of the core beliefs and practices that have been passed down from generation to generation. Our increasingly pluralistic society is stimulating an ongoing need to look seriously at training and supervision from the multiple perspectives of those previously marginalized due to social locations such as class, sexual orientation, gender, race, nationality, and abilities. There is a simultaneous feminization of CFT, as more women than men are entering the field as clinicians and becoming trainers and supervisors (Nichols, Nichols, & Hardy, 1990). There is an increase of couple and family therapists being trained in academic pro-grams in marriage and family therapy (MFT), family counseling, and family psychology, rather than in institutes or postgraduate train-ing (Touliatos, Lindholm, & Nichols, 1997). Likewise, the changing economy of mental health care and the ever-increasing global shar-ing of ideas have created new stakeholders and concerns for CFT training and supervision.

We believe there is a metamorphosis of CFT training and supervision occurring in this emerging context. We refer to training as the process of learning the basic competencies of a couple and family therapist that can occur in any context, including universities, insti-tutes, and various community institutions such as churches, hospitals, and so on. We refer to supervision as the process of men-toring and advancing the clinical abilities of a professional couple and a family therapist. Supervision can occur within any educational program, but it also refers to postgraduate supervision of individuals for licensure, credentialing, and professional growth. In this chapter, we first describe the metamorphosis, then conclude with a discussion of current debates in the emerging context.

## ENDURING CONCEPTS AND PRACTICES

After identifying what we see as enduring training and supervision concepts and practices and highlighting evidence that supports or challenges them, we make a prediction regarding their status in the future. The enduring concepts and practices included in this section have met the criteria of having endured the test of time, by being prominent in the training and supervision literature for at least two decades. We acknowledge that our conclusions are those of three European middle-class White female trainers and supervisors with degrees specifically in MFT, one of whom identifies as lesbian, whose primary experiences as trainers and supervisors are in MFT university programs (two in master's programs and one in a doctoral program).

### The Training Trinity: Knowledge, Practice, and Supervision

In the major mental health fields, there seems to be an acceptance of the training trinity of knowledge, practice, and supervision. In comprehensive reviews of research on training, Avis and Sprenkle (1990) and Liddle (1991) concluded that there was some support for the effectiveness of training in increasing conceptual, relational, and intervention skills of trainees and that sequencing of training activities may be important. However, there is a need

for research that directly assesses the effectiveness of training on therapeutic outcome. Clients' evaluations of the effectiveness of therapy provided by trainees have consistently shown that clients are pleased with services received (Crane, Griffin, & Hill, 1986; Locke & McCollum, 2001), but the research has been done almost solely in White dominated university clinics. One interesting twist is the research by Stolk and Perlesz (1990) that found clients were more satisfied with first- rather than second-year trainees. Trainees attest to the rigor of CFT training programs, citing the experience as stressful due to the high standards of the field (Liddle, 1991; Polson & Nida, 1998). Graduates of MFT university programs rate themselves as sufficiently to well prepared for practice (Hines, 1996).

Historically, the presence of a supervisor has enabled a partially trained clinician to practice, leading to supervision being a core component of training programs per se, an integral part of couple and family therapists' postgraduate experiences, and an essential component of endorsement for licensure. However, the effectiveness of supervision per se has not been studied (Storm, Todd, Sprenkle, & Morgan, 2001). The only evidence that these three components are important to the training experience is trainees'/supervisees' satisfaction with training and supervision (Hines, 1996, Ivey & Wampler, 2000) and view that supervision is a critical component for them in gaining self-confidence as clinicians (Bischoff, Barton, Thobar, & Hawley, 2002). It is highly unlikely that the components of knowledge, practice, and supervision will or should change in the near future. However, if the quest for evidence continues within CFT, we may gain much-needed direction about how each component contributes to the development of a competent couple and family therapist and what contributes to the success of each component.

## Trainers and Supervisors As Key Gatekeepers

Evaluation is a primary responsibility of trainers/supervisors, who must judge whether or not trainees/supervisees possess the appropriate level of knowledge and clinical skills. Trainees/supervisees are sheltered from providing therapy beyond the scope of their competency. The public is protected by minimal standards that are established by training programs, professional organizations, accrediting bodies, and licensure boards. This degree of oversight is critical for ensuring that couple and family therapists are providing quality services, which serves to protect the credibility of the profession. Most of the research regarding gatekeeping has been done in psychology internship sites and training programs. The findings consistently show that psychology trainers/supervisors are taking diverse actions with trainees/supervisees whom they believe lack necessary competency (cf. Forrest, Elman, Giraza, & Vacha-Haase, 1999), but that these actions are not always successful (cf. Robiner, Saltzman, Hoberman, & Schirvar, 1997).

Although research on CFT gatekeeping processes is only beginning, we believe that CFT trainers/supervisors are in a good position to meet the demands and increased challenges of gatekeeping introduced by a managed-care environment and the MFT regulation movement. CFT supervision is an intense experience, with accepted norms of 1 hour of supervision for every 5 hours of clinical contact and which frequently includes videotapes of therapy or observation of therapy sessions. Supervisors are trained in supervision per se, thus possessing background and skills in gatekeeping. As a result of this supervisory context, trainers/supervisors (1) can see early signs of difficulties, (2) have numerous opportunities to apply remediation strategies if needed, and (3) have ample data regarding trainees' and supervisees' progress to take action, such as counseling someone out of the field or dismissing someone from a training program or employment.

## Self-Awareness as Important in Learning

Trainers/supervisors have consistently emphasized the importance of developing self-awareness, or the self-of-the-therapist. Trainees/supervisees have been encouraged to explore their own families of origin, conjugal families, and other meaningful relational dynamics; emotional reactions; personal motives, values, attitudes, and philosophies; biographies or stories; and socially situated identities and contextual influences such as race, class, gender, sexual orientation, and spirituality/religion. Some training programs and supervisors emphasize the self-of-the-therapist as part of individual supervision, whereas other programs recommend, or even require, trainees to participate in self-awareness groups or therapy. A comparison of two national surveys of supervisors over more than 20 years indicates that most supervisors have considered personal therapy to be an important element of training (Nichols, Nichols, & Hardy, 1990), but that supervisors may be becoming less convinced that it is necessary. More recently, Mills and Sprenkle (1995) argued that the general shift in CFT to social constructivism requires therapists to become even more self-aware as participants in the therapeutic system.

Although there is little research in this area—trainee/supervisee and trainer/supervisor experience—theoretical rationale supports the personal common wisdom of the relevance of self-of-the-therapist exploration in training and supervision. For example, those trainers/supervisors using symbolic experiential models prompt trainees to face their own anxieties, develop themselves personally, and use their creative impulses (Smith, 1993). Thus, self-of-the therapist exploration is likely to remain central. We believe, however, that there will be a continual shift toward exploring a wide array of therapist experiences, such as multicultural influences and privilege, rather than personal therapy or extensive family-of-origin work during training/supervision.

## Importance of Multiculturalism

In the late 1970s the feminist critique of CFT led trainers and supervisors to address gender (Storm, York, & Keller, 1997), many from a feminist-informed position (Avis, 1996; Prouty, Thomas, Johnson, & Long, 2001), and ultimately to an emphasis on diversity (McGoldrick, Almeida, Preto, Bibb, Sutton, Hudak, & Hines, 1999) as a central concern. A recent study concluded that a course on gender appears to result in lower levels of sexism in interventions conducted by graduates (Leslie & Clossick, 1996). Another study demonstrated that students pay attention to gender when practicing if the study of gender is added to a curriculum (Brown-Filkowski, Storm, York, & Brandon, 2001). Most of the focus regarding diversity in training/supervision has been on (1) preparing practitioners to be culturally competent (Falicov, 1995), (2) transforming training programs and supervision to support the voice and experience of students of color (Wilson & Stith, 1993), (3) spiritual and religious diversity (Roberts, 1999), and (4) confronting racism (Laszloffy & Hardy, 2000), heterosexism (Long, 1996), and gender bias (Prouty, et al., 2001). Less specific attention has been paid to classism (Lappin & Hardy, 1997) and ableism. Recently, there is also a focus on incorporating social justice into training/supervision (McGoldrick et al., 1999; McDowell & Shelton, 2002).

We believe the trend of focusing on multiculturalism will continue. Attention will increasingly be paid, however, to the effects on supervision/training of the intersection of our many socially defined identities (such as race, class, gender, and sexual orientation) that situate us at any given time within complex social networks and result in continually shifting power dynamics.

## Isomorphism As a Key Ingredient in Training and Supervision

According to a recent study, most trainers/supervisors have been influenced by the idea of an isomorphic or similar relationship between training, supervision, *and* therapy, even though the idea of isomorphism lacks conceptual clarity (White & Russell, 1997). The concept of isomorphism initially promoted the development of training/supervision approaches based on specific models of therapy, rather than on a more general theory of training/supervision. This resulted in trainers/supervisors rarely turning to ideas outside of CFT, such as educational theory, for guidance. The overwhelming acceptance of the idea of isomorphism led supervisors to unintentionally fail to address ways that supervision is *different* from therapy and to overemphasize their own way of working (Storm et al., 2001, White & Russell, 1997). Recently, Hoffman (1998) argued for the setting aside of CFT models as a basis for training/supervision, favoring instead a focus on what trainers/supervisors and trainees/supervisees "experience within the process" (p. 148). Falicov (1988) countered that models provide needed direction to novice trainees/ supervisees. Supervisors also report isomorphism to be a highly useful concept, especially for beginners, and research studies find that most supervisors draw on several therapy models to formulate an integrated philosophy of supervision (Wetchler, 1988).

The isomorphism idea is likely to endure as an important idea in training/ supervision; however, we believe there will be an overall decrease in emphasis on isomorphism as a framework for training/supervision. There will be more attention given to limitations inherent in the concept. For example, a recent study found that an isomorphic supervisor–supervisee relationship, whereby supervisees were highly attuned to their supervisors during live supervision was associated with lack of co-operation between therapist and client (Moorhouse & Carr, 2001). There will also be more focus on how therapy differs from training/supervision and an increased consideration of other ideas about how trainees/supervisees learn. As common factors to successful training/ supervision are identified, these will be interwoven with trainers'/supervisors' preferred approaches to therapy, training, and supervision.

## The Centrality
## of the Supervisory Relationship

CFT supervisors have always believed that their relationships with supervisees are critically important, and research findings confirm that supervisees agree. A clear trend in the findings is that supervisees desire a supportive, warm, encouraging supervisory relationship (Anderson, Schlossberg, & Rigazio-DiGilio, 2000; Wetchler, 1988; White & Russell, 1995). In the last two decades many supervisors, influenced by feminist-informed supervision and postmodern ideas, have strived for more collaborative supervisory relationships. Interestingly, there is research indicating that some supervisees prefer conceptual and technical direction, if given benevolently (Anderson et al., 2000), and supervisees appreciate a hierarchical position under certain circumstances if done within a more collaborative relationship (Prouty et al., 2001).

We believe it is a given that the supervisory relationship will remain central and will have a collaborative emphasis, but that the supervision relationship will be increasingly contextualized. That is, trainers and supervisors will focus more on developing effective supervisory relationships, acknowledging the uniqueness of the supervision participants and of the professional, training, and supervision context. For example, supervisors will tailor their relationships with supervisees by using findings such as those by Hovestadt, Fennel, and Canfield (2002), where competencies needed to practice in rural settings are identified. Furthermore, innovative ways of dealing with the power inherent in the supervisory role will continue to be developed to better integrate the evaluative function with the unique needs and contributions of diverse trainees/supervisees.

## The Use of Raw Data in Training
## and Supervision

One of the most enduring methods of supervision is the incorporation of raw data of therapy into training/supervision via live, audio, and videotaped supervision; doing co-therapy with supervisees; and working with teams of therapists. Although supervisors rate videotaped supervision as more effective (Wetchler, Piercy, & Sprenkle, 1989), case presentation followed by videotaped supervision is the most frequent way supervisors access raw data (Nichols et al., 1990). But live supervision is by far the most researched. Researchers have studied the process of supervisory phone-ins during supervision (cf., Moorhouse & Carr, 2001), client reactions to live supervision (cf., Locke & McCollum, 2001), supervisee reactions to live supervision (cf., Liddle, Davidson, & Barrett, 1988), and the combination of some form of computer technology within the process of live supervision (Smith, Mead, & Kinsella, 1998). In reviewing the research on live supervision, Smith et al. (1998) concluded that live supervision seems to be an effective method for bringing about changes in supervisees' behaviors, with accompanying changes in clients' behaviors. This is especially the case when feedback given by supervisors to supervisees is done in a way that minimizes intrusion on the therapy for supervisees and clients. Reflecting team supervision creates a more collaborative training and supervision environment, while continuing the tradition of the use of raw data.

We believe that reflecting team supervision has become one of the enduring methods of CFT supervision. The training/supervision community's response is reminiscent of when live supervision emerged as an innovative method. There is a plethora of literature describing the positive experiences trainers/supervisors/ and trainees/supervisees have had with this approach (cf. Prest, Darden, & Keller, 1990); however, we predict that the constraints, as well as the opportunities, of this method for learning will be considered. In particular, we believe that trainers/supervisors will consider the intersection of clients', trainees', and supervisees' preferences and needs with specific training/supervision contexts, along with their own preferences regarding the use of reflecting teams.

## Developmental Ideas in Training and Supervision

It has been a widely held belief that trainees/supervisees acquire therapeutic skills over time and that their needs change in relationship to their level of experience and demonstrated competence. Developmental models of training/supervision generally share the premises that supervisee development is continuous, proceeding through predictable stages; that trainees/supervisees move toward increasingly complex conceptualizations; and that trainees/supervisees become more independent and self-directed over time (Anderson, Rigazio-DiGilio, & Kunkler, 1995). Supervisors have argued that numerous decisions should be based on supervisees' development, including the use of specific theoretical approaches during the early stages of training (Falicov, 1988; York, 1997), more direction and structure for novices, and increased collaboration and self-direction for more advanced supervisees (York, 1997). Although many supervisors expound the assumptions within stage models, there is evidence that this does not always influence actual supervision practice (Anderson et al., 1995; Storm et al., 2001). In fact, in a study of experienced supervisors, Fisher (1989) found no difference in their interactions with beginning and advanced supervisees. Contrary to the stage approach, other models of supervision are being proposed that rely on nonhierarchical, individual developmental concepts and on a co-constructive approach that privileges the uniqueness of the learner and the unpredictability of growth (Anderson et al., 1995). Supervisors working from a postmodern perspective promote the existing or "natural" skills and abilities supervisees bring into the therapeutic context, as well as question the supervisor's "expert" position in determining supervisee development (Gardner, Bobele, & Biever, 1997).

We believe that supervisors/trainers will continue to expect supervisees/trainees to develop conceptual and intervention skills over time, but will rely less in the future on the notion that there is a universal, sequential progression to learning CFT. Instead, it is likely that continued research will show that trainee/supervisee development is a complex, often idiosyncratic, contextually influenced process. This perspective presents a significant challenge to long-held assumptions about trainee development that trainers/supervisors will need to continue to grapple with in a more collaborative, nonexpert supervision era.

## Certain Qualities and Experience Needed in Trainees and Supervisees

It has been a long-held assumption that to learn to do therapy well, trainees must have a certain level of maturity and insight gained through life experience, along with certain personal attributes. There is a mix of opinions about which experiences and trainee attributes are the best predictors of performance (Goodman & Amatea, 1994). In a study of trainees, Lawson and Sivo (1998) found some evidence that trainees' conjugal experience and their reports of positive relationships with their own parents contributed positively to clients' perceptions of the therapist–client relationship as collaborative, caring, and accepting. Breunlin, Schwartz, Krause, Kochalka, Puetz, and Van Dyke (1989), in a study of structural-strategic training experiences, found that conjugal family experience and initial CFT knowledge were positively correlated with CFT learning and experience in individual therapy in helping trainees grasp CFT concepts but did not improve their abilities to develop CFT skills. Anderson (1992) found that prior non-CFT clinical experience had no effect on trainees' conceptual or intervention skills in an MFT master's level program. In another study of trainees in a master's level MFT program, Lyman, Storm, and York (1995) found that client satisfaction was inversely correlated with therapists' life experience, challenging trainers to rethink long-held assumptions that more life experience and professional employment leads to more competent trainees.

There is a lack of consensus on the attributes that predict how successful prospective trainees/supervisees will be in providing effective services in our diverse social context. Quali-ties such as "social skills," academic performance, and self-awareness have often been considered in choosing prospective trainees/supervisees. It is not clear if and how these factors actually influence the quality of clinical practice, leaving trainers/supervisors relying on their personal judgment to predict trainee/supervisee success and to assess individualized needs. In addition, it is important that trainers critically evaluate accepted standards and existing evidence regarding qualities shown or assumed to be positive indicators of therapist success. For example, Harris and Busby (1998) found that clients reported more comfort in disclosing problems to facially attractive female therapists. It is doubtful that this kind of evidence should prompt gatekeepers to privilege attractive candidates. Another important example is the need for trainers/supervisors in CFT training programs to carefully inspect their acceptance criteria to ensure that prospective trainees from marginalized groups are not turned away by majority culture–admitting trainers, who may inadvertently adhere to culturally bound evaluation criteria (McDowell, Fang, Brownlee, Gomez Young, & Khanna, 2002).

We believe that trainers/supervisors will continue to use critical judgment in conjunction with emerging evidence that points to factors predictive of success in developing CFT competence. There will be continued attention paid to the links between therapist and trainer/supervisor qualities, the training/supervision process, and clinical practice. We will move beyond simple descriptions of static qualities to identify crucial processes that contribute to the competence of diverse trainees/supervisees.

## Ethical Considerations in the Interactional Context of CFT

Although there is some initial evidence that mental health professionals share a common basis of an ethic of caring for making ethical decisions (Newfield, Newfield, Sperry, & Smith, 2000), numerous ethical areas have been recognized over time as unique to working relationally. For example, working with a family (or any relationship) implies a contract with and responsibility to each member (Hines & Hare-Mustin, 1978). This raises questions such as the therapist's role in making decisions regarding who should participate and who defines the problem (Gladdings, Remley, & Huber, 2001). True informed consent, as well as confidentiality, may be issues with all family members, especially adolescents and children, when therapists work with subgroups or individual members (Hines & Hare-Mustin, 1978). Concerns raised about CFT models that view the therapist as an active change agent include the control imposed by therapists over clients, who should have the power to decide what change occurs, taking away the clients' voices and initiatives, and the powerful influence of the therapist's values (Hines & Hare-Mustin, 1978). Some interventions endorsed by CFT approaches, such as the use of paradox (Gladdings et al., 2001) have also elevated ethical apprehensions. Recently, the influence of postmodern thought has led some supervisors to favor making ethical decisions more transparently, in collaboration with clients, thus likely raising new areas of ethical debate (cf. special section on postmodern ethics in the *Journal of Systemic Therapy,* edited by Swimm [2001]).

Trainers and supervisors play a critical role in preparing couple and family therapists to make ethical decisions that are often unique to the relational nature of systemic therapy. To do this effectively, they rely on state laws, ethical codes, ethical decision–making models, clinical/supervisory experience, and available research. Althgouh many concerns and controversies have been raised over the unique ethics involved in treating relationships, there is clearly a lack of evidence beyond professional experience to help supervisors and trainers negotiate this difficult territory. We believe that the divergence in state laws and ethical codes of various professional groups will in the short term make the ethical waters murkier than before. However, as CFT moves to a more unified position around training/supervision and the voices of clients are increasingly incorporated, we also believe that ethical standards will become more unified.

## DEBATES IN THE EMERGING CONTEXT

### *Reproducing the Field As Is?*

Trainers/supervisors are faced with important decisions about how to continue to pass on field knowledge, socialize new members of the field, and act as gatekeepers, while at the same time creating space for new knowledge to be generated. Furthermore, all of this must be accomplished primarily in academic institutions that have been frequently criticized for reproducing social inequalities and maintaining the status quo (Aronowitz & Giroux, 1993). In recent years, numerous debates have been raised surrounding the production and reproduction of CFT knowledge and practice. Questions such as "How is knowledge created? Who is creating and benefiting from CFT knowledge? In what ways do we, through our theories and practices, maintain the status quo of social inequity? And how might we contribute to a more just society?" have become even more frequently asked, as the challenges of diversity and social constructivism have joined the feminist critique (Smith, 1993). This has spurred a debate in the field regarding our role in social change beyond the therapy room (cf. Johnson's article [2001] and the responses to it). There are those who argue that couple and family therapists should be wary of attempting to broaden their role of helping families change to that of helping society change, and that they are in danger of imposing their own biases and exaggerations on others (Johnson, 2001). There are many therapists, trainers, and supervisors who challenge dominant, oppressive social discourses from a postmodern perspective. Still others argue that a postmodern perspective may put us at risk of abandoning a modern critique of unjust societal structures, in favor of adopting a relativist stance that fails to adequately interrogate the real, material consequences of socially constructed systems that favor members of the dominant culture and class.

We believe it is important that trainers/supervisors continue to rely on growing evidence of what is most effective in therapy, to make decisions about what and how to pass on essential knowledge and skills. At the same time, we maintain the position that it is vital for all members of the field to be truly valued as potential knowledge producers and to have a legitimate place at the CFT table. To do this, trainers/supervisors must continue to develop critical awareness and engage in initiatives that target inclusion and equity. This includes generating evidence relevant to the experiences of members of marginalized groups that is based on culturally sensitive ideology and methods, as well as the need to critically inspect the potential negative consequences of attempting to generalize research results gathered from specific gender, racial, sexually oriented, national, or class groups to those in other cultural and social locations (Parker & Lynn, 2002). In essence, we must value and teach the knowledge and skills we consider unique and necessary to CFT, including those that are supported by evidence, without limiting contributions, maintaining unequal social relations, dismissing multiple identities, supporting the myth of the monolithic family, or failing to find ways to be influenced by and to amplify marginalized voices.

## Who Will Provide the Leadership in Training and Supervision for the Next Generation?

Given the incredible complexity of the job, how do we revise standards for training/supervision and train trainers/supervisors in ways that are responsive to our emerging context? In CFT we pride ourselves in requiring high standards for persons training to be therapists and supervisors. Yet there is ambiguity regarding how professional organizations, the regulatory movement, and doctoral programs will provide leadership for training/supervision of the next generation in the emerging context. Some argue that professional organizations should take a more predominant role, with some turning to AAMFT since it has been a clear standard setter in the area of supervision over the years by designating supervisors and specific CFT supervisory training. Other trainers/supervisors argue that the regulatory movement should take the lead. Currently, the most frequent regulatory requirements to supervise couple and family therapists are a basic practice credential, which does not necessarily mean CFT, and a required number of years of practical experience (Sturkie & Bergen, 2000). However, standards set by the licensure movement are politicized, often the result of compromises among diverse groups rather than a response to evidence in the field about what constitutes effective or relevant training/supervision. Still others argue that doctoral programs should take a stronger leadership role. Presently, doctoral trainees in CFT programs are required to take a supervision course and provide limited supervision under the guidance of a supervisor, and there is no required coursework in pedagogy. Doctoral students in family counseling and psychology programs currently are not required to receive specialized training in supervision or pedagogy. It is curious that more time is not spent in them preparing individuals for training/supervisory leadership roles.

In our opinion, doctoral programs should take a central leadership role in training/ supervision. As a training ground for trainers, supervisors, and researchers, doctoral programs could be a fertile environment for promoting research of training/supervision, within and outside the confines of academia, thus providing the field with important guidance. Doctoral students could fulfill an important training, consultative, or supervising function for community supervisors who are integrally involved in the postgraduate professional development of couple and family therapists, thus serving as a link to practice outside of academia.

### Do We Fit Into or Challenge Traditional Mental Health?

There has been an ongoing debate about whether the field should train couple and family therapists to be able to assimilate within traditional mental health and offer CFT as an *additional* resource *or* to be an *alternative* resource to traditional mental health because CFT is a unique discipline. In the first choice, trainees/supervisees are taught to develop bridges between CFT and traditional mental health. Trainers/supervisors endorsing this view typically argue for including of such aspects of mainstream mental health as the understanding of individual diagnosis and psychopharmacology in order for couple and family therapists to be accepted in traditional mental health circles, to collaborate with other professionals, and to obtain employment in a wider sphere of opportunities (cf., Shields,

Wynne, McDaniel, & Gawinski, 1994). In the second choice, trainers/supervisors typically counter that it is better to devote the limited time allotted specifically to CFT, per se—theory, research, and practice. They rely on their trainees'/supervisees' creativity and abilities to navigate the larger context and often see the regulatory movement as a means of carving out increasing opportunities for employment. As Hardy (1994) queries, do we want couple and family therapists to be more like therapists in traditional mental health and "appear less like family therapists" (p. 140), or do we want them to be the best they can be as couple and family therapists, lacking in what the larger context views as foundational skills, seen by some as unimportant?

The position that is taken in this debate has fundamental repercussions for training/supervision—what content is included, what models and methods of therapy are promoted in training and during supervision, employment opportunities that graduates are suited for, and the training/supervision requirements in a particular locale, to name just few. It also has serious hidden consequences for those interested in pursuing careers as couple and family therapists. In our experience, many CFT potential trainees/supervisees do not understand the implications of this debate when they select a training program or postgraduate supervisors, often assuming that all CFT training/supervision is the same. We believe that trainers/supervisors should be more transparent about the emphasis of their training/supervision contexts, the personal stand of trainers/supervisors on this issue, and the implications of both on potential CFT trainees/supervisees.

### How Should Evidence Inform Training and Supervision?

The majority of trainers/supervisors would agree that research evidence provides useful direction in therapy, training, and supervision, and that practice and research should be mutually informing (Stith, Rosen, Barasch, & Wilson, 1991). There is controversy, however, surrounding the degree of emphasis trainers/supervisors should place on evidence, how evidence is gathered and used in training/supervision, and the type of evidence that is most important to various stakeholders of training/supervision. There is a contingency of trainers/supervisors making a passionate plea for trainers/supervisors to instill a higher value on using evidence to inform clinical work in trainees/supervisees and to use it to inform their training/supervision processes (Crane, Wampler, Sprenkle, Sandburg, & Hovestadt, 2002). They criticize the CFT field for being unfriendly to research and marginalizing it by sending a covert message that research is not important in a practice-oriented context. Some trainers/supervisors on this side of the debate question whether it is ethical to train/supervise therapists to practice from a model where there is no evidence of its effectiveness, particularly if a model exists where there is research evidence to support it. Many argue for an increased focus on evidenced-based models, such as functional family therapy, emotionally focused therapy, and the multisystemic approach in training and supervision. Still others argue for focusing on the processes that are established by research for effective therapy, training, and supervision (Blow & Sprenkle, 2001; Lebow, 2001b) and using research findings to help trainees and supervisees develop integrative models of practice (Lebow, 2001a). Finally, some trainers/supervisors believe that we must incorporate more research evidence from other areas, such as family sociology, psychology, and child development, in our training and supervision practices because this evidence is likely to contribute to our understanding of the efficacy of CFT and to support cross-disciplinary work of couple and family therapists.

Trainers/supervisors on the other side of the debate argue that using evidence as a guide to training/supervision is not only premature but may be questionable. They note that research has historically not been highly useful because it does not provide guidance for common practice settings. There is only minimal research of training/supervision in agency settings (Pulleyblank & Shapiro, 1986) and no research of supervision in the postgraduate setting. They point out that evidence models of CFT are currently highly specific to particular populations with specific presenting problems, thus not reflective of the typical internship site or employment context where highly diverse clients are treated. Lebow (2001b), reviewing the criticisms of evidenced-based practice, adds as further issues: (1) a bias toward cognitive-behavioral treatment, (2) no acknowledgment of the importance of unique therapist factors, (3) too many models for trainees/supervisees to learn, and (4) learning to do therapy according to treatment protocols and manuals as limiting trainees'/supervisees' creativity. Many trainers/supervisors argue that they do not have the luxury of focusing their training/supervision on a few select models, when they are legally accountable to providing supervision that generalizes to entire practices and that their objective is the training of generalists who develop integrated personal approaches to therapy. Another concern is that the field will prematurely popularize these models and foreclose on approaches that have yet to be adequately researched. How can we claim that recent evidence-based models are more ethical than less recent models that have longevity (e.g., structural, experiential, Bowenian), when these models have not been researched in the current context? A number of other trainers/supervisors raise important questions about what evidence is valued by whom, how and by whom evidence is acquired, and who benefits from the evidence.

Most important, we believe that more

evidence is needed on the training/supervision *process* itself. Specifically, how do trainers/ supervisors assist trainees/supervisees to learn to think critically about the therapeutic process, develop a way to incorporate advances in therapy into their practices over time, and use research as a source of information to inform their work? Second, we agree with Lebow (2001b), who recommends including prominent research findings on treatment in our training/supervision and augmenting the models we teach with the innovation and knowledge that newer evidence models have to offer. Third, we believe that evidence must reflect the common practice settings and experiences of trainers/supervisors for it to be considered relevant or useful. Clearly, there is not enough research on the common internship or employment contexts where training/ supervision actually occurs. Finally, we believe that evidence must also be sought that addresses the intersection of training/supervision with the broader context. Continued research is needed that focuses on the diverse and complex needs of those who have an interest and investment in training/supervision and influence how it evolves, such as the interface with educational institutions, mental health delivery systems, professional settings, professional organizations, regulating bodies, and participants from other countries. For example, do training/supervision standards adequately prepare individuals for careers as therapists, teachers, trainers, and supervisors in the community, and do professional opportunities exist? Whose voices are contributing to the setting of standards for CFT training/ supervision? What *specific* training/supervision is necessary for minimally effective CFT, and are these available to diverse constituencies in the training pipeline? What Eurocentric foundational ideas and practices fit within an international context? What should international trainees/supervisees be exposed to during their training in North America? (Gautney,

2002). And what methods from other cultures can work here?

*Should Training and Supervision Be Virtual?*

Whether virtual training/supervision should occur is being debated, while simultaneously being experimented with as a mechanism for supervision or as an adjunct to supervision by trainers/supervisors. Proponents of virtual supervision cite numerous advantages, including some supervisees learn best via written dialogue, writing for some supervisees promotes more openness and commitment to supervision, online exchanges build in self-reflection by supervisees, are created opportunities for supervisees/supervisors to work with a wider array of people, and some therapy and supervision approaches, such as the narrative approach, are more consistent with online technology. Most important they argue that we are no longer limited by location and see that by providing supervision globally, supervisees without access to quality supervision now have an opportunity that is sorely needed. Others argue that there are serious obstacles to virtual supervision including that definition of supervision is challenged because it is no longer face-to-face within the same room; serious confidentiality problems exist; informed consent issues are of concern; supervisors are accountable to laws in multiple locations; there are pragmatic issues such as determining the price of private supervision and time spent in supervision; there are increased expectations for participants in terms of responsiveness; and there is a need for new skills. Many supervisors see solutions to these obstacles as requiring a fundamental redefinition of the supervision process.

   In our opinion, virtual supervision will become an integral part of most supervisors' practices in the future in some form, and solutions to the obstacles cited previously will increasingly be found. Some supervisors will use virtual communication to deal with the pragmatic issues that arise in supervision (e.g., documentation, case management), whereas others will incorporate it within supervision as a means to promote reflection within the supervision process; still others will move to a virtual format for supervision. Supervisors and supervisees will routinely make agreements about when and how they will communicate online and what constitutes virtual supervision; trainers and supervisors will help supervisees figure out their stance regarding virtual therapy and online communication with clients and will supervise accordingly.

## TRAINING AND SUPERVISION IN THE EMERGING CONTEXT

We began this chapter by arguing that a metamorphosis is occurring in CFT supervision/ training, due to the forces of a changing social context. As trainers/supervisors, we feel that we are standing on shifting ground when we train/supervise. Supervision/training concepts and practices that have endured over time are being questioned via new theoretical ideas and are being critically evaluated as evidence is being gathered that interrogates their validity. This has led to important debates in the field regarding the role of training/supervision in supporting diversity and promoting social justice; the direction and sources of leadership in the field; the degree that CFT should assimilate into the culture of traditional mental health; and the place that new technology will assume in training/supervision. As a result, we are continually examining what we believe about training/supervision, and many of our prized practices are slowly changing form. In this chapter, we have attempted to describe the metamorphosis that seems to us to be occurring. We are, however, aware that

we could be experiencing the rumble of an earthquake, in which training/supervision will be completely transformed in the emerging context.

## REFERENCES

Anderson, S. A. (1992). The evaluation of an academic family therapy training program: Changes in trainees' relationship and intervention skills. *Journal of Marital and Family Therapy, 18,* 365–376.

Anderson, S., Rigazio-DiGillo, S., & Kunkler, K. (1995). Training and supervision in family therapy: Current issues and future directions. *Family Relations, 44,* 489–500.

Anderson, S., Schlossberg, M., & Rigazio-DiGillio, S. (2000). Family therapy trainees' evaluations of their best and worst supervision experiences. *Journal of Marital and Family Therapy, 26,* 79–92.

Aronowitz, S., & Giroux, H. (1993). *Education still under siege.* Westport, CT: Bergin and Garvey.

Avis, J. M. (1996). Feminist-informed training in family therapy: Approaching the millennium. *Journal of Feminist Family Therapy, 8,* 75–83.

Avis, J., & Sprenkle, D. H. (1990). Outcome research on family therapy training: A substantive and methodological review. *Journal of Marital and Family Therapy, 16,* 241–264.

Bischoff, R. J., Barton, M., Thobar, J., & Hawley, R. (2002). Events and experiences impacting the development of clinical self-confidence: A study of the first year of client contact. *Journal of Marital and Family Therapy, 28,* 371-382.

Blow, A., & Sprenkle, D. (2001). Common factors across theories of marriage and family therapy: A modified delphi study. *Journal of Marital and Family Therapy, 27,* 385–402.

Breunlin, D., Schwartz, R., Krause, M., Kochalka, J., Puetz, R., & Van Dyke, J. (1989). The prediction of learning in family therapy training programs. *Journal of Marital and Family Therapy, 15,* 387–395.

Brown-Filkowski, M., Storm, C. L., York, C. D., & Brandon, A. D. (2001). How to handle the study of gender in marriage and family therapy curricula. *Journal of Marital and Family Therapy, 27,* 117–122.

Crane, D. R., Griffin, W., & Hill, R. D. (1986). Influence of therapist skills on client perceptions of marriage and family therapy outcome: Implications for supervision. *Journal of Marital and Family Therapy, 12,* 91–96.

Crane, R., Wampler, K., Sprenkle, D., Sandberg, J., & Hovestadt, A. (2002). The scientist-practitioner model in marriage and family therapy doctoral programs. *Journal of Marital and Family Therapy, 28,* 75–83.

Falicov, C. (1988). Commentary on Hoffman: From rigid borderlines to fertile borderlands: Reconfiguring family therapy. *Journal of Marital and Family Therapy, 24,* 157–163.

Falicov, C. (1995). Training to think culturally: A multidimensional Comparative framework. *Family Process, 34,* 373–388.

Fisher, B. L. (1989). Differences between supervision of beginning and advanced therapists: Hogan's hypothesis empirically revisited. *Clinical Supervisor, 7,* 57–74.

Forrest, L., Elman, N., Gizara, S., & Vacha-Haase, T. (1999). Trainee impairment: A review of identification, remediation, dismissal, and legal issues. *Counseling Psychologist, 27,* 627–686.

Gardner, G., Bobele, M., & Biever, J. (1997). Postmodern models of family therapy supervision. In T. Todd & C. Storm (Eds.), *The complete systemic supervisor: Context, philosophy and pragmatics* (pp. 217–228). Needham Heights, MA: Allyn & Bacon.

Gautney, K. (2002). International supervisees: A different perspective on cultural competence. *Family Therapy Magazine, 1,* 44–45.

Gladdings, S. T., Remley, T. P., & Huber, C. H. (2001). Ethical considerations in the interactional context of marriage and family therapy. In *Ethical, legal, and professional issues in the practice of marriage and family therapy* (pp. 40–62). Upper Saddle River, NJ: Prentice Hall.

Goodman, R., & Amatea, E. (1994). The impact of trainee characteristics on the family therapy skill acquisition of novice therapists. *Journal of Mental Health Counseling, 16,* 483-497.

Hardy, K. V. (1994). Marginalization or development? A response to Shields, Wynne, McDaniel, and Gawinski. *Journal of Marital and Family Therapy, 20,* 139–143.

Harris, S. M., & Busby, D. M. (1998). Therapist physical attractiveness: An unexplored influence on client disclosure. *Journal of Marital and Family Therapy, 24,* 251–257.

Hines, M. (1996). Follow-up survey of graduates from accredited degree-granting marriage and family therapy training programs. *Journal of Marital and Family Therapy, 22,* 181–194.

Hines, P. M., & Hare-Mustin, R. T. (1978). Ethical concerns in family therapy. *Professional Psychology,* 165–171.

Hoffman, L. (1998). Setting aside the model in family therapy. *Journal of Marital and Family Therapy, 24,* 145–156.

Hovestadt, A., Fennel, D., & Canfield, B. (2002). Characteristics of effective providers of marital and family therapy in rural mental health settings. *Journal of Marital and Family Therapy, 28,* 225–233.

Ivey, D. C., & Wampler, K. S. (2000). Internship training in marriage and family therapy: A survey of doctoral program objectives and implementation. *Journal of Marital and Family Therapy, 26,* 385–389.

Johnson, S. (2001). Family therapy saves the planet: Messianic tendencies in the family systems literature. *Journal of Marital and Family Therapy, 27,* 3–12.

Lappin, J., & Hardy, K. (1997). Keeping context in view: The heart of supervision. In T. Todd & C. Storm (Eds.), *The complete systemic supervisor: Context, philosophy and pragmatics* (pp. 41–-58). Needham Heights, MA: Allyn & Bacon.

Laszloffy, T., & Hardy, K. V. (2000). Uncommon strategies for a common problem: Addressing racism in family therapy. *Family Process, 39,* 35–50.

Lawson, D. M., & Sivo, S. (1998). Trainee conjugal family experience, current intergenerational relationships, and the therapeutic alliance. *Journal of Marital and Family Therapy, 24,* 225–231.

Lebow, J. (2001a, October). *Evidence based training: Integrating evidence-based therapy into MFT training.* Presentation at the American Association for Marriage and Family Therapy, Nashville, Tennesee, October 18–21.

Lebow, J. (2001b). The changing face of models of marital and family therapy. *Supervision Bulletin,* Winter/Spring, 3–4.

Leslie, L. A., & Clossick, M. L. (1996). Sexism in family therapy: Does training in gender make a difference? *Journal of Marital and Family Therapy, 22,* 253–270.

Liddle, H. A. (1991). Training and supervision in family therapy: A comprehensive and critical analysis. In A. Gurman & D. Kniskern (Eds.), *Handbook of family therapy* (Vol. 2, pp. 638–697). Philadelphia: Brunner/Mazel.

Liddle, H., Davidson, G., & Barrett, M. (1988). Outcomes of live supervision: Trainee perspectives. In H. Liddle, D. Bruenlin, & R. Schwartz (Eds.), *Handbook of family therapy training and super-*

vision (pp. 183–193). New York: Guilford Press.

Locke, L., & McCollum, E. (2001). Clients' views of live supervision and satisfaction with therapy. *Journal of Marital and Family Therapy, 27*, 129–133.

Long, J. (1996). Working with lesbians, gays, and bisexuals: Addressing heterosexism in supervision. *Family Process, 35*, 377–388.

Lyman, B. J., Storm, C. L., & York, C. D. (1995). Rethinking assumptions about trainees' life experience. *Journal of Marital and Family Therapy, 21*, 193–203.

McDowell, T., Fang, S., Brownlee, K., Gomez Young, C., & Khanna, A. (2002). Transforming an MFT program: A model for enhancing diversity. *Journal of Marital and Family Therapy, 28*, 179–191.

McDowell, T., & Shelton, D. (2002). Valuing social justice in MFT curriculum. *Journal of Contemporary Family Therapy, 24*, 313–331.

McGoldrick, M., Almeida, R., Preto, N. G., Bibb, A., Sutton, C., Hudak, J., & Hines, P. (1999). Efforts to incorporate social justice perspectives into a family training program. *Journal of Marital and Family Therapy, 25*, 191–209.

Mills, S., & Sprenkle, D. H. (1995). Family therapy in a postmodern era. *Family Relations, 44*, 368–376.

Moorhouse, A., & Carr, A. (2001). A study of live supervisory phone-ins in collaborative family therapy: Correlates of client cooperation. *Journal of Marital and Family Therapy, 27*, 241–250.

Newfield, S., Newfield, H., Sperry, J., & Smith, T. (2000). Ethical decision-making among family therapists and individual therapists. *Family Process, 39*, 177–188.

Nichols, W. C., Nichols, D., & Hardy, K. (1990). Supervision in family therapy: A decade review. *Journal of Marital and Family Therapy, 16*, 287–298.

Parker, L., & Lynn, M. (2002). What's race got to do with it? Critical race theory's conflicts with and connections to qualitative research methodology and epistemology. *Qualitative Inquiry, 8*, 7–22.

Polson, M., & Nida, R. (1998). Program and trainee lifestyle stress: A survey of AAMFT student members. *Journal of Marital and Family Therapy, 24*, 95–112.

Prest, L., Darden, E., & Keller, J. (1990). "The fly on the wall" reflecting team supervision. *Journal of Marital and Family Therapy, 16*, 265–273.

Prouty, A. M., Thomas, V., Johnson, S., & Long, J. K. (2001). Methods of feminist family therapy supervision. *Journal of Marital and Family Therapy, 27*, 85–97.

Pulleyblank, E., & Shapiro, R. (1986). Evaluation of family therapy trainings. *Family Process, 25*, 591–598.

Roberts, J. (1999). Heart and soul: Spirituality, religion, and rituals in family therapy training. In F. Walsh (Ed.), *Spiritual resources in family therapy* (pp. 272–292). New York: Guilford Press.

Robiner, W. N., Saltzman, S. R., Hoberman, H. M., & Schirvar, J. A. (1997). Psychology supervisors' training, experiences, supervisory evaluation, and self-rated competence. *The Clinical Supervisor, 16*, 117–144.

Shields, C. G., Wynne, L. C., McDaniel, S. H., & Gawinski, B. A. (1994). The marginalization of family therapy: A historical and continuing problem. *Journal of Marital and Family Therapy, 20*, 117–138.

Smith, R. (1993). Training in marriage and family counseling and therapy: Current status and challenges. *Counselor Education and Supervision, 33*, 89–102.

Smith, R. C., Mead, D. E., & Kinsella, J. A. (1998). Direct supervision: Adding computer-assisted feedback and data capture to live supervision. *Journal of Marital and Family Therapy, 24*, 113–126.

Stith, S., Rosen, K., Barasch, S., & Wilson, S. (1991). Clinical research as a training opportunity: Bridging the gap between theory and practice. *Journal of Marital and Family Therapy, 17*, 349–353.

Stolk, Y., & Perlesz, A. (1990). Do better trainees make worse family therapists?: A follow-up study of client families. *Family Process, 29*, 45–48.

Storm, C. L., Todd, T. C., Sprenkle, D. H., & Morgan, M. M. (2001). Gaps between MFT supervision assumptions and common practice: Suggested best practices. *Journal of Marital and Family Therapy, 27*, 227–240.

Storm, C. L., York, C. D., & Keller, J. (1997). A genderist transforms an MFT program. *American Journal of Family Therapy, 25*, 151–168.

Sturkie, K., & Bergen, L. P. (2000). *Professional regulation in marital and family therapy.* Needham Heights, MA: Allyn & Bacon.

Swimm, S. (2001). Special section on process ethics. *Journal of Systemic Therapies, 20*.

Touliatos, J., Lindholm, B. W., & Nichols, W. C. (1997). The shaping of family therapy education: An update. *Contemporary Family Therapy, 19*, 391–407.

Twine, F. (2000). Racial ideologies and racial methodologies. In F. Twine & J. Warren (Eds.), *Racing Research and Researching Race*. New York: New York University Press.

Wetchler, J. L. (1988). Primary and secondary influential theories of family therapy supervisors: A research note. *Family Therapy, 15*, 69–74.

Wetchler, J. L., Piercy, F., & Sprenkle, D. (1989). Supervisors' and supervisees' perceptions of the effectiveness of family therapy supervisory techniques. *American Journal of Family Therapy, 17*, 35–47.

White, M. B., & Russell, C. S. (1995). Examining the multifaceted notion of isomorphism in mar-

riage and family therapy supervision: A quest for conceptual clarity. *Journal of Marital and Family Therapy, 23*, 315–333.

Wilson, L. L., & Stith, S. M. (1993). The voices of African American MFT students: Suggestions for improving recruitment and retention. *Journal of Marital and Family Therapy, 19*, 17–30.

York, C. (1997). Selecting and constructing supervision structures: Individuals, dyads, co-therapists, groups and teams. In T. Todd & C. Storm (Eds.), *The complete systemic supervisor: Context, philosophy and pragmatics* (pp. 320–333). Needham Heights, MA: Allyn & Bacon.

# PART V

# The Future of Couple and Family Therapy

## INTRODUCTION

In this section, we assess the trends in the field and attempt to synthesize the knowledge presented in this volume. Of course, we do not have a crystal ball, but certain trends have been persistently observed over the last 40 years. We also point out gaps in our knowledge, in the hope that researchers and clinicians will attempt to fill these gaps. The progress of marital and family therapy is also embedded in the larger political, economic, health, organizational, cultural, and social systems. For example, managed care and the change from the two-parent to the single-parent/blended family over the last 40 years has dramatically changed how we define families. Marital and family therapy remains intrinsically tied to psychology, counseling, social work, and other human sciences but continues to stand alone as a profession and at the organizational level. In spite of the fact that psychologists report marital and family therapy interventions as being high on their list of training, family psychology has failed to gain mainstream prominence. Psychology is still captivated by the individual cognitive/behavioral approaches. In many ways, this has given our field greater freedom to explore new ideas, unencumbered by the political factions that so often afflict psychology programs.

CHAPTER 22

# The Future of Couple
# and Family Therapy

Thomas L. Sexton, PhD

*Indiana University*

Gerald R. Weeks, PhD

*University of Nevada, Las Vegas*

Michael S. Robbins, PhD

*University of Miami*

## INTRODUCTION

More than 20 years have passed since Gurman and Kniskern (1981) edited the first comprehensive volume dedicated specifically to marriage and family therapy. In that volume they chronicled the development of a field that emerged from the early systemic notions of relationships to a range of comprehensive theories of marital and family functioning and therapeutic approaches. It described a world of couple and family therapy (CFT) that was therapeutically rich and conceptually unique, presenting a first generation of theoretical approaches to guide our understanding of couple and family functioning and therapeutic interventions. Since that time much has

changed. Our founding conceptual constructs, theoretical models, and principles of therapy have evolved and grown. The context in which family and couple therapists practice has dramatically changed. As illustrated in the chapters of this volume, CFT has retained its systemic center over time; however, the practice of CFT now looks much different than it did 20 years ago. Thus, we view the development of family and couple therapy in dynamic systems terms (von Bertalanffy, 1968)—a field has emerged and become different, while at the same time retaining a central core that remains the same. As in any evolution there are great triumphs, anxiety-producing ambiguities, and great challenges with each new development.

The purpose of this chapter is twofold. First, we hope to briefly summarize and comment on the major issues in each of the four sections of this volume, highlighting the important advances in theory research and practice and interesting questions raised in each chapter. Second, we hope to highlight the conceptual and practice-related challenges raised in these chapters that we believe exemplify the difficult questions and important dilemmas that the field of family and couple therapy will face in its next decade. We take on this task in the spirit of challenging the field to stimulate thought, debate, and the communication necessary for the evolution of family and couple therapy.

*The Current Status of Couple and Family Therapy*

When family therapy came on the scene in the late 1940s and early 1950s, it introduced a new paradigm. Over time, the epistemology of CFT has evolved in terms of underlying constructs, traditional theoretical approaches, clinical models, and specific applications. The sections of the handbook describe the current views of our founding principles (section I), our traditional theories (section II), new evidence-based clinical models (section III), and specific applications (section IV).

*Founding Constructs of Family and Couple Therapy*

To understand the "history" of the field it is critical to understand the eras of epistemology through which it has evolved, as well as the conceptual models that focus and direct its work. The chapters in section I of the handbook describe the current theoretical constructs in three different domains (epistemology, multisystemic thinking, and culture).

These domains embody the foundational constructs of the field including a history of our conceptual models, constructs of how to view families, and, finally, the most recent issues and models of thinking about culture and ethnicity within family and couple therapy.

In Chapter 1, Becvar outlines the "eras"— or three distinct periods of thinking that represent the dynamic evolution of the field. In the first era, the founding constructs of family therapy focused on a cybernetic and systemic model regarding the nature of the world, the problems within that world worthy of investigation, and the appropriate methods for investigating the particular problems identified. In the second era, the paradigm shift to cybernetic, systems models was completed, and the fundamental assumptions became defined within the theoretical perspectives of the field. Theoretical constructs such as boundaries, communication and information processing, entropy and negentropy, equifinality and equipotentiality, morphostasis and morphogenesis, openness and closedness, and positive and negative feedback arose as ways to understand relational systems. Despite its relational and holistic focus, the field lacked recognition of the role of self-reference. These epistemological limitations increased, along with the growing recognition of the influence of therapists and their role in the definition of problems, as well as in the outcome of therapy. According to Becvar, these challenges ushered in a third era, based on postmodernism. The primary challenge of postmodernism was the notion that our "reality was inevitably subjective and that we do indeed dwell in a multiverse that is constructed through the act of observation" (Becvar & Becvar, 2003, p. 91).

The foundation of our field has always been based on an appreciation of context. Robbins et al. (Chapter 2) illustrate the ways in which context has emerged from a focus on the family relational context to an ecosystemic "lens" for understanding families, couples, and the therapy process. The widening of the notion of context from an intrafamily to an ecosystemic view has emerged from the need to explain the diversity of client experience. Like the emergence of postmodern thinking, ecosystemic thinking was a reaction and a response to the singularly family-focused tradition of early cybernetic and interactional theorists. In addition, it created a contrast to the individual meaning focus of the postmodern perspective. Where the postmodern perspective emphasized individual and socially constructed "meaning," the ecosystemic perspective added systems, particulary environmental and social systems, as a way to understand and explain the diversity of clients and functioning. Ecological approaches draw heavily from the theoretical work of Bronfenbrenner (1977, 1979, 1986), in which social ecological influence is conceptualized at four levels: microsystems, mesosystems, exosystems, and macrosystems. Each of these levels either directly or indirectly influences the family and individual.

More recent articulations suggest that the relationship between these "systems" is a "cross-domain" or a "cascading" relationship. An ecological focus thus adds other important contexts to understanding the functioning of each of these smaller units (an individual, a dyad, a family). Although the family is at the core of ecological approaches, a primary focus is the important influence of peers/support networks, school/work, and the neighborhood on children, parents/partners, and other family members. Among the significant influences of this perspective are the renewed focus on the family–environment boundary, allowing for a broadening of the view beyond the family to the context around the family; a focus on individual development; and an appreciation of the need for multisystemic intervention if successful change is to occur. In fact, the ecosystemic perspective has already spawned a new era of intervention models that locate change within and outside the family.

A quite useful addition to this perspective is the metaphor offered by Robbins et al. (Chapter 2) of "built environment." Viewing the ecological world in this metaphor provides a useful example of the value of extending our view beyond the individual and the social meaning of the individual to the structure and organization of the complex world of the client. Multisystemic thinking will also force couple and family therapists, who have the challenge of learning to collaborate effectively across disciplines, to implement integrated and comprehensive treatment programs to systematically address a full range of ecological risk and protective factors. In addition, this view raises important questions regarding the roles and responsibilities of couple and family therapists as agents of ecological change, the responsibility to develop specific plans or policies to address contextual factors, as well as the potential need to play a role in dealing with issues of social inequity, particularly as research identifies ecological factors that perpetuate the status quo, which is particularly problematic for minority groups and women.

Like context, the issues of culture have been a primary theme in the founding constructs of family and couple therapy. Family therapy was among the first psychological disciplines to emphasize the critical importance of viewing culture as a central aspect of change. The focus on culture (e.g., multiculturism) has come to be an important issue across our field. It, like epistemology and ecological context, is, however, not a simple unidimensional domain. Instead, consideration of culture is complex and multifaceted (see Falicov, Chapter 3). In its simplest forms, culture is viewed as "collective identities" of groups, such as ethnic, class, gender, or social identities. Rather than normative and stable traits, gender, race, class, religion, and nationality all contribute to cultural identities and lend a sense of familiarity and community to people who share the same culture through shared experience. However, as noted by Falicov, inconsistencies, variabilities, and novelties in some of those dimensions, along with the myriad cultural blends that result, require looking at culture from a more dynamic perspective.

Falicov suggests a multidimensional-ecosystemic-comparative approach that integrates both individualistic and dynamic views of culture into the *mainstream* of all teaching, thinking, and intervening in therapy (Falicov, 1988, 1995). The uniqueness of these ideas is the perspective that every client is a multicultural person who participates and identifies with multiple groups that provide particular experiences and bestow particular values. Thus, each is more than a member of a single group that can be summarized with a single label: Latino, lesbian, Lutheran, or Black. Instead, it is the client's and also a therapist's *ecological niche* that is most useful. The "niche" requires that therapists locate individuals and families in terms of race, class, religion, sexual orientation, occupation, migration experiences, nationality, and ethnicity. Thus, therapy becomes by its very nature an encounter between the therapist's and the family's cultural and personal constructions.

The implications of a dynamic view of culture and its role in individual and family functioning are significant. As suggested by Falicov, the family and couple therapist must be comfortable with and able to connect with the universal human similarities that unite us beyond color, class, ethnicity, or gender, while simultaneously recognizing and respecting culture-specific differences, due to color, class, ethnicity, and gender. The result is that there is no list of "do's" and "don'ts" when working with ethnic, gender, racial or religious groups. There is only one "do" and one "don't"—*do* ask, and *don't* assume.

*Traditional Theoretical Perspectives*

Any review of the current status of CFT must include a description of the rich theoretical roots of the field. CFT is unique, in that in few fields of modern science have the founders and original theorists exerted such a strong and lasting influence on defining the parameters of current practice patterns. This section of the handbook includes a review of theoretical models that have had and that continue to have the broadest impact on CFT practice. The chapters in this section represent the range of traditional and current theories and practice patterns of the field, capturing the theoretical richness and clinical utility of quite disparate philosophies about couple and family functioning, intervention approaches, and the role of research.

In Chapter 4, the Scharffs present the current status of object-relations couple and family therapy (ORCFT). They describe how the object-relations approach has the flexibility, adaptability, tolerance of ambiguity, and comprehension of complexity to address today's changing family norms. In doing so, they take on the challenge of integrating different theoretical approaches from many levels of functioning (e.g., individual, family, context). For example, they review and synthesize major theoretical constructs of object-relations theory, chaos theory, and attachment theory, including significant contributions from Fairbairn, Winnicott, Klein, and Bion. Also, holding a unique stance on the etiology of clinical problems, they describe how ORCFT attends to unconscious factors in marital choice; unmetabolized marital conflict and sexual incompatibility; projective identification in families and couples; loss; sexual and physical trauma, including medical illness; multigenerational transmission of trauma, and attachment disorder; temperamental fit; holding and containment; and substance abuse.

Clinical change mechanisms consist of the therapist developing negative capability, working with transference, and countertransference, making interpretations, and setting a date for termination of treatment. Working with the therapist, the family members arrive at an improved ability to work together as a group to understand conflict, solve current problems, and deal with future developmental challenges.

In Chapter 5, Nichols presents the current status of family-of-origin models in CFT, carrying forward the tradition of understanding the nesting of individuals in families of procreation and families of origin. Nichols describes two primary and interrelated purposes of family-of-origin work: (1) individual, to help clients change; and (2) interpersonal, which includes change in interactions among family members. Major theoretical constructs are reviewed, including variables such as differentiation, object relations, contextual, operational mourning, sibling position, and family reconstruction. Most family-of-origin therapists report using clinical interviewing to assess clients and their needs; many supplement assessment with genograms and measurement scales. Because this approach supports the belief that problems are rooted in relationships and interactions that spread across generational boundaries, the ability of the therapist to deal directly with members of the client's family of origin is the most general clinical change mechanism in treatment. With today's evolving definition of family, family-of-origin treatment developments continue their efforts in answering, "What is the family?" using client definitions and preferences in emotional attachment, rather than biological kinship, to do so.

In Chapter 6, Miller, Duncan, and Sparks review brief solution-focused approaches. Influenced heavily by postmodern theory, the two approaches reviewed in this chapter, MRI and SFBT, exemplify the shift from theory-driven to client-driven, to subscribe to a relational rather than a medical model, and to commit to a personalized outcome-focused intervention delivery, rather than manualized service delivery. The MRI approach holds that two conditions are necessary for everyday difficulties to become a problem: (1) the mishandling of the difficulty and (2) continuously applying the same solution that fails to solve the problem. Assessment consists of an adequate account of the problem and previously attempted solutions, as well as an evaluation of the client's goals of treatment and position, or strongly held beliefs, values, and attitudes that influence the client's behavior in relation to the presenting problem and affect participation in therapy. MRI recognizes its most important change mechanism as any interruption of the solution pattern that results in a change in the problem cycle. Similar to MRI, in solution-focused therapy, the trademarks lie in theoretical and technical parsimony, which is illustrated in its "do more of what works" philosophy. When evaluating effectiveness and research, two key questions are asked: (1) Has behavior changed as planned? and (2) Has the complaint been relieved? The chapter includes an outstanding description of the methods of SFBT, including the "miracle question," as well as important questions about common factors research that must be addressed in the next generation of CFT research and clinical practice.

In Chapter 7, Andersen reviews the narrative approaches of CFT that use language as the primary vehicle in interventions. Continuously evolving, postmodern social construction therapies reportedly permit therapists to engage and work with a variety of populations and problems. Although they differ in regard to power, client–therapist relationships, the therapist's role, and the process of therapy, collaborative, narrative, and solution-focused therapies share common premises and values. As discussed, a common major theoretical construct is human systems as linguistic systems, which holds that we make sense of our world and ourselves through language. Furthermore, realities such as knowledge, truth, and meaning are understood to be multi-authored among a community of persons. Unique and thus unable to be predetermined, transformation is inherent and emerges in dialogue. Avoiding traditional assessment, the therapist takes a nonpathological and nonjudgmental view. Most of the information available on effectiveness is found either in anecdotal form at conferences or in books and journals.

In Chapter 8, Dattilio and Epstein review cognitive-behavioral approaches to CFT. The cognitive-behavior therapy model holds the assumption that change in family relationships involves shifts in cognitive, affective, and behavioral realms. Contrary to the narrow view many systemic models hold, CBCFT developments more fully capture circular processes that involve cognitive, affective, behavioral, and contextual factors. Clinical change mechanisms include educating couples and families about the cognitive-behavioral model, as well as interventions to modify distorted and extreme cognitions, to modify behavior patterns, and to identify deficits and excesses in emotional responses. CBCFT approaches are among the most widely practiced in CFT, either as the primary intervention, as an adjunct to other systemic strategies (eclectic), or as a critical component of integrated treatment. As the most evaluated in controlled outcome studies, CBT has been shown to be effective in reducing relationship stress.

In Chapter 9, Mitrani presents structural and strategic approaches to couple and family therapy. Unlike prior handbooks, these two approaches were included in a single chapter. This chapter attempts to specifically highlight areas of commonality and to delineate key points of divergence between these two prominent schools. Fundamental to these approaches is the view of the family as a self-correcting, homeostatic system that is innately effective. Both approaches aim to realign family organization to produce change in the entire system, and both direct attention to the hierarchical organization of the family. Family interactions are the primary focus of treatment; thus, identifying strengths and weaknesses within the family at both micro and molar levels is significant in clinical assessment. Enhanced family functioning cannot occur without symptom change, which is achieved via directive, present, and action-oriented interventions. Three decades of research have resulted in continuous findings of efficacy and effectiveness of the structural/strategic approaches, specifically with adolescents and adults presenting with drug problems and antisocial behaviors. In fact, as noted in this chapter, this area has been one of the most widely researched areas in the entire field of family therapy. Furthering the cause of closing the research-to-practice gap, studies linking process to outcome are finding that changes in family interaction are linked to improvements in measures of conduct disorder. Developments are moving toward incorporating ecosystemic interventions, as well as treating new populations.

Addressing both major theoretical constructs and prominent approaches tailored to specific problems, in Chapter 10, Lebow articulates how integrative approaches are becoming widely disseminated in practice and are accruing evidence for their effectiveness. Explaining the overlap and distinctions of eclecticism and integration, Lebow describes how both involve the application of concepts and interventions that cross scholastic boundaries, but eclecticism and integration are used to describe pragmatic case-based approaches and to describe a more extensive melding of approaches into a meta-level theory, respectively. Both refer to the process of bridging the concepts and interventions, as well as the results of the process. As noted, theoretical integration, technical eclecticism, and common factors—the three threads within integrative and eclectic therapies—are converging. Questions about how to combine session formats, when to do what in treatment, and how to judge the success of a treatment model require further research. Rather than moving toward an all-encompassing model, efforts are now directed to developing our understanding of treatment processes and how interventions fit together.

*Evidence-Based Clinical Models*

The accumulated body of research evidence in family and couple therapy is significant. The research goes well beyond the early attempts to understand whether family and couple therapy works. We now have a significant body of evidence to inform us regarding what works, who it is most likely to work for, and the circumstances under which it has a likelihood of success. Sexton and colleagues (Chapter 11) utilized a "levels of evidence" approach to organize the research-based findings of the field. This approach suggests that different types of evidence collected in different types of research studies answer different questions and serve different purposes. The "levels of evidence" model allows research to be viewed as a useful resource that can answer many different kinds of questions. Outcome research that is focused on whether an approach works is unlikely to inform a clinician about how to make a specific clinical decision when facing a client with a specific problem. Similarly, process research that discovers a useful way of approaching certain critical change moments in family therapy is unlikely to convince an agency, a state organization, or the public to utilize a particular form of couple therapy.

The key to successfully using research is to correctly match the question of interest (clinical or policy) to the appropriate type of available evidence (outcome, process, process-outcome) evidence.

Although CFT research is remarkable, it has many missing elements, many "holes" and limitations. The "levels of evidence" approach presented in Chapter 11 allows the field to be self-reflective; that is, to identify areas where we do not have systematic research to answer questions of need. Once identified, limitations can serve as the basis for further study. We suggest that the ability to identify the deficits, the limitations, and the problems in the research-based knowledge is critical to the successful integration of science into practice. It also highlights a challenge to the field to find ways to further study areas of critical need for which we have little systematic knowledge. In addition, it challenges the field to diversify the methods and strategies with which to find these answers.

These research findings have been successfully integrated into a number of clinical approaches, four of which are illustrated in section III. Two couple and two family models, described in Chapters 12 through 15, were selected to demonstrate the successful integration of process and outcome research in clinical model development, training, and practice. Within these four models, there is great diversity in theoretical constructs and assumptions of practice. Each model focuses in different ways on different aspects of the problems that families and couples bring to therapy. However, it is remarkable that these models are quite similar in what comprises them. Each model has a clear set of guiding principles, well founded in theory and research. In fact, these models are exemplars for the integration of science into practice and practice into science.

The two couple therapy models represent very different approaches to the same work.

Emotionally focused couples' therapy (EFT) is a brief, integrative approach that help partners in close relationships create secure attachment bonds by contributing on the emotional experience and the patterns of interaction that define couple relationships. EFCT provides a solid theoretical foundation by incorporating the current research regarding couple relational patterns into an explanatory framework of attachment theory. Attachment theory suggests that partners in a close interpersonal relationship need stable and significant attachments. Couple dissatisfaction occurs when one partner fails to respond at times when the other partner's attachment needs become urgent; these events will have a momentous and disproportional negative impact on the affective tone of the relationship.

Taking a very different approach, Atkins et al. (Chapter 13) describe the evolution of the most stable and enduring model of couple therapy, behavioral couple therapy (BCT). BCT is a flexible, clinically sophisticated therapy constructed from the solid science of behavioral theory. This approach has evolved in two directions that share common therapeutic principles. Traditional behavioral couple therapy (TBCT) focuses on the rule-governed behavioral skills needed to solve clinical problems. The second version of BCT is integrative behavioral couple therapy (IBCT), which emphasizes emotional acceptance and tolerating partner differences, in addition to behavior change. Both variations share a common set of principles. From a behavioral point of view, it is assumed that people form relationships because they find their partner and the relationship rewarding. In intimate relationships, being with one's partner is a reinforcing experience, to the extent that it increases wanting to be with one's partner in the future. Simultaneously, there must be relatively fewer aversive qualities in the partner. Thus, there is a positive ratio of reinforcing to punishing qualities. Therapeutic process identifies

methods to increase the ratio of rewarding qualities.

The two family approaches in section III also illustrate different routes to the same end. MST and FFT are two different models that represent powerful approaches to successfully addressing the problems of at-risk youths. Multisystemic therapy (Chapter 14) incorporates the principles of ecosystemic thinking (see Robbins et al., Chapter 2) into clear therapeutic principles that serve as parameters for practice. It has a long history of clinical trial studies that clearly establish MST as successful with a variety of youths in a variety of settings. The primary focus of MST is the "fit" between the family and the multiple systems around it. Thus, the emphasis is on the functioning of the family in the outside world. Functional Family Therapy (Chapter 15) is a more traditional, integrative family therapy approach. It has a clear and well-articulated therapeutic process that begins with engaging and motivating the family, changing specific behaviors, before attending to the family–environment fit.

What we find remarkable is the similarity between these seemingly different approaches to family and couple therapy. Each of these proposes a specific sequence and course of practice, based upon internally consistent and systemic principles. Each identifies specific behaviors that are targeted for intervention and used as measures of outcome. Finally, each of these models is much more than a cookbook; they are both systematic and clinically responsive. Thus, they represent more than four different approaches but are a template for integrative and systemic model development.

*Application of Family
and Couple Therapy*

The handbook would not be complete without an exploration of some of the special applications/special populations to which the preceding theoretical and research principles apply. The topics in the final section deserve special attention because they break new ground theoretically or empirically or are more specialized extensions of the work in the prior chapters. Unfortunately, the topics in this section cannot be exhaustive or extensively treated, due to space limitations.

S. Michael Plaut and Karen Donahey reviewed the latest developments in the field of sexual dysfunction. Sex therapy is not a new field, but many advances have been made in the last 2 decades. We included this chapter because we view sex therapy as a sub-specialization of couple and family therapy. Unfortunately, many therapists and physicians are still not comfortable with or knowledgeable about sexual issues. The authors make the point that sexual function is a truly biopsychosocial phenomenon, because healthy sexual response depends on certain functions of the nervous and endocrine systems and is subject to modification by illness, disability, and the aging process. For these reasons, sexual problems may require treatment in a multidisciplinary context. The chapter also provides a brief review of the history of modern sex therapy and describes critical elements of evaluation, counseling, and therapeutic techniques.

The last decade has seen a number of new developments in this area. There is increased interest in how men and women differ sexually. A number of new medical interventions have appeared, such as sildenafil citrate (Viagra) for erectile dysfunction, using the SSRIs for premature ejaculation, and the EROS-CTD device for female sexual arousal. Recent thinking about the pain disorders (vaginismus and dyspareunia) is that these disorders should be reconceptualized as pain disorders, rather than sexual disorders. A newly identified syndrome, persistent sexual arousal syndrome (PSAS), is also being investigated. Many in the field are concerned that it is becoming too "medicalized" as new pharmacological and medical treatments are introduced. However, rather than seeing these new treatments as a threat, sex therapists are challenged to learn how they can utilize or integrate medical and psychotherapeutic therapies— or both. Comparisons of psychological, pharmacological, and combined treatment for sexual disorders will become more necessary if we are to determine the efficacy of sex therapy.

The chapter by Ruddy and McDaniel on medical family therapy (Chapter 17) represents one of the newer applications of family therapy. The authors review the specific ways that illness challenges families and techniques family therapists have used to mitigate these issues. They note that family therapists have adapted their worldview and techniques to provide this unique application. The chapter stresses the utilization of the biopsychosocial model and the importance of acknowledging that various levels of functioning affect, and are affected by, illness. The medical family therapist must focus on more than just the relationships between family members. The importance of collaborating with medical professionals when working with a family facing illness is critical. Medical family therapists must understand the medical context, avoid becoming triangulated between the family and the medical team, and create lines of communication between the various professionals involved.

The illness is often part of the reason that the families present for therapy. In some cases, it is the immediate precursor to the family's struggle. Much like any other stressor, illness may increase problems in the family and stand in the way of resolving those problems. The primary task of the medical family therapist is to help the family recognize how medical health and illness affect families and to help families cope with the stresses an illness can cause.

Ozechowski, Turner, and Waldron discuss the success in applying family therapy to adolescent conduct disorder and drug abuse. Their chapter includes a discussion of the concepts of engagement, reframing, enactment, and multisystemic interventions. Family therapy approaches have now accumulated a body of evidence that adolescents receiving family therapy show reductions in delinquent and antisocial behaviors, as well as in drug abuse. A major contribution to family therapy has been the success of engaging families in treatment and retaining them. Researchers have also been able to identify specific therapist behaviors and clinical processes that are associated with a positive outcome. Transferring this knowledge to community service providers has led to developments of training tools or educational strategies for imparting this knowledge.

Luciano L'Abate gives us a glimpse of the future in his chapter on treatment through writing and the use of information technology. In the future, he states that the main question that will have to be answered is whether therapy will be practiced as it has been traditionally or whether it will be practiced at a distance. He suggests that therapists will be tempted to rely on mimicking what they have done verbally in the past by using unstructured treatment online. Moving into the future will require matching treatment with the presenting problem, using structured, programmed writing, especially self-help workbooks. He views the use of workbooks he has developed in three primary ways. (1) They are the software for online interventions. (2) They are to psychological interventions what medication is to psychiatry. (3) They will decrease the costs of face-to-face therapy. The use of workbooks will also allow for greater accountability. The workbook will be matched to the problem with pre- and post-tests that allow the clinician researcher to determine its effectiveness. The cost and availability of workbooks

will also help the field of prevention to flourish more than ever. Anyone with access to the Internet or a computer anywhere in the world will be able to take advantage of low-cost preventive or psychotherapeutic services.

A rapidly developing area of interest within the field is psychoeducational/preventive approaches. Rita DeMaria's chapter covers the areas of education and enrichment programs. However, she clearly places the context of these two approaches within the broader context of treatment, education, and enrichment because she believes that considerable overlap exists among all three. In her overview of the field, she discusses the confusion that has existed over the years in defining the terms. In most cases, the programs, however defined, appear to offer skill-based training and social support. DeMaria's review of the research suggests that there is little difference between couples participating in enrichment/education and therapy. Thus, she argues that a couple's therapist should be competent in all three areas and should use all three as part of a comprehensive treatment approach. Although research is still scant and diverse, given the number of programs available, it does suggest that these approaches are effective and that the effects persist over a period of time. The chapter provides a thorough overview of the types of programs available, ranging from parent education and divorce education, to enrichment.

Cheryl Storm writes about an area that cuts across the entire field of couple and family therapy. Supervision is often acknowledged as one of the core elements or integral experiences that a beginning therapist encounters. Storm and her colleagues McDowell and Long suggest that the most critical issue at this time is the use of evidence in guiding the development of training curricula and supervision. However, the entire area is still in need of much greater clarity and research. The term *supervision* is defined in the broadest possible terms because of a lack of consensus in this field. Curricular development is basically defined by the Commission on Accreditation for Marriage and Family Therapy Education and supported by the Association of Marital and Family Therapy Regulatory Boards.

Debates abound regarding the content of training programs. Many argue that training should involve a greater and more integrated focus on gender, diversity, racism, social justice, individual diagnosis, psychopharmacology, and so on. Only a couple of studies have examined this issue. The authors also review the issues of self-awareness, isomorphism, the use of raw data versus tapes, and so on, and the idea of supervision as a developmental process, as well as the ethical problems that emerge in the context of CFT. One section of their chapter is devoted to current debates in this field, including (1) perpetuating current thinking in the field, (2) determining who is prepared to provide training and supervision, and (3) questioning how CFT providers fit into traditional mental health services. The chapter concludes with a discussion of the various stakeholders and how they influence training and supervision. In the final chapter, the editors offer a new paradigm for supervision that may help to resolve some of the confusion, debates, and difficulty in researching this area.

## FUTURE CHALLENGES

The accomplishments and evolutions chronicled in the pages of this volume are significant. CFT has become more comprehensive in its conceptual foundations, in its traditional theories, and through the development of cutting-edge clinical models that have integrated both science and practice. Yet despite these great accomplishments, many challenges lie ahead. Our goal in identifying future challenges is to push the field forward, to set an agenda for the next evolution and iteration of the field. As noted earlier, these challenges are offered in the spirit of moving the field forward. From our perspective, challenges to the prevailing views of the time accompany every evolutionary step. It is how we respond to them that determines our future.

*1. Avoid the enticing comfort of simplicity—embrace the ambiguity of complexity.*

CFT is among the most complex of practices of psychology. It requires model developers, practitioners, and researchers to think and act multisystemically (individual, couple, family, extended family, community, culture), articulating the complex connections between systems and negotiating complex human relational systems. Family/couple therapists are faced with the challenge of systematically addressing multiple domains in a manner that is consistent with the model from which they work, while at the very same time responding in personal ways to the clients who sit in front of them. This requires that therapists take the multiple views and perspectives of each member of the family or the couple and find an integrated whole that represents each but describes the whole. It requires us to think of outcome and therapeutic goals in multiple ways from multiple perspectives over a period of time, with consideration of complex processes and diverse outcomes. Thus, regardless of what part of the field one works in (practice, theory development, or research), family and couple therapy is very complex.

We suggest that the complexity of family and couple therapy is actually well beyond the capacity of any single therapist, researcher, or model developer. It is hard to think in so many ways simultaneously. However, the challenge is to resist the temptation to resolve the ambiguity of complexity by embracing approaches that are enticing because of their elegant simplicity. Instead, the challenge is to embrace the inherent complexity of the field, rather than to seek simple solutions to complex problems. Responding to the challenge of addressing the complexity of systemic phenomena will require our ability to continue to increase our methodological, theoretical, and practical sophistication, rather than to resort to finding simple, unidimensional, individual-focused solutions.

## 2. Embrace the "era of evidence" and accountability.

Like any field, CFT has evolved through a number of "eras" or periods in which certain themes have shaped the development of the field. Each of these eras simultaneously shaped the practice, research, and theory of the day, while at the same time laying the groundwork for the eras to come. We suggest that a new era is afoot, an era that is being ushered in by two forces: (1) a changing landscape of practice that requires accountability, and (2) an increasing body of research evidence that is both reliable and valid. With respect to the latter, for example, Sexton et al. note (Chapter 11) that the current body of family and couple therapy literature is substantial in establishing both the efficacy of the field and the effectiveness of specific approaches to particular problems. These findings have created legitimacy of the field, allowing the services of family and couple therapy to be adopted across a wide variety of areas.

But the move to embrace research evidence as an equal partner of clinical experience and theory is a much broader challenge to the field. Embracing research evidence will require a major shift in traditional thinking. The challenge in doing so has historical roots. The early systemic models rejected the linear causal view based in the Lockean paradigm or the modernistic era. Systemic constructs were built on the tradition labeled Kantian (Rychlak, 1981). For many, evidence is still seen as information based solely on linear-causal, traditional deductive hypothesis testing–based approaches that rely on clinical trials and strict randomization and that limit difference and heterogeneity in favor of homogeneity and a lack of ecological validity. What is unfortunate is that this is not the reality of the research-proven interventions representing the state of the science of our field, such as those described in section III. For example, the field is rich with sophisticated multilevel, multimodel examinations of complex change processes (Sexton & Alexander, 2002a) that appropriately capture the complexity of clinical practice. Furthermore, the field has a growing body of evidence of common change processes linked to both distal and proximal outcomes (Pinsof & Wynne, 2002). Thus, the arguments regarding the irrelevance of research are no longer sound. That is not to say that research findings and research methods do not need to become more inclusive, be expanded to study more areas, and become even more clinically based. But those caveats apply to current theory and practice as well.

Our perspective is that the field can add research knowledge as a major partner in its clinical and theoretical domains. To be a bit more provocative, we believe that the field needs to be more accountable by including available research in theories, clinical models, and clinical decisions of the practitioner. This need is based in an ethical, moral, and professional responsibility to be accountable for our professional services. In the new era, accountability can no longer be met by subjective beliefs or claims of long-term change. Accountability must be based on the best evidence available. Evidence might be quantitative or qualitative in nature, objective or subjective, process or outcome, proximal or distal. The form is not important. What is important is that it is reliable and valid, that it represents the complexity of the domain of study, and that it is based in the most relevant method available for the specific question at hand (Sexton, Alexander, & Mease, in press).

The implications of an era of evidence will be challenging. The challenge for the practitioner is to base clinical decisions on models with demonstrated evidence. The challenge for model developers is to systematically build theoretical models through the use of outcome and process studies. The challenge for educators is to be a knowledgeable consumer and teacher of research evidence. The final challenge is to open our work to study and evaluation.

### 3. Rediscover the "relationship" in family and couple therapy.

CFT made a major paradigm shift for the entire field of psychotherapy when it asserted that relationships should be the primary focus of attention. In our early models, the "space between" people or the interactions were described in terms of a noncausal, dialectical process of mutual influence in which all parties are involved. An understanding of systems is derived from the assessment, or inference, of patterns of interaction, with an emphasis on what is happening in the here and now, rather than on why it is happening or in terms of a historical focus.

What is alarming is that since these early beginnings, so little attention has been given to understanding and furthering our understanding, either conceptually/theoretically or scientifically, of relationship and relational patterns. In fact, compared to prior volumes of this handbook, there is dramatically less attention given to relationships in this volume. The ecosystemic view acknowledges relationships but puts significantly more emphasis on multiple and ecological systems. The specific practice models that emerge from this perspective—multisystemic therapy, most notably—

focus primary attention on the "fit between" the family and the environment. The narrative and postmodern approaches described in Chapter 7 (Anderson) focus on the socially constructed meaning of the individual. Likewise, the brief solution-focused approaches described in Chapter 6 (Miller, Duncan, & Sparks) have turned our attention more to individuals than to families. Even the recent emergence of the common factors movement is based on ideas generated from individual therapy literature. Thus, it is our observation that the "relationship" has been lost as a primary focus of attention in CFT.

We think a future challenge is to embrace the ideas of meaning and subjectivity offered by the postmodern perspective, while at the same time moving the focus of attention to the relationship represented by the "space between" people. To do so, we need additional work on concepts that will describe these relationships that built on our early models of family functioning. If we do not meet this challenge, we become individual therapists working with individuals.

### 4. Identify and incorporate the common mechanisms of successful change.

One of the new advances in CFT is the development of common factors as a way of understanding the central features in all good therapy. Our perspective is that common factors are quite useful in pushing the field to think beyond our traditional "schools" of therapy (see Chapter 6). In fact, the common factors perspective seems to be the first alternative to traditional "schools" of family therapy. At this point it seems clear that good therapy shares certain elements. However, merely stating the shared areas is not enough for successful therapeutic process and treatment development, or to promote the increasing integration and diversity of our theory.

From our perspective, the future challenge will be to focus on "common change mechanisms." Change mechanisms are specific activities of the family and couple therapist that lead to specific experiences of the family/couple that result in therapeutic change in a specific direction. For example, although the relationship (a common factor) is difficult to "do" and actually more of a therapeutic outcome than an active ingredient in therapy, we might suggest that the reduction of within-family negativity and blame (a specific relationship change mechanism) is a specific goal that would result in an increase in within family alliance (working together) and the emergence of hope and expectation for change. We think *change mechanisms* is a more useful term because they are open to study (process research), they are therapeutic ingredients that can be linked to desired therapeutic goals, and they are integrated in systemic intervention programs in systematic ways, leading to a comprehensive clinical models.

The challenge for the field is to develop the range of validated "common change mechanisms" through clinical practice, research, and theory integration. The challenge will be to think more dynamically about successful change processes (change mechanism), ensuring that that theory development does not stop with the movement toward integrative models or common factors. In some sense, we view this as trading one approach for another. Instead, we suggest that the future challenge is to articulate the relationship between theory, common factors/constructs among these theories, and specific models of clinical practice. Each of these (theory, common factors, common change mechanisms, and specific models of practice) is unique and builds upon the others. The approaches outlined in section III (emotionally focused couple therapy, behavioral couple therapy, mulitsystemic therapy, and functional family therapy) approach the work differently but share an integration of theory and a basis in common factors and add much-needed attention to both the principles and the specific process "map" (change mechanisms) of how to make immediate and long-term clinical decisions in a systematic way. Thus, we see a complex relationship among theory, common factors, and specific models that is in need of discussion in the future.

## 5. Expand evidence-based models of practice that are clinically responsive and systematic.

The four models in section III represent a set of emerging clinical models that describe more than new theoretical approaches. These models, along with a number of those in section II (see Chapter 8), are comprehensive approaches to family and couple therapy that integrate theory, research (process and outcome), and clinical experience into systematic intervention programs that can guide clinicians, while remaining responsive to the needs of the client. These models are unique, in that they have truly integrated science into practice and practice into science. As such, they represent more than another choice in how to work; these models offer a template for the development of other models that have the same clear and theoretically integrated principles and specific therapeutic process, while being clinically responsive to clients.

The field is unlikely to identify evidence-based approaches to each clinical problem. In addition, evidence-based models are not likely to be appropriate for all the work done in couple and family therapy. However, we think the future challenge to the field is to broaden the range of such models to be as comprehensive as possible. We need a more varied range of comprehensive clinical intervention programs that follow the lead set by those in section III. The field must build on what has been accomplished by the current crop of comprehensive intervention programs as a basic standard for the development of new clinical models of family and couple therapy. The challenge is to expand the menu of such models such that the field can responsibly address more problem domains, different clients, in different contexts. However, in doing so, we must be careful not to rush unproven theories or interventions into practice. Each of the models discussed in this volume is the result of years of systematic theory and research. They grew, evolved, and matured. As a field, we need to develop a culture in which such growth can take place. However, we need to ensure that the growth occurs while retaining a commitment to evidence and integrated theory as the basis of practice.

## 6. Integrate diversity and culture into the core of theory, research, and practice.

Issues of diversity and context have always been a major thread in CFT. Becvar (Chapter 1) illustrates how such issues had an important impact on the historical development of our conceptual models that serve as the foundation of the field. However, as noted by Falicov (Chapter 3), though acknowledged and valued, diversity has yet to make its way into the mainstream of family and couple theory, research, and practice.

The challenge for the profession is to find a way to realize the ideas expressed by Falicov. How can we truly integrate diversity CFT theory, research, and practice in a way that allows us to maintain the founding constructs that are family and couple therapy? In the broader field of psychology and individual psychotherapy, culture has been represented by calls for sets of multicultural competencies and specialized skills. This approach does not move culture and diversity into the center of practice, but instead sets them apart as independent and distinct entities. As such, that

approach may in fact stand in the way of the very integration suggested by Falicov. As an alternative, some of the work of Ridley and colleagues (Ridley, Li, & Hill, 1998), integrates cultural competence within the broader construct of therapeutic competence. These ideas have great promise for moving the field toward centralizing diversity within our theory, research, and practice.

## 7. Disseminate effective models into the world.

Many of the serious mental health issues that clients struggle with are family- and relationally based (Sexton & Alexander, 2002). The chapters in this volume illustrate the many ways in which the current practices of family and couple therapy have much to offer clients, other fields, and practitioners. Communities, as well as individual practitioners, want new and innovative approaches to successfully respond to these problems. In fact, the profound success of CFT in specific areas (e.g., youth violence, couple violence) has had a significant impact on reforming social policy. For example, reviews by government agencies, such as the Surgeon General's report on mental health (1998) and youth violence (2002), highlight the effectiveness of family-based interventions with complex and difficult social problems. The result is that there is increasing interest in the dissemination of evidence-based family and couple models of practice in local communities, through state service-delivery systems, and through national policy. Unfortunately, as noted by Sexton et al. (Chapter 15) the technology necessary to transfer models into the community settings, while retaining high model fidelity, is only in its infancy.

We are making important steps in learning about the complex process of information and technology transfer and model dissemination.

Two of the models described in this volume (MST, Chapter 14 and FFT, Chapter 15) are now being disseminated in large-scale projects in communities across the country. Henggeler and colleagues have now disseminated multisystemic therapy in more than 125 sites, whereas Sexton and Alexander have established more than 100 community-based functional family therapy locations. What is unique about these efforts is that both disseminate through long-term (e.g., up to 2 years of training) and systematic (implementation protocols) processes that meet the stringent needs of community providers (responsive) and do so while at the same time maintaining high model fidelity. Both programs have well-developed quality assurance and quality improvement systems, focusing on both process and outcomes at the level of individual therapists. This scope and magnitude of dissemination, with a focus on high model fidelity, have never occurred before in the history of our field.

The challenge for the field is for us to put great effort into understanding the complex process of model dissemination and increasing the dissemination of other approaches. It is relatively easy to take new ideas into the field. The real challenge is to do so with fidelity as a primary objective, while at the same time meeting the unique needs of different contexts. To do so, we need additional research and the integration of theory from other areas of practice, including organization development, information and knowledge transfer, and economics, in order to identify the important constructs and processes.

## 8. Step beyond "archaeology" to the principles of effective practice in training and supervision.

The work described by Storm and colleagues (Chapter 21) illustrates the great challenges that lie ahead for training programs and for clinical supervision in family and couple therapy. Training typically focuses on the teaching of theory, skills, and traditional theories. Theories are almost always the traditional and historical models of our field, rather than the current models or practice, such as those described in this volume. In many ways, training models treat theory as a reified truth that is stable and enduring and that represents the history (or archaeology) of the profession. As Becvar persuasively argued (Chapter 1), theories are not enduringly stable but instead are inexorably tied to the era of thinking from which they emerged. When considered in this way, theories should change; they should evolve dynamically over time through the introduction of new ideas from both research and model building. Thus, traditional models are the archaeology and the history of the field and are not necessarily the most current, the most research-informed, or the most relevant principles of current practice. The challenge for the field will be to find ways to help new professionals be grounded in our history, yet well versed enough to use current models as the primary basis of professional practice and clinical decisions.

A second challenge for the field has to do with the way in which we supervise therapists. As illustrated in the work of Storm and colleagues (Chapter 21), the field of supervision, though very important to family and couple therapy, has yet to find a role in response to the emerging models of clinical practice. The constructs and purposes of supervision are varied and unclear, the role of research and clinical practice seems secondary, and the processes of supervision are not clearly defined. Supervision is often focused on the person of the therapists. Supervisors encourage therapists to find models that "fit" them, to develop and understand themselves (develop the self of the therapist), and to become the primary "lens" through which the knowledge (research, and theory) of the field is delivered to clients. With the rise of systematic models with specific goals, clearly articulated therapeutic processes, and specific change mechanisms, we suggest that a new form of supervision is needed. These new models put the model as the primary "lens" and view the therapist as bringing important strengths and skills, unique characteristics and abilities that are focused by the model into precise interventions. As such, the challenge is to find ways to organize supervision such that it is model-specific, while using the unique and individual strengths of the individual therapist. Supervision and training are the way in which the exciting work presented in volumes like this one will be imparted to those who do the work of family and couple therapy. Unfortunately, we view the current training models and supervision as critical practices in need of a comprehensive theory and direction.

## CONCLUSIONS

The *Handbook of Family Therapy* plays an important role in the field and in the profession of those who work with families and couples. The chapters in this volume represent a shift in the founding constructs of the field. The basic premise of this volume is that we are in the midst of another era of epistemological evolution. We propose that it is an era that replaces the either/or struggle of different epistemologies with the both/and perspective of another paradigm shift. The new era is not one in which the previous era is "overturned by the new one." Instead, it is a dynamic evolution from the oppositionality of one epistemology (cybernetic/systemic) versus another epistemology (postmodernism) to a more integrated one. This era represents more than integration based upon a mere mixing and joining of constructs. True integration results in a new "meta" construction of prin-

ciples that are more inclusive and wholistic than the last. This type of integration will occur when our epistemological positions come to focus on systems of relationships *and* individual meaning, clinical experience *and* scientific findings, client's perspective of their needs *and* clinician's view of the change process. We suggest that these concepts represent the inherent dialectics of CFT. Rather than being overwhelmed, clinicians, researchers, and theorists must embrace the dialectic tension through complex thinking about clients and change on multiple levels. "Savoring the dialectic" represents the new paradigm of family therapy.

As with any new era of thinking, the field is faced with challenges. The ultimate challenge is, what will we do now with these emerging ideas? Do we fall back into the either/or struggles of our era of "schools," in which one was better than another? Do we move ahead into the more ambiguous and complex world of embracing the dialectic of both/and? Can we meet the challenge of evidence while maintaining clinical responsivity? The answers to these questions will set the agenda for the next era. It is the future challenge of the field.

## REFERENCES

Becvar, D. S., & Becvar, R. J. (2003). *Family therapy: A systemic integration.* 5th ed. Boston: Allyn & Bacon.

Bronfenbrenner, U. (1977). Toward an experimental ecology of human development. *American Psychologist, 32*(7), 513–531.

Bronfenbrenner, U. (1979). Contexts of child rearing: Problems and prospects. *American Psychologist, 34*(10), 844–850.

Bronfenbrenner, U. (1986). Ecology of the family as a context for human development: Research perspectives. *Developmental Psychology, 22*(6), 723–742.

Falicov, C. J. (1988). Learning to think culturally. In H. A. Liddle, D. C. Breunlin, & R. C. Schwartz

(Eds.), *Handbook of family therapy training and supervision* (pp. 335–357). New York: Guilford Press.

Falicov, C. J. (1995). Training to think culturally: A multidimentional comparative framework. *Family Process, 34,* 373–388.

Gurman, A. S., & Kniskern, D. P. (Eds.). (1981). *Handbook of family therapy.* New York: Brunner/Mazel.

Gurman, A. S.. & Kniskern, D. P. (Eds.). (1991). *Handbook of family therapy* (Vol. 2). New York: Brunner/Mazel.

Pinsoff, W. M., & Wynne, L. C. (2002). Toward progress research: Closing the gap between family therapy practice and research. *Journal of Family and Marital Therapy, 26,* 1–8.

Ridley, C. R., Li, L., & Hill, C. L. (1998). Multicultural assessment: Reexamination, reconceptualization, and practical application. *The Counseling Psychologist, 26*(6), 827–910.

Rychlak, J. F. (1981). Will psychology ever appreciate the theory-method distinction? *Academic Psychology Bulletin, 3*(1), 13–20.

Sexton, T. L., & Alexander, J. F. (2002). Functional family therapy: For at risk adolescents and their families. In T. Patterson (Ed.), Wiley series in Couples and Family Dynamics and Treatment, *Comprehensive handbook of Psychotherapy, Vol. II: Cognitive-behavioral approaches.* New York: Wiley.

Sexton, T. L., Alexander, J. F., & Mease, A. L. (in press). Levels of evidence for the models and mechanisms of therapeutic change in couple and family therapy. In M. Lambert (Ed.), *Handbook of psychotherapy and behavior change.* New York: Wiley.

von Bertalanffy, L. (1968). *General systems theory.* New York: Braziller.

# Author Index

# Subject Index

Note: *Italicized* page numbers indicate figures or tables.

ABC Intervention Assessment Model, 416–418, *417*
acceptance, 374
acculturation theory, 43–44
accuser-defender cycle, 104–105
achieving intensity, 191
Adjunctive methods, 78
Adlerian theory, 149–150
adolescent conduct disorders, 242, 381–390, 458. *see also* oppositional defiant problems
antisocial behavior, 310, 384–385
brief strategic family therapy for, 213
core mechanisms of change, 327, 332–338
cost-effective treatment, 233
delinquency and antisocial behavior, 384–385
drug abuse, 242–243, 385–386
empirical bases of MST, 306–307
enactment, 384
engagement, 382–384, 387–388
family functioning, 386–387
family therapy effectiveness, 237
functional family therapy and, 323–326, 338–345, *339, 342*–345
mesosystemic relationships, 31, 32
multidimensional family therapy for, 211–212
multisystemic interventions, 304, 384
nature of clinical problems and, 327–329
peer-level factors, 311–312
peer relationships and school functioning, 387
reframing, 383

relational functioning of family system and, 327, 329–332
research and development, 388–390
reversed hierarchies and, 194
sex offending, 304, 309, 310
social ecological theory and, 28–29, *29*
statistical procedures for, 252–253
therapist behaviors and, 388
treatment, 387–388
violence and criminal behavior, 307–309
adolescent delinquency. *see* adolescent conduct disorders
Adoption Assistance and Child Welfare Act of 1980, 22
affect, to assess conflict, 74
African-American genograms, 92
alcohol abuse, 71, 73, 195–197, 245, 308, 309. *see also* adolescent conduct disorders; drug abuse; *individual types of therapy*
Alcoholics Anonymous, 422
alliance-based motivation, 332–334
alternation theory, 43–44
ambiguity, migration and, 42
Analytical Process, MST, *316*
anger, 267, 268
anorexia nervosa, 39–40
antilibidinal ego, 62
apology, 94
arbitrary inference, 174
architecture, 33
arousal disorders, 352, 361, 457
assessment
cognitive-behavioral couple and family therapy, 156–161
collaborative therapy, 130

family-of-origin treatment, 91–93
feedback, in CBT, 161
Mental Research Institute, 103–104
in MST, 315–317
narrative therapy, 136–137
ORCFT and, 73–75
sexual dysfunction, 357–358
solution-focused brief therapy (SFBT), 108
solution-focused therapy, 141
structural-strategic approaches, 184–188, *189*
in TBCT, 284
TBCT and IBCT, 288–291
of treatment through writing, 404–405
at-risk adolescents. *see* adolescent conduct disorders
at-risk families, defined, 398
attachment theory
adult love and, 267–269
adult relateness and, 263–264
attachment disorder, 72, 79
attachment injuries, 270, 276
emotionally focused couple therapy (EFCT) and, 248
"stonewalling" response, 266–267
attention deficit hyperactivity disorder (ADHD), 168
automatic thoughts, 152–154, 162, 163–164

balanced ledgers, 9, 88, 94
behavioral couple therapy (BCT), 11, 248, 251–252, 281–300, 456
assessment, 288–291
history, 282
IBCT interventions, 294–296